North Carolina

WILLS and INVENTORIES

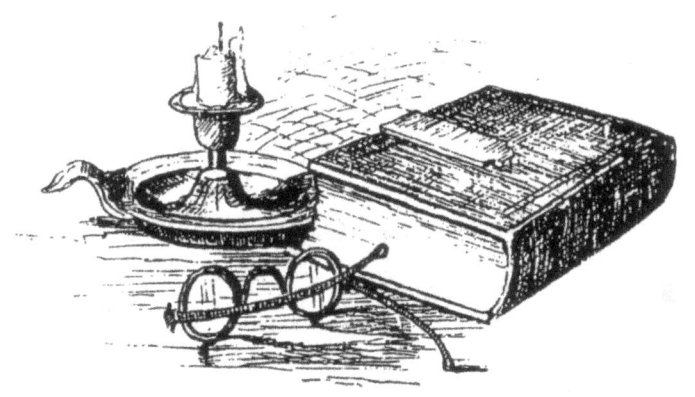

J. Bryan Grimes

HERITAGE BOOKS
2008

HERITAGE BOOKS
AN IMPRINT OF HERITAGE BOOKS, INC.

Books, CDs, and more—Worldwide

For our listing of thousands of titles see our website
at
www.HeritageBooks.com

A Facsimile Reprint
Published 2008 by
HERITAGE BOOKS, INC.
Publishing Division
100 Railroad Ave. #104
Westminster, Maryland 21157

Originally published
1912

— Publisher's Notice —
In reprints such as this, it is often not possible to remove blemishes from the original. We feel the contents of this book warrant its reissue despite these blemishes and hope you will agree and read it with pleasure.

International Standard Book Numbers
Paperbound: 978-0-7884-0853-3
Clothbound: 978-0-7884-7167-4

NOTE

In the following pages are published for the first time some of the most interesting wills and inventories filed or recorded in the office of the Secretary of State.

The wills and inventories give the most accurate illustration of industrial and social life in the colony of North Carolina that is obtainable, and will furnish to students of our history an invaluable source of information about economic conditions prior to the Revolution.

The following paragraphs taken from the introduction to a volume entitled "Abstract of North Carolina Wills," published in 1910 is applicable also to this publication:

"Occasionally is it found that a testator known to be an educated person signed his will by making his mark, it is not always an evidence of illiteracy when the will is signed by a mark, nor is the signature to the will generally a satisfactory signature of the testator, as often he was sick, weak or infirm in body at the time of signing the will. It will be observed that the terms 'father-in-law' or 'mother-in-law' often mean stepfather or stepmother; sometimes they are referred to as 'father' or 'mother.' The term 'cousin' will frequently be found to mean nephew or niece.

"It is interesting to note that in wills prior to 1752, two years are generally named for dates in the months of January, February and March; for instance, January 20, 1718/19; but this was not always the case, and occasionally only one year is given.

"On the continent and in Scotland the Gregorian Calendar is in use, but it was not adopted in England until 1751, when Parliament passed 'An Act for Regulating the Commencement of the Year, and for Correcting the Calendar now in use.' This act provided that the year begin on the first day of January, 1752, and not on the twenty-fifth of March, as was then the usage. The same act provided that eleven days be omitted in September, 1752, 'and that the natural day next immediately following the said second Day of September, shall be called, reckoned and accounted to be the fourteenth Day of September, omitting for that Time only the eleven intermediate nominal Days of the common Calendar, and that the several natural Days which shall follow and succeed next after the said fourteenth Day of September shall be respectively called, reckoned and numbered forwards in numerical Order from the said fourteenth Day of September, according to the Order and Succession of Days now used in the Present Calendar.' If this is kept in mind, it will reconcile many apparently contradictory dates."

In selecting the wills for printing it was intended to choose those that reflected most clearly the varied phases of domestic life of the colony.

Not many inventories are printed, but enough are given to throw a strong side light on economic conditions in the colony at the time the inventories were made.

The bad order and illegibility of many of the original wills make exact copying difficult, but every effort has been made to secure faithful copies.

I desire to express my appreciation of the services of Mr. W. P. Batchelor, to whom I am indebted for reading the proof and preparing the index.

J. BRYAN GRIMES.

ABRAHAM ADAMS WILL.

(Compared with Recorded Copy.)

IN THE NAME OF GOD, AMAN. The Last will & Testament of Abraham Adams, Seiner, being very Sick & weak of body, but of Sound & perfect memory, and Calling To mind ye uncertainty of This Transitory Life, hoping Through ye merits of Death & passion of my Saviour Jesus Christ to Inter in to Eternal Life, do, for avoiding Controversies after my Decease, make, publish & Declare This to be my Last will & Testamt. Revoking and Denying all other former wills by me made & recommending my Soul into ye hands of almighty God who gave it, and my body I commit to ye Earth to be Decently buried at ye Discression of my Exrs., hereafter mantioned, after all my Debts & funeral Charges are paid & Disbursed.

Item. I give & bequeath unto my Son, abraham adams, part of my Land lying on pamlico River, Beginning at ye fork of ye branch up ye Gut That parts me from mr. Thomas Ieevels, and running up noth Gut to a place Called ye Gum Going, and up along ye branch to ye back Line. Then beginning again at ye aforesd. for and running up ye Easternmost branch to a branch Called ye ISland branch: Thence up ye branch Till It Leaves ye Island, and So Still up ye branch to ye Going Over to make my Tarkiln; Thence aCross ye ridge to ye Savannah to ye back Line, Containing by Estomation Seventy Six acres of Land. which Said Land I give To my Son abraham, and To ye male heirs Lawfully begotten of his own body, wch said Land I will not have to be Sold, Let or mortgaged, but from one brother To ye other.

Item. I give unto my Son, Richd. Adams, a part of ye Land I Live on in pamlico river, Joyning upon my Son Abraham and Mr. Thomas Ieevel, being ye upper part of my Land, being Seventy Six acres more or Less to ye male heirs Lawfully begotten of his owne body, wch said Land is not to be sold, Let or mortgaged, but from brother to brother.

Item. I give to my Son, William, all of my Tools, my horse, Gun & new Coat.

Item. I give to my Son, Willoby, a Certain Cow yearling aforsd brown, white faced & her Increase.

Item. I give to my Daughter, abbia, a Certain Two year old Heifer, black pied & her Increase. one Trundled bead Stead & bed & furniture belonging to it.

I give to my Loving wife, Barthia, ye use of my plantation, Whereon I now Live, wth all ye rest of my Goods, Chattles & Estate, During her widowhood, and in Case of Death or marriage, Then my said plantation I give To my son Willoby and his male heirs Lawfully begotten of his body, not to be

Sold, Let or mortgaged, but from brother to brother, and my movebles, goods & Chattles to be Equally Divided between my Son William & willoby & abia, my Daughter. and I do hereby nominate & appoint my Loving Wife to be my hole & Sole Executrix of This my Last will & Testament, Revoking all other wills by me heretofore made.

In Witness whereof I have hereunto Set my hand and Seal. This Twenty-Third day of octobr., In the year of our Lord, one Thousand, Seven hundred and Thirty Three.

         his
      ABRAHAM A ADAMS (Seal)
         mark

Signed, Sealed, published and
Declared In the presence of us:
 PHILLIPS SHUTE.
   her
 MARY X SHUTE.
   mark
 JNO- COLLISON.

At a Court begun & held at bath Town, ye 13 day of march, 1734. Present, Wm. owen, Robert* Peyton. Henery Croston, Edward Hadley, wm. Dunbar, Esqr.

The within Last will & Testament of Abraham adams, Dec'd. was proved In open Court by ye oath of John Collison one of ye Subscribing Evidences Thereto. Ordered That ye Secretary have notice Thereof, ye Executrix having Taken Oath by Law appointed

        Test. JNO- COLLISON, Cler. Cur."
(Endorsement) Abr. Aams Will.
L'res Issd, March 27, 1734. RFDS.
Recorded.

ELEAZAR ALLEN'S WILL.

(Compared with Original Will.)

IN THE NAME OF GOD, AMEN. I, Eleazar Allen, of New Hanover County, in the province of North Carolina, being in perfect health and of sound mind & memory do make and ordain this my last will and Testament.

I most humbly bequeath my soul into the hands of Almighty God my Creator, the Infinite Father of Mercies, trusting in the alone Merits of his Son our blessed Lord & Saviour, for pardon of my Sins, and through his Mediation & Intercession hoping to be found acceptable at the last day. My Body I comit to the grave to be decently interred, attending a joyful resurrection: For such worldly goods as it has pleased God to bless me with I give and dispose of them as follows:

Imps. I will that all my just Debts & funeral Charges be first, fully paid, dischargd and Satisfyed out of my Estate.

Item. I give devise & bequeath unto my dear & well beloved wife Sarah Allen, all the rest & residue of my Estate both real

& personal, wheresoever lying & being which I am now possessed of or shall be possessed of at the time of my decease. And to her Executr:, Administrs, Assignes forever, to be disposed by her as she shall think proper. Nevertheless, It is my desire & request unto my sd Wife that she will by her last will & testamt. give devise & bequeath, unto my two Nephews, & Neice, William Daniel & Catherine Willard, Children of Josiah Willard, Esqr., of Boston, by my Sister Catherine Willard, All that part of my Estate by me accquired, (& exclusive of what she shall be possessed, by Will, deed, or any writing whatsoever, from her Mother Sarah Trott of South Carolina) which she shall dye possessed of, or the vallue thereof; first deducting my debts, and funeral Charges out of the same, to be equally divided between my said Nephews and Neice or the survivers of them, not doubting but she will fulfill this my request.

Item. I do hereby constitute & appoint my sd loving wife Sarah Allen sole Executrix of this my last will & testament, desiring my good friends, Mr. James Hassell & Nathan Rice Esqrs., to assist her in the settlement of my affairs to the utmost of their Power. And Lastly I do hereby revoke and annull all former Wills by me made.

In Witness whereof I have hereunto set my hand & Seal this first day of Janu in the year of our Lord 1742.

ELEAZR. ALLEN (Seal).

Signd, Seal'd, published & declar'd
in the presence of us,
  SUSANN HASELL,
  JAS. HASELL,
  E. MOSELEY.

These may Certifie that James Hasel, Esqr., one of the subscribing Evidences to the within will, appeared in open Court and made oath on the holy Evangelists that he was present and saw Eleazer Allen Sign, Seal & declare the within to be & contain his last will & Testament, and that the said Eleazer Allen then at that time of Sound & Disposing memory; and that allso he saw Susanah Hasel & Edward Mosely the other Subscribing Evidences, Sign their names thereto.

ISAAC FARIES, C. C.

SARAH ALLEN'S WILL.

(Compared with Original Will.)

IN THE NAME OF GOD, AMEN. I, Sarah Allen, Widow, relict of the late Eleazer Allen, Esquire, deceased, being weak in Body but of a sound Mind and Memory (thanks be to God) Do make this my last Will and Testament, hereby revoking all my former Wills.

First, I Commit my Soul to God, in humble hopes of his

Mercy through Jesus Christ, and of a joyfull Resurrection, and my body I commit to the Earth to be decently burried, at the Discretion of my Executors, as near the Remains of my late Husband as may be, so as not to hurt the foundation of his Tomb, which was bestowed on him by my beloved Niece Mrs. Sarah Frankland.

Item. It is my Will that all my Just Debts and Funeral charges be paid and satisfied as soon as conveniently may be after my Decease, hoping that Thomas Frankland, Esquire, my said Niece's husband, (whose Mortgage on the said Eleazer Allen's Estate may perhaps go near to Swallow the whole) will not avail himself of that mortgage so as to cut off the just Demands of my other Creditors. For his and their Benefit, however, and to avoid the tedious process of Law and to express the Regard I have for some other Friends and the Justice I would do them, I think it incumbent on me to make this will. And it is my Will that all the Estate, real and personal, whereof I am possessed, except what is in this will specifically bequeathed, be sold by my Executors hereafter mentioned in the manner I shall direct, that is to say, all the produce of my plantation fit for sale, and all other produce of the Labour of my Negroes, such as tar, Turpentine, Corn, and the like, all my remaining household Furniture (excepting plate, my wearing apparel and other things specifically bequeathed) and all the plantation stock of Cattle, horses and hogs, or such of that Stock as can be spared from Carrying on the Business of the plantation (which I would have continued untill advice arrives from Mr. Thomas Frankland with Direction to my Executors [or his Attorney if he appoints one], how they are to proceed in regard to the Mortgage) to be sold by public Sale to the highest bidder, allowing for enhancing the Sale a proper Credit not exceeding twelve months upon bond and Security for Sums exceeding twenty pounds. But as to the Real Estate and Negroes it is my Will that they shall not be sold but at such Time and such place, either here or in South Carolina, and in such manner as shall be directed by the said Thomas Frankland, Esquire, his Executors or Administrators having left a Letter of Advice to him on that Subject, Duplicates of which I desire may be forwarded to him by my Executors immediately after my decease, as also a Copy of my Will. And I do fully impower my Executors to make Sufficient titles for all my real Estate which they shall sell according to the Directions and Intentions of this my Will. And if there be any Surplus of my Estate after paying all my Debts as aforesaid, I do, in that case, bequeath the following Legacies. But in case there be no Surplus of my Estate after paying my Debts the said Legacies will depend upon the permission or approbation of the said Thomas Frankland, his Executors or

Imprimis. To my beloved Niece, Mrs. Sarah Frankland, my Wedding Ring (Plain Gold) as a particular Mark of my affection and a memento of my Conjugal happiness, not doubting hers is equal, and may it be as lasting.

Item. To my beloved Niece, Mrs. Mary Jane Dry, I give and bequeath my Gold Watch, not of modern Taste but an excellent piece of Mechanism, the Gold Chain and all the Trinkets belonging thereto to be worn in remembrance of her affectionate Aunt, who living or dying wishes her happiness.

Item. To my beloved Nieces, the Daughters of my Sister Moore, viz., Mrs. Sarah Smith, of Charlestown, Mrs. Mary Harlston, of the same place, and Mrs. Ann Swann, of Cape Fear, I give a mourning ring to each of them to be worn in remembrance of their affectionate Aunt, wishing to them and theirs a Series of many happy years.

Item. To my beloved grand Niece, Miss Mary Frankland, I give and bequeath my Silver chased Tea kettle and cream pot and Lamp, as also my walnut tree fineered Tea chest containing three pieces of plate chased as the Tea kettle, in the form of Urns for Tea & Sugar which I beg she will accept as a small Instance of my affection accompanied with my blessing.

Item. I give to my Grand Niece, Miss Hariet Frankland, my largest silver waiter as a small Instance of my affectionate remembrance of her, accompanied with my Blessing.

Item. I give to my Dear Grand Niece, Miss Rebecca Dry, as a small Instance of my Affection, a Dozen tea Spoons and Strainer, in a black Shagreen case, almost new, designed to accompany an eight sided silver coffee pot, put into her possession when I went to England in the year 1756 which I also give to her together with a Shagreen writing stand quite new to encourage her in that part of her Education, in which she seems to be making great progress within these late months.

Item. I give to my beloved Mrs. Mary Jane Dry my Silver sauce pan.

Item. I give to my beloved grand Niece Miss Susanah Hasell a Mohogony dressing table and a little gilt smelling bottle.

Item. I give to my beloved grand Niece Mary Hasell a little mohogony tea Chest—these I give as small tokens of my love and kind Remembrance of them attended with my Blessing.

Item. I give all the books of Modern taste which I shall die possessed of to my grand Nieces before mentioned—Rebecca Dry and Susanah Hasell, to be divided between them as equally as setts can be. And it is my further Request that the books thus bequeathed may be kept for their use and behoof only, not to be lent out and by that means the Sets may be broke before they can use them.

Item. It is my Will and desire that all my wearing apparel

of what kind soever be immoderately put into the hands of my beloved Niece, Mrs. Dry, and my much loved and esteemed Friend, Mrs. DeRossett, Senr., to be disposed of as in their Judgment shall seem meet.

Item. I give to my generous and constant Friend, William Dry, Esquire, a mourning Ring in Testimony of my Sense of his invarrying goodness to me.

Item. I Give to my loved and long esteemed Friend, Mrs. DeRossett, Senr., my Silver Etice in a black Shagreen Case as a small Instance of my affection.

Item. I ordain that the said Mrs. DeRossett and Mrs. Dry have the care of all my private papers. It is also my Request that all Mrs. Franklands Letters, which they will know by the Indorsement, may be sealed up without opening and be sent to her in England by the first safe hand. As to all my other Letters to and from my several Correspondents abroad and in America as also what Miscellanies I have of the amusing kind I commit them entirely to their Discretion.

Item. It is my Will that my Letters and Mr. Allens, of which there are several bundles, be kept sacred from the Eyes of any except these my two Friends whose inclination may perhaps lead them to peruse some of them, after this the fire will be the properest Repository for them and all the rest of my private Letters. The other Letters and papers relating to Business must be left with my Ex"ors after named.

Item. It is my Will that One Acre of Land round the Tomb of my said decd husband be reserved sacred for the use of our Cemetery or burrying Ground by my Executors when the rest of the plantation of Lilliput shall be sold and I do require my Ex"ors to cause a proper pailing to be made round the said Tombstone.

Lastly I nominate and appoint my Friends, James Murray and William Dry, Esquires, and Henry Hyrne, Gent., Executors of this my last Will in this province and in case of the Decease of one or two of them I do nominate and appoint first Frederick Jones of the Oak, Gent., and next Benjamin Hyrne, Gent., to supply the place of such Ex'or or Ex'ors decd and I do further nominate and appoint William Bampfield of South Carolina, Merchant, Executor of this Will as to that part of my Estate which lies in South Carolina.

In Testimony whereof I have set my Hand and Seal unto this my last Will consisting of two Pages this 28th. Day of January In the Year of our Lord one thousand seven hundred and Sixty one.

Signed, Sealed, published and declared by the Testatrix, Sarah Allen, as and for her last Will and Testament in presence of us who   SARAH ALLEN (SEAL) at her Request and in presence of each other have subscribed our names hereto,

   GEORGE MOORE
   ELIZ. CATH. DEROSSETT
   JAMES COLSON.

 WILMINGTON 1 April, 1761. The within written will of Sarah Allen, decd., was duely proved before me by the Oath of George Moore, one of the subscribing Witnesses thereto: At the same time James Murray and William Dry qualified before me as Executors of the within written Will.— Let Letters Testamentary issue thereon to the said James Murray and William Dry accordingly.

             ARTHUR DOBBS.

 These are to Certefy that Henry Hyrne Took the oath of an Executor to the within will before me the 21st February, 1763.

            FRED'K GREGG. J. P.

 Recorded in Will Book 8, page 193, Office of the Secretary of State.

JOHN ARDERNE'S WILL.

NORTH CAROLINA, ss.

 IN THE NAME OF GOD AMEN. I, John Arderne, of North Carolina, though in perfect health and strength of body, of thurough and Sound understanding of mind, praised be Almighty God for it; but considering ye great uncertainty of human life, ye many Contingencys of it, ye certainity of Death, have therefore made this my last will and testament, by it absolutely Revoking and disanulling all former Wills by me made, and declaring this only to be my last will and testament in maner and form following:

 Imprimis. I do in all humillity bequeath my Soul to God y't gave it, and my body to the Ground decently to be Interred as he I shall hereafter Appoint my Sole Execr shall think fitt, in hope and full assurance of a Joyful Resurection to Eternall life, through ye alone merritts and intercession of my Blessed Saviour Jesus Christ.

 And in relation to my worldly Estate; Since it is too often Seen through ye mercinary and Evil designes of many wicked men, to propagate their own Interest, many plain and interpretive Wills have had false, misterious construction put upon y'm, Directly contrary to ye Intent and designe of ye testator, I do therefore, hereby believing it as a Necessary introduction to ye particulars y't follow, and to prevent all cavells and disputes aft'r my death, most Slomnly declare in ye p'rsence of Almighty God, in Gen'er Terms, yt it is hereby my most true and Sincere intent & purpose to give and bequeath Every part and p'cell of my Estate, real and personall, whether in America, England, or any other part of ye world, unto my dearly beloved kinsman, William Duckenfield, Esqr., of ye Aforesd. Province, from whom I have Received ye greatest favours, and to whom I owe ye greatest respect of any person living upon ye face of ye Earth; I further Solomnly declare as a certain truth, as I hope for mercy at Gods hand hereafter, that were I worth Ten Thousand millions of money, and in ye same single state I am in, i would leave it Every farthing to my afores'd kinsman, but for forms sake I shall descend into ye particulars. I know myself to be possest of, and of w't I have a right to in England, and may hereafter be possest of.

Item. I therefore hereby give and bequeath after my death unto my most Dear and Affectionate Kinsman, William Duckinfield, Esqr., all that plantation and tract of Land, called and known by ye name of Salmon Creek, as likewise all ye negro, Indian, Molato Slaves I am now in actuall possesion of, and have right and title to, togeather with all ye of horses, Mares, Colts, Cattle, hoggs, young and Old, or any thing besides I have right and title to in America, England, or any other part of ye world, I hereby give and bequeath ye whole and Every part thereof, after my death, to my dearly beloved Kinsman, Wm. Duckenfield, Esqr.

Item. I further give and bequeath unto my afores'd kinsman, a massy Gold ring, with ye Essines of Death Enamelled upon it, with this Inscription Engraven: post moementum Eternitas, now in possesion of my very hon'ble Relation Sr. John Crew, of Ushkinton, in ye County of Cheshire, in England.

Item. I likewise give and bequeath unto my afores'd Dear kinsman, William Duckinfield, Esqr., a Legacy of two Guineys, bequeath'd to me by my dearly beloved Relation and Choice friend, ye Exelent Lady Crew, now in ye hand and keeping of Sir John Crew.

Item. I likewise give and bequeath unto my Afores'd. dear kinsman, all y't part of my household goods at Clayton bridge house, where my brother Ralph lives, in ye County of Lance-Shire and Parish of Manchester.

Lastly, I further appoint my dear and loving Kinsman Wm. Duckinfield, Esqr., to be my sole Exec'r of this my last will and testament, and to ye full confirmacon hereof, have hereunto set my hand and Seal, in ye prsence of three writing witnesses as ye Law Requires, this 22d of October, in ye year of our Lord 1707.

JOHN ARDERNE. (Seal)

Signed, Sealed and delivered
in ye presence of
    HENRY LYTLE,
    THO. ARNOLD,
    GEO BLAINGE,
    CHARLES BARBOUR,
    JOHN TAYLOR.

NORTH CAROLINA WILLS.

NORTH CAROLINA ss: By the Hon'ble President and councill.

We, being certified that good and lawfull proofs has been made, tl the above written is the last will and testament of John Arderne, Esq deed, a true Coppy whereof is hereunto anexed, and hath therein appoi ed and made William Duckenfield Esqr. Exec'r: These are to Impov the sd William Duckenfield, Esqr., in and upon all and Singular the Goo and Chattles, right and Creditts of the sd John Arderne Esqr., to Ent and the same into their posesion to take, and a true Inventory there Appraised according to Law, to return into the Sectys office within o Year after the date hereof, and ye same to dispose of as by ye sa will appointed.

Given under ye Collonys Seale ye 17th day of April in ye Eleventh Y of her Maj'ties Reigne, annoq Dom 1712.

THO: BOYD,
THO: PETERSON,
EDWARD HYDE,
N. CHEVIN.

Recorded in Will Book 1A, page 47, Office of the Secretary of State.

JOHN BAPTISTA ASHE'S WILL.

NORTH CAROLINA, SC.

IN THE NAME OF GOD, AMEN. I, John Baptista Ashe, Bath County, in the Province of North Carolina, Gent., bein thro' the mercy of Almighty God, of Sound Mind and Memor Do make, appoint, Declare and ordain this and this only t be my last will and Testament, revoking and making void a former Wills by me heretofore made. The Lord have Merc on my Soul for Christs Sake.

Imprimis. I will that all my Just and lawfull Debts be duel paid by My Executors hereafter named; particularly that on hundred pounds, North Carolina Money, or the Value thereq be remitted or paid to the heirs, Exors. or Admins. of Jame Nolan, of Boston, Mariner, deceased; the Sum of Sixty pound of thereabouts having laid in my hands for some years, th Widow who claimed not Complying with the Statute (in tha Case provided) for giving Security to Admtors: but I nov direct that if they cannot Comply Strictly with the Law, Ye rather than faile, their own bonds to whom the money is payable may be taken when the money is paid, to indemnify my Estat against any Creditors which may claim in this Province. Also I will that there be paid as of Debt, to Daniel Hendrick, c South Carolina, Shoemaker, his Exors. or assigns, the Sum o fourty pounds, Current money of this Province. Furthermore I will that there be paid to the Exce. or heirs of Robert Gamsby of Boston, Mariner, deceased, if such be to be found, the sum of fourty pounds, Current money of this province.

Item. I give, bequeath and devise (after payment of debts & legacies) to my three Children, John, Samuel, and Mary, all my personal Estate, to be Equally Devided amoungst them.

Item. I give, devise, and bequeath unto my Son, Samuel, 1 unto my daughter, Mary, my Lands up the north west inch of Cape Fair River, called Ashwood, which are scituate ng and being on the South side of the Said River between the ds of John Porter, of Virginia, Mercht., and the Plantation ereon Daniel Donaho, lately deceased, dwelt, Together with other Lands on the north Side of the River directly oppo- e to those aforementioned, to be equally divided betwixt em, the Said Samuel and Mary, to them, their heirs and signs forever.

Item. I give, devise, and bequeath unto my Son, Samuel, tract of land containing six hundred and fourty Acres lying Stumpy Sound, called Turkey Point; also one other tract ontaining one thousand Acres, called Stump Island or New ver Banks, to him, his heirs or assigns for ever.

Item. I give, devise, and bequeath unto my Son, Samuel, ur hundred Acres of Land lying above William Lewis's plan- tion on the Main Branch of Old Towne Creek, to him, his irs and assigns forever: unless John Russell shall personally me and demand of My Exors. a Bill of Sale for the last men- oned four hundred acres of Land, and Shall pay the ballance Accounts betwixt us, amounting be about fourty pounds oney of South Carolina, Then my Exors. are hereby directed d empowered to Convey the said four hundred Acres of land the said John Russell, to him, his heirs and Assigns for ever.

Item. It is my will that my Sons have their Estates delivered them as they severally arrive to the age of twenty and one ears, and that my daughter have her Estate at the day of Marriage, or age of Twenty and one Years, which shall first appen.

Item. I will that my Slaves be kept to work on my lands, nd that my Estate may be managed to the best advantage, so my sons may have as liberal an Education as the profits nereof afford; and in their Education I pray my Exers. o observe this method: Let them be taught to read and write, nd be introduced into the practical part of Arithmetick, not oo hastily hurrying them to Latin or Grammar, but after they re pretty well versed in these let them be taught Latin & reek. I propose this may be done in Virginia; After which et them learn French, perhaps Some French man at Santee ile undertake this; when they are arrived to years of dis- retion Let them Study the Mathematicks. To my Sons when hey arrive at age I recommend the pursuit & Study of Some rofession or business (I could wish one to ye Law, the other o Merchandize), in which Let them follow their own inclina- ions.

Item. I will that my daughter be taught to write and read some femanine accomplishments which may render her

agreable; And that she be not kept ignorant as to what appe
tains to a good house wife in the management of househo
affairs.

Item. I give to each of my Exors. a Gold Ring as a tok
of the respect which In my life I bore them.

Item. I will that a Brick Vault may be built at Grovele
and my Dear Wifes body taken up out of the Earth & broug
and laid therein; and if it should be my fortune to die in Car
lina so as my Corpse may be Conveyed thither, I desire th
one large Coffin may be made, and both our body's laid togeth
therein and lodged in the said Vault.

Item. I give, devise and bequeath unto my honoured frien
Edward Mosley, Esqr., the one half or moiety of my Land
lying near Rock Fish Creek, on the North West branch
Cape fair River, being twenty five hundred and Sixty Acr
to be equally divided between him and my heir, to him, l
heirs & Assigns forever.

Item. I give, devise and bequeath unto my Loving Broth
John Swann, Six hundred and fourty Acres of land lying
the North East Branch of Cape Fair River, which he boug
of, and of which I have not as yet made him any Conveyanc
it being land adjoining below that whereon my Brother, Samu
Swann, dwells, to him the sd. John Swann, his heirs & assig
forever.

Lastly, I nominate, Constitute and appoint my honour
friends, Edward Moseley & Nathaniel Rice, Esqrs., my goo
friend Mr. Roger Moore, my loving Brothers, Samuel Swan
and John Swann, my good friends, Messers. William Downi
and Edward Smith, to be Executors of this my last will, Test
ment, hereby desiring & praying them to see the same du
Executed.

In witness whereof, I have hereunto set my hand & Sea
this second day of November, Anno Dom., 1731.

JNO. BAPTA. ASHE. (Seal)

Signed, Sealed and Published in
the Presence of us:

    her
  MEHITTOBDE X RUTTER
    mark
  JOHN HAWKINS
  CORNELIUS DARGAN
  MICH. RUTTER.

No. CAROLINA, ss.

I do hereby make a Codicil to be annexed to this my la
will and Testament, and do hereby appoint my Loving frien
Job Hows and Thomas Jones, Executors to my last will ar

stament, and this codicil thereunto annext, together with
b several persons before named in my said last will and Testa-
nt as my Exors. And whereas their is a certain Saw Mill in
ilding between Mr. Mathew Rowan and my Self, It is my
l that my part of the Said Mill together with my part of
b lands thereunto belonging be sold by my said Exors. for
p use of my three children and the money arising by the
e thereof to be Equally divided amongst them.
n testimony whereof, I have hereunto Set my hand and
l this Sixteenth Day of October, 1734.

JNO. BAPTA. ASHE. (Seal)

}igned & Sealed In the Presence
and annext:

  JAMES INNES,
  JOSEPH WALTERS,
  ED'D SMITH.

ITH CAROLINA.

efore his Excelly., Gabriel Johnston, Esq., Captain General, Governor
'hief of the Province of North Carolina, and Ordinary of the Same.
ersonally came before me Michael Rutter, one of the Witnesses to
within Instrument, being the last Will and Testament of John Baptista
e, Esq., who being duely sworn on the Holy Evangelists, declared that
was present and saw the said John Baptista Ashe, Esq., Sign, Seal,
lish and declare the same to be his last will; and that he was at the
e time of sound and disposing mind and memory and understanding,
he best of this deponents knowledge; and that he saw John Hawkins,
nelius Dargan & Mihitobade Rutter, three other signing witnesses,
ent at the execution of the said Instrument and sign their names or
k thereunto.
ikewise, Personally appeared James Innis, Esq., one of the witnesses
he Codicil annexed to the said Instrument or Last Will and Testament
)rsd, who being duely sworn on the holy Evangelists, saith, that he
 the Said John Baptista Ashe, Esq., duely execute and publish the
Codicil as the codicil of his last Will and Testament, and that he was
he same time of sound mind and memory to the best of this deponen;s
wledge, and that he saw Joseph Waters and Edward Smith, the two
er signing Witnesses present at the Execution of * * *
iven under my hand at Brunswick, the 15th day of November, Anno
n., 1734.

GAB. JOHNSTON.

November ye 30th, 1734.

ersonally appeared before me Edward Moseley, Roger Moore, Samuel
ohn Swann, Esqrs., & took ye oath appointed by law to be taken by
cutors.

W. SMITH, C. J.

'opied from Original Will, filed in the office of the Secretary of State.

WILLIAM ARENTON'S WILL.

IN THE NAME OF GOD, AMEN. I, William Arenton, of Craven County, and Province of North Carolina, Planter, being in perfect Sound mind and Memory, thanks be to God, but Calling to mind the uncertainty of this life, do make and Declare this to be my last will and Testament, in Manner and form following.

& First, I Recommend my Soul unto the allmighty God who gave it, hoping for Pardon for all my Sins through the Merits and Mercy of Jesus Christ my Saviour and Redemer, and my body to the Earth, and as for my Temporal Estate which it hath pleased God to bestow upon me I Give and Dispose of the Same in Manner and form following:

Imprimis. my will and Desire is that my well beloved wife Mary Arenton have the use of the Plantation Whereon I now live during the time of her life.

Item. I Give and bequeath unto my well beloved wife Mary Arenton One third part of all My Estate of horses, Cattle & hoggs and Household Goods to her and her heirs for ever.

Item. I Give and bequeath unto my three Children, Rebeccah, Mary and Leah Arenton, all the rest of my Estate to be Equally Devided Amongst them when they Come to Age or Marriage.

Lastly. I Doe hereby Nominate, Constitute, Ordain and appoint my friend Henry Shippard Executor of this my last will and Testament, And I Doe hereby utterly Disallow and Make Void all and every Other will or wills, Legacys and bequests heretofore done or Made, Rattifying and Confirming this and no Other to be my last will and Testament.

In Witness Whereof he hath hereunto sett his hand and Seal this 23d Day of January, 1761.

W. A. (His Seal)

Signed Sealed Published & Declared by the Said William Arenton to be and Contain his last will & Testament in the Presence of us the Subscribers

EDMUND HATCH
MARTIN X SHIPPARD.
his mark

Copied from Original Will filed in the Office of the Secretary of State.

DAVID BAILEY'S WILL.

IN THE NAME OF GOD AMEN. This sixth day of October, Anno Dom. 1745. I, David Bailey, of Pasquotank County, in the Province of No. Carolina, Esqr., being not well in health, but of perfect mind & memory, thanks be given to God therefore, calling to mind the mortality of my body & knowing that it is appointed unto all men once to die, do make & ordain this, as my last will & Testament, That is to say:

Principally & first of all, I recommend my soul into ye hands of God that gave it, &c., and my Body to the ground, to be buried at the Discretion of my Exs. hereafter named. And as touching such worldy Estate wherewith it hath pleased God to bless me in this life, I give demise & bestow ye same, in manner & form following:

Impr. I give & bequeath to my well beloved Wife, Thamar Bailey, all the Cattle up Pasquotank River, that I had by her and also, all other Goods & Effects that were properly her own before our intermariage, also the sum of four hundred pounds Current paper money, to be paid to her by my Exs. hereafter named.

It. I give & order that my negro fellow Andrew, be sold at a publick Vendue, to help raise the afsd. money; & that my wife be not debar'd the liberty of bidding for him (if she see Cause.)

It. I Give & bequeath to my well beloved Daughter, Elizabeth Bryant, one negro wench named joney, also one Dutch Linnen wheel.

It. I give & bequeath to my well beloved son, Joseph Bailey, the Plantation whereon he now dwells, together with all the land thereunto belonging, to him & his Heirs for ever; also four steers runing on ye sd. Land.

It. I give & bequeath my negro fellow called Jones, to my son, Joseph Bailey, also my negro wench called Moll; also my negro boy called Luke; also the one half of my Whip-saw; also one Steel-Trap; also one Corn Mill; also one Walnut-oval Table besides what he has recvd. before.

It. I give & bequeath to my well beloved son, Benjamin Bailey, one negro boy called Mosee; also Two yoke of Oxen; also my old Flat; also all the Steers down ye River that shall be in being at my death.

It. I give & bequeath to my well beloved son, Benjamin Bailey, ye Land & Plantation I bought of Ebenezer Hall, containing Two Hundred & six acres, lying in this County, to him & his Heirs for Ever.

It. I give to my Daughter, Sarah Snowdon, the use & service of my negro wench called Ruth, during my sd. Daughter's life, and after her decease I give and bequeath the sd. negro wench called Ruth, and all her increase, to the Heirs lawfully begotten of my sd. Daughter Sarah's body; also three Ews & Lambs.

It. I Give & Bequeath to my well beloved son, Robert Bailey, my Land & Plantation, the Folly, to him & his heirs for Ever; also one negro boy called James; also the one half of my negro Girl Called Doll; also one feather Bed & furniture, wch is now down ye River; also one black mare, wch I Bought of Joseph Lowry, branded With E. L., Two Cows & Calves wch is down ye River; also one Case of Bottles; also the half of the new Schooner; also the half of my whip saw, one Steel Trap; one very large Iron Pot, one iron pot Trammel.

It. I give & bequeath to my well beloved Son, Simon Bailey, my plantation & Land Called Piney Point, lying at Core Sound, contianing Three hundred acres p. Patent, to him & his Heirs for Ever; also all my Cattle upon that Plantation of the Plantation mark, being a swallow fork in ye right Ear, the left Ear off; also one negro fellow called Mustipher; also the other half of my negro wench called Doll; also my Will & order is, That the increase of the sd. negro Doll, pass, the first child to my son, Robert, the next to my son, Simon, & so on, and if there be an odd one, the same to be Equally divided between them; also one bed & furniture, wch is in my Room at my son, Joseph Bailey's; also Two Cows & Calves, one young mare branded with D. B. & called Wren; also one small Trunk, & fifteen pounds in Gold & Silver in it of Virginia Currency; also all ye Hives of Bees on ye plantation abovesd; also Two Cows & Calves.

It. I give & Bequeath to my Daughter, Tamar Bailey, the work & service of my negro Wench called Hannah, during my sd. daughter's life, and after her decease, I give & bequeath my sd. negro Hannah, and all her increase, to the Heirs lawfully begotten of my sd. Daughter's body; also one bed & furniture, wch is down the River; also one young Mare called no-fail; one Trunk, one white Chest, one Case of Bottles, one Looking Glass, one Box-iron Heaters, Three Pewter Dishes, one set of Tea ware; also one Dutch Linnen Wheel, also one Woolen Wheel made at Core Sound; also Two Cows & Calves, one iron pot that I bought of Sarah Snowdon; one iron pot Trammel; also one young Horse called Button.

It. I give & bequeath to my second Wife's Daughter, Miriam Overman, one negro Girl called Hagar & her increase, to her & the Heirs of her body.

It. I give & bequeath to my second Wife's son, David Wallis, the work & service of a young negro Boy of mine, called Jeffrey, towards his maintaining & bringing up, till he shall arrive to ye age of Twenty one years; but if the sd. David

Wallis, shall happen to die before he Shall attain to that age, then the sd. negro Jeffrey, to return to me & my heirs; but if the sd. David Wallis shall live to the full age of Twenty one years, then the sd. negro Jeffrey is to be his for Ever.

It. I give & bequeath to my sons, Joseph Bailey, Robert Bailey, & my son in law, Simon Bryant, all my neat Cattle & Sheep marked with a swallow fork in ye right Ear, the loft Ear off; also all my Horses and Mares branded with D. B., wch are running upon the banks at Core Sound, Equally among them; also all the neat cattle upon Hunting Quarter, belonging to me, marked with a Poplar Leaf in ye left Ear, & a Crop & a slit in ye right.

It. I will, bequeath & strictly order, That all the rest & residue of my personal Estate, not mentioned in this will, and wch shall be found in this County, and within the Lord Carteret's line, be sold at publick Vendue to the highest bidder, and the monies thereby arising (my Wife's Legacy first discharged), to be Equally divided between my Children, Viz: Elizabeth Bryant, Joseph Bailey, Benjamin Bailey, Sarah Snowdon, Robert Bailey, Tamar Bailey & Simon Bailey; also for my Exs. to take care of my son, Simon Bailey & bring him up.

It. I nominate, constitute and appoint my son Joseph Bailey, and my son in law, Simon Bryant, Co-Executors of this my last Will & Testament, to see the same perform'd to the utmost of their power, utterly revoking, disannulling & making void all former or other Wills, Testaments, Legacies and bequests, formerly by me in any wise made, willed or bequeathed. Ratifying & confirming this & no other, as my last Will & Testament.

In Witness whereof, I have hereunto put my hand & Seal, the Day & year first afore written.

DAVID BAILEY (Seal).

Signed, Sealed, published, pronounced & declared by ye Sd. David Bailey, as his last Will & Testament, in presence of us the Subscribers:
  THOS. WEEKES, Jurat,
  PATRICK BAILEY, Jurat,
  JOHN BAILEY.

NO. CAROLINA.   March the 29th., 1746.

Thomas Weeks & Patrick Bailey, Two of the Subscribing evidences to the Within Will appeared before me and made Oath on the Holy Evangelists, that they were present & Saw David Bailey, Sign, Seal, Publish and Declare the within to be & Contain his last Will and Testament; and that the said David Bailey was then, and at that time of Sound & disposing Memory; and that they also See John Bailey, the Other Subscribing

Evidence sign his Name thereto at the Same time. Then also appeared Simon Bryan & Joseph Bailey and took the Oath by Law appointed to be taken by Exrs.

ENOCH HALL, C. J.

Copied from Original Will, filed in the Office of the Secretary of State.

HENRY BAKER'S WILL.

IN THE NAME OF GOD AMEN. I, Henry Baker, of Chowan, No. Carolina, being in good health of Body & of Sound & perfect mind & Memory, praise be therefore given to almighty God, Do make & ordain this psent. last will & testament, in Manner & form following, that is to Say:

First & principally I commend my Soul into the hands of almighty God, hoping thro' the merits, Death & Pasion of my Saviour Jesus Christ, to have full & free parden & forgiveness of all my Sins & to Inherit everlasting life; & my Body I commit to the earth to be buried at the Discretion of my Executors hereafter named; & touching all Such temporal Estate as it hath pleased almighty god to bestow upon me, I give as follows:

First, I will that all my Debts & funerall Charges be paid & Discharged.

Item. I give to my Son, Henry, all the Land whereon I now live, to him and his heirs.

Item. I give unto my Son, Henry, these Negroes, vizt: Guy, Clouse, Bobb, Ceasar, ned, Jacob, young Diner, & hagar & their increase.

Item. I give unto my Son, Henry, my watch, Seal, Desk, Six rusia Chares, ye great Glass, my Sword, one ovel table, besides what I have already or heretofore given him.

Item. I give to my Son John all my land at a place called Little Town, & my Land joining on Banks, Wynn & ascue, & the Land bought of William Garrat, all in Bertie precinct, with ye Stock thereto belonging, to him & his heirs.

Item. I give unto my Son John these negros vizt: Arthur, Juno, Finney, little Bobb & Dick & their increase.

Item. I give to my Son, Blake, my land bought of John and Thomas Wickings in Chowan, & five hundred acres thereto adjoining, wch I took up; & my land at Ahoskey marsh in Bertie & the Stock thereto Belonging, to him & his heirs.

Item. I give to my son, Blake, these negroes vizt: Cipio, Joe, Patt & Argalus & their increase.

Item. I Give to my Daughter Mary, these Negroes, Vizt: Darby, Lucey, & Peter, and their Increase.

Item. I give to my Daughter, Sarah, these negroes, Cato & Priss & their Increase.

Item. I give to my Son, David, 130 acres of Land at Meherring landing adjoining to the ferry, to him & his heirs.

Item. I give to my Daughter Ruth twenty shillings.

Item. I give to my Son Ladock (?) twenty shillings.

Item. My will & desire is that my wife, Ruth, have the use of these negroes, Vizt: Tom, Benbo, Daniel, Dinah & Joyce, Brady, during her natural life & after her Decese I give Tom & Dinah to my Son, Henry, Daniel to my Son, John, & Benbo to my Son, Blake.

Item. I give to my wife, Ruth, all the rest & residue of my personall Estate whatsoever & my will & desire is that my wife, Ruth, have & enjoy the Back room and Entry & half ye Orchard to be Divided from the house Westerly & Land adjoining to the plantation to worke on Dureing her Naturall life or widdowhood.

Item. My will & Desire is that if it so happens that my Son, John, Should Die in his Minority, that then the Land I have given him Shall go to my Son, Blake, & his heirs.

My will is that my land at ye Knuckles, in Nansemond, be Sold by my Exrs. towards ye payment of my Debts.

I do hereby nominate, Constitute, ordain & appoint my Brother, William Baker, to be my Executor; & in case of his Death, I do appoint my Brother, James Baker; & in case of his Death, I do appoint my Brother, Lawrence Baker, of this my last Will & Testament, revoaking & making null & void all former Wills.

In Witness whereof, I have hereunto set my hand & Seal, this Ninth Day of January, 1737.

HENRY BAKER, (Seal).

Signed, Sealed, publisht & Declared by the Sd. Henry Baker as his last Will & Testament in prsence of us the Subscribers,

EDWARD VANN,
JOHN BRADY,
EDWARD WARREN.

May ye 1st., 1739.

Came before me Edward Vann, John Brady & Edward Warren, & Made Oath that they Saw Henry Baker Sign, Seal and publish ye within as his last will & testament; & that he was of Sound & Disposing mind & Memory at that time & That these Deponents Subscribed as Witnesses thereto. At ye Same time William Baker took the Oath appointed by law to be taken by Executors.

W. SMITH, C. T.

Recorded in Grant Book No. 4., Will No. 81.

JOHN BARCLIFT'S WILL.

No. Carolina, Perqs. County, ss.

In the Name of god Amen, the 23d of April 1759. I, John Barclift, of the County and Province aforesd, farmer, being Weak in Body, but of a Perfect mind and Memory, thanks be to god for the Same, Therefore Calling to mind the Mortality of my Body and knowing that it is appointed for all men once to die, do make and ordain this my last will & Testament, that is to say:

Principally & first of all, I Recommend my soul into the hands of God that gave it, & my Body I Recommend to the earth to be Burried in Decent Christian Burial at the Discretion of my Executors, hereafter Named; and as for Such worldly Estate it hath pleased God to bless me in this Life, I Give Devise and Bequeath in the following manner and form:

Imprs. I Give and Bequeath to my Loving Wife Elizabeth Barclift the use of one third part of the Plantation and Land whereon I now live during her natural Life, together with the use of the outward Room & upper Chamber of my house & also the use of the Lower Room of my Brick house; also I give to my wife the use and Labour of one negro man Called Tom and the use & Labour of one Negro woman Called joan During her natural life; also the use of my large Looking Glass, during her Natural Life; also the use of my desk during her Natural Life; also the use of one Chest; and the use of one Dozon of Chairs; also the use of one large Brass Kittle; also the use of one large iron Kittle, & the use of two iron Pots, she having her Choice; also the use of one yoke of Stears, with yoke, Ring and Staple, and two Ploughs; also the use of all the she Cattle in my Stock that runs on the Plantation whereon I now live; also the use of one Feather Bed & furniture, she having her choice; also the use of one large black-Walnut Table, & the use of one 15 Bottle-Case; also one 3 Gallon jugg, & one Gallon Ditto; also the use of all my Pewter; also the use of one Black horse, also the use of Six Ewes & Lambs; also the use of 3 Iron Wedges; also the use of one falling ax, also the use of one hilling hoe & two weeding hoes and two Pr. Pot trammels & 2 Pr. Pot-hooks & Gridiron, & ho-cake-hoe; also the use of one Box iron & heaters, & one Tea Kittle, & one Sive and one Search; also two Buckets & two tubs; also one Pr. small Stilliards also one hand-mill being Cullen Stones; also Six Breeding Sows.

Item. I Give to my Daughter Eliza: Sanderson one Negro Girl called Rachel, also one Negroe Boy Called jemmy, also one Negro Boy called Toney, (being already Delivered to her) to her & her Heirs for ever; also I give to my Daughter Eliza.

Sanderson one feather Bed and furniture and one Mare, and Six head of Sheep, also one iron pot & one iron Kittle, with Sundry other things of small Value in her own Possession already deliver'd to her Since her Marriage.

Item. I Give to my Daughter Eliza: Sandersons Son John Sanderson, the first Child that my Negro Woman joan shall bring after the date of this writing to him and his Heirs for erve.

Item. I Give to my son Asa Barclift one hundred & Twenty five Acres of Land out of the Tract whereon I now live, Beginning at the head of the Line & running towards the River along Joshua Maudlins line as far as the Bridge & then up the Branch as far as is Required to make out the Hundred & Twenty five Acres holding its breadth out to the head of the Land, to him & his Heirs lawfully begotten for ever; and in Case he should Die without Heir my Will is that my Son Demson Barclift & his Heirs Lawfully begotten shall Possess & Enjoy the sd Land. I also give to my son Asa Barclift one Negro Boy Called Mosey, also one negro boy Called Luke, also one Negro Girl Called Dina, to him and his heirs for ever; Also I give my son Asa one Flax hacke.

Item. I Give to my Son Demson Barclift the remaining Part of the Plantation & Land whereon I now live to him and his heirs Lawfully begotten for ever; and in Case he should Die without Heir my Will is that my son Asa Barclift and his heirs shall Possess and enjoy the sd. Land. I also give to my Son Demson Barclift one Negro Boy Called Sampson, also one negro Girl Called Grace, also one Negro Boy Called Robin, to him and his Heirs for ever; I also give to my son Demson Barclift one Large Bible, also one young Mare, also one yoke of Stears, also one feather Bed and furniture, also one case with 15 Bottles, also one Plough Chan, also one iron Pot, also one small Gun, also my Shoemakers Tools, also one large looking-Glass and one Dozon of Chairs after my Wife's Decease.

Item. I Give to my Son Benjamin Barclift the upper part of my Land at the mark-Poplar on the North Side of the Road, beginning just above the high rooted Beach Branch at a Beach, then running a Straight Course to the Corner Trees of Frances Layden & Peter Cartwright, being an Elm & a White Oak standing about 5 or 6 Steps apart then running along Peter Cartwrights line to the Road then Down the Road to the first Station, to him & his heirs Lawfully Begotten for ever: and in Case he should Die without Heir my Will is that my Son Noah Barclift and his Heirs shall Possess and Enjoy the sd. Land; I also give to my son Benja. Barclift one Negro Boy Called Dick, also one Negro Girl called Nan, also one Negro Boy called Isaac, to him & his heirs for ever: I also give to my son Benja. Barclift one Still, one 12 Bottle Case, also one feather Bed & furniture, also one young Mare, also a Set of

Shoe-makers Tools, also one Pr. of Pot-trammels, also one Pr. of Shell-mill-Stones & one Plough Chain, also one small Gun.

Item. I Give to my son John Barclift part of my Land at the mark Poplar lying on the South Side of the Road begining at a Red Oak, Standing in the bottom of the high-rooted-Beach-Branch, then running Down the Branch to the Creek, then down Pruze Creek to a point Called Aarons point then up Batemans Creek to Batemans line, then along Batemans line to the Road, then down the Road to the first Station; to him & his Heirs Lawfully begotten for ever; & in case he Should Die without Heir, my will is that the sd. Land be Equally divided between my two Sons Benjamin and Noah; I also give to my son John Barclift one Negro Girl called Tamar, also I give my son Jno. Barclift one Negro Boy Called jo, also one Negro Girl Called Doll, to him and his Heirs for ever; also one feather Bed and furniture; also one Gold-ring, one Young mare and one Pr. of Pot Trammels.

Item. I give to my son Noah Barclift all the remaining part of my Land at the Mark-Poplar (not heretofore given,) to him and his Heirs for Ever and in Case he should Die without Heir my Will is that my Son Benjamin & his Heirs shall Possess and enjoy the sd. Land; I also give to my Son Noah Barclift one Negro boy Called George, also one Negro Girl Called Pleasant, also one Negro Girl Called Rose. I also give to my son Noah Barclift one Silver Cup after my Wife's Decease.

Item. I Give to my Daughter Mary Barclift one Negro Girl Called Esther, one Negro Boy Called Anthony, and one Negro Girl Called Judah, to her and her Heirs for ever; also one warming pan, also one Feather Bed and furniture after my Wife's Decease—being the Bed that I gave the use of to my wife.

Item. my Will & Desire is that my iron-tooth drag be for the use of all my sons, and the longest liver to keep it.

Item. My will and Desire is that my three Negro Women (that is to say) Hagar, Ruth, and Moll, and their increase, also the Increase of my Negro Woman Joan that is not already given, be Equally Divided amongst my five Sons & Daughter Mary, when the youngest of them comes to age.

Item. I Give to my son Asa Barclift one Negro woman Called Joan after my wife's Decease, she having the Labour of her during her Life.

Item. I Give to my son Noah Barclift one Negro man Called Tom after my wife's Decease, she having the Labour of him during her Life.

Item. My Will and desire is that my negro man Peter be sold at the discretion of my Executors and the Money arising be apply'd towards paying Debts and Charges, & also I desire that such a part of my Estate as my Excrs shall think Perishable may likewise be sold & the money apply'd as aforesaid.

Item. My Will is that after my Wife's Decease all that I have given her the use of (Except what I have already Disposed of) may be Equally Divided Amongst my five Sons & Daughter Mary.

Item. My Will and Desire is that all the remaining part of my Estate not already given, together with the overplush of the money arising by the Sale of any of my Estate (if any there be) be Equally divided between my wife and Six Children, that is to say, Demson, Benjamin, John, Asa, Noah, and Mary as they come to Age.

And I do hereby nominate, Constitute & Appoint Samll. Sutton & Thomas Stevenson, to be my whole & Sole Executors of this my last will and Testament and I do hereby utterly disallow, revoke and Disannul all and every former Testaments, Wills, Legacies, Bequests and Excrs. by me in any way before named, Willed, and Bequeathed: Ratifying and Confirming this and no other to be my last Will and Testament.

In Witness whereof I have hereunto set my hand & Seal the day and year above Written.

JOSEPH BARCLIFT (Seal).

Signed, Sealed, Published, Pronounced and Declared by the sd. Jno. Barclift as his last Will and Testament In Presence of

  JAMES GIBSON, Jurat,
  SAMLL. BARCLIFT, Jurat,
  MATHIAS JOHNSON, Jurat.

No. CAROLINA, PERQMS. COUNTY.   July Court, Anno Dom. 1759.

Present his Majestys Justices, & This Certifies that James Gibson & Samll. Barclift, two of the Subscribing Evidences to the within will, appeared In Court and made Oath that they were Present and Saw John Barclift Sign, Seale, Publish & Declare the within to Be and Containe his Last will and Testament and that they also saw Mathias Jonston Sign his Name thereto at the same time. Then allso appd. Samuel Sutton & Thomas Stevenson Executors In Court, take & took the Excrs oath In Due form of Law.

Ordered that the Hon. Richd. Spaight, Esqr., Secrtry of this Province have notice thereof that Lettrs. Testamentary Issue thereon as the Law Directs, &c.

    (Test) MILES HARVEY, Clk cr.

Copied from Original Will filed in the office of the Secretary of State.

WILLIAM BARROW'S WILL.

IN THE NAME OF GOD AMEN, I, William Barrow, of ye precinct of Hide, in ye County of Bath, in ye Prov°. of North Carolina, being Sick & weak of Body but of sound and perfect mind & memory and Calling to mind ye Certainety of Death and not knowing when it may pleas ye Lord to Call mee out of this life do make and ordaine & appoynt this my last Will and Testament, in maner and forme following:

Imp: I give, devise & bequeath to my three Sons, William, John & Richard Barrow, my Plantation whereon I now live, Containing ffouerteen hundred Acres of land more or les, to be Equally devided between my afsd. three Sons, that is my Eldest Son William Barrow to have ye maner Plantation whereon I now live after my Wifes Dec: to be held of them & Every of them their heirs and assignes in fee simple for ever.

Itm. I give devise & bequeath to my Other three Sons, Samuel, Joseph and James Barrow, all my Tract of Land lying & being upon Broad Creeke Containeing one Thousand Acres of land more or les, to be Equally devided between my sd. three Sons namd: Samuel, Joseph & Jams. Barrow to be held of them, their heirs & assignes Severally, In fee simple for ever.

Itm. I give and bequeath to my Son, William Barrow, all and every part of my Smithe tools, and my longest Gun or fouleing peace to be at his disposall when he shall attaine to ye: age of one & twenty years.

Itm. I give and bequeath to my Son, John, all & Every part of my Coopers tooles, and my Shortest gun to be at his disposall when he shall attaine to ye age of twenty one years.

Itm. All the rest & residue of my Estate over & above ye legasies before given So Comeing & remaineing boath personall & reall, the one third part of which so riseing I give to my Loveing wife Eliz. Barrow, and ye remaineing part after her full one third part so taken oute I give & bequeath to my six Sons before named & to my two Daughrs Ann & Sarah Barrow to be Equally Divided among my sd. Six Sons & two Daughs. to be at their disposall, that in my sd. Six Sons afsd. as they shall respectively attaine to ye age of twenty one years & my two Daughs: to have at ye age of Eighteen Years or ye day of marriage.

Itm. My Will & desire is that my Lov. Wife, Eliz. Barrow, have the use and ocquepation of my plantation whereon I now live together with all houeses, orchards & all other Conveniances there unto belonging with oute Molestation or Incumbrance dureing her naturall life and after her dec: then to my son, William Barrow, his heirs for ever more as afsd. that is, my will & desire is that my sd. three Sons, William, John and Richard Barrow, Shall not be hendered or debarred fron Seat-ing on Conveniant parts of ye sd. Lands so given them when they shall attain Respectively to ye age of twenty one Years.

Itm. I doe appoynt my Loveing wife, Eliz. Barrow, and my Son, William, to be Joynt Execs. of this my last will & Testament as witness my hand & Seal this 8th. Day of Jan'ry, 1715.

THOS. BONNER,   W. BARROW. (Seal)
THO. MARTIN,
JNO. PORTER.

This may Certifye That on the 23d. Day of Octo., 1716. The above written will was proved by the Oath off John Porter.

before me,

GALE, Ch: Just.

Eliz. Barrow one of Exrs. within & above mencond took the Oath for prformance of ye before written will in presence of:

GALE, Ch: Just

Copied from Original Will filed in Office of the Secretary of State.

EDWARD BATCHELOR'S WILL.

IN THE NAME OF GOD AMEN. I, Edward Batchelor, of the Town of New-Bern, in the State of North Carolina, being Sick, and weak in Body, but of Sound Mind, memory and understanding, do make and publish this my last Will and Testament in manner and form following, to wit: first I recommend my Soul into the Hands of almighty God; and my Body I commit to the Earth to be decently buried at the Discretion of my Executors hereafter Named; and as touching the Disposition of all my temporal Estate, I give & Dispose thereof as followeth:

Imprimis. I Will that my Debts and funeral Charges shall be paid and Discharged.

I give and bequeath unto my well beloved Wife, Francis Batchelor, all my household Furniture plate and every Article of Kichen Furniture &c; I also give and bequeath unto my Said Wife one Negro Wench named Cordera, and a negro man Named Frank for and During her natural Life and after her Decease my Will is the Negro Wench Corderia shall go to my Daughter Elizabeth and the Negro Frank shall go to my Son John to him and their Heirs and assines.

I also give to my eldest Daughter, Elizabeth, the increase of the above mentioned Negro Wench Cordera in case She has Children; and my Gold Watch.

I also give and bequeath unto my Son, John Batchelor, a Tract of Lying on Susquehanna in Pensilvania, and my wearing apparel.

I also give and bequeath unto my Son, Edward Batchelor, a negro Boy named Moody, and also my Stock Buckel and Sleve Buttons.

I also give and bequeath unto my Daughter, Frances Batchelor, a negro Wench and child, the Wench Named Judah and her Increase & that my estate to be charged for these two Negros, and Credit given the Partnership of Assheton & Batchelor for the Value of them when they came into the Country.

It is my Will and Desire that my good friend, Thomas Assheton, shall have the Management and is Impowerd hereby, to Receive all Debts due and Owing to me on my private account in Pensylvania and the Jerseys for the use of my private account and family, and that if my Said Thomas Assheton should Die before such Settlement is finished that then and for the Same purpose, I do hereby apoint my Good friend, John Chevilear, Esquire, to do the Bussiness for the purposes aforesaid.

And it is my Will and Desire that as soon as it may be convenient after After my Decease, that the Accounts of the Partnership of Assheton & Batchelor may be Generally Settled, and for that purpose all the Goods on Hand, and Negros, the following Vessels in which the partnership of Assheton and Batchelor is concerned with other people in Interest of Vessels and Cargo, Vizt: one half of the Sloop Betsey in partnership with Seamore Hood; One quarter of the Schooner Called the Patrick Henry, in partnership with Stacey Hebum & Seamore Hood; One Sixth part of the Sloop Lydia, in company with Jno. Wright Stanly & others. Those Vessels being now on their Voyages at Sea to be Sold on their Return, that is to say, that part of the Said Vessels & Cargoes which is above Mentioned belonging to the Comp^y of Assheton & Batchelor. Three Quarters of the Ship Called Harmony Hall, now lying in the Harbour of New Bern with a Cargo on Board bound to France, whereof John Darcius is One Quarter Owner, who was to get the Said Ship Insured at Charles Town, if so, I would not have Our part Sold untill she has made the Voyage and returned, But if the Insurance Shou'd not be made, I do in that Case Will & require that the three Quarters of the Said Ship belongin to the partnership of Assheton & Batchelor may be Sold immediately after my Decease before the Voyage is made. The new Ship Called the Harriot, now lying at my warf, also a small Sloop called the Dolphin, and the Schooner Called the Lively, now lying in the Dock at my Wharf, all belonging the partnership of Assheton & Batchelor, my desire is that those three last Mentioned Vessels be also Sold for the Account of the Said Partnership. And my Will and Desire is that the Concerns of the Partnership of Assheton and Batchelor may be as Soon as convenient Generally and finally Settled, and that

After the partnerships Debts are paid and Satisfied the Amount of My Share of the Stock in trade my Will and Desire is that the Same bed is posed of in the following manner, that is to say:

I give and bequeath unto my well beloved Wife, Francis Batchelor, fifteen hundred pounds, to be paid unto her After the Settlement is made by my Executors.

I also give and bequeath to each of my Children the like Sum of fifteen hundred pounds each, to be put out at Interest untill the Boyes Shall arive to the Age of Twenty one, and the Girls to the Age of eighteen years old, and do appoint my well beloved wife Guardein to my Said Children, with the Advice of my Executors. And it is my Will and desire that if After a Settlement of Partnerships Concerns there Shou'd remain more money then is required to pay the sum of fifteen hundred pounds to my wife and the like Sum to each of my Children according to the above bequists, that then the Overplus be equally devided between my wife and Children. And if my Interest Shou'd fall Short of the Sum of fifteen Hundred pounds each, then each of them to have as much less in proportion so that what they are to receive may be equal to each. And it is my Will & request that my children be kept at school and that they may Virtuously brought up in the Fear of God, and the Interest of the money shall be applied to Defray the expence of Education; And it is my further Will and Desire that if any of my Children shou'd Die before they arive at age that then their part of money &c., shall be Equally Devided among the Survivors.

I also give and bequeth unto my Beloved wife, my Horse and two Chairs, Harness, Saddle, &c., to her only Sole use, benefit & behoof and also all the Rest and Residue and remainder of my Worldly Goods and effects whatsoever I give devise and bequeath unto my Said Wife.

And I hereby Nominate and Appoint my good friends Thomas Assheton of Philadelphia, Dr. Thos. Hasline of New Bern, & Frances Batchelor my Wife, Executors and Executrix of this my last Will and Testament hereby revoking all former Will and Wills by me heretofore made.

In Witness whereof I have hereunto Sett my hand & Seal this——day of November, 1777.

Signed, Sealed, published and Declared by the Above Named Edward Batchelor as and for his last Will & Testament in the presence of us who have hereunto Subscribed Our Names as Witnesses thereto, and in the presence of each other:

(Seal.)

N. B. The Words interlined, between the Tenth and Eleventh Lines & to the end of that paragraph (for and during her Natural life and after her Decease my Will is the negro Wench Corderia shall go to my Daughter, Elizabeth; and the negro Frank shall go to my Son John to them their Heirs and Assignes) were entered so before Signing & other words Interlined, to wit: My, her,

NORTH CAROLINA, CRAVEN COUNTY ss.

This day about Seven o'Clock after noon, personally appeared before me, Joseph Leech, one of the Justices for said County, Richard Cogdell, Esqr., Who being Sworn on the Holy Evangelists Declareth, that on tuesday the twenty first, Instant, November, a Messenger came and told him Mr. Batchellor was very Ill and desired to See him, that he went to Mr. Edward Batchelor's, who sayed he had Been for some time very Sick and in a bad State of health, and was desirous of making his Will and wanted the favour of his assistance to do it. In Compliance thereto said Cogdell took down in writing several Instructions from said Mr. Batchelor about the Same and after having prepared the same, the next day waited on Mr. Batchelor with it, and read it to him, with which he approved, and then gave him some further directions for finishing and compleating his said Will, all but the naming of an Executor, which he desired him to Leave a Blank for, as he had not spoken to the person he wanted to nominate, which said further directions said Cogdell also took down in writing, and the next morning, which was yesterday morning, he finished the said Will according to Mr. Batchelor's directions as above mentioned, and Carried it to him and read it, all of which he the said Mr. Batchelor approved off, but desired him to call again in the Evening, to fill up the blanks for the Executor, as he had not yet spoke to the person he wanted to ask, and then to have the Will Executed, Which the said Cogdell accordingly did, but finding him asleep, did not care to have him disturbed, but went the next morning again, which was this morning about ten or Eleven o'Clock, with the Said Will What is the Will hereto annexed, and which is the Will he drew from the said Mr. Edward Batchellors own Instructions and read to said Batchellor which he approved off as his Last Will and Testament, and then desired him to fill up the blank for the Executor with the name of Doctor Thomas Haslen as one of his Executors, which he did. And the said Batchellor was afterwards in the afternoon twice raised up in the bed to Sign it, but being taken with Such violent pains could not Set up Long Enough to do it, and about five o'Clock this afternoon died away, to all appearance in Sound Mind and perfect Sences, and further this deponant Sayeth not.

RD. COGDELL.

Newbern, November 27, 1777.
Sworn to Before me:
JOSEPH LEECH, J. P.

NORTH CAROLINA, CRAVEN COUNTY. ss.

This day about Seven o'Clock after noon, also Personally Appeared before me, Joseph Leech, one of the Justices for said County, Mr. Michael Gorman, who being Sworn on the Holy Evangelists Declareth that he well knows that Richard Cogdell, Esqr., attended every day at Mr. Edward Batchellor's for several days before he died for the purpose of drawing his Will, and that he this Deponant, with Mr. John Flynn, were both called up between five and Six o'Clock this afternoon to Mr. Batcheler's room where he was Laying sick to be Evidences to his Signing his Will, and that the Said Batchelor was twice Lifted up in his bed to Sign it but was taken with Such violent pains he could not keep up Long Enough and died away before he could Sign it, Seemingly to him in Sound Mind and perfect Sences, and that the Will hereto annexed is the Same Will that Richard

Cogdell, Esq., had in his hand which Mr. Batchelor was then going to Sign which they were called to Evidence and further this deponant Sayeth not.

MICHL. GORMAN.

Newbern, November 27th., 1777.
Sworn to before me,
JOSEPH LEECH, J. P.

NORTH CAROLINA, CRAVEN COUNTY. ss

This day also, about Seven o'Clock after noon, Personally appeared before me, Joseph Leech, one of the Justices for the Said County, Mr. John Flynn, Who being Sworn on the Holy Evangelists Declareth, that on tuesday morn the twenty fifth Instant November, Mr. Edward Batchelor of Newbern, Merchant, Since deceased, Sent him to Richard Cogdell, Esqr., for the purpose of desiring him to Come to draw his Will for him, which Mr. Cogdell did and hath been every day Since at Mr. Batchelors about the Same, and that this afternoon between five and Six o'Clock he and Mr. Michael Gorman were both called up to the room where Mr. Batchelor Lay Sick to be Evidences with Richard Cogdell Esqr to the said Will which Said Cogdell then held in his hand and which Mr. Batchelor was twice raised up to Sign, but was seized with such violent pains that he could set up to sign it, and then Soon after died away, Seemingly to him in his Sound Mind and perfect memory, and that the Will hereto annexed is the Will Mr. Cogdell then held in his hand which Mr. Batchelor was then going to Sign and further this Deponant Sayeth not.

JOHN FLYNN.

Newbern, November 27th., 1777.
Sworn to before me,
JOSEPH LEECH, J. P.

STATE OF NORTH CAROLINA, NEW BERN, 4th., December, 1777.

Personally appeared before me, Richd. Caswell, Esqr., Governor & Commander in Chief of the said State, Richard Cogdell, John Flynn and Michael Gorman, and being sworn upon the Holy evangelists, Severally declared that the foregoing affidavits by them respectively made before Joseph Leech, Esqr., and Certified by him and Signed by the said Richd. Cogdell, John Flynn and Michael Gorman, are true, that is to say, each of the said Witnesses declare that the affidavit signed by himself is true.

At the Same Time Doctor Thomas Haslen and Mrs. Frances Batchelor appeared and Qualified as Executor & Executrix to the said Last Will & Testament by takeing the Usual Oath before me. Of the premisses the Secretary is required to take Notice and issue Letters Testamentary Accordingly.

RD. CASWELL.

Copied from Original Will filed in Office of the Secretary of State.

HENRY LAWRENCE BATE'S WILL.

IN THE NAME OF GOD AMEN, the Twelf day of may, 1740. I, Henry Lawrence Bate, being very sick & weak in Body, but of Perfect mind & memory, Thanks be given Unto God, Therefore Calling Unto mind The mortality of my Body & Knowing That it is appointed for all men once to die, do make & Ordain This my Last will & Testament: That is to say,

Principally & first of all, I give & recommend my soul Into The hands of God that gave it; and my Body I recommend to The Earth, to be buried In decent Christian Burial at the discretion of my Executors, Nothing doubting but at the generall resruection I shall receive the same again by the Mighty Powers of God; And as Touching such worldly Estate wherewith it hath Pleased God to bless me In this Life I Give demise & Dispose of the same In the following manner & form.

Imprimis. I Give & bequeath to my Loving son, Augustine Bate, my Lands & Plantation whereon I now Live To him & his heirs for ever.

2dly. I Give & bequeath to the Child my wife is Big with, One hundred Acres of land joyning to the Land I now Live on (the sd Land I hold By deed from Jonathan Taylors), to that & its heirs for Ever.

3dly. I Give & bequeath to My son, Augustine Bate, & the Child my wife is Big with, One Negro woman Named Janny & her Encreas, to be Equally Divided between them when they are at ye Age of twenty one years, To them & Their heirs for ever.

4thly. My will is that if Either of my Above mention children Should Die before they are of Age, the Other Shall have all I have given them.

5thly. I Give & Bequeath to my Loving Brother, Humphry Bate, one sorrold horse with a white blaze In his face, Called Spark, all my wearing apparil Except one hat at the hatters; one hackny saddle & Bridle, And one fifth Part of All my stock of Hogs which was Raised Last Winter, he Taking Care of the Stock till market presents.

6thly. I Give & bequeath to my Loving Sister, Ann Bate, one gold Ring of fifteen shils price Virginia Currency.

7thly. I Give and Bequeath to my Loving wife Martha Bate the Use of my Plantation I now Live on and One Negro woman Named Janney During her Natural Life.

8thly. I Give & bequeath to my Hond. mother, Sarah Sanders, the Use of one hundred Acres of Land I hold By deed from Jonathan Taylor, During her natural Life; & One hundred Pounds in Publick Bills to be raised out of my Personal Estate, to be paid her towards Building a house on ye sd. Land.

9thly. After all my just Debts & funerall Charges & Legacies are paid, I Give & bequeath the remaining Part of my Personal Estate to be Equally divided between my Loving Wife & Children.

Lastly, I Constitute & appoint my Loving wife Martha Bate my Executrix & my Loving Brother, Humphry Bate, & my Loving Brother in Law, Thomas Whitmell, Executors To this my Last Will & Testament & I doe hereby revoke & Disanull all former wills By made and acknowledge this to be my Last will & Testament.

In witness whereof I have hear Unto set my hand and seal the day & Year above written.
Enterlind before signd with the word, Die.

HENRY LAWRENCE BATE. (Seal)

Signs, Sealed & Delivered
In Presence of us:
   WILL CATHCART,
   HENRY HUNTER,
   SARAH HUNTER.

Then proved before me.   Eden House, July 9, 1740.

GAB. JOHNSTON.

Copied from Original Will filed in the Office of the Secretary of State.

THOMAS BELL'S WILL.

NORTH CAROLINA, SS.

IN THE NAME OF GOD, AMEN. I, Thomas Bell, of Albemarle County, Gentn., being of Sound and Perfect mind and memory, doe make, Ordaine, constitute and declare these presents to be and contain my last Will and Testiament, hereby revokeing & makeing Null and Void all former and other Wills by me heretofore made or declared.

Imprimis. I give devise and bequeath unto my Cousen, William Bell, and to his Heirs for ever, all my Tract of Land called Matthew's Point in Perquimains Precinct.

Item. I give devise and bequeath unto my Cousen, Thomas Bele, Son to my Brother, John Bele, and to his Heirs for ever Fifteen Acres of Land out of my Tract of Land joyning on Kendricks Creek, it being the Tract of Land on which I now live, and to be laid out according to the discretion of my Execut's hereafter named, so as to take in & include the Plantation that is cleared & the House now built at the Back Landing; Also Two hundred Acres of Land more to be laid out by my Executo's as aforesaid so as to joyne on the deep Runn & Swamp or division between my land and Mr. Cullen Pollocks & so as not to take in or include my Plantation that is Cleared at the deep Runn.

Item. I give devise and bequeath unto my Cousens, Ann & Jane, the Children of my Brother, John Bell, the Sum of Fifty Pounds (the currancy of this Country) to each, to be paid unto them Severaly as they shale arrive to full age or day of Marriage which shall first happen.

Item. It is my Will that my Execut^s. hereafter named or the survivor of them doe see that out of the profitts annualy arriseing by my Estate, they doe maintain & Educate my

Cousins, Thomas, and Anne, Children of my Brother, John, in as handsome and good a manner as may be.

Item. Is my Will that ale the residue of my Estate boath real & personal be and remain unto my Loveing Wife, Elizabeth, dureing her life, and after her dcease unto my Cosen, William Mackey, & his heirs for ever. Provided & be it hereby understood that if my Cousen, William Mackey, shall depart this life before my Wife; or dye without Heirs lawfully begotten by him, that then all my said Estate boath real & Personal be and remain (after the Decease of my Wife) unto my Cousen, Thomas Bell, the Son of my Brother, John Bell & his Heirs for ever.

Item. It is my Will that no Sale be made of any Slaves or Stock, but that my Estate be kept intire as it now is as near as possible dureing ye life of my Loving Wife, Elizabeth, excepting my Sloop which I leave to the discretion of my Executors hereafter named to employ or dispose of as they shall think most proper.

Lastly, I doe make Nominate & appoint my Loveing Wife, Elizabeth, and Loveing Cousen, William Mackey, to be Executrix & Executor of this my Will & Teastiament whome I desire to see all Parts of this my Will performed.

In Testimony whereof, I, the said Thomas Bell, have hereunto put my hand & Seale this Eleventh day of December, One thousand, Seven hundred & Thirty three.

THOS. BELL. (Seal.)

Signed, Sealed, Published & declared to be my last Will & Testiament (being Interlined, with ye words [after ye Decease of my Wife]) in Presence of us.

SAML. DURRANCE.
W. DOWNING,
HANAH H̬ GIRKIN.
marke

CHOWAN, Sc. January Court, 1733.

The within Will of Thomas Bell was in Open Court proved by the Oath of William Downing, one of the Subscribing Evidences thereto.

Test. MOSELEY VAIL, Cler. Cur.

Copied from Original Will filed in the Office of the Secretary of State.

WILLIAM BENBURY'S WILL.

NORTH CAROLINA. SS.

IN THE NAME OF GOD AMEN. I, William Benbury, of ye prcinct. of Chowan, in ye Govermt. of No. Carolina, Planter, being Sick & weak in Body, but of Sound and perfect mind & memory (praised be God) Do make, ordaine, Constitute & Declare These presents to be & Containe my last will & Testamt., Hereby revokeing & annulling all former & Other wills or Testamt. by me heretofore made or Declared.

I will that all my just debts & funeral Expences be paid by my Executrix hereafter named.

I give & bequeith ye plantation whereon I now live, together with my other plantation whereon my Son In Law, James Watch, now liveth, unto my loving wife, Jane, for & During ye term of her Natural life; & after her Decease, I Give & devise ye plantation whereon I now live to my Son, William, & his heirs & Assigns for ever; & my other plantation whereon James Watch now liveth, after ye Decease of my sd. wife, I Give, devise & bequeith unto my Son, Jno., & his heirs & assigns for ever.

I Give & bequeith unto my loving wife, Jane afsd. ye Use, Occupation of all my personal Estate wtsoever, for & duering ye terme & time She Shall remaine Sole; And I hereby Authorise & Impower my Sd wife at any time During her life, or by her last will Testamt., to Give, Devise or bequeith all my personal Estate to Such of my Children now unmarried, & in Such parts & portions as She shall think fitt; but if it so happens that my Sd. wife, Shoud after my Decease marry, Then & In such Case I Give, devise & bequeith ye two thirds of my personal Estate to be Equally Devided att Such time of marrage, amonge my Children now unmarried, Vizt: William, John, Martha, and Hannah, & ye other third to my wife afsd., Except & always reserved to my Son, William, ye Mill now Standing in my house, & to my son, Jno., As much money as Shall purchas another, & lastly

Doe make, Constitute & appoint my loveing wife, Jane my whole & Sole Executrix of this my last will & Testamt.

In Testimony whereof, I, ye Said William Benbury, have hereunto put my hand & Seal, this thirteenth Day of July, Anno Dcm., 1709.

WM. BENBURY.
W. B.

Signed Sealed, published And declared in presence of:
    HENRY BONNER.
    ANN MOSELY.
    EDWD MOSELY.

Recorded in Will Book 2, p. 39, Office of Secretary of State.

JOHN BENNET'S WILL.

IN THE NAME OF GOD AMEN. I, Jno. Bennet, of Coratuck P'cinct, in ye Albemarle, In ye province of No Carolina, being of perfect mind & remembrance, praised be almighty God, Doe make this my last will & Testamt. In manner & forme following:

First, I freely Surrender my Soul unto almighty God who Gave itt unto me hopeing to receive free pardon & remission of all my Sins through ye Infte. mercy of my Infitly. Gracious Jehovah, in & through ye merits of my precious Redeemer; & for my body to be decently buried att ye Discretion of my Extrs. or Extx. hereafter nominated.

I Give & bequeith unto my son Joseph one half this tract of land I now live upon, being three hundred & Twenty four acres, with appartenances; also from ye break to ye back ridge, Except two acres for a Chappel upon ye Back Ridge joying to Jno. Robs Land.

I Give unto my Son, Benjamin, ye other moiety or half pt. of ye sd. Tract I now live upon with ye appartenances also & furthermore I freely fully & absolutely Give unto my sd. Sons, I manner & forme afsd. & to ye heirs of their Body lawfully begotten; & for want of such issue to revert, Decend & Come to my Bro^r Joseph Bennet & to ye heir of his body lawfully begotten; & for want of Such Isue to revert, Decend & Come to my Couzan, William Jones of —————, In No Hampton Shire & to ye heirs of his body lawfully begotten; & for want of such Isue to remaine & be for ye use of poor old men or woamen that have been honest & laborious & so to Continue to ye worlds End, always provided & Excepted & So reprised that my lawfull & loving wife, mary, shall have hold possess & quietly Enjoy my plantation I now live upon with all Conveniences & appartinances thereunto belonging or in any wise appertaineing During her Natural life. & then to revert & be as Is limited & appointed afsd.

I Give & bequeith to my Son, benjamin, half that Tract I bought of Jonh Nicker joyning on ye line of ye afsd. Tract on ye South Side & on ye line of Edward Jones Senr. on ye North Side. I freely fully and Absolutely Give unto my sd. Son ye sd. half with ye appertenances & to ye heirs of his body lawfully begotten; & for want of Such Isue to revert decent & Come to my Son, Joseph, & ye heirs of his body lawfully begotten & for want of such Isue to revert, decend, & come to my Brother, Joseph Bennet, & to ye heirs of his body lawfully begotten; & for ye want of Such Isue to remaine & bee for ye use & bennefitt of poor Children To pay for their Schooling & to remaine unto ye worlds End.

Now for ye other moiety of half pt. on ye North Side adjoyning to ye land of Edward Jones, Senr., I freely, fully & absolutely give unto my Son, Joseph, & to ye heirs of his body lawfully begotten, & for want of Such Isue to revert, decend & Come to my Son Benjamin & to ye heirs of his body lawfully begotten, & for want of Such Isue to be lett by ye Elders of ye Parrish to Dispose to Charitable uses & so to Continue to ye End of ye worlds End.

For my Island I Doe freely & absolutely Give unto my two Sons, Jos. & Benjamin, for ye breeding young Cattle & horses & to be undevided to them & their heirs lawfully begotten, & for want of such Isue to revert, decend & come to my Couzan Towers frith & to ye heirs of his Body lawfully begotten, & for want of such Isue to remaine & be for ye use & benefit of ye poore of ye No west River & so to Continue to ye worlds End.

Now for my Tract of land Lying on ye East Side Moyoke Creek, being three hundred & fifty acres my whole mind & will is that itt shall be Sould & ye money laid out to buy Servants by my Executris & my wife to have ye use & benefitt of themm During her Natural life, & then to be equally devided between my abovesd. two Sons, provided always, & my further will is, that if either of my two Joseph & Benjamin or ye heirs of either of them Doe attempt or Goe about to doe any act, or acts, thing or things to alien or discontinue ye lands, Tenements & hereditamts. or any pt. or parcel thereof, to them, either or any of them by me Given & bequeithed in manner & forme afsd. *either by Testment, fine, recovery or otherwise by any ways* or means so that ye same lands & every and parcel thereof, Can not, or my not, decend, Come, remaine, revert, & be in manner & forme before this my will limited, declared & appoint & according to ye true Intent & meaning of this my Gift, will and last Testamt. yt then Immediately & from thence froth ye Estate, Enterest & Title of him or them so attempting Doeing or Going about any Such act or acts, thing or things, as afsd., then Immediately & from thence forth ye Sames shall remaine & be to such person or persons as by this my last will is limited & appointed in manner & forme & upon ye like Condition or Conditions as though he or they so attempting or Going about any act or acts, thing or things, in forme afsd. near & Indeede any thing in this my p'sent last will afore mentioned or declared to ye Contrary notwithstanding * * * (Illegible).

* * * (Illegible) Estate with in ye province of No Carolina my whole mind & will is that my Wife Shall have ye one half During her Natural life & then at her Decease, to Give itt to one of my Sons or both of them or to one Grandchilde of mine or to all of them or to Either during (?) one as afsd according to their Care of or Kindness to her. Now for ye other half of my afsd. Estate my whole & mind & will is that itt be equally devided between my above sd. two Sons, furthermore my whole

mind & will is that my Wife shall have anything Except Cattle & hoggs of my Sons pts. paying them for what she shall Chuse for her use being Duely appraised, & my further will is that forty Shillings be taken of my whole Estate before any devesion be made to pay for ye Schooling of two poor Children for one whole year.

Now for my house & land & houshold Goods with all other Goods & Cattle arriving (?) to my wife by a legace of two hundred & fifty pounds Given unto her by her Grandfather Mr. Richard Nesent (?) of South pedeeton in Sumenersett Shire, with in ye realme of old England, my whole mind & will is that my wife shall have ye one Moiety or half pt. & ye other Moiety or half pt. to be equally Devided among all my Grand Children.

& what is my proper rite house, Cisterne, houshold Goods, & other things I Give to my afsd two Sons, Joseph & Benjamin, yt is to say that wch. was left in Burmodas att my first wifes Coming away to me Into Corowtuck: & my further mind will is that thay my adopted Son, Sampson Goldard, shall have land upon either of my Sons Tracts by me Given with in one Quarter of a mile of either of my sd Sons plantations During his Natural life; & one heifer wth. Calf & one sow with pigg, provided he live with my wife untill he be of ye age of one & Twenty & behave himself Dutifully towards her.

And I Doe make ordaine & appoint my wife, mary, my Sole Executrix of this my last will & Testamt. If She doe live to prove this my last will & Testamt. & it Please God to take her out of this Sublunary world before ye afsd probation then my whole mind & will is that my son Joseph shall be my Executor, & my Son Benjamin to succeed my Son Joseph in his Executorship if Death so Cause a necessity & I revoke & make void & null all other wills & Testamts.

In witness whereof I have hereunto Sett my Seal this Tenth of December, Anno, 1710.

JOHN BENNETT.

GEORGE THOMSON.
ANN THOMSON.
EDWARD E C COB.
EDWARD E S STAFFORD.

Recorded in Will Book 2, Page 49, Office of the Secretary of State.

RICHARD BLACKLEDGE'S WILL.

IN THE NAME OF GOD AMEN. The 20 Day of February, in the yeare of Our Lord, one thousand Seven hundred & seventy Six, I, Richard Blackledge, Senr., of Craven County, in the provance of No. Carolina, being in Parfect Health, Sound mind

& memory, Do make and ordain this my last Willl and Testement in manner and form following:

Imprimis, I give unto my Loving wife, Ann Blackeldge, the use of the following Negroes Slaves, Viz.: Tanner Joe, and his wife Hannah, and her Son Nedd, negro woman Jean, and her Daughter Sebinah, and Boy Moses, & man Fryday, for and During the Term of her Natural Life, provided they are not Carryed out of the County (without Security given for thire Return, at the Decease of my said wife,) I also give unto my said wife, a negro Gairl Named Mille & her Increase for Ever, I allso give to my said wife the use of the Land Called Handcocks Plantation, with all the Land I Bought of Joseph Crispin, for and During her natural Life; & allso the Benefitt of one hundred and forty apple Trees to be laid of on the Back of the old Orchard on my manner Plantation, for the Term of Ten Yeares, after my Decease; I allso give unto my wife Sixty pounds, in money, to be laid out by my Executors for Building a house on the said Lands, and my will and Desire is, that a Sufficient Quantity, of Scantlery and Plank be furnished, for the said House, and other out houses Nessery, from my uper Saw mill, I allso give to her my said wife the Laboure of five (?) good negro men, for the Space of three months, Imediately after Crops laid by, to help Cleare ground on said Plantation.

Item. I give and Bequeath unto my Said Loving wife, Ann Blackledge, Six Cowes, & Calves, and fifteen head of Dry Cattel, the Choice of my Stock on my Manner Plantation (working oxen Excepted), and all my Stock of Sheep, Excepting Six yewes and Lambs, that I Reserve for Mr. Spyers Singleton; allso all my Stock of Hoggs in Fork of Nuce and Contenteny, one half of my Crop of Corn, pees, Flax, and Cotton, & Pertatoes, and all my Household Furniture one yoak of Oxen, a good Cart, and a Sufficient of Plantation Tools for the working her Plantation; allso my Riding Chaire, maire, womans Saddle, Two horses, the Choice of what I have, to her and her Heirs and assigns for Ever.

Item. I give and Bequeath unto my Son, Richard Blackledge, the Plantation where on I now Dwell, and all that part of Andrew Basse's Patent for foure hundred and fifty Acres Lying to the westward of the Allegator Branch and a line to be to be Drawn from the mouth of the said Branch, Lower Corner on the River side; allso, all that part of my Patent for Six hundred and forty Acres, Joining Brantons, Jones, and Phillipes, which lyeth to the westward of the head of Said Branch, & Joining last mentioned old Patents; and One half part of all my Lands and mills on Batchelders Creek, Subject to the Reservation hereafter made, to him and his Heirs and assigns for Ever.

Item. I give and Bequeath to my said son, Richard Blackledge, The One undivided half part of Two hundred and seventy five Acers Land on the north side of Nuce River at Pecosen Point, Taken up and Patented in the Joint names, of Chistopher Neale and Richard Blackledge; also the northern Quorter part of the Lott one hundred and Eight, with the Proper Front of the said part, Lying in the Town of New Bern; Allso one Lott of Land in the said Town, on Frunt Street, Number forty Six, to him my said Son Richard Blackledge and his heirs, and assigns for Ever; allso one sett of Smiths Tooles to be kept for the use of the mills at Batchelders Creek, and all my Library of Books, and my wearing apparel, and one peare of Gold Sleve Buttons that I ware, & my watch; I allso give & Bequeath to my Said son, Richard Blackledge, The uper half of Six hundred and Forty Acres of Land, being the uper Survay for that Quantity of Land on Mosleys Creek; allso Six hundred and forty Acres of Land Patented by John Fowler & Richard Blackledge Jur., & Son William Blackledge and Son Benjamin Blackledge Jur., now an Infant, Two hundred Acres of Land, Patented by mySelf Eleventh of March, 1775, Lying on the Eastermost Branch of Mosleys Creek, for the mutual use and benefitt, of a Reservoy of water, for all ye Lower Lands I hold on Said Creek: & this I strictly forBid and Disere may Never be Sold to any person Out of the Familey while theres one of the name that hold a foot of Low grounds on Mosleys Creek.

Item. I give and Bequeath to my Son, Thomas Blackledge, Blackledge, all that Tract of Land I Bought of William Farmer and wife, (Daughter of Caleb Mattcalf, Deceased), and One hundred Acres Land lying on the Beever Dam, Patented by Andrew Bass, Joining the above; and one half part of all my Lands, & mills on Batchelders Creek (Subject to the Reservation heare after made) to him his heirs and assigns for Ever. I give and bequeath to my said son Thomas, The Southermost Quorter part of-Lott Number One hundred and Eight, in New Bern, with the Proper Front of Said part of Said Lott; allso one Lott in said Town, Number Foure Hundred and four; and the One half of my One third part of Fifty Acres of marsh Land on Trent River, Neare New Bern, Joining the Town Line; allso One Negro Man Named Quomino, and Foure Cowes and Calves, to him my Said Thomas, and his Heirs and assigns for Ever.

Item. I give and Bequeath unto my Son William Blackledge all That Tract of Land I Bought of Benjamin Keith, together with that part of Andrew Basse's Patent, for four hundred and fifty Acres of Land, which Lyes on the East Side of the Alligator Branch, and a line to Be Drawn on Run from the mouth of Said Branch to the Lower Corner of said Patent of Andrew Bass'es; Together with a Patent for Seventy Acres;

and one other Patent for Thirty Seven Acres on the Front of Keeths Place; and all the Lands I hold or own on The East side of the head of the allegater Branch, Joining caleb Wiggines, and John Phillips; allso one hundred and Eighty Acres of Land I Bought of Richard Gibbs; and one Other Tract of Land for one hundred & Eighty five Acres on the Egle Swamp Joining Phillips; & one Other Tract that Joins Bothe these Last Patents, in my own Name; also One Tract Patented by me, for five hundred and fourteen Acres Opposite Coxes Ferry; allso Two Tracts of Land I Bought of John Browning; and one Tract of Land, of One hundred Acres that I Bought of Henry Darnall & wife, these three Last Tracts Lays in Contenteny Neck; allso half of all my Lands On Mosleys Creek, Excepting whats before given & allso Excepting one Tract for Six hundred and Forty Acres of Land that I Bought of Wm. Russell; this I Desire may be sold, by my Exec. (if Peter & David Golstrap Dont take itt as they & I Partly agreed, & youl find ye memorandon made in the Day Book); But the half of all ye other Lands, pine Trees that I have Reserved on Lands Sold by my Self, & Trees I Bought of Leve Trewhett, I give to my Son William his Heirs & assigns for Ever. I allso give and Bequeth to my said son William one half of a Front Lot in New Bern which I Own with Christopher Neale, whare the Slaughter house Stands; and one half of my One third part of fifty Acres of marsh Land on Trent, neere New Bern, Together with the Saw and Grist Mills, Erected on the Bever Dam near my Home plantation, with Two good yoak of Oxen, one peare of Timber wheels, Screw & Chane and Ox Cart, four Cowes and Calves and The following negroes: Sip's son George, Boy Jack, a Tanner by Trade, & Augustus Ceasar, negro wench Lucy and Daughters Dina and Temp, and thire futer Increse; which said Lands, Lotts, Slaves & thire Futer Incress To him my said son William, and his Heirs, and Assigns for Ever.

Item. I give and Bequeath unto my son, Benjamin Blackledge, The Lands and Plantation given to my Said wife her Life time; allso Two hundred Acres of Land on Stonington Creek in Dobbs & Craven County; allso that Tract of Land on the south Side of Nuce River known by the Name of Trewhetts old Place, with all the Lands Joining the Same and one half of all my Lands on mosleys Creek not heretofore given away, or Ordered to be Sold with the half of the pine Trees Reserved & Purchased, in order if it shold be agreeable to my Two Sons, William & Benjamin, that thay might Buld a saw & grist mill on Some Conveenant place on Said Creek; I allso give unto my said son Benjamin Blackledge, The following negroes, Dick, Fourtain, & Lidea, and half the negroes I willed to my wife Ann Blackledge her life Time, to be Delivered to my son Benjamin Imediatly after my Wifes Deceas, to him his Heirs and assigns for Ever; allso foure Cowes & Calves, and one Lott in The Town of New Bern, Number foure hundred and five to him his Heires and Assigns for Ever.

Item. I give and Bequeath to my Son in Law, Spires Singleton, to hold in Trust for any Children he may have by my Daughter Elizabeth, his wife, The One half of all my Lands at Mattemeskeet, Patented By Christopher Neal & Self, John Jones and Edward Spencer; allso one half of half of a Tract of Land Patented by mr Christr. Neal in Quanitty and Quallity, so as to give the Equil One half in Value; allso one half of my One third part in a Tract of Land Bought at mattemeskeet Betwen Cap Chris^r. Neale, Capr John Jones, and Self, all these Lands Lays at Mattameskeet; allso the following Slaves, one Indean or Mustee Garle Named Amelia, One negro man Named Cuff, one negro woman Floro, one negro Boy Frank, One Negro Gairl Violet, and there futer Increase, To them, there Hiers and assigns for Ever; Allso four Cawes & Calves, & six yewes and Lambs, I give and Bequeath my Said Son in Law, his heirs and assigns for Ever; I allso give my said Son in Law to hold in Trust as afore said, Eighty pounds to be laid Out as soon as it Can be raised by my Execr. to Buy for my Said Daughter Elizabeths Children one Young Breeding wench, for her & her Increase to be Divided Amongst my grand Children, if any, as follows, Viz.: I first Disere my Daughter, Elizebeth, now wife of Mr. Spires Singleton, may have the use & Benefitt of the Laboure of said negroes & Rents of said Lands, if any, for and During her natural Life; the Lands to go all to her oldest Son, if She hath any Lawfully begotten, if none, then to be Equilly Devided amongst all her Children; & ye negroes and there future Increase to be Equilly Devided amongst her Children, or the Survivers of them, there Heirs and assigns for Ever; I allso give my Daughter Elizebeth Ten pounds to Buy her a morning Ring, and a pair of Gold Buttons. The aforesaid Lands and negroes to be Devided amongst my Grand Children, if any, Imediately after the dcease of my said Daughter Elizebeth, & not before unless itts agreeable to her: And in Case She Dies with Out Leiving any Children or grand Children alive behind her, then I give the afoesd. Negroes & Land to Equilly Divided amongst my Other Children Or there Heirs or assigns for Ever.

Item. I give and Bequeath to my Said son in Law, Spires Singleton, the Half of one Lott of Land in the Town of New Bern that I Bought of Joseph Hall, Number four hundred and Six, to him, his Heres and Assigns for Ever.

Item. I give and Bequeath to my son in Law, Cap John Jones of Lower merian, in Penselvania, to hold in Trust for any Children he may have by my Daughter Ellenor, his wife,

The One half of all my Land that I hold at mattemeskeet, Patented By Capt Christo' Neal, Self, John Jones, & Edward Spencer; allso One Lott of Land in New Bern, No. Two hundred and thirty Six; as allso One half of my one third part of a Tract of Land Bought by Chris' Neale, Said John Jones, & my Self, according to Quanitty and Quallity, I Desere the said Lands my be Devided, the said John Jones & Spyres Singleton, to hold in trust for the Children of my Two said Daughters; I allso give into my Said son in Law John Jones, to hold in Trust for the Children he may have by my Daughter Ellener, now his wife, the following Slaves, Viz.: negro man Simon & his wife Hannah & her son Pollepus & gairl Rachel, Besides the Gairl Penney which She haith with her now, and thire futer Increas, to them thire Heirs & assigns for Ever; I allso Give & Bequeath, unto my Said Son in Law, John Jones, in Trust as afoesaid for the Children he may have by my said Daughter Ellenor, the Sum of Eighty pounds, to Layd Out by my Exec'. as soon as it Can be Raised out of my Estate, to buy a young Breeding negro wench with, for her and her futer Increas to be Devided amongst my Grand Children that my Said Daughter Ellenor haith by the said John Jones, if any if Shes none by him, any Other Children She may Lawfully have by any Other Husband. First, I Desire my Daughter Ellener wife of the said John Jones, may have the use & Laber of the aforeSaid Slaves for and During her natural Life; allso the the Rents and Benefitts of Said Lands &c. Then I Desire the Lands & Lotts Given to Said John Jones in Trust as aforeSaid, may all of it go to the Oldest son My Said Daughter Ellener may have by Said John Jones, his Heres and Assigns for Ever, or if she Shold have non by him, & shold she have any other son Lawfully begotten or to be begotten, I give the said Lands & Lotts to him, his Heires & assigns. Secondly I Disere the negores & there future Increas, after my said Daughters Death, be Equilly Devided amongst her Children, or the Surver of them, that She may have by the Said John Jones, or any Other Husband, and there Heires and assigns for Ever. The Said Lands and negroes to be Imediately Divided after the Decase of my said Daughter, amoungst her Children & my Grandchildren, if She hath any Left alive, if not, then My will and Disere is that the aforesaid Lands & negroes, may be Equilly Devided amongst the Rest of my Children or the Survivers of them, thire Heeres and assigns for Ever.

Item. I give and Bequeath to my Daughter, Ann Blackledge, The following negroes Viz.: negro man Called Miller George, Boy Daniel, & girle matha, & one negro wench to be Bought out of my Estate, thats young, & will Bread; allso, I give to my Said Daughter, Ann, the One half of the negroes willed to my wife, Ann, Dureing her Life time, to be Delivered to my Said Daughter, Ann, Imedially after my wifes Death, to her her Heeres and assigns; allso, One Tract of Land I hold on the Loosing Swamp, of three hundred Acers, and Two Other Tracts of Lands that I hold in Dobbs County, one Neare David Jarnigan Jur. on the No side of Nuce River, that I Bought of mr peter Knights, & One Other Tract of Land that Lays On the So. Side of nuce, Neare David Jarnegan, the younger, that Mr Andrew Bass gave me; I allso give Ten pounds a peace to my Daughters Elenor Jones, & my Daughter Ann, allso Ten pounds to my Loving wife Ann Blackledge, to Each of them to Buy a morning Rings & a pair of gold Buttons; the afore Said Lands & negroes I give to my Daughter Ann, here Heeres and assigns for Ever.

Item. I give and Bequeath to any Child, or Children that my wife may now be pregnant with, or that She may have Nine months, after my Decease; the following negroes Viz.: Monday a Cooper, Corneliah, & Bay Cane, & girl Tabitha, And one other young Breeding wench to be Bought Out of my Estate as soon as the money Can be Raised, with thire futer Increase to him, her or them, there Heers and assigns for Ever.

Item. I give and Bequeath to my son, Richard, the following negroes, Scipio, Tayler, Jack, Begg, Jem, wench Persillah and hir Daughter Silve; Two yoak of Oxen, Two peare of Timber wheels, one Ox Cart, half of all the Tooles Belonging to the mills & half the Stock of Cattel and Hoggs that Runs on Batchelders Creek & Jumping Run; & half the Boates Belonging to the said Mills on Batchelders Creek, or places adjacent: and my will and Desire is that Two yeares proffitt of the aforesaid mills, at Batchelders Creek and the negroes Given to my son Richard, allso with what I have and shall heare after give my son Thos. or so much of them as is sofeecent, Shall be Imployed, Imedially after my Decease, to the Bulding of a Saw & Grist mill, up Batchelders Creek, wheare I Cleare'd to make the Dam Last Summer, a littel Below the forks of said Creek or neare that place, whare my Execr. thinks itt Can be best & most Convently be Don; & when Said mills are Bult & Desire the Neat Proffs of all ye mills on Batchelders Creek with this to be Erected may be Equilly Devided betwen my Two Son Richard, and Thomas, & thire Heirs and assigns for Ever.

I give and Bequeath to my Son, Thomas, The Other half of my Stock of Cattel & Hoggs on Batchelders and Jumping Run with ye Boates and utensils at sd. mills, to him my Sd. Son, Thomas, His Heres and assigns for Ever, or the Survivers of them, the said Richard and Thos. thats In Case Either of them Shold Die with Out Coming to the age of Twenty one or Leaving Children alive behind them Lawfully begotten.

And my will and Desire is, that if Either of my said Sons shold Disagree in Continuing the said mills at work that they shall not have power to Convay to others, but that the Valuation there of shall be left to the Determenation of Two or more skilfull Honest men and Draw by Lots for the Chance of selling or Buying the said mills with all the Lands I hold on the said Creek & Jumping Run the shares of the Parties Contending and the Purchaser shall have Twelve months Credett free of Intrust.

Item. I give and Bequeath to my son, Thomas, the following negroes Besides the one heretofore given, Tony & his wife Combe, man Industry, & Boy Grigg, to him his Heers and assigns for Ever,

Item. I give to mrs. mary Neal, Ten pounds to Buy a morning Ring and a pair of Gold Buttons.

Item. I give to Miss Betsey Baker, Ten pounds to Buy her a Mourning Ring and a pair of gold Buttons.

Item. I give and Bequeath to my Honourd Feather, Benjamin Blackledge Senr., Ten pounds P Annum During his naturl Life, and the Labour of my negro man Ceazer.

Item. I hereby Impower my Executors or any Two of them to Sign Seale and Execute any Deed or Deeds of sale for Lands to be Sold in Vertue of this will, or heretofore Sold by me and Deeds not Executed or fulfiled or perform, any Contract or Covenant in as full a manner as I Cold, ware I in Being.

And to the End that my Heires, or Legatees may see how Earnestly I Recommend it to them to Shun Law Sutes, it is my will and Desire, & I hereby order that if any Misunderstanding, or Dispute shold arise conconing or Relating to this my will, that the Parties Contending Shall Imedially make Choise of Two or more Skillfull Honest men, whoes Determination shall be final, and if any Legatee or thire Hiers or assigns Shall Refuse to Comply with Such Settlement, I hereby Declare him her or them, to be for Ever Barred from the Injoyment of Such Contested Legacy or Intrust in Dispute.

Item. All the Rest of my Real Estate not hereby Devided I give to be Equilly Devided amongst my Children or the Survivers of them, According to Quanitty and Quallity in Such manner as my Exec. may think most Just & Equitable to them and thire Heirs and assigns for Ever; and all the Remaining part of my Personal Estate I Desire may be Sold Imideally after my Decease for Twelve months Credett with Intrust from the Day of sale and the money Ariseing thereby to pay of my Debts and Legacyes in this my will mentioned; allso all Debts Dew me to be Collected as soon as possible and the Residue to be Equally Devided amongst all my Children, or the Survivers of them, thire Heres or assigns for Ever.

Lastly I mominate, Constitute and Appoint my Freind

Jacob Blount, Esquire, Christopher Neale, my Son Richard Blackledge Jur., and my Son in Law Spyers Singleton, to be Executors, to this my will, allso Guardians of all my Children, of whome I Request that my Children, be well Educated, thire Plantations well Rented, and negroes hired out to advantage.

In Witness whare of I, the said Richard Blackledge, have hereunto Sett my hand, to this my will Contained on Two Sheets of paper and affixt my Seal, the Day and year first above Written.

RICHD BLACKLEDGE (Seal)

Signed, Sealed, Published and Declared by the Testator as his Last will and Testament in the Presents of us who Signed Our Names as Evidences at the Request of the Testator, in his Presence and allso of Each Other.

  J. G. BLOUNT.
  HANRY CANNON.
  READING BLOUNT.

STATE OF NORTH CAROLINA.

These are to Certify that on the fifteenth day of October, Anno Dom., 1777. Personally appeared Henry Cannon, one of the Subscribing Witnesses to the foregoing instrument of Writing, Before me, Richard Caswell Esquire, Governor & Commander in Chief of the said State, And being Solemnly Sworn upon the Holy Evangelists Declared that He saw Richard Blackledge, the Testator, Sign, Seal publish and declare the said foregoing instrument of Writing, Comprised in three Sheete of paper, to be and Contain his Last Will and Testament, that to the best of the said Witnesses knowledge and belief the Testator was at that Time of Sound and disposing Mind and Memory; And that he also Saw John Gray Blount & Reading Blount, the other Subscribing Witnesses Evidence the same with him in the presence of the Testator and of each other. At the same Time Jacob Blount, Christopher Neale, Richard Blackledge & Spyers Singleton, the Executors in the said Will named, Appeared before me and Qualified as such. Ordered that the Secretary have Notice of the premises and that Letters Testamentary issue accordingly.

RD. CASWELL.

Copied from Original Will filed in Office of Secretary of State.

BENJAMIN BLOUNT'S WILL.

NORTH CAROLINA.

IN THE NAME OF GOD AMEN. The first Day of febuary, 1739, I, Benjamin Blount, Sen; of Terrill County and Province Aforesaid, Planter, being Very Sick and weak in Body But of perfect Mind and Memory, Thanks be Given unto God; Therefore calling to mind ye mortality of my Body And knowing that itt is appointed for all men once to die, do make and ordain this my last will and Testament, that is to Say: Principally and first of all I Give and Recommend my Soul into ye Hands of God that Gave itt and my Body I recommend to ye Earth to be Buried in Christion Burial att ye Discretion of my Executors, nothing Doubting but att ye Generall Resurrection I Shall Receive ye Same aGain by ye mighty Power of God; and as touching Such worldly Estate Wherewith It hath pleased God to bless me in this life I Give Demise and dispose of ye Same in ye Following Manner and form:

I Desire that my Whole Stock of Cattle That is in my Proper mark may Be Equily Divided Between My Son, James and Jacob and Isaac and my Daughter Esther, and Each of Them one Bed and one Iron pot and Each of them one ew.

Item. I will that my Son, Edmund, and my Daughter, mary, and my Daughter, Sarah, may have five Shillings Each.

Item. I Give to my Sone, Benjamin, my manner Plantation.

Item. I will yt if any of my Children Dies without heirs Lawfully Begotten of them to fall then To ye youngest Son Either Land or Movables.

I will and bequeath to my beloved wife, Elisabeth, ye Remainder Part of my Estate Both of Goods and Chattles and Movables, Whome I likewise make my Executrix with my son, Benjamin, Executor, of This my Last will and Testament of all and Singular my Lands and tennem'ts, and I do hereby utterly Disalow and Revok all other former Testaments, Wills, Legaces and Excet (?) by me in any ways Before named willed and Bequeathed, Confirming this and no other to be my last Will and testament.

In witness whereof I have hereunto set my hand and Seal ye day and year above written.

BENJ. BLOUNT, (Seal)

Signd: Sealed Published and pronounced in presence of us:

ANN X HOLLIS.
her mark

ZACARIAH X GURKIN
his mark

June ye 1740.

Came before me Eliz. Blunt, Ex'x & Beiaman Blunt, Ex'r to Ben. Blunt, Decesed, being duly Sworn promis to fulfill Eavery part of the within will. Sworn before me, JAMES TURNBULL, J. P.

TYREL COUNTY ss. June Court, anno Dom, 1740. Present His majestys Justices:

These may Certifie that the within will was proved in open Court according to Due form of Law:

Test, THOS. LEARY, D Cl. Cur.

Recorded in Grant Book 4, Will No. 114, Office of Secretary of State.

EDMUND BLOUNT'S WILL.

IN YE NAME OF GOD AMEN, the 12th. Day of Febuary, In ye year of our Lord, 1754, I, Edmund Blount, of ye County of Tyrrell, Being very Sick and weak in Body but of perfect Mind and memory, thanks be given unto god for ye Same, and Calling to mind ye mortality of my body & Knowing that it is appointed for All men once to die, do make and ordain this my Last will and Testament, that is to Say principally and first of all I Give and Recommend my Soul into ye hands of god that gave it and My Body I Recommend it to ye Earth to be Buried in a Christian Like and Decent Manner at ye Descretion of my Executors Nothing Doubting But at ye General Resurrection I Shall Receive ye Same again by ye mighty power of god, and as touching Such worldly Estate wherewith it hath pleased god to Bless Me in this Life I give Devise and Dispose of the Same In ye following manner and form:

Imprimeses, I Give to my well Beloved Son, Edmund Blount, my manner plantation with all ye Land Belonging to it.

Item. I give and Bequeath to my well beloved wife, Elisabeth, one third part of all my movable Estate.

Item. I Desire that Each of my Children Excepting my Son, Edmund, may Have one Cow and Calf apeice, and ye Remainder part of my Estate I will that it Go to ye maintainence of my Children.

Item. and I do make ordain and appoint my wife, Elizabeth, Executrix, and Benjamin Blount Executor of this my last will and testament, and I do hereby utterly Disalow, revoke and Disanull all and Every other former testaments, wills and Legacies, Bequests and Executors by me in any ways Before this time named, willed, and Bequeathed, Ratifying and Confirming this and no other to be my last will and Testament.

In witness whereof I have hereunto Set my hand and Seal ye day and year above written.

his
EDMUND E BLOUNT.
mark

Signed, Sealed and Delivered by ye sd. Edmund Blount as his last Will and testament in ye presents of us ye Subscribers, Viz:
    BENJAMIN BLOUNT.
    JACOB BLOUNT.

NORTH CAROLINA, TYRELL COUNTY. SS.   June Court, 1754.

These may Certify that Jacob Blount, one of the Subscribing Evidences to the within will appeared in Open Court and made Oath on the Holy

Evangelists of Almighty God that he was present & Saw Edmund Blount, Deceased, Sign, Seal, publish, pronounce & Declare the within writing to be & Contain his Will and Testament, and that he was then and at that time of sound & Disposing Memory; & that he also Saw Benjamin, the other Subscribing Evidence, sign his name thereunto at the Same time. Then Also Appeared Elizabeth Blount, wife of the Deceased, and Quallified as Executrix by taking the Oath by Law Appointed for the Quallification of Executors. Ordered that the Honble. James Murray, Esqr., Secretary of this Province, have notice thereof that Letters Testamentory issue thereon as the Law Directs.

Test, Evan Jones, Cler. Cur.

Copied from Original Will filed in the Office of the Secretary of State.

ELIZABETH BLOUNT'S WILL.

North Carolina, sc

In the Name of God Amen. I, Elizabeth Blount, of Chowan Precinct, Widow, do make & Declare these presents to be & Contain my last Will & Testament, hereby Revoking all former & other Wills by me heretofore made & Declared.

Imprs. I Give and bequeath unto my Son, John Blount, Ten shillings in Publick Bills of this Province.

Item. I Give unto my Son, Thomas Blount, Ten shillings in Publick Bills of this Province.

Item. I Give unto my Son, James Blount, the Negroe Woman named Cushaba and one third of the Cattle at Morattoke, the Bed I comonly ly on, a Rugg, Bolster & pair of sheets.

Item. I give unto my Daughter, Ann Worley, Thirty Pounds in Publick Bills of this Province.

Item. I Give unto my Son, Joseph Blount, my Negro man Nam'd Hector.

Item. I Give unto my Son, Charlesworth, my Negro man Nam'd Dick.

Item. I Give unto my Daughter, Rachell, my Negro Man Named ffrank, my Side Sadle & all my wearing Cloathes.

My Will & Desire is that my Land at Bare Swamp & the Land my husband puchased of Henry Haughton be Equally Divided between my two Sons, Joseph & Charlesworth, And that the Land at Barrows hole be sold by my Executors & the Doctor to be paid out of ye money Arising by the Sale thereof.

All the rest of my Estate I Give unto my two Sons, Joseph & Charlesworth, & my Daughter, Rachell, to be Equally Divided between them.

Lastly I hereby Constitute & Appoint Jno. Lovick, Esq., Samll. Pagett & Jonathan Jeacucks, Executors of this my Last Will & Testament.

& in Testimony thereof, I have hereunto putt my hand & Seal this 8th ffebry, 1732.

the mark of
ELIZ. X BLOUNT. (Seal)

Sign'd, Seal'd Publish & Declar'd in presence of:
R HICKS.
the mark of
MARY X COLESON.

NORTH CAROLINA. SS.

This Day came before me Robert Hicks, and made Oath on the Holy Evangelists that he saw Mrs. Elizabeth Blount, lately deceased, Sign, Seal, publish and declare the within Writeing to be her last will and Testament the day therein mentioned, & that he, the said Robert Hicks, did Witness the same, and that he saw Mary Coleson the other Witness thereunto put her Mark as Witness also to the same. Given under my hand att Edenton the 12th. of March, Anno Domini, 1732-3.

GEO. BURRINGTON.

Copied from Original Will filed in the office of the Secretary of State.

JAMES BLOUNT'S WILL.

IN YE NAME OF GOD AMEN. I James Blount, of Chowan precinct, in ye County of Albemarle, in ye Province of Carolina, Esqr., well knowing the uncertainty of this life, Do make, Ordain & appoint this to be my Last Will & Testament, hereby Revoking & Adnulling all former Wills by me Made, and this Only to be taken & reputed as my Last Will.

Imp. I Bequeath my Soule to God who gave it; & my body to ye Earth to be Decently Interrd; & as for that Worldly Estate wch it hath pleased God to bestow upon me in this Life; My Just Debts, funeral Expenses & Legaties being first payd, i give & bequeath as followeth:

Item. I give unto my son, James Blounte, one Shilling in Countrey Commodities to be pd him by my Executrix hereafter named, w'thin one year after my Discease.

Item. I give unto my son, Thomas Blounte, & to my two Daughters, Ann Slocom & Eliz. Hawkins, Each of them twelve penc a peice in Country Comodities to be paid them within one year after my Dissease.

Item. I give & bequeath unto my Grand Children, James & Sarah Blounte, the Children of my Son Thomas Blount, & to Ann Slocum ye Child of my Daughter Ann Slocom, & to John Hawkins ye Son of my Daughter Eliz Hawkins, Each of them a Cow & Calfe to be paid to their several parents w'thin three years after my Discease in some sort of Stock to run for ye use and behoofe of ye Sd Children, till they Severally Com of age or by Mariage Capacitated to receive ye Same.

Item. I give & bequeath all ye Remainder part of my Effects Reale & personall whither it Consist in Lands, houses, negroes, Servants, Stock, household goods, or any other Kind of Specie w'tSoever, unto my Loving wife Ann Blounte for her to have, hold, Occupie & enjoy, During her Naturall Life w'thout Lett or Controule, and att her Death to Dispose out of ye Same to ye Value of Sixti pounds in Countrey Comodities to Whoever She Shall think fitt. And after her, my D Wifes Disease, I give ye whole remainder of my Estate to my Son, John Blount, and his heirs for ever; And I do hereby appoint and ordaine that my said son John Shall be Decently Maintained out of ye Estate During his Minority. And in Case my said Wife, Ann Should Live till after my Said Son John Should come of Age, then if he Should Happen to Marry, or to go to Live in some Other place from my Sd Wife, then Shee to pay him thirty or forty pounds wch Shee please, in Country Comodities.

Lastly, I appoint my Loving Wife, Ann Blounte, my whole & Sole Executrix of this my last Will & testament, Desiring her to be carefull in every Article & Clause thereof; & for Confirmation of ye Same I have hereunto sett my hand & Seale, this 9th day of July, In ye year of our Lord God, 1685.

March ye 10th &c. Before signing sealing or Publishing I do hereby Appoint yt, in Case My Son Jno Should Dye w'thout heirs Male, then I give & bequeath all my lands & houses to ye Heirs Male, of My son Thomas Blounte & so successively do Entaile the Same on their Heirs Male of my Son Thomas forEver; But in Case the heirs Male, of my Said Sons John & Thomas should both fayle, then I Intayle ye Same on ye heirs genall of my Son Jno. first, then of my Son Thomas, & if both Should fayl, then of the heirs of My Daughter Ann Slocum & Eliz Hawkins.

JAMES: BLOUNTE (Seale)

Signed, Sealed & Published as his Last Will & Testam't in presence of

her mark
JANE X MILLER
JNO BAILY
WILLIAM DOBSON
JNO WETTINHALL

This Will Proved by Jno Hall and Jane Miller on ye 17 Day of July, 1686, And by Will'm Dobson on the 11th of July, 1686, who upon their Oaths before me Duely administerd did Attest that they See ye Testator above named, James Blounte, Signe & Seale And heard him Declare the Above written to be his last Will and Testament.

SETH SOTHELL.

Recorded in Will Book No. 1 p. 120, Office of Secretary of State.

JAMES BLUNT'S WILL.

IN THE NAME OF GOD, AMEN. The twelf day of ffebuary, In the year of our Lord God, 1716. I, Jeamse Blunt, in the Prcinct Chowan, in Nor. Carolina, Being very Sick and weak of body but of perfect mind and Memory, Thanks be to God, Do make and Ordain this Last Will and Testament, In manner following, That is to say:

First and Chefest, I give my Sole To the hands of Allmighty God who Gave It me; and my body I Commend to the Earth to be Decently Buried in Christan Buriel, at the Discretion of my Executors, nothing doubting but at General Resurection I shall recave the Same again by the Mighty poure of God.

As Touching Worldly Estate wherewith It hath pleased God to bless me with, I give, Devise, Bequeath and Dispose of the same in manner and forme following:

I Leave to my Loving wife, Elizabeth Blunt, all my personal Estate During her Life, porvisardly that She, the Sd Elizabeth doth remain wedow, otherwaise, no longer then She the Sd Elizabeth Shall marry; at that time of her maredge to returne to my blovd Daughter, Anne, and her heairs for Ever.

I make my well beloved wife, Elizabeth Blunt, and my Daughter, Anne, full and whole Executrix, and after my Loving wife, Elizabeth, Desease, I give to my Loving Daughter, Elizabeth Yelverton, a yong mare; and to my Two grand Children James Yelverton and Jon (?) Yeltverton, to Each of them a Cow yearling after the Desease of my loving wife, Elizabeth Blunt; and

My Son, John Yelverton, I make over Seare of my Estate; And to my Daughter, mary, five pounds, She or her heairs;

And to my Granddaughter, Sara Philips, Two Cows with ther Calvs, to be Left in the porseon of my Daughter, anne, till the Day of her maredge, the Sd. Sara Philips.

Give to my Son, John Blunt, a Shilling; and to my Son James Blunt, I give a Shilling; and to William Nea—(?), a cow yearling and Iron pott and Two puter Dishes.

And I Give and bequeath to my Daughter, Anne Blunt, the plantation that I now Live appone with Two hundred[240] acers of Land, with all my Cows, Calves, Stars, Buls, Sheep, horses, mars, or Mills with all watter Crafts, with all housall gods, with all mannor of Implements whatsoever belongen unto me, rale or personal; and at the Day of my Daughter, anne, marredge, She may Seate (?) apon any part of the Sd. Land with out the least trouble of her, the aforsd Elizabeth Blunt, or any persone, or persons whatsoEver.

If It may please the allmighty God that I Desease att this presents, that I give to my Daughter, anne, the half of my

Lether that, I, the Sd James Blunt, have by me now this psents, to her and her disposal.

And I do utrly deny, disalow, revoke, annulle and Evry other formar Testament, wills and Legacies, bequests and Executors.

And I give and bequeath to my Son, John Yelverton, fifty Shillings, to be paid in Starling money England.

I utrly deny all maner wills, Testemt. as aforSd mad befor this time named, willed and bquathed, ratifying this and none other to be my last will and Testement.

In witness, I have heareto Sete my hand, Seale the of the Yeare above Written.

JAMES BLUNT (Seal)

Signed, Sealed, published and pronounced by the Said James Blunt, as his last will and Testement:

    F. TURNER.
         her
    ANNE N DUGLES.
        mark
    JOHN YELVERTON.

March the 27th, 1717.

The within Will is provd. by the Oath of Jno. Yelverton in Open Court.

R. HICKS, CLK. Cur. Gen:

Copied from Original Will filed in the Office of the Secretary of State.

JOHN BLOUNT'S WILL.

NO. CAROLINA SC.

IN THE NAME OF GOD AMEN. I, John Blount, of Chowan precinct Esq., Do make and declare these presents to be and contain my last Will and Testament, hereby revoking all former and other Wills by me heretofore made or declared.

Imprimis, I Give, Devise and Bequeath unto my well beloved Wife, Elisabeth, all and Singular my Lands, Tenements and Hereditaments whatsoever within this Government for and during the Term of her Natural Life if she so long continues Sole.

Item. Whereas the Land I now dwell on containing Six hundred and forty acres, fronting on Albemarle Sound is Intailed Land, It is my Will and Desire that the one half thereof, or Such part thereof being the Westernmost part as in this my Will is hereafter described, shall be my Son, John, the Heir at Law, be vested in my Son, Thomas, and the Heirs of his Body Lawfully begotten, either by Act of Assembly or by some other Lawfull way or means, or that in Lieu thereof my Son John shall have such part of my back Lands as is hereafter described. But if some Expedient shall not be found out, by my Son, John, either by Act of Assembly, or otherwise, to vest the Westernmost part of the Land whereon I now dwell, to and for the Use of my Said Son, Thomas, and the Heirs of his Body lawfully begotten, then it is my Will that all my Said back Lands containing by Estimation Twelve hundred and Sixty Seven Acres, be the Same more or less, shall be and remain to my Said Son Thomas and the Heirs of his Body lawfully begotten; And in Case a Division of the Said intailed Lands can be Effected, then my Will is that my Eldest Son, John, and his Heirs lawfully begotten shall have the Easternmost part of all the Lands as well intailed as those I have taken up myself, and my Son, Thomas, and his heirs lawfully begotten to have the Westernmost part of the Said Land, all which Lands are to be divided after this Manner, Vizt: The Breadth of the Land belonging to the plantation whereon I now dwell on Chowan or Albemarle Sound, to be equally divided on the Front to the Water, and when the Middle is found, then to Set a Course which will take the Branch or Valley on the Back of my now dwelling House where is a Sort of a Spring of Water, and Mulbery Trees planted; and from thence down the Branch 'till it comes to a Bridge (which goes over the Swamp behind the House unto the neck called poplar Neck), which Bridge is now the Main Horse Road to Yawpim, and that Bridge to be the Division across the Swamp, So along the Swamp on the West Side of the Bridge 'till it comes to the Mouth of the Branch where there is a piece of Ground cleared, and a puncheon House built at the Head of the Branch, and that Branch to be the Division 'till it comes to the North west Corner of the Said cleared Ground; then Such a Course as will go to a Hickory, in both Patents called a Poplar, marked with this Mark *; and from that Tree the division to be according to the patents 'till it comes to the Northernmost End of the Beech Island Land, and so to divide each Ways according to, and agreeable with the Patents: But if my Son Thomas cannot by any lawfull wayes or means have the part of all the Lands allotted him according to the Division mentioned in this Paragraph, then my Will is as before Exprest, that all my back Lands, containing by Estimation Twelve Hundred and Sixty Seven Acres, be the Same more or less, shall go to my Said Son, Thomas, and the Heirs of his Body Lawfully begotten.

Item. My Lands lying on Welches Creek Vizt: Six hundred and forty Acres that I bought of Roger Snell, and One hundred & Ten acres adjoinging thereto surveyed for me by Mr. William Gray, I Give, devise and Bequeath unto my

Two Sons, James & Charles, to be Equally divided between them; my Son James to have the Lowermost half; and my Son Charles to have the uppermost half, To have & to hold the same unto the said James & Charles, and the heirs of their Respective Bodies Lawfully begotten, by Moieties in Severalty and not in Joint Tenancy.

Item. I Give, devise & Bequeath unto my Son, James, and his Heirs & Assigns, Two hundred forty five acres of Land, commonly called Ticers rich neck, lying on the back of Welches Creek land, he paying the Sum of Thirty pounds to my Son, Joseph, within One Year after my Son, Joseph, shall arrive to full Age, but if my Son, James, shall not think fit to accept of that Land on this Condition, then I Give the same unto my Son, Charles, and his heirs and Assignes, on the like Condition of his paying to my Son, Joseph, Thirty pounds within Eighteen months after my said Son, Charles, shall come to Age: But if neither my Said Sons, James and Charles, shall pay unto my Said Son, Joseph, the aforesd Thirty pounds as exprest in this Paragraph of my Will, then I Give, Devise and Bequeath the said Two hundred forty five Acres to my Said Son, Joseph, and his heirs and Assigns for ever.

Item. I Give, Devise & Bequeath unto my Son, Joseph, all my Lands at Matchapungo, known by the name of Goshen, where Thomas Davis lately dwelt, to him the said Joseph, and the heirs of his Body lawfully begotten.

Item. It is my Will, and I do hereby order the same, that in case either of my Sons John, Thomas, James, or Charles should dye without Lawfull Issue, the first of them so dying, his Lands in this Will given, shall go to my Son, Joseph, and to the Heirs of his Body lawfully begotten forever. And if any other of my Said Sons shall Dye without Issue after my Son Joseph shall be possest of any Lands by Virtue of this paragraph of my Will, then my Will is that the part of such so dying without Issue, shall go to the next heir at Law, and the heirs of his Body Lawfully begotten forever.

Item. I Give, Devise & Bequeath unto my Dearly beloved Wife, Elisabeth, all my Lands at Bear Swamp and at Barrow Hole & that piece of Land which I bought of Henry Haughton, to her, and her heirs & Assigns forever.

Item. I Give, Devise and Bequeath unto my Dearly beloved Wife, Elisabeth, the use and occupation of all and Singular my Personal Estate during the time she shall continue Sole, and at her Decease (if sole), to dispose thereof as she shall think fitting, to all, or any of my Children; But in case my said Wife shall Marry, then it is my Will that my Personal Estate shall be equally divided into Three parts, whereof my said Wife shall have one Third part, and the other Two third parts to be divided by my Said Wife among my Children, as she shall think most proper and convenient.

Item. I Bequeath unto each of my Daughters Vizt: Mary Jacocks, Elis^a. Paget, Sarah Lovick, Martha Worsley, and Hester Worley, a Gold Ring.

And I do hereby make & Constitute my said Wife, Elisabeth, Executrix of this my Will, and also do request my respected friends John Lovick & Thomas Pollock Esqr., to be assistants to my said Will to see every Clause and article in this my Will performed.

Lastly, It is my Will that my Sons, John & Thomas, shall have Liberty to Build & Settle on each of their respective Tracts of Land when they shall come to Age or sooner with their mothers Consent, and that they may have Liberty to clear Ground, Fence & Tend it & make Pasture of the clear Ground where I dwell, without too much incommoding their Mother, to whose advice & direction I recommend them and all my Children.

In Testimony whereof I have hereunto Set my hand & Seal this twenty Seventh day of January Anno Dom. 1725–6.

JOHN BLOUNT (Seal)

Signed Sealed published and
declared in presence of
  SAMLL. WARNER.
  WM. BENBURY.
    his
  MAGNES Z PLOWMAN.
    mark

NO. CAROLINA Sc.

Be it known to all Men by these presents, That whereas, I, John Blount, of Chowan precinct, Esq., have made and declared my last Will and Testament in Writing, bearing date this twenty Seventh Day of January Anno Dom: 1725–6, I, the Said John Blount, do by this present Codicil, confirm and Ratify my Said last Will and Testament, and in Consideration that my Daughters, Ann, and Rachel, are not mentioned in my Said Will, I do hereby desire that my Said Daughters should have a Gold Ring each, as in my Will is directed to be given to the Rest of their Sisters, and that they also shall receive of my Estate as their Mother shall see convenient.

And I also do request Christopher Gale, Esq., to be an Assistant, together with Jno. Lovick, and Thomas Pollock, Esq. mentioned in my Said Will to See every Clause and Article of my will performed. And my Will and meaning is that this Codicil be, and be adjudged to be, a part and parcel of my Said last Will and Testament, and that all things herein Contained be as truly performed as if the Same were so declared and Set down in my Said last Will and Testament.

In Testimony whereof I have hereunto Set my Hand and Seal, this twenty Seventh Day of January, Anno Dom. 1725-6.

          JOHN BLOUNT (Seal)
Signed, Seald, published and (Coat of Arms on Seal)
declared, in presence of
  SAMLL. WARNER.
  WM. BENBURY.
     his
  MAGNES Z PLOWMAN.
     mark

NO. CAROLINA SC. Sir Richard Everard, Barrt., Governor, Capt General, and Admiral.

These may Certify that Samuel Warner, Gent., personally appeared before me and made Oath on the holy Evangelist, that he Saw John Blount, Esq., Sign, Seal, publish and declare the within written to be his last Will and Testament, and that he was then of a Sound disposeing mind and Memory; and that he saw the other Evidences that have witnessed the Same, Sign their Names to it at the Same time; and further that he Saw the Sd John Blount, Sign & Seal the Codicil annexed to this Will, and that he was then of perfect mind & Memory, and Witnessed the Same together with the other Evidences thereto.

In Witness whereof I have hereunto Set my Hand, this 18th day of May 1726.

Letters Granted May ye 18th, 1726.   RICHD EVERARD.

Copied from Original Will filed in the Office of the Secretary of State.

JOHN BLOUNT'S WILL.

NORTH CAROLINA.

IN THE NAME OF GOD AMEN. I, John Blount, of Chowan County, do make and declare These Presents to be and contain my Last Will and Testament, hereby revoking all former and other Wills by me heretofore made or declared.

Imprimis, I give, Devise and bequeath unto my beloved Wife, Sarah, the Use of the East part of the Land whereon I now Live, to begin on the Sound side, Twenty Feet to the Eastward of the North East Corner of the Barn; from thence such a Course as shall take one Third part of the Lands and Tract, during her Natural Life or Widow-hood, And I Likewise give to my Loving Wife the Use of Three Negroes, Vizt: Fortune, Gregory, and York, during life or widow-hood. I Likewise give to my Loving Wife the Use of all my House-hold Goods, Excepting my writing Desk, she paying to my Three Sons, James, Frederic, and Wilson, one Feather Bed and Furniture, To Each of them when they come to the Age of Twenty One Years. I Likewise give to my well beloved Wife the Use of one fourth part of all my Cattle, Hogs and Sheep, and my Riding Horse, called Trooper, and one young Horse, called Dart, one young grey mare about Three Years Old, during her Natural Life or Widow-hood, and after her Marriage or Decease to be Equally Divided amongst all my Children with the Increase thereof. I Likewise give to my beloved Wife the Use of Two Negroe Wenches, called Venus and Doll, reserving their Increase to be Equally Divided amongst all my Children, and at the Marriage or Decease of my said Wife, the Two aforesaid Negroes, Venus and Doll, to be given to my Children as my said Wife shall think proper.

Item. I give to my Loving wife, fifteen Barrels of Indian Corn.

Item. I give, devise and bequeath to my Son, James, my Plantation and Tract of Land whereon I now Live (he not barring his Mother of her Third Part during her Natural Life or Widow-hood), to him and his male heirs Lawfully begotten of his Body, for Ever, and in case of failure of such Heirs of my Son, James, then to my Son, Frederic, and heirs male, Lawfully begotten of his Body for Ever, and in case of failure of Male Heirs of my son, Frederic, then to my Son, Wilson, and his male Heirs, Lawfully begotten of his body for Ever.

Item. I give and bequeath to my Son, James, Three Negroes Viz: Sharper, Finn, and Tom, with all my Brewing Kettles, Tubbs and Fats, and all my brewing works, and my writing Desk, To him, his Heirs or Assigns.

Item. I give and bequeath To my Son, Frederic, Four Negroes, Viz: Potter, Frank, Charles, and Will, his Heirs or Assigns for Ever.

Item. I give and bequeath to my Son, Wilson, Three Negroes, Vizt: Boston, Jack, and Mustipher, and as my Sister in Law, Mrs. Mary Moor, desires to have the care of my Son, Wilson, my Will and desire is that she should have the Care of his Education and bringing up, and in case that she should Die and not provide sufficient for him, then to come under the Care of my Executors herein after mention.

Item. I give and bequeath To my Daughter, Elizabeth, one Negro wench, call'd Dinah, and her Increase.

Item. I give and bequeath to my Daughter, Martha, one Negroe wench, called Jane, and her Increase.

Item. I give and bequeath To my Daughter, Mary, one Negroe wench call'd Sarah, and her Increase.

My Will is that five or Six of the likelyest of my breeding Mares, that is now on my Plantation or that can be rais'd, should be kept for the use of my Children, and Likewise I would have all my other Stock of Cattle, Hogs and Sheep, to be kept on my Plantation To raise on, for the Use of my Children.

My desire is that my Chaise, Boat, Blacksmith's Tools, watch, and other Tools, or anything Else that is Likely to perish, should be sold at Public Vandue, Excepting Sufficient Tools for the Use of the Plantation.

Item. I give and bequeath To my Brother, Charles Blount, my best Broad Cloth Suit of Cloaths, my best Beaver Hatt & Wigg.

My will is that none of the Timber should be cut or Sold, Excepting for the Use of the Plantation, and that no Stranger shall be admitted to Live on any part of the back Land to Destroy the Timber, and that no Person shall on any Consideration whatsoever be admitted to Live on any part of my Land Excepting an Overseer, my Will is likewise that all my Negroes should be kept to work on my Plantation, and that no other Negroes shall be admitted to work on my Plantation, Excepting they are the property of my wife or Children. And my Will is that all the money that shall arise out of my Estate, after all Reasonable Expences is paid, should be Laid out to purchase Likely young Negroes, at the Discretion of my Executors hereafter mentioned, for the use and Benefit of my Children, and my will and Desire is that my Executors, hereafter mentioned, should take great Care to have my Children Educated and brought up in a Christian Like manner, and in case any one or more of the Children's Negroes should Die before they come into their Possession, then my desire is that they have others bought, of the same value as they would have been at the Devision, out of the remaining part of my Estate which is not perticularly before given, my Will and desire is, that when the Estate of my Children that is Liveing shall come to ye Age of Twenty one Years, that if any of my Children should have lost any of their Negroes, that they should be made up to them in full Value, then all the principall part of my Estate, with the Profits arising thereon, in the Hands of my Executors to be Equally Divided between my Children.

And Lastly, I do nominate, constitute, and appoint my trusty and Loving Brothers, Joseph and Charles Blount, and my Two Sons, James and Frederic Blount, after they come to the Age of Twenty one Years, my Executors, to see every clause and Article of this my last Will and Testament fulfill'd.

Dated the Eight Day of December 1753.

           JOHN BLOUNT (Seal)
Signed, Sealed, Publish'd, and   (Coat of Arms on Seal)
Declar'd in Presence of
  J. HALSEY Jurat
  JOHN BEASLEY
  JNO SMITH
  RICHARD DUNBAR

NORTH CAROLINA, CHOWAN COUNTY, ss: April County Court, 1754. Present, His Majestys Justices.

These may Certify that John Halsey, Esqr, appeared in open Court & made oath on the Holy Evangelists of Almighty God, that he Saw John

Blount, Esqr., Sign, Seal, Publish, and Declare the within to be & Contain his Last Will and Testament, and that he was then and at that time of sound & Disposing mind and memory, and that he also Saw John Smith, John Beasley, & Richard Dunbar, Sign their names thereto at the Same time.

Test: WILL HALSEY, Cler. Cur.

CHOWAN COUNTY, ss. May the 9th: 1754.

Then Appeared before me Mr: Charles Blount, one of the Executors of the Last Will and Testament of John Blount, Esqr., deceased, and was duly Qualified as Executor thereto, by taking the Executors oath by Law appointed to be taken by Executors.

JAS: CRAVEN

Copied from Original Will filed in the office of the Secretary of State.

THOMAS BLOUNT'S WILL.

NORTH CAROLINA.

IN YE NAME OF GOD AMEN. I, Thomas Blount, being in perfect health and sound Memory, Do make this my last will & testament, thereby Revoke all former Wills & testements wtever in manr. & form following, viz:

Impr. I Do give & Bequeath my soul to God yt gave it, Hopeing throw yr mercy & Merett of our Ld. & Saviour Jesus Christ. to receive a full & Genl. pardon of all my Sins; and my body to ye earth, there to be Desently Intered, acording to ye rits of ye Church of Engl., by my Execr. hereafter Named.

Item. Whereas, by a former Will I have given Half my moveable Estate, & two plantations, known by ye names of Midle plantation, & yt whereon I now live at ye mouth of Hendricks Creek, to my ever loving wife, Mary Blount, & her issue (provided it be to ye children Begotten of her body by me Thomas Blount), after her Death, I Do confirm and make good ye same unto her, by this my will, in man'r. as is above expresst.

Item. As to ye Part of my Estate, both real and personal, I give and bequeath as following: unto my son, James Blount, his Chare of two negroes out of ye other halfe of my sd Estate, and my shoope of smith tooles, with ye anvell, belows, & all other tooles thereunto belonging, wt. the Iron & Steel & filles, and half ye tract of land Called Cobbin Necke, yt is to say, ye Northerly part of ye plantation, to be included in ye part belonging to him & ye boye Bonner.

Item. I do give & bequeath all my whole stocke of Cattle, to be equally Devided between my children begotting of sd. Mary Blount, my daughter, Billah, who has maryed to kellem tyler, to be excepted out of this gift, she having received her portion allready.

Item. I give and bequeath to my daughter, Billah, aforesd. one silver spoon.

Item. As to ye rest of my Estate, tis my will & Desire yt it should be brought to an apprismt & out of it pay unto my three daughters, Sarah Peirce, Christian Ludford, & Ann Wilson, these sums hereafter named, yt is to say, unto my Sarah tenne pound Sterl. to be paid in Country Commodity; to my daughter, Christian, twenty Pounds Sterl. to be pd. as aforesd. & to my daughter, Ann, twenty Pounds Sterl. to be paid in like manner: and in case of the death of any of my aforesd daughters, ye same to be pd to either of their heirs: & to each of them one silver spoon: & further I Do give unto either of my two daughters last named, being, Christian, & Ann, too yews and a Ram, to each of them, and in case my sd Estate so appraised, after the things before giving away, do not amounted to ye sd sumes of money, by me giveing them, my said daughters, to be paid proportionable out of w't it is apraised to: but if it shall amount to more then it my further will & Desire yt my two sones, John and Thomas, shall have each of them a negro, & for want of negroes to have each of them five & twenty Pounds Sterl. apeace, to be pd in Country Comodity.

Item. I do give and bequeath ye other half or Moitye of ye tract of land, called Cobbin Necke, unto my son, John, and his heirs; & for want of heirs, it to come to my sone, James, & his heir; and if my son, James shall dye w'tout heirs, his part to com to my son John & his heirs.

Item. As to ye rest of my Estate, after my wife's half paid and Delivered her, and my Above Legacys being paid as herein expressed, I Doe give & bequeath unto my son, James Blount, & his heirs forever, whom I make my full and sole Executer of this my last will and Testiment, Declaring & Publishing this to be soe: as,

Witness my hand & seal, this third Day of September, in ye year of our Lord, Seventeen hundred & one, & in ye 13th. year of ye reign of our Soveraign L'd. William ye 3rd, King of England, &c.

Thomas Blount (Seal)

A Codicil to my Will: This is my further will & pleasure, yt ye legacys within my said Will giving & exprest, shall be pd. w'thin eighteen months after my decease. as, witness my hand & seal ye year and day abovesd.

Thomas Blount (Seal)

Signed & seald in presence of
  Wm Wilkison.
  John Blount.
  Thomas Green.

March 28th 1706.

The within will was proved before me the Honble: Thos. Cary, Esqr., D: Gov:, by ye oathes of Tho: Green & John Blount, who upon their oathes Say that they did see ye within Tho: Blount, Sign, Seal, & acknowledge ye within written, to be his last Will & Testamt.

THOMAS CARY.

Copied from Original Will filed in the Office of the Secretary of State.

WILLIAM BLOUNT'S WILL.

My Desire is that my True and Loving wife, Elizabeth Blount, may be In, and hold possession of my whole Estate dureing her natural Life, and To make what Improvements She Can for the good of my Children, and To observe alsoe my derections, as near as possible Can be Complyed with, in This my Last will and Tastament.

Item. I give and bequeath To my Eldest son, John Blount, the Eastermost part of halfe of the Land I now Live on, with part of my Beech Island Tract, and a tract Containing 403 acres, Lying Eastward from Sd. part of the Beech island Tract, and northward from a peece survaid by Thomas Luten, Junr. and bounds upon the percorsson.

Item. I give to my son, Thomas, the westermost part of the Land I now Live on, and the Remaining part of my Beech island tract, which is not given to my son John, The Devision to be made between them as follows: the Bredth of The Land upon the River to be Equally devided upon the Sound side, and when the middle is found upon the Sound, then to set a Corse which will Take the Branch or valley, on the Back of The houses I now Live, at where is a Sort of a Spring and mulberys planted; and from Thence down that branch tell It come To the Bridg which goes over the swamp on the Back side of the house, Into a neck which is Called popler neck, which Bridg is now the main horse Road to Yapim, the Brig to be the devision acrause the swamp; then the Swamp on the west Side of the Brig, Till It Come to the mouth of the Branch whereon is a peece of ground Cleared, and a Small punchin house built, at the head of the Branch; that Branch to be the devision Till It Come to the Cleared peece of Land; then from the northwest corner of which peece of Land Cleared, toward a Line drawn 110 E, or there abouts, as I suppose the Corse to Bear, to a popler marked In both pattents with this mark*; Then from that popler the devision to be acording To both patents, Till It Come to the nothermost End of the Beech Island and soe to devide Each way as the Lines of Both pattents Runs. I alsoe desire that what orchards there is at my death upon the plantation they may

Both have Equal benefit, and be at Equal Charg. of fencing and manuring or pruning and If They, or Either of Them, Should Settle before there mothers death, To have Equal benefit with her of the orchards, or If they Should Live with her on the plantation after my decease They may have Liberty to Keep a stock * * * Each of their own Land, and Liberty To settle and Build, Clear, fence or Tend, or make pasture of part of the old field, not preiudging ther mother, on there own part, when they Come to the age of Eighteen years, and when they Come to that age to have foer Cows and Calves, six breeding Sows, three Ews, and a young mare, To be delivered To them on the plantation, and to Run for their use, with their Increas. And my desire is they may not hender Each other In any Common Conveniance, as a Tree for Timber when It groes Convenant, Either oak, siprous, or pine, or springs, or Cart Roads, Soe It be not two much to dammage.

I give To my son, James, all my Land upon welchs Creek, up moratock, that is To say, Six hundred and forty acres, bought of Roger Snell; Tow hundred and forty five, Called Ticers Rich Land; and one hundred and Ten acres Survaied by mr. wm. gray, down the Creek from that of Snells, as the severall pattents will Show, with halfe the stock of Cattle and hogs that shall be on the plantation at my death, and three Ews and a young mare, to be delivered on the plantation when Comes to the age of Eighteen years.

I alsoe give To my son, Joseph Blount, all my Land at machapungo, known by the name of goshan, where Thomas davis, Lives with all the stock that shall be upon It at my death & their increase.

Alsoe, I give my wife Liberty to settle a Tennant on some part of the Land Every where she hath any Stock, doeing as Little preiudice To the owner as may be, with Liberty of Clearing, fencing, or tending part of the Land (the plantation Excepted), and I alsoe desire my boys may all have there Liberty at the age of 18.

I alsoe give my Land at bear swamp To be Equally devided between my Son, John, and James, after there mothers death, and alsoe that I bought of Coll. maule, at barrows hole, known by the name of Tom williamses, unto my son, Thomas and Joseph to be Equally devided after there mothers death; with Liberty to them all In her Life time, to settle a stock and Tennant If they be minded, not preiudiceing there mothers If she should have any Stock or Tennant there after they Come to the age of 21 Years.

I give unto my foor daughters, Sarah, Easter, ann, and Rachel, Each of Them, at the age of Twenty years, or a twelve month after marrage, Twenty barrills of pork, to be paid them by my Executrix, or Fifty five each in Some Vendabl Speceie of the Country.

I give To my daughter, mary Jacocs, and my daughter Elizabeth paget, and my daughter, martha west, to Each of them a gold Ring, of Twenty shillings pric, In bauston or Elsewhere to be got, to be paid them within a year after my decease.

And w^t Remains of my Estate, I Leave the use of It to my wife E. B. dureing her Life, To bring up the Children upon, and maintain them with, and at her death To be disposed of at her discrestion to some or other of my Children or amongst them as she thinks best, Soe It be some of them, whome I make my Executrix.

Mrs. Blount Sole Ex. Thos. Pole, John Toons, Trustees, unles she Marries, then Joint Exrs.

Copied from Original filed in Office of the Secretary of State.

JOHN BOND'S WILL.

NORTH CAROLINA, BEAUFD COUNTY.

IN THE NAME OF GOD AMEN. I, John Bond, of ye. County afforsd: This Eight Day of July, 1749, being Sick and weak in Body, But of perfect mind and memory, thanks be to god therefore, Calling unto mind the Mortality of my Body and Knowing that it is appointed for all men once to Die, I Doe therefor make and ordain this my Last will and Testament, that is to Say, Principally and first of all, I give and Recommend my Sole into ye hands of god that gave it, and as for my Body I Recommend it to ye Earth to be buried in a Christian Like and Desant manner, Nothing Doubting but at ye general Reserection I Shall Receive ye. Same again through ye. mighty power of god; and as to touching Such worldly good wherewith it hath pleased god to Bless me with in This Life, I give and Devise in manner and form as followeth: Viz,

Itam. I give to my Son, William Bond, all that part of a Tract of Land yt. he now Lives on, that is, all on the west Side of ye middel Swamp of ye head of ye Creek, to him & his Heirs for Ever.

Item. I give to my Son, John Bond, the Remainder part of ye. sd: Tract of Land, from the middel Swamp of ye sd. Creek on ye East Side, to him and his Heirs for Ever.

Itam. I give to my Son, James Bond, all that Tract or percel of Land Call'd huddies, Likewise Lying on ye: sd: Side of pamlico River; Likewise I give to my James Bond, all that Tract or percel of Land Call'd Roberts, Lying on ye: north Side of South Dividing Creeks, to him and his heirs for Ever.

Itam. I give to my Son, Robt. Bond, this Plantation that I Now Live on, and all the Land that belongs to ye: sd: Plantation on this side of ye: Creek up to ye: Second Large Branch that Ruins out of ye: main Branch of y^e: head of y^e: Creek; and Likewise I give to my Son, Robert Bond, the one half of a Tract or percel of Land that I have on ye. South Dividing Creeks that Joyns to this sd: Plantation, and my Desire is the sd. Robt: Bond Shall have the one half of ye: sd: Land next to and Joyning to this sd: Land that I now Live on, ye. which Land after my Son, Robt. Shall Come to Thirty years of age, I to him and his heirs for Ever, and my will and Desire is that ye: sd: Robt: Bond Shall have ye: full use and profet of ye: sd: Land in ye: mean Time fully and absolutley in all Cases, Excepting making Sale of ye. sd: Land.

Itam. I give to my Son, Richard Bond, all the Land that now belongs to me over this Creek, which Land was formally Calld: Piners; and Likewise what Land Is on this side of ye. head of this sd: Creek that above ye. Second great Branch as mentioned before which was Robt. Bond Bounds; & Likewise I give to ye: sd: Richard Bond the other half of that Land below on ye: sd: Dividing Creeks Which Robt Bond had the one half of, ye: which sd: Land I give to ye: sd: Richard Bond and his heirs for Ever

Item. I Lend to my Loving wife, the use of this Plantation and house that I Now Live in and all the furinetur in or belonging to ye: sd: house During of her Life, & Likewise I Lend to my wife the use of Two negroes Viz: one negro man Call'd Shippy, and one negro woman Call'd Hannah, During of her Life.

Itam. I Land to my wife the use of Ten Cows and Calves, & forty head of Dry Cattel, and half ye: Sheep yt: I now have, Excepting three During of her Life.

Itam. I give to my Son, James Bond, two Negroes, Viz: one negro man Call:^d Ned, and one Negro woman Call:^d Sarah, to him and his heirs for Ever.

Itam. I give to my Son, Richard Bond, one Negro Boy, Call:^d Littel Jack, to him and his heirs for Ever.

Itam. I give to my Son, Robt. Bond, one negro Boy, Call:^d Sam, and one Negro garl Call^d airly, to him and his heirs for Ever.

Itam. I give to my Daughter, Marey, one Negro Boy Call^d Domina, to her and her heirs for Ever.

Itam. I give to my Cosen, martha Spring, one Negro man Call^d Jack, to her and hir heirs for Ever.

Itam. I give to my son Robt Bond, Three Small putter Dishes & for puter Plates, two Deep ons & two Shallow. ones, puter pottel Bason, to him and his heirs for Ever.

Itam. My will and Desire is that all ye. Remainder of my Cattel, after my Death, Should be Eaquilley Divided betwen my Children, Viz: James, Richard, Robt. Sarah, & anna, & Marey, Excepting what I Shall hereafter mention.

Itam. I give to my Cosen, martha Spring, Two Cowes and Calves, and Eight head of Dry Cattel, to be Delivered to her by my Exc: before there is any Division made, and Likewise I give to my Cosen, Martha Spring, one feather bed, & two Sheets, & two Blankets, & one puter Dish, & one puter pottel Bason, and one pint puter Bason, & one pint porringer & two puter plates.

Itam. I give to my Son, James Bond, one feather bed & two Sheets & two Blankets.

Itam. I give to my Son, Richard, one feather Bed & two Sheets & two Blankes.

Itam. I give to my Son, Robert, one feather Bed & two Sheets & two Blankes.

Itam. I give to my Daughter, anna, one feather Bed & two Sheets & two Blankes.

Itam. I give to my Daughter, marey, one feather Bed & two Sheets & two Blankes.

Itam. I give to my son, John Bond, one Chest and one Looking Glass.

Itam. I give to my Son, William Bond, my Desk & one puter Dish.

Itam. I give to my Son, Robt. my gun that I Commonly use.

Itam. I give to my Son, Richard, my Swoard.

Itam. I give to my Son, Richard Bond, one Black mare.

Itam. I give to my Son, Robt., one Black Colt and I Leave my Bay horse Call^d Buet, for ye: use of the Sd: Plantation.

Itam. I give ye. use of my whipsaw Eaquilley between my Sons Wm., John, James, Richard, & Robt.

Itam. I give all my Carpentes Tools and Coopers Tools to be Eaquilley Divided between my sons, James & Richard.

Itam. I Leave my wife, ye use of all ye: hogs that I have to my wife During of her Life, & after her Death to be Eaquilly Seared amongst my Children, James, Richard, Robt:, & Sarah & anna & Marey.

And my will and Desire is that these two Negroes as I Leave ye: use of to my wife, Viz. Shippy and Hannah, Shall be Keep on this Plantation for the use of ye: Sd: Plantation till my Son Robt. Shall Come to ye age of Twenty one Years, and as much Longer as my wife Shall Live, and I Leave my Son, Robt., and what I have given him under the Ceare of his Brother, James, but then if there Shall be aney Complaint of misusage by him, Then I Impower any of his Brothers to take ye. Sd: Robt. and what belongs to him out of ye: sd: Jameses Ceare, and my will and Desire is that my Son Robt. Shall Come to ye age of twenty one years and my wifes Death, that then these two Negros afforsd: Shippy & Hannah Shall be Eaquilley Divided my Chilldren Viz: Wm:, John, James, Richard, Robt.,

Sarah, Anna, & Marey, and Likewise my Desire is yt. after my wifes Death, that What Cattel, Sheep and Household Goods, She has ye: use of, be Eaquilly Divided betwen Ja.ues, Richard, Robt., & Marey and my Meaning is that my Daughters, Sarah & anna Shall have an Eaquill Shear of ye. sd: Cattel which my has ye: use of; and my will and meaning is that if Either of my Children that is now unmarried Should Die without an Heire, then my meaing is that what I have her given him or them in this will, Shall be Eaquilley Divide amongst the Surviours of my Children, Wm:, John, James Richard, Robt., Sarah, anna, & Marey.

And I Doe hereby Constitute and appoint my Son, Willia Bond, and my Son, John Bond, and my Son, James Bon Executors of this my Last will and Testament

his
JOHN X BOND (Seal)
mark

Signed, Sealed, and Published,
In the Presents of us, Interlined
before signed ye: word (or them)
betwen ye 102 and 103 Line.

  ABRAᴹ PRITCHETT.
  JOHN TURNER.
  PHILIP PRITCHETT.
  JOSHUA PRITCHETT.

BEAUFORT COUNTY, ss. Septr. Court, 1749. Present His Majesties Justices:

These are to Certify that the Last will and Testament of John Bond, late of the aforsd. County, decsed., was proved in open Court by the oath of Abᵐ. Pritchett, one of the subscribing evidences, who Saw that the other Subscribing evidence witness the Same; whereupon Wm. Bond, John Bond, & James Bond, were herein named, Qualified according to Law. Ordered that the Secretary have notice thereof.

           Test. JOSIAH PRATHEX. Clk.

Copied from Original Will, filed in the Office of the Secretary of State.

VINYARD BOND'S WILL.

IN THE NAME OF GOD AMEN. I, Vinyard Bond, of Beaufort County, and Province of North Carolina, Being Very weak in Body but of Perfect mind and memory, and Calling to mind That it is appointed for all men once to Dye, Do make, ordain, Constitute and appoint This and no other to be my Last Will and Testament, in manner and form following, That is to say:

First, I give and Bequeath unto my Beloved Wife, Sarah Bond, the Plantation I now live on, and one other Plantation ajoyning to it on Core Point, with all my Houshold goods, furniture, Stock and Negroes, in order to support, Educate and maintain my son, Sweeting Bond, and my Daughter, Sarah Bond, untill my said son arives at the age of Twenty one years and then I Desire that all my furniture, Houshold goods and stock Remaining on the Said Plantation, be sold and the money arising from the sale thereof to be Equally Divided Between my said Wife, My said Son, and Daughter; But if it should happen that my said Son should Dye Before he arives to the age of Twenty one years, in such Case I Desire that the Sum of one Hundred Pounds Proclamation money to be Paid to my Wife out of the Estate that my said son Dyes Possest of, over and above what I have Already given her.

Item. I Desire that in Consideration of my giving to my said Wife, The Several Sums of money above mentioned, my Will and Desire is that the Estate of Mr. Southey Rew Deceased, When Settled and a Division Thereof made, whatever Part of that Estate that shall or may Come to my Said Wife, after my Decease, be Equally Divided Between my Said Wife and my Son and Daughter.

Item. I Desire that soon after my Decease, the goods then Remaining in my Store, Consisting of Lining and Stockings and all other goods whatsoever in the said store, may be sold and the money arising from the sales thereof, be applyed to the use of my said Wife and son and Daughter within mentioned, According to the Directions of my Executors herein after mentioned.

Item. I Desire that my Exors. herein after mentioned may Sell and Dispose of my Negro man Angus, and my Negro man Harrey, and the money arising from the sale thereof to be layd out to such Proper Uses as my Executors shall think Proper for the Support of my said Wife and Son and Daughter.

Item. I Desire that my Plantation on the north side of Trent River, Containing two hundred Acres; and Likewise my Plantation near Bath, on Town Creek, may be sold and the money arising therefrom the sale thereof, be let out on Interest for the use of my said Wife and son and Daughter, untill my son arives to the age of Twenty one years, and then to be Equally Divided Between my said Wife and Son and Daughter.

Item. I Desire that If my Son, Sweeting Bond, Should Dye Before he arives at the Age of Twenty one years, my will and Desire is that all the Household goods, furniture, and Stock, remaining on the Plantation at Coor Point at the Time of his Decease, may be sold and the Money Arising from the Sale thereof Be Equally Devided Between my said Wife, and my Daughter, Sarah Bond.

Item. I Desire that after my Decease, if it should Happen that my said Wife should marry and Dye without Issue, then and in such Case it is my will and Desire that the one half part of what I have given and mentioned to be given to my

Wife, shall be given to my said Son and Daughter, and Equally Devided Between them.

Item. I Desire that all my Just Debts shall be paid out of the Book Debts that are due and owing to me, and the over Plus, if any, to be Equally Devided Between my said Wife and Son and Daughter; and as to the Negroes Remaining of my Estate, to be sold with my Houshold goods and furniture as Before Mentioned, and the money arising from the Sale thereof to be Equally Divided Between my said Wife and Son and Daughter.

Item. My Will and Desire is that if my said Son, Sweeting Bond, and my said Daughter, Sarah Bond, should Dye before they come of age, then and in Such Case, my will and Desire is that my Sister, Susanah Kershaw, shall have out of the Portion I have Left my said son and Daughter, fifty Pound, Proclamation money, and the Remaining Part of their Estates to go to my Wife, Sarah Bond.

Item. I give and Bequeath to my there other Sisters, Sarah, Mary, and Margaret, Each of them, one Shilling, Sterling money, to them and their heirs forever.

And I further Nominate, Constitute and appoint my Beloved Wife, Sarah Bond, Executrix, and her Brother, John Carruthers, Executor of this my Last Will and Testament, Revoking all former Wills by me made.

In Witness whereof, I have hereunto Set my Hand and Seal, the Twenty fifth Day of March, in the year of our Lord, one Thousand, Seven Hundred and Sixty two.

Signed, Sealed, Published and Declared by the within named Vinyard Bond, to be his last Will and Testament, In the Presence of us who have hereunto Put our Names as Witnesses in the Presence of the Testator:

VINYD. BOND (Seal)

    WILLM. PEYTON.
    WILLM. TRIPPE.
    HENRY LOCKEY.
    THOMAS LEE.

NEWBERN, November, the 8th, 1762.

This day Personally appeared before me Thomas Lee, and made oath on the Holy Evangelists of Almighty God, that he Saw Vinyard Bond, the Testator, Sign, Seal, Publish and Declare the Above to be and Contain his Last will and Testament; and that to the best of his knowledge he then was of sound mind and Disposing memory; and that he also saw Wm. Peyton, William Trippe and Henry Lockey, sign as Concuring Evidence with him. At the same time John Carruthers, Executor therein name qualified as such agreeable to Law.

Let Letters Issue thereon.   ARTHUR DOBBS.

Recorded in Will Book 8, page 263, Office of the Secretary of State.

WILLIAM BOND'S WILL.

NORTH CAROLINA, BUFORD COUNTY, ss.

IN THE NAME GOD AMEN. I, William Bond, of ye County aforsd, This six Day of Novmber, 1757, Being Sik and weak in Body, But of parfet mind and memory, thanks be to god for it, Thearfor Calling mind the Morttillity of my body and Knowing that it is Apinted for all men once to Die, I doe therefore make and ordain this my Last will and testament, that is to Say, Principly and first of all, I Give and Recomend my Soall into ye hand of God that give it; and as for my Body I Recomend it to the Earth to be Bueried in Chirstien Like and Disint mener; nothing Doubting but at ye Generall Reserection I Shall Recive ye same again through ye Mighty Pouer of God: and as touching such worly goods wharewith it hath Pleased God Besto me with in this Life, I give and Divise in this maner and forme as foloweth, Viz:

Itim. I give to my Son, John Bond, the Plantation whearone now I doe Live, and all ye Land blonging therto, Excepting fifty acors up ye werstermost Swamp; lik wise I give to my son, John Bond, half the old Box Neak, to him and his Hears for Ever, and one Negro Boy named Seasor, and one Negro grall named amey, to him and his Eirs for Ever, and it is my Disier that the first Child that ame has, that my Son, William Bond, shall have to him and his Eirs for Ever, and my Disier that my Son John Bond Shall have one par of Silver Shue Bockells and Silver Stock Clasps, and one Small gun, and one fether Bad and fornetud and one Dask Viz.

Itim. I Give and Bequeth to my Son, William Bond, one ———— of land, ware Samull Daves, Lives and fifty acors, ware Sarves Smith Did Live, and one Negro boy named Limes, and one par of Silver Shue Bockells, and par of Silver nea Bockells, and one Stock Buckell, and one fether bad and fornetud, to him and his Eirs for Ever.

Itam. I give to my Dafter, Rebaker, one Negro garll, named Rose, and one par of Silver Shue Bokels, and one fether Bad and furnetud, to her Ears for Ever.

Itam. I give to Kniga (?) Erkman, one Negro Boi, named Bristor, to him and his Eirs for Ever.

Itam. I give to William Smith, one Cow and Calf to him and his Eirs for Ever.

Item. I leave my two old Negros, Sip and Easter, to be Sold to pay my Lofell Debts, and the rest of my Movebll Estat to be Equilly to be Divided betwen my Son, John, and mary Erkman, and her Ears for Ever.

And I Do Apint James Bond, and Richard Bond, and Samuell Davis, Executors of this my Last Will and tastiment.

WILLAM BOND (Seal)

Sign, Sealled and Delivered,
Published In the presents of us,
    FRS. GILBURT.
    FRANCES WARNER.
    ANN MAYO.

BEAUFORT COUNTY, ss. Decr. Court, 1757. Present: his majesties Justices:

This certified that the within last will and testament of Wm. Bond, was exhibited into Court and proved by the Oath of Ann Mayo, one of the subscribing witnesses thereto, who swore that she saw the said William Bond, sign, seal & publish the same as his last will and testament, and that she also saw Fra. Gilbert and Francis Warner, the other subscribing witnesses set their hands thereto. And at the same time James Bond, one of the Executors thereto, qualified by taking the Oath by law appointed.

Ordered that the Secretary have notice that Letters Testamentary may issue.

    Test. WALLEY CHAUNCEY, Cl. Clk.

Copied from Original Will filed in the Office of the Secretary of State.

HENRY BONNER'S WILL.

IN THE NAME OF GOD AMEN. I, Henry Bonner, of Chowan precinct, in the province of north Carolina, planter, Calling to mind the uncertainty of this life, Do make and ordain this Insturment of Writing to be and purport my Last Will and testament, and as to what Estate it hath pleased God to bless me with here, I Give and bequeath in the manner and form following, to wit:

I Give and bequeath to my son, Henry Bonner, all that my plantation, tract, or seat of Land Lying in the precinct aforesaid, and whereon I now Live, with the Appurtenances, to him and his heirs forever. I give and bequeath all that my plantation, tract, or seat of Land Lying in Greenhall, in the precinct aforesaid, and the appurtenances, to my said son, Henry Bonner, and his heirs forever.

I give and bequeath to my son, Thomas Bonner, all these my three plantations, tracts, or seats of Land Lying in the precinct aforesaid, Comonly called and known by the names of Brin's, Holes's, and Jones's plantation, with their appurtenances, to him and his heirs forever.

I give and bequeath all that my plantation, tract, or seat of Land Lying in the precinct aforesaid, comonly Called by the name of Bayes's plantation, to my Grandson, Richard Lewis, and his heirs forever.

I give and bequeath unto my said son, Henry Bonner, all the Stock of what nature or kind soever that is now on and belonging to the aforesaid plantation in Greenhall, and Six Negroe Slaves Called, to wit: Sam, James, Maria, priss, Kate and Bob, One new feather bed and furniture, one Oval table, one brass kettle, six new peuter dishes, four peuter basons, six peuter sup plates, six peuter flat plates.

I give unto my said son Thomas Bonner all and every of the stock that is now on, and belonging to the aforesaid two plantations Called Brin's and Holes's, and five Negroe slaves called, to wit: Cush, Suew, Cudjoe, Tomboy and Doll, One new feather bed and furniture, One Oval table, six new pewter dishes, four pewter basons, six sup plates, and Six flat plates, and One mare.

I give and bequeath to my Daughter, Elizabeth Lewis, One Negroe woman slave, Called Grace, One new feather bed and furniture.

I give and bequeath to my Grandson, Richard Lewis, a Negroe girl slave called, Nann.

I give and bequeath to my Daughter, Deborah Bonner, One new feather bed and furniture, and three Negroe slaves Called, Minge, Simon, and phebe.

I give and bequeath unto my Daughter, Mary Bonner, One new feather bed and furniture, and three Negroe slaves Called, Daniel, Dinah, and Jane.

I give and bequeath to my Grand daughter, Sarah Lewis, One Negroe Slave Called Joan.

I give and bequeath unto my Grand daughter, Deborah Lewis, one Negroe slave Called, Moll.

I give and bequeath all the rest and residue of my personal Estate unto my said Children, to wit: Henry, Thomas, Elizabeth, Deborah, and Mary, to be Equally divided amongst them.

And all the rest and residue of my real Estate, I Order and direct my Executor, hereafter mentioned, to dispose of, and the moneys arising therefrom to be Laid out for the Educating and maintaining my two Daughters, Deborah, and Mary, in their minority, and that they Live with my Daughter, Elizabeth, and that she have the Care and management of them.

And further it is my Will and pleasure, that my son, Henry, before the Negroes are Divided between him and his Brother Thomas, do make or Cause to be made upon One of the plantations herein bequeathed unto the said Thomas, which he, the said Thomas, shall direct sixty thousand bricks for building a house thereon.

It is my Will and pleasure that my said son, Thomas, do Live with my son Henry, during his minority, and I appoint my friend John Benbery to take care that the Estate herein bequeathed to the said Thomas, be not in the mean time be embeziled or wasted.

And I do hereby nominate and appoint my said son, Henry Bonner, to be Executor of this my Last Will & testament, Revoking and annulling all former Wills by me heretofore made, and pronouncing, publishing and Declaring this to be my Last Will and testament.

In Testimony whereof I have hereunto set my hand and Seal, at Chowan precenct aforesaid, the twenty first day of September, 1738.

HENRY B BONNER. (Seal)
his mark

Sealed, pronounced, published, and Declared in the presence of:

    JOS. ANDERSON.
    ABRAM. BLACKALL.
    JAMES POTTER.

October ye 7th. 1738.

Came before me Dr. Abraham Blackhall, & James Potter, & made oath that they saw Coll: Henry Bonner, sign, seal & publish ye within as his last will & testament, that he was of sound & disposing mind & memory, & that Mr. Joseph Anderson subscribed as a witness thereto.

At the same time, Mr. Henry Bonner took ye oath appointed by law to be taken by executors.

W. SMITH, Clerk.

Copied from Original Will, filed in the Office of the Secretary of State.

JOHN BONNER'S WILL.

IN THE NAME OF GOD AMEN. The Eleventh Day of November, and the year of our Lord God, One Thousand, Seven Hundred and fifty Three. I, John Bonner, of Chowan County, in the Province of North Carolina, Planter, being very Sick and weak in Body, but of perfect mind and Memory, Thanks be given unto God for it, Therefore calling unto Mind the Mortality of my Body, and knowing that it is appointed for all men once to Die, do make and Ordain this my last Will and Testament, That is to say, Principally and first of all, I give and recommend my Soul into the Hands of God that gave it; and my Body I I recomend to the Earth, to be buried in decent Christian Burial at the Discretion of my Executors, nothing doubting but at the general Resurrection I shall receive the same again by the mighty Power of God: and as touching such Worldly Estate wherewith it hath pleased God to bless me in this life, I give, demise and dispose of the same in the following manner and Form:

Imprimis. I Give and bequeath unto my God Son, Thomas Ecleston, Two Negroe Boys, Jack, and Cato., Six Cows and Calves, & my Riding Horse, to be deliver'd him when he comes to Age, and if he should die without Heir Lawfully begotten of his Body, the same to return to my Brother, Thomas Bonner.

Item. I give and bequeath to my Cousin, William Howcott, one Negroe Boy Named, Bob. and if he should Die without Heir, the said Negroe Boy to be Divided between his Two Sisters, Elizabeth and Mary Howcott.

Item. I give and bequeath to my Cousin, Edward Howcott one Negroe Girl Named, Grace. and if he should Die without Heir, the said Girl, to be divided between the aforesaid Elizabeth and Mary Howcott.

Item. I Give and bequeath to my Sister, Sarah Howcott, One Gold Ring.

Item. I Give and bequeath to my Sister, Martha Howcott, One Gold Ring.

Item. I give and bequeath to my Brother, Thomas Bonner, my Plantations whereon I now Live, and all the Land that I have now in my Possession, Likewise all the Rest and Residue of my worldly Estate. (Except such as is herein before mentioned.)

I Likewise constitute and Appoint the aforesaid Thomas Bonner, my Sole Executor of this my Last Will and Testament; I Likewise leave John Benbury and Henry Bonner as Trustees to see that my Will is fulfilled according to my Desire. And I do hereby utterly disallow, revoke, disannul all and every other former Testaments, Wills, Legacies and Bequests, and Executors, by me in any ways before Named, Willed and bequeathed; ratifying and Confirming this and no other to be my last Will and Testament.

In Witness whereof I have hereunto set my Hand and Seal, the Day and Year above written.

JOHN BONNER. (Seal)

N B—The above word (my) was Interlined before the Signing & Sealing of this Will.

Signed, Sealed and Declared by the said John Bonner, as his last Will and Testament, in the Presence of us:

JERE^H. MICHENER.
JNO SMITH X.
GEORGE LILES. Jurat

Thos. Bonner Qualified.

NORTH CAROLINA, CHOWAN COUNTY ss. January Court, 1754. Present His Majestys Justices:

These may Certify that George Liles, appeared in open Court and made oath that he Saw John Bonner, Sign, Seal, Publish and Declare the within to be and Contain his Last Will & Testament, and that he was then and at that time of Sound & Disposing mind and memory, and that he also Saw John Smith, & Jeremiah Mitchener, Sign there names thereto at the same time. Then appeared Thomas Bonner, Exr. to the within Will and was duly Qualified by taking the oath by Law Appointed.

Ordered that the Secretary of sd. Province have notice that Letters testamentary issue thereon as the Law Directs.

Test. WILL HALSEY, Cler. Cur.

Copied from Original Will filed in the Office of the Secretary of State.

THOMAS BONNER'S WILL.

NORTH CAROLINA, BERTIE COUNTY, Nig'l.

IN THE NAME OF GOD AMEN. I, Thomas Bonner, of the County and provence aforesaid, being in my perfect Senses and Memory, I do to prevent disputes in my Family after my desese, do make this my Last Will and Testament in manner and form following: first and principally, I comend my soul to the hands of glmighty God that gave it; and my Body to be Buried in a Christian like maner.

Secondly, I give to my well beloved son, Thomas Boner, and his heirs, one hundred acres of Land, be the same more or less, Lying and being, bounded the rode by hog pen Branch and knee Branch.

3'ly. I Give to my well beloved Dafter, Esther More, two hundred ackers of Land, to her and hir heirs, bounded by the rode and hintons Line and Blithehenden Line.

4'ly, I give my Son, henry Bonner, the Sum of one Shiling, sterling Money of Grate Britain.

5'ly, I Give my Dafter, Elsebeth Wheeler, the sume of one Shiling, Starling Money of Great Britain.

6'ly. I Give my Dafter, anna Byrde, the sum of one Shiling, Starling money of Grate Britain.

7'ly. I Give my Dafter, Sarah wharton, the sum of one Shiling, Sterling money of Grate Britain.

8'ly, I Give my Dafter, patchnce Byrde, the Sume of one Shiling, Sterling Money of grate Britain.

9'ly, I Give to my son, Moses Boner, the sum of one Shiling, Starling money of grate Britain.

10'ly, I give to my well beloved Wife, Elsebath Bonner, all the Rest of my Estate, both Real and personal of all kinds whatsoever, to her disposal for Ever; I also appoint my said Wife whole and sole Ex'cutrix of this my Last will and testament.

In witness whereof, I have set my hand and Seal, this Eleventh day of november, in the Year of our Lord Christ, one thousand, Seven hundred and fifty five.

           his
        THOMAS X BONNER. (Seal)
Sined, Seled and delivered Mark.
in the presants of us:
     his
   MOSES M BONNER, Jurat.
     Mark.
     his
   EDMON E BYRDE.
     mark.
   ARTHUR MOOR, Jurat.
   ABRAHAM BLITEHENDEN.

BERTIE COUNTY, ss.   April Court, 1756.
 The before Written will was Exhibited into Court and Proved by the Oaths of Moses Bonner and Arthur Moore, two of the Subscribing Witnesses thereto, which was ordered to be Certifyed.
        Test. BENJN. WYNNS. Cler. Cur.

BERTIE COUNTY, ss.
 This day Personally appeared before me Elizabeth Bonner, and was duly qualified as Executrix to the Last Will and Testament of Thomas Bonner, Decd.
 Certifyed under my hand this 4th. Day of April, Anno Dom., 1757.
          WM. WYNNS, P. J.

Copied from the Original Will, filed in the Offic e of the Secretary of State.

JAMES BOON'S WILL.

IN THE NAME OF GOD AMEN. I, James Boone, of the precinct of Bertie, being Sick and weak of Body, but of Sound and perfect mind & memory (thanks be to God for the Same), calling to mind the frailty of my Body & the mortality of my Body, and that it is appointed for all men once to die, do make and ordain this to be my last will and Testament in Manner and form following, that is to say: first & principally, I recommend my Soul into the hand of almighty God who gave it, hoping through the merits, death & passion of my Saviour, Jesus Christ to have and receive full and free pardon & forgiveness of all my sins, and to Inherit Everlasting life; after death; my Body I commit to the Earth from whence it came to be Burryed in Dacent and Chritain like Manner at the Discretion of my Excrs. hereafter named; and as Touching the disposal of all Such Temporal Estate It hath pleased almighty God to bestow upon me (beyond my Diserts) in this Transitory life, it is my will that it shall be Disposed as followeth:

 Imprs. First I will that my Debts and Funerall Charges Shall be paid & Discharged.

 Secondly, I give and bequeath to my Son in Law, John Early, my Negro woman Called Rose, to be Delivered after the Decease of my Loving wife Eliza. Boone, and fifty apple trees to be Delivered on Demand.

Thirdly, I Give and bequeath to my Son in Law, John Wynns, my Negro man called Charles, to be Delivered after my wifes Decease, and my Cross Cut saw and my writing Desk to be Delivered upon Demand, and half the benefit of my Apple Orchard (which I Leave under his care) untill his Son, George Augustus Wynns, come to full age, and also my Black Walnut Table to be Delivered after my wifes Decease, and 1000 foot of new plank to be Delivered Imediately.

Fourthly, I give and bequeath to my Son in Law, cullineur Sessums, My Negro man Adam, to be Delivered after my wifes decease.

Fifthly, I give, bequeath & Demise to my Grandson, George Augustus Wynns, My manner plantation whereon I now Live, and four hundred acres of Light woodLand adjoyning to it, in fee Simple to him, the said George Augustus, his heirs and (and) assigns for Ever. And in case he die without any heir, or assignee, Then it is my will that the Same fall to the next heir of My Daughter, Mary Wynns' Body, to his, her, or their heirs or assigns for Ever, & in Case my sd Daughter, Mary Wynns, Die without such heir, Then it is my will that the same Decend to the heirs of My Daughter, Eliza: Early Body, Lawfully begotten & to his or her heirs or assigns for Ever.

Sixthly, I Give and bequeath to my sd. Grandson, George Augustus Wynns, my Baldfaced mare Branded W, and the Choise of all the Children my negro Girl Judey brings, after the first.

Seventhly, I give to my Grandson, James Early, my negro man Called Sam, to be Delivered after my wifs Decease.

Eightly, I Give to James Burk, my negro woman called Moll and her Son Coaffe, and all her futer Increase and 100 Publick Bills and £21: 12s in Gold, and my great fether bed and its furniture, or his Choise of any of my beds w'ch shall be Imediately after my wifes Decease, and my Gray young mare wch came of my Bush Mare, and a Yearling filly, and a young Gray horse wch now runs in my Pasture, and my new riding Sadle and Bridle and my Buckineer gun and Cutlash, and my new Chest, and one Learge Iron pot and pot hooks, and my own Wareing apperill to be maid in to apperill for him, All wch I Leave in the care and trust of my Son in Law, John Wynns, with him as his Tutor and Guardian untill he arive at ye age of Eighteen years, and then the sd. Estate to be Delivered to him, but not to his own Disposal untill he arive at the age of Twenty one years, without the advice and Consent of him the sd. Wynns.

Ninthly, I give unto william Burk, my Negro Girl Judey

and her increase (Except the Child before given to my Grandson, George Augustus Wynns) and £100: Publick Bills and £5: cash and £25 in Bills (for his Education), and one Sorriel Mare filly runing in my pasture, and a Large Gray mare Called the Bush Mare, and my Little Gun, and one Iron pott and pott hook, All which I Leave in the care & Trust of my Son in Law, John Wynns, (reserving the Service of Judey to my wife dureing her life) untill he arive at ye age of Eighteen years and then the sd. Estate to be Delivered by the sd. Wm., but not at his Dispossial without the advise and Concent of the sd. John Wynns (whom I appoint his Tutor and Guardian) untill he be at ye age of Twenty years. Reposing only the trust of his person to my wife while she Lives.

Tenthly, And in Case Either of the sd. Brothers, James or William Burke die under age, Then it is my will that half of the Deceased Estate be Delivered, when due, to the other brother, and the other half thereof to be Devided Equilly between the Children of my sons in Law, John Early and John Wynns.

Eleventhly, I give to John Asskew, two Cows and Calves, and fifty apple trees to be Delivered on Demand; & two Ews & a Ram to be Delivered next Spring; and £20 Currt. Bills on Demand.

Twelfthly, I give to my God Daughter, Martha Davis, one mare colt to be Delivered next Spring.

Thirteenthly, I give to my Loving Wife, Elizabeth Boone, my two horses Jock & Shavers, and my Large Sorrel Mare, and my new England Saddle, and Five pounds cash, and my great kill of lightwood: and all the remainder of my Light wood I give to her and our Son in Law, John Wynns.

Fourteenthly, It is my will that after my wifs Decease in whose hands I leave ye Remainder of my personal Estate what shall be remaining thereof shall be equilly Devided between the sd. John Wynns and John Early and James Burke.

Fifteenthly and Lastly, I Constitute, ordain and appoint my Loving wife, Elizabeth Boone, Executrix, and my Trusty and well beloved Sons in Law, John Wynns and John Early, Execrs. of this my last will and Testament, and I do hereby revoke, disanul and make void all former wills and Testaments by me heretofore made.

In Witness whereof, I, the said James Boone, have hereunto Set my hand and Seal, this Eighth day of June, annoq Domini, 1733.

JAMES B BOONE (his seal)
his marke

Signed, Sealed, published and declared in the presence of us:
  JOHN WILLSON.
  THOMAS LEE.
  JAMES J MARTIN.
   his mark

NORTH CAROLINA.

Before his Excelly. Gabriel Johnston, Esqr., his Majestys Govr. of the Province, and Ordinary of the Same: Personaly appeared Thos. Lee, who being duely Sworn, Sayeth that he was present and Saw the deceased James Boone, Sign, Seal, publish and Declare the within Instrument as his last will & Testament & that he was then of Sound & Disposing mind & Memory: And that he Saw John Willson and James Martin, the two other Subscribing Witnesses present & Sett their Names as Witness thereunto.

Likewise appeared John Wynns, one of the Execrs. appointed by the Above Last will & Testament, & took the Oath of Executor as required by Law.

Given at Edenton, under my hand the 31st of March, Anno Dom: 1735.

GAB. JOHNSTON.

Copied from Original Will, filed in the Office of the Secretary of State.

RALPH BOOZMAN'S WILL.

IN THE NAME OF GOD AMEN. The fift Day of January, In the Year of Our Lord, 1744-5: I, Ralph Boozman, in the County of Perqs., Husband Man, being In good Health and of Perfect Mind and Memory, Thanks be given unto God therefore, calling to mind the mortality of my Body & Knowing that it is Appointed for all men to Dye, do make & Ordain this my Last Will and Testiment: that is to Say, principally, and first of all, I give & Recommend my Soul Into the Hands of God yt gave it; And for my Body I Recommend it to ye: Earth, to be Buried In a Christien like & Decent Manner, at the Discretion of my Exs. And as Touching Such Worldly Estate wherewith it hath pleased God to Bless me with in this Life, I Give, Devise, & Dispose of the Same In the following manner and firm:

Imprimis. It is my Will & I do Order, That in the first place, all my Just Debts and Funeral Charges be paid & Satisfied.

Item. I Give and Bequeath unto my Dearly beloved Sister, Mary Bullock, all & Singular the Lands, Messuagis and Tenements, to her, and after her Decease, to the Children of Joseph Bullock, and Thomas Bullock, (That is to Say) the Heirs of the sd: Joseph Bullock & Thomas Bullock, Whom I Likewise Constitute, make and Ordain my Sole Exs. of this my Last will & Testament.

Item. I Give & Bequeath unto Sarah the Daughter of my Sister, Mary Bullock, five pounds, Current money of this Province, & a Cow & Calf.

Item. I Give & Bequeath unto my Beloved Sister, Mary Bullock, all my Household Goods and Moveables, and after her Decease to the Children of Joseph Bullock & Thomas Bullock as aforesd: And I do hereby Utterly Disallow, Revoke, and Disannul all and Every Other former Testaments, Wills, Legacies, Deed or Deeds of Gifts, and Exs: by me In any Ways before this Time Named, Willed and Bequeathed. Ratifying, and Confirming this and No Other, to be my Last Will and Testament.

In witness whereof, I Have hereunto Set my Hand and fixt my Seal the Day and Year above Written.

the mark of RALPH R BOOZMAN. (Seal)

Signed, Sealed, Published, Pronounced, and Declared by the Said Ralph Boozman as his Last Will and Testament, In the presence of us the Subscribers, Vizt:

JOSHUA HOBART. (Seal)
Jurt. JAMES SITTESON, Junr. (Seal)
her
Jurt. HANNAH H SITTESON. (Seal)
mark

NORTH CAROLINA, PERQUIMANS COUNTY. ss. January Court, anno Dom, 1750. Present His Majestys Justices:

Then was the within will proved in Open Court by the Oaths of James Sitterson, and Hannah Sitterson, in due form of law and at the Same time Thomas Bullock, Executor to the Within will, was duly Qualified by taking the affirmation by law appointed to be taken by Executors.

Ordered that the Secretary or his Deputy of said province have Notice that Letters Testamentory issue thereon as the law Directs.

Test. EDMUND HATCH, Cler. Cur.

Copied from Original Will filed in the Office of the Secretary of State.

WILLIAM BOYCE'S WILL.

IN THE NAME OF GOD AMEN. The Eleventh day of June, Seventeen hundred and three. I William Boyce, Merch't. of Pequimins, in the County of Albemarle, in the Proprietorshipp of North Carolina, being Sick and weake in body but of Sound and Perfect memory, (praise be given to God for the Same), and knowing the Uncertainty this life on earth, and being desireus to Settle things in order, doe make this, my last will & Testam't, in Manner and forme following, That is to Say: First and Principally I Commend my Soul to Almighty God my Creator, assuredly believing that I shall receive full pardon and free remission of my Sins, and be Saved by the presious death and meritts of my blessed Saviour & Redeemer Christ Jesus; and my body to the earth from whece it was taken, to be buryed in such decent christian manner as to my Executrix hereafter named Shall be thought meet & convenient;

& As touching such worldly estate as the Lord in mercy hath lent me, my will & meaning is, the Same shall be Imployed and bestowed as hereafter by this my will is Expressed. And first I doe revoke, renounce, frustrate and make void all wills by me formerly made, and declare and appoint this, my last will & testam't. And first, I will that all those debts and dutyes as I owe, in right or Conscience, to any manner of Person or Persons whatsoever, shall be well and truely Contented and payd, within Convenient time after my decease, by my Executrix hereafter named.

Item. I give and bequeath unto my Mother, Mary, of Yarmouth in the County of Norfolk, in England, the Summe of fifteen Pounds, Sterling, to be remitted to her by bills of Exchange.

Item. I give and bequeath unto my Brother, Robert, of the towne and County Last Named, the Summe of Twenty Shillings, Sterling, to be payd & remitted as aforesd.

Item. I give and bequeath unto Mrs Juliana Lakers the Sume of five pounds currt. money of Carolina, to be payd in Convenient time after my decease.

Item. I give and bequeath unto Mr Robert Bradley, of Prince Georges County, Maryland, the Summ of five pounds Currt. money of the Said place.

Item. my will & pleasure is y't my Executrix, hereafter Named, doe Send & buy or cause to be purchased, bought & delivered, Eight Gold Burial Rings, which shall cost four & twenty Shillings Each, which are to be given & Distributed in manner & forme following, (to witt), To Mrs Juliana Lakers, my Executrix hereafter named; Coll Wm. Wilkison; his wife; James Stodart in Prince Georges County in Maryland; his wife; Mr John Cobb; & Peter Godfrey.

And Lastly, I give & bequeath unto Mrs. Joanna Taylor, all the rest & residue & remainder of all my Goods & Chattles, wheresoever or howsoever legally belonging or Due unto me, and Doe hereby make, Constitute & ordaine the Sd Joanna Tayler, my only & Sole Executrix of this my last will & testmt., to see the same performed according to the true intent & meaning thereof.

In Witness whereof, I have hereunto Sett my hand & Seale, the day & year above written.

WIL BOYCE (Sigill)

Sealed & Delivered in presence of:

DAVID X HARRIS.
his marke

ELIZ. ELIZ STUART.
her marke

J. GODFREY.

NORTH CAROLINA W—By the Hon'ble Deputy Govern'r Et. (Sigill)
Whereas good & lawfull proofs have been made, that the above written is the last Will & Testmt. of Mr. William Boyce Deced. A true Coppy whereof is hereunto annexed, & hath therein appointed & made Mrs Joanna Tayler Executrix of the Same.

These are to Impower the Sd Joanna Tayler, in & upon all & Singular the Goods & Chattells Rights & Creditts of the Sd William Boyce, to Enter wheresoever in this Governm't to be found, and the Same into her possession to take, and a true Inventory thereof to return into the Secretaryes office within one year after the Date hereof, & the Same to Dispose of, as by the Sd Will is appointed.

Given under my hand & Seale the First day of December, Anno Dm. 1703.

ROBT. DANIELL.

Recorded in Will Book 1A, pages 26 & 19, Office of the Secretary of State.

THOMAS BOYD'S WILL.

No. CAROLINA, ss.

I, Thomas Boyd, of Bath County, in No. Carolina, remembering the uncertainty of this frail & Transitory Life, And the Necessity that all human Flesh are under of departing this Life, Do make, publish and ordain this, my last Will and Testament, hereby revoking and annulling all other Wills or Testaments or either of them heretofore by me made, either by Word or writing. First & Principally I recommend my Soul to Almighty God, assuredly expecting Forgiveness and Redemption from all my Sinns thro' the precious Blood of my blessed Saviour Jesus Christ: And as to what wordly Estate the Lord heth bestowed upon Me, I give and dispose of in manner following:

Imprimis, I give and bequeath unto my Wife, Katharine Boyd, my best Bed and all it's Furniture, Six Cows and Calves, four Sows and piggs, three two Year old Stears, my greatest Iron pott and Hooks, my Greatest Brass Kettle, one frying pan, Six Soop plates, Six other new plates, Two of my best pewter Dishes, Six black Chairs, my best Table, my best Chest, and the Chest of Drawers, I say to her and her assigns for Ever.

Item. I give unto my Said Wife, Katharine, the profits and occupation of my plantation at Broad Creek, where I now dwell, during her Widowhood (without Suffering or making any waste thereon), in full of Her Dower and demand on all or any of my Land; But if she shall marry my Will and Desire is that she have only one third of my Lands during her Life and no more.

Item. I give unto my Said Wife, the Labour and Service of my two Slaves, Betty which I bought of Mr. Tho. Martyn, and Transway which I bought of Mr. James Robins, upon the plantation afsd. during her Widowhood. PROVIDED, my Wife do first give good Security to the Court that the Same two Slaves, Betty and Transway shall be delivered to my aforesaid Son, John Boyd, or his Order (Mortality in the said Slaves excepted) when she shall marry or dye, whichsoever shall first happen.

Item. I give and bequeath unto my Kind Friend Coll. Edward Moseley, of Albemarle County, five pounds to buy him a Ring.

Item. I give unto my loving Friend, Mr. Robt. Turner, of Bath County, five pounds, to buy him a mourning Ring.

Item. I give and bequeath unto my loving friend, Capt. Simon Aldersoan, of Bath County, my Smallest Case of Bottles, my writing Desk or Buroe, and five pounds to buy him a mourning Ring.

Item. I give devise and bequeath unto my dutyfull and well beloved Son, John Boyd, my largest Case of Bottles, and all other my personal and real Estate of what Kind or Nature soever or wheresoever to be found or Had. And it is my Earnest Desire and Will that all the Cattle and Hogs which shall belong to my aforesaid Son be put on some Land belonging to my Said Son at the Descretion of my Exec., there to breed for his only advantage and profit, And that all the Moneys arising from the Sale at Vendue of all the personal Estate which shall belong to my Son (except the Case of Bottles aforesaid and his Slaves) after all my just Debts are paid, and Legacies Satisfied, be applyed to buy Slaves for my Said Son; And that the Slaves so bought together with all those Slaves I leave him be constantly kept at Work on Lightwood on my Sons Land, thereby to raise money to buy more Slaves, with what convenient Speed my Exec. can, and to educate and School my Said Son.

Lastly I do hereby nominate and appoint my trusty and loving friends Coll. Edward Moseley, & Capt. Simon Alderson, my whole and Sole Exec. of this my last Will to see the Same performed.

In Witness whereof I have hereunto Set my Hand and Seal, this 17th. Day of December., Anno Dom., 1725.

THOMAS BOYD* (Seal).

NORTH CAROLINA, BEAUFORT C. Hyde P.cinct ss. April Court 1726.
Present James Leigh, Samll. Slade, Joshua porter & Jno. Martyn, Esqr, justices of ye. Said Court:

The last Will and Testament of Thomas Boyd, Gent., deceed, bearing Date ye. 17th of Decembr., 1725, was exhibited in open Court by Simon Alderson, one of the Exec. thereof, and the Same being in his own Hand Writing without any Subscription of Witnesses, was proved by parity of Handwriting it being compared with other writings of his, and Some of the Justices members of this Court being well acquainted with the Said Boyd's

Handwriting are of the Opinion it is the Said Thomas Boyd's Handwriting. Likewise Capt. Jno. Tripp & Giles Shute Esqr. being Summoned and Sworn deposed that they were well acquainted with the Said Boyd's Handwriting, And that they verily believed the Said Will to be his the Said Thomas Boyd's own Handwriting, Moreover as a further adminicular proof Samuel Poyner, being Summoned and Sworn declared that Thom. Boyd, afsd., Came to Him on Friday, about one by the Clock, being the 17th. of Decembr. last past, and told him that Night he would go in and make his Will And his shewing great apprehensions of Dying in a little Time made the said Poyner Conceive he was in Liquor tho. from no other Reason he Saith he conceived it. Likewise, Mary Christmass, being Summoned and Sworn declared that on the Said 17th. of Decembr., in the Evening the Said Boyd came to her Husband's House and enquired for Her Husband, And the next Day came to the Said House three times and was desirous of her Husband's being Evidence to a Will which he said he had made, at the Same time burning One which he said was a former Will of His, adding that he had been a Week contriving that Mr. Moseley and Mr. Alderson might have the Management of his Affairs after his Death to His Child's Benefit. And that the Said Boyd then Said that tho He should be disappointed of His Witnesses yet the Court well knew his Handwriting and that he knew if he could have the Management thereof Himself he could make it Stand for a good Will without Witnesses. Also Jonathan Christmass, being summoned and Sworn, declared that the Will aforesaid was delivered to him by Mrs. Catharine Boyd, Relict of the Said Thomas Boyd, to be kept 'till She demanded it. She taking it out at that Time of a Chest of Drawers, but he further Saith That he Saw the Said Mrs. Boyd, before that time open the Desk or Buroe in which Mr. Boyd aforesaid kept his papers of Moment, and that the Deponent by her Direction looked over his papers for a Will but found none.

This Court being of the opinion that the said Will has been Sufficiently proved Ordered that the Secretary have notice thereof. And for the Satisfaction of Such as it may concern this Court Has caused the foregoing proofs exhibited into Court to Support and maintain the Will afsd. to be thereunto annexed, which together with the Said Will, the Motion of Simon Alderson afsd. are ordered to be recorded.

Then Came Simon Alderson One of the Exec. of the Said Will into Court and took the Exec. Oath To perform the Said Will of the Deceed. aforesaid, as the Law directs.

Testis Thos: Jones Clr. cur.

Recorded in Will Book 3, page 95, Office of Secretary of State.

ANNE BRYAN'S WILL.

In the Name of God Amen, the 25th. Day of October, 1767. I, anne Bryan, of Craven County, & Province of North Carolina, being Sick & weak in body but of Perfect mind and Memory, Thanks be Given Unto God therefore, Calling Unto Mind the Mortality of my Body & Knowing that it is Appointed for all Persons Once to Dye, Doe make & ordain this my Last Will & Testament, that is to say Principally, and First of all I Give and Recomend my Soul into the hands of God That Gave it; my Body I recomend to the Earth to be buried in a Desent Christian Like buriel, at the Discretion of my Executors,

Nothing Doubting but at the General Reserrection I shall Receave the same by the Mighty Power of God: And as Touching such Worldly Estate where with it hath Plessed God to bless me with in this Life, I Give, Demise & Dispose of the same in the Following Manner & Form:

Item. I Give & bequith to my Well beloved Son, William Bryan, One Negro Woman Named Venis, One horse Called Bull, One Large Looking Glass, One Silver spoon, One Large Ovel Table, a Safe, & the half of my Cattle on Hatterass Banks, to him and his heirs.

Item. I Give & bequeath to my Well beloved Son, John Bryan, One Negro Man Named Kent, One Peace of Land Laying on the No. Side of Neuse River & West Side of Island Creek, Containing 40 Acers, be the same More Or Less, which I Bought of John Starkey, Known by the Name of Fort Neck, One Mair Colt Bonney, One Cow & Calf, spise Morter & Pessell, One Silver Table spoon, the half of my Cattle on Hatterass Banks, & the Labour of One Free Born Negro Boy Named Asa, Tell his Indentuers shall be Exspierd, to him & his heirs for ever.

Item. I Give & bequeath Unto my Well beloved Son, Jesse Bryan, One Peace of Land Containing 150 Acers which I Bought of Thos. Carraway, Laying on the No. Side of Neuse River & East side of smith Creek; 100 Acers which I Bought of Samuel & Isaac Easlick, on the No. Side of Neuse River & head of Orchard Creek; One Negro Man Named Seasor, One Boy Named Will, Two Negro Wimen Named Rose & Jane, & the Labour of Two Free Born Negro Boys Tell there Indentuers is Exspierd Named. Aron & David, & Two horses Called, Frolick & Poilet, to him & his heirs for Ever.

Item. I Give and bequith to my Well beloved Daughter, mary Cook, One shilling Sterling, to her & hier heirs For Ever.

Item. I Give and bequith to my Well beloved Daughter, Elizabeth Dawson, one Shilling Sterling, to her & her heirs.

Item. I Give and bequith to my well beloved Grandson, Joseph Stockley, one Shilling Sterling, to him & his heirs.

Item. I Give and bequith to my Well beloved Grandson, John Dawson, one Shilling Sterling, to him and his heirs.

Item. I Give and bequith to my Well beloved Son, Jesse Bryan, all the Remainder Part of my Estate, to him and his heirs.

I Likewise Constitute, make & orDain my Loveing Sons, William Bryan, John Bryan, & Jesse Bryan, Executors, of this my Last Will and Testament, and I Doe here by Utterly Disallow of and Revoke and Disanull all Former Wills by me made, Confirming this and Noe other to be my Last will & Testament.

In Witness whereof, I have here Unto Sett my hand & seale, the Day and Year above Written.

ANNE BRYAN (Seal)

Signed, Sealled, Published, Pronounced, and Delivered, by the said Anne Bryan, as her Last will & Testament, in the Presents of us the Subscribers:

 JAMES CARRAWAY.
 ANN CARRAWAY.
 ELIES JUSTES.
 GIDEON CARRAWAY.

The above last Will and Testament of Ann Bryan, was proved before me this 9th. day of March, 1773, by the Oath of Gideon Carraway, one of the subscribing Witnesses thereto, who swore that he saw the Testatrix sign, seal, publish & declare the same to be her last Will and Testament, and that at the time thereof she was of sound and disposing Mind & Memory.

And John Bryan one of the Executors therein named, having taken the Oath appointed for his qualification, It is ordered that letters Testamentary issue thereon

W. MARTIN.

Copied from Original Will filed in the Office of the Secretary of State.

EDWARD BRYAN'S WILL.

IN THE NAME OF GOD AMEN, This 28th Day of January, In the Year of our Lord, 1745, I, Edward Bryan, being In perfect mind and memory, blessed be God for his Mercy, calling unto Mind that it is Appointed for all men to Die Doth make this my Last Will and Testemt, and Dispose of my Worldly Estate wherewith God hath blessed me With, as followeth:

Imprimis. Unto my Eldest Son, John Bryan, I give and bequeath to he and his heirs lawfully begotten of his body and their bodies, for Ever, Two hundred Acres And Twenty Acres of Land, being part of the Land which I bought of Martin Frank, and Edward Frank, called New Germiny, beginning at the begining bounds of the Deed, On Jacks cabin branch, and Runing the bounds of the Deed for the Two hundred and Twenty Acres, which shall be Marked out by the Exs: or Some other Appointed person; Unto my Son, Edward Bryan, I give and bequeath To him and his Heirs Lawfully begotten of his Body and of their Bodies, for Ever, Two hundred & fifty Acres of of Land being part of the Land wch. I bought of Martin Frank and Edward Frank, call'd New Germany, begining on the Left bounds of his brother John's and Runing Up Towards Cyprus Creek within the Deed, For the Compliment to be

Marked out by the Exs. or some other Appointed person, in any shape or Course as they shall see fit & proper.

Item. I Give and bequeath to my son, William Bryan, and his Heirs Lawfully begotten of his Body and of their Bodies for Ever, three hundred Acres of Land, more or Less, being the Remaining part of the Two Deeds as I bought of Martin Frank and Edward Frank, called, New Germany, the Four hundred and Seventy Acres given to his Two Brothers Excepted, to them, and if any one of my Three Sons should Die without Heirs lawfully begotten of their Bodies, his portion bequeathed as affsaid shall be Equally Divided between the two living Brothers and their heirs lawfully begotten of their bodies for Ever; Also I give and bequeath to my Son, John Bryan, One lot In Newburn Town, to him, his heirs or assigns.

Item. I Give and bequeath unto my son, Edward Bryan, one Lot in Newburn Town, to him, his Heirs or Assigns; and I give and bequeath to my son, William Bryan, one lot in Newburn Town, to him, his heirs or Assigns. These three lots shall be Divided by my Exs., of other appointed persons, when my son, John Bryan, shall be at Age; Also I give and bequeath to my Daughter, Penelipy Bryan, One lot in Newburn Town, The lot and Storehouse, the same lot whereon the storehouse now Stands; Also I give and bequeath to my Daughter Penelipy Five Hundred Pounds, in bills, instead of a Portion of Land, to be paid out of my Money which lies in stock of Trade, at Age, or at the Day of Mareage; also I give and bequeath One hundred pounds in bills out of my Stock of Money in Trade, to buy her a bed and furniture, to be paid out at the Executors Discression before he comes to Age if Need be for it.

Item. I Give and bequeath to my loving Wife, Ann Bryan, One Plantation and all the Survey of Land belonging to it, lying on the West side of swifts Creek, Surveyed for me in One Thousand Seven hundred and forty four-five, called paradice, to her, her heirs or Assigns. And all the Rest of my Lands as is Not Given by Will or Deed, I give and bequeath to be Sold at the Exs. Discression, and the Sale and title shall be good to whomsoever shall buy it: also I give and bequeath to my Loving Wife One Negro Women called, Agey, and One Negro Man called Will, One Negro man called, London, One negro Man called Simon; also two plowhorses; also Five Riding horses; also all my stock of Cattle, sheep & hoggs, Except Twenty four Cows and Caves, Seven Stears only also I give all my household Goods as beding, Cetchen Wair, and all Vessels of Iron, brass, Copper, or puter, or Wood, and all other Vessels of any Kind, as ar generally Used in the house.

And I give and bequeath to my Three Sons, and Daughter, John, Edward, & William Bryan and Penelipy Bryan, Twelve Negroes Named as follows: Melatto, Tener, Sary, Nancy and little Egey, Tom, Cesar, George, Joseph Called Joe, Jack, Frank, & Robin, & Primas; and also I give and bequeath to them Twenty four Cows and Calves, and four Mairs. The said Negroes & Cattle and Mairs to be at their own proper Resque & Not to be Divided nor any Division made between my four Children of Neither Negroes, nor Cattle, nor horse-kind, until my Eldest son John shall be of Age, that is to say, of Twenty One Years, and then there shall be a Devision made by the Exs. and three other Men chosen by the Court. The Negroes and their Increase the Cattle and horse Kind & their Increase, The Cattle and horse Kind and their Increase shall be Equally Divided between my four Children and shall be at Each ones proper Resque.

Also I Give unto my Three sons, Each, One hundred Pounds in bills to buy Each of them a bed and Furniture, and this Three hundred Pounds shall be paid out of my Stock of Money that lies in Trade.

And my Desire is that my four Children should have Seven Years schooling and between the Age of seven Years old and Seventeen Years old, to be given in such Siencies as the Exs: shall think proper, and the Cost of their Cloathing, Washing, lodging, and schooling and Vittling, shall be paid out of their Negroes Labor put to Use as the Executors shall agree and think proper.

Also I Give my loving Wife the Use of my Childrens Negroes the first Two Years after my Decease, she paying the Childrens Expences, and when the Two Years is out the Children to have the Vallue of their hire for the time to come.

Also I Give the Money that lies in Trade, the Remaining part that is Not Given already, to be Divided, my Loving Wife to have One Third part, and the Two Third parts to my Children, to Equally Divided. Likewise I leave four Stears at Wiggines, One at Grimes, two at Goose Creek, and One of my Riding horses to be sold, to pay Jane Hand the Money Due to her Upon the books.

I likewise Constitute and Ordain my Loving Wife, Ann Bryan, and my Loving Brother, Hardy Bryan, and my Loving Brother, Lewes Bryan, to be my true and Lawfull Exx. & Executors of this my last Will and Testament.

As Witness my hand the Day and Date above mentioned.

EDWARD BRYAN. (Seal)

Signed, Sealed & Published before Us:
    WM. WHITFORD.
    JANE HAND.
    RICHARD HART.

May 9th, 1746.

These are to Certifie that Richd. Hart, and Jane Hand, came before me, Enoch Hale, Esqr., Chief Justice of North Carolina, and made Oath that they saw the w'thin nam'd Edwd. Bryan, in his Lifetime, Sign, seal & Publish the w'thin Wile & Testamt., and that he, the said Edwd. Bryan, was of sound mind and disposeing Memory at the time thereof, as also that Wileiam Whitford was a Concurring Evidence with them.

Test. E. HALL, C. J.

And The said Enoch Hale, Do further Certifie, that Hardy Bryan & Ann Bryan Exr. & Exx. to the wth. Wile, Qualified themselves According to Law by taking the Oath appointed.

Ord^d that Letter's Issue Accordingly.

E. HALL C. J.

Copied from Original Will filed in the Office of the Secretary of State.

HARDY BRYAN'S WILL.

IN THE NAME OF GOD AMEN. I, Hardy Bryan, of the province of North Carolina, & Craven County, Planter, being sick in Body, but of sound Mind & Memory, do make my last will & Testament in the form & Manner following, that is to say:

It is my will that the plantation on which my son Thomas now lives, consisting of about Two hundred & Seventy acres, be divided by the ash Branch, & then I give & bequeath that part of it lying on the North Side of the ash Branch to my said Son Thomas, to him & his Heirs for ever. I further give & bequeath to my son, Thomas, one Negroe man named Edinburgh, & one negroe Girl named Lucy, which said Lucy is already in the Possession of my son Thomas.

I give & bequeath to my son William, to him & his heirs forever, two hundred & seventy acres of Land, be the same more or less, which I bought of my Brother Lewis, & is adjoining to the Land of Frederick Isler. I further give & bequeath to my son William to him & his heirs for ever one hundred Acres of Land which I bought of Frederic Jones, & lying on the West side of Trent River. I further give & bequeath to my son William, One Negroe Boy named Cain, which I have already delivered into his Possession.

It is my will & desire that the Plantation or Survey of Land on which I now live be equally divided, & then I give & bequeath to my son, Hardy, to him & his heirs for ever, after the Marriage or death of his affectionate Mother, the upper half of the said Plantation or Survey, or that half of it on which the houses are now erected.

And I give & bequeath to my Son, Nathan, to him & his heirs for ever, the other or lower part of the said Plantation or Survey of Land. But if my son Nathan shou'd (die) without Issue or before he arrives at the age of Twenty one Years, then I give & bequeath the whole of the said plantation or survey of Land I now live upon, to my son Hardy, to him & his heirs for ever, after the Marriage or Death of his affectionate Mother; or if my Son Hardy shou'd die without Issue, or before he arives at the Age of Twenty One Years, then I give & bequeath the said whole Plantation or Survey of Land on which I now live, to my Son Nathan, to him & heirs for ever, after the Marriage or death of his affectionate Mother. But if both of my Sons Hardy & Nathan should die without Issue, or before the Age of Twenty One Years, then whatever Land I have given & bequeathed to my Sons Hardy & Nathan, I give & bequeath to my Son Lewis, to him & his heirs for ever.

I give & bequeath to my Son, Isaac, to him & his heirs for ever, one half of the plantation or Land on which my Son, Thomas, now lives, namely, that half of it which lies on the South Side of the Ash Branch.

I give & bequeath to my Son, Lewis, to him & his heirs for ever, one front Lot in the Town of Newbern, lying upon Nuce River, & one of my Two front Lots in the said Town lying upon Trent River, it being my will that my son Lewis, shall take his Choice of the said Two Lots lying upon Trent River. But if my Son, Isaac, should die without Issue or before he arrives at the age of Twenty One years then I give & bequeath to Son, Lewis, to him & his heirs for ever, all the Land which I have given & bequeathed to my Son Isaac; But if my Son Lewis shou'd die without Issue or before he arrives at the Age of twenty one Years, then I give & bequeath to my Son, Isaac, to him & his heirs for ever, all the Lots in Newbern which I have given & bequeathed to my Son Lewis.

I give & bequeath to my Daughter, Mary, to her & her heirs for ever, one Front Lot in the Town of Newbern Lying on Trent, after My son Lewis has taken his Choice of the two Lots as before mentioned.

It is my will & desire that my loving wife, Sarah, so long as she shall continue my Widow or live unmarried, shall have one half of the plantation or Survey of Land on which I now live, particularly, the upper half, or that half or part on which the houses are now erected. And it is further my will & desire, that as long as my loving Wife, Sarah, shall continue my widow or live unmarried, she shall have the Use & profits of the following five negroes, namely, one negroe Man named David, one negroe Man named Pomp, one Negroe Man named Frank, one negroe Man named Ben, & one Negroe Girl named Scylla; But then it is my Will & desire that my loving wife Sarah, shall find Meat, Drink, Washing, Lodging, & Schooling for my Children till they are married or arrive at the Age of Twenty One Years, out of the profits arising from the plantation & the Labour of the five Slaves abovementioned. And it is further my Will that the said Five Negroes, David, Pomp, Frank, Ben & Scylla be equally divided among all my Children, at the Marriage or Death of my loving Wife Sarah. I likewise give & bequeath to my loving Wife, Sarah, all my Stocks of cattle, Hogs, Sheep & Horses, all my household furniture, all my Plantation Tools & Implements of Husbandry.

It is further my will & desire that my following Six Children, namely, My sons, William, Hardy, Nathan, Isaac & Lewis & my Daughter, Mary, or the Survivors of them, shall have, & be equal Sharers of, all the rest of my Negroes not mentioned in this will, in the Manner following, that is to say, the rest of my Negroes not mentioned in this Will shall not be immediately divided, but each of my said Children, namely William, Hardy, Nathan, Isaac, Lewis & Mary shall have & receive his or her Share of the said Negroes & their Increase on the Day of Marriage or at the Age of Twenty one Years, And it is my Will that when any one of my said Six Children shall have received his or her Share of the said Negroes as before directed; he or she so receiving his or her Share shall not have any Claim or Title to the remaining Slaves or their future Increase.

I do hereby nominate & appoint my Sons, Thomas & William, Executors, & my loving Wife, Sarah, Executrix, of this my last Will & testament, & I do hereby revoke & disannul all other Wills heretofore by me made.

Witness my hand & Seal, this Twenty Eight Day of February, in the Year of our Lord, One thousand, Seven hundred & Sixty.

HARDY BRYAN (Seal)

Signed, sealed & acknowledged in the Presence of (the words "for ever" being first interlined in the Second page of this will):

  JAMES REED.
  SHADRACH ALLEN.
  MATTHEW X ARTER.
    his
    mark

NEW BERN, 6. May, 1760.

The foregoing last Will and Testament of Hardy Bryan, deceased, was duely proved before me, by the Oaths of James Reed and Matthew Arter, Evidences thereto. At the same Time Thomas Bryan, one of the Executors within named, and Sarah Bryan, named Executrix in the foregoing Will, qualified before me by taking the Oath of Executor and Executrix.

Let Letters Testamentary issue to the said Thomas Bryan, and Sarah Bryan, on the foregoing Will accordingly.

ARTHUR DOBBS.

Copied from Original Will, filed in the Office of the Secretary of State.

JOHN BRYANT'S WILL.

IN THE NAME OF GOD AMEN. The fourteenth day of Sept., one thousand, Seven hund., Thirty and four, I, Jno. Bryant, of Edgecombe precinct, in North Carolina, being very weak in body but perfect of mind and memory, thanks Be to Almighty God for it, And knowing that it is appointed for all Men once to die, Do Make, Constitute and appoint this to be my Last will And Testament, Revoking and Disanulling all other Wills and Testaments Ever before me made: And as for the worldly Inheritance the Almighty God hath Endowed withal, I Leave and Bequeath in manner and form following:

Imps. I leave and Lend to my well Beloved wife, Elisabeth Bryant, During her natural life, A Molatto wench Called Bess, and her Own bed and furniture, as also another bed and furniture wch. hath Oznabrigs Tick to it, One black walnut Safe, and half Adozn. turnd frame Rush chairs, And one trunk, And A Large Iron pot wt. A Still made upon it, and A Small Iron pot, One Brass Skellett, five tongs and Shovel, and Box Iron & Chaffing dish, as also A grey gelding, Bridle and Saddle, & A Mare & Colt called Diamond, & twenty five head of cattle, Young & old, and four Sheep, as also two Basons of putre & two dishes, four plates & half a Dozen Spoons And an Iron Spit.

Item. I Leave and Bequeath to my Son, Wm. Bryant, his heirs & Ass^s. for Ever, A tract of Land Beginning in the Marsh where ye. Line Crosses it, So running thro ye. pasture along ye. water course to another tract of Land, and then Continuing ye. water course to the Lower Line. I further give & Bequeath to him another tract of Land in Cupress Swamp known by the name of Ballards; I also Leave as afforsd. My other tract of Land Lying & Being in ye. East side of Deep Creek, Upon the Indian path; as also another tract of Land Lying in a Bever Dam Swamp, that Leads out of fishing Creek, known by the name of Polluck's Bever Dam; as also two Negroes, the One Named Robbin, the other Mingo, One New feather Bed wt. furniture, Called his bed, One Large Iron pot & a smal one, One Black walnut Round table, and four Leathern chairs, One new Case of Bottles, two putre Basons, two putre dishes, Four putre plates, & half A Dozen Spoons, One Buckaneer Gun, and whatsoever Cattle, hogs, horses and Mares that now Are Called his, and fifteen head of my own Stock here at Home, and four Steers that are at Canahoe, and all the rest of My Cattle at Canahoe, to be Divided betwixt he and Jno. Fort. I Further Leave & Bequeath to him A Bay horse called Spot, wt. A new Saddle and Bridle, and four other horses & mares And four Sheep; I also Leave him Seven pounds, Currant.

Item. I Leave and Bequeath to my Son, Arthur Bryant, his Heirs and ass[es]. for Ever, the plantation whereon I now live, joyning To the Land wch. I gave to my Son William, and another plantation On Deep Creek, where Richd. Camp now Liveth, And One hundred Acres of Land Lying in Cahukee Swamp. I also Leave & Bequeath to him a Negro Boy, Called Tom, and A Negro girl Named Jenny, I also give him a Large feather Bed wt. new furniture, I also Give him A Black walnut Square table, and four Leather Chairs, two Iron pots, two putre Basons, two Do. Dishes, and four plates, and One Iron Spit, and Six head of horses & Mares, And all the Stock of Cattle and Hogs in ye. plantation where Richd. Camp now Liveth, to be Divided Betwixt Camp and he, And twenty five head of Cattle, Young and old, of my home Stock, And four head of Sheep. I also Leave and Bequeath to him Seven pounds Currant Money of Virginia, and One Silver Sack Cup, and One Small trunk, and an Iron Bound Case of Bottles.

Item. I Leave and Bequeath to My Son, Davie Hopper, A hundred and Sixty Acres of Land Lying in the fork of the Bever Dam Swamp, joyning the Land I gave to My Son, William, I also Leave & Bequeath to him twenty pounds Currt. Money of Virginia, due to me pr. James Barns, By a note under his own hand, appeareth to be paid at Mr. Theophilus Pughs. As also to my Son Hopper Two thousand weight Of pork to be paid at his own house.

I also Leave and Bequeath to my well Beloved friend, Jno. Pope One hundred Acres of Land in A place On Cahukee Line, below ye. place where Robt. Wright Now Liveth.

I also Leave and Bequeath to James Turner, Living in Virginia, the Remainder of the tract of Land I Left to my Son Hopper.

I Leave and Bequeath all the rest of My Moveable Estate, to be divided Betwixt my wife, and my Son Wm. and Arthur, at the discretion of my Executors, Whom I Constitute and appoint who are My Sons, Davie Hopper and Wm. Bryant. Publishing, Declaring and pronouncing this and no other to be my last will and Testament.

Sealed wt. my Seal and dated the 14th day of 7 E., 1734.

JOHN BRYAN (Seal)

ROBT BEDFORD,
ARCHBALD THOMPSON,
ANN X TRAZIER.
her
mark

No CAROLINA. EDGECOMB ss. At a Court held for the Said Precint. on the third Tuesday of May, anno Dom. 1735. Present His Majesties Justices:

These may Certifie, that Anne Frazier, one of the Subscribing Evidences to the within Will, Appeared in Open Court and made Oath on the Holy

Evangelists that he was present and Saw, John Bryant, Sign, Seal & declare the within to be and Contain hie Last Will & Testament, & that the Said John Bryant was then and at that time of Sound and disposeing Memory; & that he Saw Robt. Radford, and Archd. Thompson, the other Subscribing Evidence Sign their names thereto at the Same time. Then also Appd. Davis Hopper, and William Bryant, Executors, in Open Court, and took the Execu. Oath in due form of Law.

Ordered that the Secrey have notice thereof, that Letters Testamentory Issue there on

Test. J. W. Mer——(?) Cler. Cur

Copied From Original Will filed in the Office of the Secretary of State.

SIMON BRYAN'S WILL.

N. Carolina, Bertie County.

In the Name of God Amen. I, Simon Bryan, being in my perfect Sences but in a Very bad State of health, do make this my Last will & testament, revoking all former wills whatsoever by me heretofore made, Constituting & appointing my wife Ann, My Bror. Edward Bryan, & my Son, David, my Sole Exors. First my Soul to almighty God in Sure & Certain hopes of a resurection from the Dead through the merits of my Lord & Saviour Jesus Christ, my Body to be buried at the discreation of my Exors., my Worldly goods in the following manner:

Imp^{rs}. To my Dear & Loving wife, I bequeth one third part of all my personal Estate after my Just debts are paid (there being nine Negros belonging to my Children, Some of wch came by the death of their Bror. Jno. Armour, the rest they hold by deed of gift; the negros are named, viz: Perry, Hannah, Feb, Dina, Ben, Lyd, Joe, Jupiter & Pina).

Item. To my Son, David, I bequeth, that tract of Land I bought of Michell & Henry Kings, to him, his heirs & assigns; the other two thirds of my personal Estate to be equally divided amongst my three children, but if my wife is with child now, my will & pleasure is that it have one Equall Share with my other children.

As witness my hand & Seal this 26, Nov^r., 1751.

Simon Bryan (Seal)

Signed, Sealed & published befor us:

Martha Bryan.
Isabel X Deal.
her
mark
Jas. Lockhart.
Lillington Lockhart.

BERTIE COUNTY.   May Court, 1753.
The within Will was Exhibited into Court by David Bryan, One of the Exors. therein Named, and Proved by the Oath of James Lockhart Esqr. and Lillington Lockhart, Two of the Subscribing Witness's thereto; & at the same time the said Exor. Quallifyed for said office according to Law, which was Ordered to be Certifyed.

Test. BENJN. WYNNS, Cler. Cur.

Copied from Original Will filed in the Office of the Secretary of State.

WILLIAM BRYAN WILL.

IN THE NAME OF GOD AMEN, the Twelfth Day of December, 1746. I, William Bryan, of Craven County, & Provance of North Carolina, being Sick and weak In Body but of Parfect mind & Memory, Thanks be given unto God Therefore, Calling unto Mind the Mortality of My Body, and knowing that it is appointed for all men Once to Dye, Dow make & Ordain this my Last Will & Testament, That is to Say, principally & first of all, I Give & Recommend My Soul into the hands of God That Gave it, & my Body I Recommend to the Earth to be Buried in a Desent & Christian Like burial at the Discretion of My Executors, Nothing Doubting but at the General Resurrection I Shall Receive the Same aGain by the mighty Power of God; and as Touching Such Worldly Estate Wherewith it hath pleased God to bless me with in this Life, I Give, Demise & Dispose of The Same in the following maner and form:

Item. I Give & Bequeath to Anne, My Dearly beloved Wife, one third part of my Negrews, and Likewise one third of all ye Rest of my Movable Estate, and the Use of the plantation I now Dwell on Dureing her Natureal Life.

Item. I Give & Bequeath the Remaining part of my Negrews & movable Estate to be Equally Devided amongst my Six Children, William Bryan, Elizabeth Bryan, Lewis Bryan, John Bryan, Anne Bryan, Jess Bryan, to them & their heir for Ever.

Item. I Give & bequeath to my well beloved Son, William Bryan, One hundred & Twenty five acors of Land the plantation I Now Dwell on, to him & his heirs for Ever.

Item. I Give and bequeath to my well beloved Son, John Bryan, One Hundred & Twenty five acors of Land, the one half of the Tract of Land I now Dwell on, known By the Name of kits Neck, begining at the Gut which the Cart bridge is Over & So Runing up to the head Line, to him and his heirs for Ever.

Item. I Give & bequeath to my Well beloved Son, Lewis Bryan, One hundred acers of Land Lying upon the head of

Smith Creek, which I Bought of Gunston Allen, known by The Name of Holley Neck, to him & his heirs for Ever.

Item. I Give & bequeath to My well beloved Son, Jesse Bryan, one Tract or persell of Land Lying upon the head of Goose Creek, Joyning upon Cohoons Savanah, Which I had of John Bryan, to him and his heirs for Ever.

I Likewise Constitute Make and Ordain My Loving Wife, Anne Bryan, and my Brother, Joseph Bryan, and my Son, William Bryan, Executores of this my Last will & Testament, & I doe hereby Uterly Disallow of & Revoke & Disanull all former wills by me made, Confirming this & No Other to be My Last Will and Testament.

In witness Whereof, I have here unto Set My hand & Seal, the Day & Year above Writen.

WILLIAM BRYAN. (Seal)

Signed, Sealed, published, pronounced, & Delivered by the Sd. William Bryan, as his Last will & Testament, In the Presents of us the Subscribers:

    LAZARUS PEARSE.
    JAMES CARRAWAY.
    WILLIAM CARRAWAY, JUN.

CRAVEN COUNTY, SS.

At a Court of Comon Pleas begun & held at New Bern, the third Tuesday in June, Anno Domini, 1747, then the within will was Proved by the Oath of a Concuring Evidence thereto, & Joseph Bryan, Executor & Ann Bryan, Executrix of the said Will Came into Court & took the Oaths by Law Appointed for their Qualification. Ordered that they have Letters Testamentary thereon

WILL: HEDGES: S: C. Cur.

Copied from Original Will filed in the Office of the Secretary of State.

BENJAMIN BUNDY'S WILL.

IN THE NAME OF GOD AMEN, the fift day of october, one thousand, Seven hundred and tWenty Eight. Beniamen Bundy, of pascuotank, in the province of North Carolina, being Sick in body, but of Good and perfect memory; thanks be to Allmity God; And Calling to remembrance the uncertenty of this transitory Life, and that all flesh must yeld unto death when it Shall plese God to Call, Do make, Constitute, odain and declare this, my Last will and testament, manner and form following, Rovoking and adnulling by thes presents all and Every testament and testaments, Will and wills, heretofore by me made and declared, Eigher by ward or writing, and this to be taken only for my Last will and testament, and none other, I Do Gieve and dispose the Same in manner and form following: that is to Say,

First, I Will that all those debt and dues as I owe in Right or Conscience, to any manner of person or persons What So Ever, Shall be well and truly Contented and paid, within Convenient time after my decese, by my Executors hereafter named.

Item. I Give and bequeve in witness unto my Loving wife, hannah bundy, the plantation whereon I now Lieve, together with a tract of Land Containing two hundred Eakers adioyning unto my Sd. plantation, during her naterell Life: and in Case my wife, hannah, die without Ishue begotten by my own body, then I will and bequeive the Said Land unto my Loving brother, Samuell bundy, to him his heirs and assigns for Ever.

Item. I give and bequieve unto my Loving brother, Samuel bundy, a certain tract of land Sirvaid by william Norris, Sinaor, Liing in griffens Swamp, to him his heirs and assigns for Ever.

Item. I gieve and bequieve to my Sd. brother, Samll., one negro named tom, to him his heirs & assigns for Ever; and allso one young horse; and furthermore, in Case my wife Should marry After my decese, then I will and bequieve to my Sd. brother, Samll., one feather bed and furniture.

Item. After the decese of my now wife, I give and bequieve my negro Jack, unto my Sd. brother, Sam^{ll}, him his heirs for Ever.

Item. I gieve and bequieve unto my Loving wife all my parsonable Estate, both goods and Chattles, that Came to me by her; and the Rest of my personible Estate att the decese of my Sd. wife, to go to my Sd. brother Sam^{ll}., his heir or Assigns.

Item. I Except onn mare Coalt for my Cosen, mary Jons.

Item. I gieve and beqeieve Unto my loveing Brother, Sam^{ll}., all my Right and title to a tract of land Survaed by me and Tho:^m Jesup, Lieing in griffens Swamp, To him, hie heirs or assigns for Ever.

Item. i do appoint my Loving wife, hannah bundy, and my brother, Sam^{ll}. bundy, my Sole Executors.

In wittness I have here Set my Seal.

BEN^N + BUNDY. (Seal)
the mark of

Signed Sealed and delivered In the presents of Us:

ZACHARIAH FIELD
THOMAS WOODLEY
JOHN X PHITT
the mark of

No. CAROLINA, ss. Oct^br 26th, 1728.

Thomas Woodley & John Phitt, Two of the Evidences to the aforewritten will came before me & made Oath on the holy Evangelists, that they Saw Benjamen Bundy, decd., seal & Execute the same as his last will & Testamt., he then being of perfect mind & Memory.

GALE, C. J:

Copied from Original Will filed in the Office of the Secretary of State.

JOHN BUTLER'S WILL.

IN THE NAME OF GOD AMEN, the 24th day of december, 1772. I, John Butler, of the County of Tyrrel, Farmer, being weak in body but of perfect mind and memory, thanks be given unto God therefore, calling unto mind the Mortality of my body and knowing that it is appointed for all men once to die, do make and ordain this my last will and Testament, that is to Say, principally and first of all, I give and recommend my Soul into the hands of Almighty God that give it, and my body I recommend to the Earth, to be buried in decent Christian burrall at the descretion of my Executors, nothing doubting but at the Generall Resurrection I shall recive the Same again by the mighty power of God; and As touching such worldly Estate wherewith it hath Pleased almighty God to bless me in this life, I give, demise and despose of the Same in the Following manner and Form:

Imprimis. I Lend unto my dearly beloved Wife El^h: five negroes, Viz: Jack, Zepero, Nan, mereen, and mark, with this plantation we now live on, with the horsess, hoggs and Cattle, and all the house hold Furniture. In Case there Should be any money It must be divided Equally, my Wife, William, John & James Butler: I Lend, I Say, to my dearly belov'd Wife, Elizabeth, all the Aforsaid Articles dureing her Widowood.

Item. I give to my Son, William Butler, the plantation he now lives On, and fifty pounds prock. money, to Leved out of my Estate, and Four Cows & Calves or the Value thereof, to him and his Lawfull heirs for ever.

Item. I give unto my Son, John Butler, Six negroes, Vizt: Jack, Zeperoh, Rose, Ben, Bristo and dick, after the decease or marage of my Wife Elizabeth, To him and his Lawful heirs for ever.

Item. I give unto my Son, James Butler, the plantation he now lives On, lying on Turkey Swamp, on the South Side the Sd. Swamp, Containing three hundd. acres of of Land more or less, to him and his Lawfull heirs for ever. I Likewise give to my Son, James Butler, four negroes Vizt. Dinah, Mark, Little Jack, and Nan, with one Still, one desk, and Ten pounds prock. money, after the Deceas. of my Wife, Elizebeth, or marrage, to him and his heirs for ever.

Item. I give unto my Daughter, Phereby McHenry, the manner Plantation or the Land I now live, On dureing her Naturall Life, after the Decease or marrage of my Wife Elizebeth, then to my two grand Daughters, Sarah ann McHenry, and Susanna McHenry: I Likewise give to my grand Daughter, Wineford McHenry, one Negro Garl Named Mereen, to her and her heirs for ever, all to be rec^d: in mater and Form As before mentioned, at the Deceas or marrage of my wife, Elizebeth.

Item. I give to my Grandson, James Butler Cherry, the Son of Martha Cherry, A piece of Land Joyning to the Gum Log, and from the gum Log up to Wheatleys Old Field. I Likewise give unto Sd. James Cherry, the Son of Martha Cherry, two Negroes Vizt: one garl, named Charity, one Boy named Nedd, the Son of Negro Nann, I give it to him to be rec^d: at the years of twenty one, in matter and Form as before mentiond. I give unto Sd: James Cherry, one Feather Bead and Bedstead, four Basons, two dishes and Six plates, one Iron pott: in Case he should die without a Lawfull heir it must return to John and James Butler my two Sons to be Equally devided between them.

Item. I give unto my Grandson, James Gainer, the Son of Arther Gainer and Sarah, his Wife, one hundred Acres of Land from the flag branch up to the head line, Joyning to his fathers Land, Likewise One negroe boy named Tom, to him and his heirs for ever: if in Case he should die without heirs to return to John and James Butler left in manner and form As before mentiond.

Item. I give unto my daughter, Mary Leggett, twenty pounds prock money, To be Levied out of my Estate, to be paid unto her; and her heirs for ever.

Item. I give unto my grand Daughter, Elizebeth Cherry, Daughter of Arther Gainer and Sarah, his Wife, one negro boy named Isaac, also one Feather Bedd and Furniture or forty Shillings prock, to be rec^d. in matter and form as before mentioned, to her and her Lawfull heirs for ever.

Item. I give unto my Daughter, Elizebeth Johnson, Ten shillings Sterling, to be Levied out of my Estate.

Item. I will and desire that after my Deceas., and my Wife, that all the Resedue of my Estate may be Equally Divided amongst my four Children, Vizt: Wm., John & James Butler, and Phereby McHenry, the Wife of George Augustin McHenry, to them and there heires for ever.

Item. I give unto my two grandsons, Simon Butler, the Son of John Butler, and John Butler, the Son of James Butler, a Tract of Land or plantation Lying the north Side of Trenten

Creek, Containing 640 Acres, formerly known by the name of Joseph Messers Land, To them and and their heirs for ever.

Item. I give unto my Son, James Butler, the Land Whereon Mary Cage now Liveth, to him and his heirs for ever.

I Likewise Nominate and appoint my loveing Wife, Elizebeth Butler, and my two Sons, John and James Butler, my Sole Executors and Exx: of this my Last will and Testament, revokeing and making void all other former wills, Lagacies formerley by me made, Ratifying and confirming this and no other To be my Last will and Testament.

In Witness whereof I have hereunto Set my hand Seal, the day and date first Above Mentiond.

JOHN BUTLER X (Seal)
his mark

Signed, Sealed, pronounced, and declared, by the Sd John Butler to be his Last will and Testament in Presence of us:

EDMUN ANDREWS,
JOHN WHITEHURST,
SOLO WILSON,

BE IT KNOWN TO ALL MEN BY THESE PRESENTS. that, I, John Butler, Senr., of the County of Tyrrell, planter, have made and declared my last will and Testament. in writing, Bearing date the 24th. day of December, 1772. I, the Said John Butler, by thise presents Codicil do ratify and confirm my Sd. Last will and Testament, and do give and bequeath unto my Grand Son, Andrew Butler, the Son of James Butler, the Herring gut Land, from the Gum Logg Branch Down to the river. I do Likewise revoke the Bedd and Furniture which I give to my grand Daughter, Lizabeth Cherrey, mentioned in my will. I give to my Daughter, Pherebe McHenry, one Bedd and Furniture which I now Lay On, after me and my Wifes Decd. And my will and meaning is that this Codicil or Schedule be Adjudged to be a part and parl· of my last will and Testament, and that all things therein mentioned and Contain'd be Faithfully and truly performed, and as fully and amply in every Respect As if the Same were So Declared and Sett down in my Last will and Testament.

Witness my hand this fift day of march, 1773.

JOHN X BUTLER (Seal)
his mark

JACOB MORRISS.
SOLO WILSON.

The within last Will and Testament of John Butler, deceased, and the Codicil thereto annexed, were proved before me this fourteenth day of

October, 1773, By the Oaths of Edmund Andrews, and John Whitehurst, two of the subscribing Witnesses to the said Will, and Jacob Morris one of the Subscribing Witnesses to the said Codicil, who severally, and not one for the other, swore that they were present and did see the said Testator sign, seal, publish and declare the same to be and contain his last Will and Testament with his Codicil thereto annexed; and that at the several times of executing his said Will and Codicil he was of sound and disposing Mind and Memory. And John and James Butler, the Executors therein named, having taken the Oaths and qualified as the Law directs, It is Ordered that Letters Testamentary issue thereon accordingly.

Jo. Martin.

Copied from Original Will filed in the Office of the Secretary of State.

CALEB CALLAWAY'S WILL.

Pequimons in North Carolina:

I, Caleb Callaway, being Sick And weak of body, butt, through the marcy of the Lord, in Sound and perfect mind And memory, And Considering ye Certainty of Death and not Knowing the time it may pleas him to take mee hence, Doe make and Ordayne this my Last will and testament, first revoking All former will or wills by mee made, Doe Ordayne this only to Stand & remaine As my Last will And Testament As follows:

Itm. I Give and bequeath Unto my Son, Josua Callaway, the first Child that Shall bee hereafter borne by my negrow girle named Ruth, (wch negrow Girle is wth my Daughter, Rachell, And her husband, John Wiatt) that Lives to bee two years and Half, and the Sd mother being to nurse the Sd Child tell it is Come to that Age, & then to bee Delivered to my Sd. Son, Josua, or his assins, by John Wiatt.

tt. I allso give to my afore Sd. Son, Josua, All my Coopers tools.

It. I Give Unto my Grand Daughter, Eliz: Wiatt, the Daughter of John Wiatt, when Shee Come to Age, Or Att the Day of marriage, her Choyse of Any one of the rest of the Children that shall bee born one my afore Sd. negrow Girle, Named Ruth. I allso give to my Sd. Grand Daughter, the first mare fould that Either of my two mare brings, to run for her Use and to bee in her Fathers Custody. And In Case Any of the Increas of the Sd mare fould Shall Grow Up fitt for saile, my will is that my Son in Law, John Wiatt, Shall have liberty to Sell the Same for Good Housold Stuf, for my Afore Sd. Grand Child Use.

It. It is my will that my aforeSd. negrow Girle named Ruth, bee and remain wth my Daughter, Rachell, and her Husband John Wiatt, for & During theer naturall Lifes, And yt they Shall Have ye whole profit of hir Labour, and After theare Deces, then if the Sd negrow Girle Shall bring more Children then is before Given, then Shee and Those Children to bee Equally Devided Among Such other Children as shall bee beegat hereafter one my aforeSd Daughter, Rachell, by her Husband John Wiatt.

It. I Give to my Loving wife, Elizabeth, if Shee stands to this my will, All my Stock of sheep and one mare, And Hors, her Choyse out of my stock of Horses.

It. I Give to my Son, Josua Callaway, one full third partt of All the rest of my Personal Estate yt remains, besides wt is already Given. It is also my will yt in Case my Son Josua, will him Self in p'son Come And Live One my Plantation in Yawpim Creek, that he Shall now forth wth have ye one Half of Cleare ground, and half ye Barn, & Half ye Benefitt of ye Orchard, butt in Case yt my Son Dus nott Come himself, then he Shall nott putt a tennat theare During his mothers Widowhood.

It. The Other Half of my Plantation, wth All the rest of the Houses thereon, & Half the Orchard, I appoynt And Hereby Ordr. that my Afore Sd wife, Eliz:, Shall have the Use of During her widowhood; butt in Case yt my Sd wife Shall marry a Husband, then it is my will yt my Plantation bee Indeferantly Devided into three parts, my Sd wife to Choos one third part During her naturall Life, And my Son forthwth to Enter on the other two Third parts.

It. I Allso hereby Apoynt yt ye other two third parts of my Personal Estate not Already Given, Shall bee and remain in the hands of my Sd Lo: wife, Eliz:, So long as Shee remains a widow, butt in Case Shee marries a Husband, then my will is yt my Son, Josua Callaway, Shall Have one third part of those two Thirds in her Hands. And in Case that my Sd wife Shall Die a widow, Soe yt the two thirds of my Sd personall Estate lies in her Hands Dureing her naturall life, then my will is yt those two thirds of my Estate in my Sd wifes possesion Att her death, Shall bee my Son Josua Callaways, And his Heys: for Ever, together wth all my reall Estate of Lands, Houses &:

It. I Do Appoynt my Son, Josua Callaway, my Sole Executors of this my Last will and testament, hereby requiring him to See All my Just Debts in the first place Satisfied Oute of my Estate.

In Confermacion of wch, I have here Unto Sett my hand And Seale, this 10 Day of Jun., Ano:, 1706.

CALEB SALLOWAY. (Seal)

Sealed & Delivered in presents of:
 THOMAS LONG I his mark.
 JOHN BARROW.
 ANTHONY A WHERRY.
    his mark

parte Enterlined by me, Caleb Salloway.

Memd. added: It tis my will that my Daughter, Elizabeth, have a yong Cow delivered to her Father, for my grandaughter owne estate, and her Father to have the same Liberty to dispose of the Increas of the Cow, as of the mairs Colt.

As witness my hand, this 13 day of June, 1706.

CALEB SALLOWAY.

Proved in Court by the Oaths of Thomas Long & Anthony Wherry. This 13th Day of July, Anno Dom. 1706.

Test. THO: SNODEN, Cl. Cur.

Copied from Original Will, filed in the Office of the Secretary of State.

WILLIAM CARR'S WILL.

IN THE NAME OF GOD AMEN. I, Willaim Carr, of the County of Duplin, & Province of North Carolina, Am Sick in Body, but perfect In Memory and of a Sown Judgment, Blessed be God for It, and having Called to Mind the Scertainty of Death and of a future State, and that it is appointed for all Men Onest to Die Do hereby Recommend My Soul to God, and my Body to the Earth to be Buried at the Descration of my Executors, whome I shall hereafter Name, And in hopes of a Glorious Resurraction through the Merits of My Lord and Saviour Jesus Christ; Do hereby as far as Almighty God Enabels me in this My present Condition, Do Renounce the World & the Things of this Life, and by these Presents Do Constitute and Ordain, this to be my last Will & Testament, Revocking all other Wills and Testament by me Made, Either by Word or Writing, and this only to Stand and remain for my last Will & Testament: Therefore Doth Order, Settle & Leave what Woreldey Estate God hath Blessed me with, In the following Manner, Viz:

Itam. I Order that all my Just Debts & Funeral Expenses be first Pay'd out of my Estate That Almighty God hath Now Blist me with, And the rest of my woreldey Substance I leve and Bequeath In the following Manner, Viz:

Itam. I Leave & Bequeath to my Beloved Wife, Hannah, The one third part of all my Moveable Estate after my Lawful Debts & funeral Expences is pay'd, together with the Houses & plantation where I now live to Such times as My Son, Archibald Carr, comes to ye age of Twenty one years, and then the Sd. Houses & Plantation to be his for Ever. But In falure of him to ye Nixt Heir In Law & so on; And the rest of my Goods & Chattles, after my Just Debts and Funeral Expences is pay'd, and the one Third of ye rest of ym. taken off to my Wife, as afsd., then ye remainder I leave & Bequeath to be

Divided Equaly In it's kine Amongs my other Children, Viz: Archibald Carr, Jane Carr, & ye one that is yet unborn if it Should pleas God that it comes to the woreld; and In case that any of ye children Should Die before that they arive to age; I order that the part of the Deceased shall be Equally Devided Amongst the rest of the Surviving Children.

To Which Last Will & Testament, I Do hereunto set my Hand and fix my Seal, this fifth Day of December, In the year of our Lord, One thousand, Seven Hundred and fifty Three;

I order & appoint my Beloved Wife, Hannah, Executor of this my Last Will and Testament.

WILLIAM CARR. (Seal)

Signed, Sealed, and Declared
In presents of Us:
    JOHN DICKSON.
    WILLIAM McREE.
    SUSANNAH McALEXD.

NORTH CAROLINA, DUPLIN COUNTY, ss.   October Court, 1754.

This Day Hannah Carr, Executrix of the last Will & Testament of William Carr, Deceased, Came Into Court & proved the sd. Last will & Testament of ye Deceased, And Took ye Oath of An Executrix as by Law prescribed. And produced an Inventrey Upon Oath of what Goods & Chattels & Debts Due to ye Estate of the Deceased, and Pray'd Letters Testamentorey upon the Same &c.

The Court then and There Ordered that the Above proceedings of Sd. Executrix be given to ye Secretarys Office In Order to the Obtaining of sd. Letters.

The Above Certified by me, October ye 9th, 1754.
    JOHN DICKSON, C. C.

Copied from the Original Will, filed in the Office of the Secretary of State.

WILLIAM CARTRIGHT'S WILL.

IN THE NAME OF GOD AMEN, the second day of fabury, in the year of our Lord, one Thousand, Seven hundred and Thirty and one. I, William Cartright, being very sick and Weak in body but of perfect mind and Memory, Thanks be given unto God therefore, Calling unto mind the mortality of my body and knowing that it is appointed for all men once to Die, do make and ordain this my Last will and Testament, that is to Say: principally and first of all, I Recomend my body to the Earth to be buried In a Christian lik and Dacent Manner at the Discrestion of my Executors, nothing Doubting but at the Genrell Resariction I shall Recive the Same again by the might power of God that gave it; and as Touching Such worldly Estate whare with it hath pleased god to bless me in Life, I give and Dispose of the Same In manner following, Viz:

Itm. I give unto my friend, Hannah Staford, all my Land and plantation whereon I now Liveth by her freely to be possessed and Injoyed During The Term of her natural Life, and at her Death then I give it to my god Son, Joseph Stockley, to him and his heirs for Ever, freely to be possessed.

Itm. I give Hannah Staford, three Cowes and a Fowe year old hefer and Two Two year old Steers, and Eight yards of Seven Eight Lining.

Itm. I give unto my Sister, mary Rees, four yards of Seven Eight Lining, and one Large pertor Bason.

Itm. I give unto my brother, Robert, one bason and a Dish.

Itm. I give unto my brother, Thomas, one pottel bason and one Dish.

Itm. I give unto Owen Rees, one gun and a new Chest, and Two Sows and pigs, and one young horst.

Itm. I give to my Brother Thomas, Two Sows and piggs, and one beaver hatt.

Itm. I give unto Hannah Staford, my horse Sadel and bridle, and one Little Pott and pot hucks, and one Chest, and one white mug, and two bolltes, and one hive of bees.

Itm. I give my Brother Robert, Two Sows and piggs.

Itm. I give to my brothers, Robert, Thomas, and Owen Rees, Each of Them, one Earthen Mugg and a glass bottle to Each of Them.

Itm. I give unto my weel beloved friend, Ann Stockley, one frieing pan and one Eight Squiar bottle, and one behive of bess, and Two sows and piggs.

Itm. I give unto hannah Staford, Two Sows and Piggs.

Itm. I give unto John Makdaniel, Two sows and piggs.

Itm. I give unto Owen Rees, one fether bed and boulster.

Itm. I give unto my brother, Thomas, one Rugg and blanket.

Itm. I give unto hannah Staford, one Large new Rugg.

Itm. I give my ax, and Two hows unto my Brothers, Robert, Thomas, and Owen.

Itm. I give to my Brothers, Thomas and Owen, one young mare bhay, giveing unto Elisabeth Clark the first Colt of the sd. Mare.

And I doe make and ordain Jeremiah Murding and Stephen Delemare, my full and Sole Executors of this my Last will and Testament, and I doe hereby Revoke and Disanull and make viode all former wills and Testaments Whatsoever.

In Witness Wharoof, I have hereunto Sett my hand and seal.

his
WILLIAM WW CARTRIGHT. (Seal)
Marke

Signed, Sealed, published and pronounced, by the sd. William

Cartright to be his Last Will and Testament, in ye presence of us:

ELISABETH X̲ CLARK.
        her

JONATHAN HIBBS.
   mark.

MARY MURDEN.

NORTH CAROLINA, PASQOUTANK PREC'T. SST.

This foregoing will recorded in ye Register Book of pasquot'k, June ye 7th, 1732.
        Test. WM. MINSON, Regist.

February, 6, 1730.
Proved this Will be fore me,
        RICH. EVERARD.

NO. CAROLINE, CHOWAN, SC.

These may Certify that Stephen Delemarr, personally appeared at Edenton, in the precinct aforesay'd & took his Solemn affirmacon well & Truly to perform the above written Will of Wm. Cartright, Deced. This 16th day of February, Anno D'ni, 1730. Before me,
        W. BADHAM, Just. Peace.

Copied from the Original Will, filed in the Office of the Secretary of State.

WILLIAM CARTRIGHT'S WILL (Senior).

IN THE NAME OF GOD AMEN, the fifteenth Day of January, in the year of our Lord, one thousand, Seven hundred & thirty three. I, William Cartright, of North Carolina, In the County allbramall, in the precinct of pasquotank, planter, being Sick and weak, But of perfect sence and memory, thanks be to God therefore, Calling to mind the Mortality of my Body, and knowing that it is apointed for all men Once to Dey, do make and ordaine this my Last will and Testament, that is to say: principally and first of all, I give and ReCommend my soule Into the hand of God that Gave it, and my Body I recommend to the Earth to be buried In Decent and Cristone maner at the discrision of my Executricks, nothing Doubting but at the Generill Resurrection I shall Reseive the Same aGain by the allmighty power of God; and touching Such worldley Estate where with it hath pleased God to Bless me with In this Life, I Give and Demis and dispose of the Same, in the following maner and forme:

Item. I Give and Bequeath unto my Son, Thomas Cartright, the sum of tenn shillings, speasuea.

Item. I Give and Bequeath unto my Son, Robert Cartright, a small of land aJoyninn unto his Land.

Item. I Give and Beqeath unto oen Rese, Teen Shillings.

Item. I Give and Bequeth unto my son, Joseph Cartright, my plantation whare one now I Dwell, after the desess of my wife, Sarath Cartright, begin att my Sons, Robert's line, up as fare as the pigg pens, and my will Is that neither he nor his mother molest one and other Dureing hir natrell Life and after hir Desese then my plantation to fall to him and his heirs Lawfully Begotten of his bodey for Ever.

Item. I Give and Bequeth unto my Daughter, hannah Cartright, all the Remaner part of the Land Belongin to my plantation patern, that Is above the pigpens and to his heirs for ever.

Item. I Give and Bequith unto my Daughter, Tamer Cartright, a tract of land called the Little, for a Bove Oen Rese and to his heirs for Ever.

Item. I give and Bequeth unto my two Sons, Caleb Cartright, and David Cartwright, my tract of Land Cominley Called Sandey run to be Eakqeley Devided betwene them and to their heirs for Ever; But In case Either of my two Sons Should Dey without heirs, then my will is that the longest Liver to porscs the hole tract of Land Called Sandy run.

Item. I give and bequeth unto my son, Joseph Cartright, my hunting gun.

Item. I give and bequeth unto my son, Caleb Cartright my new gun.

Item. I give and bequeth unto my son, David Cartwright, my two letle Guns.

Item. I Give and bequeth unto my Daughter, hannah Cartright, one young Black Mare Called rose, and my will Is that the first horse Colt she brings for my Son Joseph, and the first mare colt for my Daughter, tamer.

Item. I give and bequeath unto Elizabeth Cartright, to my son John Cartwright Desesed, one two year old heffer.

Item. I give and Bequeth to my Loving and lafull wife, Sarath Cartright, all the rest of my personell Estate, During her widowhood, but in Case the should marry, then att the Day of marig, all the Rest of my Goods and Chatles to be Eakqley Devided amongst my five Children, Joseph Cartright, Caleb Cartright, hanah Cartright, David Cartright, Tamar Cartright.

Item. I Give and Bequeth unto my Daughter, hanah Cartright, one likely Cow and Calfe, to have the sam Cow and Calfe this Insewing Spring after the Date hereof.

Item. I Give and Bequeath unto my two Sons, Caleb Cartright and David Cartright, one negrow man, If your mother Continues a widow she shall have the use of him Dureing the natrell Days of hir life, but If she shall marey, then the said negrow to be between Caleb Cartright and David Cartright, And the said David Cartright to have his Labour three Months, and Caleb Cartright to have his labour one month and so to Continew as Long as he shall Live.

Item. I Give and Bequeath unto oen Rese, a Serten tract of land Containing one hundred and Eighty akers of Land, begining att a Beach one the west Side of a Branch Called anauerell Branch, and from thence Runing verioas Corses to the (to the) horn Beame to the Lithe fork swamp, soever the swamp to a mayple which is over Deviding line, which said tract of Land I now live one, to him and his heirs for Ever.

Item. I give and Bequeath unto Elizabeth Cartright, Daughter to John Cartright, Desesed, fortey akers of Land lying one the South side of the Creeke swamp Known and Calld. by the name of maverts, which Said land I Give for more or Less, to hir and hir heirs for Ever.

Leaving my loving wife, Sarah Cartright, hole and Sole Executricks of this my Last will and testament, and after hir Deses, the Rest of my Estate to be Eaquelly Devided amongst my five Children.

WILLIAM ^{his} XX _{mark.} CARTRIGHT (Seal)

Signed, Sealed, published & Delivered in the presents of us:
EDWARD ^{his} E _{mark.} WHORTEN
JOHN ^{his} J _{mark.} RICHARDSON.
JAMES GREAVES.

NORTH CAROLINA. PASQUOTANK PREC'T. SC.

At a Court held for the sd. precinct, at the court house in Broomfield, the 19th Day of aprill, ano. Domi., 1734. Present His Majesties Justices:

These may Certifie that Edward Wharton & John Richardson, two of the Subscribing Evidences to the within Will, appeared in Open Court and made Oath on the Holy Evengilist, that they were present & saw William Cartwright Sign, Seal & declaire the within to be & Contain his last will and Testament, & that the Sd. Wm. Cartwright, was then and at that time of sound & Disposing memory; and that they also saw James Greaves, the other Subscribing Evidence Sign his name thereto at the Same time.

Then also appeared Sarah Cartwright, Extrix. in Open Court & took the Exctors. Oath in due form of Law.

Ordered that the Secretary have notice thereof that letters test'ry Issue thereon as the Law Directs.

By Order, JOS: ANDERSON, Cler: Cur:

Copied from the Original Will, filed in the Office of the Secretary of State.

JOHN CARRUTHERS' WILL.

NORTH CAROLINA.

IN THE NAME OF GOD AMEN. I, John Carruthers, of the County of Craven, and Province of North Carolina, merchant, Being of perfect mind and memory and Calling to mind and Duly Considering the unsartainty of humane life, Do make this, my last will and testament. First and Principally I Commit my Soul into the hands of my blessed maker, trusting in his mercy and in the merits of my Dear Redeemer for the Remission of my Sins; and my Body I Commit to the Earth to be Interred in such Decent and Christian like Manner as to my Executors That seem meet, In hopes of the glorious Resurrection of the last great Day; and as for such worldly goods that providence hath blessed me with, after my Just Debts and necessary Expenses are Contented, Discharged, and payd by my Executors, Which I will shall be first honestly done, then the Remainder I Bequeath in the following manner:

Imprimis. I Give and Bequeath unto my Daughter, Rocksolnnah Witherinton, one Lott of Land lying in Newbern town, and joining Pollocks Streat and Eding Streat, and known in the plan of the Sd. town, by number 98, together with all Houses and appurtenances to the same belonging, and my Deask, unto her, the said Rocksolanah Witherinton, her Heirs and assigns for Ever.

Item. I Give and Bequeath unto my Daughter, Frances Hodges, one Negro girl Cald Carolina, and one feather Bed and one Boulster, 2 pillos, one Blanket, two Steats, and one Countarpen, it being the Bed that I Commonly Lodg on, and all the Cattal that I have yousing at the Francis Hodges Cow Pen, unto her, the Sd Frances Hodges, her Heirs and assigns for Ever.

Item. I Give and Bequeath unto my Son, John Carruthers, my Riding Sadal and Bridal, and gun, and one pr. large money Seals, and my Silver Shubuckels and Knee Buckels, to him, his Hairs and assigns for Ever.

Item. I Give and Bequeath unto my Son, Joseph Carruthers, Six large Silver tea Spuns, and one Silver tea tongs, and Silver Straner, and fore large Silver Spuns for table use, to him and his Heirs and assigns for Ever.

Item. I Give and Bequeath unto my Daughter, Sarah Rice, my gould Buttons I wear in my Sleeves, and one Brase Warming Pan with a wooden handal to it, to her and her Heirs for Ever.

Item. I Give and Bequeath unto my two Sons in law, Frances Hodges, and John Witherinton, all my wearing close of all Sorts, Except the Buckels and Buttons before menchan'd, to be Equaly Devided Betwen them.

Item. I Give unto my well beloved Wife, Content Carruthers, the Labar or Serves of one Negro man, Coled Hannabal, Dewering the time of her natril Life or the time of her Wedowhud, and at the time of her death or the day of her marrage, my Will and desier is that my Executors, hereafter Menchand, may taek the foreSd Negro, Hannabel, into thear Cear and Persestion, and my Will is that thay may Set him up at Publick Vander to be Sould to the highest bedar for Redy money, and the money arising by the Sale of the fore Sd Negro to be Equaly devided amung my Chilldring that may or shall be then Liveing, and my Will and desier is that the above menchand Negro man Hannabel, may not be Carried out of Craven County with out the Leve or Consent of my Executors.

Item. I Give unto my well beloved Wife, Content Carruthers, the Labar or Sarvis of one Negro woman Coled Enow, dewering the tim of her, ye Sd. Content Carruthers, her Natril life, and at her Deces I Give and Bequeath the fore Sd Negro Woman Coled Enow, to Rebekah McCarthy, to her and her Heirs for Ever.

Item. I Give and Bequeath unto my well Beloved Wife, Content Carruthers, one Negro Woman Coled, Baranton, and all my Horses and all my Cattal that youses on trent, or anyways Belongs to my Cow Pen at my home House, and all my hoggs and Sheep and my Cart and Plows, and axes and hows, belonging to the Plantation work, and all my Howshould goods of all Sorts, Except them before gaven to my Chilldrin, unto her, the foreSd. Content Carruthers, her Heirs and assigns for Ever.

Item. My will and Desier is that my Executors hearafter menchand may and Shall sell all my Lands, and all my Lotts and Houses, and appurtenences thear unto belonging, in New Bern town, and all my trading Stock of goods of all Sorts, to be Sould at Publick vandew to the highest biders, alowing three months Credit, the Purchesars giveing good security for the Payment of the moneys. My will and Desier is that Evry Lott Should be set up Singal, Except them two whear the Long house stands, and with the money arising by the fore menchand Sales, and What Redey money I may have by me, and what money may be Recved of my outstanding debts, my will and desier is that my Executors may pay all my Just Debts and my fewnarl Exspences, and What is Remaning of the above menchand money when my debts are payd, my will and desier is that that Remandar of money may be Equely devided between my three sons, William Carruthers, John Carruthers, and Joseph Carruthers, and my daughter, Sarah

Rice, and if my son William Carruthers Shuld not be at the devistion of the money, I desier his Part of the money may Continue in the the hands of my Executors tell he, the fore Sd William Carruthers, Cums for it.

Lastly. I do nominate, Constitute and appint my two sons, John Carruthers, and Joseph Carruthers, Executors of this my last Will and testament, and do hereby utterly Revoke, disallow and disanull all former Bequests, Wills and Legacies, by me heretofore made, Ratifying and Confirming this, and no other, to be my last will and testament.

In Witness whereof, I have hereunto set my hand and seal, the Twentieth day of September, the year of our Lord, one thousand, seven Hundred and fifty one. (and my desk interlined before Assigned in the lour line of the first Side).

JOHN CARRUTHERS: (Seal)

Signed, Sealed, Published and Declared, by the within named tastator, John Carruthers, to be his last will and testament, in presence of us the Subscribers:

SARAH X BETSWORTH.
(her mark)

ABIAH BANGS.
SOL: REW.

CRAVEN COUNTY.   February Court, 1752.

These are to Certify, That the within Will of John Carruthers, Deceased, being Exhibited into Court, was Proved by the Oath of Solomon Rew, one of the Subscribing Evidences to the same, Who swore That he saw The Testator sign, Seal & Declare the same to be his last Will and Testament, and to the best of his knowledge was of sound Mind and Disposing Memory; and that he also saw Sarah Betsworts, and Abiah Bangs, the other Subscribing Evidences, sign as such in Presence of the Testator. At the same time John Carruthers, one of the Executors therein mention'd appeared in Court and Qualified according to Law.

Ordered that Mr. Secretary have Notice that Lres may issue &c

Test. PHIL SMITH, Cl. Cur.

Copied from Original Will filed in the Office of the Secretary of State.

EDMUND CHANCEY'S WILL.

NORTH CAROLINA, the Fifteenth day of March, 1753.

I, Edmund Chancey, of Pasquotank County, and province aforsaid, being in perfect mind and memory, thanks be Given to god, and Calling to mind the mortallity of my body and knowing that it is appointed for man to die I do here make and ordain this my Last will and Testament, that is first of all, I will that all my Just debts and funeral Expences be well and Truly paid by my Executor and Executrix hereafter named.

Item. I Give and bequeth unto my Grand Son, Edmund Chancey, Son of Stephen Chancey, the Easternmost part of my Plantation and for a Division to begin in and by the Southeast Side of the Branch which Runs through Laurance Retons pattent then Runing north fifteen degrees west through the middle of an Island that Lies in an Elbow of the Said Branch four hundred and Ten yards then north thirty five degrees west through my Land Granted to me in two pattents and a Convayance from Laurance Retons pattent and a Deed from nathinel martin according to the Divison aforsaid Give to my Grand Son Edmund Chancey Son of Stephen Chancey to him his heirs and assigns.

Item. I Give and bequeth unto my Grand Son, Edmund Chancey, Son of Jacob Chancey, the middle most part of my plantation adjoining to the Eastermost part begining at the Divison aforsaid, then Runing down the Branch to the mouth of it with a Streight Corse to the main Swamp of newbegun Creek, then Runing up and Joyning to the said Swamp Various Corses to the mouth of a Cypruss Branch which Runs out of the main Swamp, aforsaid, Just below the narrow Sandhills, then Runing up and Joining to the middle of the main fork of it then north Six Degrees west through my Land I Give to my Grand Son, Edmund Chancey, Son of Jacob Chancey, to him his heirs and assigns.

Item. I Give and bequeth unto my Grand Son, Edmund Chancey, Son of Zachariah Chancey, my Sandhills Land adjoining to the west Side of my Grand Son, Edmund Chancey, Son of Jacob Chancey, begining at the mouth of the Cypruss branch aforsaid, then Runing up and Joining to the East Side of the main Swamp, I Give to my Grand Son, Edmund Chancey, Son of Zachariah Chancey, to him his heirs and assigns, but if my Grand Son, Edmund Chancey, Son of Jacob Chancey, Should die without Esue, then it is my will that the Land Should fall to my Grand Son, Edmund Chancey, Son of Stephen Chancey, to him, his heirs and assigns; and it is my will that my Daughter in Law, Rachel Chancey, Shall have the Liberty to Dwell on the Eastermost part of my plantation, and to Enjoy the benefits of it with all the appurtenances thereunto belonging, untel my Grand Son, Edmund Chancey, Son of Stephen Chancey, doth Come to the age of Twenty one years, and for her to pay the yearly Quitrents for the Same, and it is my will also, that my Daughter in Law, Rachel Chancey, Shall have full previlleg and use of the middlemost part of my plantation, and for her to pay the yearly Quitrente for the Same, untill my Grand Son, Edmund Chancey, Son of Jacob Chancey, doth Come to the age of Twenty one years.

Item. I Give and bequeath unto my Son, Daniel Chancey, five pounds, Virginia money, and my Two Servants, Jack Spanyerd boe and Spanyoll Boe, During the time of their Servitud, by their Indenters, and Two feather Beds and Bolsters, and and Two Ruggs, and all my wearing Cloths, and my Riding Saddle and Bridle, and Sorrel mair, and Three young horses, and Two Large pewter Dishes, and Two Small ones, and Two Large pewter Basons and one Small one, and one Dozn. of Spoons, and Two midling Iron pots, and a full pot, an one Gun, and my Large Bible, and a pair of Brass Scales, and five weights, and one Iron Skillet, and Ten pounds of woll.

Item. I Give and bequeth unto my Son, Zachariah Chancey, one Shilling, Sterling money, to Cut him off from my Raiel and personal Estate, because of the wickedness that he Committed in my house in the time of my absence.

Item. I Give and bequeth unto my Daughter in Law, Rachel Chancey, my white mair, and yearling horse named Trip and go, and my mair named Trim and her Encreas, and a Spice morter and pestel, and Currying knife, and all my Coopers and Carpenters and Shoe makers Tools, and my Stakle, and Three Iron weges, and all my home Spun Linning, and wolling Cloth, and all my Thread thereunto Relating, and one Brass Candle Stick, and one box Iron, and Two heters, and Three Supe plates, and all my Sifters, Three Iron pots, one Large and Two midling and a brass kittle, and a Iron Skillet, and one frying pan, Two pair of pot hooks, and Two pair of Tongs and one pair of Stilerds, and a Tin funnel, and Three Vhests Two in the outward Room and one heigh Chest, and half my Leather, and Two feather beds, and Two Bolsters, Two Ruggs and one pair of Blankets, one pair of Sheets, and Two Bedsteads and Cords, and a Large Dish and Two middling ones, and one Lare pewter Bason, and a midling one, and one Small one, and Six pewter plates, and one full pot, and a par of Talers Shears, and a Looking glass, and one Dozn. of Spoons, and one pewter Chamber pot, and all my Chears, and Two Juggs, and all my Round Bottles, and a Gun, and my wolling and Linning wheals, and Sixteen Barrels of Corn, and four hundred and fifty pounds of Dryed Meat, and Three Galllons of fatt, and Two Bushells of Salt, and my Sope, and one Quarter part of my Sweetning, and my work horses Named Rone and Roney, and Baul and Huzzes Two year old horse, and all my plows, hoes and axes, with the gears, and on grind Stone, one pair of mill Stones, and my woll Cards and Eight Cows and Calves or yerlings, and four Stears, one Quarter part of my hoggs, and my wheat patch, and all my black peper and all my flax and woll and Sheep, and also my Servants bob boe, and Rachel boe, and frank boe, and her Two Children, Durin the time of their Indenters.

Item. I Give and bequeth unto my Grand Daughter, Mary Chancey, Daughter of Jacob Chancey, one feather bed and a Bolster, and a Rug, and a blanket and a Sheet and Six Spoons, and Two Iron pots, and a full pot, and a brass Candle Stick, and Three pewter plates, and a pewter Bason, and a frying pan, and Three Sheep and Two Cows and Calves, Two Saws and Six Shotes, and one dish.

Item. I Give and bequeth unto my Grand Son, Edmund Chancey, Son of Jacob Chancey, Two Cows and Calves, and Two Sows and Six Shotes and Three Sheep, Two pots and a Pewter Bason, a Dish and Three plates, & two Razors and a hone.

Item. I Give and bequeth unto my Grand Daughter, hannah Chancey, Daughter of Zachariah Chancey, one yearling mair Colt and one Iron pot.

Item. I Give and bequeth unto my Grand Son, Edmund Chancey, Son of Zachariah Chancey, one Cow and Calf, and Two Iron pots, and my will is that my grand Daughter, mary Chancey, and my grand Son, Edmund Chancey, and my grand Daughter, Hannah Chancey, and my grand Son, Edmund Chancey, Son of Zachariah Chancey, Shall have their Legacies which I have Given them Delivered to them within Three months after my Deceas, and they Shall Run all Resks and hazards of Loses of whr I have given them.

Item. I Give and bequeth unto James Furbish, my Book no Cross no Crown.

Item. I Give and bequeth unto my Grand Son, John Bakor, all the Remainder part of my Books.

Item. I Give and bequeth unto mulato Jack Ten Shillings Cash.

Item. I Give and bequeth unto my Daughter Ruths Children, viz: John Bakor, mary Degrafenred, Blake Bakor, Sarah Bakor, Ruth Bakor, and Zadock Bakor, all the Remainder part of my personal Estate to be Eaqually Divided among them.

Item. I do hereby Constitute, make and ordain my Grand Son, John Bakor, to be my Executor, and my Daughter in Law, Rachel Chancey, to be my Executrix to this my Last will and Testament and I do hereby utterly Disallow Revoke and Disanul all and Every other former will by me in any wise made Ratifieing and Constituteing this to be my Last will & Testament.

In witness whereof I have hereunto Set my hand and Seal, the day and date above Ritten. EDMUND CHANCEY (Seal)

Sined and Sealed by the Said Edmund Chancey, as his Last will and Testament in the presents of us the Subscribers:
 Test. JONATHAN REDING.
    ROBERT HALL.
    WM. SWANN.

NORTH CAROLINA, PASQUOTANK COUNTY. ss July Court, Annoq Dom, 1753.
   Present His Majesties Justices.

   These may Certifie that Jonathan Reding and Robert Hall, Two of the Evidences to the within Will, appeared in open Court and made Oath on the Holy Evangelist that they ware present and Saw Edmund Chancey Sign, Seal, publish and declare the within to be and Contain his last will and Testament, And that he, the said Edmund Chancey, was Att that time of sound and disposeing Memory. And that they also Saw William Swann, the other Evidence Sign his Name thereto att the same time. Then appeared Rachel Chancey, Executrix, and was duly Qualified as Such.
   Ordered that the Honorable James Murray Esqr Sec. have Notice that Letters Testamentory issue &c.
   dated att the Clarks office the 18nth day of July, Annoq. Dom., 1753.
                Test: THOS: TAYLOR Ck Co

   Copied from Original Will filed in the Office of the Secretary of State.

RICHARD CASWELL'S WILL.

   IN THE NAME OF GOD AMEN. I, Richard Caswell, of Dobbs County, in the State of North Carolina, Do this second day of July, in the Yiear of our Lord, one thousand, Seven hundred and eighty seven, make and declare this to be my last Will and Testament as the one I made on the death of my dearly beloved son, William Caswell, will not withe my present circumstances, I declare that and all former Wills and Testaments by me made, null and void, holding this and this only for firm and effectual, which is as follows:
   First, I reserve for the use of a burying ground for all those of my family and Connections who may choose to bury their Relations and friends there, one half acre of Land where the Bones of my dear father and Mother lie, at a place called the Hill, to be laid out East, West, North, and South so as to leave those Bones near the centre of the said half Acre of Ground, and I also reserve in like manner, one half Acre of Land where the Bones of beloved wife (and) and son, William, now lie near the red house, to be laid out in the same manner and for the same purpose as the above half Acre is directed; and these two half Acres to be reserved for the uses afores'd for ever. And its likewise my Will that those who wish to bury their Dead at either of the said places and coming with in the meaning of the description above, shall always have liberty of Egress, Ingress and regress to, at and from the said respective burying grounds to bury the dead or repair or raise an enclosure to the same.
   Secondly, To prevent any kind of Dispute which might arise between my Brother, Martin Caswell, or his heirs or Assigns with those claiminge under me, I declare all the Land comprised within his Title from Samuel Caswell or the Title to Samuel

Caswell or Nathaniel Bird, I have no claim to, notwithstanding my patent may be of a Younger date, than the Deed I granted to Nathaniel Bird for the same.

Thirdly, Whereas, my Brother, Samuel Caswell, in his life time and myself, agreed for two hundred acres of Land whereon he lived, immediately before his death, which was to begin at Mackilwean's (corner) corner next the river, near Mrs. Skiners dwelling and run up Mackilweans to Dosiers out corner, then with his line to the flat branch near the end of Mr. Coasts feild, then with the side of the said Flat and high Land down to where a small branch empties into the said Flat branch, which runs through Keilings old field, then a direct line to the mouth of the Cypress Gut, then down the river a small distance to Boxes corner, then with his line out to my corner, and then to the Beginning, which included part of Dosiers, Keilings, Boxes and my own former claims, for three hundred pounds and notwithstanding a very small part of that Sum was paid me in my said Brothers life time, and knowing it would very much distress his family was I to require the remainder, therefore, I leave the use of the Land aforesaid with the plantations and appurtenances to my Sister, Eleanor Caswell, the widow of said Brother, untill her son, Shine Caswell, arrives to the age of twenty one Years, at which period I give and devise the same to him, the said Shine Caswell, his heirs and Assigns for ever.

Fourthly, I give to my Grandson, Richard William Caswell, a negro boy named Boson, and his assigns for ever.

Fifthly, I give to my Grandson, Richard Francis Mackilwean, a Negro boy named Daniel, and to his Assigns forever.

Sixthly, If Jonathan Morris chooses to take the Land whereon old Jack lives, which I bought at the vendue of Richard Caswell, Junrs: estate at the price I gave for it, I desire that the Title may be made to him for the same.

Seventhly, Whereas, I purchased at the Vendue of the Estate of my Son, Richard Caswell, one Lot and half a Lot of Land in Kinston, with the house wherein Mrs. Caswell now lives, and the appurtenances, one Negro Woman named Sarah, one Negro girl named Sall, one Negro boy named Charles, and one Negro boy named Jim, which Lot and Half and premisses, with the said Negroes, I leave the use of to my Daughter in Law, Mary Caswell, untill my Neice, Sarah Caswell, her duaghter, arrives to the age of eighteen Years, if my said Daughter should so long live, and at that period or at the time of my said Daughters Death, if it should happen before my said grand Daughter arrives to the age aforesaid, I give, devise and bequeath the said Lot, half Lot, and premises with the said Negroes, to my said Grand Daughter, her heirs and Assigns forever, to be delivered over to her free of any charges or incumbrances on account of the maintenance and support of my said Grand Daughter. And as it is uncertain into whose hands she may fall, or it may so happen that she may fall into distress unless provided for by me, I therefore desire the Executors of this will in such case to find her reasonable and decent support, in cloathing and board, and attend to her Schooling and Education, which they shall thenselves pay to those who may be intitled to receive the expences of the same, without its going through other hands, and shall be a charge against my Estate, which Support in the case aforesaid, I direct shall be made and continued to her untill she arrives at the age of eighteen years or marries.

Eighthly, And, as I have heretofore virtally given to my Daughter, Anna Fonvielle, the land I hold on the East side of the Atkin branch from the road down to the river and down the same to the mouth of the Cypress gut, bounded by the lines, from thence, of the Land herein given to Shine Caswell, and John Coasts lines and my own lines to the road, and then with the road to the Beginning, including all the Land I claim adjoining the atkin and Neuse, below the road, is what is called the walnut Hill and contains about three hundred acres. I have also verbally given to my said daughter, Anne, Negroes, Peter and his wife Barbara, and Doll, these verbal gifts I now confirm to the said Anna Fonveille, her heirs and Assigns for ever.

Ninthly, Whereas, I am engaged to pay very considerable Sums of Money on Account of purchases made of my dear son, Richard's estate, and as the articles then purchased will by no means bring a sum sufficient, and as I cannot now discriminate what of my property may be best to dispose of, to raise money sufficient to pay all my debts, I hereby direct the Executors hereof or such of them as may be acting at the time it may become necessary to dispose of such part of my real or personal estate, as he or they Judge necessary and on such terms, tho I think twelve months credit will be best, may appear most for the advantage of my Estate and I hereby empower such Executor or Executors to make Legal and authentic conveyances to the purchasers for the same.

Tenthly, After my Debts are paid and the expences of my household, and Schooling of my children, with every other incidental charge so as a fair and just inventory of the remainder of my estate can be made, of both real and personal property, I require my Executors or acting Executor to return such inventory with his or their Account of the whole transactions relative to my estate, to my friends, Spyers Singleton, Robert White, John Herritage, Jesse Cobb, Francis Childs, Simon Bright, Joshua Croom, Benjamin Caswell and John Coart, or the majority of them or of the Survivors of them, and I request such majority, will arange the personal estate into five equal divisions or parts as near as may be, of which parts, I give my wife, Sarah Caswell, one, which I request she may be allowed to choose, at the same time I request such majority of my friends may set apart for my said wife, in lieu of her dower of my Lands, as she may choose to live on, and such part I leave her the use of during her Natural life; the other four remining parts of my personal property, I request may be drawn for by my three sons, Winston, Dollam, and John, and my daughter, Susannah, and such part as they shall respectively draw I give to the drawer of the same forever. The remainder of my real Estate, I give in like manner, and recommend an appraisment to be made by my friends or a majority of them, or the Survivors of them, so as to assertain the value, and then to put them in four Lots as nearly equal as may be, those Lots to be drawn by my aforesaid four children, Winston, Dallam, John and Susannah, and such Lot I give to the respective drawers, his or her heirs and Assigns forever.

Lastly, I nominate and appoint my said Sons, Winston, Dallam, and John Caswell, Executors of this my Last Will and Testament, that is to say, Winston to act alone untill Dallam arrives at twenty one Years of age, then those two to Act untill John arrives to the age of Twenty one years, after which the whole to act as Executors 'till the business is compleat, and I appoint my good friend James Glasgow, in trust to advise and direct the due Execution hereof, which I beg he will attend to.

In Testimoney of the premises, I have hereunto Set my hand and Seal, the day and year first herein written, contained on five sides.

R. CASWELL, (Seal).

Executed in presence of us, who have subscribed our names as Witnesses in presence of the Testator, and of each other:
 SIMON BRIGHT.
 JAMES BRIGHT.

A Codicil to the foregoing last will and Testament of Richard Caswell, made and executed the same day of the will and is to be considered as a part of the same, that is to say, I give to my son, Winston Caswell, Negroes Venus and Diamond, and to his Assigns for ever, to be appraised in like manner and by the persons named in my will, and the Value deducted from his one fourth part, with my Sons, Dallam and John, and Daughter, Susannah.

It is further my Will, that in case of the death of any of my now living children, to wit, Winston, Anne, Dallam, John and

Susannah, before marriage, arriving at lawful age or legally disposing of any of the property, herein given, then, that such property shall go to my surviving children and their heers and Assigns, to hold for ever.

Witness my hand and seal which is affixed to the string that binds these two sheets together.

R. CASWELL. (Seal)

Executed in presence of:
SIMON BRIGHT.
JAMES BRIGHT.

STATE OF NORTH CAROLINA, DOBBS COUNTY. January Court, 1790.

Then was the within Last Will and Testament of Richard Caswell, deceas'd, exhibited into Court and proved by the oaths of Simon Bright and James Bright, the only Subscribing witnesses thereto, who swore that they saw the Testator sign, seal, publish and declare the same to be and contain his last Will and Testament, and that they also say him Sign and Seal the Codicil thereto, and acknowledged it to be apart of his Will; and to the best of their knowledge, he was at that time of perfect mind and memory.

At the same time, Winston Caswell, one of the Executors therein named, appeared and Qualified as such. Ordered that Letters Testamentary issue accordingly.

Test. W. CASWELL, Clk. C.

STATE OF NORTH CAROLINA, LENOIR COUNTY.

I, Simon Bright, Clerk of the County Court Aforesaid, do hereby Certify that the foregoing is a true Copy from the Original Will & Probate thereof, now remaining in my Office. And that Dallam Caswell, one of the Executors therein named, is the only (now) Surviving Executor to said Will.

Given under my hand and the Seal of the County, at Kinston the 20th. day of July, 1799.

SN. BRIGHT, Cler.
(Official Seal)

Copy of Original Will, filed in the Office of the Secretary of State.

MATTHEW CASEWELL'S WILL.

IN THE NAME OF GOD AMEN, this Twenty Fourth Day of March, Seventeen Hundred and Fifty Four. I, Matthew Casewell, of Tyrrell County, in the Province of North Carolina, planter, Being sick and weak in Body, but of Sound and perfect Memmory, thanks be Given to God for the Same, Therefore calling to Mind the Mortality of my Body & knowing that it is appointed for all men once to Die; do make and Ordain this my Last will and Testament, In the form & Manner Following, That is to say: principaly and First of all, I Recomend my Soul unto the hands of God who gave it me & my Body to the Earth to be Buried in a Decent Christian Buriall at the Descresion of my Exers. hereafter Named; And as Touching Such Worldly Estate wherewith it hath ben pleased God to Bless me in this Life, I Depose of the Same in the Manner & Form following:

Imprimis. I Give & Bequeath unto my Beloved son, Matthew Casewell, the plantation and Two Hundred and Twenty Acres of Land, being the Land formerly Belonging to Edward Phelps; and Likewise Twenty two Accres of Land out of the Loghouse Survey Joyning on Samll. Spruill Line, Known by the Name of the Back Ridge, Unto Him & His Heirs & Assigns for ever.

Item. I give and bequeath to my beloved Son, Samuell Casewell, my Log House plantation with Two Hundred Acres of Land Belonging to the same.

Item. I Give and bequeath to my Beloved Son, Elisha Casewell, my Manner plantation which I Live on, with one Hundred Thirty And Six Acres, more or Less, to him, his heirs and Assigns for Ever.

Item. I Give and Bequeath to my Beloved Daughter, Joanna Casewell, the Land Called ye Red Banks, with one hundred acres of Land Joyning the plantation, to her, her Heirs and Assigns for Ever, with Twenty Two Acres of Land in the Log House Survey, Joyning her Brother Matthew.

Item. I Give and bequeath to my beloved Daughter, Eiza. Casewell, the plantation and Land belonging to the Same, known by the Name of Briffits Island, to her & Her Heirs & assigns for Ever.

Item. I Give and bequeath to my Beloved Daughter, Jemima Casewell, the plantation and Land Belonging to the Same, Known by the Name of Addesons Island, and Likewise my part of the Tract of Land Surveyd between me and James phelps, Sen., Lying on the East Side of Scuppernung River &c., To Her, And Her Heirs and Assigns for Ever.

Item. I Give and Bequeath to my Daughter, Tabitha Casewell, Two Hundred acres of Land known by the Name of the Log House Land, Joyning my Son, Samuell, to Her and Her Heirs and Assigns for Ever, or forty Pounds, Proc'l., my Son Matthew haveing the Refuise, Then Samuell.

Item. I Give and Bequeath to Casewell Hassell, one Cow, Calfe & Her Increase.

Item. I give and Bequeath to my well Beloved Wife, Elizabeth Casewell, One Third part of all my personall Estate, The Remainder to be Equily Devided between my Children, to be Divided at the Descresion of my Exrs.

Item. I make, Constitute and Ordain my Beloved Wife, Elizabeth Casewell, Executrix, and my beloved Father in Law, Samuell Spruill, and my Son, Matthew Casewell, Exrs. of this my Last will & Testament, Utterly (Disannuling all other)

Allowing this and no Other to be my last Will and Testament.
In Witness whereof, I have hereunto set my Hand & Seal, the Date above written.

        MATTHEW M C CASEWELL (Seal)
           his Marke.

Signed, Sealed, published, pronounced and Declared by the sd. Matthew Casewell as his last Will and Testament, in the Presence of us:

  JOSHUA TURNER, Jurat.
  ROBERT ELTON.
  EDWD. PHELPS.

NORTH CAROLINA, TYRREL COUNTY, ss. June Court, 1754, Present his Majesty's Justices:

These may Certify that Joshua Turner, one of the Sibscribing Evidences to the within Will, came into Open Court and made Oath on the Holy Evangelists of Almighty God, That he Saw Matthew Casewell sign, seal, pronounce & Declare the within Writing to contain his last Will & Testament; and at the same Time he saw Robert Elton, & Edward Phelps, sign their names as Evidences to the same. Then appeared Samuel Spruel & Mathew Caswell, Executors & Qualified themselves as Exec'rs., by taking the Oath as the Law in such Cases Directed.

Ordered That the Hon'ble James Murray, Esqr., Secretary of this Province have notice thereof, that Letters Testamentary Issue accordingly.

      Test. EVAN JONES, Cler. Cur.

Copied from Original Will, filed in the Office of the Secretary of State.

THOMAS CLIFFORD'S WILL.

No. CAROLINA SC.

IN THE NAME OF GOD AMEN. I, Thomas Clifford, Esqr., late of Charles Town in South Carolina, but at present residing in New Hanover Precinct, in North Carolina, Do Make and declare these presents to be and contain my last Will and Testament:

Imprimis. I Will that all those Debts which I owe in Right or Conscience be truly and Justly paid by my Executrix hereafter named within some reasonable time after my decease.

Item. I Give, Devise & Bequeath unto my Loving wife, Mary, all the rest & Residue of my Estate whether Real or personal, to her and her heirs and Assignes for ever.

Hereby naming, Constituting and appointing my said wife, Mary, Sole Executrix of this my Last Will & Testament, Revokeing all other Wills by me heretofore made or Declared.

In Testimony whereof I have hereto put my hand and Seal, this Nineth day of October, Anno Dom., 1735.

        T. CLIFFORD (Seal)

Signed, Sealed, published and
Declared In presence of:
  M: MOORE.
  ELIZA: SWANN.
  E. MOSELEY.

NORTH CAROLINA:
Personaly appear'd Maurice Moore, Esqr., one of the Evidences to the within Last Will and Testament, who being Sworn on the holy Evangeist of Almighty God, saieth, That he saw Thos. Clifiord sign, Seal a declare this to be and contain is Last Will and Testament, and that he was of sound mind and disposing memory, and that he saw Eliz: Swann and Edward Moseley sign as Evidences thereto at the same time.

GAB. JOHNSTON.

Copied from Original Will filed in the Office of the Secretary of State.

JOHN COLLINS' WILL.

IN THE NAME OF GOD, AMEN, the 27 Day of Dissember, 1749, I, John Collins, of Bartee County, in the Province of North Carolina, Being sick and weake in body, but of Perfect mind and memory, thanks be unto God, therefore calling unto mind the mortality of the Body, knowing that itt is appointed for all men once to Dye, do make and ordain this my last will and testament, that is to say, principally, and first of all, I give and recommend my sole into the hands of God that gave itt, and my Body I recommend to ye Earth to be buried in a decent christan Burell, at the discretion of my Executors, nothing doubting but at the General Resurrection I shall recive the same by the mighty power of God, and as touching such worldly Estate, warewith itt hath pleased God to bless me in this liffe I give, demise and dispose of in the following manner and form:

Imprimis. I give and bequeath to my Son, William Collins, all that track of land lying on Casshi River, a plantation purched of Jonathan Standlye containing two hundred Eakers, to him and his hears and asigns for ever, and a pare of Iron pot Racks.

Eitom. I give to my Granson, John Collins, a bras kitell, to him and his hears for ever.

Eitom. I give to my two Sons, John and David Collins, each of them a Bible.

Eitom. I give and bequeath unto my Son, Joseph Collins, a Plantation lying the north side of Guy hall Swamp, purtered of hardy Keele, containing one hundred and fifty Eakers at the beginnin, End to him and to his Ears and asigns for Ever. all so, I give him my Cooper Tools and two Ews and Lambs, an a Cow and Calfe.

Eitom. I give and bequeath unto my Son, Mikell Collins, my Surva that lys on Red bud, containg three hundred Eakers, to him and his Ears for ever. Also, I give him a neagro Boy named Robin, and if my said Son should die without hears of his body, then I give the Neagro to my Son Jessee and to his Ears. all so, I give to Son Mikell a black Warnut table, and a Cow and Calfe and a puter dish, except two Days in weak for my Wife.

Eitom. I give and bequeath unto my Son, Demsee Collins, a plantation that henry Ballentin formerly lived on, parte of the tracte of land that I bote of Hardy Keele, lying on Gie hall Swamp by at the lower Ende of the said lane Contain one hundred and fifty Eakers to him and to his Ears and signs for ever. also, I give him an Ovel Table, mad of Maple. also, I give him Cow and Calf, and a puter dish, and a neagro man called toney, to him and his Ears for Ever, an in Case my said Sone should die before he hath anny lawfull Ears, then this Neagro I give to my Son Joseph, an to his Ears, two days every weak to worke for my Wife duering life.

Eitem. I give and beques to my Son, Jesse Collins, my Plantasion I now live on with three hundred Eakers of Land, to him an his Ears an asigns for Ever. also, I give him a Case with fifteen botells, an a feather Bed and furnetude, an two Cows an Calves, an puter dish to him and his Ears for Ever.

Eitem. I give and bequeth to my Son, Absolum Collins, two hundred and forty seven Eakers of land, part of the survaye that I now live on, begining on the deep Branch an so runing to the head line, itt tis the Eastard side of my plantasion, an so to the patine line for breath. all so, I Give him a neagro garl, named Venus, and in case my said son should dye befor he Come to age of twenty one years, then I give this negro to my Son Jessee. I Give the first Child this negro girl bring, if itt live tell one yeare old to my Son Jessee. I all so give my son, absalom, a feather bed and furnetude, an a Cow an Calfe, a bel, metell morter and pessel, and a puuter dish an my Sorell Mare.

Eitem. I Give and bequeth to my well beloved Wife a fether Bed and furnetude, and my horse and hur Sadle, one Pott, two basens and dishes two, and a Chist to Shee and hur Ears for ever, and two days qorke of my two neagro fellows du life.

Eitem. All the Remainder of my Estate within and without, that is after my Just debt is fully satefide and paide, I give to my Wife and six Sons, William, Joseph, mikell, Demsee, Jessee an sbsalom, to be Eacally devid among them all, and my Will and desier is that my Estat shall lie in the hands of my Executors tell the youngest come to the Eage Eighteen years, and not to be sold but to have thare Estate as they come to age of Eighteen years. I doe apint my well beloved Wife and my Sone Mikell to be, I Leave my whole and Sole Exectricks and Execetor, and I do Revke, disanull and disalow of all other Wills made by me or in my name, Ratefying and confirming this to be my lasy Will and testament.

In Witness whareof I have hereunto set my hand and Seale, interlined before asined. JOHN COLLINS (L. S.)

  MOSES HILL,
  JETHRO ROUNTREE.

EDENHOUSE, 18th March, 1752.

This Day Moses Hill & Jethro Rountree, the two Sunscribing Evidences of the last Will & Testament of John Collins, appeared before me & made Oath that they saw the Testator Sign, Seal & Deliver the same as and for His last Will & Testament, and that at the signing thereof He was of sound & disposing mand & memory. At the same time Michael Collins & Mary Collins, Executors appointed by the said Will qualified themselves as Executors by taking the Oath appointed by Law for that Purpose.
              GAB. JOHNSTON.

Copied from Original Will filed in the Office of the Secretary of State.

MARY CONWAY'S WILL.

NORTH CAROLINA.

IN THE NAME OF GOD AMEN. I, Mary Conway, of the Town of New Bern, in the province aforesaid, Widow, being sick and weak in body, but of sound and disposing mind, memory and understanding, thanks be to God for the same, Do make and publish this my last Will and Testament, in manner and form following: (that is to say), First and principally, I recommend my Soul to Almighty God that Gave it, and my body to be decently interr'd at the Discretion of my Executors hereafter named; and as to the little worldly Estate which it hath pleased God to bless me with, I Give and dispose thereof as follows:

I Give and bequeath unto Margaret Gordon, Daughter of Mrs. Mary Gordon, One large Gold Ring, and my clouded silk sack and petticoat, as a token of my friendly regard to her.

Item. I Give and bequeath unto Susannah Wrenford, Wife of Edmund Wrenford, and Elizabeth Elmsley, all the rest and residue of my wearing apparel, silk and Linen, she the said Susannah Wrenford, first making choice of such part thereof as she shall think proper.

Item. It is my will and desire that my Executors hereafter, Do and shall sell and dispose of all my Household ffurniture, together with a Lott of Land in the said Town of New Bern, bought of John Fowler, in order to pay and satisfy my just Debts and Funeral expences, but if the same is found not sufficient for that purpose, that in such case they sell and dispose of such other parts of my personal Estate as may be most useless to my Son, William Conway, when he shall attain the Age of Twenty one Years, or they shall in their discretion think proper, earnestly recommending to them, if possible, to preserve and keep together all such Negroe Slaves as I may die possessed of, to the intent that they may be hired out for the benefit of my said son, and defraying the charges of his maintenance and Education during his Minority.

Item. I Give and devise and bequeath unto my said Son, William Conway, all and singular, my plantations, Lands, Houses and Lotts, in the Town of New Bern, aforesaid, and also my Negroe Slaves, male and female, together with two pair of Gold Buttons, and the residue of my Gold rings, when and as soon as he shall attain the Age of Twenty one Years, but if my said Son, William Conway, shall happen to die before he shall so attain the Age of Twenty one years as aforesaid, I Give, devise and bequeath unto my Esteemed Friend, Edmund Wrenford, All and Singular, my said plantations, houses and Lotts in the Town of New Bern, as aforesaid, to Hold to him, his Heirs and Assigns for ever. And I do earnestly intreat my Executors to pay a strict regard to the Educating of my said Son in such manner as shall be necessary to qualify him for such Business or profession as his Genius shall most incline to.

Lastly, I do hereby Nominate, Constitute and appoint my Good friends, John Hawks; Esquire, and the said Edmund Wrenford, Executors of this my last Will and Testament, hereby revoking all former Wills by me made, declaring this to be my last Will and Testament.

In Witness whereof, I have hereunto set my hand and seal, this Seventeenth day of August, in the Year of our Lord, One thousand, seven hundred and seventy four.

MARY CONWAY. (Seal)

Signed, Sealed, Published and declared by the said Testatrix, as and for her last Will and Testament, in the presence of us who in her presence, and at her request, and in the presence of each other, have subscribed our Names as Witnesses hereto:

    JOHN BONNER.
    JOSEPH DOWSE,
    HENRY VIPON.

The above last Will and Testament of Mary Conway, was proved before me, this 26th day of August, 1774, by the oaths of Joseph Dowse and Henry Vipon, two of the subscribing Witnesses thereto, who swore that they were present and did see the said Testatrix sign, seal, publish and declare the same to be and contain her last Will and Testament; and that at the time thereof she was of sound and disposing mind and memory. And Edmund Wrenford, one of the Executors in the said Will named, having taken the oaths of Executors, and qualified agreeable to Law. It is Ordered that Letters Testamentary issue thereon accordingly.

Jo. Martin.

Copied from Original Will filed in the Office of the Secretary of State.

JOHN COTTON'S WILL.

In the name of God Amen. I, John Cotten, of Bartie Precinct, in North Carolina, Gent., being Sick in body but of perfect Sence & Sound memory, blessed by God, doe mak and ordaine this to be my Last will and & Testament, in manner and forme folowing, Viz: first,

Item. I Give to my Son, John Cotten, Three Hundred and twenty acors of Land, be it more or Less, whar he now Lives, on the west Sid of Ahorskey Marsh, to him and his heairs for Ever.

Item. I Give to my Son, William Cotten, one hundred and fifty acors Land, be it more or Less, lying in the oserow (?) Meadows, whar he now Lives, beginning at a Marked hickory at my upermost Line, So runing down a line of Marked Trees to the Lower most line, to him and his heairs for Ever.

Item. I Give to my Son, Samell Cotten, a Neack of Land whar he now Lives, be the Saime mor or Less, and parte of a Survay that I bought of Charles Stevenson, being a hund. acors mor. or Less, to him and his heairs for Ever.

Item. I Give to my Son, Thos. Cotten, all the Remainder of my Land bought of Charles Stevenson, it is northerdly of william Cotten, and Containes Three hund and forty acors, being a neck Called, the Green pond neck, to him and his heairs for Ever.

Item. I Give to my Sons, arthur Cotten and James Cotten, my Lowermost Survay Land on fishing Creek, to Eaqualey devided betwixt ym, to them and their heairs for Ever.

Item. I Give to my Son, Joseph Cotten, to hundred acors Land and to be taken oute of my uper Survay on fishing Creek, to him and his heairs for Ever.

Item. I Give to my Son, Alexand^r Cotten, one hundred acors Land out of my uper Survay on fishing Creek, to him and his heairs for Ever, and the other three hundred acors to be Equaley Devided be twen my my Sons, John Cotten, william Cotten, and Samll. Cotten, to them and their heirs for Ever.

Item. I Give to my Son, Arthur Cotten, one Neagerow Man Naimed Meingo, butt Except the Labour and Sarvice of the sd. Neagerow, to be preformed and don for my Loveing wife, Martha Cotten, deureing her widowhood, and my sd Son, arthur Cotten, to be and Goe for himSelf when he Shall arrive at the age of 18 Years.

Item. I Give to my Son, James Cotten, one Neagerow boye Naimed peter, to him and his heairs for Ever, and that my Son, James Cotten, May Goe and for himself when he Shall arrive att the age of Eighteen Years.

Item. I Give to my Son, Thos. Cotten, one Neagroe Gerlle Naimed Rose, To him and his heirs for Ever, but Except the Labour and Sarverce of the sd Neagrow Geirll to be for and with my Loveing wife, Martha Cotten, deureing her widowhood, and that my Son, Thos. Cotten, be free and and Goe for him Self when the sd. Thos. arrive at the age of Eighteen Years.

Item. I Give to my Son, Joseph Cotten, one neagerow boy naimed Toney, to him and his heairs for Ever.

Item. I Give unto my daughter, presseler Cotten, one Neagerow woman, named Mooll, to her and her heairs for Ever, butt Except the youse and Labour of the sd Neagerow to be for my Loveing wife, Martha Cotten, Dewering her widowhood.

Item. I Give to my Son, alexander Cotten, one Neagerow man, naimed Guge, butt Except the Sd. Neagerows Labour and Survice to be for my Loveing wife, Martha Cotten, During hur widowhood.

Item. I Give to my Son, william Cotten, one new feather bead and a woosted Sett Ruge, and one Large fine blanket, and a Sheate, to pewter bassons, and to pewter dishes, three Cowes and Calefes, to yearlings, and one three year ould heifer, and Eight Soues with their In Creese, and one baye Gelding horse, and one Large barow or Spayed Sow, and a pateran of fine druged for a Sute of Close, Coate, bretches and Jacket and Triming answreable, and fifty bushalls of oyster Shells. And all that parsell of plank that wase Sawed for the meill work, to Euqualie devided betwene my Sd. Son, william Cotten, and my Son, Samll. Cotten.

Item. I Give to my Son, Samll. Cotten, a p'terne of fine druged to make him a sute of Close and Triming answrable, which Cloth and triming is to be answare and Euqualey devided betwixt my Sonn, william and Samll Cotten.

Item. To my Son, Samll. Cotten, I Give one feather bead known by the naime of the Trundle bead, and a blew wostde Sett Rugg, and one blanket and Sheate, and one Square fraimed warnut table, and three Cowes and Caveles, and an in broke hors of to years ould, to puter bassons, and to puter dishes, and fifty bushells of oyster Shells, and to Each of my Sons, Samll and wm Cotten, a large Sheare, to purches Ym nails to buld them a howse, Each &.

Item. I Give to my Son, Alexander, Eight Sowes with their increese, and Three Cowe, one heifer yearling, and one to year ould Steare, and one three year ould Steare.

Item. I Give to my Son, John Cotten, all the Stock of both hoggs and Catte that is now in his persesion of my Marke, and fifty bushalls of oyster Shells.

Item. I Give to my daughter, Susanah Cotten, the feather bead whar on She lyes with all its furneture.

Item. I Give to my Son, Thos: Cotten, one Sute of new Courteins of ablew Couller, one Large fine bead Tick, one wosted Sett Rugg, and one Large fine blankett. I Give and bequeath to my Loveing wife, Martha Cotten, my bead whar on I lye with all its furneture, Courtens, Rugg, blankets, Sheates, pelowes, and one Large new fine blanket and Quelt, beSides, and one bead Stead Corde and matt. and,

Item. I Give to my Son, alexander Cotten, as much dewroys which is now by me, as will make him A sute of Clothes.

Item. I Give to my Sons, alexander and Samll. Cotten, as much Striped holan, as will Make Each of ym a Jeacket and Bretches and Trimeing to it. And I give & bequeath to my Loveing wife My Rideing horse, Calling his Name blaise, and a Sid Sadle.

Item. I Give to my Son In Law, John Tomas, one puter dish.

Item. I Give to my Son in Law, Capt. John Spears, one puter dish.

Item. I Give to my daughter, Mary holand, one puter dish, and the use of the above neageroes is Left to my Sd wife for hur own and my Sd fower youngest Childrens Maintaneance during her widowhood.

Item. I Give to my Son, Joseph Cotten, three wethers and a Ramm, to yewes and a Lam.

Item. I Give to my Daughter, Martha Benton, Late widow of frances Benton, decesed, Three Ewes with their inCrease.

Item. I Give to my Sons, wm. and Samll. Cotten, 20 pound of feathers, to be Equaly devided Inlargen their beads.

My will is furder, that my mill Stones, Spindle, Jaks and peecks, to be Sould for Silver Money, and that to be Equaley devided betweixt my fower Small Children, arthur, pesseller, James, and Thos. Cotten, and all the Rem^d. of my Estate, both with in and with oute dores, I Leave to my wife and fower Small Children above named, to be Eaqualey devided.

Item. I Give to my Daughter, Susanah, as Much fine Silk Stufe as will mak hur a Sute of Clothes, and my will is that my mair that Runes in Tormenteing nack, the first Coult She Bringes, may be for my Son, arthur Cotten, and if the Sd mair lives to bring Aney more Coultes may be for my Son, James and Thos Cotten. and,

Lastly, I doe apoint My Loveing wife to be Exetrs. of This my Last will and testment, butt Nomonate and apoint My Loveing friend, Thos Bryant, and wm Benet to be over Sears, and have power, In case my wife Should again Marey, and hur Covetor prove unhapey to hur and my fower Small Children, to Remove and Secure them and their Estate att their desc.

In witness war of Asigne this to be my Last will and testement.

JOHN COTTEN. (Seal)

Test. THOS. BRYANT, Jurat.
THOMAS STRANGE.
MAREY M PARKERS. Jurat.
hur
marke

BERTIE Sc.   May Court, 1728.

The above Will was Exhibited by Martha Cotton, Widow and Sole Executrix of John Cotton, Deced. and was proved by the Oaths of Capt. Thomas Bryant, and Mary Parker, in Open Court, in due form of Law, who were Evidences thereto. And then the sd. Martha took the the Exrs: oath in Open Court.

Test. RT. FORSTER, Cler. Cur.

Copied from Original Will filed in the Office of the Secretary of State.

JOHN COTTON'S WILL.

NORTHAMPTON COUNTY.

The Deposition of ye under Subscribers first Sworn on The Holy Eveng * * * * * 1741. John Cotten who Deceast this Life ye 2d of feb., 1741; as aforsd Did make, * * * under his hand and Seal, & the Subscriber were Wittness Thereto, which * * * was by ye sd. Cotten Delivered Into ye Care of John Dawson, one of the Subscribeing Wittnesses, who by misfortune hath Lost ye sd will with Sundrey of his own papers, but ye sd subscribers being well assured in their Consciences that they Can Remembr The whole Substance of the sd will Declared it was as followeth, Viz: After funeral Expences Discharged and Debts paid, I give & bequeath my Estate as followeth:

Itim. I give & bequeath To my son, John Cotten, my plantation whereon I now Dwell, to him & his heires forever, only my wife to Live thereon and to Injoy the Use thereof During her natural Life; also one gun, one feather Bed and furniture, Two Cows & Calves, Two Ews and Lambs. My will and Desire is that my Crosscut Saw & whipsaw be Equalley between my Two Sons. also, I give my Son John one Iron pot.

Itim. I give & bequeath to my Son Benjamin Cotten, my plantation whereon phillip Edens now Dwells, to him & his heires forever, only the sd Edens to Live thereon and Injoy the Use thereof During his Natural Life. My will & Desire is that my Land belonging to my sd plantations be Divided as Equal as Possible, one half to ye one plantation and ye Other half to ye other; also I give my sd. son my black horse, bridle and Saddle and Cane, one feather Bed and Firniture, one Iron pot, Two Cows and Calves, Two (?) Ews and Lambs.

Itim. I give and Bequeath to my Daughter, Mary Breecle Two hundred acres, be ye same more or Less, Lying at at a place Called Blue water, to her and her heires for Ever; also one feather Bed & firniture, one Dish, and one Bason, one Iron Pott, one Cow and Calf, Two heiphers, and three Ews and Lambs, Ten Sows and pigs, one Iron Pot.

Itim. I give and bequeath to my Daughter, Anne Cotten, one bey Mare & her Increase, Two Cows and Calves, Two Ews and Lambs, and one feather Beed and firniture, and one Iron pot.

Itim. I give & bequeath to my Daughter, Sarah Cotten, my Negroe wench, Called Rose, and her Increase, only, my wife to have ye Labour of ye sd wench During her natural Life; also, I give my sd Daughter, Two Cows and Calves, Two Ews and Lambs, one Iron pot.

Itim. I give and bequeath to my Loving wife, anne Cotten, my Negroe fellow Mingo, to Maintain and School my small Children; also, give my sd wife, my working oxen for the plantation use; also, I give my sd wife, my Grey Horse and Side Saddle, and all my working Tools not alreadey given.

Also, I Do nominate and appoint my Loving wife, Executrix and my Loving brother, William Cotten, Executor of this my last will & Testament, Revoking and Disalowing of all other wills by me heretofore Made.

In will: hereof I have hereunto Set my hand & Seal, 17th of Jan: 1741.

& further we Say not

JNO. DAWSON.

RICHD. BERFIELD, his R mark.
THOS. COWMAN. W his mark

* * * * within Deposition * * * * Richd, Berfield & Thos. Cowman * * * * on oath before Isaac Hunter * * * * * Justs of the County within Mentioned as witness my * * * * & Date * * * written.   ISAAC HUNTER.

NORTHAMPTON COUNTY, SC.   May Court, 1742.

The within written Nuncupative Will of John Cotten, Deceased, was proved in open Court by the Oaths of John Dawson, Richard Barefield, & Thomas Cowman, ye subscribing evidences thereto, & on Motion of William Cotten, praying Administration on ye sd Deceased's Estate with ye Will Annexed, which was granted, he having given Security as ye Law directs

Test. J. EDWARDS, Clk. C.

Copied from Original Will filed in the Office of the Secretary of State.

JEAN CORBIN'S WILL.

IN THE NAME OF GOD AMEN. I, Jean Corbin, of New Hanover County, Widdow and Relict of Francis Corbin, late of Chowan County, in the Province North Carolina, Esqr., being weak in body, but of perfect Sound & disposing Mind and Memory, do make this my last Will and Testament in Manner following: And first I resign my Soul in to the hands of my all mercifull God, in hopes of a Joyfull resurrection thro' the Mediation of a Blessed Redeemer; And as to my worldly Goods and Estate I Give, Devise, and Bequeath in manner following:

First. Whereas, by a certain Marriage Settlement, or Indenture Trepartite, bearing date the Twenty eight day of October in the Year of Our Lord one Thousand Seven hundred & Sixty one, and Executed between me and my said late Husband Francis Corbin and Samuel and John Swann Trustees named in the sd Indenture, I have an absolute and disposing right in and of a Moiety of three plantations, Tracts or parcels of land, Lying and being on the Eastermost Branch of Long Creek in New Hanover County containing in the whole Twelve hundred and Sixty Acres, Also One Other plantation Tract or parcel of Land, lying and being on the North East Side of the North West branch of Cape Fear River, Joining the upper side of the late Henry Simmon's Land; Also One Other Plantation Tract or parcel of Land containing One hundred & eighty Acres lying and being in Bladen County on the West side of the North west branch of Cape Fear River, Joining Mcknight's land; Now I Give Devise & Bequeath to John Rutherfurd Junier, William Gordon Rutherfurd and Frances Rutherfurd (Children of my good friend of my good friend John Rutherfurd of New Hannover County Esquire) and their respective Heirs and Assigns forever, to be equally devided between them, the Moieties of the said several Plantations Tracts or Parcels of Land. And it is my Will, Intention, and direction, that in the partition of the said Parcels of Land,

JEAN CORBIN.

regard be had as well to the Value as the quantity, so that each Devision be in Value & quantity nearly equal.

Item. I Give and Bequeath to the said John Rutherfurd Junior, William Gordon Rutherfurd, and Frances Rutherfurd, All my Negroe Slaves, wch I hold and Possess or am entitled to, as well by Virtue of the aforementioned Indenture or Otherwise, (and not Otherwise disposed of by this my Will) and wch I may at the time of my decease, hold, possess have, or be entitled to, together with all my Stocks of Cattle Horses, Sheep & Hogs, with All my Plate, Houshold & Kitchen furniture,

Plantation Tools, and implements of Husbandry of whatever kind or Sort they may be wch I shall die possess'd of.

Item. I Give and Bequeath to the said John Rutherfurd Junier, Wm Gordon Rutherfurd, and Frances Rutherfurd all arrears of money due or growing due to me, as my Jointure or annuity of One hundred & Twenty Pounds per Annum from the Death of my said late Husband, Francis Corbin, and provided to me, by the aforemention Marriage Settlement.

Item. I Give and Bequeath to my Good Friend Thomas Holloway, the Use of my Negroe boy Exeter (wch he now has in his possession) for and during the Term of his Natural Life, and after his decease I Give the said Negroe to John Rutherfurd Junier, William Gordon Rutherfurd, and Frances Rutherfurd.

Item. It is my Will and desire, that my old Negroe fellow Peter, who hath Long & faithfully Served me, be, at the time of my death. Liberated & Set free, and it is my further Will and direction that my Executors herein named, pay him Eleven pounds proc money pr Annum during his natural Life, as a reward of his fidelity, and for his Support and Maintenance.

Item. Whereas I have advanced & paid several sums of my own Monies, for and upon Amount of the Estate of my late Husband, Francis Corbin, wch said sums are still in Ar-

JEAN CORBIN.

rear & unpaid to me; it is therefore my Will and desire that all the accts between the sd Estate & myself (wch shall be unsettled at my decease), be settled, as Soon as the same can be done; and the balances & monies due me thereon recovered; All wch balancies & Monies, I Give to the sd John Rutherfurd Junier, William Gordon Rutherfurd and Frances Rutherfurd.

Item. Whereas my good friend John Rutherfurd Esqr: has had, at different times the Labour & Service of several of my negros Slaves; now my will and desire is, that no Accts. or charge, be made or brought against him for the Same And my Will & meaning is, that he be acquitted & discharged of & from any demand therefor; And Also that he be acquitted exonerated & discharged from all Other Debts, dues, demands, or Claims of what nature or kind soever wch I may have against him.

Item. It is my Will and direction that all my Just debts be first paid as soon as may be, either by the hire, work & Labour of my Slaves, or by the Sale of so much of the most perishable part of my Estate, and wch may be of the best use and benefit to the sd John Rutherfurd Junier William Gordon Rutherfurd and Frances Rutherfurd; or by both, as my Executors shall Judge necessary.

Item. I Give Devise & Bequeath to the sd John Rutherfurd Junier William Gordon Rutherfurd and Frances Rutherfurd All the rest residue and remainder of my real and Personal Estate, not herein particularly devised, of what nature or kind soever or wheresoever it may be found.

Item. And for the more Clear, and better Understanding of this my will, and to prevent disputes and contraversies thereon, I hereby declare my design to be, that all the Several Slaves, Stocks, Plate, houshold & kitchen furniture together with ever Other article or Articles, thing or things Devised, Given and bequeathed, or intended to be Devised Given and

JEAN CORBIN.

bequeathed by this my Will to the said John Rutherfurd Junier, William Gordon Rutherfurd and Frances Rutherfurd, be equally divided among them, share and share alike, and in Case of the death of either of them, the Share to have fallen to such party, to goe to the Survivors or Survivor.

And further, my Will and positive directions are, that All the Lands, Stocks, Plate, houshold & kicthen furniture, together with every Other Article or Articles Thing or Things, Devised, Given & Bequeathed by this my Will to the sd John Rutherfurd Junior William Gordon Rutherfurd and Frances Rutherfurd shall be, and remain in the keeping, and Under the direction Care & management of my sd good friend John Rutherfurd Esqr.; and after the payment of my Debts, he to receive all the profits, emoluments and benefits ariseing and accruing therefrom, to enable him the better to Educate, Support, and Maintain his said Children, without being further accountable for the Same, untill the Marriage of the sd Frances Rutherfurd, at wch time the said Frances to have her Share or Portion thereof; And the Residue or the Remainding parts or Shares, to continue and remain under the Care, direction and Management of the said John Rutherfurd Esquire, and he in like manner to receive all the profits, emoluments, and benefits ariseing and accruing from the sd residue or remainding parts or Shares (to enable him to Educate, Maintain & Support the sd John Rutherfurd Junier, & William Gordon Rutherfurd) without being accountable therefor, for such time, and so long as he shall think proper; to retain & keep the same.

Lastly. I do nominate, constitute, and appoint, my good friends Lewis Henry Derosset and John Rutherfurd Esquires and Mr Thomas Holloway Executors of this my last Will, contained in Six pages, each page being Signed at the Bottom with my own hand; revoking all former Will and Wills by me heretofore made.

JEAN CORBIN.

In Witness Whereof I have hereunto Set my hand & Seal the 10th February 1775

JEAN CORBIN (Seal)

Signed Sealed & Published by the said Jean Corbin for and as her last Will and Testament in the Presence of
SAM ASHE
DANIEL MORGAN
DAVID MORGAN

This the last Will and Testament of Jean Corbyn deceased was proved before me this third day of April 1775 by the Oath of David Morgan one of the subscribing Witnesses thereto who swore that he was present and did see the Testatrix sign seal publish and declare the same to be and contain her last Will and Testament and that at the time thereof she was of sound and disposing mind and memory and John Rutherfurd one of the Executors in the said Will named having taken the Oaths of an Executor and qualified agreeable to Law.

It is Ordered that Letters Testamentary issue thereon accordingly.

JO. MARTIN

STATE OF NORTH CAROLINA   New Bern 23d. April 1778

Personally appeared Mr. Thomas Holloway one of the executors in the within Will named Before me Richard Caswell Governor of the said State, And qualified as Executor to the said Will of which the Secretary is required to take Notice & certify the Same accordingly.

RD CASWELL

(Endorsement): The Last Will of Mrs. Jean Corbin.

ROBERT COURTNEY'S WILL.

IN THE NAME OF GOD AMEN, the Seventeenth day of January, in the year of our Lord, one Thousand, Seven Hundred and fifty. I, Robert Courtney, of the County of Onslow, and province of North Carolina, planter, being sick in body but of Good and perfect Memory, thanks be to Allmighty God, and Calling to Mind the Uncertain Estate of this Life, and that all flesh must yeild Unto Death when it shall please God to Call, Do make, Constitute, ordain and Declare this, my Last will and Testament in Manner and form following: that is to Say, first, being penitent from the Bottom of my heart for my Sins past, Most Humbly Desireing forgiveness for the same, I Give and Commit my Soul Unto Allmighty God my Saviour and Redeemer, in whom and by the Merits of Jesus Christ, I trust and beleave assuredly to be saved, and to have full Remission and forgiveness of all my sins, and that my Soul with my Body Shall Rise again with Joy at the General Resurection, and through the merits of Christs Death and passion, possess and Inherit the Kingdom of heaven prepared for his Elect and Chosen: and my Body to be Decently buried as it shall please my Executors hereafter Named: and now for my Temporal Estate, and such Goods Chattels & Debts as it hath pleased God, far above my Deserts to bestow Upon me, I Do order, Give and Dispose in Manner and form following, that is to say, I will that my funeral Expences and Just Debts be paid and Satisfyed.

Item. I Give and bequeath Unto my well beloved wife, hannah Courtney, the bed and furniture whereon we now Lye, one Chest, one pot which formerly belonging to her, one pair of worsted Combs, Eight Cows and Calves, as Likewise and Equal Share of what young Cattle shall be when they Cone to be Divided, betwixt her, my Sons, Robert, Jonathan, and Rowland, as Likewise and Equal part of what houshold Goods, beds and beding, Excepted one Silver head for a Cane, one Iron Kettle and one third part of the Increase of the plantation [of the plantation] I now Live on Dureing her Natural Life, and one Mare and Colt.

Item. I Give and bequeath Unto my well beloved son, John Courtney, one Shilling, Sterling money of Great Britain.

Item. I Give and bequeath Unto my well beloved Daughter, Phebe Curtis, one Shilling, Sterling money of Great Britain.

Item. I Give and bequeath Unto my well beloved Son, Robert Courtney, a Tract of Land Lying on the East Side of the Northwest beach of New River, on the half moon Creek, Containing on Hundred and fifty acres, Known by the Name of Wallins, one Riffle Gun, one Mare Sadle and bridle, one bed and furniture, one half of a Case of bottles, and Equal Share of the Implements of Husbandry and houshold Goods, (and what Cows and Calves Shall be Left after my wife has had hers as above Mentioned, and my Son Rowland, three as will be hereafter Mentioned), to be Equaly Divided between him and my son, Jonathan, as Likewise and Equal Share of the young Cattle, as Likewise and Equal Share of my wearing Apperal, one half of my petiauqua, to him and his heirs for Ever.

Item. I Give and bequeath Unto my well beloved Son, Jonathan Courtney, the plantation I now Live on, (one Hundred Acres at the Lower End Excepted) a Quantity of feathers, one horse for the use of the plantation, one Mare Sadle and bridle, one Gun, and Equal Share of what houshold Goods, Implements of Husbandry, young Cattle, and what Cows and Calves, shall be to be Devided between him and my Son Robert, after my wifes and my Son Rowlands Shall be taken out, as Likewise one half of my petyauqua, to him and his heirs for Ever.

Item. I Give and bequeath Unto my well beloved son, Rowland Courtney, one Hundred Acres of Land, at the Lower

End of the plantation I now Live on, three Cows and Calves, an Equal Share of the young Cattle acording to what Cows shall be to be Devided), one two year old Mare, To him and his heirs for Ever.

I Likewise Desire that my Son in Law, Richard Curtis, and my Good friend, Benjamin Easom, in Case any Difference Should arise in Shareing of my Estate, that they Should be the persons to Decide it and No other person to Interfere, Unless Desired by the parties Concerned, as Likewise to be as Overseers in the Distribution.

I Likewise Constitute and apoint my well beloved Sons, Robert Courtney, and Jonathan Courtney, to be my Sole Execu^r. of this my Last will and Testament, Utterly Revokeing all former wills and Testaments by me Made.

In witness whereof, I have Set my hand and affixed my Seal, the Day and Date as above.

ROBERT COURTNEY. (Seal)

Signed Sealed published and pronounced by the sd Robert Courtney as his Last will and Testament, in presence of us:
MATHEW LEWIS.
JOS: STURGES.
BENJAMIN EASON.

NORTH CAROLINA, ONSLOW COUNTY. ss.

At a Court begun & held at Johnston, on New River, in and for the County of Onslow, on Tuesday the Second of April, anno Dom. 1751, Before John Starkey, Esqr. & the Rest of the worshipful Justices &c.

The Within Will of Robert Courtney, was proved by the Oath of Mathew Lewis, & Jonathan Courtney, One of the Exers. therein Named, Qualified. by Taken the Oaths appointed by Law.

Ordered that the sd. Courtney have Letters Testamentory.

THOS: BLACK, C. Cr.

Copied from Original Will, filed in the Office of the Secretary of State.

JAMES CRAVEN'S WILL.

IN THE NAME OF GOD AMEN. I, James Caraven, late of Droughton, near Skipton, in Craven, in the County of York, in Great Britain, but now of Edenton, in the Province of North Carolina, Esqr., being sick and weak of body, but of Sound & perfect mind and memory, trusting & Confiding in the Mercy of Almighty God, through the Merits of Jesus Christ my Saviour for Pardon and Redemption of my Sins and frailtys, for a happy Eternity in the World to Come; And Touching my

Estate wherewith it has pleased God to bless me with in this World: After Payment of all my just Debts and funeral Charges, I give, Devise, Bequeath and Dispose of the Same as followeth, That is to say:

First, I give, Devise and Bequeath to my Loving Wife, Penelope Craven, her Heirs and assigns for Ever, all those Lands, Tenements and Hereditaments with their appurtenances which I purchased of her before our Intermarriage, the Particulars whereof will Appear in a Deed, Dated the Eighteenth day of February, in the Year of our Lord, One Thousand Seven Hundred and fifty Two, & Executed by her by the Name of Penelope Hodgson.

Item. I give and Bequeath to the said Penelope Craven, all the Black Cattle, Sheep and Hogs, and Plantation Tools whatsoever, I shall Dye Possessed of at the Brick house, and the Old Plantation Commonly calld. Pagetts Plantation, and in the Range Commonly Calld. the Great Marsh.

Item. I give and Bequeath to the said Penelope Craven, Ten Negro Slaves and my Will is, that she have her Choice out of all the Slaves I shall Dye Possessed of.

Item. I give and Bequeath to the said Penelope Craven, Silver Plate and Household Furniture to the Amount of One Hundred Pounds, Sterling, first Cost, the whole to be appraised and Valued by the Majority of my Executors, she afterwards to take her Choice to that Amount of the Plate and Furniture, Furniture so Appraised as Aforesaid.

Item. I give and Bequeath to the said Penelope Craven, Fifty Volums of Books to be Chosen by her out of all my Books I may Dye Possessed of.

Item. I give and Bequeath to the said Penelope Craven, the Horse I bot. of Mr. Richmond, with her Side Saddle and furniture; and all the Provisions and Liquors that shall be in my Dwelling house or Cellar in Edenton at the time of my Death.

Item. I give to each of my God Children, one Pound proclamation Money.

Item. I give to each of the Children of John Hodgson Esqr., Deceased, the Sum of Twenty Shillings, Proclamation Money as a token of my friendship to them.

Item. I give to Dockter Abraham Boulton, my Brother, Ten Pounds.

Item. I give to Thomas Craven Hodgson, Fifty Pounds, Proclamation Money, and my Large Gold Seal.

Item. I give my Godson, William Badham, Six Silver Spoons Marked W. B., and Also Ten Pounds Proclamation Money.

Item. I give to each of my Executors hereafter named the Sum of Three Pounds Proclamation Money to buy each of them a Ring as a Testimony of my Regard for them.

Item. I Leave the use of the house wherein I Dwell, and the Six Lotts thereon, to the said Penelope Craven until all my Affairs are Settled by my Executors, and by them so Declared, She Commiting no Waste.

Item. I Will and Ordain that the Executrix & Executors of this my Last Will and Testament, And their Executors or Administrators for and towards the Performance of this my said last Will and Testament shall as Soon as they have Settled my Affairs after my Decease, bargain, sell and alien in fee Simple all the Residue of my Real Estate not herein before Absolutely give and Bequeathed for ever, for the Doing, Executing and perfect finishing Whereof, I do by these Presents give, grant, Will and Transfer to my said Executrix and Executors and to their Executors and Administrators, or the Majority thereof, full power & Authority to Grant, Bargain, Sell, Convey and assure all my Said Real Estate, that is to say, all my said six Lotts and Houses thereon, & my Dwelling House, the use of Which I have before Left to my Loving Wife, Penelope Craven, untill my Affairs are Settled by my Executors; and also all my Lands not hearinbefore Absolutely Given & Bequeathed for Ever, to any Person or Persons and their Heirs for Ever, in fee Simple by all and Every such Lawfull ways and means in the Law as to my said Executrix and Executors or their Executor or Executors, Administrator or Administrators or their Councel Lerned in the Law, Shall Seem fit or Necessary and the Moneys Arising by such Sale to be applyed towards payment of my just Debts.

Item. I Order and Derect, and my Will and Pleasure is, that my Executors or the Majority of them, do make Sale of all my personal Estate, not herein Specially Given & Bequeathed at Publick Vendue or by Private Sale at the Discretion of my said Executrix & Executors, or the Majority of them, and the money arising by the Sale of my Real & Personal Estate aforementioned, after my just Debts are paid, I give and Bequeath to my said Loving Wife, Penelope Craven, Doctor John Craven, and my Sister, Mary Leeming, to be Equaly Divided between them, the said Penelope Craven, Doctor John Craven and Mary Leeming. If my Executors shall think giving a Certain Day for Payment of the Moneys Arising, or that may arise, by the Sale of my Said Real and Personal Estate will advance the Price thereof (as I think it will), they may, and my Will and Desire is that they do so, otherwise not.

Item. I give unto Mr. Peter Leeming, all my Wearing Apparell and Linenn of what Sort Soever.

Item. I Nominate and Appoint my Loving Wife, Penelope Craven, Executrix and my Good Friends, Frances Corbin, Wyriot Ormand and William Heritage, of North Carolina, Esqrs., and John Watson, of Suffolk, in Virginia, Esqr., Executors of this my Last Will and Testament & to see the Same duly Executed and Fullfill'd According to it's true Intent and Meaning, hereby Revoking all Other Wills by me heretofore made, Ratifying, allowing & Confirming this to be my last will and Testament & None other.

In Testimony Whereof, I have Set my hand & affixed my Seal, this Twenty Eighth day of September, in the Year of our Lord, One Thousand, Seven Hundred and fifty five, (1755).

JAS. CRAVEN. (Seal).

Signed, Sealed, Published and Declared by the said James Craven, as and for his Last Will & Testament in the Presence of us the Subscribers, who at his Request & in his Presence put our Names as Witnesses to the same:
SARAH BLOUNT.
JOSEPH HARRON.
JOHN WILLIAMS,
JOHN PINDAR.

NORTH CAROLINA, NEWBERN, SS.

The Execution of the within last Will & Testament of James Craven, Esquire, deceased, was proved before me, Arthur Dobbs, Esqr., Governor & Commander in Chief of North Carolina, and Ordinary of the Same, by the Oath of John Williams, One of the Subscribing Witnesses thereto, the 11th Day of October, 1755: at which Time and Penelope Craven herself, The Executrix within named, qualified herself pr. the sd. Office, by taking the Oath appointed to be taken by Executors.

ARTHUR DOBBS.

Recorded in Will Book 7, page 12, Office of the Secretary of State.

NICHOLAS CRISP'S WILL.

NO. CAROLINA. SC.

IN THE NAME OF GOD AMEN. I, Nicholas Crisp, of Chowan precinct, in North Carolina, Gentn., Do make and declare these presents to be and contain my Last Will and Testament, hereby Revoking and making Null and void all former & other Wills by me heretofore made or Declared.

Imprimis. I Will that all my Just Debts and Funeral Expences be paid and Satisfied by my Executors hereafter named.

Item. I Give, Devise and bequeath unto my Grandson, Richare Crisp, and his Heirs and assignes for ever all that my Lands and plantations in Chowan Precinct whereon I now dwell, Together with the plantation commonly called or known by the Name of Windlys; also my Lot and Ware house in Edenton.

Item. It is my will, that my Daughter in Law, Elisabeth Crisp, shall have the use and benefit of my Grandson's plantations untill my Grandson shall arrive at the Age of twenty one years, or day of Marriage, which shall first happen; And that my Executors hereafter named shall have the use & benefit of my Ware house & Lots in Edenton for three years after my decease, And then my aforesd. daughter in Law to have the use thereof, until my Grandson shall arrive at the age of 21 Years or day of Marriage.

Item. I Give, devise and bequeath unto my Said Grandson, Richard Crisp, and his Heirs and Assigns for ever, my Land in Pequimans precinct, known by the name of Fendals, also the Island called Batts's Grave.

Item. I Give, Devise and bequeath unto my Granddaughter, Mary Durant, and her Heirs and assignes for ever, all that my plantation & Lands in Pequimins Precinct, lying on Albemarle Sound between Norcombs & Coll. Harveys, Together with all the Live Stock that shall belong or appertain thereto at my Decease; Also a Mulatto Boy named Billy.

Item. I Give, Devise and bequeath unto my Grand daughter, Sarah Durant, and her Heirs & Assignes for ever, all my Lands lying on Moratoke River in Bertie Precinct, at and near Skauwaukee and Hennunteh, containing in the whole by estimation Eleaven hundred & twenty Acres of purchased Lands, be the same more or less, together with a Girl named Maria.

Item. It is my Will, That in case either of my said Grand daughters, Mary or Sarah, shall depart this Life before arrival to the Age of twenty one Years or day of Marriage, that then Such Legacy before in this Will given to such of my said Grand daughters, shall go to the Survivor of them, my Said Grand daughters & their heirs and Assignes for ever.

Item. I Give & bequeath unto my daughter in Law, Elisabeth Crisp, Widow and Relict of my son John Crisp, lately deceased, One large Silver spoon guilt with Gold.

Item. I Give, devise & bequeath unto my Grand son, Richard Crisp (son of my son John Crisp, deceased, to whom I advanced largely & Sufficient during his Life Time), unto my Grandson, George Durant, to my Grand daughters, Ann, Mary, Sarah & Elisabeth Durant, Children of my daughter Hagar, All the Rest and Residue of my Personal Estate, to be equally divided among them my said Six Grand Children, and the Survivor or Survivors of them as they shall severally

& respectively attain the Age of twenty one Years or day of Marriage.

Lastly, I do hereby nominate & appoint my good Friends, Edward Moseley and Jeremiah Vail, of Chowan Precinct, to be Executors of this my Last Will and Testament.

In Testimony whereof, I have hereunto set my hand and Seal, this Twenty Second day of March, Anno Dom. 1726-7.

NICHOLAS CRISP. (Seal)

Signed, Sealed, Published & declared in presence of:
    WILLIAM WILLIAMS, Jurat.
    HUMPHRY ROBINSON, Jurat.
    JAMES BUSH.

No. CAROLINA. ss.   May 23d., 1727.

Came before me William Williams & Humphry Robinson, Evidences to the afore written Will of Nicholas Crisp, decd., And made oath on the holy Evangelists, That they saw the sd. Nicholas Crisp, Seal, Sign, publish & declare the Same to be his last Will & Testamt, he then being of perfect mind & Memory to the best of their apprehension.

Also, That they saw James Bush, the other Evidence, Sign the Same as an Evidence thereto.

GALE, C. J.

Recorded in the Will Book 3, page 93, Office of Secretary of State.

MOSES JOHN DeROSSETT'S WILL.

IN THE NAME OF GOD AMEN. I, Moses-John DeRosset, of Wilmington, in the province of North Carolina, practicner in physic and Surgery, being of sound and disposing mind and memory, do make this my last will and testament, in manner and form following, that is to say:

First of all, I order that my executors hereinafter named do pay all my just debts and funeral expences; Also I give, bequeath and devise all my estate, both real and personal, of what kind or quality soever, to my beloved wife, Mary, and to my daughter, Magdalene-Mary & my son, Armand-John, their heirs and assignes forever, to be equally divided among them, share and share alike; and I do make my said wife executrix, and my brother, Lewis-Henry DeRosset, and my friends, John DuBois, James Moore and Marmaduke Jones, esquires, executors of this my last Will and testament, hereby revoking all wills by me heretofore made.

And I do also nominate and appoint my said executors to be guardians of my said son and daughter until they shall arrive at the age of twenty one years of age respectively. And in case both my children should die before they shall arrive at age, or the day of Marriage, then it is my will that my whole estate should belong to my said wife, to hold to her heirs and assigns forever.

In witness whereof, I have hereunto set my hand & seal & published this as my last will and testament, the thirtieth day of November, in the year of our Lord, one thousand, seven hundred and sixty seven.

MOSES JNO. DEROSSETT (Seal)

Signed, sealed, published and declared by the above named testator as & for his last will and testament, in his presence, in the room where he was, & in the presence of each other: (the words "their heirs & assigns forever" being first interlined).

ANN MOORE.
E. JUSTICE.
A. MACLAINE.

WILMINGTON, the 1st of March, 1768.

Ardhibald Maclaine, Esquire, one of the Subscribing Witnesses to the within Will personally appeared before me and made oath that he saw the within mentioned Moses John DeRossett, the Testator, Sign, Seal, publish, pronounce and declare this to be his Last Will and Testament; and that at the Time thereof he, the Testator, was of sound and disposing mind & Memory according to the best of this Deponents knowledge and belief.

WM. TRYON.

Copied from the Original Will, filed in the Office of the Secretary of State.

ARTHUR DOBBS' WILL.

IN THE NAME OF THE ALMIGHTY GOD AMEN. I, Arthur Dobbs, of Brunswick, in New Hanover, Governor and Captain General of the Province of North Carolina, in America, injoying a moderate state of health and having by the blessing of the infinitely perfect and good God the Father Almighty, a perfect and sound mind and memory, do make this my last Will and Testament in manner following:

First, I recommend my soul to the Almighty Triune God, Jehovah Elohim and his only Begotten son, Jesus Christ my God and only Saviour and Redeemer and to his Holy Spirit Blessed forever; and my Body to the Earth to be decently and privately interred, in an assured and full hope of a Glorious and happy Resurection with the Just, at the first Resurection and a Blessed immortality in the Heavenly Kingdom of Christ the Messiah, untill he shall deliver up his Mediatorial Kingdom to God his Father when he shall be all in all his Creatures; and instead of immoderate Funeral Expenses, I desire that one hundred pounds, Sterling Money, may be paid and distributed proportionally among the Housekeepers of the Parrishes of Ballynure and Kilroot in the County of Antrim, and Kingdom of Ireland, and one other Hundred pounds like Money among the poore Freemen House keepers who reside within the County of the town of Carrick fergus, in the said Kingdom, to be paid out of my Personal Estate which I may be intitled to at the time or my Decease out of my Demesnes at Castle Dobbs, or out of the arrears of Rents I reserved out of a Moiety of my Lands in that Kingdom during my Life, at the Discretion of my Executors hereinafter to be named; desiring that my Body may be Buried in the parish or place where it pleases God that I shall die:

And as to the Disposition of the Worldly Estate which I may die possessed of, my funeral Espences and Debts being first paid, I give, devise and bequeath as followeth, that is to say:

First, I do confirm in the most ample manner the Settlement made on my son, Conway Richard Dobbs, on his Marriage in July, 1749, in which is included the several remainders and Fortunes to my Younger Children and to his and their Issue.

Item. I confirm unto my Younger Son, Edward Brice Dobbs, (over and above his fortune secured in that Marriage settlement, which I hereby limit and Ascertain to be One thousand pounds, Lawful Money of Ireland, is mentioned in my Marriage settlement upon my intermarriage with my first Wife) all the Lands in America, which are Specified in a Deed or Deeds which I made to him and his Heirs since my Setling at Brunswick; together with all the Slaves, goods & Chattles, therein mentioned.

Itim. I give, devise and bequeath unto my beloved Wife, Justina Dobbs, and her Issue, by me Begotten, in case she shall have any or be pregnant at the time of my Decease, all the Slaves and other Chattels which was or shall be hereafter given her by her Father.

Item. I give, devise and bequeath unto my said beloved Wife, all my Slaves, goods and Chattles, Plate, Money and other Effects of what Nature of kind soever in America (not already settled by deed upon my son, Edward Brice Dobbs), which I now have or hereafter shall have at the time of my Decease, in which is included the money and Interest due, or which shall be due to me by the General assembly for the

Lands Called Tower hill, in Johnston County, purchased from me by the public.

Itim. I give, devise and bequeath unto my said beloved Wife, Justina Dobbs, after the payment of my D^bts, Funeral Charges, and Legacies, all arrears of Sallery which now are, or shall be due to me at the time of my Decease, by Virtue of my appointment by his Majesty to the Government of North Carolina.

Item. Whereas, I have a right to the Moiety of Two hundred thousand acres of Land, Granted to me by the Crown, in Sixteen Patents of Twelve thousand, Five hundred acres each, in Mecklenburgh (late Anson) County, as one of the associates of Huey and Crymble, the other Moiety having been settled by me upon my eldest son, Conway Rirchard Dobbs, upon his Marriage, I do hereby impower and direct my Executors, or Either of them, as soon as convenient may be after my Decease, to sell in parcells (to the present Occupants or to such others as shall incline to become purchasers), the said moiety of Lands, and that the Money arising therefrom (except so much thereof as shall, together with the Money hereinbefore bequeathed to my said wife, make up the sum of Two Thousand pounds, Sterling Money of Great Britain) shall be laid out by my Executors in Negroes for the sole use and benefit of such Issue by me as my said Wife shall have living, or be pregnant with at the time of my Decease, and their heirs forever; And in case my said Wife shall have no Issue by me alive, or be pregnant at the time of my Decease, then, and in that case, I will and devise the said undivided Moiety of Land shall be and remain to my son, Edward Brice Dobbs, and his heirs, upon this special provisor, that he makes up and pays so much Money to my said Wife, Justina Dobbs, as together with the sums herein before bequeathed to her, shall amount to the sum of Two thousand Pounds, sterling Money of Great Britain, which I Will and Desire that my said beloved Wife may have and receive out of the Estate I shall die possessed of.

Item. I bequeath to each of my Children who shall be alive at the time of my Decease, fifty pounds Sterling.

Item. I bequeath to my beloved Brother, the Reverend Doctor Richard Dobbs, Twenty pounds Sterling, which two last Mentioned bequest is to buy them Mourning and Rings.

Item. Whereas, I am intitled to a Moiety of Twelve Thousand Acres of Land by a purchase from Mr. Patrick Smith, of Waterford, Merchant, (for which) for which a Patent was Granted to him as an associate of Huey and Crymble, Subdivided from the Great Tract Number 4, the heirs or assigns of Mr. James Benning, of Lisburn, In Ireland, being intitled in equity, to the other Moiety of the said Patent. Whatever part of the same as may remain unsold at the time of my Decease, I devise to my Executors, to be sold for the payment of my Debts and Legacies herein bequeathed.

Item. I give and Bequeath unto my son, Conway Richard Dobbs, after his Discharging my Debts, Funeral Charges, and Legacies which shall be due in Europe at the time of my Decease, all my Plate, Goods, Household Furniture, arrears Rents, and other Chattles whatsoever which are now belonging or hereafter may belong to me, at my Decease, which now are or hereafter may be at Castle Dobbs, in the County of Antrim, and Kingdom of Ireland.

Lastly, I do appoint my Beloved Wife, Justina Dobbs, and my Sons, Conway Richard Dobbs and Edward Brice Dobbs, my Residuary Legatees and Executors of this my last Will and Testament; hereby revoking all former wills by me heretofore made.

In Witness whereof I have hereunto set my hand and seal, this 31st. day of August, in the Year of our Lord, 1763.

ARTHUR DOBBS (Seal)

Sign'd, Seal'd, Publish'd and declar'd to be the last will and Testament of the Testator in presence of:

> JAMES HASELL,
> LEWIS DEROSSET,
> JOHN SAMPSON.

NORTH CAROLINA. Wilmington, 24th, April, 1765.

Then personally appeared Before me James Hasell & Lewis DeRosset, two of the subscribing Witnesses to the foregoing Will and made oath on the Holy Evangelists of Almighty God, that they saw Arthur Dobbs, sign, seal and publish the foregoing as and for his last Will and Testament; and that the said Arthur Dobbs was at the same time (to the best of their Knowledge and Belief) of a sound and disposing mind and Memory, and that they, the said James Hasell & Lewis DeRossett, together with John Sampson, subscribed their Names as Witnesses thereto, in the Presence of the Testator.

At the same time, Justina Dobbs, Executrix before mentioned, took the Oaths by Law appointed for Her Qualification. Let Letters Testamentary issue thereon accordingly.

WM. TRYON.

Recorded in Book 8, page 290. Office of Secretary of State.

JAMES DOUGLASS' WILL.

IN THE NAME OF GOD AMEN. I, James Dougless, of Bartie County, of North Carolina, being not well in health of Body at this Present, but of Perfect and Sound Memory, Praised be Almighty God for the same, do Make and ordain this to be my only last will and Testament, revoaking all other heretofore by me Made, holding and Declaring this only to stand as in Manner following: That is to say, first and Principally I recommend My Soul to Almighty God who gave it me, hopeing Through the Merits and Death of my Savior Jesus Christ, to have a Gloryfull Resurrection; and my Body to be Decently Buried at the Discretion of my Executriss hereafter Named; And as for my Temporall Estate, I give and Dispose of as followeth, vixt:

That first I will That my Debts and funerall Charges Shall be Discharged and paid.

Item. I Lend to my Loving Wife, Eliza. Doughless, all my land and Personall Estate During her time of her widdowhood or life, And after her Death I give my Said land and Plantation whereon I now live, to my Loving Son, Kesia, and the heirs of his Body Lawfully begotten for ever.

Item. I give to my Daughter, Ann, Two hundred Acres of my land over Hoske Swamp, which I bought of one Cocks at which end She pleaseth to have it.

Item. I give the reamining part of the sd. Land to my loving Son, Kesia, and his heirs for ever, and the rest of my personal Estate after my wifes Death, to Equally Divided Between my son, Kesia and my Daughter, ann.

Item. I give to my Son, James, five Shills. to be pd. him out of my Estate for his part.

Item. I give to my Grand Daughter, Elizabeth Dougless, the Daughter of my Son, James, Ten Pounds, Virginia Currency to be pd her out of my Estate at the age of Sixteen years old and in case She should Die before that time appointed, That the next heir lawfully begotten to have the same.

Item. my will and Desire is my loving wife have accasion to sell or Dispose of any of my land over Hoskie, She shall have full power to doe the same only after her Death my Son Kesia and Daughter Ann to have answering what I left them of the sd. Land or rest of my Estate after my wife's death.

And I Constitute and appoint my Loving Wife, Elizabeth Duglass, my whole & sole Excrs. of this my last will and Testament in Truth whereof, I have interchangably set my hand and Seal, this 6th: of October, 1750.

JAMES DOUALL (L S) (Seal)

Test.
 JOHN BROWN.
   her
 ELIZABETH X ROBERTSON.
    marke
 JOSEPH I MADLIN.
  his marke.

NORTH CAROLINA.

This Day Personally appeared before me, John Brown & Elizabeth Robertson, two of the Subscribing Evidences of the last Will & Testament of James Douglass, & made Oath that they saw the Testator sign, Seal & Deliver the foregoing, as and for his last will & Testament & That at the time of his signing thereof, He was of sound & disposing mind & memory; and that they saw the Joseph Medlin, the other Evidence Sign his name thereto.

At the same time Elizth. Douglass, the Executrix appointed by the sd. Will, tooke the Oath by Law for to be taken by Executors.

Given at Eden house under my Hand this 11th. July, Anno Dom. 1752. (61-2 C. S.)

Memorandum. The above Will was proved before his late Excelly' Governor Johnston, according to the Tenor of the above Certificate & Letters were Issued, but his Excelly being at that time indisposed he did not sign the sd. Certificate.

Given under my Hand, this 16th September anno. Dom., 1752.

SAML ORMES, Secretary to the late Governor.

Recorded in Will Book 6, page 61. Office of the Secretary of State.

JOHN DUBOIS' WILL

IN THE NAME OF GOD AMEN. I, John DuBois, of Wilmington, in the province of North Carolina, Esquire, being of sound & disposing mind and memory, do make this my last Will and testament in manner and form following, that is to say:

First of all, It is my Will that all my just debts and funeral expences be first paid.

Also, I give unto my eldest son, Peter, ten pounds sterling, which tho, he merits an equal proportion of my estate, will I flatter myself be more agreable to him (as he is already blessed with a plentiful fortune), than an equal distribution with my other children.

Also, I give unto my son, Walter, forty pounds, current money of the province of New York, a year to be paid him half yearly out of my estate by my executors hereinafter named during his natural life; I also give to my said son, Walter, my silver watch.

Also, I give and devise unto my son, John and his heirs and assigns my upper brick tenement in Dock street next to the house of Wm. Campbell, with the ground thereto belonging, together with my plantation on Smith's creek containing three hundred acres of land. I also give unto my said son, John, my fowling piece, my silver hilted sword and my case of pistols, I likewise confirm unto my said Son, John, a large diamond ring which was formerly given him by captain Dekan.

Also, I give and devise unto my daughter, Magdalene-Margaret, & her heirs and assigns, my middle brick tenement in

Dock street with the ground thereto belonging. I also give unto my said daughter, two diamond rings which belonged to her mother.

Also, I give and devise unto my Daughter, Margaret, and her heirs and assigns, my lower brick tenement now occupied by Doctor Eustace, with the ground thereto belonging.

Also, I give and devise unto my son, Isaac, my wooden tenement in Dock street adjoining to the tenement where Doctor Eustace lives together with the small tenement thereto adjoining & the ground belonging to the said two tenements, to hold to him, the said Isaac, his heirs and assigns forever.

Also, I give and devise unto my beloved wife, Jean, the house in which I now live, with the lott of ground belonging thereto and all the houses and improvements thereon, together with the lott of ground adjoining, during her widow hood and after the expiration of that term, then to my daughter Anna-Jean and her heirs and assigns forever.

Also, I give and devise unto my son, James, my lott of ground in front street and running thence to the river with the two tenements, bake house, and all other houses and improvements thereon with their appurtenances, together with my land and the Wind mill erected thereon adjoining to Wilmington, to hold to the said James, his heirs and assigns forever.

Also, I give and devise unto my daughters, Magdalene-Margaret & Margaret, and their heirs and assigns my lott of ground on the North side of Market street between the house of Alexander Ross, deceased, and Samuel Swann's lott, share and share alike as tenants in common.

Also, I give unto Caleb Grainger, son of Colonel Caleb Grainger, deceased, a monthly clock which I had with my third wife his aunt, but if the said Caleb Grainger should happen to die under age or unmarried, then I give the said clock to his brother Cornelius.

Also, I give unto my beloved wife, Jean, all my silver plate, household and kitchen furniture and utensils, the said clock excepted.

Also, All the residue of my personal estate in North Carolina not heretofore disposed of, I give and bequeath unto my beloved wife, Jean, and my children, John, Magdalene-Margaret, Margaret, Isaac, Anna-Jean, and James, to be equally divided among them by my executors herein after named.

And whereas I am intitaled to a proportion of lands or personal estate, or lands and personal estate, in the province of New York, in right of my Grand-mother or other wise, I therefore give and devise the said estate whether real, personal or both to my executors herein after named to be sold, and the money arising from such sale to be equally divided among all my children hereinbefore mentioned.

Also, It is my will and so the same is to be taken and understood, that the legacies hereinbefore given to my said wife be in full of her right of dower and all other demands on my estate, and if she pretends to claim her dower that, then, and in that case, I hereby give and devise the house and lotts where I now live to my Daughter, Anna-Jean, immediately after my decease, and the other legacies herein given to my said wife, in that case I give to my children, John, Magdalene-Margaret, Margaret, Isaac, Anna-Jean and James, to be equally divided among them.

Also, It is my will that my children, John, Magdalene-Margaret, Margaret, Anna-Jean, Isaac, and James, shall not be intitaled to the profits of the tenements & lands respectively devised to them, till each of them shall arrive at the age of twenty one years, or day of Marriage, but that the same shall be received by my executors herein after named and applied towards the education of my said children and the maintenance of my family, and improvement of my whole estate for the joint benefit of my said Last mentioned children and my wife.

And it is also my will, that the bake house divised to my son, James, be kept employed for the benefit of my said wife, and last mentioned children, & my boats and negroes kept employed in the usual manner for the same purpose, until my son, James, shall arrive at the age of twenty one years or the day of Marriage, and that such child or children who shall happen to marry, or may have arrived at the age of twenty one years, shall draw his or her proportion of the profits of the said boats and negroes.

And in case of the death of any of my said last mentioned children before such child or children shall have attained the age of twenty one years or day of Marriage, then it is my will that the share or shares hereby given to such child or children so dying, both real and personal, shall go to the survivor or survivors of my said last mentioned children, to be equally divided among them, if more than one and that such part of my real estate as shall go to any of my children by the death of the others or any of them shall, be held by such children as as a tenancy in common. And in case of the death of all my said last mentioned children before marriage, then I give and devise such part of my estate as is herein given to them, to my beloved wife Jean & her heirs and assigns forever.

And lastly, I do make, nominate and appoind my beloved wife, Jean, my sons, Peter, Walter and John, and my friends, Lewis-Henry DeRosset and Moses-John DeRosset, esquires, to be guardians of my children and their respective estates during their minority, and also executors of this my last will and testament: hereby revoking all wills by me heretofore made.

In Witness whereof I have hereunto set my hand to this my will, written on four pages of paper together with my seal and published the whole as my last Will and testament, this thirteenth day of September, in the year of our Lord, one thousand, and seven hundred and sixty seven.

Before publishing this my last will, I hereby order and direct that my said executors shall purchase out of the profits of my estate, able negroes in number four, fit to go in my boats, & that the number then on my estate shall be kept up by my said executors as often as necessary in case of death or otherwise. (The words "then on my estate" being interlined.)

JOHN DUBOIS, (Seal)

Signed, sealed, published & declared by the above named, John DuBois as and for his last will and testament in presence of us whose names are hereunder written, who did each of us subscribe our names as witnesses thereto at his request, in his presence, and in the room where he was (the words "of twenty one years" being first interlined in the third page.)
  J. EUSTACE.
  EDWARD CHIVERS.
  A. MACLAINE.

WILMINGTON, April 9th, 1768.

John DuBois, one of the Executors named in the within will, appeared before me, and took the Oath appointed by Law for the Qualification of an Executor.
          BENJ. HERON, Sec.

Wilmington, the 1 March, 1768.

Archibald Maclaine, Esq., one of the subscribing Witnesses to this Will personally appeared before me and made oath that he saw the above mentioned John DuBois, the Testator, sign, Seal, publish, pronounce and declare this to be his last will & testament; and that at the Time thereof he, the Testator, was of sound & disposing mind & Memory according to the best of this Deponents knowledge & belief. Jean DuBois, The Executrix & Lewis Henry DeRossett, Esq., one of the Executors therein mentioned, took the oaths appointed by Law for their Qualification.

Whereupon it is ordered that Letters Testamentary issue.
            WM. TRYON.

Copied from the Original, which is filed in the Office of the Secretary of State.

CHRISTOPHER DUDLEY'S WILL.

IN THE NAME OF GOD AMEN. I, Christopher Dudley, of the County of Onslow, planter, being aged and infirm, but of Sound mind and good memory (thro mercy), do make this my last will and testament, in form following: Cheife of all Commend my Soul into the hands of almighty god, as a christian ought to do, and my Body to the Earth, to be intered at the discression of my executors hereafter named; and as for such worldly goods as providence has trusted me with, I dispose of the same as followeth:

First, I will and Bequeath unto my Grandson, George, Son of my Son, Edward Dudley, after my Wifes decease my plantation whereon I now dwell, together with one halfe of all my Lands adjoying to it, with all its appurtenances, to my said Grandson, George Dudley, and the heirs Lawfully begotten of his Body for ever; and in faillure of his heirs, then I Bequeath the said land unto my Grandson, Christopher, Son of my Son, Thomas Dudley, and his heirs Lawfully Begotten for ever; and in failure of such heirs then to my right heirs forever; also I will and Bequeath the other halfe of all my Lands, that part highest up the River, together with the appurtenances, to my Son, Christopher Dudley, and his heirs and assigns for ever; also I bequeath unto my Son, Thomas Dudley, my negro girl called flora, and to his heirs and assigns for ever; also I Bequeath to my Daughter, Ann Houston, my negro man Called Luke, and to her heirs and assignes for ever; also I Bequeath to my son, Christopher Dudley, my negro woman called penny, and to his heirs and assignes for ever; Also, I bequeath unto my Son, William Dudley, one Shilling, Sterling, I also give or forgive rather, what debt he owes me in full for his childs part.

Also, I Bequeath the one halfe of my stock of Cattle and horses (except the mare and her encrease that is called my wifes), to be divided betwixt my Sons, Thomas and John, and their heirs and assignes for ever; also, I will and Bequeath my negro Luvenieh, to work on my plantation and to belong to my wife during her Life, and then to go with the plantation to which ever has the reversion. My will further is, that in case I should die after a Crop is pitched, that no negroes as legacies shall be delivered till the crop shall be compleated and finished.

Also, I will and Bequeath to my wife, Mary Dudley, the use occupation and possession of all my lands during the term of her naturall life without any impeachment of waste; I also will and Bequeath unto my Said Wife, for her Comfort and Support, she paying all my debts, all the rest and remainder of my negroes, goods, Chattles, Rights, Creditts of what kind soever or wheresoever, and to her heirs and assignes for ever.

Lastly, I do constitute and appoint John Starkey and my wife, Executors of this my last will and testament; Revoking all other or former wills by me at any time before made, and declaring this only to be my last will and testament.

In witness whereof, I have hereunto set my hand and seal, this 19th. of March, 1744-5.

CHRISTOPHER DUDLEY, (Seal)

Signed, Sealed, published and Declared by Christopher Dudley as his last will and testament in presence of us:

JANE X SIMPSON, alias Watts.
her mark

JOHN X SIMPSON
his Mark.

MARY X TROTT
her mark.

NEWBERN, Feby. 26, 1746.

Then prov'd and John Starkey Qualified before me as Executor.

GAB. JOHNSTON.

Recorded in Book 5, page 29, Office of Secretary of State.

NATHANIEL DUCKINFIELD'S WILL.

IN THE NAME OF GOD AMEN. I, Nathaniel Duckinfield, of Utkinton, in the County of Chester, Esqr., being of sound mind and Memory, but in a Very infirm state of health, or rather an Almost Cessacion of health, waiting for a Comfortable Dismission from my Afflicted Painfull Body and from all the Sorrows, Troubles and Evils I have been Subject to in this Transitory, Vain Life; but that I may leave nothing undone that Ought to be done, that my Mind may free from all Earthly incumbrances, I do make, Publish and Declare this to be my Last Will and Testamt., in manner and form following:

Imprimis. I give, Devise and Bequeath all my Messuages, Lands, Tenements, Hereditaments and Premises, with their and every of their Appurtenances that I am Now Seized or Possessed of, Scituate, Lying and being in the County of Chester, unto my Dear Wife, Margaret Dukinfield. To hold to her and to the Heirs of her Body by me Begotten, that is to say, my Will is, That my Dear Wife, Margaret, shall posssess, enjoy, Receive and take the Rents, issues and Profits of all the said Messauges, Lands and Tenements for and During the term of her Natural Life, if she shall so long Continue my Widow, unmarried, and if it shall so happen that she should have no Child living by me Begotten, and she Continues my Widow During the Term of her Natural Life, then my Will is, and I do hereby give to my said Dear Wife, Margaret full Power to make a Will and to Devise, Bequeath and to give by Virtue of such Will, the full sume of Three Hundred Pounds, Sterling Money of Great Britain, to Such of her own Relation or Relations nearest in Blood as she may think fit, or that she may think most Deserving of her Favours, the said Sume to be Raised out of the Rents, Issues and Profits Arising from my Messuages, Lands and Tenements aforesaid; but if my Dear Wife, Margaret, shall marry again, I then give and Devise all my Messuages, Lands, Tenements, Hereditaments and Premises with their Appurtenances in the County of Chester aforesaid, unto my Brother, John Chorley, and my Nephew, Samuel Duckinfield, Son of the Late John Duckinfield, of Bristol, Esqr., and their Heirs to hold to them and their Heirs upon the Several Trusts hereinafter Mentioned, that is to say, upon trust from from and after such Marriage, and not Otherwise, to Pay her one third only of the said Rents, issues and Profits Arising from my said Messuages, Lands and Tenements for and During the term of her Natural Life, and to Apply the Remainin two thirds of the said Rents, issues and Profits, or so much thereof as my said Trustees in their Discretion shall think Reasonable, for the Maintenance and Education of such of my Children or Child by my said Wife as shall be Living at such Marriage; and if there shall be Any such Children or Child Living at her Death, then upon Trust my said Trustees shall Apply the Whole rents Issues and Profits of the said Premises, or so much Thereof as they shall think Reasonable, for the Maintenance and Education of Such Children or Child untill the Eldest of such Children or only Child shall attain his or her age of Twenty One Years, and from and after his of her Attaining such Age, Upon Trust, that my said Trustees and their Heirs shall as soon as conveniently may be, make a Proper Division of Equal Proportion and of Equal Value of the said Premises, According to the Number of Such Children then Living, the Whole in Equal Share and Parts, to be Divided and Given to them. The Necessary Expenses and Charges the said Trustees may be at in Making such Division to be first Paid to them; but if there should Happen to be but one such Child, then my Will is that my said Trustees shall Convey the said Premises unto such Only Child on his or her attaining such Age as Aforesaid and his or her heirs or Assigns for Ever; but if there should be no such Child or Children living, by me Begotton on the Body of my said Wife and she shall Marry again, I Will that my said Trustees shall Receive and Take two Thirds of the said Rents, issues and Profits of the same Premises unto them, the said John Chorley and Samuel Duckinfield, Equally Between them, and Pay the remaining one third unto my said Wife for and During the term of her Natural Life, and from and after her Decease, I give & Devise my said Messauges Lands and Tenements unto my Nephew, John Chorley, Son of my Sister, Jane Chorley, to him and to his Heirs Lawfully Begotten, he Paying to my said Nephew, Samuel Dukinfield, one third only of the rents, issues and Profits of the said Premises, untill such time that my said Nephew, Samuel Dukinfield, should Obtain such a Support by his Profession in the Law as may rais him Above the Misfortune of Necessity, or should Come into Possession of the Hereditary Title and Estate Successive in the Duckinfield Family, or by any other Means should Obtain the Comfortable supports of Life, And no longer.

I give and Devise unto my Worthy Friend, Mr. Joseph Collett, all my Plantations, Negroes and Estate of What kind or Nature soever, Scituate in North Carolina, in america, upon trust; that is to say, my Will and Desire is that the said, Mr. Collett would not Refuse taking upon him this Last Request from me, that as Soon as Conveniently, he Would sell and Dispose of the said Estate, both real & Personal, to such Person and Persons at and for such rate or Price as he Can Best Obtain, and do and shall Apply the Purchase Money to Arise from such sale thereof, as I by any Writing Signed and Sealed by me in the Presence of one or More Credible Witnesses, shall Direct or Appoint.

I Give and Devise to my said Dare Wife, Margaret, all my Leasehold Estate in Ludgate Street, London, and also all the rest and Residue of my Personal Estate Whatsoever and Wheresoever.

Finally, I Constitute and Appoint my said Dear Wife, as long as she Continues my widow, Unmarried, my Executrix, but in case of Marriage, I Constitute & Appoint my Brother, John Chorley, and my Nephew, Samuel Dukinfield afsd., my Executors of this my Will; and I do hereby enjoyn them to be as assistant and as Servissable to her as they Possibly can, to Act and to do upon her Request, with as much Sincerety, faithfulness and Chearfulness in all things be best and most Comfortable manner for her Well being in Life, as if I had Particularly Nominated them to be joint Executors with her During her Continuance my Widow unmarried.

I Constitute and Appoint my Dear Friend, Mr. Joseph Collet, my Executor of all my Affairs in North Carolina, to Act and to do, Dispose and Sell every Part and Parcel thereof in the Best Manner he Can; and this trust I know he is best Qualified for.

But if my Brother, John Chorley and my Nephew, Samuel Dukinfield, should not Behave with that Relative Affection and

Regard that is sutable and Due to her as being my Wife, or should refuse to Act for her in the best Manner they can, or Jointly With her whenever She either Desires or Requiers such Assistance, then in this case, I Will, impower & Authorize my sd. Dear Wife, Margaret, to make her Will and to Devise and Give every of the Premises aforesaid unto such of my Relations, Nearest in Blood, that shall Behave with a Much Superior Degree of Sincere Affection and Respect Suitable to the Near Relation she stands in to them by being my Wife, than they have really shewen to her in my life time; but if such Respect and Esteem be not fully Given to her, then my Will is that my said Dear Wife, shall Devise, Bequeath and Give by her Will all the sd. Premises, to any of her Own Relations, nearest in Blood, that my best deserve such favour from her, Provided, she Continues my Widow Unmarried, During her Natural Life. I know no Reason to Subject a Good & Dear Wife to the Insults and Precarious Humours of Relations.

I Will that my Dear Wife shall Bury me in the same Grave where my Dear family lies, in Bun hill burying Burying Ground, London, without the least Pomp or Show, Which to me is a Strange Absurd Vanity, to Tarry Death Victories over Mortals in Triumph to the Grave; my Desire is to be Buried With as much Privacy as Consists With Decency, and when Pleas God, my Dear Wife Departs this Life, it is my Desire that she should be Buried in my Grave.

If any one should Pretend to Dispute this, my Last Will and Testament, in order to Give Uneasy Disturbances to my Dear Wife, in my real intention of preventing such a Vise Wicked Practice after my Death, I require and Charge my Executors aforenamed if they Continue faithfull Assistance to my Dear wife, and if otherwise, I desire my friend, Mr. Joseph Collet, Will lay this my Last Will and Testmt. Before the Right Honourable Lord High Chancellor, Who will Determine it agreeable to my sincere intention which is the Plenory Cumfort and Welfare of my Dear Wife, and that she may possess all that I have given her Without the least molestation. I have not studied Law Phrases but have Used Words without guile, Suitable to the Simplicity and integrity of my Own mind and With Intire Approbation of my own Reason and Consideration of things.

I revoke and make Void all former Wills by me made, and I hereunto set my hand and Seal to Each side of this Paper wherein this my last Will is Contained. Written with my Own hand this fourth Day of July, in the Twentieth Year of our Most Rightfull Lord Sovereign, George the Second, King of Great Britain, France and Ireland &c. and Glorious Defender of the faith and the Libertys of Europe, Annoq. Dom., 1746.

N. DUKINFIELD.

Signed, Sealed, Published and Declared by the said Nathaniel Dukinfield, the Testator, and for his last Will and Testament in the Presence of us Who Subscribed our Names as Witnesses hereto in the Presence of the Testator:

   WILLIAM PRIOR
   JOSEPH COLLET.
   DOROTHY POTTS.

 Thomas, by Divine Providence Archbishop of Canterbury, Primate of all England and Metropolitan, do by these Presents make known to all men, that the tenth Day of May, in the Year of our Lord, One Thousand, Seven Hundred and fifty, at London, before the Worshipfull Robert Chapman, Doctor of Laws Surrogate to the Right Worshipfull John Bettesworth, Doctor of Laws, Master keeper or Commissary of our Prerogative Court of Canterbury, Lawfully Constituted the Last Will and Testament of Nathaniel Dukinfield, Late of the Parish of St. George, in the County of Middlesex, Esqr., Deceased, hereunto Annexed, was Proved, approved and Registred. The said Deceased, having Whilst living and at the time of his Death, Goods, Chattles or Credits in Divers Dioceses or Jurisdictions, by Reason Whereof The Proving and Registering of the said Will and Granting Administration of all and Singular the said Goods, Chattles and Credits, and Also the Auditing, allowing and final Discharging the Accompt thereof, are Well known to Appertain Only and Wholy to us and not to any inferior Judge; and that Administration of all and Singular, the Goods, Chattles and Credits of the said Decd. and any way Commencing his Will was granted to Margaret Dukinfield, Widow, the Relict of the said Deceased, and Sole Executrix Named in the said Will, being first Sworn well and faithfully to Administer the Same and to make a true and Perfect Inventory of all and Singular the said Goods, Chattles and Credits, and to Exhibit the same into the Regestry of our said Court on or before the Last Day of November, Next Ensuing; and Also to Render a just and True Accompt. thereof.

 Given at the time and Place aforesaid and in the third year of our Translation.

             WM. LEGARD
(The Seal of London)   PET: J. ELOY
             HEN: STEPHENS
              Deputy Register.

 TO ALL TO WHOM THESE PRESENTS SHALL COME: I, Joseph Collett, of London, Merchant, send Greeting:

 Whereas, Nathaniel Duckinfield, late of Utkinton, in the County of Chester, Esqr., decd., did in his Life time, Duly make and Publish his last Will and Testament in Writing, bearing Date, the fourth day of July, One Thousand, Seven Hundred and forty Six, and thereof Constituted and appointed his Wife, Margaret Dukinfield, as long as she continues his Widow Unmarried, His Executrix. But in Case of Marriage, the said Testator Constituted and Appointed his Brother, John Chorley, and his Nephew, Samuel Duckinfield, Executors of his said Will; and the said Testator did also by his said Will Constitute and Appoint me, the said Joseph Collett, To be his Particular Executor of all his Affairs in North Carolina, To Act and to do, Dispose and Sell every Part & Parcell thereof,

Which said Will has been Duly proved by the said Margaret, the sole General Executrix thereof in the Prerogative Court of the ArchBishop of Canterbury as by the said Will and the Probate thereof, Relation being thereunto Had, may more fully and at large appear.

Now, Know ye, that I, the said Joseph Collett for Divers Good Causes and Considerations me hereunto especially moving, do hereby Refuse to take upon me the Executorship for the Affairs of Nathaniel Duckinfield, the Testator, in North Carolina, or Elsewhere, or to intermedle in Any Manner therewith; And do Absolutely Renounce the Probate of the said Will and that this my Refusal and Renunciation may have its due Effect, I do hereby Name, Constitute and Appoint the said Margaret Dukinfield, the Widow and Relict of the said Nathaniel Dukinfield, to be my Procurator and Attorney for me and in my Name to Appear before the Governor of North Carolina aforesaid, or any other Competent Judge in that behalf, to Exhibit this my renunciation and to do whatever Elce shall be requisite or Necessary to be done in and About the Premises for the Purposes Aforesaid; and I do hereby Promise and agree to ratify and hold for firm and irevocable, all and Whatsoever my said Procuratrix or Attorney shall Lawfully do, or cause to be Done, in and about the Premises, by Virtue of these Presents.

In Witness whereof, I, the said Joseph Collett, have hereunto set my hand and Seal, this 29th. day of July, 1755, and in the 29th. Year of the Reign of George the Second, King of Great Britain and soforth.

JOSEPH COLLETT (Seal)

Sealed and Deliverd, being first Duely stamped, in the Presence of us:
SAMUEL DUKINFIELD.
BENJAMIN ROSEWILL.

NORTH CAROLINA, BERTIE COUNTY, ss. January Court, 1756. Present His Majestys Justices:

Mrs. Margaret Dukinfield, Widow of Nathaniel Duckinfield, Esqr., Late of the Kingdom of Great Britain, Deceased, appeared in Court and Produced duly proved and Certified under the corporation Seal of the City of London, A renunciation and Refusal of Joseph Collett, of London, Merchant, to Act as Executor of the Last Will and Testament of the said Nathaniel Duckinfield, in which Office by the said Testator as to that Part of his Estate which is in this Province, and also Produced a Copy of the Will of the said Testator duly proved and Certified in the Prerogative court of the Arch bishop of Canterbury, which Renunciation and Will are Ordered to be Recorded.

The said Margaret Dukinfield then Moved the Court to Letters of Administration on the Estate of the said Nathaniel Dukinfield, with the Copy of his Will Annexed, which is Granted on her Giving Security in the Sum of One Thousand Pounds, Proclamation Money, and Ordered that Letters Accordingly Issue.

Whereupon, Samuel Ormes, Esqr., and David Ryan, Gent., offered themselves as Security for the said Administration and Were Approved of by the Court, Which was Ordered to be Certifyed.

Test. BENJN. WYNNS. Cler. Cur.

Recorded in Will Book 7, page 144, Office of Secretary of State.

WILLIAM DUCKENFIELD'S WILL.

No. CAROLINA. Sc.

IN THE NAME OF GOD AMEN. I, William Duckenfield, formerly of Cheshire, in Great Britain, but now of Chowan Precinct, in North Carolina, Esq., being of sound & perfect mind & memory, Do make & declare these presents to be & containe my last Will and testamt: hereby revoking all former & other Wills & Testaments by me heretofore made or declar'd.

First, I will that all my Lawfull Debts be well & truly paid & satisfied by my Executor or Executors hereafter named, within convenient time after my Decease.

Item. I give & bequeath unto my Loving Brother, John Duckinfield, the Sum of fourty pounds P. Annum, during the Term of his naturale Life, to be paid unto him Yearly by me Executor or Executors hereafter named, out of my Estate which I shall leave at my decease, the first payment to become due & payable at the Expiration of one Year after my Decease & to be paid in Pork, Indian Corn, Pitch or Tarr, at the prices now Currant. I also Give & bequeath unto my sd. Brother, John Duckinfield, the the Bed he now lies on, together with the Furniture to the same belonging.

Item. I give & bequeath unto my Loving Cousin, Charles Barber, of North Carolina, one Young Horse & one Mare & twenty pounds.

Item. I give & bequeath unto my Loving Friend, Edward Mosely, of Chowan Precinct, Gent., the Sum of Twenty pounds to buy him & his wife each, a Suite of Mourning.

Item. All the rest & residue of my Estate whether Reale or personale, Of what Nature, Kind or Quality Soever or wheresoever, that is now due & belonging to me, Or which hereafter shall become due unto me by any manner of waise or means whatsoever, I give, devise & bequeath ye Same unto my Loving Cousin, Nathaniel Duckinfield, Son of my Brother, Sr. Robert Duckenfeild, Baronet, and to his Heirs & Assignes for ever. And in case my sd. Kinsman, Nathaniele Duckinfeild shall depart this Life before me having no Lawfull Issue, then & in such Case I give, devise & bequeath the Estate which I have intended for my sd. Kinsman & his Heirs, unto Mary, Anne, Susanna, Jane, Sarah, Katherine & Judith Duckinfeild, the Sisters of the Sd. Nathaniel of ye whole Blood & to their Heirs & Assigns for ever. But if my sd. Kinsman, Nathaniele Duckinfeilfd, shall depart this life before me & Leaving Lawful Issue, then my Will, true Intent & meaning is, that ye Estate before mentioned & every part & parcele thereof shall come, remaine & be unto ye Lawfull Issue of my sd. Kinsman, Nathaniele, & their Heirs forever.

Lastly, I do hereby Nominate & appoint my sd. Kinsman, Nathaniele Duckenfeild to be Executor of this my Will & of all other Wills & Testaments whereof I am Executor, particularly the Will of John Arderne, late of North Carolina, bearing date ye twenty second day of October, Anno Dmi. one thousand seven hundred & seven, & to have, take & receive all which shall of right appertain unto me by force of such Wills, to him ye sd. Nathaniele Duckinfeild & his Heirs for ever. But if the sd. Nathaniele, shall depart this Life before me without having Lawful Issue then I will that my nieces aforsd, Mary, Anne, Susanna, Jane, Sarah, Katherine & Judith Duckinfield, shall be Exors., of this my Will & of all other Wills & Testam'ts whereof I am Executor, particularly the Will of John Arderne aforsd. And then the sd. Mary, Anne, Susanna, Jane, Sarah Katherine & Judith Duckinfeild to have, take & receive all wch shall of right appertain unto me by force of such Wills, to them, my said Neices & their Heirs for ever.

In Testimony whereof, I the sd. William Duckenfeild, have hereunto sett my hand & Seale, this Seventeenth day of May, Anno Dmi., 1720.

WILLIAM DUCKENFEILD (Seal)

Sealed, Published & declared
In the Presence of us:
  THOMAS ASHLEY.
  JNO. POWELL.
  BENJ'N SOAMES.
    his
  JOHN I C CHERRYHOLME.
    mark.
  JOHN DUCKENFEILD.
  ED. MOSELEY.

NORTH CAROLINA. ss. Charles Eden, Esqr., Governor.

The within Will of William Duckenfeild, Esqr., was prov'd before me by the Oaths of Thomas Ashley & John Cherryholme, two of the Evidences thereto.

In testimony whereof, I have hereunto set my hand this 27th day of Feb'ry, 1721.

C. EDEN.

Letters Granted the 1st of March, 1721.

Recorded in Will Book 2, page 311, Office of the Secretary of State.

ALEXANDER DUNCAN'S WILL.

No. CAROLINA ss.

IN THE NAME OF GOD AMEN. I, Alexander Duncan, of Wilmington, Merchant, Intending, please God, going Soon for Great Britain & knowing the uncertainty of Human Life, in Case of my death do make this my Last Will and Testament for the ordering & Disposing of what Worldly Estate or Personal Interest which it has pleased God to Bestow upon me.

In the First place, I give and bequeath unto my Brother, Robert Duncan, if allive, the Sum of three hundred Pounds Sterling money,. to him or his heirs; In case of his death or having no heirs, this Legacy to be divided equally between the Surviving Children of my Sisters, Elizabeth Ronaldson, Deceased, & Margaret Henery, now Supposed to be in Edinburgh, if not there, Let enquiry be made where my said Nieces & Nephews do Live; I Also Will & bequeath to Said Children of my said Sisters, as many as there may be of them, the sum of Seven hundred pounds Sterling, to be equally divided among them, Share & Share alike, to them & their heirs. These Legacys I desire to be made to Alexander Purves, Esqr., in Edinburgh; or to John Clark, Goldsmith there; in Case of their death, to Mr. Thomas Smith, Merchant there, as soon as my Executors Can, not Exceeding two years at Farthest.

I Give & Bequeath to John Rutherfurd, Esqr., of this Province, the Sum of One thousand pounds Sterling money, by him to be disposed of as he pleases, the same to be Remitted to his order in London, as soon as the Circumstances of my affairs will permitt, not exceeding three years, to him & his heirs.

My Will & Desire is also, that my Executors may within two years after my decease, if Circumstances will permitt, purchase four young Negro Men & as many young Negro women that are likely, which I desire them, my Executors, to make a present of to James Moore, Esqr., for his use during his own life; in case of his death before his wife the said Negroes are to decend to her, and their Increase to be willed & Disposed of as she pleases.

I Also give & bequeath to Thomas Cunningham, Junior, who has Lived with me with great fidelity, the sum of four hundred Pounds, Proclamation money, to assist him to follow Trade, if he pleases, which if he does, I desire That my Executors may procure for him in England, Credit to ammount of five hundred pounds, Sterling, for the payment of which they are to be his Security. To Ammount of the Four hundred pounds, Proclamation money, my Executors are to Remitt for him, it being the sum I give him & his heirs, the rest he to make payment of himself.

I Give & Bequeath towards the finishing, if finished, towards Adorning Wilmington Church, the sum of four hundred pounds, Proclamation money, to pay which the Executors of my Will are desired to make over to the Judge of the Superior court for the time Being, the ammount of that sum in some Sufficient Bond or note due to me at the time of my death, to be Recovered for this purpose.

I Give & Bequeath, Frances Rutherfurd, daughter of John Rutherfurd, Esquire, the Same Legacy as I have given to Colonell James Moore, above mentioned, in Case she returns to this Province & Marys here; But in Case of her Living in Europe & Marying there then I Leave to her four hundred Pounds, Sterling, to be paid to her when she Marys or is of Age, to her & her heirs forever.

I Give & beqneath to the Daughter of John Walker, a Carpenter in Wilmiugton, by his wife, Isobell Walker, being his Last Marriage, (this girl Lives or did Live at Richard Lyons at Cross Creek) if allive at my death, three Negro Girls to be purchased in Like manner as the Others I Leave above mentioned, which Legacy is to be in Trust for this Girl till she Comes of Age or is married, with the Wife of Thos. Cunningham, in Wilmington, if dead, young Thomas Cunningham to take care of them for her use forever.

My desire also is, that the following Sums may be paid Soon after my Decease as a token of my friendship & Esteem for the following persons, either to purchase mourning Rings &c in Remembrance of me, at their option, or disposed of as they think proper, Cornelius Harnett, Twenty Pounds, Sterling, His wife the same Sum; Mary Grainger, widor of Caleb Grannger the same sum; Mr. Maurice Moore the same sum, His wife the same sum; Captain John Forster the same Sum, His wife the same sum; & to Alexander Chapman the same sum; All which is to be understood if these persons are allive at the time of my death and are in North Carolina.

Having an opinion of the good qualitys of Arthur Benning, of Wilmington, and Considering him as unfortunate in this part, I will & Bequeath that my Executors make over to him for his Sole use if allive, the Sum of Five hundred Pounds, Proclamation Money, out of such debts in this Province as may be due to me at the time of my death, to him & his heirs or Assigns.

I Will and bequeath to Robert Schaw, my now Partner, after my debts and the afforesaid Legacies are paid, one half of all the Outstanding Debts that may be my part in this Province or in America at the time of my Death, as also one quarter part of all the Ready Effects, or Negroes that are now my part in Company with him & Mr Ancrum to him and his heirs forever.

And Lastly, I give & Bequeath to John Ancrum, my now Partner, all the rest of my Real or Personal Estate not before given, to him & his heirs forever, Who with Robert Schaw, I Constitute & Appoint my Executors of this my will, to see it Executed as it means without any form of law, which they know I never Choose to have any thing to say to, on which Account I make this will more for their Government in the distribution of my Effects, than to have it conformable to law, & I desire that they may Construct it as such knowing this to be my hand writing without even a Witness as the Law in all Wills directs, therefore desire that they may agree in all things Like Brothers, Live together in Harmony to perform their friend's Will & Remember him only as he has deserved.

Given under my hand as my Last Will and Testament at Wilmington, the 11th. May, 1767.

ALEXR DUNCAN.

P: S: Mrs. Elizabeth Hall may be in Ordinary Circumstances, in Case of her being so, my Will is that during her Continuance as such, that my Executors pay her yearly the sum of Thirty Pounds, Proclamation money, for her assistance.

NORTH CAROLINA.

The Within last Will and Testament of Alexander Duncan, deceased, was proved before me this 18 Day of May, in the Year of our Lord, 1768, by Thomas Cobham and William Lord, who swore that they were well acquainted with the Handwriting of the said Alexander Duncan, the Testator, and that they verily believe the said deceases Name, as well as the whole Body of the Will, is of his, the said Testators own proper Handwriting. The said Thomas Cobham and William Lord further declare, that they were both before and since the Date of the said Will, well acquainted with the said Alexander Duncan in his Life Time, and were often in his Company, & that they believe at the Time of the date the Said Will He was of sound and disposing mind & Memory.

John Ancrum and Robert Schaw the Executors therein named took the Oaths appointed for their Qualification.

Ordered That Letters Testamentary issue thereon accordingly.

WM. TRYON.

(Endorsement)
Alexr. Duncan's Will. Recorded.

This is the Will of Alexander Duncan of Wilmington, merchant at the time of Leaving North Carolina, going for England, which is not to be Opened till Accounts are Certain of his Decease.

Copied from Original Will filed in the Office of the Secretary of State.

GEORGE DURANT'S WILL.

IN THE NAME OF GOD AMEN, the ninth day of october, 1688. I, George Durant, of the Countie of Albemarle, in the Province of Carolina, Marriner, being in perfect health and memory, thanks bee to Allmighty God for the same, and calling to mind the uncertain state of this transitory life and that all flesh must yeld unto Death when it shall please to call and being desirous to Settle things in order, Doe make this my las will and Testament in Manner and forme following. Revoking and Absolutly Un willing by these presents, all and every testament and testaments, will and wills, heretofore by me made and declared, either by word or by wrighting, notwithstanding any promise to the contrary or clause derogatory in the same, and this to bee taken only for my last will and testament and non other.

First, I bequeath my soule to God my maker and to Jesus Christ my Redeemer and to the Holy Ghost my sanctifier; and my bodie to the Earth from which it came, to bee buried in such decent and Christian manner as to my Executor shall bee fitt and convenient, there to rest untill my body and Soul shall meete again at the Joyfull Resurection; and for my worldly estate I give and bequeath as followeth:

1st. I bequeath to my son John Durant my plantation wheron I now live with the eaquall part of on half of the tract of land belonging thereto to him and his Heiyrs male, lawfully begotten of his own bodie for ever, and the other half of the said tract of land I give to my son Thomas Durant, and to his Heiyres male, of his bodie lawfully begotten, forever, and in case of failing of Heiyrs as Aforesaid, that then the of * * either of them is * * (Illegible). My will is that my Nephew George Durant, the son of my brother John Durant, of London, Shall enjoy the whole tract of land, to him and his Heiyrs male, of his own body begotten, for ever and for want of such Heyers as aforesaid, that then the said plantation and land to fall to Henry Durant, the son of my Brother John Durant aforesaid, and for want of Heyre male as aforesaid in him, then my other Nephew John Durant, the sone of my Brother John Durant aforesaid, and his Heyres male as aforesaid, to have hold and enjoy for ever. and for want of Heyers in him I doe give and bequeath my said plantation and tract of land thereto belonging * * * (Illegible). Rights and priveledge for ever.

2ly. I doe give and grant to my loving wife, An Durant, my Said plantation, with all benefitts and profitts during hir naturall life, without controule or any molestation whatsoever, and that all the remainder of my estate be equally divided between my loving wife, An Durant, and my Daughters Sarah, Matytya, Pertyenia and Ann Durant, and likewise I doe here make my loving wife, An Durant, to bee my whole and Sole Executrix to see this my last will performed, leaving her the trust of my Children untill they shall come to age or maried.

In Witness whereof I have hereunto sett my hand and seale the day and year first above written.

GEO. DURANT (Seal)

Signed sealed and delivered in presence of
   JOHN PHILPOTT.
    The marke of
   FRANCIS X HOSSTEN.
    The Marke of
   JOHN C CULLY

Proved in Court by the oath of Mr John Philpott and Mr Francis Hossten, ye 6th day of Feby 1693-4
    Attested EDWARD MAYO Cler

Recorded ye 26th day of Feby, Anno Do: 1693–4,
    EDWARD MAYO Cler.

Copied from Original Will filed in the Office of the Secretary of State.

GEORGE DURANT'S WILL.

IN THE NAME OF GOD AMEN, ye Twenty Fifth Day of May, 1730. I, George Durant, of ye County of Albemarle, in the Province of North Carolina, being very Sick and weak in Body, but of perfect mind and Memory, thanks be to Almighty God for the same, Therefore calling to mind the Mortallity of my Body, and knowing that it is appointed for all men Once to Dye, doe Make and Ordain this my Last will and Testament, That Is to Say:

Principally, and first of all, I give and Recommend my Soul Into the Hands of God that gave It; and my Body I Recommend to the Earth to be Buried In decent and christian manner at the Discretion of my Executors, nothing doubting but at the Generall Resurrection, I shall receive the same again by the Almighty Power of God; and as touching Such worldly Estate Wherewith it hath pleased God to bless me in this life, I Give, Demise and Dispose of the same in the Following manner and Form:

Imprimis: I order one moyety or Tract of Land Containing Five Hundred Acres, It being and Lying on the South Shore, to be Sold by my Executors, and the one half of the Money to Paid to Anthony Hatch's Estate.

Item. I give and Bequeath to my well Beloved Son, George Durant, one Bible, one Silver beeker with G. D. A. upon It. And Further, I Desire my Executors to Build one Barn on the Plantation I now Live on and the Charge to be Paid out of my whole Estate. And Likewise, I Order one Brick Chimney to be Built to my Daughter, Mary Durant House.

Item. I Give to Anne Longlarther, Five Pounds, Currant

Money. And also, my Will is that my Son, George Durant, should have as good Learing as can be had In this Government.

And after my Lawfull Debts being Paid, Then my whole Estate to be Equally Devided Between my Five Children, Anne Durant, Mary Durant, Sarah Durant, Elizabeth Durant and George Durant, and that each Child to be paid as they Come of Age; and In Case of Death Before They Injoys their Estate, That then their part to be Equally Divided between the Survivors.

And Likewise, I Doe hereby make my Loving Brothers, Zebulun Clayton and Richard Whidbee, to be my whole and Sole Executors to see this my last will performed. Leaving them the care and tuition of my Children Untill they Shall come to age or marryed.

In witness whereof, I have hereunto Sett my hand and Seal, the Day and year first above written.

GEO. DURANT (Seal)

Signed, Sealed and Delivered
In presence of:
   THOMAS J^{his mark} SNOWDEN.
   ELIZABETH GIBSON.
   JOHN STEVENS.

Sept. 29, 1730.
Proved this will by the Oath of Mr. John Stephens.
RICHD. EVERARD.

Copied from the Original Will, filed in the Office of the Secretary of State.

RICHARD EAGLES' WILL.

IN THE NAME OF GOD AMEN. I, Richard Eagles, of the County of Brunswick and Province of North Carolina, Gentleman, being weak in body but of sound mind & memory, and Considering the uncertainty of this Life, do make this my Last Will and Testament in manner and form following, that is to say.

Imprimis: It is my will and desire that all my just Debts be paid out of the Profits of my Estate, by my Executors hereafter named.

I Give and Bequeath to my son, Joseph Eagles, son of Margaret Henrietta Eagles, my wife, formerly Call'd Marg't Henrietta Bugnion, his heirs and Assigns forever, the House, Plantation, Saw & Grist mills, where I now Live, together with all the lands I am now possessed of, Except such as is hereafter given to my Daughter, Susannah Eagles, or otherwise; Also

I give to my Son Joseph, son to my wife Marg't Henrietta Eagles, formerly Called Marg't Henrietta Bugnion, fifteen Negroes, Big and little, as their families shall be; also, his Choice of four Lotts of Land in the Town of Wilmington, together with two thirds of all the stock I am Possessed of, Cattle, Horses, mares, hogs, sheep, &c.

Item. I Give and Bequeath to my Daughter, Susannah Elizabeth Eagles, Daughter to my late wife, Marg't Henrietta Eagles, formerly Called Marg't Henrietta Bugnion, Six hundred and forty Acres of Land Adjoin'g the Bank'd piece now Intend for a rice field & Bought of Hugh Blenning. Also, one third part of all the Land I now owne on the Island Commonly Call'd Eagles's Island, together with one half the number of Lotts in Wilmington, that I am possessed of Except such as are already given to my Son, Joseph; Also, one third part of all the stock I am possessed of Viz: Cattle, Horses, Mares, Hogs, Sheep, &c.

Item. I Give and Bequeath to my Two Cousins, Jean & Elizabeth Davis, one young Negro each, about their owne Age, to them & their Heirs for ever.

Item. I give and Bequeath to my Sister, Elizabeth Davis, the House she now lives on the no. side of the mill Pond, with the field that is fenced in, as long as she Lives, after her Death, to return to my son, Joseph Eagles.

Item. I Give and Bequeath to Jeanet McFarling, for and in Consideration of her faithfull and Diligent Care & Attendance in Mrs. Eagles's life time as well as since; two Negroes, Vizt: a wench Called Caelia, and a Boy Call'd Peter, to her & her heirs forever; And it is my Desire that she, the sd. Jeanet McFarling, be and remaine in the house I now live, to have the Care of the Stock, Poultry, &c., and that my Execut'rs pay her the sum of Thirty five pounds, procl., Yearly until she is married or my son, Joseph, Come to the Years of Eighteen; Afterward as long as he shall think proper & no longer.

Item. I Give and Bequeath to John Eagleson, my Negro boy Jack, also, I do hereby Assign over to him the Mortgage of Price's Land, Commonly Call'd Judy's Branch, & four Mares & Colts.

It is my Desire that my two Molatto Boys, Natt & George, both have their freedom, when they arrive to the Age of thirty five Years. And Also that my Negro fellow, old Larry have his freedom, as soon as my son, Joseph, Comes of age, 'till which time to be and remaine on the plantation as usual, without being turn'd into the feild or other hard Duty.

Item. It is my will & Desire that all my Negroes, Except those already Bequeathed away, together with all my household Furniture, Plate, Beds, Bedding &cs., be Equally Divided between my Son, Joseph & Susanna Elizabeth Eagles, Son & Daughter of my late wife Marg't Henrietta Eagles, formerly Marg't Henrietta Bugnion, and that the remaining half of the Lotts of Land in Wilmington be the property of my Son, Joseph.

Lastly, I do hereby Nominate & Appoint, John Gibbs, Robt' Shaw, John Ancrum, & Thos. owen, Executors of this my last will & testament, revoking all other former wills by me made, ratifying & Confirming this, & no other.

In witness whereof, I have hereunto set my hand & seal, this Twenty third day of March, in the year of our Lord, one thousand, seven hundred & Sixty Nine.

RICH'D. EAGLES ( )

Sign'd, Seal'd & Publish'd & Declared to be the last will and Testament of Rich'd Eagles, In Presence of:
(The Date alter'd before Sign'd.)
  JOHN, WALKER.
  JNO. FERGUS.
  MARY WALKER.

Codicil of the Last will & Testament of Rich'd Eagles.

'Tis my will and Desire that Mr. Wm. Dry, has a Title for a Certaine piece of Land Bo't of my Father, Rich'd Eagles & never yet Confirm'd lying and being on the Island near the sd. Wm. Dry's Brick house, he making my Heirs a Title for one Square acre out of the same, on the Side next Wilmington.

RICH'D EAGLES.

Sign'd Seal'd, Publish'd & Declar'd in the Presence of us, this 23d March 1769.
  MARY WALKER,
  JOHN WALKER.
  JNO. FERGUS.

The within last Will and Testament of Richard Eagles, with the Codicil Annexed was proved before me this thirty first day of March, 1769, by the Oaths of John Walker and John Fergus, two of the subscribing Witnesses thereto, who swore they say the Testator sign, seal, publish and declare the same to be and contain His last Will and Testament; and that at the Time thereof, He was of sound and disposing Mind & Memory.

John Gibbs and Robert Shaw two of the Executors therein named took the Oaths appointed for their Qualification.

Ordered that Letters Testamentary issue thereon accordingly.

WM. TRYON.

Copied from Original Will, filed in the Office of the Secretary of State.

WILLIAM EATON'S WILL.

IN THE NAME OF GOD AMEN, February 19th, 1759. I, William Eaton, of Saint John's Parish, in Granville County, do make & Ordain this my last Will and Testament, in Manner and form following: to wit, First I bequeath my Soul to God that gave it, trusting in Merits and Advocacy of my ever blessed Lord and Saviour, Jesus Christ, for a Remission of all my Offences, and my Body I commit to this Earth to be decently intered at the Discretion of my Executors herein after named. And as for such Worldly Estate as it have been pleased almighty God to commit to my Stewardship, I give, dispose and bequeath the same in Manner following: That is to say:

Imprimis: I give and devise unto my beloved Son, William Eaton, and to his Heirs and Assigns for ever, all my Lands, Tenements and Hereditaments in the Counties of Dinwiddie and Brunswick, in the Colony of Virginia, except the Land and Plantation I received of Willian Scoggan as Heir to John Scoggan, and my Lot and House in the Town of Petersburgh.

Item. I give and bequeath unto my Daughter, Jane Edwards, Wife of Colo. Nathaniel Edwards, all the Negro Slave which I possessed her in the Lifetime of Her former Husband, Anthony Haynes. And it is my Will and Desire that they, with all their Increase, shall descend, pass, go and remain according to the disposition made of them respectively by the last Will and Testament of the said Anthony Haynes. Also I give to my said Daughter, Jane, five Shillings, Virginia Currency.

Item. I give and bequeath unto my Daughter, Anne Haynes, Relict of Andrew Haynes, deceased, all the Negro Slaves of which I possessed her in the Lifetime of her said Husband. And it is my Will and desire that the said Slaves respectively, with all their Increase, shall pass, go, descend and remain according to the disposition made of them by the last Will and Testament of the said Andrew Haynes. Also I Give to my said Daughter, fifty Pounds Virginia Currency, of the Debt owing to me by Colo: Richard Kennon.

Item. I Give and bequeath unto my Daughter, Mary Jones, Wife of Robert Jones, jun: three Negroe Slaves, to wit, Aggey, Annaca & Bob, and all their Increase, which said Negroes are now in the Possession of the said Robert Jones. Also I give to my said Daughter one hundred and eighty Pounds, Virginia Currency.

Item. I give and bequeath unto my Daughter, Sarah Johnson, Wife of Charles Johnson, all the Slaves and Personal

Estate whereof I Possessed her in the Lifetime of her former Husband, John Thornton, And it is my Will and desire that the said Slaves with their Increase, and personal Estate, shall go, descend, pass & remain according to the disposition made of them respectively, by the last Will and Testament of the said John Thornton. Also I give to my said Daughter five Shillings, Virginia Currency.

Item. I give and bequeath my ten Negroe Slaves, namely, Beck, Nell, Lucy, Oustom Son of Lucy, Jenny & Jenny, Daughter of Hannah, Haster, Rachel, Aggy & Essie, now in the possession of my Son in Law, Daniel Weldon, being formerly lent him, unto my Son in Law, Robert Jones, Junr. and my Son, Thomas Eaton, and their Heirs and Assignes in Special Trust and Confidence nevertheless and to and for the Uses, Intents and purposes following; and to or for no other Use, Intent or purpose whatsoever, that is to say to permit and suffer my Daughter Elizabeth Weldon for and during the Term of her natural Life to take, receive and dispose of at her Will and Pleasure exclusive of any power, authority, Interest or controul of her said Husband, and to and for her Sole separate Use, all and singular the profits arising from the Labour of the said Slaves and their Increase; so that it shall not be in the Power of her s^d Husband to release, Charge, Change, alter or Incumber the same or any part thereof. And from & immediately after the decease of my said Daughter, I give and bequeath the said Slaves and their Increase, unto such Children as She shall have living at her Death, equally among them to be divided. But in Case any Child or Children of my said Daughter Betty shall depart this Life in her Lifetime leaving Children which shall survive her, then such Children shall be admitted to Share in the s^d Slaves, with the Children of my said Daughter which shall be living at her Death vizt: to receive the same proportion of them as the Parent or Parents of such Grand-Children would be intitled to had they been living. And in Case all the Children of my said Daughter Betty shall depart this Life before her Death, then I bequeath the said Slaves and all their Increase, unto such Grand-Child or Grand-Children of my said Daughter as shall be living at her decease. And if it shall so happen that my said Daughter Betty shall have no Children, or Grand-Child. living at the Time of her decease, then I give and bequeath the said Slaves and their Increase to be divided into five equall parts among my Daughters and Grand Children and their Assignes for ever, to wit: One fifth part to the Children of Anthony Haynes, deceased, equally among them to be divided, one fifth part to my Daughter, Anne Haynes, one fifth part to my Daughter, Mary Jones, one fifth part to my Daughter, Sarah Johnson, and one fifth part to my Daughter, Martha. Also I give to my said Daughter, Betty, five Shillings, Virginia Currency.

Item. I give and devise unto my Son, Thomas Eaton, and to the Heirs of his Body lawfully begotten for ever, the Land and plantation in Granville County, whereon I now live, including my reSurvey adjoining thereto; And for default of such Heirs, I give and devise the same unto my Son, Charles Rust Eaton, and the Heirs of his Body lawfully begotten for ever; And for default of such Heirs I give and devise the same unto my Son, William Eaton, and the Heirs of his Body Lawfully begotten for ever; And in default of such Heirs I give and devise the same to my next Heir at Law. Also I give and devise to my said Son, Thomas Eaton, and his Heirs and assignes for ever, my Plantation and Tract of Land in Granville County, commonly called Bowser's; Also my Two Tracts of Land whereon Lewis Ballard & Cormelial Earls live, being adjacent to the s^d Tract of Land called Bowser's; Also my Tract of Land in Northampton, commonly called Cumboe's; All which said four last mentioned Tracts of Land I give and devise unto my said Son, Thomas, his Heirs and Assignes for ever, upon Condition that he pay & Satisfy to my Grand-Son Eaton Haynes, twenty Pounds, Virginia Currency.

Item. I give and Devise unto my Son, Charles Rust Eaton, and to his Heirs and Assigns for Ever, all my Lands, Tenements and Hereditaments Situate in the County of Halifax, except my Lots in the Town of Halifax.

Item. I give and devise unto my loving Wife, Mary Eaton, for and during the Term of her natural Life, my Tract of Land whereon Granville Court-house is built, with all and Singular my other Tracts of Land and Surveys of Land on Tabb's Creek and the branches thereof; and from and immediately after the decease of my said Wife, I give and devise the said Tracts of Land and the remainder and Remainders, Reversion and Reversions of each of them, unto my Son, Charles Rust Eaton, his Heirs and Assigns for ever.

Item. I give and devise unto my two Sons, Thomas, and Charles, and their Heirs for ever equally to be divided, my Lot of Land in the Town of Petersburg, to wit, my Son Thomas's part to include the Houses built thereon.

Item. I give and devise unto my Son, Thomas Eaton, & his Heirs for ever, my Tract of Land in Granville County, commonly called Gould's.

Item. I give and devise unto my Executors, herein after mention'd, my Tract of Land on little fishing Creek, commonly Called Youngs; my Tract of Land on Anderson's Swamp; and my two Tracts of Land on Smith's Creek, the one Called Hughe's and the other Rayborn's, to be by them Sold for the best price that can be got, and the money arising from the Sale thereof be applied towards discharging the Legacies by this my Will bequeathed.

Item. I give and devise unto my Son, Thomas Eaton, & to his Heirs for ever, my Lot in Halifax Town, adjoining the Market place and main Street, and desire that it may be saved at the Expence of my Estate.

Item. I give and devise all my other Lots in Halifax Town, unto my Son, Charles Rust Eaton, and his Heirs for ever, and do desire that such of the said Lots as are not already built on, shall be saved at the expence of my Estate.

Item. I give and bequeath unto my Daughter, Martha Eaton, my three Negroes namely, Pud, Sarah & Suckey & three hundred pounds, Virginia Currency; Also such Horses and Mares as are commonly called hers.

Item. It is my will and desire that my negroe Girl, Nanny, Daughter of Dido, now in the possession of Daniel Weldon, be returned unto my my Estate, And all and singular the residue of my Estate of what Nature or Quality soever, I give and bequeath in Manner following: to wit, one third part thereof to my beloved Wife, Mary, one third part to my Son, Thomas Eaton, and the other third part to my Son, Charles Rust Eaton. And that my s^d Wife shall and may possess and enjoy her said proportion therein, for and during the Term of her natural Life & take and receive the profits arising therefrom to her own Use, and from and immediately after her decease, I give and bequeath the same to be equally divided into nine equal parts, to wit, one ninth part thereof to my Son, William, and his Assignes, one Ninth part to the Children of Anthony Haynes, deceasd, equally among them to be divided, one ninth part to my Daughter, Anne Haynes, and her Assignes, one ninth part to my Daughter, Mary Jones, and her Assignes, one ninth part to my Daughter, Sarah Thorton, one ninth part to the Children of my Daughter, Betty, which she shall have living at her death, equally among them to be divided, one ninth part to my Son, Thomas Eaton, and one ninth part to my Son, Charles Rust Eaton, and one ninth part to my Daughter, Martha Eaton.

Item. If either of my Sons, Thomas and Charles Rust, shall depart this Life before they shall attain the Age of twenty one Years, or are married, its my Will and desire that the Survivor shall have and enjoy the proportion of the residuum aforementioned of such of my s^d Sons as shall so happen to die. And if both my s^d Sons shall happen to die under the Age of twenty Years, and before marriage, then I give and bequeath their s^d two Shares in the s^d Residuum as follows: to wit, one seventh part to my Son, William Eaton & his Assignes, one seventh part to the Children of Anthony Haynes, deceased, equally among them to be divided among them, one seventh part to my Daughter, Anne Haynes, one seventh part to my Daughter, Mary Jones, and her Assignes, one seventh part to my Daughter, Sarah Thornton, one seventh part to the Children of my Daughter Betty Weldon, equally among them to be divided, and one seventh part to my Daughter, Martha Eaton, and her Assignes.

Item. It is my Will and desire that my Negroes belonging to my Plantation on Tabb's Creek be alloted in part my Wifes proportion of the residuum of my Estate afores^d, And that my Negroes at Mush Island be alloted in the proportion of my Son, Charles Rust Eaton. And that each of my said Sons, be put in Actual possession of their Estates at the Age of eighteen.

Item. In Case either of my said Sons, Thomas or Charles Rust, shall depart this Life under the Age of twenty one Years and before Marriage, its my Will and desire that the Survivor of them, his Heirs and Assigns for ever, shall have, possess and enjoy the respective Lands and Tenements by this my Will devised to such of my s^d Sons, as shall so happen to die, in Fee Simple. And if both my said Sons shall die before marriage and under the Age of twenty one Years, then I give and bequeath the said Lands & Hereditaments by this my last Will & Testament devised to them in Fee Simple, unto my Son, William Eaton, his Heirs and Assigns for ever.

Item. It is my Will and desire that my Daughter, Martha, be allowed a Suitable Maintainance out of the Profits of my Estate until she Attains the Age of twenty one Years, or is married, And that the profits arising from the Estate herein bequeathed to my Sons, Thomas, and Charles Rust, untill my Son Thomas shall Attain the Age of Eighteen Years, be applied in educating and maintaining my said Sons and discharging the pecuniary Legacies by this my Will bequeathed.

Item. I do hereby Constitute, nominate, and appoint my beloved Wife, Mary Eaton, and my Son in Law, Robert Jones, junior, to be ye Executors of this my last Will and Testament, hereby revoking, disannulling and making void, all other Wills and Testaments heretofore by me made;

In Witness whereof have hereunto set my hand and affixed my Seal the Day & Year first above written.

WILLIAM EATON (Seal)

The foregoing Contents contained in pages one to eight inclusive was published, declared and pronounced by William Eaton, Gent. to be his last Will & Testament in presence of,
    WM. PERSON
    JAS. PAINE
    RICHD. COLEMAN

At a Court held for Granville County, 20. March 1759.

This Will was proven by the Oath of William Person & James Paine, two of the Subscribing Witnesss thereto, to be the Act & deed of William Eaton, Gent. late deceas'd., then Mary Eaton & Robert Jun: the Executors in this Will named, Qualified as such according to law.

Teste. DANL. WELDON C. C.

Copied from Original Will, filed in Office of the Secretary of State.

CHARLES EDEN'S WILL.

IN THE NAME OF GOD, AMEN. This twenty Sixth day of December, in the Year of our Lord one thousand seven hundred and twenty one, I, Charles Eden, Esqr. Governor of the Province of North Carolina, being in a very weak & languishing Condition, but thro' the Mercy of God in a sound, perfect, & Disposing Mind & Memory, do make & Ordaine this, my last Will and Testament, hereby revoking all other & former Wills & Testaments heretofore by me made, & Confirming this to be my last Will.

Item. It is my Will and Desire, and I hereby order the same, that all my Just Debts in Great Britain be very speedily & punctually paid, after my Decease, according to a list of ye Same left in my Execut'rs Possession.

Item. I give to my Dear Niece, Mrs. Margaret Pough, Youngest Daughter of Robert Pough Esqr. Decsd. Five hundred pounds Sterling Money, of Great Britain, to be paid here at London, which is to be raised out of my Estate, as soon as possible after my Debts are paid and Satisfied.

Item. I give & bequeath unto my very Dear Friend, John Holloway, Esqr., of the Province of Virginia, my Negro Boy nam'd David, and my Gold Watch, to be delivered soon after my Decease.

Item. I give & bequeath to Daniell Richardsaon Esqr., his Choice of my Swords & Belts, the Mourning Ring left by Col. Hecklefeild, my horse called Taffy, my second best furniture, with my Boots & Silver Spurrs.

Item. It is my Will, that presently after my Decease, my Exr. remitt out of the Money in the House, to Authur Trevor, Esqr., as much as will pay the interest of one hundred pounds at 6 pr. Cent. p. Ann. for eight Years, the Principal being already paid.

Item. I give & bequeath unto Mr. James Henderson, Twenty pounds, Currant Money, and one hundred Acres of Land lying on Deerham's Creek, in Pamplicough, formerly belonging to John Lilington, to him & his Heirs for ever w'ch sd Land is bounded upon Sparrows Plantion.

Item. I give, devise & bequeath unto John Lovick, Esqr.,

Secretary of this Province, & to his Heirs & Assignes, all my Estate, both Reale & Personall, to raise Money to pay off my sd. Debts & Legacies, whom I also Nominate, Constitute & Appoint Exor. of this my Will.

In Witness whereof I have hereunto Sett my Hand & Seal the day & Year before Written.

CHARLES EDEN (seal)

Signed, Seal'd, Publish'd & Declared to be his last Will & Testam't in Presence of:
 MARY BADHAM.
 H. CLAYTON.
 W. BADHAM.

Proved in open Court by the Oaths of Henry Clayton & W. Badham, the Evidences thereto. April the 2d 1722.
 Test. W. BADHAM C. Cur Genl.

Mem'dum, this 9th day of February, 1721.

It's my Will & Desire that the Legacy of Twenty Pounds and one hundred Acres of Land, given & bequeathed to James Henderson, that the Same be not paid, he having had from me already what I think Sufficient, and this I desire may be as firm as any other part of my Will.
 Witness my hand.   CHARLES EDEN.
Witnesses:
 GEOR. ALLEN.
 KATHER LINCH.

Proved in Open Court by the Oaths of George Allen one of the Evidences hereto. April the 2d 1722.
 Test. W. BADHAM, C. Cur Genl.

Letts Granted April the 3rd 1722.

Recorded in Will Book 2, page 299, Office of the Secretary of State.

HENRY EBORN'S WILL.

IN THE NAME OF GOD AMEN, The twentieth Day of October, Anno Domini, 1732. I, Henry Eborn, of Matchapungo, in the County of hide, and in the Province of North Carolina, being very sick and weak In body, but of Perfect mind and memory, thanks be given unto God, Therefore calling unto mind the mortality of my body, and knowing That it is appointed for all men once to dye, I Do make and ordain This my last will and Testament, That is to say, the Principally and first of all, I Give and Recomend my Soul Into the hands of God that Gave it; and my body I Recomend to the earth to be buried In a decent, Christian Burial at the Discretion of my Executors, Nothing Doubting but but at the General Resurection I shall Receive the Same again by ye mighty power of God;

and as touching Such worldly Estate where with It hath pleased God to bless me In this Life, I Give and Demise and Dispose of the Same In the following manner and form:

Imprimis. I Give and bequeath unto Nathaniel Eborn, the son of Henry Elizabeth Eborn, a trak of Land butted and bounded by George Mixon on one side, and William Cambal on the other side, Joyned on the Creek of Matchapungo; and two three years old steers, two killable hogs, and a Greate Coate and herling heifer to the said Nathaniel Eborn, son James Eborn.

Item. To Henry Eborn, my Dear Son, I Give and bequeath him my plantation, the Said Henry Eborn, The son of Henry and Elizabeth Eborn is to let the said Elizabeth Eborn, his Mother have the said plantation till the said Henry Eborn comes to age, and then the said Elizabeth is to Delivered up the said plantation to the said Henry Eborn, her Dear Son, and the said Elizabeth Eborn, the mother of the said Henry Eborn, is to hold half of the said plantation for her Widowed, the horse, Mill & all things In General as belongs to the said plantation, all Chattle That are his In Generall, and two young Cows acalfs, and one old Gun, and the said Henry Eborn my Dear Son a negro man man Jack.

Item. I Give and bequeath to my Dear Son, Littletun Eborn, a plantation with Chattel situated one the west Side of Broad Creek, with all the Sheep, two heifers of his marke, and a Plantation Pantego, on the East side, and if the said Henry Eborn, the son of Henry and Elizabeth Eborn, Dyes without heir lawfully begotten of his body, It falls to Littletun Eborn, the Brother of the Said Henry Eborn Plantation, and if the said Littletun Eborn enjoyed the saide Plantation of Henry Eborn, he is to Give Salathyel Layson, Son of Evens Rhoda Layson, The said Plantation of Broad Creek; and the other Plantation laying on Pantego to James Eborn the son of Nathaniel and Anne Eborn.

Item. I Give to my Dear Son, Littiltun Eborn, a black wonut table and Lignumvite Punch bowle, and a large bible, a Great brass kittell, and the new Gun & a Negro Man, named Jupiter, and a Bed and a bolster; And if the Said Elizabeth Eborn Marries, the Said Henry Eborn and Littiltun Eborn, her sons, are to have all ye plantation and Stock and household Good, to be Delivered at 18 years of Age.

Item. I Give to Henry Eborn, My Dear Son, three ewes to be Delivered next Spring.

Item. I Give to my Dear wife, the work of the Negro Man named Jack as long as she Continues a wedower.

Item. I Give to my Dear Daughter, Rhoda Layson, a Bed, Two Sheets, two Blankets, a Rog and bolster, and a small Chest, a puder Dish, two basons, a horse named byard, to have at her

Mother Marriage or other husband Comeing again, two plates and three ewes, all her chattel that was called hers, two heifers, three years old and a four years old one, and a Large Cheare.

Item. I Give to my Dear Daughter, Mary Eborn, a bed, a bolster, two sheets, and two Blankets, and a Rug, and all the Chattel as was hers, two Plates, two Basons and a Dish, and a Iron pot & three ewes, a large chare and a Linnen wheel.

Item. I Give to my Daughter, Rhoda Layson, a Iron pot.

Item. I give to my Dear Daughter, Elizabeth Eborn, a bed, a bolster, a pair of Sheets, a pair of Blankets and a Rugg, a Iron pot, a Small Chest, a Chear, two basons and a Dish, and two plates, three ewes, all her chattel that are hers, a young Cow, a Calf, and a horse called fox, to be Delivered at the day of her marriage.

Item. I Give to my Dear Daughter, Anne Jones, one shilling.

Item. I Give to my dear Daughter Rebecker Deedan, one Shilling.

Item. I Desire that William Barrow and Nathaniel Eborn and Thomas Smith, May see that they may be over Seer for me the said Henry Eborn.

Item. I Give to my Dear wife, Elizabeth Eborn, all the Chattle that is not the Childrens, and all the Remainder of the sheep, two working horses named Jack and Dobing, a plow and harness, a cart wheels, and a new pair of wheels, and all the Remainder of the houshold Goods.

Item. I Give unto my wellbeloved wife, and Henry Eborn, my Dear Son, whome I likewise make and ordain my Sole Executors of this my will and testament by her and himself freely to be possessed and enjoyed. and I Do hereby Utterly Disallowe, Revoke and Disannul all and every other former Testament, Wills, legacies and bequests and executors by me, In any way was before named, willed and bequeathed, Ratifying and Confirming this now to be my last will and (and) Testament.

In witness whereof, I have hereunto Set my hand and Seal the Day and Year above writing. HENRY O EBORN (Seal)
his
marke.

Signed, and Sealed, publick, pronounced and Declared by the said Henry Eborn, as his last will and testament, In the Presents of us the Subscribers:

GEORGE N MIXON.
his

ELIZABETH WILLIAMSON.
mark

CHARLES JOHNSON.

BEAUFORT, SC. March Court, 1732.
The within Will was Proved in Open Court by the Oath of George Mixon.
Test. JNO. COLLISON, Cler: Cur.

Copied from the Original Will, filed in the Office of the Secretary of State.

NATHANIEL EBORN'S WILL.

IN THE NAME OF GOD AMAN. I, Nathaniel Eborn, of Hide County, and Province of North Carolina, being very Sick and weak in body but of a Sound and perfect memory of mind, Thanks be to God for ye same, Calling to Mind the mortality of my body, knowing That it as appointed for all men once to Die, Do make and ordain This my last will and Testament, That is to say, and first of all I Recommend my Soul into the hands of God that Gave it; and my body to be DeSently buried at the Descretion of my Executors hereafter mentioned, nothing Doubting but at the General Resurrection at the last Day, I shall Receive the Same, Through the Merits of Jesus Christ; and as to what Worldly Estate it hath pleased God to Endue me with, I Dispose of in manner and form following:

Imprimis. I Desire that all my Debts and funeral Charges be fully Contented and paid.

Item. I Give and bequeath to my well beloved Wife, Rebecca, the Lent of my Negro Woman Jane, During her widowhood.

Item. I Give and bequeath unto my well beloved Son, James Eborn, my Plantation and Land whereon I live, to him and his Heirs for ever; and also one negro Man named Jefery, upon Condition that he Doth with his brothers, and his and their Negroes, work Clear my Estate of Debt, and also Raise up two young negroes named Quako and Hagur.

Item. I Give and bequeath to my well beloved Son, Littleton Eborn, my plantation on the South Side of Matchapungo Creek with Two Hundred and Forty four Acres of Land, being the lower half of the sd. Land, and half the Cattle of the Stock on the South Side of ye Creek, and one young horse which I bought of John Paretree, and one negro boy named Elijah, to him and his heirs forever.

Item. I Give to my well beloved Son, William Eborn, one Mesage, plantation or track of Land, lying on the North Side of ye above sd. Creek, between my land and Henry Eborns holden by a bond under the hands of Thomas Barrah, George Barrah and Zacheria Barrah, bearing Date ye 19th. of July, 1753, To him and his heirs for ever; and one negro boy named Quock, to him and his heirs for ever, and one black Mare which I bought of William Winly and her Encrease.

Item. I give unto my well beloved Daughter, Elizabeth Eborn, one negro Girl named Hagur, to her and her heirs Lawfully begoten of her body, and if She Die without Issue, then the Said negro Girl Return to my heirs; and one mare Colt and her encrase.

Item. I Give and bequeath to my well beloved Son, Aaron

Eborn, Two hundred and forty four acres Land on the South Side of Matchapongo Creek, binding upon Thomas Barrah's Line, To him and his Heirs for ever; and one negro boy, Named Ishmeal, to him and his heirs for ever; and One Roan Gray Mare and her encrease.

I Desire that after my well beloved Wife, Rebecca Eborns Discease, or end of Widowhood, Then my Son, Littleton Eborn Shall take into his possession untill my youngest Son arive to the age of twenty one years, my negro woman Jane, and Divide her and her encrease between my four youngest Children, be it to them and their heirs for ever.

Item. I Give and bequeath unto my well beloved Wife, Rebecca Eborn, a third part of all my Goods and Chattels which I have not Given, to her and her Heirs for ever.

Item. I Give and bequeath all the Rest of my Gods and Chattels to be equally Divided between my five Children.

I Desire that my Son, William Eborn, may be kept under the care and Tusion of his brother James Eborn, untill he arive to the age of Eighteen years and then to possess his Estates, not bargaining or Selling without the advice of his said Brother; and I Desire that my Son, Aaron Eborn, may be under the Care of his Brother, Littleton Eborn, untill the Age of eighteen years, then to possess his Estate, not bargaining or Seling without the advice of his brother.

I Do hereby make, Constitute and ordain my two Sons, James Eborn and Littleton Eborn, Executors of this my Last Will and Testament, and I Do hereby Revoke all other Will or Wills, Testament or Testaments, and I do hereby publish, Declare and pronounce this to be my last will and Testament.

Whereunto I have set my hand and fixed my Seal, This first Day of October, 1753.   NATHANIEL EBONE (Seal)

    his
ISREAL I WINDLY.
   mark.
     her
ELIZABETH X WINDLY.
     mark.
JOHN HOUZEN.

HYDE COUNTY, SS. March Court, 1754.

The last will and Testament of Nathall. Eberne, Dece'd, Exhibited into Court, and proved by the Oaths of Isreal Windly and John Houzen, and that they Saw the Testator, Sign, Seal and acknowledge it to be his last Will and Testament, and that the Testator was of sound and Disposing Mind and Memory at that Time. Ordered that Mr. Secretary have notice thereof.

And at the same time James Eberne and Littleton Eberne, was Qualified as Executs. under the said last Will and Testament according to Law in that Case made and provided.

Veria Copia, pr. STEPHN. DENNING, Dep. Clk. Cot.

Copied from the Original Will, filed in the Office of the Secretary of State.

GEORGE EUBANK'S WILL.

NORTH CAROLINA SS. March ye 2d., 1732—3,

IN THE NAME OF GOD AMEN. I, George Eubank, of Bertie precinct, and Society parish, being Sick of bodey but of perfect health, Memorey, and judgment, praise to Almighty God, do make this my Last Will and testament.

Imprimis. I will and bequeath to my brother, James Eubank, and my Sisters, Elizabeth and Isabell Eubanks, all my personall and real Esteat in the Kingdom of Great Britain, to be Joyntly devided among them.

Secondly, after paying my debts and funerall charges, I will and bequeat all the resedue of my esteat, excepting forty pounds, Sterling, to Thomas Whitemell, Juneor, and Twenty to Elizabeth Whitemell, Juneor, and fifteen to Martha Whitemell, and fifteen pounds, Sterling, to William Gray, Juneor; and all the resedue of my esteat as aforesd, except fifteen pounds Sterling, to William Castellaw, I will and bequeath to my Brothers and Sisters as aforesd., and there heirs for ever.

And lastly, appointing James Castellaw, Thomas Whitemell and John Gray, Executors to this my last will and Testament, I do revock all other wills and testaments.

In witness whereof, I have put my hand and Seall to this date and delivered it in the presents of:
GEORGE: EUBANK (Seal)

   his
JAMES X BULOCK.
  mark.
  his
JOHN B BARTON.
  mark.
ELIZ: WHITMELL.

NO CAROLINA, SC.   March 13th, 1732.

John Barton & James Bulock, Two of the Subscribing Evidences to the within written Instrument, personally appeared before me and made Oath on the holy Evangelist, That they Saw George Eubank, Sign, Seal, publish & Declare the within Written as his Last Will and Testament, in their presence & in the presence of Eliza. Whitmell, the Other Subscribing Evidence.

Sworn to before me.   GEO. BURRINGTON.

Copied from Original Will, filed in the Office of the Secretary of State.

BARWELL EVANS' WILL.

IN THE NAME OF GOD AMEN. I, Barwell Evans, being sick of Body, but of perfect mind and Memory, thanks be to Almighty God for it. I Recommend my Soul to God that Gave it; and my Body to the Earth, to be Buried in a Christion

Manner at the Discretion of my Executors; and as touching such worldly Goods as it hath pleased God to Bless me with, I bestow in following manner, to wit:

Item. I give and bequeath to my well beloved Daughter, Sarah Evans, all the Land and plantation whereon I now live, with all ye Appurtenances and Priviliges thereunto belonging, only excepting as follows: My Will is that my well beloved Wife have ye Use of ye Land and Plantation and all priviliges thereunto belonging till my Daughter, Sarah, comes to age or Marries; and then, that ye Land, Plantation be Equilly devided betwixt my said Wife and Daughter Sarah, with all Priviliges deuring my Wifes life, ye Houses only excepted, which my will and pleasure is that my wife have ye use of all the Houses on my sd. Plantation deuring her Life, and after her Desease, I give it Hole and Intire to my said Daughter, Saroh. I likewise give and bequeath to my said Daughter, Saroh evans, forty Acres of land on ye South side of the creek whereon I live, Joining the Above bequeath Land, with all the benefits and privileges thereunto belonging.

Item. I give and bequeath to my well beloved Daughter, Susanah Evans, all that Land and Plantation whereon Thomas Brantly now lives, lying up Evans' Creek, Containing two hundred Acres with all Benefits and privilliges thereunto belonging. I likewise give and bequeath to my well beloved Daughter, Susannah Evans, Three hundred Acres of Land on ye mil Creek, Joining Edward Williams Land, with all the Privilliges and benifits thereunto belonging.

Item. I give and bequeath to my well beloved Wife, Susanah Evans, the use of my Negro Man peter dewring her life.

Item. I give and bequeath my friend, William Stokes, Two hundred Acres of Land Joining ye Little Fork of Edward Williams Branch & running up Edward William's line for ye Compliment, Including ye Plantation whereon he now lives, with all ye Benefits and Privilliges thereunto belonging, to him and his heirs or assings for ever.

Item. I give and bequeath my Negro Man Peter, after my Wifes decease, to my well beloved Daughter, Susanah Evans, to her & her heirs & assigns for ever.

Item. I give and Bequeath to my Well beloved Daughter, Saroh, my negro man Isaac, & my Negro wench hannah, to her or her heirs and Assigns for ever.

Item. I give and Bequeath to my well beloved Daughter, Susanah Evans, my Negro Boy Sezar & my negro Gall cresey and my Negro Man jack, to she, her heirs and Assigns for ever.

Item. I give and bequeath to my well beloved Nefew, Jacob Evans, all my Black Smiths Tools, to him, his heirs and Assigns for ever.

Item. I give and bequeath to my well beloved Nefew, Berwell Evans, Three pounds, Current Money of Vergenia, to be paid by my Executors out of my Estate.

Item. I give and bequeath to my well beloved Nefew, Berwell Evans, Son of Benjamin Evans, Three pound, Current Money of Virginia, to be paid out of my Estate as abovesaid.

Item. My Will and Pleasure is, that all the Residue and remainder of my Estate, Real and Personal, be Equilly Devided betwixt my well beloved Wife, Susanah Evans, my well beloved Daughter, Saroh Evans, & my well beloved Daughter, Susanah Evans.

Item. I Constitute and Appoint my Well beloved Wife, Susannah Evans, my Executrix, Also my Three Brothers, Jacob Evans, Benjamin evans and charles evans, Executors, to this my last Will and Testament.

In witness whereof, I have hereunto set my hand and Seal, this first Day of Aprel, in the Year of our lord god, 1756.

BARWELL EVANS, (Seal)

Signed, Sealed and Delivered in presence of:
> GEO. SUGG.
> PETER HULL.
> RICHARD X HURLEY.
> his
> mark.

BEAUFORT COUNTY. ss.

This certifies that at a court Held at Bath Town, on the second tuesday in June, Ann. Dom., 1756, Present his Majestys Justices: the last Will and Testament of Barwell Evans was Exhibited into court and proved by George Sugg, one of the Subscribing witnesses thereto, who Swore that he saw the said Barwell Evans Execute the sd. Last Will & Testam't, & that he was at the time of Sound & Disposing mind and Memory; & that at the same time he saw Peter Hull and Richard Hurley, the other Subscribing witnesses, set there hands thereto; whereupon Susanah Evans, Jacob Evans, Benja. Evans & Charles Evans, Qualified as Ex'ors to the sd. Will.

Ordered that the Secretary have notice that Letters Testamentary may issue.

Test. WALLEY CHAUNCEY, Cl. Cur.

Copied from Original Will, filed in the Office of the Secretary of State.

RICHARD EVANS' WILL.

IN THE NAME OF GOD AMEN. I, Richard Evans, Gentleman, of Beaufort County, being of a low Estate of Body, But of perfect Sound Mind and Memory, praised be almighty God, and Calling to Ming that its appointed for all men once to Die, Do make and ordain in this my Last Will and Testament, in manner and form following, that is to say, I recommend my

Soul into ye hands of almighty God who gave it, and my body to the Earth, to be Decently buried at the Decretion of my Exeuctors hereafter to be named. And as to the worldly Goods whereof I am possest, I Give and Bequeath in Manner and form Following, that is to say:

1. I give and Bequeath to my Eldest Son, Richard Evans, three negro slaves, to witt: Balam, flora & maria.

2. I Give and Bequeath to my Daughter, Mary Evans, one mollatto Slave, and two negro Slaves, to wit: Nell and nimrod and Rue.

3. I give and Bequeath to my Youngest Son, George Evans, Three negro Slaves, to witt, Robin, and Nan and Jenny.

Item. I will that my negros, Trinkelo, Bossen and Blanford, Judah and Bess, be and remain undivided untill the marriage or Lawful age of Either of my said Children which first shall happen, and then to be Equally Divided among my aforesd. three Children. My Land lying and Being in Onslow county, on ye Mouth of New river, on The North side, I Give and Bequeath to my Daughter, Mary Evans. My Cattle of the Neats kind, I will and Desire that they be and Remain undivided untill the Marraige or Lawful age of Either of my Children which shall first happen, and then to be Equally Divided among my aforesd. Three Children. My horses and mares I give and bequeath To my two Sons, Richard and George, to be Equally Devided Between them. To my Daughter, Mary, I give and bequeath all my China ware and Tea Spoons; ye rest of my household Goods, Plantation tools and Provisions to be and remaine undivided untell the marraige or Lawful age of Either of my Children which shall first happen, and then to be Equally Divided among my aforsd. three Children.

Lastly, I do Nominate and appoint Mr. Michael Cautanche, and my Son, Richard Evans, to be Executors to this my last Will and Testament.

RICHARD EVANS.

Signed, Sealed, Published and Declared in the presence of us, Twenty Sixth Day of December, one thousand, Seven hundred and fifty two. EDMUND PEARCE.
JOSHUA PEARCE.
READING BLOUNT.

BEAUFORT COUNTY, ss.

At a Court held for the sd. County, at Bath Town, on the second tuesday in June, 1753: Present his Majesty's Justices.

This Certifies that Reading Blount, one of the subscribing Evidences to the within Will, appeared in open Court and made Oath, on the holy Evangelists, that the sd. Richd. Evans was of sound & disposing mind & memory at the time he executed the sd. Will; and that he also saw Edmond

Pearce & Joshua Pearce, the other subscribing Witnesses, set their names thereto. At the same time Mich'l Cautanche, appeared in Court & Qualified as Excr. unto the same.

Ordered that the Secretary have notice thereof.

Test. WALLEY CHAUNCY, Cl. Cu.

Copied from Original Will filed in the Office of the Secretary of State.

THOMAS FALCONER'S WILL.

IN THE NAME OF GOD AMEN. I, Thomas Falconer, of Chowan County, this 31st. day of Janry., 1756, being Sick & weak in body, but of perfect mind & Memory, thanks be to God for the same, & calling to Mind the Uncertainty of this Life, & the Certainty of Death, do make & appoint this my last Will and Testament, in Manner and Form following:

Imprimis. I give & restore my Soul to God from whom it came, hoping for a full Remission of all my Sins thro' the Merits & Satisfaction of Jesus Christ; and my Body I leave to be decently buried at the discretion of Executors hereafter mentioned.

Item. I will that my Funeral Expences, & all my just Debts be paid & discharg'd, in convenient Time after my Decease.

Item. I give and bequeath to my Loving Wife, Sarah, the Plantation whereon I now live, with all the land thereunto belonging, during her natural Life, and after her Decease, I give & bequeath the aforsd. Plantation with the Land thereto belonging, to my loving Nephew, James Beaseley, to him & his Heirs for Ever.

Item. I give & bequeath to my loving Wife, Sarah, two Cows and Calves, two heifers, one Bull, two Steers, all of them to be of her own Choosing. I also give and bequeath her my riding Gray Mare & side Saddle, as also all my Hogs both great and small, one Loom & all the utensils for Weaving, one linnen Wheel, one Long Wheel, and all the Cards; the best bed, two pair of Sheets, one Rug & one Blanket, All of her own choice; fifteen Gallons of Malasses, all the cotton pickt and unpick't, my Chest with the Lock & Key, one Tea kettle with all its Appurtenances, with all the Earthen Ware, one Flower Sifter one Search, one Walnut Table & Table Cloth, with all the Knives & forks, two Red Leather Trunks, one Box Iron, four Heaters, one Looking Glass, six chairs, six pewter plates, two Dishes, two pewter Basons, two pewter porringers, all of her Own Choice, two Iron pots, one frying pan, two Earthen fat Pots, with all the fat in them, the Potts to be of her Own Choice.

Item. I give and Bequeath to my Loving Wife, Sarah, all the wool, one Candlestick, one bible, one common Prayer Book, All the wheat, two Juniper Tubs, one Large & one small, one

Stone Butter Pot, all the Provision of what Sort soever, except one barrel of Port & two Hogs to be kill'd to discharge Capt. Silvester. I also give her all the corn, two Stone Jugs, One 8 Gall. Cag, one seven Cag, 1 Bolster, two Pillows, four towels, one Case & six bottles belonging to the Case, 1 bucket with all the Sugar in it, the Loaf Sugar, all her wearing Clothes.

Item. I give and bequeath unto Sarah Freeman, Daughter of Thomas Freeman, one Cow & Calf, and two Yearling Heifers, and three pound, ten Shillings, Proclamation Money.

Item. I give and bequeath unto Richard Leary, Senr., of Tyrrell County, one close bodied Coat, two home spun Shirts, two White Shirts, one Great Coat, and my Gun.

Item. I give and bequeath unto John Beasley, Son of James Beasely, 2 home spun Shirts, & one White Shirt.

Item. I give and bequeath to my loving Wife, Sarah, the Hand Mill & Frame, one small Canoe, & my bedstead.

Item. My Will & Desire is, that all the Residue of my Estate be sold at publick Vendue, and after my Debts be paid to be equally divided betwixt James Beasely, son of John Beasely, and Thomas Beasely, Son of James Beasely, and Mary Pain, Daughter of James Beasely.

And I hereby appoint my Friends, Col. John Halsey, and Cornelius Leary, Executors to this my last Will and Testament, requesting and desiring of them to make a title to John Rowsum, his heirs & Assigns, of 100 Acres of Land, his father bought of me, beginning at the mouth of Blount Creek & running up ye Courses of ye Creek to the Head so far as to conclude 100 Acres.

And I do hereby Revoke & Disannul all former Wills by me made.

As Witness my hand & Seal, this 31st. day of January, 1756.

THOMAS FALCONER (Seal)

Sign'd, Seal'd and Acknowledged
In presence of:
    ROBT. BEASLY.
    JAS. FRANS. EDWD. ROBINS.
    ELIZABETH E̲ ROWSUM.
             mark

Whereas, Col. Jno. Halsey agreed with me for a certain parcel of Land, being part of the Land belonging to the Plantation whereon I now live, at the rate of five Shillings, Virginia Currancy, Pr. Acre, the sd. Parcel of Land being bounded as follows: beginning at a Hickory & running 60 Pole to the River, thence East and by North, 36 Pole, thence South East by South, 54 Pole, Thence a straight Line to the first Station. Now, by this Codicil annex'd & dated the 1st. of Febry., 1756, My Will and Desire is, that Cornelius Leary, one of my Executors, do make a good and lawfull Title of the sd. Parcel of Land to Colo. Jno. Halsey, his His Heirs or Assigns upon his or their paying five Shill. Pr. Acre, according to the aforesd. Agreemt., and this Codicil I would have to be held & taken in as full, large & ample power & Vertue, as the Will to which it is annexed.

Sealed with my Seal, and dated this 1st. day of Februry, 1756.

THOMAS FALCONER (Seal)

Sign'd, Seal'd and Pronounced,
I' Presence of
    THOMAS PEIRCE.
          his
    JOHN I CREECY
       mark
    JAS. FRAS. EDWD. ROBINS.

CHOWAN COUNTY. ss. April County Court, 1756: Present his Majesty's Justices.

These may Certifie that James Francis Edward Robins, Appeared in Open Court and proved the Within Will in due form of Law. Then also Appeared John Halsey, Esquire, and was duely Qualivied as Executor to the Within Will, by taking the Oath by Law Appointed for the Qualification of Executors, and thereupon Ordered that Letters Testamentary Issue thereon as the Law directs.

Test. THOMAS JONES, Cler. Cur.

Copied from the Original Will, filed in the Office of the Secretary of State.

JOHN FENDALL'S WILL.

IN THE NAME OF GOD AMEN. I, John Fendall, of Pequimons Prcinct, being very Sick and weake in body tut of perfect mind and memory, God be praysed, doe make and Ordeyne this my last Will and Testament in forme following:

First, I surrender my Soul into the hands of Almighty God my maker & unto Jesus Christ my only Saviour & redeemer trusting in his merritts and prcious Death to have pardon of all my Sins; & my Body to the Earth from whence it came to be decently Interred according to the Discretion of my Executor; And for the Worldly Estate God hath given me, I bequeath as followeth:

Imprimis. I give unto my Brother, Robert Fendall, all my wearing Cloathes; And all the rest of my Estate whatsoever, be it real or personall, in any kind whatsoever, I give to my loving Wife Elizabeth Fendall, and to her heyrs forever.

And I make & Ordayne my loving Father in Law, Alexander Lillington, Executor of this my last will and Testament. And I revoake all former Wills by me in any wise made.

In wittness whereof, I have hereunto sett my hand & Seal, the Seventeenth Day of December, 1695.

JOHN X FENDALL

Signed, Sealed, published & declared (after the word Lillington interlyned) in Presence of:
    JOHN DIX.
    ANN WALKER.
    HENDERSON WALKER.

Att a Court held for the preinct of Chowan, the first Monday in April, 1696, this will of Capt. John Fendall was proved by the Oathes of Captn. Henderson Walker, Mrs. Ann Walker & John Dix.

Attested by NATH. CHOWIN Cler.

No. CAROLINA. The Hono'ble the Palatines Court.

Whereas, Captn. John Fendall, of Pequimons, is Deceased having made by his Last Will and Testament, Major Alexander Lillington, his Executor, a true Coppy whereof is hereunto annexed, These are to impower the said Alexander Lillington, to Enter in and upon all and Singular the Goods & Chattles, Rights and Creditts of the sd. John Fendall, and a True Inventory thereof to return, & within one year after the Date hereof, and the Same to dispose of as by the sd. Will.

Dated the Eighth Day of April, 1696.
                        THOS. HARVEY,
                        DANIEL ABELHURST.
                        FRANCIS TOMES
                        SAM'L SWANN.

Recorded in Will Book 1, page 81, Office of the Secretary of State.

BARTHOLOMEW FIGURES'S WILL.

IN THE NAME OF GOD AMEN, I, Bartholomew Figures, of Northampton County, being in Perfect sence and Memory, prased be God for it, do make this my Last Will and Testament, in Manner and form following, Viz: First and principally, I recommend my soul to the Hands of Almighty God that gave it, hoping through the Meritorous Death and Passion of my only Saviour Jesus Christ to have full pardon and free Remission of all my Sins; and my Body to be decently Buried by my Executors hereafter Named; and for such Worldly Estate as it hath pleased God to Bestow on me I Dispose of as followeth, Viz:

    Imprimis. I give and Bequeath unto my son, John Figures, One tract of Land Containing Two Hundred Acres, and is part of that Patent Granted to Henry Wheelor and One Hundred & Ten Acres of Low ground which I have taken up and a Deed taken out for the same, with Four Hundred Acres of Pine Woods, on the West End of that Tract which I purchased of John Bond;

and likewise the after Named Negroes, Sam, Sambo, Nan, Jude; and one Case of Bottles, to him and his Heirs or Assigns for ever.

Item. I give and Bequeath unto my son, Richard Figures, Two hundred and Seventy five Acres of Land, it Lying Above my Plantation and part of the tract whereon I now live and to be taken from the Islands on the pasture Side, beginning Midway Between the Lightwood Stake and My Lower fishing place, and thence up the Island Side to the fishing place, thence up the River so far as to come a strait Course to the first Station, and to contain the Above Number of Acres (One Half Acre at Each fishing place which I desire may be thus Disposed of to my three Sons, John, Richard and Bartho'w Figures, with three Sains which I Desire be Equally Devided amongst the sons Above Named, and to be neither Sold nor leased) and to Richard, Two Negroes Named Ned and Harry, to him and his Heirs forever.

Item. I give and Bequeath unto my Daughter, Robekak Derring, One Negro Girl called Sal, to she and Heirs and Assigns, And likewise One Negro Boy Named Ben, I lend the Use of During her life, and if She deceased without Issue, to fall to my Lawful Heir.

Item. I give and Bequeath unto my Daughter, Mary Mosson, one Negro Girl Named Jenny, and one Boy Named Dick, to she and Heirs for ever.

Item. I give and Bequeath unto my Son, Bartholomew Figures, the plantation whereon I now live, and all the land in the two Patents Except what is above given, and likewise Three Hundred Acres of pine Woods to be laid of part on the North end and part on the Southend, to be laid of by my son, John and Richard Figures; and three Negroes Named, George, Natt and Annaca; and One Bed and furniture as it now Stands, and three pewter Dishes, 6 plates and six spoons, and one Iron pot and frying pan, and three Cows and Calves, to him and his Heirs and Assigns for ever.

Item. I give and Bequeath unto my Son, Joseph Figures, One Survey of Land whereon he now lives and Money to take out the Deed, and likewise one Hundred and twenty Acres on the South side of Old tree Swamp, joyning to that whereon he now lives; with two Negroes Named Jemmy and Hanner, and to Cows and Calves and one Heifer, to him and his Heirs and Assigns forever.

Item. I give and Bequeat unto my Son, William Figures, Seven Hundred acres of Land which is the Remainder part of parcel of Land Which I purchased of John Bonde, and three Negros, Peter, Jacob and Lucy, and one feather Bed and furniture as it now Stands, and three Cows and Calves, and three pewter Dishes, Six plates and Six Spoons & Iron pot and one pan, to him and his Heirs and Assigns forever.

I give and Bequeath unto Elizabeth Lewis, My Daughter, Two Negroos Named Sal and Jenny, to She and Heirs and Ass. forever &c.

Also I leave my son, John Figures, and son, Bartholomew Figures, whom I do likewise Constitute, make and Ordain my only and Sole Executors of this my Last will and testament, and Desire that the remainder part of my Estate may be thus Dis (Over leaf Brought forward) Disposed of that the Other part of my Moveable Estat not mentioned to be Equally Divided, by these four men or any three of them to Equally Divide it Among my Children then living; and My will is that these three men shall offer every Child his part Allotted for him or her, and on the refusal of the Same to be taken and Divided amongst the rest of the Children, and he Quite Excluded from any part or Right thereof; the men Named, Wm. Sherrod, Wm. Taylor, Joseph Dew and Charles Dew; and I also give my Son, John Figures, the Liberty or Use of all the Said Negros all intire as the now are to finish the Crop now begun. And I do likewise Desire that their be no Appraisment nor Sale made of my Estate, but Divided as above mentioned, and my Desire is these my Exec'rs do see that the above Legacies and Shares be Equally Divided & Disposed of as heretofore mentioned.

And I do hereby Utterly Disallow, Revoke and disannull all and every Other former Testaments, Wills and Legacies, Bequests and Executors, by me in any ways before this Time Named, Willed and Bequeathed, Ratifying and Confirming This and no Other to be my last Will and Testament.

In Witness whereof, I have hereunto Set my Hand and Seal, This the Sixteenth Day of March, One Thousand, Seven Hundred and Fifty Eight.

BARTHOLOMEW B FIGURES (Seal)
his
Mark.

Sign'd, Seal'd, Published, Pronounc'd and Declar'd by the Said Bartho'w Figures, as his Last Will and Testament, in the Presence of Us the Subscribers, that is to Say:

JOSEPH DEW, } Jurant
CHARLES DEW
WILLIAM SHERARD
JOHN DEW.

Be it known to all Men, by these Presents, That I, Bartholomew Figures of the County of Northampton, Planter, have made and Declared my Last will and Testament in Writing, Bearing Date the Sixteenth Day of March, 1758. I, the Said Bartho'w Figures, by this present Codicil do ratify and Confirm my Said last Will and Testament; and do give and Bequeath unto my Son, John Figures, One Copper Still, Cap and Worm and pump and likewise the Benefit of all the Crop now made, for paying my Debts, and likewise all the Cash and proclamation Money in hand or Due to me to be kept for this Service; for paying the Levies and Quitrence now Due.

And Likewise I give and Bequeath unto my Son, Bartholomew Figures, One Brass Bottle, A Whip Saw and One Cross Cut Saw; And my Will and Meaning is, that this Codicil or Schedule be Adjudged to Be a part and Parcel of my last Will and Testament, and that all things therein Mentioned and contained Be faithfully and truly Performed and as fully and Amply in every Respect as if the Same were so Declared an Set down in my Said last Will and Testament.

Witness my hand this the Nineteenth day of March, 1758.

BARTHOLOMEW B FIGURES (Seal)
his
Marke.

Signed (*Ut Supra*)
   JOSEPH DEW, Jurat,
   CHARLES DEW, Jurat.
   WILLIM SHERRAD.

No. HAMPTON COUNTY, ss. July Court, 1758.

The within written Will of Bartholomew Figures, Deceased, with the Codicil annexed, were Exhibited into Court and severally proved on the Oath of Joseph Dew & Charles Dew, two of the subscribing witnesses thereto; at the same time John Figures and Bartholomew Figures were Qualified Executors thereof; which on motion was Ordered to be Certified.

               Test. J. EDWARDS, Cler. Cur.

Copied from Original Will, filed in the Office of the Secretary of State.

JOHN FONVIELLE'S WILL.

IN THE NAME OF GOD AMEN. I, John Fonvielle, of Craven County and province of North Carolina, Being in perfect mind and Memory and Calling to Mind my Mortality do make and ordain this my Last Will and Testament in Manner and form following: (That is to say),

Imps. I give and Bequeath unto my Loveing son, John Fonvielle, two Hundred and forty Acres of Land where he now Lives, and a Hundred and Twenty two Acres of land Between Isaac Fonvielles And Arthur Blackman, and a Lott of Land in Newbern Town known by the no. 6 Except that part is in my Yard; and I give my said son, John, the front of the said Lott where Mrs. Hay's Now Lives; and also three negroes, (viz) Tim, Simon and Rachell, And two Beads, and Thirty five pound weight of pewter, with the House Furniture and my Riphell Gun which I delivered to him at his going to House Keeping, to him, his Heirs and Assigns for ever.

Item. I give and Bequeath to my Loveing son, William Brice Fonvielle, Six Hundred and Forty Acres of Land, where he now Dwelle, and a Lott of Land in Newbern Town, known by the No. 5, Except that part that is in my Yard where my two Houses Stands with the pailling between his house and mine, Including the Shopp and Love Oaks as the pailling of my Yard now Stands, being of John's Lott Excepted; also, I give my said son the front Lott of No. 5, Joyning to my son John's front Lott and three Negroes, (viz.) Joe, Sam and Dina; and two Beads, and thirty five pound weight of pewter, and that house and furniture which I Delivered to him when he went to keep house, to him, his Heirs and Assigns for ever.

Item. I give and Bequeath unto my Loveing son, Francis Fonvielle, five hundred and Ten Acres of Land where he now Lives and a Lott of Land in the Town of Newbern, where Mr Buckston now Lives, known by the No. 7, as in the Deed or plan of said Town, and Three Negroes (viz) Abram, Tom, and Doll, and thirty five pound (pound) of pewter, and a gun, and a bead and, his House Furniture Delivered to him when he went to House Keeping, Except the Lott, to him his Heirs and Assigns for ever.

Item. I give and Bequeath unto my Loveing son, Frederick Fonvielle, the Land where he now Lives (Except the Eastermost side of the Branch that Devides myself and him, which I Reserve for my beloved wife, Mary Fonvielle, During her Widdowhood and and Then to be His), and also a piece of Land I have taken up Between Mr. Cornells Land and the said Land, and a Lott in the Town of Newbern, where Sigley formerly did Live, and a Bead and furniture, & Thirty five pound weight of pewter, and a gun, and three Negroes, (viz) Bull, Grace, and Quacko, and sum House Furniture all Delivered But Negro Bull and the Lott, to him, his Heirs & Assigns forever.

Item. I give and Bequeath unto my Loveing son, Stephen Fonveille, five Hundred Acres of Land where he now Lives on New River, and part of my Lower Tract on Stone Bay, to begin at the Lower part, so up the River Half way, so to Run the Course of the Patent till It comes to the Road and not to Cross the Road that goes to Mrs. Walters, so that Lower part to be my said son Stephen, and I give unto my said son, Stephen, that Half Lott of Land in Newbern Town, that Mrs. Snead formerly Lived on, and with a Straight Course to Hatches Line, being that where Hendrick did Live on; and I give my said son, Stephen, a Bead, a Gun and three Negroes (Viz), Robin, Jenny, and Southey, and the Furniture I Delivered him when he went to keep house, to him, his Heirs and Assigns for ever.

Item. I give and Bequeath unto my Loveing Son, Jeremiah Fonville, Seven Hundred and Seventy Acres of Land on the

Mouth of Stone Creek, where I am aBuilding, and the upper part of the Lower Tract on Stone Bay to Run Down the River Half way, and then with the Course of the Patent till it comes to the (road) Road that goes to Mrs. Walters, and so with the Road till it comes to Mrs. Walters at the Corner tree; also a Bead and furniture, & all the tools on The said Plantation, and a gun, and all the Hoggs and Cattle Belonging to The said place and five Negroes (viz), Charley, Muck, Priss and Isaac, and also part of a Half Lott in the Town of Newbern, Begining at the Stone that Devides Samuell Hatch and him, so with the Course of the said Lott till it comes to Stephens Line, and also my Yard and Houses, Being the two peices I Excepted out of John's Lott and Brices; and Thirty five pound wieght of pewter, to him, his Heirs and Assigns for ever.

Item. I give and Bequeath unto my Loveing Daughter, Mary Hatch, two Half Lotts of Land in Newbern Town, which I have given a deed for, and posession of the same, and two hundred Acres of Land on the North side of Nuce River, and Samuel Hatch Hath sold it to my son Francis; and I also give my said Daughter, two Negroes (viz), Sipp and Phillis, and thirty five pound weight of pewter, and a Bead and furniture, all Delivered at her Marrage to her, her heirs and Assigns for ever.

Item. I give and Bequeath unto my Loveing Daughter, Eliz- Hatch, a Lott in Newbern Town, by the West gate as No. in the Deed of the sd. Lott and in the Plan of the said Town; and three Hundred and Sixty Acres of Land in New-hanover County as per the Patent; and three Negroes (viz), Amey, Will and Pegg, and Thirty five pound weight of pewter, and a Bead and Furniture, all Delivered at her Marrage, to her, Her Heirs & Assigns forever.

Item. I give and Bequeath unto my Loveing Daughter, Ester Fonvielle, a Lott in Newbern Town Joyning Mrs. Shingleton, known by the No. in the Deed of the sd Lott and plan of the said Town, and four Negroes (viz), Moll, Joe, Beck and Abram, and a Bead & Furniture, and Thirty five pound weight of pewter, to her, her Heirs and Assigns forever.

Item. I give and Bequeath unto my Loveing Grand Daughter, Elizabeth Fonvielle, Daughter of Frederick Fonvielle, one Negro named Silvey, to her, her Heirs and Assigns for ever only reserving the use of the (said) Said Negro Silvey, unto my Beloved Wife, Mary, During her Widdohood.

Item. I Leave unto my well beloved wife, Mary, the use of the plantation where I now Live the East side of the Spring Branch with Liberty of pasterage as far as the Little gate by the Road, During her Widdowhood and no Longer; I also leave her the Use of three Negroes (viz), Dunk, Sarah & Patience, during her Widdowhood; I also give unto my well beloved wife, the Bead and furniture that she & I Beded when we were Married, and also thirty weight of pewter which she is to take her first Choice out of my pewter in the house, & two potts; a frying pan, also my Mare, & Six Cows & Calves, and three Sows & piggs, and one Table & a Tea Table, half a Dozen of Silver Tea Spoons & tea Tongs, a sett of Tea Cups & Saucers, & a Tea kettle, all these to be Delivered to her by my Executors without trouble & have a quiet and peaceable possesion till her Marrage or Death, Then said Land to be Frederick Fonveilles, and the three Negroes to be Equally Devided amongst all my Children; the Negroes to be valied or Sold & the Money Devided.

Item. I give to the Church in Newbern, twenty pound, proclamation money; and it is my will & Desire that all my Lands not already Disposed of & all moneys, Cattle, Horses and Hoggs, and all my plantation tools and Household Furniture, and all the Rest & Residue of my whole Estate that is not already Bequeathed (Except Jeremiah to have his Choies of a horse & Mare), Except a horse Called Forister and that sd Horse to be sold toward paying my debts, and also Easter to have a Mare, and my wife to have a years provision of Either sort of Meat & all the Rest & Residue to be Equally Devided among my Children, or theirs, after my Lawfull Debts is paid.

And I do Nominate & Appoint my Loving Sons, John Fonvielle, William Brice Fonvielle, and Francis Fonvielle, Executors to this my Last Will & Testament, hereby Revoking all other wills heretofore by me made.

In Witness whereof, I have hereunto Sett my hand & Seal this 25th Day of January, in the Year of our Lord, one thousand, Seven Hundred and Seventy three.

JOHN FONVIELLE. (Seal)

Signed, Sealed, published & Declard in the presence of:
    JOHN TURNER.
    WILLIAM BALLARD.
    ISAAC ESLECK.

The last will and Testament of John Fonville, hereunto annexed, was proved before me this twenty seventh day of January, 1773, by the Oath of Isaac Esleck and William Ballord who swore that they saw the Testator sign, seal, publish and declare the same to be and contain his last Will and Testament, and that at the time thereof he was of sound disposing Mind and Memory.

And John Fonvielle, William Brice Fonvielle, and Francis Fonvielle, Executors therein named, having taken the Oath appointed for their Qualification. It is Ordered that Letters Testamentary issue thereon accordingly.
    Jo. MARTIN.

The Annexed last Will and Testament of John Fonvielle, Deceased, is Recorded in the Clerks Office of Craven County, this 10th. September, 1773.
    By CHRIS'R NEALE C. J. C.

Copied from the Original Will, filed in the Office of Secretary of State.

MARY FORTSEN'S WILL.

Whereas there is a patent Granted unto mee, Mary Fortsen, wife to Fredrick Fortsen, for a divident of twoe thousand acres of land for mee, my heirs or assignes, ye said Land Lying & being att Paspetank, of w'ch divident there is disposed by ye Said Fredrick Fortsen & my Self nine hundred Acres, my right title and intrest of w'ch I doe by these presents assigne & sett over unto my Said Husband, to enable him to give bills of Sale for ye Same nine hundred Acres of land.

Now, know yeu, That I, ye said Mary Fortsen, being Sicke, yet having my perfect senses, considering ye cartainty of death & ye uncertainty of ye houre thereof, I comitt my Soule Unto God Almighty; & my body to ye Earth whence it came; Desiring to dispose of ye remainder of ye said divident of land beinge elleaven hundred acres;

I doe by these presents, give & bequeath unto my son, Theophilus Fortsen, all ye Said P'cell of Elleaven hundred Acres of Land, to have & enjoy ye Same after, ye decease of my said Husband, for my will & intention is y't my Said Husband shall enjoy ye same during his life. But if my said son shall come to dye before my said husband, then he to dispose of ye sd. land according to his pleasure.

And it is also my intention & will, y't if my said husband shall think fitt to dispose of any part or p'cell of ye sd. land, it shall be lawfull for him to doe it. Soe yt the proceed thereof be imployed in Cattle for & to ye behoofe of my Said Son, Theophilus Fortsen. Provided allwaise yt. if it shall please God to send me safely delivered of ye child I goe wth, all yt ye same shall have Equall Share wth ye said Theophilus.

In witness whereof I have hereunto set my hand & Seale, the 20th day of June, 1663.

          MARY FORTSEN. (seal)

Testrs.
  ye marke I of JNO. LAWRENCE.
  ye mke W of WILLIAM EMLY.
  ye mark O ELIZABETH ROSY.
  ye marke O of ELLINOR WADELL.

Recorded ye 15th novemb'r 1665.
       Test. THOMAS HARRIS Cle: Co.

Copied from Original Will, filed in the Office of the Secretary of State.

JOHN MARTIN FRANCK'S WILL.

IN THE NAME OF GOD AMEN. I, John Martin Frank, of Craven County, in the province of North Carolina, being in good health of Body and of sound and perfect mind & memory, praise be therefore Given to God, doe make and ordain this my laste will and testament in manner and forme following: that is to say, first and principally, I Commend my soule to almighty God that Give it me; and my Body I Commit to ye Earth to be decently buried at the discretion of my Executors heare after Named, and as touching the Disposal of such temporal Estate as it hath pleased God to bestow me I Give and dispose thereof as followeth:

First, I will that my Just Depts and funeral Charges be paid and satisfied.

Item. I lend and bequarth to my loving wife, Sevil Frank, one plantation called by ye name of Chinpin, with foure hundred Acors of Land, moore of less, for and Iniuren her Natural Life, and after her discease to My son, John Frank, to him and his heairs for Ever; like wise, I lend and bequarth to my loving wife three Negrous (to wit). toney, and Rachel his wife, and filles, one feather Bead and pare of pillers, one pare of sheets, one Rug, one Blancit and Boulster, and after her disease to fall to her heairs lawfully begoting of her Body with me. Further, I Give to my loving wife wife, one pare of Curtins, and twelve Cowse and Calves, the fifth Parte of ye dry Cattle, half of ye hogs, ye fifth parte of ye Sheep. Like wise, I Give to my loving wife, one sorrel horse Named brass, one white maire branded with G K, and Colte, and an Equal parte of ye Depts that is Come in after my Lawfull Depts is paid, and one lite Gray horse Called friday Branded M F; like wise, I Give to my loving wife, two small spinning wheales and one Grate spinning Wheale, and one smale Bell mettle skillet one Large Copper Cittle I Bought from Celley, and one bell mettle Mortor, and one potrack, one Silver peper box, and one Gray horse.

Item. I Give and bequarth to my Son, Edward Franck, Three Negrows (to wet), Bungy, antoney, and tom; and twelve Coues and Calves, an Equal parte of the dry Cattle after my beloved wife, Sevil Franck, has her parte out, one feather Bead, one Rug, one pare of Sheets, one Boulster. Like wise, I Give to my Son, Edward Franck, thre youse and one Ram, and one Silver Wach he has Rec'd alridy. Further, I Give to my son, Edward Franck, one Maire Called plesant, one Bay horse Called frollik, and one horse Called Bay, and and an Equal part of my Depts that is Due to me after my beloved wife, Sevil Franck, has her share out, and all my lawfull Depts is paid, and an Equal parte of ye moveable that is to be sould

After my beloved wife, Sevil Franck, has her shere out of it; one Warnote Dask.

Item. I Give and bequarth to my son, John Franck, Three Negrow (to wet), tobey, farow; and one feather bead, Boulster, Rug, one pare of sheets, one silver wach, one silver Wach that I sente out with Mr. Godfree to be mended, and one Clock, and an Equal parte of ye Drie Cattle, and twelve Coues and Calves, an Equal parte of ye Sheep after my beloved wife, (wife) sevil Franck, has her share out, and one mare and Colte Called flie, and Equal parte of ye Deapts that is Due to me after my lawfull Depts is paid and my beloved wife has her share out, an Equal parte of ye hogs, and an Equal parte of ye Movables after my beloved wife has her share out, and two plow horsis, one Gray horse and one Bay horse.

Item. I Give and bequarth to my Daughter, susanna Franck, Three Negrows (to wet), James and his wife Cate, and Jack, and twelve Coues and Calves, and an Equal parte of ye Drie Cattle, one silver spoone, and an Equal parte of ye Sheep after my beloved wife, sevil Franck, has her share out, and one feather Bead, one pare of sheets, one Rug, one Boulster, one pare of pillers, and an Equal parte of ye Depts that is Due to me after my Lawfull Depts is paid, and an Equal parte of ye Movables, an Equal part of ye Land that is to be sould after my beloved wife has her share out, and ye first Choice of all ye young horses. Likewise, I Give to my Daughter one young maire that Came of plesent, one little Warnote Dask.

Item. I Give and bequarth to my Daughter, sevil Franck, two Negrows (to wet), little Cate and Samboe, one feather Bead one pare sheets, one Boulster, one pare of pillers, one Rug and one silver spoone, and twelve Couse and Calves, and an Equal parte of ye Land that is to be sould after my Lawfull Depts is paid, and Equal parte of all ye Movables; like wise, I Give to my Daughter, Sevil Franck, ye second Choice of ye young horsis and one young maire Came of Bonney, and an Equal parte of ye sheep after my beloved Wife has had her out, and an Equal parte of all ye Movables.

Item. I Give and bequarth to my Daughter, Barbara Franck, two Negrows (to wet), little Rachel, little pater, Twelve Couse and Calves, one silver spoone, one feather Bead, one Rug, one pare of sheets, one Boulster and an Equal parte of ye Drie Cattle, an Equal parte of ye Movables after my beloved wife has her share out, and an Equal parte of my Deapts that is due after my law depts is paid, and an Equal parte of ye land that is to be sould, and one young maire three years ould.

Item. I Give and bequarth to my Daughter, Cathrine Franck, two Negrows (to wit), Joseph and Sammuel, and Five hundred Acors of land, moore or less, lying upon ye North side of trente River, Joining unto ye Land Called Chinpin, Running up ye Crick to ye Complemint. Like wise, I Give to my Daughter, Cathrine Franck, twelve Couse and Calves, and one feather Bead, and one Rug, one paire of sheets, one Boulster, and one silver spoone, an Equal parte of ye Drie Cattle after my beloved Wife has her share, and an Equal parte of the movables, an Equal parte of ye Land that is to sell after all my lawful Depts is paid, and one young maire Abought two or three yeare ould.

Item. I Give and bequarth to my Daughter, Mary Worsley, one Negrow man (to wet), Johnno, and an Equal parte of ye Drie Cattle after my beloved Wife, Sevil Franck, has her share out like wise, I Give to my Daughter, Mary Worsley, six hundred and forty Acors of upon wine swamp, Commonly Called James Marchels plantation, and an Equal parte of Depts that is Due after my Lawful Depts is paid, and an Equal parte of ye Land that is to be sould after my lawfull Depts is paid.

Item. I Give and bequarth to my Daughter, Elizabeth Harrold, one Negrow man (to wet) Hector, and an Equal parte of ye Drie Cattle, and an Equal parte of the Depts after my beloved wife, Sevil Franck, has her share out, and an Equal parte of ye Land that is to be sould after my Lawfull Depts is paid.

Item. I Give bequarth to my Gran Children, that is, John Worsleys Children, Every one of them, one two years old heffer apease. like Wise, I Give and bequarth to my two Granchildren, Thos. Harrolds, Every one of them, one two yeare ould heffer apease.

Lastly, all the Rests and Resedue of my Estate, Both Reale and parsonal, my will is that it be sould and ye money Ariseing therefrom to pay and satisfie my Just depts And funeral Charges, and the surpluss money ariseing by the sd. soale to be Equailly Devided betwen my loving Wife, sevil Franck, and my Children before menchened, (to wit) Edward Franck, John Franck, susanna Franck, Sevil Franck, Barbara Franck, Cathrine Franck, Mary Worsley, Elizabeth Harrold; and I appoint my loving Wife, Sevil Franck, my son, Edward Franck, and my loving frind, Frederick Isler, my Executrix, Executors of this my Last will and tastamente, heareby Revoking all other and former will and testamente by me heareto fore maid, Ratifying, allowing and Confirming these two sheets of paper to be my laste will and testamente.

In Witness whereof, I have Heare unto seet my hand and seals, This Third Day of November in ye yeare of our Lord, 1744.

JOHN MARTIN FRANCK. (Seal)

Sined, sealed, published, purnounsed and Delivered by ye sd. John Martin Franck, to be his last will and Testament in ye presents of us:

Chrestian CE Isler. his mark.
Melcher Remm.
Fredrick Isler.

(Endorsement) Martin Franks Will 1745.
Copied from Original Will, filed in the Office of the Secretary of State.

THOMAS FRY'S WILL.

In the Name of God Amen. I, Thomas Fry, late of London in Great Britain, now of Bath County in North Carolina, Mariner, being well in bodily health, as also if sound & sane mind & memory (Praise be unto God) but calling to mind the uncertain State of this fleeting, transitory life, and willing to prepare for a future State against that unknown hour in which It shall please God to call me hence, Do (hereby revoking all and all manner of former Wills & Testaments by me made), make, appoint, ordain & declare this, and this only, to be my last Will and Testament.

Imprimis. Into the hands of Almighty God I recommend my Soul, hoping for Salvation through the Merits & Mediation of the blessed Redeemer and Saviour of Mankind, Christ Jesus the Son of God. My Body I desire may be committed unto and interred after a Christian like Manner in the Earth, there to lye in Expection of the General Resurrection; And as to the Disposition of Such Worldly Estate and riches, as it has pleased God to bless me with in this World, I give, devise and bequeath them in manner following, Viz.,

After all my Just & lawfull debts are duly and truly paid by my Executrix hereafter named, I give, devise & bequeath unto my honoured Mother, Elizabeth Fry, of Milton, in Sothton, all such Effects, Goods, Interest or Moneys of mine, as now are in her own hands and keeping.

And all the rest and Residue of my Estate, both real & personal, of what nature or kind soever, in this Province of North Carolina, or wherewoever else, It, or any part thereof shall, or may, be found, I give, devise, and bequeath unto my true & loving wife, Elizabeth, to her & her heirs for ever.

Lastly, I nominate, appoint, & ordain my aforesaid Loving Wife, Elizabeth Fry, Sole Executrix of this my last will & Testament.

In testimony hereof, I have hereunto set my hand and Seal, this 18th. Day of March, 1724/5.

          THOS. FRY. (Seal)

Signed, Sealed, Publish'd and declared, in presence of:
 PAT. MAULE.
 THOMAS HARDING.
 SARAH SWANN.
 JNO. BABTA. ASHE.

NORTH CAROLINA, BEAUFORT AND HYDE PRECT'S. ss. Jan. Court, 1726.

 The Within Will was Exhibited in Open Court, by Eliza. Fry, the within mentioned Execrx., And proved by the Oaths of Patr. Maule and Jno. Bapa. Ashe, Two of the Subscribing Evidences thereto, who likewise Deposed that they Saw Thomas Harding & Sarah Swann, the other Evidences Sign the Same; and she likewise took the Execxs. Oath by Law Appointed.

       Testis. THO. JONES. Cler. Cur.

Copied from the Original Will, filed in the Office of the Secretary of State.

ALEXANDER GOODLATT'S WILL.

IN THE NAME OF GOD AMEN. I, Alexander: Goodlatt, Younger Sone to Abbottshaugh, in Sterlingshire, in that part of ye Kingdom of Great Britain formerly Called Scotland, Now of North Carolina, Merch't, Doe make, Ordeyne, Constitute and declare these presents to be and Conteyne my last Will and Testam't, hereby revokeing & makeing void all former and other wiles or Tes'am'ts. by me heretofo e made or Declared.

 Impris. In case it shall Soe happen that I shall Dye without Issue by my loveing wife, Elizabeth Goodlatt, I Give, Devise & bequeath unto my said Loveing wife, Eliza Goodlatt, All my Estate of w't Nature, Kind or quallity soever, which is in North Carolina, but if it shall happen that I shall have Issue by my said Wife, then it is my will, true Intent & Meaning, that four hundred pounds of my Estate in North Carolina be paid unto such Issue as I shall have by my said wife, at and upon his, or her, Arrivall to ye Age of Twenty Years.

 Itm., all ye rest of my Estate whatsoever in America, together w'th ye Sume of three hundred and thirty pounds sterl. Money, Due from my bror:, James Goodlatt, Younger, of Abbottshaugh, as appears by accounts made up by John Cunninghame, writer, to ye Signett in Edinburgh, the Second of ffeby., 1708/9, And Deposited in ye hands of John Cunninghame, Sone of ye above Named w'th twenty pounds Sterl. to raise & Process on ye Same, I Give, Demise & Bequeath unto ue Issue I shall have by my sd wife to be paid, at and upon his Arrivall to ye Age of Twenty Years. But, in Case I shall dye without Issue, then to my next of Kin.

Lastly, I doe Nominate and appoint my sd. loveing wife, Eliza. Goodlatt, Sole Executrix of this my last Will & Testam't.

In Testimony whereof, I have hereunto put my hand & Seale (after erasing ye two last lynes of ye first Article) this 12th. of Octor., 1710.

ALEXR. GOODLATT (Seal)

Sealed, Signed, and Declared
In ye presence of:
  ELIZA HECKLEFIELD.
  CORNELIUS RATSLITT.
  EDW. MOSELEY.

NORTH CAROLINA. By the Honble. the Presid't, &c.,

It being Certifyed to me that Alexr: Goodlatt, late of this province, Merch't, is Dead, and hath made & put his last Will & Testam't in writeing, a true Copy whereof is hereunto annex'd and hath therein appointed Eliza Goodlatt, widow & Relict of ye said Alexr., his Sole Excx., These are therefore to Impower her, ye sd. Elizabeth Goodlatt, to Enter in & upon, all & Singular, ye Goods & Chatles, rights & Credits of ye said Alexandr. Goodlatt, wherever in this Governm't to be found and ye Same into her possession to take, and a true Inventory thereof, Appraised according to Law, to returne into ye Sectys. Office within One Yeare after after ye Date hereof, and ye Same to Dispose of as by ye Said Will is appointed.

Given und'r my hand & ye Seale of ye Collony this 1st. day of Augt., Ano. Dni., 1713.

THOMAS POLLOCK.

Recorded in Will Book 2, page 4.

CALEB GRAINGER'S WILL.

NORTH CAROLINA, SS.

IN THE NAME OF GOD AMEN. I, Caleb Grainger, of New Hanover County, in the Province of North Carolina, Esquire, being in Perfect health and of Sound and Disposing mind and Memory, but knowing the Incertainty of human Life do make Ordaine and Declare this to be and Contain my Last Will and Testament, hereby Revoking all former And Other Wills by me at any time heretofore made.

Imprimis. I give and Bequeath my Soul to Almighty God, the Giver of all things, hoping at the Last day to Inherit Eternal Life; And as to Such Worldly Substance wherewith it hath Pleased God to Bless me with, I Give, Devise, And Bequeath in Manner and form following, that is to Say:

I Give, Devise and Bequeath unto my Loveing Wife, Mary Grainger, and to her heirs and Assign's for ever, one fifth Part of all my Personal Estate after My Just Debts is Paid off and discharges, Except what or Such Part as I hereinafter give and Bequeath to my Daughter, Mary Grainger, which Fifth Part as aforesaid is for and in Lieu of Any Thirds or Dower, She, my said wife, May Claim out of My Estate herein Devised and Bequeathed.

Item. I Give, Devise and Bequeath Unto my son, Caleb Grainger, all my Houses and Lands on Smiths Creek, and the No. Et. River on the Northermost side of the Main or Kings Road that leads frcm Smiths Creek Bridge to Blakes Ferry, which said Land as aforesaid, I give, Devise and Bequeath unto him, my said Son, Caleb, his heirs and Assign's for Ever, But my will is that my said Son shall not sell said Land untill he arrives to or at the Age of Twenty five Years, which will be in the Year of of Our Lord One Thousand, Seven Hundred and Seventy three, on the 20th day of April.

Item. I Give, Devise and Bequeath unto my son, Cornelius Harnett Grainger, all my Houses and Lands on Smiths Creek on the Southermost side of the Main Road that Leads from the Bridge to Blakes ferry, that is to say, all my Lands between said Road and Mr. Sam'l Swanns Land on said Creek, which said Land as aforesaid, I Give, Devise & Bequeath unto my said Son, Cornelius, to him, his heirs and Assigns for Ever. But my will is that my said Son, Cornelius Harnett Grainger, shall not sell said Land Untill he arrives to, or at, the Age of Twenty five Years.

Item. I Give, Devise and Bequeath unto my son, William Grainger, all that Tract of Land on the Sound which I purchased from Charles Harrison, where I have Settled a New Plantation, to him, My son William, his heirs and Assign's for Ever.

Item. I Give, Devise and Bequeath Unto my Daughter, Mary Grainger, Two Negro Wenches and what Children they now have, or May hereafter have, the Names of which Wenches is, Little Hager and Venice, which Said Negroes as aforesaid, I give, Devise and bequeath to my said daughter Mary, to her, her heirs and Assigns for Ever. My farther Will is, that in Case either of said Wenches Hager of Vence should die before my said daughter comes to the Age of Seventeen of day of Marriage, that then, and in such Case my Executors shall replace such Negro or Negroes out of My General Stock of Negroes, and said Negro or Negroes, so replaced, to be a Breeding Wench or Wenches.

Item. I Give, Devise and Bequeath unto my Daughter, Mary Grainger, one Lott of Land in Wilmington, Containing Thirty feet front upon the Street, and the Common Debth of Lotts which I have sold upon said Street, Unto her, her heirs and Assigns for Ever; which said Lot as aforesaid my Will is shall be laid off and given to her, my said Daughter, by My Executors hereinafter Named, in Such Street or Part of the Town where they thing most Proper that is to say, where I own the Land: I also give, devise and Bequeath to my said Daughter, Mary, one Good Bed & Furniture, two Mahogany Tables, Six Mahogany Chairs, one Large Mahogany fraimed Looking Glass, and Such of my Plate as I shall leave a List of Inclosed in my Will; all which things as aforesaid shall be delivered to her at the Age of Seventeen Years, or day of Marriage.

Item. My Will is that My Exec'rs sell my House and Land at Masonborough for the Use of my three Sons.

Item. My Will is that my Bridge on Smiths Creek, be keep in repair and in Case of a New One being wanted that it be built out of my Personal Estate, and that the Money Arising by the Rent of the Same go towards the Victualing, Clothing & Educating my Children, and that my wife have her Proportion of the Same dureing her remaining My Widdow.

Item. All the rest an Residue of My Estate, both real and Personal, I Give, Devise and Bequeath, Unto and Between, my three Sons, Caleb, Cornelius (Harnett), and William Grainger, to them Respectively, and to their several and Respective Heirs and Assign's for Ever, to be Equally Devided Between them, Share and Share Alike, by my Executors or the Survivors of them, when or as soon as my son Caleb, shall arrive to the Age of (Twenty) Twenty One Years; and in Case of the death of either of My said Children, before they or either of them shall come of Age or Day of Marriage, that then, such Part of my Estate, both Real and Personal, hereby intended for such Child so dying, I give, Devise and Bequeath to the three surviving Children, to them, Their Heirs and Assign's for Ever, and in Case of the Death of any two of My said Children, before they shall come of age or Marr'age that then such Part intend (that is to say of my Estate both real and Personal) for such Children dying I Give, Devise & Bequeath to the two Surviveing Children to them their heirs & Assign's for Eever; And in Case any Three of my Children should die before they become of Age, That then Any Part of my Estate, both Real and Personal, intended for such three deceased Children, I Give, Devise and Bequeath to the One Surviving Child, to him or her heirs and assigns for Ever.

Item. It is my Will and Desire (after my Debts is Paid) that then my Executors Pay over and Deliver unto my Wife, Mary Grainger, all and every Part of my Estate herein Before given and Bequeathed unto her, and it is my Will, that my said wife have the Use of My Household goods untill my son, Caleb Grainger, is of Age, she giving Security to my Executors (if required), to return the same in good Order, all that does not fall to her share, and I hereby begg and desire my Executors to take an account of my Plate, Other furniture, Stock of Cattle &c. My farther Will is, that after my Wife has had her Share of Negores and Slaves, that then the Negroes and Slaves remaining I do hereby Order, direct and Appoint shall be kept to work together or hired, wherever or which ever, my Executors shall think Most Advantagious and the Money arising from their Labour and the rent of the Bridge, I would have laid out in board, Cloathing and Education of my Children, either in this Province or wherever my Executo s May thing most Propper, and if any Overplus Remain of the Profits Arising from the Negroes Labour, & Rent of the Bridge, as afores'd, that the same shall be laid out in buying young Negroes to add to the General Stock, for my Children.

Item. It is my farther will, that my Wife have the use of My Plantation till my Son Caleb, become of Age. Provided she remains my Wddow Solong, but She is not to have it Any Longer than her Remaining so.

Lastly, I——Nominate, Constitute and Appoint Maurice Moore, Cornelius Harnett, Saml. A—e and Alexander Duncan, Esquires, Executors to this my Last Will and Testament, And My Wife, Mary Grainger, Executrix dureing her Remaining my Widdow; hereby revoaking all other and former Wills by me at any time heretofore made, and Acknowledge this, Containing two Sheet of Papper, to be my Last Will and Testament.

In Witness whereof I have hereunto set my hand and Seal this   day of   in the   Year of His Majestys Reign and in the Year of Our Lord, One Thousand, Seven hundred and Sixty Three

CALEB GRAINGER (Seal)

Signed, Sealed Published and declaired by the Testator, Caleb Grainger, as and for his Last will and Testament in Presence of us, who in his Presence and at his request have hereunto Set And Subscribed Our Naims as Witnesses, the word (Creek) between the tenth & Elevent lines from the bottom of the first Page being first intelined and the word "Cornelius" between the Seventh & Eights lines from the bottom of same Page interlined, and the word "Harnett" between the Sixth & Seventh lines interlined from the bottom, And the Naim "Cornelius" Putt in the Margin of the Same Page. The Word "Bequeath" interlined between the fifth and Sixth lines from the bottom of the Second Page interlined, all the above before sealing.   SAM'LL GREEN.
ANTH'Y WARD.
JOSEPH STOCKLEY.

Account of Plate Left my Daughter, Mary Grainger.
1 Doz. Table Knives & forks, Silver Handles.
1 Doz. Desart Ditto Silver Handles.
1 Silver Butter Boat,
1 Do. Tea pott.
1 Ditto Milk Pot.
1 Dz Silver Salts & Shovels.
1 Silver Salver.
1 Set of Casters with Silver Tops.
1 Soop Spoon, Silver
Half a Dozen Silver Table Spoons, Tea Spoons
August 23d., 1760.

CALEB GRAINGER.

Test.
    JOSHUA FORMER.
    THOS. WRIGHT.

(Turn Over) As it will be of no Real Service to my Friends, the giving of Scarfs &c (I desire that I be Buried in a Decent Manner and as a Mason), with a Plain Blacked Coffin, not Covered with Cloth, And that my Dear and ever Worthy Friend Mr. Corn. Harnett have purchased out of my Estate a neat Mourning Ring which I begg he may wear in remembrance of his Sinciar Friend & Brother,

CALEB GRAINGER.

Feb'ry 16th., 1761.

Be it known unto all men by these presents, that I, Caleb Grainger, of New Hanover County, in the Province of North Carolina, Gentleman, have made a declared that my Last Will & Testament In Writing bearing date the   day of   in the year of our Lord, One thousand and Seven hundred and sixty three to which said will, this Codicil is annexed.

I, the said Caleb Grainger, Do by these presents Codicil, Confirm & ratify my said Last Will and do give & bequeath unto the Child My wife, Mary Grainger, is now Pregnant with whether it be a Male or a female, his, or her heirs & Assigns forever, all my Moiety of the Land on Smiths Creek adjacent to the Saw Mill & Grist Mill now building by my friend, Cornelius Harnett & myself, together with a proportionate part (with the rest of my children), of my personal Estate. It is also my Will that the said Saw mill, to wit, my Moiety, be compleated & finished by by Executors out of the Proffits of my Estate; the proffits arising from the said Mills, to go to the use of my Estate until the said child come of age or day of Marriage; and my will is that this Codicil be adjudged a part of my said Will.

In Witness whereof, I have hereunto Set my hand & seal this fifth day of October, in the Year of our Lord, One thousand Seven hundred & Sixth five.

CALEB GRAINGER (Seal)

Signed, Sealed, delivered, published & Declared, to be a Codicil to the said Caleb Graingers Last Will & Testament, (the words "his or her assigns for ever" being first interlined) in presence of:
MARY GRAINGER.
MARGARET DOUGLASS.
EDMOND FOYER.

BRUNSWICK, 31st. Octb., 1765.

Sir: This day personally appeared before His Honour, the Lieutenant Governor, Mr. Anthony Ward, one of the subscribing Witnesses to the Will of Caleb Grainger, dec'd, & made Oath on the Holy Evangelists of Almighty God, that he saw the said Caleb Grainger sign, seal and publish the said Will as for his last Will and Testament, & that the said Caleb Grainger was at the same time (to the best of His Knowledge and belief) of a sound and disposing mind & Memory; & That he the said Anthony Ward, together with the other Witnesses, subscribed their names to the said Will in the Presence of the Testator.

At the same time appeared before His Honour, Miss Mary — Grainger, subscribing Witness to the Codicill Annexed to the said Will, who also made Oath According to the above Meaning in Respect to the said Codicill.

Also appeared at same time Mary Grainger, Widow & Executrix to the said Will who took the Oaths by Law Appointed for her Qualification. Lett Letters Testamentary issue thereon Accordingly.

I am, Sir, Your most Obed't Servant.

FOUNT'N ELWIN.

Copied from the Original Will, filed in the Office of the Secretary of State.

JOHN GRAY'S WILL.

NORTH CAROLINA. SS.

IN THE NAME OF GOD AMEN. I, John Gray, of the County of Bertie, Surveyor, being in good health & perfect and sound in my mind do make & Ordain my last Will & Testament in manner and form following: that's to say, first I Commend my soul to God that gave it; and my Body to the Dust; as to my worlldy goods I distribut as follows:

Imprimis. I give and Bequeath to Anne, my loving Wife, three feather Beds and their Appurtenances, all my Houseld Furniture belonging to the lower Rooms, except one Desk, all my pewter and brass Pots &c. at her own Disposal; allso, the meal, Cattle belonging to this Plantation, and fifteen Cows & Calves, and my Hoggs, two Horses at her choice, and a Mare and one half of the Sheep as afors'd; allso, the use of my Plantation were I now live as its bounded wt. a branch called

Aunt Sarah's, by estimation four hundred Acres; and all the working Tools for the Plough or field; the use and labour of my Negroe Men Charles and Ned, and a woman called Sarah.

I give and bequeath to my eldest son John, all and singular my Lands lying in Northampton and Edgecombe Countys; three hundred Pounds of this Currency. I do not get him a Negro man before this will's proved a negroe girl called Frank, the remaining part of my Sheep, half the Cattle on the Plantation after his mother gits her quota, a feather bed and the appurtinances; a Desk in the North Room, a doz. of new pewter Plates, ditto of Spoons, two dishes, all my bred of horses at Needhams Marsh.

I give and bequeath to my son, William, my Plantation where I now live, containing by es imation eight hundred acres, begin at the broad Branch runnin ; up to a branch opisit to the Plantation knowen by the name of Aunt Sarahs, y'n runing up that Branch to the Line that Divides the Land I bought from Robert Hicks, y'n running West to the next branch, y'n down the branch to the broad branch, y'n up the broad branch to the East Line, then along that to a Pine on Cashia River side, then doun the River to the first Station, to him and his Heirs for ever. If he dies before he arives at the Age of twenty one, or has not a child living in lawfull wedlock, in such case the land & all I bequeath him, is to be sold by my executors by and with the consent of my Daughters, Anne and Barbaras husbands, if they have any, but nothing to be disposed of before my Wifes death, nor in less than Six Months after, and after Sold the Money arising from the seal of the Land and Chattles, to be divided equally amonges my five youngest daughters, Viz: Barbara, Anne, Lucretia, Amelia & Louisa. I furhter give him a Negro Boy called Jamey, and after the Decease of His Mother, a negroe Wench Called Sarah, A Horse, two Mares, twenty Head of Cattle, my Gun and Saddle and Bridle.

I give to my Daughter, Janet McKinzie, one Shilling, Sterling, having already given Her a portion. To my Grand son, John Mc.kenzie, a breding Mare, to be delivered him Six months after my deceas.

I give and bequeat to my daughter, Barbara, five hundred Acres of Land lying in Bertie county, on the West Side of Cashia River, joining her brother Williams, begining at the mouth of the broad branch running wt. his boundarys to the Line of the survey, from thence to Thomas Turner's corner, y'n along his Several lines to make up the complement, to witt: one hundred pole along his line South to an Oak in His line, y'n East to the River, then up the River to the 1st. Station; also, A Negro Girl Called Thomasin, to Her and Her Heirs for Ever.

I give and bequeath to my Daughter, Ann, and her heirs for ever, a l the residue of my Land lying in Bertie County, on the West Side of Cashia river, begining at Her Sister Barbara's corner, running thence west to Her other, then along Thomas Turner's line South to William Grigoreys corner, then along his line to the river, then up the river to the first Statione; and a negroe girl called Moll.

I give and bequeath to my Daughter, Lucretia, and Her heirs for ever two hundred acres of land lying in Craven County, joyning Maules branch, and Six Cows and Calves and a breeding Mare upon it, and a Negroe Girl called Pat.

I give and bequeath to my daughter, Amelia two hundred and fifty Acres of Land, lying in the County of Bertie, in the Indians Woods, and a negroe boy called Cooper, to her and her heirs for Ever.

I give and bequeath to my daughter, Louisa, a negro boy called Marke, and a Negroe Girl called Linda.

My Will, and I do hereby order, that six Months after the deceas of my Wife, all my negroes not here bequeathed, cattle horses or any kind or manner of Goods whatsoever, be got together by my Executors and my Children, at any time or times & to be divided into Six equal parts and each of my Six youngest children is to have one, viz: Barbara, Ann, William, Lucretia Amelia and Louisa, and John and Janet is to have no share either of the Negroes left to their mother during her natural life, or those not mentioned in this Will, each to have there part the day of Marriage of the girls & Boys the same.

Revoking all former Wills by me made I do constitute and appoint my loving Br. Edward Bryan, and my loving Nephew, Thomas Whitmell, to be Joyn Executors, and Anne, my loving Wife Executrix, to this my last Will and testament.

In wi ness whereof, I have hereunto set my Hand and afixed my seal, this 20th. day of September in the eighteen year of the Reign of our sovering Lord, King George, the 2d. Annoq. Domi. 1745.

JOHN GRAY. (L S)

Signed, Sealed and published as the last Will and Testament of John Gray in Presents of:
DAVID GRAY.
JAS. WATSON, witness.
DUGALD McKICHEN.

NORTH CAROLINA. ss., 1750.   Nov'r. 16

This day the within Will of John Gray, Decd., was proved before me. And Ann Gray, relict of ye sd. John Gray, and Thomas Whitmell, an Executrix & Executor to the sd. Will qualified by taking the Oaths according to Law.
GAB. JOHNSON.

Recorded in Will Book 6, page 1, Office of the Secretary of State.

FARNIFOLD GREEN'S WILL.

IN THE NAME OF GOD AMEN. I, Farnifold Green, in County of Bath & Province of No. Carolina, Planter, being of a Sound & perfect memory, but Seriously Considering ye Frailty & uncertain State of ye Life at all times, Especially Especially in ye dreadfull times of Almighty God's Visitation by Sword & fier under which we tremble & to wch. do humbly submitt, I do make & Ordain and Constitute ys my last Will & Testament, In manner & form following, Vizt:

First, I render my Speritt in ye hands of Almighty God my Creator, stedfastly trusting in Jesus Christ, my Redeemer, for ye free remission of all; my Body to be buryed after ye discretion of my Executrix hereafter mentioned.

I give, Devise & bequeath all yt Tract of Land whereon my now Dwelling House stands w'th all its buildings Improvem'ts & appurtenances, beginning at a Live Oak w'th Severall Forks Standing at ye upper Side of ye first long Gutt below my house, near ye Mouth of ye Gutt being w'th severall marks; thence runing up ye River to a Corner Pine betwixt me & ———— Dawson, Esqr., Standing near a small Marsh & by ye Dawsons old Corn feild fence, & runing from ye forementioned Live Oak up ye afsd. Gutt; thence into ye woods No. untill three quarters of a mile from ye River be Compleated; thence by a Line run an equal Distance from ye River to ye afsd. Dawsons Line. And also, one Plantacon and all my lands Lying ye Lower side of broad Creek of ye No. side of Neus River, neer to Piney pointe & near ye mouth of ye sd. River, unto my Son, Thos. Green, & to ye heirs of his Body for ever.

I Give, devise & bequeath a Plantacon, with a Tract of land Begining at a Live Oak neer to ye mouth of ye Gutt aforesd. so runing down ye sd. River of Neus three quarters of a mile, thence No. Cross into ye Woods half a mile, and from ye aforementioned Live Oak No. One mile, And from there to ye End of ye Lower half mile Line, with all the Improvem'ts & Appurtenances thereto belonging; And also, my Entry and right to one Tract of Land Lying and being on ye lower side of ye first broad Creek above Captn. Jams. Beards Creek, begining a quarter of a Mile above ye Indian landing, by Computation thence down ye sd. Creek half a mile, with all ye Priviledges & appurtenances thereto belonging unto my Son, John Green, & to ye Heirs of his Body for ever; And for want of such Heirs to my Son, Farnifold Green, & the heirs of his Body for ever; & for want of heirs of ye sd. Farnifold Green, to my son, James Green, & ye Heirs of his body for ever; & for want of Heirs of ye sd. Jams. Green, to my two Daughters, Elizabeth & Jane Green, & their Heirs for ever.

I give, devise & bequeath a Tract of Land begining at my upper Corner Tree, on ye Creek, & runing down ye Creek to ye first branch below the Plantation whereon his Brother, Titus Green now Lives; thence to ye fork of ye sd. branch, & thence up ye Westermost parts of ye branch to ye head a line parale'll ye head line quite a Cross to ye aforesaid Dawsons Line, unto him ye sd. Titus Green, and his Heirs for ever.

All ye rest of my land in Greens Neck, whereon I now Live, I Give, divise & bequeath my two Sonns, Farnifold & Jam's Green, to be divided into two Equall parts by a Line Drawn from ye No. Most Corner of Jno. Green's Land to ye, Vizt: the upper part to Farnifold & ye heirs of his body for ever, and ye other part to James & ye heirs of his body for ever, reserving to James Egress & Regress into ye Woods through Farnifolds parts. And also, I give, divise & bequeath unto my Son, Farnifold, One Tract of Land Lying in Green point neck on ye No. Side of Neus River & unto ye Heirs of his body for ever.

I Give, divise & bequeath ye Lower survey of Land wch. I made in Greens bay of ye No. Side of Neus River to him & ye heirs of his body for ever, Provided yt in my Will, yt In Case my Son Farnifold should dye without Heirs of his Body, then all ye land hereby Divided unto him shall decend, be & remain unto my sd. Son, James & ye Heirs of his Body for ever; And In Case my sd. Son James should dye without heirs of his Body as aforesaid, then all ye Land Divided unto my Sons, Farnifold and James, shall Descend and be, remain unto my Two Daughters, Elizabeth & Jane, & to their Heirs for ever.

I Give, Divise & Bequeath unto my Daughter in Law, Ann Smithick, one Tract of Land Lying on ye No. side Neus River, Called Nottingame points, yses: Two hundred & fifty Acres, to her & her Heirs for ever.

I Give, divise & queath all ye rest of my Lands, Tenements or hereditam'ts, not hereby before Divided I Give, divise & bequeath unto my Loving Wife, Hannah Green, & her heirs for ever.

I Give & bequeath unto my Son, Thos. a Young black Mare branded with F G & a Young gray Horse branded with F G on ye neer Butlock, and my bullet Gun, one Feather Bed & boulter, one Pillow, one Rugg & two blanketts & two sheets.

And unto my son Jno. One Negro Woman Called Fillis, one Trumpett mussell Gun, One Grey Mare ab't two Years olf, branded w'th F G on ye neer butlock.

And unto my Som, Farnifold, One Bay Mare branded w'th F G & her Coult w'ch is now by her Side, & one half of a Sixty pound Bill of Exchange now sent to Virginia, In Order for to be sent for England, & a Couple of Cows w'th Cow Calves, & my black Gunn, to be mark'd in his proper Mark ye next

Spring after my Decease; ye Guns to be deliver'd to each of them well fixt & in good Order.

And to my Son, James, One Sorrell Mare branded w'th F G on ye near buttock, and her Coult by her Side, & one Negro man Call'd Nick, and ye other half of ye afsd. Sixty pound Bill of Ex. as aforsd.

And my Will is yt my sons abovemention'd shall be Deem'd at full Age when they shall arrive at ye Age of Eighteen years respectively. And to my two Daughters, Eliz. & Jane Green, I give & bequeath four young Cows w'th Cow Calves with their female Increase to mark'd in their proper marks ye next Spring after my Decease.

All ye rest of my goods & Chattells, rights & Creditts, my Debts being pd. & funerall Charges Defray'd, I Give, & Bequeath unto my Loving Wife, Hannah Green, whom I also make & appoint my Sole Executrix of ys my last Will & Testam't & utterly making Void all Wills & Testamt's by me hereafter made.

In Testimony whereof, I have hereunto fixt my hand & Seale, this 26th. day of October, Anno Dom., 1711.

(Interlined in ye 36th. Line, ye words Call'd Nottingame point).

FARN. E'G' GREEN

Sign'd Seal'd & Publish'd in ye Presence of us:
    TITUS GREEN.
    RT. BRUCE.
    EDWD. BREDY.
    ———(?) FISHER.

Recorded in Will Book 2, page 10.

EDWARD GRIFFIN'S WILL.

IN THE NAME OF GOD AMEN, The Twenty Seaventh Day of aprel, 1753. I, Edward Griffin, of the County of tyrrel, plantor, being Very Sick and weake in body, but of perfect mind and menory, thanks be given unto God Therefore, Calling unto mind the mortality of my body, and Knowing that it is appointed for all men once to Die, Dow Make and ordaine this my Last will and testament, that is to say, principally and first of all, I Give and Recommend my Soul into the hands of God that Gave it, and my body to the Earth to be buried in Decent Christian buriall at the Discretion of my Executors, Nothing Doubting but at the Generall Resurrection I shall Receive the same again by the mighty power of God; and as touching such worldly Estate wherewith it has pleased God to bless me in this Life, I Give and Demise and Dispose of the Same in the following manner and forme:

Imprimis, I Give and bequeath unto my two Soons, Edward Griffin and William Griffin, a sertain Tract of Land in beartey County, Lying on a branch Called Croofoot branch, and Joining Mikell Hills Line, the Same to be Equalley Devided betwene my two Soons at the Discretion of two persons appointed by them or my Selfe, so that each of them Ma have an Equall part of the Good Land.

Item. I Dow Likewise Lend to my beloved wife, Grace Griffin, the servis of my Negro man Roben as long as she Remains a Widdoe, and if the Negro Should prove Obstinant and Cross in the family, that they Can not Rule him, that then, he shall be sold and the moneys arising by that Sale to be Equalley Devided betwene my son, Edward Griffin, and my Soon, William Griffin, and my youngest Daughter, Ann Griffin.

Item. I Give and bequeath to my Soon, Edward Griffin, my Gun and Cutlass, and one yearling horse to his proper use for Ever.

Item. I Give and bequeath to my two Daughters, one Mare Called the old mare to Mary and Sarah Griffin, the mare is branded with the brand 22 to their uses forever.

Item. I Give to my Soon, William Griffin, my Daughter, Ann Griffen, one mare Called the young mare male and female, to their use for Ever, Excepting the first Mare Colt the Young mare Rase, to Rhoda Coopers, to her proper use for Ever.

Item. I Dow Likewise Give to my son, Edward Griffin, one horse Colt wich Came of the mare branded 22.

Item. I Give unto John Griffin, ye Soon of Sarah Griffin, one Yearling heffor to be marked for him in the Spring 1754, to Run on male and female, to his use for Ever.

Item. I Give and bequeath to my Son, William Griffin and Ann Griffin, my youngest Daughter, Each of them one Iron Pott.

Item. I Give and bequeath to my Daughter, Elisabeth Cooper, my Loome and the Geare belonging, to hir for Ever.

Item. I Give and bequeath unto my beloved wife, Grace Griffin, all and Singuler my my household Goods not all Ready bequeathed, to hir Dispose During hir Life, and if any Remains at hir Death, to be Equaly Devided amongst my Children, one and all; and allso, I Give to my Wife my Riding horse to her use for Ever.

Item. I Give and bequeath unto my two Daughters, Mary Griffin and Sarah Griffin, the Benifit of a Note of hand of the Valew of twelve pounds, ten Shillings, Virginia monyy, to their sole use, benifit for Ever, and to be paid to them by Edward Cooper in the year 1757.

Ratifying and Confirming this to be my Last Will and testament and Dow hereby Constitute my well beloved brother, John Griffin, and Edward Cooper, to be my Lawfull Executors to this my last Will and Testament and Do hereby Utterly Disallow, Revoke and Disannul, all and Every other former testaments, wills, Legacies, and bequests, and Executors, by me in any wais named, Willed, and bequeathed, Ratifying and Confirming this and no Other to be my Last will and testament.

In Witness whereof, I have hereunto set my hand and Seale, the Day and year above Writen.

Sined, Sealed and Delivered in
the presents of us:

EDWARD GRIFFIN. (Seal)

Testis,

WILLIAM GARDNER, Jurat.
JOHN GRIFFIN.
EDWARD COOPER, Jurat.

TYREL COUNTY. ss.   March Court, 1754.

Then was the Within Will Duly Prov'd in Open Court by the Oaths of William Gardner, and Edwd. Cooper, Two of the Subscribing Witnesses thereto; and at the Same time John Griffin and Edward Cooper were Duly Qualified as Executors thereto, As the Law Directs. Ordered that the Honourable Jas. Murray, Esqr., Secr., have Notice thereof that Letters Testamentary Issue thereon Accordingly.

Testis. EVAN JONES, Clk. Cur.

Copied from Original Will, filed in the Office of the Secretary of State.

RICHARD GRIST'S WILL.

IN THE NAME OF GOD AMEN. I, Richard Grist, of the County of Beafort, In province of North Carolina, planter, being of a weak and Lo Condition of boddy, but of a sound mind and memory Praised be Allmighty God; but Caling to mind the uncertainty of This Life, and knowing that It is apointed for all men once to Die, do make, ordain, Constitute and apoint this to be my Last will and Testament, That is to Say, my Soul I Bequeath to God that Gave it to me, my Boddy I Commit to the Earth from whence It was taken To be Interred In a Christianl'ke maner at the Discretion of my Executors, nothing Doubting but at the Generall Resurection at the Last Day I Shal Receive The same again by the myty power of God; and now Touching such Worldly Goods as has been pleased God to Bless Me In this Life,

Principally and first of all I do order and Desire that all my Just Debts and my funerall Charges be fuly paid, Discharged and Satisfied, and Legeases paid, Which I Depose of In the following manner.

Item. To my well Beloved Wife, frances Grist, I Do Give and bequeath the use of one feather bed and furniture, and one bay horse Caled Robin, for and During her Widoohod.

Item. To my Daughter, frances Nouell, I Do Give and Bequeath one Shilling, Sterling monney of Great Britton, and no more.

Item. to my Son, John Grist, I do Give and Bequeath one hundred and fifty acres of Land at the Beginning, being part of a mesage or track of Land purchased by me; and one negroe man named Dublin, being now In the posesion of the aforesaid John Grist, and one negroe man named Dublin.

Item. to Elizabeth pinor, I Do Give and Bequeath one Cow and Calf.

Item. to my Grandaughter, mary Grist, I do Give and Bequeath one two year old hefer.

Item. to my son William Grist, I Do Give and Bequeath one negroe man named Quamana.

Item. to my Duaghter, Elisabeth Wall, I Do Give and Bequeath one negroe Wench or forty pounds proclatation Money, to be paid after the Decease my Beloved Wife, aforementioned.

Item. to my son, Richard Grist, I Do Give and Bequeath my manner plantation and forty five pounds, ten Shillings, proclation money, and one Gray horse Caled tobey.

The rest, Remainder and Residue of my Estate and Worldly Goods, Chatels, Tenements, negroe Slaves, Cattel, house hold Goods, and all other Goods and Chattels to me In any Wise Belonging or apertaining, It is my will should be Equally Devided Between my two sons, William and Richard Grist, aforementioned.

Farthermore, It is my will that my Legases afore mentioned, be Justly paid, the Rest, Remainder and Residue of my Estate and Worldly Goods not Given by Legases, my Beloved Wife, frances, should keep the Use During her Widoohod.

I Do nominate, Chose and apoint my Beloved wife, frances to Executrisse, and my Beloved son, William Grist, and my Beloved son, Richard Grist, to be Executors of this my Last Will and Testament,

RICHARD GRIST. (Seale)

Sined, Sealed, Published and Declared this first Day of June, In the year our Lord God Everlasting, one thousand, seven hundred, fifty and two In the presence off:

WILLIAM WILLIS,
WILLIAM LANIER,
The mark X of ELISABETH HILL.

BEAUFORT COUNTY. ss.

At a Court held for the said County, at the Court house in Bath Town on the second Tuesday in March, and 13 day of the same Month, Anno Domoq, 1753. Present his Majesty's Justices.

These are to certify, that William Willis, one of the subscribing Witnesses to the within Will appeared in Open Court & made Oath on the holy Evangelists, that he was present & saw Richard Grist Sign, Seal and Declare the within Insturment of writing to be his last Will & Testament, & That the said Richard Grist was at that time of Sound and disposing mind and Memory; and that he also saw William Lanier & Elizabeth Hill the other subscribing Witnesses, sign their names thereto at the same time

Then William Grist & Richard Grist Exors. of the said Will appeared in open Court & Took the Oath of an Exor. in due form. Whereupon I was Ordered by the said Court that Mr. Secretary have Notice thereof that Letters Testamentary Issue thereupon as the law directs.

Test. WILL ORMOND Cler. Cur.

Copied from the Original Will, filed in the Office of the Secretary of State

EDWARD HARE'S WILL.

IN THE NAME OF GOD AMEN. I, Edward Hare, of North Carolina, in Hertford County, Being in Perfect Sence and memory, I Do make and ordain this my Last Will and Testament, first I Give and Recommend my Soule to God that Gave it; and my Body I Commit to the Earth to be Buried in a Christianlike manner, and I am in hopes of a joyful Resurrection; and my Worldly Goods and Estate, I Give and Dispose of in the following manner and form:

Item. I Lend unto my Mother, Mary Hare, the Use and Profits of all my Lands and all my Negros, and all the Remainder Part of my Estate, Except money, for and During the Term of her Natural Life.

Item. After my mother, Mary Hares, Decease, I Give and Bequeath unto my Brother, Thomas Hare, one Negro man Named frank, and one Negro man named arthar, and one Negro man Named Ben, and one Negro Boy named Jo, and one Negro Boy named Dave, and one negro Boy named Sam and one Negro woman Named amy; and allso, all my Stock of Cattle, and all my Stock of Hogs, and all my Stock of Sheep and all my Stock of Horses, and all my Household furniture and a Debt that is Due to me from Colonel Benjn. Wynn. by bond, to him and his heirs and assigns.

Item. I Give and Bequeath unto Mary Hare, Daughter of Thomas Hare, one Negro Boy Named nimrood, to her and her heirs and assigns.

Item. I Give and Bequeath unto Wynne West, Daughter of Peter West, one Negro Girl Named Rachal, and one Par of Silver Sleave Buttons, and one Gold Brouch, to her and her Heirs and assigns.

Item. I Give and Bequeath unto my Sister, mary Burges, One Negro mand Named Isaac, and one Negro Boy Named Tom, to her and her heirs for Ever.

Item. I Give and Bequeath unto my Sister, ann Scost, one Negro man Named Bob, and one Negro Girl Named Daphny to her and her heirs for Ever.

Item. I Give to Luke Lewis, Son of John Lewis, the money that is Due to me from Jesse Barnes for the Hier of a hors, the Said Barnes is to Pay one Shilling Pr. Day, Virginia money, for Evry Day he hath him in use, the said Money to be Delivered to the Said Luke Lewis, by my Executors hear after mentioned.

Item. I Give and Bequeath unto Lucretia Hare, Daughter of Bryan Hare, four Dollars in Silver, to her and her heirs and assigns.

Item. I Give and Bequeath unto Edward Bryan Hare, Son of Bryan Hare, one Gun and one Ewe and Lamb, to him and his heirs and assigns.

Item. I Give and Bequeath unto John Pipken, Son of Isaac Pipken, one Gun, to him and his heirs and assigns.

Item. I Give and Bequeath unto (Bra) Warren, Son of Joseph Warren, one Par of Pistols and Holstens, to him and his heirs and assigns; and also one Brinded Three year old Heffer to him and his heirs and assigns.

Item. I Give and Bequeath unto Eff Lewis, Son of John Lewis, one Red Three year old Heffer, to him and his heirs and assigns.

Item. I Give and Bequeath unto John Miller, one Large Dressed Buck Skeen and ——Pounds Proclamation Money, to him and his heirs and assigns.

Item. I Give and Bequeath unto Edward Warren, one Large Church Bibel, and one four year old Stear, to him and his heirs and assigns.

* * * (torn) Bequeath unto my Brother, John Hare, one Silver Tancard, to him and his heirs and assigns forever.

Item. I Give and Bequeath unto Mills Lewis, Sone of John Lewis, Two Silver Dollars, to him and his heirs and assigns.

Item. I Give and Bequeath unto William Warren, Son of Edward Warren, Deceased, Two * * * (torn) Dollars, to him and his heirs and assigns.

Item. I Give and Bequeath unto Phillip Lewis, Son of John Lewis, Two Silver Dollars, to him and his hirs and assigns.

Item. I Give and Bequeath unto John Gatteleen Two, Silver Dollars, to him and his heirs and assigns.

Item. I Give and Bequeath unto Isaac Pipken, one Pistol in Gold, and one Brown Holland Coat, to him and his heirs and assigns.

Item. I Give and Bequeath unto Jesse Barnes, Two Silver Dollers, to him and his heirs and assigns.

Item. I Give and Bequeath unto Francis Speight, Son of Joseph Speight, Tenn Shillings Cash, to him and his heirs and assigns.

Item. I Give and Bequeath unto Henry Speight, Son of Joseph Speight, Teen Shillings Cash, to him and his heirs and assigns.

Item. I Give and Bequeath unto John Goodman, Son of William Goodman, Two Silver Dollars, to Him and his heirs and assigns.

Item. I Give and Bequeath unto Benjn. Wynne, Junr. Teen Pound Proclamation Money, to him and his heirs and assigns.

Item. I Give and Bequeath unto Solomon King, forty Pistreens Silver, to him and his heirs and assigns.

Item. I Give and Bequeath unto William West, Son of Peter West, Two Pounds, Proclamation money, to him and his heirs and assigns.

Item. I Give and Bequeath unto my Brother, Thomas Hare one Large Trunk and—— Small Trunk, and all that is in them to him and his heirs and assigns.

Ite. I Give and Devise unto my Brother, Thomas Hare all may Land With all its appurtinances to him and his heirs and assigns for Ever—and also I Give and Bequeath unto my Brother, Thomas Hare, all the Remainder Part of my Estate to him and his heirs and assign forever.

Lastly. I Constitute, make and ordain my Brother, Thomas Hare, my Soul Executor of this my Last Will and Testament I hear by Revoke all other former Wills Executed by me any ways before this time Named, and Confirming this and no other to be my Last Will and Testament.

In Witness Whereof, I have hear unto Set my hand and Seal, this Sixteenth Day of May, one Thousand, Seven Hundred and Seventy Two.

EWD. HARE. (Seal)

Signed Sealed and Pronounced and Delivered by the Said Edward Hare as his Last Will and Testament in the Presence of us:
Interlined befor Signed
SOLOMON KING.
JOHN LEWIS.
ISAAC PIPKIN.
EDWARD WARREN.

NORTH CAROLINA. NEW BERN, 22d. April, 1777.

I, Richard Caswell, Esqr., Governor, &c., of the State of North Carolina Do hereby Certify that Isaac Pipkin, one of the Subscribing Witnesses to the within last Will & Testament of Edward Hare, Deceased, this day appeared before me and being Sworn upon the Holy Evanjelist Ddeclared, that he saw the Testator sign, Seal, publish & declare the said Writing to be & Contain his Last Will & Testament; that he also saw Solomon King, John Lewis and Edward Warren, Sign as concuring Witnesses with him, but that he cannot declare the Testator was of Sound Mind; that John Miller was present when the said Will was executed, who being also Sworn declares that He verily believes from many circumstances which he mentioned that the said Edward Hare was at the Time of the execution of the said Will of Sound & Disposing Mind & Memory.

Thomas Hare also appeared & Qualified as Executor to the said Will. The Secretary is therefore required to issue Letters Testamentory Accordingly.
Rd. Caswell.

Copied from Original Will, filed in the Office of the Secretary of State.

JOHN HARRELL'S WILL.

In the Name of God Amen, the Eight day of November, 1755. I, John Harrell, jun., of Bertie County, in the Province of North Carolina, being Very Sick and Weak in Body but of Perfect mind and memory, thanks be to God therefore, Calling to mind the mortality of my Body, and Knowing that it is appointed for all Men Once to Die, do make and Ordain this my Last Will and Testament, that is to Say, Principally, and first of all, I Give and Recommend my Soul into the hands of God that gave it; and my Body I recommend to the Earth to be Buried in a Decent Christian Burial at the Discretion of my Executor, nothin Doubting but at the General Resurrection to Receive the same again by the mighty Power of God; and as Touching my Worldly Estate, I Give, Demise and Dispose of the same in The following Manner and form:

Imprimus. I Give and Bequeath to my Well beloved Son, George Harrell, to him and his Heirs for Ever, One Negro boy Named Cato, and one Mare and Two Colts, and one horse and Three Cows, and Two Calves, and Three Two Years old Heffers, and One Year Old Steer, and all the Hoggs that Are of his Mark, Except two Grown Sows, all Which Creatures are Called his. I also give and Bequeath to the Above said George Harrell, to him and his Heirs for Ever, a Certain Peice or Parcel of Land lying between Thomas Williams and John Rhodes, beginning at a Pine my Own and Thomas Williamsis Corner, then along a line of Marked Trees To John Rhodses Corner, Near a Place known by the name of Rhodses hogg Pen, then along Rhodes's Line a Cross the road to a Corner of Rhods's, then along his line to a Read Oak John Rhodes's Corner, and formerly was Robert McClarys Corner, then along Rhodes's line to the Center of Three White Oaks near Burks branch, then along my line and Thomas Williames to the first Station, Containing One Hundred and Thirty five Acres, more or Less.

Item. I Give and Bequeath to my four Sons, Vizt: George, and Jesse, and Elisha, and Benjamin, to them and their Heirs for Ever, a Certain Peice of Parcel or Land lying in the Low Grounds of the river, Beginning at a Gumb in a Swamp, known by the Name of Conaquina Swamp, then along Norflets road to a live Oak in the Marsh to Norflets line, then along Norflets line to James Browns Corner, then along Browns line to the Swamp aforesaid, then up the Water Course of the sd. Swamp to the first Station, Containing One Hundred Acres, more or less, to be Equally Divided Between my four sons aforsaid, at their Coming to Age,

Item. I Give and Bequeath to my Three Sons, Jesse, and Elisha, and Benjamin, to them and their Heirs for Ever, a Certain Peice or Parcel of Land beginning at Thos. Williamses and Nicholas Skinners, then along Williamsis Line to a Pine Williams's and my Corner, then on the North side of Cashi, then along the afsd. George Harrells line to John Rhodes's Corner, then along Rhodes's line to Samuel Andrews's Line, then along Andrews's Line to James Browns and my Corner, then along Browns and my line a White Oak On the North side of Cashi, James Browns Corner, then along Browns and my line to my Corner, a White Oak, then along my Old Patent to against James Seays Corner at a White Oak in a New Patent line of mine, then along the said line to my Own and James Seays Corner in Richard Williams's Line, then along Williams's Line to John Glasses Corner, then along Glasses line to little John Harrells Corner, then along his Line to Nicholas Skinners Corner, then along Skinners line to the first Station, Containing Seven Hundred and Seventy five Acres, more or Less, to be Divided Between my Three Sons aforesaid after the following Manner: to Jesse Harrell a Peice of Land binding On James Seays's Line, then along my line to James Browns line, then along my line and Browns aCross the Willow branch to the North side, then a line of Marked Trees from the aforesaid Branch to a Place known by the name of the Saw Scaffold, from thence a Continued Line of Marked Trees to a Pine, a Marked Tree, standing John Glasses line, then Down Glasses Line to Richard Williams's Line, then down Williams's line to James Seays, aforesaid, Containing Two Hundred and Twenty Acres, more or less; To Elisha Harrell, a Peice of Land Binding on the aforesaid Jesses line, then along my line and James Browns to a White Oak, Browns Corner then, along a line of Marked Trees to a Place known by the name of John Skinners Spring, in the Mill branch, then Down the Water Course of the Branch aforesaid to Nicholas Skinners and Little John Harrells Corner, then a ong my line and John Harrells aforesaid to John Glass's Line, then along Glass's line to a Pine the aforsaid Jess's Corner in Glass's Line aforesaid, Containing Two hundred and Twenty

Acres more or Less; To Benjamin Harrell, my Plantation on Where I now live & all my Land joyning to it, Except What I have already Disposed of to my Three Sons aforesaid, Containing Three Hundred and Thirty five Acres, more or Less.

Item. I leave my Mill and all my Land joyning to it for the use of my four Sons aforesaid, and if my Executors and my Sons that is of Age shall at any time think it Proper that the said Mill and land Should be sold, that my Executors shall Act in Behalf of my Sons Which are not of Age, and shall sell the said Mill and Land, and if Either Peice of land which I have left to my Three Sons, Vizt: Jesse, Elisha, and Benjamin shall Prove or be thought by my Executors not so Good as the Other two, or if any Two of the aforesaid peices shall Prove not so Good as the Other one, that they shall be made up to an Equal Value out of the money Which the aforesaid Mill and land shall be sold for, and if any of the Money afsd. shall be left, to be Equally Divided Between my Wife and all my Children.

Item. I Give and Bequeath to my four Sons aforesaid, to them and their Heirs for Ever, all my Smith's Tools, and neither of them shall buy or Sell their Part of them till they shall Come to Age.

Item. I give and Bequeath to my Son, Jessee, to him and his Heirs for Ever, my Negro man Sam, and one Bed and furniture, and One Young mare, and Two Cows, and Calves, and all the Hoggs that are Called his Hoggs, and One Iron Pot.

Item. I Give and Bequeath to my Daughter, Mary, to her and her Heirs for Ever, one Small Black mare and Colt, and One Bed and furniture, and three Cows and Calves, at the Day of her Marriage, and one Iron Pot.

Item. I Give and Bequeath unto my Son, Elisha, to him and his Heirs for Ever, One Bed and furniture, and four Cows and Calves, and five Sows and Pigs, And One Iron Pot, and one Young likely Mare of Three or four Years Old.

Item. I Give and Bequeath to my Son, Benjamin, to him and his Heirs for Ever, One Negro Boy named Ned, and one Bed and furniture, and four Cows and Calves, and One Likely Young horse of Three or four Years Old, and five Sows and Pigs, and one Iron Pot, and the Second Child that my Negro Girl Jude shall bring.

Item. I Give and Bequeath to my Son, George, to him and his Heirs for Ever, The first Child that my Negro Woman Phillis shall bring, and one Bed and Furniture, and One Rifled Gun, and One Iron Pot.

Item. I Give and Bequeath to my Son, jesse, to him and his heirs for Ever, the Second Child that my Negro Woman Phillis shall Bring, and my Old Gun.

Item. I Give and Bequeath to my Son, Elisha, to him and his Heirs for Ever, the first Child that my Negro Girl Jude shall bring, and my Negro Woman Phillis.

Item. I give and Bequeath to Daughter, Mary, to her and her Heirs for Ever, my Negro Girl Jude.

Item. I lend unto my Well Beloved Wife, Mary, all my Land and Negroes and Stock and household Goods during her natural Life, after her Decease, to be Equally Divided between all my Children at the Discretion of my Executors, I also, Constitute, make and ordain my Son, George Harrell, and my Brother, Jesse Harrell, and my Brother, Israel Hardis Harrell, and Richard Williams, Thomas Williams and William Andrews and John Rhodes, my Sole Executors of this my Last Will and Testament, and Every thing mentioned in this my Last Will and Testament to be fully settled and Determined by my afore mentioned Executors, and I Do hereby utterly Disalow, revock and Disanull, all and every other former Testament, Wills, legacies, and Bequeaths and Executors by me in any Ways before named, Willed and Bequeathed, ratifying and Confirming this and no Other to be my Last Will and Testament.

In Witness Whereof I have hereunto set my hand and Seal, the Day and Year above Written.

JNO. HARRELL (Seal)

Signed, Sealed, Published, Pronounced, and Declared by the sd. Jno. Harrell, as his Last Will and Testament in the Presence of us the Subscribers:
    THOMAS WILLIAMS.
    WILLIAM ANDREWS.
    his
    JOHN Z SKINNER.
    mark

BERTIE COUNTY. ss.   Jany. Court, 1756.

The Before Written Will Was Exhibited into Court by Jesse Harrell and Israel Hardy Harrell, Two of the Executors therein Named, and Proved by the Oaths of William Andrews and John Skinner, Two of the Subscribing Witness's thereto, and at the same time the said Executors were Qualifyed &c, Which was ordered to be Certifyed.

Test. BENJN. WYNNS, Clk. Cur.

Recorded in Will Book 7, page 164.

JOHN HARRELL'S WILL.

NORTH CAROLINA, BERTIE COUNTY.

IN THE NAME OF GOD AMEN. I, John Harrell, of the County and Province aforesd., being of Body but of Perfect and Sound Mind and Memory (Thanks be to God), Do make, Ordain, Constitute and Appoint this my last Will and Testament, Hereby Revoking and Disannulling all others heretofore by me made, & this only to be made & held as my last Will and Testament, in manner and form following &cᵃ:

Imprimis. I Leave to my Beloved Wife, Grace Harrill, Dureing her Natural life or Widowhood, the Use of the Plantation whereon I now live, & all the Land thereunto Belonging, and all my Stock of Horses, Cattle, hoggs & Sheep, & all my Houshold furniture & Plantation utensils; and the use of the following Negroes, (to wit) Patt, Bett, Rachel, Sambo, Jemmy, Jenny, Phillis, & Jack, and after her Decease or Marriage, to be Given & Divided in the following Legacies.

Item. I Give and Bequeath to my Son, Jesse Harril, his heirs and Assigns for ever, the Plantation whereon I Now live, and all the Land thereunto belonging, and two Negroes (to wit) Patt & Jack.

Item. I Give and Bequeath to my Son, David Harrell, his heirs and Assigns for ever, the Plantation whereon he now lives, Containing One hundred & Sixty Acres, being part of the Tract of Land I bought of Mr Thomas Barker, and One Negroe Girl Nam'd Fillis.

Item. I Give & Bequeath to my Son, Josiah Harrill, his heirs & Assigns for ever, the Plantation whereon he now lives, containing One hundred & Sixty Acres, being part of the Tract of Land I bought of Mr. Thomas Barker; and One Negroe Wench Named Bett.

Item. I Give and Bequeath to my Son, Ezekiel Harrill, his heirs and Assigns forever, the Plantation whereon he now lives, Containing One hundred & Sixty Acres, being part of the Tract of Land I Bought of Mr. Thomas Barker, and One Negroe Boye Named Jemmy, and all the Cattle that is of his Deceas'd Brother Hardys Mark.

Item. I give and Bequeath to my Grandson, Esias Harrill, son of Esias Harrell, Dece'd, the Plantation whereon Jonathan Spivey now lives who married the Widow of the said Esias Harrill, Deceas'd, it being part of the Tract of Land I Bought of Mr Thos. Barker, Which sd. Land I give to my sd. Grandson, Esias Harrill, his heirs and Assigns for ever.

Item. I give and Bequeath to my Grand Daughter, Sarah Harrill, Daughter of Esias Harrell, Dec's'd, one Negroe Girl named Jenny, only, Reserving that my Grandson, Esias Harrill above Mentioned, shall have the first Child that the sd. Negroe Girl Jenny brings and Raises to the Age of Two years old. and in case my said Grand Daughter, Sarah Harrill, die without Lawfull Issue of her Body, then my Will and Desire is that the said Negroe Girl Jenny and he Increase, fall to my sd. Grandson, Esias Harrill, his heirs and assigns forever.

Item. I give and Bequeath to my Grand Children, the Children of my Son, John Harrill, Deceased, the Sum of Thirty Pounds, Virginia Currancy, to be paid after the Decease of my Wife, Grace, and then to be Equally Divided among them share and share alike.

Item. I give and bequeath to my Grand Children, the Children of Sarah Williams, Dec'd, the Sum of Twenty four Pounds, Virginia Currancy, to be paid by my Exors. after the Decease of my Wife, Grace, and then to be Equally Divided between my sd. Grand Child'n Share and Share alike.

Item. My Will and Desire is that my Two Sons, David & Josiah Harrill, Pay the above Sums of Money to my Grand Children above Mentioned, and that my son, David, for Paying his part of the Money shall have one Negroe Girl named Rachel, for which he is to pay Thirty Pounds Virginia Money & my Son Josiah shall have One Negroe Boy Named Sambo for which he is to pay Twenty four Pounds, like money, only in Case the sd. Negroes or either of them shall die before my Wife, Grace, dies then, and in that Case, the sd. Money is to be paid out of my whole Estate, and my sd. Grand Children shall allow a Proportionable abatement with the Rest of my Children.

Item. I give and Bequeath the use of my Copper Still, to my four Sons, only, that they shall still all their Mother Liquor during her life, and after her Decease, I give the sd. Still to be Equally Divided Between my said four sons & their Heirs

Item. I give and Bequeath my whole Estate that is not above Given in Legacies, After the Decease of my Wife, Grace to be Equally Divided Between my four sons, Jessee, David Josiah, and Ezekiel Harrill, and there Heirs & Assigns forever

Lastly, I Nominate, Constitute & Appoint my three Sons Jessee, David, & Josiah Harrill, Executors to this my last Will and Testament.

In Witness whereof, the sd. John Harrill hath hereunto set his hand and Seal, the first Day of November, Anno Dom., 1756.

JOHN HARRELL. (Seal)

Sign'd Seal'd Published & Declared by the sd. John Harrill, to be his Last Will and Testament in Presence of us:
Witness. WM. WILLIAMS.
EDWARD TOOLE, Jurat.
JONATHN. X TOOLE his mark, Jurat.

Memorandum, Octr. 10th., 1758.

Whereas, in this my Will above Written, I have not given any Legacies to Elizth. Spivey, formerly wife to my Son, Esias Harrill Deceas'd, nor to Thomas Williams, who Married my Daughter, Sarah Harrill, now Deceas'd, nor to Mary Harrill now widow of my son John Harrill, deceas'd; But what I intended for my said Deceas'd Children in case they had lived, I have given to my Grand Children, the Children of my said Deceas'd Children above mentioned and I do by these presents Declare that it is my Will and Desire that Eliz. Spivey, Thomas Williams nor Mary Harrill shall have no part of my Estate of any Kind mentioned in this my last Will and Testament above written.

JOHN HARRELL.

Witness. WM. WILLIAMS.
EDWARD TOOLE, Jurat.
JONATHAN TOOLE, Jurat.

BERTIE COUNTY, SS.   April Court, 1759.

The Annexed Will and Testament of John Harrell, Decd, with the Codicil thereto, was Exhibited into Court by Jesse Harrell and Josiah Harrell, two of the Executors therein appointed, and Proved by the Oaths of Edward Toole and Jonatham Toole, two of the Subscribing Witnesses thereto, and at the same time the same Exors were duly Qualifyed. Which was Ordered to be Certifyed.

Test. BENJN. WYNNS Cler. Cur.

Copied from Original Will, filed in the Office of the Secretary of State.

JOHN HARRIS' WILL.

IN THE NAME OF GOD AMEN. I, Jno Harris, in ye County of Albemarle, in ye precinct of Chowan, in ye province of North Carolina, planter, being sick & weak in body, but of perfect sound mind & memory, Doe make this my last will & Testimony, revokeing all other wills, verbal or writeing, made before by me. I Commit my Soul To almighty God that Gave itt me; & my body to ye Dust from whence itt came, to be Decently buried according to ye rules of ye Christian burial, in full & certain hopes of ye Glorious resurrection att ye last day; & as for all my personal & real Estate wch itt hath pleased God to Endew me withall I bequeith & bestowe as followeth, after my Debts is paid & my funeral Expences is Discharged.

I Give & bequeith unto Harris, ye Son of Sarah Tiner, ye plantation whereon I now Dwell & all ye land belonging to itt, after my wifes Decease, when he shall Come to ye Age of twenty one years, to him ye sd. Harris, & to ye heirs of his Body lawfully begotten for ever, not to Sell any part or parcel w'tsoever, Likewise, I Give unto Harris, ye Son of Sarah Tiner, my Gunn & also my proper marke after my Decease, which is a crope & Slite in ye right year & a swallow forke in ye left yeare.

I Give & bequeitt unto William, ye son of Sarah Tiner, two plantations leying on ye head of Machacomack Creek, call by ye name of ye holes, with all ye land thereunto belonging, to ye sd. William, & the heirs of his body lawfully begotten for ever, to be possessed when he shall Come to ye Age of twenty one years, not to Sell no pt. nor parcel of it w'tsoever; & if any one of these Sons of Sarah Tiner, Either Harris or William, Dye before they Come to ye Age of twenty one years without heirs of their Body lawfully begotten, then it is my Desire ye land of him that Dyes Shall to Sarah, ye Daughter of Sarah Tiner, for a legace to ye said Sarah & to ye heirs of her body lawfully begotten for ever; & if ye said Sarah, ye Daughter of Sarah Tiner, Dye without heirs lawfully begotten, then ye land to fall to ye son that's living & to ye heirs of his body lawfully begotten for Ever. Likewise, I Give unto Sarah, ye Daughter of Sarah Tiner, one young Gray mare runing in rockahock neck, with all her Increase, to ye sd. Sarah & her heirs for Ever.

I Give & bequeith unto Sarah Tiner one plantation & all ye tract of land belonging to itt, lying in Rockahock neck, is nowne by ye name of Jno. fryers, to ye sd. Sarah Tiner & her heirs for Ever; & as for my personal Estate, my stock & housall Goods I bestow as followeth:

I Give & bequeith unto my loving wife, Mildred Harris, ye one half of my Estate During her life; & all ye rest of my Estate moveables & Immoveables, I Give & bequeith as legace unto Harris & William, ye sons of Sarah Tiner, to be equally & farely devided between them ye sd, Harris & William when they Shall arive to ye age of Eighteen years.

& I Doe here Impute Constitute & appoint my true & Trusty friends, Jno Mixon & Sarah Tiner, to be my whole & Sole Exectr. & Extrx. of this my last will & Testamt.

As wittness hereof, I have fixed my hand & Seal this 16th(?) Day of December, 1711.

JOHN X HARRIS

Signed Sealed & Delivered in ye p'esence of us:
  EDWARD E PATCHET.
  JOHN X WELLS.
  MARY M TINER.

Recorded in Will Book 2, page 48.

HUMPHREY HARRINGTON'S WILL.

IN YE NAME OF GOD AMEN, ye Second Day of November, in ye year of our Lord, 1713. I, Humphrey Harrington, of North Carolina, in perquomons Precinct, Black Smith, being very sick & weak in body, but of perfect mind & memory, thanks be Given to God therefore, calling to mind ye mortality of my Body & knowing it is appointed for men once to dye, doe make & ordain this my last will & Testament, that is to say principally & first of all; I Give and recommend my Soul into ye hands of God that gave it, hopeing through ye Merits, Death & passion of my Saviour Jesus Christ To have full & free pardon & forgiveness of all my sins, & to inherit Everlasting life; And my Body I commit to ye Earth, to be decently buried at ye discretion of my Executrix hereafter named, nothing doubting but at ye Genll. resurrection I Shall receive ye same again by ye mighty power of God; & as touching such worldly Estate as it hath pleased God to bless me with in this life, I demise & dispose of ye same in ye following manner & forme, that is to say:

I will that all those debts & duties as I doe owe in right or Conscience, To any manner of person, or persons, whatsoever shall be well & truely contented & paid, or ordained to be paid, in Convenient time after my decease, by my Executrix hereafter named.

I Give & bequeith unto my daughter, Ann, my Plantation that I now live on, with one hundred and twenty of land, & to ye heirs of Body lawfully begotten, & She to be posesed at ye age of Sixteen years.

I Give & bequeith Unto my daughter in law, Ann Majour one hundred & twenty acres Joying to ye aforesd. Plantation of a Tract of land of 340 Acres, & to ye heirs of her body lawfully begotten.

I give unto Elizabeth Major, whom I have taken to be my wife, whom I likewise Constitute, make & ordaine my onely & Sole Executrix of this my last will & Testamt., by her freely to be posses'd & enjoyed, & I doe hereby utterly disallow, Revoke & disannul all & every other Testaments, will & legaces beqts. & Exts. by me in any ways before this time named, willed & bequeithed, Ratifying & Confirming this & noe other to be my last will & Testament.

in witness whereof, I have hereunto Set my hand & Seal, ye Day & ye year above written.
                                          HUMPHREY HARRINGTON.

Signed, Sealed, published, Pronounced & declared bye sd. Humphrery Harrington, as his last will & Testament in ye presents of ye Subscribers, Vizt:
    RICHARD MORRIS.
    FRANCIS P. THOMAS.

Recorded in Will Book 2, page 18.

THOMAS HARVEY'S WILL.

In the Name of God Amen. I, Thomas Harvey, of ye County of Albemarle, in ye Province of North Carolina, Esqr. being of sound and perfect memory, but considering ye un certainty of this life, Doe make and Publish this my Last Wil and Testament as followeth, Viz: I Humbly render my Sou unto Almighty God my Creator whensoever he shall in hi Mercy call me out of this transitory life, Stedfastly beleevin ye free remission of my Sins through ye pr'tious Meritts o Jesus Christ my Lord and my Redeemer; And my Body I giv to ye Ground from whence it was taken, decently to be burie at ye discretion of my Executrix hereafter named.

And I doe hereby appoint and make my beloved Wife, Saral Harvey, Executrix of this my last will and testament. Willin that all my just Debts be paid as soon as possibly may be afte my death; And ye rest of my Personal Estate, I give one thir part to my Sd. Wife, and ye rest to be devided between my Son Thomas Harvey, and my Daughter, Mary Harvey; And i it shall happen that my Sd. Wife, shall after my decease bea to me a Child, my Will is that Such my poshume Child shal have equal share of ye two thirds of my p'sonel estate w'th m son and Daughter above named; and my will is that ye part or portion above bequeathed to my Children, shall be pai to them respectively, viz: to my Son or Sons at ye age o twenty one yeares, and to my daughter or daughters at y day of their Marriage or age of twenty one yeares, w'ch shal first happen; and if it shall hapen that one or any of my Childre shall depart this life before ye time hereby appointed for th receiving of his or their part or portion above mentioned the I Will that the Survivor or Survivors Shall have ye Whole; an if all my Children die as aforesaid, then I Give all my p'sone Estate to my said loving Wife, Sarah Harvey.

Ite. I give, Devise and Bequeath my Land and plantatio which I purchased of Roger Snell, and my land called Faulk Point, containing in all five hundred acres of land, w'th y appurtenance, lying upon Pequimons River, in ye Count aforesaid, unto my Daughter, Mary Harvey, and to ye heir of her Body for ever, and for want of Such heirs to my Son Thomas Harvey, and ye Heirs of his Body for ever, and fo want of Such heirs to such issue as is hereby appointed.

Item. I give, Devise and Bequeath my plantation whereo I live w'th five hundred acres of Land thereunto adjoying, w't all and Singular, ye appurtinances unto my Loving Wife, Saral Harvey abovenamed, for and During the Terme of her natural life, and I will that the houses and fences thereupon be Kep in good and Sufficient repair.

Item. I Give, Devise and Bequeath my Plantation Called ye Quarter, w'th all my land not Bequeathed and the Remainder of ye Plantacon and land whereon I Live, to my Son, Thomas Harvey, & to ye Heirs of his Body for ever, and for want of Such Heirs to my Daughter, Mary, and the heirs of her body for ever. And if it shall happen that there remain none heires of ye body of my said son or Daughter then I give, Devise and Bequeath all my lands and tementents above said (reserving to my Wife her estate for life as is above mentioned), unto ye next heirs of my own body if any Such Shall be, And for want thereof to my Nephew, Thomas Harvey, Son of my Brother, Richard Harvey, late of London, Currior, and to ye Heires Male of his Body for ever; and for want of such heires to his Brother, John Harvey, and ye Heires Male of his body for ever; and for Want of Such heires to ye Eldest Son of my Brother Robert Harvey, of ye Heath in Sinter field Parish, in Warwick Shire, and to ye Heires male of his Body for Ever; and for Want of Such heires to his next eldest Brother and the Heires male of his brother; and for want of Such heirs to ye next Brother in like manner, and if noe Brother remain to ye next heir Male of my Sd. Brother, Robert Harvey, forever. (and)

And it is my Will that if I shall have more Children than my Son and Daughter w'thin mentioned, then my personal estate to be devided equally between my Wife and Children.

And I doe Give to my Sd. Loveing Wife, Sarah, my Silver Tankerd over and above her part of my personal estate. And I Doe hereby make void all wills by me formerly made.

In testimony Whereof, I have hereunto Sett my hand and Seale, ye 31 day of March, Ano. Domi., 1696.
    THOMAS HARVEY, (Coat of Arms on Seal)
Signed, Sealed and Published
in presence of:
    Signum
  HENRY HA NORMAN
  ROBERT FENDALL.
  JOHN PIERT,
  W. GLOVER.

Item. A Codicil. I do make & appoint Coll. William Wilkinson, Executor in my room as I am an Executor unto the Estate of John Harvey, Esqr., deceased, and this I do ordain to be my last will to be joyned to the above, written March 23d. Ano Dom., 1698/9.
    THOMAS HARVEY (Coat of Arms on Seal)
Signed and published in the
presence: RICHD. FRENCH.
  RUTH LUKER.
        November, y't 2d, 1699.
The Coddicell proved by the Oaths of Mr. Rich. French & Mrs. Ruth Luker before me.   HENDERSON WALKER.

Copied from Original Will filed in the Office of the Secretary of State.

THOMAS HARVEY'S WILL.

NORTH CAROLINA, SS.

IN THE NAME OF GOD AMEN. The 10th. Day of Aprell, in ye year of our Lord, one Thousan, Seven hundred & Twenty nine I, Thomas Harvey, of ye precinck of perquimens & Province o: North Carolina, Gent., Being of perfickt mind & memory Thanks be to Allmitey God. Thare fore, Calling unto mind ye Mortality of my Body & knowing yt it is apointed once for al men to Dye, do make & ordain this my last Will & Testement, yt is To Say, Principally & ferst of all, I Recomend my Soul into ye hands of God yt Gave it; & my Body I Recomend to ye Earth to be buread in a Decent & Cristeon maner, at ye Des cration of my Exetors. Hareafter named, nothing Doubting but Genarll. Resuration, I shall Receive ye Same aGain by ye Power of Allmitey God; and as Touching Such Worldly Estate wherewith it hath pleased God to bless me with in ys. Life,] Give & Demise & Dispose of ye Same in ye following maner & Forme:

Imprimis. I will & Desire yt as Sune as my Death, all my Just Debts yt in write or Conchinnces I owe To Eney persor or persons be Deschard. & payd, with Justes.

Item. I Give to my Dear beloved wife, Elizabeth Harvey ye one thuerd part of my personell Estate, to be Equally Taker out of ye Hole, both in quantity & Qualety of ye Same, after all my Just Debts are payd. But all Legeaseys to be payd out of ye other Two Thurdes of my Estate.

Item. I Give to my Beloved wife aforesaid, my Negro Mar Called Jamey.

Item. I Give To my beloved Wife aforesaid, My Plantatior whareon I now Live, dureing her Natrall Life & at hur desse. To be Injoyd by my soun, Thomas Harvey, and his aires for Ever. My Will is, That ye Said Thos. Harvey, shall not be debard or hindread from bulding or leiving on Eney Part of ye Lands so Sune as he Shall arive to ye Age of Twenty one yers, Ye Clear'd land & Dwelling house Exceptd.

Item. I Give To my Soun, Thomas Harvey, my Negro Boy Callead Ned, and my Negro Gall, Called Dinear, to be Injoyd by him & his ares for Ever.

Item. I Give to my Soun, John Harvey, my Negro Boy called Frank, and my Negro Gall, called Marey ann, To be Injoyed by him & his ares for Ever.

Item. I give to my Son, Benjn. Harvey, my Negro Boy Callead Willcock & my Negro Gall Callead Hannah, To be injoyd by him & his ares for Ever.

Item. I Give to my Soun, Miles Harvey, my Negro Boy Callead Jack & my Negro Gall Called filles, & my Negro Gal Callead Pegg, To be inJoyed by him & his ares for Ever.

Item. I Give To my fore Souns, namely: Thomas, John, Benj'n. & Miles, My fore plantions or Pasealls of Land; To my Soun Thos. Harvey, My Plantion whareon I now live, after his Mothers Desese as above said, To be in Joyd for Ever; To my soun, John Harvey, My Plantion, Callead ye Quarter, with ye Lands beLoing thare to, To be inJoyd by him & his ares for Ever; To my Son, Bejn. Harvey, my Plantion Called Foleks Pint, with the Lands belonging thareto, To be Injoyd by him & his ares for Ever; To my Soun, Miles Harvey, all my Lands on Chowan River, ling in Rockahock neck, ye lands I Bought of Samuel Woodard, To be InJoyd by him & his ares for Ever.

Item. I give to my Brother, Miles Gale, of Boston, in Newengland, one Quarter or forth part of the Slupe Called The two Brothers, whare at this Time I own Three partes & he one.

Item. I Give To Each of Collo. Robad Wests Dafters, which he had by my Sester, marey Harvey, Namely: Mathe, Sarey & Marey, one Gold Ring, To Each of them, to ye valey of fortey Shillings Each. And I likewise Give to my two Sisters, Elizabeth Clayten, and Penelopy Lettell, Wife of Mr. Willm. Lettell one Gold Ring apes, or fifty Shillings each.

Item. I Give to The Children, or so many of them as is now Living, Belonging to ye Wife of James Settersen, & ye Wife of Willm. Tetterten, fortey Shillings a pese, or to ye Valey of ye Said Money in what my Exceters. hareafter named Shall Tink fitt.

Item. I Give to John Cole, Soun of John Coles, of Nancesmun in Virieny, one tree year old Hores.

Item. I Give to Josway Wherey, Soun of Antoney Wherey, one Bed and Furneture, To ye Valey of Tenn pounds.

Item. I Give to Elizabeth Wherey, Dafter of Antoney Wherey, one feather Bed, To ye Valey of Ten pounds, & Ten pounds in Current Money of North Carolina.

Item. I Give one Hundred Pounds, Current Money of North Carolina, To be Emplid & Lade oute for ye youse & benefett of ye pore & pore Children beloing to ye precinck of Perquimons, Such as are Mentanead by ye paresh Excepted out. But ye money to be Ametadatly Layd out at ye Descretion of my Excetr. hareafter namead, but to ye youse aforesaid.

Item. I Give To Mr. Willm. Lettell of North Carolina, & my Friend, Collo. Edward Moseley, & my Friend, Mr. Thos. Pollock, & To Each of Them, one Gold Ring a pesese to ye Valey of Ten pounds, Currant Money of North Carolina, Each Ring to be purched out of my Estate by my Excetrs. hareafter named.

Item. I Give all ye Rest & Residue of my Estate, Both Reall and Persnall, be it in North Carolina or Eleswhere, be it in wot

kind or maner SoEver, To my foure Sounes, namely; Thom[a]
Harvey, John Harvey, Bejn. Harvey, & Miles Harvey, To [be]
Equally Sheard & Devided betwene them & To them & tha[t]
ares for Ever. And If Either or Eney of Them shall Diye befo[r]
thay ARive to ye age of Twenty one Years, that then, & in Suc[h]
Case, that part of ye Estate as beloingd to ye Desesead, to [be]
Equally Devided among ye Sirvivrs & thare ares for Eve[r]
both rell and persnall. And my will is that the Money arisei[n]
out of my Estate, Either by ye Sale of Good, Hire of Negroes, [or]
by Eney ways or menes wot Ever, To be Emplid in Trade [or]
Lett To Entrest for ye Benefett of my Children after an alown[e]
for thare Edecation.

And Lastly, I do aPint my Brother, Miles Gale, of Bost[o]
in Newengland, & my Knnsman, Mr. Willm. Lettell, My Frien[d]
Collo. Edward Mosley, Mr. Thos. Pollock, Excters. & my Lo[v]
ing Wife, Elizabeth Harvey, Excetres, of this my Last Will
Testement, To Se it Strickely fullfilld in all its parts, Revockii[ng]
& disallowing all other will or wills by me mayd, Ratefying
confirming This To be my Last Will & Testament.

In Witness whareof, I Have hareunto Sett my Hand & Se[al]
ye Day & Year above written.

THOS. HARVEY, (Seal).

Sind, Seld, Publeshid, pronounced & Declared by the Said
Thos. Harvey, To be his Last Will
& Testement, in presences of us
ye Subskribers:

    THOS. NORCOM. (Seal)
    RICHARD SUTTON. (Seal)
    JOHN WIAT, Jurat. (Seal)

I, The Thomas Harvey, doth further apoint my friend t[he]
Honble. John Lovick, Esq., one of my Executors to this my abo[ve]
will, Provided my Kinsman, Mr. William Little is not Capa[ble]
Of Acting, In the proformance of this my will, and tis my w[ill]
that my Sd. friend, John Lovick, Esq., have one gold Ring
the Vallue of ten pounds, current money of No. Carolina.

THOS. HARVEY (Seal)

Singd. Seald, and Delivered In
presence of:

    CHARLES DENMAN,
          his
    JOHN X MITCHEL
        mark

Memd. That about Three Dayes before his Death Th[e] within M[en]
tiond, Thos. Harvey, payd me to take notice that it was his desire th[at]
Mr. Lovick shoud Act with the other extrs., notwithstanding the man[ner]

of Expression as to Mr. Little's Illness or incapacity of Acting, mentioned in the Codicil as a condition wch might imply the contrary.

GALE.

Novbr. 10th, 1729.
Proved This will before me,   RICHD. EVERARD.
Copied from Original Will, filed in the Office of the Secretary of State.

ANTHONY HATCH'S WILL.

IN THE NAME OF GOD AMEN, This first Day of august, Anno, 1726. I, Anthony Hatch, of the precinct of pequimons, in the County of Albemarle and province of North Carolina, Gent., being of Sound Mind & perfect Memory, Doe Declare, make & ordain this to be my Last Will and Testament, Revoking and disannulling & making voyd all & every other Will & Wills by Me at any time heretofore made, in any kind whatsoever, in manner & form following, that is to Say, first and principally I Recomend my Soul into the hand of god almighty, who first gave it, Hoping for Salvation through mercy & the Merrits of Jesus my Saviour; & my Body I Commit to the Earth from whence it was Taken to be decently bruied at the discretion of my Executors hearin after mintioned & appointed; And to what Worldly Estate it has pleased god to bestow upon me (after my Debts & Funeral Expences thereout paid and Sattisfied), I give and bequeath, order and dispose of as follows:

Imprimis, I give & bequeath all that my plantation & Lands thereunto belonging or appertaining, Lying in Neuse, in the County of Bath in the province afforesaid, in as full and ample man as I my Selfe now doe, might or Could hold & enjoy the Same, unto my Two Sons, Edmond Hatch and Lamb Hatch, to he equilly devided between them, to their Heirs and assigns for ever.

Item. I give and bequeath all this my plantation & lands thereunto belonging or appertaining lying in perquimons afore sd. and where I Live, in as full & ample manner as I my Selfe now doe, might or could hold, occupie & enjoy the Same, unto my Dear & Loving wife, Elizabeth Hatch, for and During the Term of her Natural Life, and from & after her Decease, I give and bequeath the Same plantation and Lands in Like Manner as afforesaid, unto my Son, Anthony Hatch, his Heires and assigns for Ever.

Item. I order and Direct that all that my moyety or halfe part of a tract or parcel of land lying in Alligator, and by me held in partnership with my brother in Law, George Durant, to be Sold by my Execut's as soon after my Decease as Conveniently may be, & to the best Advantage, & the Money or

Commodities the Same shall be for, to be Devided, Disposed of in the very same manner as the rest of my personal Estate is to be, by this my Last Will & Testament.

Item. I give and bequeath my great Bible unto my Son, Anthony Hatch, after his Mothers Deceases, and it is my Will and Desire and I doe hearby order and direct the Same accordingly, that all my personal Estate in any Kind or Respect whatsoever, belonging unto me at the time of my Decease, shall be equally devided between my sd. Dear wife, Ellizabeth Hatch, my three Sons, Vizt: Anthony Hatch, Edmond Hatch, & Lamb Hatch, and my Daughter Ellizabeth Hatch, to be and Remain, to them, and their heirs for ever, and her & their proper use and behoof.

And Lastly, I doe nominate, Constitute and appoint my afforesaid Dear & Loving Wife, Ellizabeth Hatch, my true & Loving Brothers in law, Richard Whidbey and George Durant, to be my Executrix and Executors of this my Last Will and Testement.

ANTHO. HATCH. X

Signed, Sealed, published, pronounced, and declared to be the Last Will & Testament of Anthony Hatch, in presence of:

J. SWEENY,
THOMAS T PENRICE,
 his
 mark
JOHN STEVENS,
PARTHENIA L STEVENS.
 her
 mark

NORH CAROLINA SS. SR. RICHD EVERARD Barrt. Governor and Ordinary.

The above Will was proved before Me by the Oaths of Thomas Penrice and John Stephens, Evidences thereto, in due form, this 16th. Day of Novr. 1726.

RICHD. EVERARD.

Copied from Original Will filed in the Office of the Secretary of State.

JOHN HAYWOOD'S WILL.

IN THE NAME OF GOD AMEN, the twenty third Day of July, in the Yeare of our Lord, one thousand, Sevin hundred & fifty Six. I, John haywood, of the County of Edgcomb, in the Province of North Carolina, being Sick & weake of Body but of perfect mind and memory, thanks be Given to God therefore, Calling unto mind the mortalety of my body & Knowing its appointed for all men once to die, do make and ordaine this my laste will & testament, that is to say, principally & first of all, I give and Recommend my soul into the hand of God that Gave it; & for my body, I recommend it to the earth, to be buried in a Christian manner, and as touching such worldly Estate whare with it hath pleased God to bless with, I Give, devise and dispose of the in following manner & form:

Imprimis, I give & bequeath unto my son, William haywood, ten Shillings, Sterling for his Birth Right, he having already Land, and Chattles.

Item. I give and Bequeath to my Daughter, mary haywood, hur heirs & assigns for ever, a bond of thomas Davis, dated the Sixteenth day of febrary, 1754, by which the Sd. Davis stand bound in the sum of forty pound, Conditionally, for the making a title for two hundred, thirteen acres & half of land.

Item. I give & bequeath one half of the two tracts of land I now live on, witth the new house, milk house & 1 Corn Crib, to my two daughters, Deborah & mary haywood, to be by them possesed as long as they or either of them shall Continue Singal & after that to my son, Egbert haywood, his heirs & assigns for ever.

Item. I give the other half of the two aforesd. tracts of land to my son Egbert haywood, his heirs & assigns for ever, he paying out of the sd. Land when he Comes In possestion of the whole, ten pounds Sterling to his brother, John haywood.

Item. Its my will that all other my Estate, Reile & personal, be Eqully Divided between my Six Children, that is to say, Deborah haywood, mary haywood, William haywood, Herwood haywood, John Haywood, Egbert Haywood; further, that each Render an account of what they have alresdy Received in part of thare potion &c.

And Lastly, I appointe all my aforSaid Six Children, Excrs. of this my laste will & testament.

           JNO. HAYWOOD. (Seal)

Signed, Sealed, Published, and pornouneds by the John Haywood as his last will & testament In presents of:
  EDWARD CROWELL.
  WM CAMPBELL.
  THOMAS MERRIT.

EDGECOMBE COUNTY. SC.   December Court, 1758.

The within Will was in open Court Exhibd. on oath by the Excors, & prov'd by the Oath of Edward Crowell & Thomas Merrit, Two of the Subscribing Witnesses; & at the same time William Haywood & Egbert Haywood, two of the Exors. within mentioned were duly Qualifyed for that Office, which is ordered to be Certify'd.
        Test. JOS. MONTFORD, Cler. Cur.

Copied from Original Will, filed in the Office of the Secretary of State.

JOHN HECKLEFEILD'S WILL.

IN THE NAME OF GOD, AMEN. I, John Hecklefeild, of the Precinct of Pequimmons, in the County of Albemarle, in the Province of North Carolina, Gent., being sick & weak of Body, but of sound mind & memory (Blessed be God for the Same) & Knowing ye Certainty of Death, to hereby make, Ordain, Constitute & Appoint this to be my last Will & Testament, hereby revoking & making void all former Wills by me made, & this only to stand & be of force in Law. First & principally I recommend my Soul to God that gave it, hoping and Assuredly trusting in & thro' the Meritts of my Blessed Lord & Saviour Jesus Christ, to obtain full & free pardon of all my Sins; My Body I commit to the Ground to be decently interr'd at the discretion of my Executors hereafter mentioned, according to the manner I buried my last Wife. As for w't worldly Goods it hath pleas'd God to bestow on me in this Life, I give, devise & bequeath the Same in manner & forme following:

Imprim. I give to the Hon'ble Charles Eden, Esqr., Governor, my Mourning Ring w'th a Death's Head & y'e Christall

Item. I give to Mr. Edm'd Gale, ye Diamond Rign I formerly us'd to wear, being all Diamonds.

Item. I give to Mr. George Durant one Mourning Ring, value thirty Shillings.

Item. I sett at perfect freedom from all Slavery to be claimed by my Heirs, Executors, &c., my Negro Woman Jane, for her diligent care had of me in my Sickness.

All the Rest, Residue & Remainder of my Estate W'tsoever & wheresoever to be found I give & bequeath to my Son, Hecklefeild, & I further Nominate, make, constitute & appoint Mr. Edmond Gale & Mr. George Durant, Executors of this my last Will & Testam't, & Guardians to my sd. Son, John Hecklefeild, that they my afors'd Executors shall have the Tuition & Education of my sd. Son until he arrive at the age of Twenty & one years after the best thought manner this Country will admit.

What Negroes he hath Capable of it, I desire they may be hired yearly to Good paymasters for the better Support of my Sd. Son. And I further desire, that watsoever of his Estate will not be thought Serviceable to him when he shall come of Age, may be disposed of for good pay & converted into Young Negro Women for his use.

But if my sd. Son do die before he be of the Age of Twenty & one years w'ch (by Gods blessing) will be in the year one thousand, Seven Hundred & Thirty seven, then w't Estate I have by this Will given to him, I give & bequeath as follows, viz: the one half p't thereof to my Sister in Law, Mrs. Mary

Cox, or her heirs, living near Essex Bridge, in Dublin, in Ireland; the other half p't to Mr. Edm'd. Gale.

In Witness whereof, I hereto set my hand & seal this thirtieth day of May, in ye year of our Lord, 1721.

JOHN HECKLEFEILD (Seal)

Sign'd, Seal'd, publish'd & Declar'd by the Testat'r to be his last Will & Testam't in Presence of:

> WILLIAM BURCLIFT.
> his
> DARBY O O'BRYAN.
> marke
> ENOCH FLOWER.

NORTH CAROLINA ss. CHARLES EDEN, Esqr., Govern'r &c.

Darby O'bryan this day came before me & made Oath that he saw Collo. John Hecklefield, Seal & declare the within Will to be his last Will & Testam't & y't Wm. Berclift & Enoch Flower, the other two Evidences thereto were then Present; that ye Sd. Hecklefeild was then of Sound Memory & sign'd the same without any Constraint or compulsion.

In testimony whereof, I have hereunto sett my hand at Chowan, Aug'st ye 8th, 1721.
CHARLES EDEN.

Recorded in Will Book 2, page 305, Office of the Secretary of State.

PETER HENLEY'S WILL.

IN THE NAME OF GOD AMEN. I, Peter Henley, Esquire, Chief Justice of the Province of North Carolina, Do make this my last Will and Testament in Manner & form following, Viz:

Imprimis. I direct all my just Debts & funeral Expences to be paid; And whereas, just before my leaving England I was on the point of being married to Agnes Tucker of Corytown, near Honiton, in the County of Devon, Spinster, & Some Money was wanting to make the necessary preparations for that purpose which money, amounting to £400 Sterling, she advanced out of her own private fortune, & a short time after, to the great Disappointment of us both, the Marriage was postponed to be compleated at a future Day, after w'ch Marriage so postponed I gave her my bond bearing Interest after the rate of £5 per Cent per Annum for the sd. Sum of £400. which yet remains unpaid. My Desire is that the said Bond may be discharged Out of any Moneys that may be in my posession, or the first that shall or may be collected after my Decease, with all the Interest that shall be found due thereon according to the Tenor of the Sd. Bond.

There is also a Bond of mine of £40: to Mr. Simon Bunker, of Axminster, in the County of Devon, attorney at Law, of which I am informed he has received part by a Cask of Indigo weighing 137l, but how much I cant tell, because I have never had the Account of Sales.

There is also a trifling Debt to Mr. Benjamin Mayberry, Taylor, of Craven Buildings, near Drury Lane, London, All which I desire may be paid & the Bonds cancelled.

I Know of no others, & the first of these would not have been at all necessary but upon the critical Occasion on which it was advanced.

With Respect to the rest of My Estate, Plantations, Negroes & Moneys with w'ch it has pleased God to bless me (except hereafter excepted) I hope they will be so managed & expended as to be most for the Interest and Advantage of my Son John Henley, to whom I devise all my Lands, Tenements & Hereditaments, and all my personal Estate that shall not be disbursed for the payment of my Debts, Investing them however in John Campbell of Lazy Hill, Esqr., for whose humanity & Integrity I have the highest Honour & Regard. In trust, nevertheless to & for the Only Use & behoof of my sd. Son, John Henley, His Heirs and Assigns forever. And I earnestly entreat the sd. John Campbell, whom I hereby appoint Executor of this my last Will & testament to forward the Education of my Son as much as he can, & to endeavour to make him an useful Member of Society.

And, whereas I have a great Deal of Good furniture, w'ch it will be better to Dispose of than keep, as also sundry parcells of Liquors, Molasses & Sugar, I wo'd chuse they should all together with my Chariott, be sold at publick Auction some Day During the Supreme Court at Edenton, which shall be held next after my Decease, for ready money only, (I mean all except my plate, w'ch I would have reserved), after having been first advertised for some time in the Carolina & Virginia Gazettes. And the moneys arising from such Sale to be applied for the purchasing of Negroes for the better stocking & improving my plantations.

And as I have observed great Losses & Damages arising to Orphans from the Buildings upon their plantations being suffered to run to decay, My desire is that every Edifice or Building upon my plantation in the county of Edgecombe, be kept in due repair at the Expense of my Estate, and that the Negroes w'ch I now have or w'ch hereafter may be purchased, May be constantly employed upon it under a proper Overseer, so as to make it turn to most account, & whatever money it may annually produce, the expence of my Sons Education and other Disbursements being first Deducted, my Executor to apply the Overplus most beneficially for my sd. Son, either in the purchase of young Slaves or any thing else he shall judge most proper.

Item. I beg my said Executor would accept of 20l proclamation Money, for Mourning & a Ring & I hereby revoke all & every other Wills or Wills by me heretofore made.

In witness whereof, I have hereunto set my Hand and Seal, this 23d. Day of November, 1757.

PETER HENLEY (Seal)

Signed, Sealed, published & declared as & for the sd. Peter Henley, Esqrs. last Will & Testament. Also in Our presence & We in the presence of each other have subscribed our names as Witnesses the 23d Day of November, 1757:

SARAH McCULLOCH.
JOSEPH MONTFORD.
RICHD. BROWNRIGG, Jurat.

NORTH CAROLINA, CHOWAN COUNTY. ss   July County Court, 1758.

Present His Majesty's Justices.

The above last Will & Testament of the Honourable Peter Henley, Esquire, deceased, was duely proved in open Court by the Oath of Mr. Richard Brownrigg, according to Law; and at the Same time John Campbell Esquire, Qualified as Executor to the said Last Will and Testament, by taking the Oath Prescribed by Law for the Qualification of Executors. Ordered that the Secretary have notice that Letters Testamentory may Issue thereon.

Test.   THO. JONES, Cler. Cur.

Endorsement on Back of Will.

The Last Will & Testament of Peter Henley, Esqr., who departed this life on Tuesday the 25th. day of April, 1758, about nine O'clock in the morning, & was interred in the church in Edenton on the evening the 27th. of Same month, at six o'Clock in the evening, in a Decent manner, and much Lamented by his Acquaintance.

Copied from the Original Will, filed in the Office of the Secretary of State.

WILLIAM HERITAGE'S WILL.

IN THE NAME OF GOD AMEN. I, William Herritage, of Craven County, in the Province of North Carolina, Gent., Being Weak in Body But of Sound and Disposing Mind and Memory, Do this Eighth Day of March, in the Year of Our Lord, One Thousand, Seven Hundred and Sixty Nine, make and Declare this to be my Last Will and Testament in manner and Form following, that is to say:

Imprimis. I Will and require that my Body be Decently Interred at the Discretion of my Executors hereinafter named; and that my Just Debts and Funeral Charges be first paid and satisfied.

Item. I give and Devise to my Son, Heneage Herritage, the Land and Plantation where on I Dwell, commonly called

Springfield, on the East Side of Jemmys Creek; the Land I bought of George Metts, lying on the West side of Jemmys Creek; and Fifty Acres of Land, which I took up in the front of the said Land I bought of George Metts, and Patened in my own name. Also, the Land I had of Adam Moore, Grand Father to my said Son, Heneage, called Jemmys Neck lying on the East side of Jemmys Creek, at and below the Mouth thereof; and Five hundred and twenty Acres of Land joining the above mentioned Land, Called Springfield, and the Lands of Adam Moore & others as per. the Patent for the same will at large appear, And to his Heirs Male Lawfully Begottn; and in default of such Issue, to my right Heirs forever. I also Give and Devise to my said son, Heneage Herritage, one Lott of Land lying in Newbern Town, and known in the plan of the said town by the number (21) to him and his Heirs and Asignes forever.

Item. I Give and Bequeath to my said Son, Heneage Heritage, One Negro Man Named Mingo, One Negro Man Named Sherbro, One Negro Woman Named Tamer, One Negro Man Named Ben, One Negro Man Named Bill son of a Negro Woman named Bettress, One Negro Man Named Sam, one Negro Woman named Betto, one Negro Woman Named Kate, and all the Children she, the said Negro Woman Named Kate now ha¹h or hereafter shall have, one Negro Woman Named Tortola and one Negro Child named Phebe, And to his Asignes forever.

Item. I Give and Devise to my Son, John Heritage, all that Tract of Land or Plantation Called Harrow, Situate in Dobbs County (but formrly Called Johnson County); and also my other Lands adjoining or lying or being within three miles of my said Plantation called Harrow; and also my Land on the North side of Neuse River called Atkins Banks, containing as per Patent, Six Hundred and Forty Acres: be the same more or less, and whereon the Town of Kingston now is Situate And to his Heirs Male Lawfully Begotten Forever and In Default of such Issue to my Right Heirs forever.

Item. I give and Devise to my said Son, John Heritage, one Lott of Land situate lying & being in New Bern Town, and known in the plan of the said town by the number (79), and to the Heirs Male lawfully begotten of his Body forever; and in Default of such issue then to my Right Heirs forever.

Item. I Give and Bequeath to my said son John, Heritage, One Negro Man Named Pompey, one Negro Man Named Joe, one Negro Man Named Peter (a cooper), one Negro Man Named Jack, who once belonged to John Williams, One Negro Woman Named Venus, Daughter of my Negro Woman Named Phillis, one Negro Woman Named Maria, one Negro Boy named Solomon, one Negro Boy Named Jacob, one Negro Girl named Moll, one Negro Woman Named Lucy, and one Negro Boy Ben, her son, and also the Money due me by Bond from Stephen Lee for a Negro Woman Named Venus, which I sold to him, to the said John Heritage and His Asignes forever.

Item. I Give and Devise to my Son, William Martin Heritage, all that Tract of Land or Plantation Situate in Craven County, Commonly Called Fort Barnwell, and also all my lands Contiguous and adjoining thereto, and within three miles of any part thereof, which I now have or hereafter may have take up or purchase; And also, four hundred Acres of Land I Bought of Robert Hays, Situate in Dobbs County (but then called Johnston County), and alsc, all the Land I have, Or shall take up, or Purchase, adjoining the same, and to his Heirs Male, Lawfully Begotten forever; and in Default of such Issue to my Right Heirs forever. I also Give and Devise to my said son, William Martin Heritage, one Lot of Land Situate In the Town of New Bern, and known in the Plan of The said Town by the Nimber (22) and also the Front of the said Lot, to hold to him and his Heirs Male Lawfully Begotten, forever, and in Default of such Issue to my Right Heirs forever.

Item. I Give and Bequeath to my said son, William Martin Heritage, one Negro Man Named Scipeo, One Negro Man Named Caesar (a cooper), one Negro Man Named Tom, one Negro Man named London, One Negro Woman Named Jude Daughter of my Negro Woman Named Phillis, one Negro boy named Tom, one Negro Boy named Stephen, one Negro Man Named Balaam, one Negro Girl Named Suse Daughter of my Negro Woman Named Judith (Stephens Wife), one Negro Girl Named Winifred, and one Negro Girl Named Abigaal, two others Daughters of my Negro Woman Named Big Bess, and one Negro Boy Named Virgil son of my Negro Woman Named Priss, and to his Asignes forever.

Item. I Give and Devise to my Son in Law, Richard Caswell, a Piece or Parcell of Land, Situate in Dobbs County near Bear Creek, and above the Land Commonly Called Judge Smiths, on the North side of Neuse River, at or near a place called Herritages's Banks and the Lot or Land Situate in New Bern Town on the North Side, whereon Mary Dupree lived, and is known in the Plan of the said Town, by the Number (190), to him and his Heirs and Asignes forever; and also one Negro Man Named Prince, one Negro Woman Named Big Rose, one Negro Woman Named Phillis, one Mulatto Boy Named Hesketh, one Negro Boy Named Isaac, one Negro Girl Named Sabina and one Negro Man Named Stephen, and to his Asignes forever for the use and subject to the Incumbrances herein mentioned that is to say; That He, the said Richard Caswell, his Executors or Administrators, shall Annually pay to my Daughter, Susanna, and During her Nateral life the Sum of

Forty Pounds, Proclamation Money, one Fourth part thereof to be paid to her once in every three Months in each Year, during the Time of her life, Which said Forty Pounds to be paid as aforesaid, I Give to my said Daughter for her seperate Maintenance and Support, without being subject to the payment of Debt or Debts now due, or which may hereafter become due, to any person or persons from the present Husband of my said Daughter, or to his will or demand in any Respect Whatsoever; And the said Negro Man Named Stephen to be Employed in Tanning and Making of Shoes for my several Children herein mentioned and their Families and Slaves.

Item. I Give and Devise to my Daughter, Elizabeth Heritage, one Lot of Land Lying in NewBern Town whereon Mary Dupree formerly Dwelt, being a Corner Lot and Numbered in the Plan of the Said Town (191), and also one other Lot of Land lying in the said Town of NewBern and Numbered in the Plan of the said Town (84), and to her Heirs Male Lawfully Begotten forever and for Default of such Issue then to my Right Heirs forever.

Item. I Give and Bequeath to my said Daughter, Elizabeth Heritage, one Negro Man Named Jack, which I bought of Mr. John Campell, one Negro Woman Named Clarinda, one Negro Woman Named Judith (Stephens wife), one Negro Man named Harry, one Negro Boy Named Carolina, one Negro Man Named Mercury, one Negro Woman Named Big Bess, one Negro Girl named Jenny, Daughter of Big Bess, one Negro Girl Named Moll, Daughter of Clarinda, one Negro Girl Named Amy, and one Negro Boy Named Sam, the Two Children of Tamer, one Negro Boy Named Jupiter, one Negro Girl Named Hannah Daughter of Tortola, and one Negro Woman Named Priss, and to her Asignes forever.

Item. I Give and Devise to my Son in Law, Richard Caswell, Thirty Eight ft. of Land in Front, lying in NewBern Town running Easterly and Westerly and Southerly Down or across near the mouth of Trent River, which said piece of Land I bought of Nicholas Routledge, and is the same whereon my two Stores are situate, opposite the Lot Known in the Plan of the said Town by the Number (15) with its Appurtenances, to hold to him his Heirs and Asignes forever.

Item. I Give and Bequeath to my Daughter, Anna, now Wife of George Lovick, Esq., One Negro Woman Named Little Rose, one Negro Man Named Cado, son of my Negro Woman Named Clarinda, one Negro Man Named Frank, one Negro Girl Named Sall, Daughter of my Negro Woman Named Judith, and one Negro Man Named Billey, my late Waiting Man, and to her Asignes forever.

Item. I Give and Bequeath to my Daughter Sarah, Now Wife of Richard Caswell, one Negro Man Named George, one

Negro Man Named Moses, his Brother, one Negro Man Named Cato son of my Negro Woman Named Phillis, one Negro Boy Named Daniel son of my Negro Woman Named Tamer, one Negro Woman Named Judy Mother of my Negro Woman Named Tamer, and one Negro Woman Named Rachel, And to her Asignes forever.

Item. It is my Will and Desire that my Son in Law, Richard Caswell have the Tuition and Guardianship of my Daughter, Elizabeth Heritage, and my Son, William Martin Heritage, and I do appoint the said Richard Caswell Guardian to my said Daughter and Son accordingly during their Minority.

Item. I will and Ordain that the Executor of this my last Will and Testament shall, with all convenient speed for and toward the performance of this my last Will and Testament (after my Decease) Bargain, Sell and Alien all those my Lands I shall be possessed of at my Death, except such as are by this Will Specially Given and Devised, and for the Doing, Executing and perfect finishing whereof I do by these Presents Give, Grant, Will, and Transfer to my said Executors and the Survivors or Survivor of them full power and Authority to Grant, Alien, Bargain, Sell, Convey, and Assure all my said Lands Except as before Excepted, to any Person or Persons and their Heirs forever, by all and every such Lawfull Ways and Means in the Law, as to my said Executors or Survivors or Survivor of them, as their Council Learned in Law shall think Necessary.

Item. I Will and Desire That all the rest of my Personal Estate not herein particularly Given, be sold at Public Vendue to the Highest Bidder at twelve months Credit, the Purchaser or Purchasers to Give Bond with Sufficient Securities, on Interest, before the Delivery of the Article or Articles, he, she or they, may or shall Purchase, and the Monies arising therefrom, together with the Monies arising from the sale of my Lands above directed to be sold, together with my outstanding Debts be Divided Equally among my Children hereafter Named, that is is to say: my Son Heneage Heritage, my son John Heritage, my son William Martin Heritage, my Daughter Sarah Caswell, wife of Richard Caswell, my Daughter Anna Lovick, wife of George Phenny Lovick, and my Daughter Elizabeth Heritage, they first paying thereout to the Children my Daughter Susannah may, have Lawfully Begotten before she shall be a Widow if it shall so happen, on the arrival of the Eldest of them to the age of Fourteen Years, the sum of Fifty Pounds Proclamation Money with Interest from the Sale of my said Estate above mentioned until the same shall be paid to the said Children of my said Daughter Susannah, but in case she shall * * * * * arrive to the age of Fourteen, that then and in such case the said Fifty Pounds above mentioned shall be paid to her my said daughter Susannah with the Interest due to the time the same shall be paid her, for her own proper use and behoof forever.

Item. I Will and Direct that my Executors hereafter named, out of the Monies arising by and out of the sale of my Lands and Personal Estate above directed to be sold, pay unto the Servant I may have living with me as a House keeper at the time of my Death, the sum of Ten Pounds Proclomation money Unto whom I give and Bequeath the same forever, to be paid within Six months after my Decease.

And Whereas I, the Said William Heritage, some time between the Years of our Lord, one thousand seven hundred & forty four, and One thousand seven hundred and forty eight, did by four several Deeds of Gifts Give to foure of my Children, to wit: Heneage Heritage, Sarah Heritage, Anna Heritage, and Susannah Heritage, Sundry Pieces or parcels of Land lying in Craven and Johnston Counties; and also sundry Goods and Chattels, Which said Several Deeds I kept in my own Custody not having suffered them or any of them to be proved or acknowledged in order to Alter, Destroy, and Revoke, or other wise to make void the same as I thereafter should or might think proper, Since the Execution of which said Deeds, the same are lost, mislaid or privately taken out of my Custody so that I could not now cannot Alter, Revoke, Destroy and make void the same as my intention is to do could I find and get Possession of them, Wherefore, to prevent any Disputes or Law Suits which may arise Between my Children after my Decease, for or by Reason of, the Gift to them, or any of them of any Lands, Goods or Chattels, contained or mentioned in the above mentioned Deeds, which said Deeds I do hereby Revoke, Disannull, and Make Void, to all intents and purposes as if the same had never been made, Therefore, it is hereby, Provided always, and my further Will is, and I hereby Expressly Declare, that if my Son or Sons, Daughter or Daughters, Legatees, and Divisees herein mentioned or their or either of their Husbands, or their or either of their Heirs, or other Legal Representative or Representatives, shall at any time hereafter Controvert or Oppose any Part of this my Will, or shall Obstruct or hinder the admittance of all or any of the before mentioned Legatees and Devises or their Heirs, or any other Legal Representatives or Representative, of, in, or to, any of the Hereditaments, Lands, Tenements, Goods or Chattels, or other the Premises hereby Respectively given them as aforesaid, or shall at any time after such their, or any of their Admittance and Possession either in Law or Equity or otherwise Molest, Sue, or Trouble any such Legatee or Divisee whereby, to put him, them, or any of them, out of or get, or take possession of the same Premises or any part thereof, for or by Reason of the Deeds of Gifts as aforesaid Made and above mentioned, or for, or upon account of my not having cancelled or otherwise made Void the same * * * but not otherwise, & I hereby Revoke and make Void the Legacy, Estate, Share, and Interest of her, him or them, my above mentioned mentioned Son, or Sons, Daughter, or Daughters, Legatees or Devisees aforesaid. or her or their Respective Husbands, and of their Respective Heirs, Executors and Adminstrators, and other Legal Representative or Representatives, of, in and unto, the before mentioned Legacies and Devises so given to them as aforesaid, and then, and in such case, but not Otherwise, I hereby Give, Devise, and Bequeath all such said Estate & Estates, Legacies, and Bequests hereby given, from such of them, my said Son or Daughter, or their, or either of their, Legal Representative or Representatives as shall so Contrevert, Obstruct, oppose or Molest all, or any of the before mentioned Legatees or Divisees in manner aforesaid, unto such Legatee or Legatees, Devisee or Devisees, who by Means thereof shall be Prejudiced or suffer thereby, the same to go and be paid to * * * use of, and be paid to such Legatee or Legatees, Devisee or Devisees so Prejudiced, and to their Respective Heirs, Executors and Administrators, or other Legal Representative or Representatives proportionably according to His Her, or their, loss or damage sustained by means thereof. Provided, nevertheless, that if my said Son or Sons, Daughter or Daughters, Legatee or Legatees, aforesaid and all other persons Lawfully Claiming Any Estate, Right or Interest of in or to the Premisses by, from or under them,—either of them shall and do as soon as may be, or can be after my Decease Ratify and confirm this my Will, and also Release unto the said other Legatees or Devisees Respectively all their Estate Rights Title and Interest of, in, and to the several Estates, Monies, Legacies, Devises & Premises so by me hereby Respectively Given as aforesaid, then;—and in that case, the last before mentioned Proviso shall be void and of none effect, anything therein contained to the contrary in any wise Notwithstanding. And Lastly, I hereby Make, and Ordain, and Appoint, my Son in Law, Richard Caswell, and my Sons, Heneage Heritage and John Heritage, Executors of this my Last Will and Testament, which is comprised in three sheets of paper Wrote on Every side thereof, hereby Revoking all other and former, Wills by me heretofore made, and Ratifying and confirming this to be my Last Will and Testament and none other.

In Witness whereof, I have hereunto put and affixed my Hand and Seal the day and year first above written.

        WILLIAM HERRITAGE (Seal)

Signed, Sealed, published and
Declared by the said William

Heritage as and for his Last Will and Testament, in the presence of us who have Subscribed our Names as Wittnesses, and not only Wittnesses to the signing on this Sheet but also to the Testator affixing his Name to Two other sheets which are to this annexed and the whole complete his Will.

———— BAYLEY (?)
WILL, BANKS.
DANL. BARRY.

CODICIL.

I, William Heritage, of Craven County, Gent., do this tenth day of April in the year of Our Lord, One Thousand, Seven Hundred and Sixty Nine, make and Publish this Codicil to my last Will and Testament, in manner following, that is to say

I Give and Bequeath to my Son, Heneage Heritage, my Gold Watch and One Negro Girl named Bella and to his Asignes forever. Also, I Give and bequeath to my Son, John Heritage, my Silver Watch, commonly worn by my Son, Heneage Heritage.

And whereas, in and by my last Will and Testament I have Given and Devised to my aforesaid Son, Heneage Heritage, the Land a Plantation whereon I Dwell commonly called Springfield on the East side of Jemmys Creek, and sundry other Tracts or Parcels of Land Situate in Craven County adjoining the same, which are Particularly described in and by my said last Will and Testament and to his Heirs Lawfully Begotten, and in Default of such Issue to my Right Heirs forever; and whereas, I am Apprehensive it will be for the Benefit and Advantage of my said Son, to have a Fee Simple Estate in all those Lands, I do therefore give and Devise to my said Son, Heneage Herritage, all those Lands commonly called Springfield and other Tracts or Parcels of Land Adjoining the same, which are Particularly mentioned and Described in my last Will and Testament to be given and Devised to him, in manner aforesaid, To hold to him and his Heirs and Asigns forever, without any manner of Limitation or Condition whatsoever, any thing in my said last Will and Testament to the Contrary Notwithstanding.

And lastly, it is my Desire that this Codicil be annexed to and made part of my last Will and Testament to all intents and purposes.

In Wittness Whereof, I have hereunto set my Hand and Seal the Day and Year above written.

WILLIAM HERRITAGE, (Seal)

Signed Sealed Published and Declared by the above named William Herritage, as a Codicil to his last Will and Testament in the Presence of us:
>DAVID GORDON.
>MARGARET her X mark WIGGINS.
>ELIZABETH BLOUNT.
>RD. CASWELL.

Copied from Original Will, filed in the Office of the Secretary of State.

HARMAN HILL'S WILL.

IN THE NAME OF GOD AMEN, the 4th of December, 1752. I, Harman Hill, of the County of Beaufort, in the Province of North Carolina, being very Sick and Weak of body, but of Perfect mind and Memory, thanks be to God therefor, Calling unto mind the Mortality of my body and knowning that it is Appointed unto all men once to Die, Do make and Ordain this my last Will and Testament, that is to say, Principally and first of all, I give and recommend my soul into the hands of God that gave it and for my body, I give to be buried in a Christian like and Decent manner at the Discretion of my Executors, Nothing Doubting but I shall receive the same again at the General resurect'n, by the Mighty Power of God; and as touching such worldly Estate wherewith it hath Pleased God to bless me in this life, I give, Devise and Dispose in the following manner and form:

Imprimis. It is my Will, and I do order, that in the first Place all my Just Debts and Funeral Charges be Paid and Satisfied.

Item. I Lend unto my Dearly and well beloved wife, Sarah Hill, two Negroes Named Scipio and Sarah, with two Large Feather beds and Furniture, One Desk and Four Chairs, one Chest. I likewise lend unto the said Sarah Hill, one fourth of my Plantation, and two Horses Named Ball and Primas, One Middle Siz'd Table, Two Pewter Dishes and one Dozen of Plates, one Small Wallnut tree fram'd Looking Glass, 6 Oecamy Spoons, Four Cows and Calves, Two Sheep, Namely, one Wether and one ram, untill the Decease of the said Sarah Hill, then after to Descend to the heirs, only my Desk to return to my Son, Harman Hill. I also Lend unto my Wife, one Middling iron Pot and one brass Kettle, During the term afores'd, then to descend to my heirs.

Item. I give and bequeath unto my said Wife, four of my best Steers for ever.

Item. I give and bequeath unto my Dearly and Well beloved son, Harman Hill, A Tract or Parcel of Land lying and being in the County of Beaufort, formerly Called Callums Creek, the said Land Containing Four hund'd and Thirty Acres and taken in Cary's time, only, Near about Thirty Acres of the said Land belonging to Capt. Richard Evans, and Joyns his Land and one Negroe Boy named Jack, one Duck Gun, and a Mare Called Chance, and one Cow and Calf, two New Club Axes, One Iron Pot, Four Plates, unto him for ever, Excepted, that the said Harman Hill dies without Issue, then the said Land to be equally divided among my heirs.

I Likewise give and bequeath unto my Son afores'd, One Silver Stock Buckle, and one fifteen Bottle Case and Bottles, and one Beaverett Hat, and one Small Oval Table, and my Chest, to him, his heirs and Assigns forever.

Item. I Lend unto my Daughter, Elizabeth Hancock, one Negro boy Named Cuffy During her Life, and after the Decease of the said Eliz. I give the said Negroe to be Devided between her two Sons, (Viz), James & William, to them for ever.

Item. I give and bequeath unto the said Eliz. Hancock one Mare Called Faney, Two Plates, to her, her heirs and Assigns for ever.

Item. I give and bequeath unto Sarah Rice, One Negroe boy Named Cezar, One Feather bed and Furniture, Two Cows and Calves, One Mare Called Jenny, Two Plates, one Small Iron Pot, to her and her heirs & Ass'gs for ever.

Item. I give and bequeath unto my beloved Daughter, Ann Slade, One Negroe boy Named Quacko, and one Large Feather bed and Furniture, to her, her heirs and Assigns for ever. I likewise give and bequeath unto my afr'sd Daughter, Ann Slade, a Tract or Parcell of Land, Containing Three hundred and fifty Acres, Lying and being on the South side of Pamplico River, begining at a Poplar and running So. 35 D. wt. 290 Pole to a Pine, and the Lines as is in the Patten. Provided, that the Husband, Joseph Slade, does in Consideration of this Gift, build a House 25 foot long, 16 foot Wide, where the Wife of me shall appoint, then within two years after the Decease of me, then the the said Land to be and remain forever, Otherwise the said Gift to be Void, and Descend to my heirs; I Likewise give unto the said Ann Slade a Trading Gun for ever.

Item. I give and bequeath unto my beloved Daughter, Mary Smith, One Negro Girl Named Pegg, Two Cows and Calves, one Iron Pot now in her Possession, Three Plates and one Large Pewter Dish, one Walnut tree Fram'd Looking Glass, one Case of Nine Bottles, to her, her heirs and Assigns for ever.

Item. I give and bequeath unto my beloved Daughter, Rachel Hill, One Negro Girl Called Sall, One Large Oval

Table, two Cows and Calves, one Mare Colt, Six Pewter basons, Three Plates and one Pewter Dish, to her, her heirs and Assigns for ever.

Item. I give to my Wife and Children £32—12s—11d, Virg'a Money, to be equally Divided to them, their heris and Assigns for ever; and all the remaind'r Part of my Estate to be equally Devided among my heirs afors'd to them for ever.

I Likewise make and Ordain and Constitute my Wife, Sarah Hill, and Joseph Slade, and Mr. John Barrow, my Whole and Sole Executors of this my last Will and Testament, and Do Deny, Revoke and Disanul all other former Wills, Legacies, Testaments by me in any Wise before Named, Will'd and bequeath'd, Ratifying and Confirming this, and no Other, to be my Last will and Testament.

In Testimony hereof, I have hereunto fixed my hand and Seal the Day and Year afors'd.

HARMAN HILL (Seal).

Sign'd, Seal'd, Pronounc'd and Declared by Harman Hill, to be his last Will and Testament in Presence of us:
    EDMUND PEARCE,
    JOSHUA PEARCE,
    GRIFFETH HOWELL.

BEAUFORT COUNTY. ss.

At a Court held for the sd. County, at Bath Town, on the second tuesday in March, Anno Dom., 1755. Present his Majesty's Justices.

This certifies that the last Will & Testament of Harman Hill, decd., was exhibited into Court & proved by Edmond Pearce, one of the subscribing witnesses, who swore that he saw the sd. Harman Hill execute the same and publish it as his last Will & Testament, & that he was then of sound & disposing mind and memory; & also that he saw Joshua Pearce & Griffeth Howell, the other subscribing Witnesses, Set their Hands thereto at the same time.

And Sarah Hill, Joseph Slade & John Barrow, qualified as Exor's thereto, by taking the Oaths according to Law.

Ordered that the Secretary have notice that Letters Testamentary may issue.

Test. WALLEY CHAUNCEY, Cl. C.

Copied from the Original Will, filed in office of Secretary of State.

ISACK HILL'S WILL.

IN THE NAME OF GOD AMEN. The Third Day of March, in ye year of our Lord God, One thousand, Seven hundred & Ten, I, Isack Hill, of Chowan prcinct, in ye province of North Carolina, planter, being sick of Body, but of Good & perfect Memory (God be praised), Doe Make & ordaine this my last will & Testam't (& I utterly revoke & Disannull Every other former Testaments, Wills, legaces, & bequeiths, Executer & overseer by me in any wise before this time, made, named, willed & bequeithed), in manner & forme following: First, I Commend my Soul into ye Hands of God my maker, hopeing assuredly through ye onely merits of Jesus Christ my Saviour, to be made partaker of life Everlasting; & I Commend my Body to ye Earth where It is made, to be Decently buried by my Executors hereafter named; & what Estate God Allmighty has been pleased to bless me with in this world I will Give & bequeith in manner following, Vizt:

My Tract of land I now live upon, Containing Six hundred & forty Acres, to Be Equally Devided between three of my Sons, Vizt: Michal, John & Isack, that is two hundred & Thirteen Acres & one third part of one Acre to My Son Michal (which he now lives upon) & ye same quantity of land Adjoyning to my Son Michals (which he now lives upon his land) I Give to my Second Son, Isack, & ye other Devidend of ye tract I Give to my Third Son, John. & to my Youngest Son, Nathaniel, I Give three hundred & twenty acres of land I bought from Thomas Pollock adjoyning to that part of ye foresd Tract I have Given to my Son Michal. Ye above quantity of land I have Given to Each of my Sons by this my last will & Testam't, I intale on them, their heirs & assigns for Ever, & when it shall please God to Call one or any of them, haveing no Issue, males then their land to be equally Devided among their Surveying Brothers, & having Given my Eldest Son, Michal, his Share of ye Cattle & hoggs, ye remaining part, that is those that Shall be found properly belonging to me at my Death, I Give unto my three Sons, Isack, John, & Nathaniel, & my Dear Daughter, Martha, shall have her choice of ye Cattle & Hoggs for her share, not Exceeding ye Same Number her Brother has, & their Shares I leave to be Given them by my Executor, & I further will that ye hand mill shall remaine for ever were she now is, & that all my Children shall have equal previledge to use her were she now stands, & this Dwelling house & all ye other houses on this plantation to me, I Give to him whose land they happen to be upon, & Commit ye Emediate Care of my hand Mill to him.

I will that all my houshold furniture to be Equally Devided between my three, Sons Isac, John & Nathaniel, & my Daughter, Martha, always letting he Chose for her Share, & theirs to be Given them according to ye pleasure of my Executors.

I will that my horse & mare remaine at ye Plantation were they now are for ye use of ye Same till they Increase to four, & then to be Devided to my three Sons last named, & my Daughter, Martha,

& I appoint Capt. Robt. west, Executor of this my last will & Testam't, likewise, I leave to his Care my youngest Son

Nathaniel till he be Capable to provide himself a livelihood, or till he be Majour, & Desire he may Endeavour to keep my two sons, Isack & John, on ye plantation where their Sister Martha, till they Can better provide for themselves.

In wittness whereof, I have hereunto Subscribed my name & Seal, to this my last will and Testament, before these wittnesses: Edward Bryan, William Maule & John Hale.

ISACK HILL X (Seal)

    WILLIAM MAULE.
    EDWARD BRYAN.
    JOHN HALE.

Recorded in Will Book 2, page 33.

JOHN HASSELL'S WILL.

IN THE NAME OF GOD AMEN. John Hassell, of the Province of North Carolina and County of Tyrrel, being Sick and Weak of Body but of Sound and perfect Mind and Memory, thanks be to almighty god for the Same, and Calling to Mind the Mortality of my body, and knowing that it is appointed for all men once to die, Do make and ordain this to be my last will and testament, first and principally I Recommend my Soul to God that gave it, and my Body to the Earth to be Buried in a Deacent and Christian like manner, at the Descretion of my Executors hereafter Mentioned; And as Touching such Worldly Estate wherewith it hath pleased God to bless me with In this life, I give and Dispose thereof in manner and form following:

Imprimis. I give unto my Dearly beloved Wife, Rachel Hassell, all my movable Estate of what Nature & Kind soever, to her proper use forever, Except Such legacies as are particularly otherways mentioned and Disposed of.

Item. I give and bequath unto my wellbeloved Son, John Hassell, a Plantation on the West Side of Scupperlong River, Containing one Hundred acres and known by the Name of the Plains, unto him his heirs and assigns for ever.

Item. I give and bequeath unto my well beloved Son, Joseph Hassell, one hundred acres of Land on the East Side of Scupperlong River lying on the North Side of the Leading Swamp, Begining at the head of the Leading Swamp at a goom, from thence to the popler Line, unto him and his Heirs and Assigns for ever.

Item. I give and bequeath unto my well beloved Son, Isaac Hassell, one hundred acres of Land on the East Side of Scupperlong River, on the north Side of the Leading Swamp, begining at the popler line, from thence to the three marked pins at Phelpsis Swamp, to him & his heirs and assigns for ever.

Item. I give and bequeath unto my well beloved Son, Benjamin Hassell, my Manner Plantation and the Said Land belonging to it, after his Mothers Deceas, to him and his heirs and assigns for ever.

Item. I give and bequeath unto my two Sons, Isaac Hassell & Beniamin Hassell, a negro man named Robin, after their Mothers Decease, to them and their Heirs and Assigns for ever.

Item. I give to my Daughter, Mary Wynne, Five Shillings Currant money of virginia, to her & her Heirs and assigns for ever.

Item. I give to my Daughter, Rachel ward, Five Shillings, Currant Money of Virginia, to her and her heirs and assigns for ever.

Item. I give to my Daughter, Sarah fox, five Shillings, Currant Money of virginia, to her and her heirs & assigns for ever.

Item. I give to my Daughter, Esther Hassell, five Shillings, Currant Money of virginia, to h'r and h'r heirs & assigns for ever.

Item. I give unto my fore Sone before mentioned, my Saws, and Carpenters tools, & Coopers tools, and Shoemakers tools, after their Mothers Deceas, to them and their Use for Ever. Lastly, I Constitute, ordain and apoint my beloved Wife, Rachel Hassell, whole & Sole Executrix of this My last will and testament, Utterly Renouncing and Revoking all former Wills by me heretofore made, Ratifying & Confirming this to be my last Will & Testament.

In witness whereof, I the said John Hassell, have hereunto Sit my Hand and Affixed my Seal, the Twenty fifth day of March anno: Domini, 1754.

Signed Sealed Pronounced and Declared by the said John Hassell in the Presents of us:

JOHN HASSELL, (Seal)

    THOS. WYNNE.
    JEREMIAH WYNNE, Jurat.
    PETER WYNNE.
Exrs Qualifd.

NORTH CAROLINA. TYRRELL COUNTY, ss.   June County Court, 1754.

    Present his Majestys Justice's:

These may Certify that Jeremiah Wynne, One of the Subscribing Evidences to the Within Will, personally appeared in open Court and made Oath on the Holy Evangelist of almighty God, that he was Present and Saw the within named John Hassell Sign, Seal, publish, Pronounce and Declare the within to be and Contain his last Will and Testament, and that he was then, and at that time, of sound and Disposing Memory; and that he also saw Thomas Wynne and Peter Wynne Sign their Names thereto at the same time; Then also Appeared Rachel Hassell and Qualified as Executrix by taking the Oath by Law appointed for the Qualification of Executors. Ordered that the Hon'ble James Murray, Esqr., Secretary of this province, or his deputy, have notice thereof, that Letters Testamentary Issue thereon as the Law Directs.

Test. Evan Jones, Clk. Cur.

Copied from Original Will, filed in the Office of the Secretary of State.

JAMES HODGES' WILL.

In the Name of God Amen, the Second Day of February, one thousand, Seven Hundred, fifty Eight. I, James Hodges, of Pasquotank, North Carolina, being very Sick & weak in body but of Prefect mind & Memory, thanks be therefore given unto God, Therefore calling unto mind the mortality of my Body and knowing that it is appointed for all Men once to Dye, do make and ordain this my last Will & testament, that is to say, Principally and first if all, I give & recommend my Soul, into the Hands of god that gave it; and my Body I Recommend to ye earth to be Buried in decent order, at ye Discretion of my Executors.

Item. I give & Bequeath to my Son, Josiah, that Plantation & Islands on the N. E. Side pasquotank River Bridge to him & his heires for ever.

Item. It is my Will & Desire that if my loving Farther, Joseph Hodges, as Willed any part or Parcel of his Estate to me, I humbly beg him to give & Bequeath it to my well beloved Son, Jams. Hodges, Jun., to him & his heires for Ever, & farther, it is my desire yt my loving Brothers, Joseph & Stephen Hodges shall collect all my Debts on the Great Bridge Books, and to Pay all my Just Debts that I owe in Norfolk & theire Lawfull Commissions.

Item. I give & Bequeath to my Son, Willis Hodges, wt. over Rush of my Book debts, if any Remaining, to him & his Heires for Ever.

Item. I Give and Bequeath to my loveing Son, Samuel Hodges, Negro boy named Peter, to him & his Heires for ever.

Item. I also give a bequeath to my Loveing Son, Willis Hodges, Negro boy Named Sam, to him, & his heires for Ever.

Item. I give & bequeath to my well beloved Wife, my writing Desk & bigest ovel Table, my Painted Chest & Seal Skin trunk, one Set of Silver Teaspoons & Tong's, & all my Pewter I brought out of Virginia, Two Frying pans, five Iron pots, & all ye Plantation utensiels, & Sufficiant of household Meat to Support ye Family untel New years day, & fat.

It is my Will that my Estate shall Pay for ye Building of a New Kitchen, w'th one small Brick Chimney in room of the old wood Chimney. And farther, I give & Bequeath to my loveing wife all Small Furniture, such as Earth'nware & Coopers, &c., and ten old chairs and Six red Do., & one Safe Bought of Timothy Hickson, one Iron Chafeing dish, & all ye aforsd. mentioned, to her and her Heires for ever. I likewise desire that none of my Children shall lay any Clame to any Part or parcel, or any part, of my Wifes Estate that she was Posest of before I married her.

Item. I give & Bequeath to my Loveing Son, James Hodges, my lot of Land & Marsh on the west Side of the road going to the Great Bridg accord'g to ye bounds that Thomas Manning formerly held by, & give him my Storehouse standing by brick hous formerly belonging to Mr. Charles Sweny, and I give him my Roan horse called Rock, & a dark bay Horse wch. I had in Swop of Solomon Timple, & my Riding Sadle and housing.

Item. I give, bequeath to My loveing Wife, the use of my Negor Woman call'd Phebe, tell my Son, Portlock attains to the age of Twenty one years, and then the sd. negro Phebe & her increase to return to ye sd. Portlock & his heires for Ever. I likewise give him ye Horse I bought of David Cook, Call'd Ball, to be sold by Ferebe Hodges & the Money Laid out in Goods to support ye sd. Portlock.

Item. I give & Bequeath to my well beloved Wife, my horse call'd Dultage, to her & her Heires for ever, & the use of Sam & Peter tell my two Sons, Willis & Josias Hodges comes to Lawful age; & it is my desire that my two sons, Josias & Willis Hodges, shall not in any wise disanul my part of the sd. Clause before mention'd.

Item. I Give & bequeath to my daughter Kesiah Curlin, Negor girl call'd Sarah, & one feather bed & furniture, spining wheel, pewter, one chest deliver'd to her when Marri'd, in full of her Portion, to her & her heirs for Ever.

Item. I give & Bequeath to my Daughter, Molly, the Negro Girl call'd Rachel, to her & her heirs for Ever.

Item. I give & bequeath to my Daughter, Frances Hodges, one negro Girl Call'd Hannah, to her & her Heirs for Ever, I likewise give to ye use of my wife, ye use of the two Negro Gerles Hannah & Rachel, tell my two Children, Molly & Frances Hodges Comes to Lawful age.

Item. I give & bequeath to my Son in Law, Joseph Stokely, my new Survey over ye River on ye N. E. side Pasquotank River, & I give him Cash to Purchase a grant for ye sd. Survey of Land, to him & his heires for Ever, & I desire that my Exe'or or Executors to take out the grant Soon after my decease.

Item. I give & bequeath to my Daughter, Miriam Hodges, one Negro Girl call'd Nan, to her & her heires for Ever.

Item. I give & bequeath to my loveing Son, James Hodges, my negro man Call'd Boatswain, to him & his heires for Ever.

Item. I Give & bequeath, & it is my Will & desire, that my Brother, Joseph Hodges, Pay to Colo. Robert Tucker, thirty Pound wch. I owe him upon Balce. of old Bond, & ye Joint Bond Brother Joseph Hodges & I ower ye sd. Robert Tucker, in Part of Eighty five Pounds that Brother Joseph Hodges owes to me, & uppon Settlem't wn. I was Last in Virginia in December last; & I further desire, that my loveing Brother, Joseph Hodges, shall Com in here & take all ye Invoics that is in PardonShip between him & I, at Spraules, Newtons, Atchison, & Sum them up & see wt. the Amounts is, & then go to ye sd. Sproules, Newtons & Atchison, & take true Copys of what we have Paid in company & see if I fall in Debt to pay it, giveing me Credit for ye one half of all ye money he pays away of mine, in my Old Book list; all ye Moneys that can be got in, Brother Joseph Hodges must have one half & ye other half to my well beloved Wife, Miriam Hodges in Concideration of Supporting & Schooling ye Children, & after my beloved Wife, Miriam Hodges & Brother Joseph Hodges & Mr. Andrew Miller, Merch't, if any remains to be Equal Divid'd between my two Sons & Daughters, Lamb, Portlock, Molly & Frances Hodges.

Item. I give & bequeath to my loving Wife, Side Saddle & my longest Gun, Some wite &nd Brown Sugar Bought of Capt. Headly and Part of a Barr'l Molasses.

Item. I give & bequeath my short Gun I brought from Virginia, to my Son, Lamb Hodges, & one pair of hand Mill Stones being now in Possession of Solomon Temple.

Item. I further give strict orders that no Person or Persons shall Pretend to make Publick vandue of any Part or Parcel of my before Mentioned Estate, under Penalty of one hundred Pounds, proc. Money.

Item. I give & Bequeath to my loving Wife, Mariam Hodges our feather beds and furniture I brought out of Virginia, to her & her heires for ever.

Item. I give to my Daughter, Molly Hodges, three new Black Chairs, & one small Ovel Table, to her & her heires for Ever.

Item. I give & bequeath to my daughter, Frances, three new black chaires, & one Square Table.

I do hereby appoint my real friend, Colo. Robert Murdon, & ferebe Hodges, my whole & Sole Executors of this my last Will & Testament. And I do hereby utterly disallow, revoke and disanul all & every former testaments, Wills, Legacies & bequests & Exers., by me in any ways before bequest, and Executors by me in any ways before named, Willed, & bequeathed, Ratifying & Confirming this & no other to be my last Will & Testament.

In Witness whereof, I have hereunto set my hand & Seal the day & year above Written.

JAMES HODGES, (Seal)

Signed, Seal'd, published, Pronounc'd & Declared by the sd. Jams. Hodges as his Last Will & testament in ye Presence of us ye Subscribers:

 Test. JOHN HARRIS, Jurat.
   DANIEL KOEN.
    the mark
   JOHN J. M. MURDEN.
    of

NORTH CAROLINA, PASQUOTANK COUNTY. March Court, 1758.

Present His Majesties Justices:

Theses may Certify that John Harris, one of the Evidences to the within Will, Appeared in open Court and Made Oath on the holy Evangelist, that he was present and James Hodges, sign, Seal, publish and declare the within to be and Contain his last will & Testament, and that he was at that hime of Sound & disposing memory, and that he also saw Danial Coin & John Murden, the other two Evidences, Sign their names thereto at the same time. Then appeared Joseph Hodges, Exe'r in Virginia and was duly Qualified. Ordered that the Honle. Richd. Spaight Esq., Secretary, have notice that Letters may issue.

         Test. THOS. TAYLOR, Clk. Cou.

Copied from the Original Will, filed in the Office of the Secretary o State.

JOSEPH HOLEBROUGH'S WILL.

IN YE NAME OF GOD AMEN. The Eighteenth day of October 1711. I, Joseph Holebrough, of ye County Bath, & Pamlicoth precinct, Being very Sick & weak in Body, but of perfect mind & memory, Thanks be Given Unto God. Therefore calling to mind ye mortality of my Body & knowing that It is appointed for all men once to dye, Doe make & ordain This my Last will & Testament, That is To Say, principally, & First of all, I Give & recommend my Soul into ye hands of God That Gave it, & my Body I recommend To ye Earth, To be buried in decent & Cristian manner at ye discretion of my Executor nothing doubting but at ye General Resurrection I Shall receive The Same again by ye mighty power of G d; and as touching Such worldly Estate wherewith it hath pleas'd God To bless me in This Life, I Give, devise And dispose of ye Same in ye following manner & forme:

I Give bequeith unto My dearly beloved friend, Alexander Avera, One Gun, one Chest, one white Coat, & all my Carpenters Touls.

I Give & bequeith into Elizabeth avera one Gold Ring, one peuter dish & four plates.

I Give unto my beloved friend, Swan Swanson, Two Cows & Calfs which did run this Summer at Mr. price Plantation, & one heifer at Mr. Holms.

I Give & bequeith unto my well beloved Brother, John Holebrough, fourteen Shillings Due me, from Martenquam, deceased. I Give & bequeith unto my Brother, John Holebrough, 1 younge horse. I Give & bequeith unto my Brother, John Holebrough, all my wearing Cloths, only one white Coat excepted.

I give & bequeith unto my Brother, John Holebrough, two Ewes, one ram & all my Cattle in Generall; only, two Cows & Calves & one heifer Excepted. I Give & bequeith unto my Brother, John Holebrough, Seventeen Shillings and Six pence due upon accompt. from Patrick Pendal.

I Give my well beloved Brother, John Holebrough, whom I likewise Constitute, make & ordain my Sole Executor of this my last will & Testam't, all & Singular my lands, messauges & Tenements, & wills, legacies & bequeits, & Executors by me in any ways before named willed & bequeithed, & ratifying, & Confirmeing this & noe other To be my last will And Testam't.

In witness whereof I have hereunto Sett my hand & Seal ye Day & year Above written.

JOSEPH H HOLEBROUGH (Seal)

Signed, Sealed, publishd, pronounced & declared By ye Sd. Joseph Holebrough as his last will Testament, in ye presence of us ye Subscribers:
DANIEL HALLSEY.
JAMES LEIGH.

THOMAS HOSKINS WILL.

IN THE NAME OF GOD AMEN. The 24th. of October, 1733. I, Thomas Hoskins, of The precinct of Chovan, in the County of Albemarl being weak in body but of perfect mind & memory, Thanks be To God Therefore, Calling to mind ye mortality of my body & knowing yt it is appointed for all men once to Diee, do make & ordain This my Last will & Testament, That is to Say, principally, & first of all, I give & recommend my Soul into ye hands of God That Gave it; and my body I recommend to ye Earth to be buried in a Decent & Christian Manner at ye Discression of my Exrs., nothing doubting but at ye General Resurrection I Shall receive ye Same again, I Shall receive ye same again by The mighty power of God; & Touching such

17

Worldly Estate wherewith it hath pleased ye Almighty to bless me with in This Life, I give, Demise & Dispose of ye same in The in ye following manner & form:

Impr. I give to my daughter, Sarah Charlston, one Gold ring, I give to willm. Luton, husband to my Daughter, Ann, Deseaset ten Shillings.

Item. I give to my Son, William Hoskins, whome I Likewise Constitute, make & Ordain one of my Exrs. of This my Last will & Testament, All my Estate Excepting These few articles Here mentioned. I give to my Daughters, Mathew the Stone Called fib, and one fether bed and furniture, one hundred pounds province bills, one pot, one pan, one Table, Two Dishes, four basons & Six plates, four Cows & Calves, Three Ews and Lambs. I give to my Daughter, mary, one negro to her Liking, Which is to be raised out of The Estate, & one hundred pounds province Bills, one feather bed, one pot, one pan, one Table, two Dishes, four basons, & Six plates, four Cows and Calves, Three Ews & lambs, Which is to be raised & Levied out of ye Estate;

And I do hereby Disallow, revoke & Disanul all & Every other former wills, Legacies & bequests & Exrs. by me in any ways before named, Willed, & bequeathed, Ratifying and Confirming This & no other to be my Last will & Testament.

In witness whereof I have hereunto Set my hand and Seal ye Day & year above Written, & Lastly I do make Constitute ordain & appoint my Son, William Hoskins, and John Benburry Exrs. of This my Last Will and Testament.

In Witness Whereof I have hereunto Set my hand & Seal.

THOMAS HOSKINS, (Seal)

Signed, Sealed, Delivered in ye presence of us:
JOHN MITCHENOR,
JAMES SMITH.

CHOVAN. SSC. April Court, 1734.

The Within Will of Thomas Hoskins was proved In open Court by ye oath of John Michneor, an Evidence Subscribing Thereto, who deposed he saw James Smith Sign ye sd. Will as an Evidence.

Test. MOSELEY VAIL. Cle. Cour.

Recorded in Will Book 3, page 304.

ISAAC HUNTOR'S WILL.

IN THE NAME OF GOD AMEN. I, Isaac Huntor, of Chowan County, Being of perfect Memory and minde and Calling to minde the Uncertainty of this Transitory Life, Do make and ordain this my Last will and Testament, in manner and forme following, first, I Bequeath my Soul to almighty God; and my Body to the Earth to be Buried at the Discretion of my Execut'r, hereafter named; and as for my worldly Estate which it hath pleased God to Bestow upon me, I Give and Dispose of as followeth, Vizt:

First, my will and Desire is, that all my Just Debts be Trewly paid and Discharged by my Execr.

Item. I Give and Bequeath to my Son, Elisha Huntor, my plantation whereon I now Live, and the plantation whereon he now Lives, together with all the Land thereunto Belonging, I Say to my sd. Son, Elisha Huntor, and his heirs and Assignes for Ever. I also give to my Sd. Son, Elisha Huntor, my Negro man named Duke, to him and his heirs for Ever.

Item. I Give and Bequeath to my son, Jesse Huntor, all my Land and plantation Purchased of Thomas Morris as Pr. (Deed) Deed of Sale Containing three hundred Acres, be it more or less, I Say to my son, Jesse Huntor, and his heirs and assignes for Ever. I also give to my sd Son Jesse Huntor, my Negro boy named Toney, I Say to him and his heirs and assigns for Ever.

Item. I Give and Bequeath to my son, Isaac Huntor, all my Land in Bartea County, as by a pattent Dated the twenty Eighth day of Febuary, 1744/5, for one hundred and fifty acres; also, a Deed of Sale for 170 acres, Dated April, 20, 1745, and Joyning to Elisha Huntors Lands, I Say to my Son, ISaac Huntor, and his heirs and assignes for Ever; I also give to my sd. Son, Isaac Huntor, my Negro Girle named Venus, she and her Increase; also, one Good feather Bed and furniture there unto belonging; also three medle Sized puter Dishes and one puter Bason, and one Iron pott of forty pounds weight, one frying pan, and two Cows and Calves, to him and his heirs for Ever.

Item. I Give to my Son, Daniel Huntor, Seventy five pounds, Currant Money of Virginia, to be Raised out of my Estate, it being in Consideration as I have not Given him any Land or negroe, I also Give to my sd. Son Daniel Huntor, one Good feather Bed and the furniture thereunto belonging, also three Medle Sized puter Dishes, one puter bason, and one Iron pott of about forty Pounds weight, one frying Pan, and two Cows and Calves, I Say to him and his heirs for Ever.

Item. I Give to my Daughter, Alce Perry, my Negro man named Tobey, to her and her heirs for Ever.

Item. I Give to my Daughter, Hannah Riddick, my Negro Girle named Lucey, She and her Increas, to her and her heirs for Ever.

Item. I Give to my Daughter, Elizabeth Perry, my Negro Girle named Kate, provided She pay to my Daughter Alce five pounds Currant money to make the Vallue of Tobey Equill with her negro Kate, and then I Say to her and her heirs for Ever.

Item. I Give to my Daughter, Rachell Walton, my negr[o] woman named Hagor, to her and her heirs for Ever.

Item. I Give to my Daughter, Sarah Huntor, my Negro Girle named Tresea, also my Side Saddle, and my Leather Trun[k] with a Date of 1734 on it, and a Horse or mare of four pound[s] Vallue, and three Meddle Sized puter Dishes, one puter Baso[n] one Iron pott, one frying Pann, two Cows and Calves, and on[e] Good feather bed and the furniture thereunto belonging, Say to her and her Heirs for ever.

Item. I Give to my Grand Children, ye Sons and Daughte[rs] of my Daughter, Jean Deceast, namely Jesse Phillip, & Mar[y] Perries & Sarah field, to Each and Every of them the Sum [of] five pounds, Currant money of Virginia, to them and their hei[rs] for Ever.

Item. I Give to Zilphea Parker, Daughter of Jonatha[n] Parker, one Good feather Bed and furniture, and two Put[er] Dishes & three puter plates provided, that if She Stays an[d] Lives with me or in my family till She Cumes to the age [of] Eighteen years and Behaves well, or at ye day of Marriag[e] if to my, or friends Satisfaction, then I say, to her and h[er] heirs for Ever.

Item. All the Rest and Residue of my Estate not befo[re] given, be it of what nature or Kindsoever, It is my Will an[d] Desire that it be Equally Devided between my Sons an[d] Daughters Namely: Elisha, Jacob, Jesse, Isaac, Daniel, Alc[e] Hannah, Elizabeth, Rachell, and Sarah, Share and Sha[re] a Like; it is also my Desire that my Son, Jacob Huntor, have [to] injoy all my Right of the Water Mill.

Lastly, I Nominate and appoint my Son, Elisha Hunto[r] my whole and Sole Executor to Se this my Will duly fulfile[d] and performed, and I do hereby Revoak and Make Null & Voi[d] all former or other will or wills heretofore by me made, pu[b]lished, or Declared, Either by word or wrighting, and if my So[n] Elisha Should happen to Die before this my will be fulfile[d] then, and in that Case, I Do hereby appoint my Son, Jaco[b] and John Gordon, or Either of them, to Se this my Last Wi[ll] and Testament Duly fulfiled.

In witness whereof, I have hereunto Sett my hand and fixe[d] my Seal this Seventeen day of aprill, 1752.

Signed, Sealed, published, and
Declared by the Testator to be his
Last Will and Testament in the
presents of us:

                                                              ISAAC HUNTOR (Seal)

        MOSES SUMNER.
        SAMUEL SUMNER, Jurt.
        JOHN SUMNER, Jurt.

CHOWAN COUNTY, ss.   April Court, Anno Dom., 1753.
Present His Majestys Justices:
These may Certifie, that the within Will was Duly Proved in Open Court, by the Oaths of Samuel Sumner and John Sumner, two of the Subscribing Evidences thereto; and at the same time appeared Elisha Huntor, Executor, in Open Court and was Duly Qualified thereto by taking the Executors Oath by law appointed. Ordered that the Secretary of Said Province have Notice thereof that Letters Testamentary issue thereon as the Law Directs.
Test. JAMES CRAVEN, Cler. Cur.

Copied from the Original Will, filed in Office of Secretary of State.

HENRY HYRNE'S WILL.

NORTH CAROLINA SS.

IN THE NAME OF GOD AMEN. I, Henry Hyrne, of New Hanover County, in the Province aboves'd, Gentleman, being in an Ill state of health but of a sound mind and memory, blessed be God, Do make, Declare and Publish this my last Will and Testament, hereby revoking and Declaring Null and Void all former or other Wills by me heretofore made. First, I recommend my Soul to almighty God, hoping and believing a remission of my sins and the Errors and failings of my life through his mercy and the mediation of my Redeemer, Jesus Christ; And my body to the Earth to be Decently buried at the discretion of my Executors herein first after Named. And as to my Worldly estate with which it hath pleased God to bless me, I Give, Bequeath, devise and dispose of it in manner and form following:

Imprimis. I Give, Devise, and Bequeath to my Nephew, Henry Walters, and his Heirs and Assigns forever, all that my plantation and six hundred & fourty acres of Land whereon I now dwell in New Hanover County, called New Hyrnham, together with the five hundred and fifty three Acres of Land adjoyning and contiguous thereto, devised to me by my Honoured Father, Colonel Edward Hyrne, being Part of a larger Tract of Land belonging to my said Father in his life time (as by a Plan thereof Annexed to his last Will and Testament may at large appear).

Item. I Give, Devise and Bequeath to my said Nephew, Henry Walters, and his heirs and Assigns for ever, all that my other Plantation containing about Seventeen hundred and fourty seven Acres of Land in New Hanover County whereas * * * * * (Illegible) and Devised by me said Father to my said Brother, George Hyrne (as by a Plan thereof annexed to the last will and Testament of my said Father may at large apear) and by the death of my said Brother George descended to me.

Item. I Give and Bequeath to my said Nephew, Henry Walters, my negroe man Call Casar and my Negroe Girl called Hannah.

Item. It is my will that my House, plantation and lands be rented out by my Executor first Named, for the benefit and advantage of my said Nephew, Henry Walters, at a moderate rent with a covenant in the lease that the person renting the same shall, at the Expiration of such lease, leave the Said Houses & plantations in the same good repair they are in when he leases them, or any of them he shall so lease.

Item. I Give and bequeath to my Neice, Elizabeth Walters my Negroe Girls Betty and Calia.

Item. I give and Bequeath to my Nephew, Joseph Walters and my Nephew, George Walters, Ten pound, proclamation money, to each of them.

Item. I Give and Bequeath, I give and Bequeath to my Nephew, Moses Britton, my Gold Sleeve Buttons.

Item. Item. I Give and Bequeath to my Niece, Mary Britton, my shagarene case of Silver Instruments, also my Six Silver Tea spoons, silver Tea Strainer and Tongs.

Item. I Give and Bequeath to my Nephew, Henry Britton my silver Watch and Silver pepper Castor, in rememberance of his regard and kindness shown me, in coming to see me and staying some time with me.

Item. I Give and Bequeath to my Nephew, Francis Britton, my Gold Stock Buckle (and) And my six silver table Spoons in remembrance of his regard and kindness Shuon me in coming to see me and staying some time with me.

Item. Whereas, I have been greatly aflicted with Sickness and thereby rendered incapable of going about or transacting my own business, except for about fourteen months, for more than twelve years past, and since my making a former Will. And my Good Friend and Neighbor, Frederick Jones, Esquire, having all the said time (except the said fourteen months) Transacted my business, settled my accounts, and also as my Attorney during my absence when I went to Philadelphia for the recovery my health managed and directed my Whole Affairs and business to my satisfaction and the benefit of my Estate, I therefore Give and bequeath to the Frederick Jones, and his Assignes, my Negro Called or Named Tobey. I also Give and Bequeath to the said Frederick my Negroe Woman called old Lucey, he paying into my Estate so much proclamation money for the Said Lucey as she shall be appraised at, by three honest and credible persons to be worth, the said Lucey having been a good Slave, it is my desire my said friend, Frederick Jones should have her, as I am Sensible his humanity is such that he would treat her well.

Item. I Give and Bequeath to my said Friend, Frederick Jones, my stand of Cruits I bought of Mr. Smith, also my two volumes of Chambers Dictionary, and such of my other books as he shall choose to have.

Item. It is my further Will, and I do hereby Qrder and direct that my Executor, the said Frederick Jones, shall have and take five per centum Commission on all moneys that shall arise the by sale of such of my Estate as is or shall be in—my Will ordered is to be sold * * * (Illegible).

Item. I Give and Bequeath to my God Daughter, Elizabeth Jones, Daughter of my Friend, the said Frederick Jones, my Negroe Woman called Flora, wife to my Negro man call Toby, together with her three children by Name, Bessy, Toby & Guy.

Item. It is my Will and I do hereby order and direct that all my Negroe Slaves, household Goods, Stocks of weak ? Cattle, horse, Hoggs, Sheep, Geese, Turkeys, Ducks and Fowls of every kind, Carts, Waggon and Plantation Tools of every kind, and all the rest and Residue of my Estate of what kind or nature Whatsoever, not in this my will by me before bequeathed and disposed of, be sold by my Executor, the said Frederick Jones; and in case of his death by my Nephews, Moses Britton & Frances Britton, and the money arising by the sale thereof, after payment of my just debts and Funeral Expenses & the Commission aforesaid before Given & Orderd to my Executor the said Frederick Jones, I give and Bequeath to my Nephews, Moses Britton, Francis Britton, Henery Britton & my Niece, Mary Britton to be Equally distributed among them, Share & Share Alike.

Item. It is my Will & I desire my Executor, Frederick Jones do imediately after my decease, send my Negro man Cato with an anon'mt of my death to my Nephews, Moses Britton & Francis Britton, and is is my desire that my will be not opened till they have such Notice.

Lastly, I Nominate & Appoint my aforesaid Friend, Frederick Jones, Esquire, Executor of this my last will & Testament & after his death I Nominate & Appoint Moses Britton & Frances Britton, Executors thereof.

In Testimony whereof, I have, to this my last Will & Testament, set my hand and seal this nith— day of September, in the year of our Lord, one thousand and seven hundred and Seventy two.

      HENRY HYRNE (Coat of Arms on seal)

Signed, Sealed, Published and declared by the said Henry Hyrne, as, and for his last Will & Testament in the presence of us.
  SAML. GWANN.
  JOHN BUFORD.
  BENJAMIN WILLIAMS.
  WILLIAM BUFORD.

N. B. The words "and fourty" between the thirteenth and fourteenth lines from the Top of the first page, first interlined; and the Words "fourty" in the twenty second line, and Hannah, in the twenty nith line of the said first page blurred, before the Signing of the Will on the other half of this Sheet, by the said Henry Hyrne in the presence of us.

    SAM GWANN,
    JOHN BUFORD,
    BENJAMIN WILLIAMS,
    WILLIAM BUFORD.

NORTH CAROLINA. SS.

CODICIL. I, Henry Hyrn, of New Hanover county, in the Province abovesaid, Gentleman, Do this day make and declare this my Codicil in manner following, that is to Say,

Whereas, In my Will bearing date this ninth day of September, in the year of our Lord, one thousand, Seven hundred and Seventy two, I have forgot to dispose of my wearing apparell I Do now by this my Codicil Give and Bequeath all my Wearing apparel to my Nephews, Joseph Walters, Henry Walters & George Walters (except my Shirts or Wearing Linnin) to be Equally divided among them. And my shirts or Wearing Linnin, I Give and Bequeath to my said Nephews, Joseph Walters, Henry Walters Gorge Walters, and my Neice, Elizabeth Walters, to be equally   * * *   (Illegible) I Give and Bequeath to my friend * * * (Illegible) in transacting my Law business the sum of Ten pounds proclamation money, to be paid him out of the money arising by the Sale of the residuum of my Estate.

And Lastly, It is my Will and desire that this present Codicil, wrote in the same Sheet of paper whereon my will is wrote, be made a part of my Last Will & Testament to all intents and purposes.

In Witness whereof, I have hereunto put my hand and Seal, this ninth day of September, one thousand Seven hundred and seventy two.

                HENRY HYRNE (Coat of Arms on Seal)

Signed, Sealed, Published & declared in presence of us: (The word "Elizabeth Walters" between the tenth & eleventh line from the Top of the Codicil first interlined).

    JOHN RUFORD.
    BENJAMIN WILLIAMS.
    WILLIAM BUFORD.

The within last Will and Testament and Codicil thereto, of Henry Hyrne, deceased, was proved before me this 26th. day of October, 1773, by the Oath of William Buford, one of the subscribing Witnesses thereto, who swore that he was present and did see the within named Testator Sign, Seal, publish and declare the same to be and contain his last Will and Testament, and that * * * (Line Illegible).

And the Said Frederick Jones, the Executor in the said Will named, having qualified by taking the Oaths of an Executor agreeable to Law. It is Ordered that Letters Testamentory issue thereon accordingly.

Jo. Martin.

Copied from the Original Will, filed in the Office of the Secretary of State.

JAMES INNES' WILL.

In the Nam of God Amen. I, James Innes, of Cape Fear, in North Carolina in America, Coll. of the Regement of sd. Province, (Raised for His Majestys imediate Service and Commanded in Chief of this Expedition to the Ohio, Against the French & there Indeans, whoe have most unjustly Invaided & fertified Them Selves on His Majestys Land), Being now readdey to enter upon Action & of Sound minde, Memory & Understanding, Do make this my Last Will & Testament, in Manner & Forme following, viz:

I recomend my Soul to the Almighty God that gave it, relying on the merits of Jesus Christ for Mercy at the last day. My Bodie, I most freely Offer to be disposed off as God in His wise providence shall please to direct.

I recomend the paying of all my Just & Lawful Debts, instantly or when demanded. I direct a remittance may be made to Edinburgh, Sufficient to pay for a Church Bell for the Parish Church of Cannesby, in Caithness, agreeable to my Letter to mr. Jams. Broadee, Minister there.

I also appoint and direct, that there may be a furder remittance made of one hundred Pounds, Sterll., for the Use of the Poor of the said Parish of Cannesby, and the said summ of One hundred Pounds, to be put to Interest for the use of the Poor of Said Parish, as formerly directed by me.

I also give & bequeath, att the Death of my Loving Wife, Jean Innes, my Plantation Called Point Pleasant, & the Opposite mash Land over the River, for which there is a Separate Patent, Two Negro young Women, One Negro young Man, and there Increase; all the Stock of Cattle and Hogs, halfe the Stock of Horses belonging att the time to that Plantation With all my Books, and one hundred Pounds Sterling, or the Equivalent thereunto in the currency of the Country, For the Use of a Free School for the Benefite of the Youth of North Carolina. And to see that this part of my Will be dewly Executed att the time, I appoint the Colonell of the New Hanover Regiment, the Parson of Willmington Church & the Vestrey for the time being, or the Majority, of them as they Shall from time to tim be Choised or Appointed.

The Residue of my Estate, both reall and personall, I lav to the Sole disposall of my Loving Wife and companion of m; Life, Jean Innes, whome I appoint to be Sole Executrix of thi my last will and Testament, which I desire may be recorded ii the Publique Regester.

In testimony hereof, I have put my hand and Seall, thi fift day of July, and in the Year of our Lord, God, One thousand Seven hundred, fifty and four.

JAMES INNES (Seal).

Done at Winchester, in Virginia, in presence of us, Sign'd, Sealled, & published:
  JOHN CARLYLE.
  W. COCKS.
  CALEB GRAINGER.

The foregoing Last Will and Testament of James Innes, Esquire, wa duly proved before me by the oath of Caleb Grainger, who made Oath o: the holy Evangelists, that he saw and heard the said James Innes, sign seal and publish the foregoing as, and for, his last Will and Testamen in the presence of the said Caleb Grainger, John Carlyle, and Williar Cocks, who subscribed their respective Names as Evidences thereto, i: presence of the Testator, who was at the same time of sound and Dis posing Memory and Understanding.

Let Letters Testamentary Issue hereof to Jean Innes, Executrix in th foregoing Will named.

Brunswick, 9th., Octor., 1759.

ARTHUR DOBBS.

Copied from the Original Will, filed in the Office of the Secretary c State.

CHRISTIAN ISLER'S WILL.

IN THE NAME OF GOD AMAN. The Fourth Day of octobei one Thousand, seven Hundred and forty Seven: I, Chrystiai Isler, of the County of Craven, In the provins of North Carolina Blander; being Very Sick and Weak In the Body, but of perfec Mind and memory, thanks be given unto god, therefore Callin; unto Mind the Mortality of my body and knowing that it I appointed for all men once to die, do make and ordain this m: Last Will and Testament, that is to Say, principally and firs of all, I Give and Recomment my Soul Into the hands of Go(that Gave it; and my body I Recomment to the Earth, to b buried in decent Christian Burial at the Descretion of m: Executors, not doubting but at the General Resurrection Shall Receive the Same again by the mighty power of God and ;touching Such worldly Estate wherewith it hath please(almighty god to bless me in this Life, I Give, Demise an(dispose of the same in the following maner and form:

Imprimis, I Give and bequeath unto Elizabeth Isler, my dearly beloved Wife, one negro man Callit Cato, and one negro women Callit judee, two plow horses under Ceers and one plow and fluck, one pay Mare Callit jan, and one three year old horse; and the third of all my Houshold goods, and of all my Chattle, to her, the Said Elizabeth Isler, my Wife, her heirs, Executors or asministrators or assigns for Ever, and her Widow Sead on the blantation I now Life on by her freely to be possessed with out ang Interruption & * * *

Item. I give and bequeath to my well beloved Sonn, John Isler, one negro man Callit Embero, and one horse Callit Zany, with my Sadle and bridle, and five four year old Steers, five three year old heafers with Calvs, and one Yearling horse, I give to him, his heirs, Executors, administrators and assigns for Ever.

Item. I Give and bequeath to my well beloved Son, William Isler, my land and blantation I now Live on, and one negro boy Callit Simon, and one maladder boy Callet Scot, and four Ews and lambs, and one Ram, and Eight Sows and picks, I give to him, the said William Isler, his heirs, Executors, administrators, and assigns for Ever.

Item. I give and bequeath to my well beloved Daughter, Elizabeth Isler, one feather bed, one negro boy Callit Nooris, and one Sorrel mare and Cold, all of which I Give to her, the Said Elizabeth Isler My Daughter, to her, her heirs, Executors, administrators and assigns for Ever; and also, the third of all my household goods, and the third of all my Chattle, to her for Ever.

Item. I Give and bequeath to my well beloved Daughter, Susanna Isler, one negro boy Callit Charles, and one Two year old mare that Came of old Jan; and also, the third of all my Houshold goods, and the third of all my Chattle, all of which I Give to her, her heirs, Executors, administrators and assigns for Ever.

Item. I to Elect and Choose my well beloved brother, Frederick Isler, and John Isler, and William Isler, my Sons, for my Executors, to act acording to this my last will and Testament, and I do here by utterly disallow, Revoke and disanul, all and Every other former testament, wills, Lagacies and Requests and Executors by me in any ways before named, Willed and bequeathed, Retifying and Confirming this, and no other, to be my Last will and testament.

In witness whereof I have hereunto Set my hand and Seal the day and year above written.   his
                               CHRISTIAN C E ISLER (Seal)
                                        mark

Signed, Sealed, published, pronounced and declared, by the Said Christian Isler, as his Last

will and testament, In the presence of us the Subscribers:
>MELCHER REMM.
>JAMES MARSHEL.
>SARAH X LICKBLAT.
>her marke

On the Oaths of Melcher Remm and Sarah Lickblat, of the due Execution of this Will, Let it be Registered. The within named John Isler and William Isler having taken the oath of Extors. Dated this 7th day of November, 1747. E: HALL, C: J:

Copied from Original Will, filed in the Office of the Secretary of State.

JOSEPH JENORE'S WILL.

IN THE NAME OF GOD AMEN. I, Joseph Jenore, Surveyor Generale of North Carolina, being Sick and weak, but of Sound mind and memory, do make and ordain this my Last will and Testament, desiring my body may be decently buryed, And recommending my Soul humbly to the mercy of God.

Impris. I will That all my Just Debts be payed as soon as Conveniently may be, and after my funeral Expences & Debts are payed, I Devise & bequeath all my Estate, real & personal whatsoever and wheresoever, to my Dear wife, Anne Jenore, to her, her heirs & assigns.

And I do hereby appoint my sd. wife sole Executrix of this my last will and Testament. My son being already provided for & under the Care of his grandfather, I give him one Shilling only, not doubting but due Care will be Taken of him. And I do hereby revoke all other wills by me made.

In testimony whereof, I have hereunto Set my hand & Seal. This 30th. (30) day of Sept., 1732.

>JO. JENORE.

Signed, Sealed, published & declared, to be his last will and Testament in presence of us:
>WM. LITTLE.
>R. FOSTER.
>———— WILLIAMS.

NO. CAROLINA. SSC. Jan'ry 13th., 1732.

Ayleffe Williams Personally appeared before me and made oath on the holy Evangelist, that he Saw Joseph Jenoure, Esqr., Sign, Seal, publish & Declare the within written Instrument to be & contain his last will and Testam't, and that he Saw William Little & Robt. Forster sign as Evidences at the same time. GEO. BURRINGTON.

Copied from the Original Will, filed in the Office of the Secretary of State.

GABRIEL JOHNSTON'S WILL.

NORTH CAROLINA.

IN THE NAME OF GOD AMEN, This is the last will and Testament of Gabriel Johnston, Esquire, Governor of North Carolina.

Imprimis, I give and bequeath unto my Dearest Wife, Frances Johnston, a Plantation called Possum Quarter, lying and being in Granville County. I also give and bequeath unto her another Plantation Called Conahoe, with the Three Hundred Acres lying near it by Gainers Plantation, both in Tyrrel Countys, together with a small Plantation lying on Salmon Creek in the County of Bertie, which I lately purchased of Lamb Hardy, to her & her Heirs for Ever.

Item, it is my Will that the said Frances Johnston shall at a Time she Shall Think proper and Convenient for her own Interest and that of my Daughter, Purchase for her own Use, and in Order to Manage and Stock the aforesaid Plantation, Twenty Working Negroes, Seventy Head of black Cattle, and a Proportional Quantity of Hoggs, which Purchase I allow her to make Either all at Once or Gradually as it shall best Suit her Interest; or if it can't be done Easily to take the said Negroes out of the Estate of my Daughter, Penelope, and take Care to have the Gradually Replais'd.

2° I give & bequeath unto my Dearest Daughter, Penelope Johnston, all my Lands lying the Counties of Bertie, Northampton and Granville which I had by her Mother, to her and her Heirs for Ever, and all the Slaves I had by her Mother when I married her, Together with their Increase. And in Case my Wife shall Choose to Remain in North Carolina and Reside upon the Lands of, and live with my Daughter (which is my Hearty Wish), my will is that she, my said Wife, shall have the Use of all my said Daughters Plantations, and for her Encouragement to Cultivate & Improve these Plantations, Especially in Raising Silk, and she, my said Wife, shall Receive and Enjoy for her own Proper Use, One Half or Moiety of the Yearly Produce of the said Plantations, untill the Time of my said Daughters Marriage, or her Attaining the Age of One and Twenty, I likewise give my Daughter all the live Stock which shall be on my said Plantations at the Time of my Decease. And I Earnestly Request my Dearest Wife to be a kind tender Mother to my Dear little Girl, and to bring her up in the Fear of God and under a deep Sense of her being always in his Presence, and in Sobriety and Moderation Confining her Desires to things Plain, neat and Elegant, and not aspiring after the Gayety, Splendor and Extravagances; and Especially, to take Care to keep within the Bounds of her Incomes, and by no Means to Run in Debt.

And in Case it shall please Almighty God to remove my Daughter without her leaving any Children behinde her, it is my Will that the Above Estate shall go to my Brothers Sons and their Heirs Heirs forever; and that in such Case my Dearest Wife, Frances Johnston, may Enjoy, Possess and live upon any One of my Plantations she shall Choose Within Twelve Months after my Decease, and my Brother, Samuel Johnston, may in like Manner Choose any other of my Plantations to be Enjoyed during their Natural lives.

It., I give and bequeath unto Henry Johnston, now at School in Newhaven, in the Colony of Conecticut, a Tract of One Thousand Acres of Land Lying on Cypress Creek on the South Side of Trent River in Craven County; and a Tract of Nine Hundred and Eighty Acres lying on the South Side of Trent, to Carolina Johnston, his Sister; and a Tract of Four Hundred and Odd Acres lying on the Head of Trent and New Rivers to my Neice, Penelope Johnston, to them and their Heirs for ever. All which Lands formerly belonged to William Smith, Esqr., Chief Justice of this Province, and were left to me by his Will.

Item, I give and bequeath unto my Brother's Two Son, Samuel Johnston and John Johnston, a Tract of Land of Seven Thousand Acres lying on Deep River in Bladen County, which I hold under the Name of Edward Griffith, Esqr., to be Equally Divided between them, to them their Heirs, Executors for Ever.

It, I give unto my Daughter, Penelope, all the small Islands lying in Roanoke River, and in the neighbourhood of Mount Gallard.

It., I do will, and hereby Impower my Executors hereafter Named, to Sell all the Remainder of my Real Estate to the best Purchaser within Two Years after my Decease, and the Monies arising from the Sale thereof, I do hereby Order to be applied to the Payment of my Just Debts.

I leave all my Houshold Furniture, Plantation Tools and Necessaries to my Wife and Daughter in Case they Remain in this Province; My Books, I leave to William Cathcart, Esqr., after my Wife and Brother have Choose out them any Number not Exceeding Forty Each.

It, To my Sister, Elizabeth Smear, of the County of Fife, North Britain, my large Repeating Gold Watch after it has been put in Order at the Expence of my Estate. To Carolina Johnston, so be she settles at her Plantation, Ten Cows and Calves, with Hoggs in Proportion, and Five Negroes, And to Each of my Brother's Daughters, at the Day of their Marriage, Two Negroes. And all that Distressed poore Family I Recommend to the Kindness and Protection of my Dear Wife, not Dareing to leave more to my Brother least it should

be Seized to his Creditors, and his Family have no Benefit by
it. As for all the Remainder of my Estate, after Payment of
my Just Debts as above Directed, I Order all may be sold
and my Credits and Arrears of Sallary to be Divided in Five
Parts; One Fifth to my Wife, Two Fifths to William Cathcart
in Trust for my Brother for the Education of his Family, One
Fifth for my Sister, Elizabeth Smear and her Heirs, and One
Fifth to Henry Johnston.

It., I give unto my Dearest Wife, One Negro Female Child
Called Titty, and leave her Sole Executrix of this my last
Will; And in Case of her Death or Absence, Samuel Johnston
and William Cathcart, Esqr., Executors, Done at Edenhouse
this Sixteenth Day of May, 1751.

GAB: JOHNSTON. (Seal)

This last Will and Testament
all written with my Own Hand
and Contained in this & the Two
Preceeding Pages was signed,
Sealed and Declared to be my
last Will and Testament in Presence of:
> ANDW. LEAKE.
> SAML. ORMES.
> THOS. WHITMELL.

NORTH CAROLINA.

I, Matthew Rowan, Esqr., President & Commander in Chief in and over the said Province, Do hereby Certify that this Day Samuel Ormes Personally appeared before me and made Oath that he saw his late Excellency Gabriel Johnston, Esqr., late Governor of the said Province, sign, seal and Declare the above Instrument of Writing as & for his last Will and Testament, and that at his Signing thereof he was of sound & Disposing Mind and Memory; and also, that he saw Andrew Leake and Thos. Whitmell sign their Names at the same Time as Evidences thereunto.

Given at Newbern under my Hand, this Fourth Day of April, Anno Dom., 1753.

MATH: ROWAN.

NORTH CAROLINA.

This Day Frances Johnston, Widow, Relict of the late Gabriel Johnston, Esqr., late governor of this Province, Personally appeared before me as Executrix appointed by the Will of said Gabriel Johnston, Esqr., and took the Oath appointed by Law to be taken by Executors.

Given under my Hand this 16th. Day of April, Anno Dom., 1753.

JAS. HASELL C. Sc.

BERTIE COUNTY. May Court, 1753.

The within written last Will and Testament of his late Excellency, Gabriel Johnston, Esqr., late Governor of North Carolina was further proved by the Oath of Thomas Whitmell, One of the Subscribing Witnesses thereto, Ordered to be Certified.

P Order of Court.

Copy, SAML. ORMES, Cl. Cur.

Recorded in Will Book 6, page 153.

SAMUEL JOHNSTON'S WILL.

NORTH CAROLINA, } ss.
ONSLOW COUNTY,

IN THE NAME OF GOD AMEN, This is the last Will and Testam' of Saml. Johnston, of Onslow County, in the Province aforesaid.

Imprs., after paying my lawful Debts both in Great Britain and here, I give and bequeath to my Son, Samuel and John, Six thousand, five hundred Acres of land lying on the NorthEast of Capefear River, contained in four Patents.

Item, I give and bequeath unto my Daughter, Jean, Penelope Isobell, Ann, Hannah, all my lands on Tuckahoe, and Two hundred Acres on Beaver Creek including the Mouth thereof both in Craven County, and all my lands on the Branches of New River, in Short all my real Estate except what is given away above.

Item, I Give and bequeath unto my said Daughters Jean penelope, Isobel, Ann and Hannah, all my Personal Estate my Nigers to be Divided among them in Manner following (Vizt.) one Wench Named bigless and her increase to my Daughter Jean, I mean Dinah and Lydia bess her two Children; to Penelope, little Bess and Susannah; to Isobel Inda and Sall; to Ann, Juno and peter; to my Daughter Hannah Sapho and her Daughter Cary and Black Hannah. The Negro Men to be divided amongst my Daughters, Vizt. Fordune, Frank, Cato, Lewis and Dundree, My Stock of Horses, Black Cattle and Hoggs, Houshold Goods, Plantation Tools, and every other thing belonging to my Personal Estate as if they were herein Particularly Mentioned, to be divided amongst my Daughters; and in Case any of them Should be called of by Death, that their portion Shall go to the Surviver or Survivers of my Daughters. It is my Will that my hands may be kept at work on my plantation for payment of my Debts so far, or be hired out, at the Discretion of my Executors after mentioned, and it is my desire that my Daughters should Stay wth. Mrs. Pheebee Warburton as long as She lives and is willing to keep them, or till they are Married.

lastly, I declare this to be my last Will and Testament, Making Void all former Wills, and I hereby appoint John Starkey, Esquire, my Exr.

In witness whereof I have hereunto put my hand and seal before Cary Godbe, William Williams and John Melton, Subscribing Evidences, this 13th. Day of November, in the Year of Our Lord, one thousand, Seven hundred and fifty Six Years, and in the 30th. Year of our Sovereign Lord the King, his reign.   SAML. JOHNSTON. (Seal)

 CARY GODBE.
 WM. WILLIAMS.
 JNO. MILTON.

NORTH CAROLINA, ONSLOW COUNTY.
At a Court begun and held at the Court Hous on New River, the first Tuesday in Janry. being the 3d. Day, in and for the County of Onslow, Before John Starkey, Esquire, & the rest of the Justices, the within Will was proved by the Oath of John Milton, and John Starkey the Exor. therein Named, Qualified by takeing the Usual Oath.
Ordered that he have Letters Testamentary

WILLM. CRAY, C. C.

Recorded in Will Book 8, page 133.

FREDERICK JONES' WILL.

No. CAROLINA. SC.

IN THE NAME OF GOD AMEN. I, Frederick Jones, of the Precinct of Chowan, in No. Carolina, Esqr., being sick and weak in body, but of Sound and perfect mind & memory, Do Make and Declare these Presents to be and contain my Last Will and Tesament.

Imprimis, I Give, devise and bequeath unto my Eldest daughter, Jane, My Indian Girle named Nanny, My Negro woman named Dinah, together with her three Children, and all the increase that shall be borne of any of them; Her Mothers Diamond wedding ring, and large pair of Diamond Ear-rings, Gold Watch, with the Chain, Seal & other things fixed thereto; All her Mothers wearing Apparrell Such as is already made up & Such things as was designed for her but not made up, All her Mothers Child bede Linnen, with white silk Damask Gown; All the China ware and Tea furniture, with the Dressing Table and furniture; also, a Dozen of my finest Damask Napkins and Table Clothe, a Dozen of fine Diaper Napkins & Table Clothe, One pair of my finest holland Sheets with Pillow Cases; and one other pair of holland Sheets with pillow Cases.

Item, I give, devise and bequeath unto my Daughter, Martha, four young Negroes, two male and two female not under ten years of Age, to be set apart from the rest of my Estate for the use of my said daughter, together with the Increase thereof; Also, the smaller pair of Diamond Ear-rings, one Diamond ring, her Mothers Gold Shoe Buckles, thimble & Bodkin; one Dozen of my finest Damask Napkins and table Clothe; one dozen of fine Diaper Napkins & Table Clothe, One pair of my finest holland Sheets & pillow cases, and one other pair of holland Sheets with Pillow Cases. Also, the Sum of one hundred and fifty pounds, Boston Money.

Item, I Give, devise and bequeath unto my daughter, Rebeckah, four young Negroes, two male & two female, not under ten years of Age, to be set apart from the rest of my Estate for the use of my said daughter, together with the Increase thereof; One Diamond Ring, One Dozen fine Damask Napkins and Table Clothe, One Dozen fine Diaper Napkins and Table Clothe, Two pair of fine holland Sheets and pillow Cases. Also, the Sum of Two hundred pounds, Boston Money.

It is my Will, True Intent & meaning, That these Three Legaceys before given unto my three Daughters, be paid and delivered unto them as they shall respectively attain the age of twenty one Years, or day of Marriage, which shal first happen, and if it shal happen that either of my said Daughters shal depart this life before Marriage or Age of twenty one years, Then it is my Will, true Intent and meaning, that the Legacyes so given shall go to the Survivors or Survivor of my Said Daughters.

Item, I Give, Devise and bequeath unto my Eldest son, William Harding Jones, all my Land on the South side of Moratoke River, being part of a large tract of nine Thousand, one hundred Acres by me taken up. Also, all my Lands in Hyde precinct, To have and to hold the aforesaid Lands on the South side of Moratoke River, and in Hyde precinct unto my said Son, William Harding Jones, and the heirs male of his body lawfully begotten; And for want of such heirs Male, then to my Son, Frederick and the heirs Male of his body lawfully begotten; And for want of such heirs Male, then to my Son Thomas, and the heirs Male of his body lawfully begotten; and for want of such heirs Male, then to the Right heirs of my Son, William Harding Jones.

Item, I Give, devise and bequeath unto my said Son, William Harding Jones, All the rest of my Lands in Albemarle County, and in Beaufort and Hyde precincts, as well what I shal hereafter Purchase, as what I am now possessed of, (Excepting my Lands near and adjoining to Meherrin Creek, and my Lands on the North side of Moratoke River). To have and to hold ye Same, Excepted as before Excepted, unto my said Son, William Harding Jones and his Heirs and assigns for ever.

Item, I Give, devise and bequeath unto my Son, Frederick Jones, all my Lands in Craven precinct, To have & to hold the same, unto my said Son, Frederick Jones, and the heirs male of his body lawfully begotten; and for want of such heirs male, then to my son, William Harding Jones, and the heirs male of his Body lawfully begotten; and for want of such heirs male, then to my Son, Thomas Jones, and the heirs male of his body lawfully begotten; and for want of such heirs male, then to the right heirs of my said Son, Frederick Jones.

Item, I Give, Devise and bequeath unto my Son, Thomas Jones, all my Lands at, or near, Meherrin Creek, in Chowan Precinct; Also, those Lands belonging to me on the North side Moratoke River, in the Precinct aforesaid, being part of the tract of nine thousand, one hundred acres by me taken up, To have & to hold the same unto my said Son, Thomas, his heirs and assignes for ever.

Item, After the Slaves before in this my Will given to my Daughters, are set apart, I Will, That all the rest of my Slaves be equally divided as near as may be according to age and goodness, among my three Sons aforenamed, to be delivered them by my Broth'rs as they shall respectively attain the age of twenty one Years or day of Marriage, which shall first happen, this Clause to be understood of what Slaves I shal hereafter purchase, as well as what I am now possessed of.

Item, I give unto each of my Sons one Diamond Ring.

Item, I Give unto my three Sons, to be equally divided among them, all my Library of Books, Except those books commonly used by my wife, which I have ordered to be put into her Closets; which books I give unto my Daughter Jane.

Item, all my Plate, and household Furniture, with the Appurtenances belonging to the Plantation whereon I now Dwell, I give unto my Son, Wm. Harding Jones, he paying to my two Sons, Frederick and Thomas, to each of them, one third of the value thereof as it shal be adjudged by my brother, when they shall attain the Age of twenty one years or day of Marriage.

Item, I give unto my Son, William Harding Jones, all my Stock of Cattle, horses, Sheep and hogs, he paying & delivering unto my son Frederick, fifty Cowes & Calves & twenty Steers, not under four Years old when my said son, Frederick, shall attain the Age of twenty one Years or Day of Marriage.

Item, If any of my Sons, shal depart this life before they attain ye age of twenty one years or day of Marriage, Then it is my Will, true Intent and meaning, that the Portion of my Personal Estate given in this my Will to such Son or Sons, shal go to the Surviving Son or Sons.

Item, If any Doubt shal arise about the Construction of this my Will, or any part thereof, It is my Desire that the Same be referred to the Decision of my Brother, to be by him determined without going to Law.

Item, I do hereby Authorize, Impower & Appoint my Loveing Bror., Thomas Jones of Virginia, Gentn., to make Sale and dispose of all my Lands lying in King William County in Virginia, commonly called Horns Quarter, to such person or persons in fee Simple as he shal think fit, And the moneys ariseing by such Sale to Appropriate to the benefit of my three Sons, as he in his discretion shall think fit.

Item, I Give unto my Loveing Brother Ten pounds, Sterling, to buy a Suit of Mourning.

All the rest and residue of my Estate of what nature, kind or quality soever, I give, devise & bequeath unto my three Sons, to be equally divided among them by my brothers aforesaid.

Lastly, I do hereby Nominate & Appoint my Loveing

Brother Thomas Jones, of Virginia, Gent., and my Two Sons, Wm. Harding Jones & Fredcrick Jones, to be Executors of this my Last Will & Testament, hereby Revokeing all former & other Wills by me heretofore made or Declared.

In Testimony whereof, I, the said Frederick Jones, have hereunto Set my Hand & Seal, this Nineth day of Aprill, Anno Dom., 1722.   FRED. JONES, (Seal)
(Impression of Coat of Arms on Seal)

Signed, Sealed, Published &
Declared In the presence of:
mark of
SARAH X STEWART Jur.
ROGER HAZARD.
JOHN ANSLEY, Jure.
E. MOSELEY, jure.

No. CAROLINA, SS.

 Memd. That the afore written will was proved before me by the Oaths of Sarah Stewart, John Ansley, & Edwd. Moseley, Evidences thereto, March the 26th., 1723.

 At the Same time Thomas Jones, Gent., one of the Exrs. therein appointed, came before me and tooke the Oath of an Exr. as pr. Law required.
              GALE, C: Just:

No. CAROLINA. SC.

 A Codicil to be annexed to the Will of Frederick Jones, Esqr.

 I Give and bequeath unto my daughter, Jane, My wives Side Saddle and furniture thereto belonging, with the horse called Blaze. To my daughter Martha, a Set of Silver tea Spoons, double guilded. To my daughter Rebeckah, to pair of filigreen gold Shift buckles, and all the gold rings and Earrings.

 To my good friend and Neighbour, Edward Moseley, of Chowan precinct, my pair of Pistolls, mounted with Silver Caps, &c., with bridle Locks and stocked with Englis Walnut.

 In Testimony whereof, I, the said Frederick Jones, have hereunto set my Hand and Seal, this thirteenth Day of Aprill, 1722.
            FRED: JONES. (Seal)

Sealed, Published & Declared
to be annexed to the Will, In
presence of us and was annexed
before Witnessing.

SARAH X STEWART, Jur:
ANN MOSELEY,
E. MOSELEY, Jur:

No. CAROLINA, SC.

 Memd. That the above Codicil was duely proved before me, by the Oaths of Sarah Stewart & Edward Moseley. March the 26th. 1723.
              GALE, Ch: Just:

 Copied from the Original Will, filed in the Office of Secretary of State.

JAMES JONES' WILL.

IN THE NAME OF GOD, AMEN. I, James Jones, of the Province of North Carolina and in the County of Tyrrell, Cooper, being at Present in sound Mind and memory, thanks be given to God for it, and caleing to mind the mortality of my Body and Knowing that it is appoynted for all men once to Die, Do make and ordain this my last will and Testament, that is to say: Principaly and first of all, I give and Recomend my soul into the Hands of Almighty God that gave it and my body I Recommend to the Earth to be Bureyid at the Discretion of my Executors, Nowthing Doubting but at the general Resurrection, I shall Receve the same again by the mighty Power of God; and as Touching Such worldly Estate, wherewith it hath Pleased God to Bless mee in this Life, I give and Dispose of in the Form and Manner Following:

Imprams., I give and bequeath to my Loveing wife, Mary Jones, Dureing her Naturall Life, one Hundred and Fifty Acres of Land, Including my uper Plantation.

Item, after the Death of my said Wife, my Will and Desire is, that the said one Hundred and fifty Acres of Land, including my Said uper Plantation, be my Son, James Jones, to him and his heirs for Ever; and in Case my Son, James, should Die in his menority, then my Will and Desyer is, that the sd. upper Plantation, with one Hundred and fifty acres of Land, be my Son, Traley Jones, to him and his heirs for Ever.

Item, I give and bequeath to my son, Benjamin Jones, one hundred and fifty acres of Land, being the Remaining Part of the Land belonging to my sd. uper Plantation, to him and his Heirs for Ever: and in Case my son Benjamin should die in his Menority, then the sd. Hundred and fifty Acres of Land to be my Son, Traley Jones, and his Heirs for ever.

Item, I give and Bequeath to my Daughter, Mary Drapir, one young Mare.

Item, I give and Bequeath my Personal Estate to my Severall Children hereafter mentioned, only, my wife to have the use thereof Dureing her Life; and in Case she mary again, then to have the use of my sd. Personall Estate During her Widohood. my Said Personall Estate I Desyer should be Equally Devided Betwen my Children after the Death or Marage of my said Wife, To wit: Evan Jones, James Jones, Traley Jones and Benjm. Jones, and Ann Jones and Elizabeth Jones.

Item, I give to John Ray the Liberty Dureing his Life and his Wifes WidoHood, the Privilege of Dewlling on Part of my Land Called the folley.

I do herby appoint and constitute my Loveing Wife, Mary Jones, Exectrx. Together With my Two Sons, Evan and James

Jones, Hole and soul Executors of this my Last Will and Testement, and I Do hereby utterly Disalow, Revoke and Disanull all and Every other former Testaments, Wills, Legaces and Bequests and Executors by mee in any Ways before Named, Willed and Bequeathed, Ratifying and confirming this and No other to be my Last Will and Testament.

In Witness whareof, I Have hereunto Set my hand and Seal this third Day of August, in the year of our Lord, one thousand, Seven Hundred and fifty.

JAMES JONES. (Seal)

Signed, Sealed and Delivered
in the Presence of us:
    JOHN RAY.
            his
    WILLIAM MC HOWARD, Jurat,
            mark
    ELIZABETH && HOWARD.
            her Mark
JAMES JONES Qual'd Exer.

Copied from the Original Will filed in the Office of the Secretary of State.

WILLIAM HARDING JONES' WILL.

To All Christian people, To whom this present writing Shall Come, I, Wm. Harding Jones, of ye Eastern Parish of Chowan, and Precinct in Allbemarle County, Send Greeting in our Lord God Everlasting:

Know ye, That I, the said Wm. Hard: Jones, as well for and in Consideration of the Tender Love & good will wch I have & do bear unto my well beloved wife, Ann Jones, As also for diverse other good causes and Consideration me at This present Especially moving, have given & granted and by these presents do give, grant & confirm unto the said Ann Jones, my wife, her heirs and assigns for ever, one certain piece or parcel of Land containing four thousand Acres on Roanoak river in Bertie Precinct, it being That Trackt of Land out of Wch, I have sold three hundred to Ellis Hodges of the same precinct; I also give to her during her natural Life, the house & plantation whereon I now live, with all & Singular, the rights, heridatements, appertenances & appendants whatsoever, to the said peice or parcel of Land in any wise appertaining; with all Cattle, hoggs, horses, Sheep, belonging to the sd. plantation, with one third part of the Negroes I now possess; also, all my houshold goods belonging to the sd. house, Excepting the family pictures and Court of Armes, which I give to my well beloved brother, Freddick Jones; & likewise all my books in ye sd. house, I give to my brothers, Freddick and Thomas Jones, Equally to be divided. All the residue of my Estate, I give to my two well beloved brothers aforesaid, both real & personal, after a discharge of all Just Debts.

To have and To hold all and Singular, the above mentioned premises to the said Ann, Frederick & Thomas, and to their heirs for ever, in as clear and ample manner to all intents and purposes, as a pure and indeazable Estate in fee Simple and Absolute can be held or Enjoy'd, and such an Estate in and To ye premises I bind my Self, my heirs for ever, to warrant and defend unto the said Ann, Frederick & Thomas, and Their Assignes for ever.

In witness whereof, I have hereunto affixed my hand & Seale, this Second day of January, in the year of our Lord God, one thousand Seven & Thirty.

WM. HARDING JONES. (Seal)

Sign'd, Seal'd & deliver'd in
Presence of us:
    GEORGE ALLEIGN.
    SAMLL. SNOWDEN.
    MATTHEW YOUNG.

Proved before me by ye oath of George Alleyn, and Samuel Snowden and that they also Saw Mathew Young, Sign as an Evidence to the Same. The 27th. day of July, 1732.

JNO. PALIN, Ch: Just:

Copied from Original Will, filed in the office of the Secretary of State.

LEWIS ALEXANDER KNIGHT'S WILL.

IN THE NAME OF GOD AMEN. I, Lewis allexr. Knights, of pasquotank, in the province of North Carolina, being sick and weake in body but of perfect mind & Memory, Thanks be unto ye almight God for the Same, & knowing that all men Must Certainly Die, doe in order Thereunto make This last will & Testament, in manner & form following, (Thats to Say), first and principally, I give and bequeath my Soul into the hands of almight God that gave it, trusting in the merits of my blessed Saviour Jesus Christ; and my body to the Earth from whence it was taken, at the discressions of my Executors hereafter named; and as Touching Such EstAte as the allmighty god hath bestowed upon me in This Life, I give and bequeath the same as followeth:

Impr., I give and bequeath unto my Loving Wife, ann Knight, this my plantation whereon I now live, during her natural Life; and after her Decease, I give and bequeath unto my Son, Emmanuel Knight, this part of my plantation on the River; and the other part Joying to Thomas Armours, I give to my son, Lewis Knight, devided at the middle of the piney ground, to them and the heirs of their body Lawfully begotten for Ever.

And alsoe, my will is that my two Sons before mentioned, Shall be at their liberty at the age of Eighteen years from the Command and Service of any manner of persons Whatsoever, as also the Rest of my Children to be there own men at the age aforesaid.

Item, I give and bequeath unto my son, Emmanuel Knight, my Chest.

I give and bequeath all the rest of my Estate unto my wife, whom I appoint and Nominate my whole and sole Executrix of This my Last will and Testament, Revoking & Renouncing all other wills and Testaments by me heretofore made or nominated.

Witness my hand and Seale, this 17th. Day of March 1731/2.

       LEWIS: ALEXND: KNIGHT. (Seal)

Signed, Sealed, published, pronounced, declared to be the Last
will & Testament of Lewis Alex.
knight, in presence of:
  JER—. SWEENY.
  TIMOTHY MEADES.
     her
  MARY X SWEENY.
     mark

PASQUOTANK PRECINCT.   Aprile Court, 1732.

The above will was proved in open Court by ye oath of Timt. Meades and That he say mary Sweeny & Jerame Sweeny, Sign ye same.

      Test: W. MINSON, Cle: Cou:

Copied from Original Will, filed in the Office of the Secretary of State.

JOHN LAWSON'S WILL.

No. CAROLINA.
BATH TOWNE.

IN THE NAME OF GOD, AMEN, ye 12th. day of August 1708. I, John Lawson, of Bath Towne, in the Province of North Carolina, Gent., being of perfect mind & memory, thanks be given unto God therefore, calling to mind the mortality of my body & knowing that it is appointed for men once to dye, Doe make and Ordayne this my last will and testament, that is to Say, principally & first of all, I give a recomend my body to ye Earth, & my Soul to Allmighty God that gave it.

Impris., I give & bequeath to my Dearly beloved Hannah Smith, the house & Lott I now live in, to enjoy the same during her Naturall life & also one third part of my Personale Estate in No. Carolina to her own proper Use & behoofe & for her to dispose of ye Same as She Thinks fitt.

Item, I give ye remainder of my Estate, both Personall & reale, to my Daughter, Isabella, of Bath Town and to the brother & sister (which her mother is w'th Child off at this present) to them Equally to Enjoy (vizt.) that Each of them two shall Enjoy & inheritt alike an Equall part of all my Estate that I dye Possessed of, the Land to be parted & devided when they shall arrive att twenty one years of age or Marry. And if it shall please God that her Mother, Hannah Smith, shall have more than one Child at a Birth, which she is now with Child off, that then, every Child of hers by me shall Enjoy an equall part of my Estate.

And Doe hereby Constitute, make & Ordayne ye Commis' of ye Court of Bath County w'th Mrs. Hannah Smith, the Exr's. of this my last will and Testament all & Singular my lands tenem'ts & Messauges, & I doe hereby utterly disallow, revoke & disanull all & every other former Testaments, Wills, Legacy's & Bequests & Exrs. by me in any way before named, Willed & bequeathed, ratyfying & Confirming this & no other to be my last will & testament.

In Witness whereof, I have hereunto Sett my hand & Seal ye day & Year above Written.

JOHN LAWSON. (Seal)

Signed, Selaed, published & declared by ye sd. John Lawson, as his last will & testament in the presence of us ye Subscribers:
WM. W. HAWKOCK.
RICH'D SMITH.
JAMES LEIGH.

Recorded in Will Book 2, page 98, Office of the Secretary of State.

JOHN LEAR'S WILL.

IN THE NAME OF GOD AMEN, The twenty first day of November in ye year of our Lord, one thousand, six hundred, ninty and five. I, John Lear, of ye county of Nancemond in Virga. being weak in body and in good and perfect memory, thanks be to God, Doe make this my last will & Testament in manner and forme following, That is to Say, first I bequeath my Soul and Spirit unto ye hands of God, my heavenly father, by whome of his mercy and only grace I trust to be saved and received unto eternal rest through ye death of my Saviour & Redeemer Jesus Christ, in whose precious blood I sett ye hope of my salvation; and my body, in hope of a joyfull resurection

I committt to ye earth to be buried decently as my deare relation shall think fitt. And touching ye disposition of my worldly goods, I dispose of ye same as followeth: First, I will that all such debts as I owe shall be truely paid.

Imprimis, I give to ye widow Pitt, my Sister, besides what she owes me, five pounds.

Item, I give ye poor widow Perdue of ye Isle of Wight county, five hundred pounds of tobaco a yeare, so long as she lives.

Item, Ye bottles of all sorts, Silk, Silver & gold fringes, as all dresses fitted and made—now in ye house w'th —— belonging to my widow and daughter, as also New wearing linen, I Give to be Equally devided betwixt my daughter —— Burwell and my daughter, Elisabeth Lear, widow of my deceased son, Thomas Lear.

Item, I give and bequeath my Grandaughter, Elizabeth Lear, all that tract & devidend of Land w'ch I leased to Coll. James Jewell and is now in possession of Capt. Robert Randall, for her life, and after her death to ye heirs of her body lawfully begotten, and for default of such heirs, I give ye said tract of land, being aboute two hundred & fifty acres, lying in Narrowsquick bay to John George, and ye heirs of his body; & in default of such heirs I give ye same to my grand Son, John Lear, to him and his heirs lawfully begotten for ever.

Item, I give unto Charles Goremge, all my lands in Surry County w'th I was about selling to William Brown, as per pattent about three hundred & thirty acres, to him & his heirs for ever. and I also give ye said Charles Goremge, ye negro boy Charles at Kerotan, and ye negro girle Fanny there also, & Six Cows and A bull.

Item, I give unto John George, ye negroes Jack & Fido & to use & plant, if he see good, only, point land whereon ye said negroes are till his own land, given by Coll. George, shall come into his hands, & I also give him what cattle is on ye said point belonging to me.

Item, I give my buff suit with fringe jacket & Silk hose unto James Mountgomery, in full compensation of his trouble from first to last. All other my wearing clothes linen & woolen I desire may be devided between John George & Charles Goremge.

Item, I give & bequeath unto my grand son, John Lear, all other my landes, tenements & hereditements —— nature, quality, together with what leased & for tearme of years, to him & his heirs of his body lawfully begotten.

As to all other my accompts, estate, whether merchantable goods, household goods, plate, money, bills, lands and accompts, or any other goods, wares, or merchandizes, of what nature soever, either here or in England, Carolina or elsewhere, my will and desire is, that it be equally shared after a true accompt taken in three parts. The first parte, I give to my grand son, John Lear, for ever. ye second third part thereof to my two grandaughters, Elizabeth & Martha, children of my only son, Thomas Lear, deceased, and in case of mortality ye survivors to enjoy ye deceased or deceases's parte; & ye third and last parte I give betwixt my daughter Martha Burwell & her children she had by Col. Cole & to ye survivors of them.

And ye land I bought of George Powell and adding ye plantation whereon John Mackwilliams did live, & containing aboute three hundred & fifty acres, with all houses, orchards, tenements, hereditaments to ye Same belonging, to her, her heirs for ever, anything to ye contrary notwithstanding.

And Lastly, I doe appoint my son in law, Maj. Lenoard Burwell, & my good friend Capt. Thomas Godwin, my absolute, whole & Sole Executo'rs of this my last will & Testament, & every parte & Clause therein contained, making null & Void all other wills & Testam'ts whatsoever, & this only to be my last will & Testament and no other.

In witness whereof, I have hereunto sett my hand & fixed my Seale ye day & year above written.

JNO. LEAR (Coine Sigilli)

Signed, Sealed & delivered in
ye presence of:

Signum

WILLIAM W COFFEILD

JOHN LOWE.

ELIZABETH BRIDGERS.

signum

ANN A COFFEILD.

Copia Vera. Test. ANDREW ROSS, dept. Cl. Court.

At a court held for Nansemond County, Feb'y ye 12th. 1695, proved by ye oathes of mr. William Coffield, Mr. Jno. Lowe & Mrs. Ann Coffeild, and by ye affiemation of Mad'm Elizabeth Bridgers with order to record & it recorded.

Test. ANDREW ROSS, dept. Cl. Court.

Copied from Original Will, Filed in the Office of the Secretary of State.

FRANCIS LEYDON'S WILL.

IN THE NAME OF GOD AMEN, This Twenty Third Day of february, In the Second year of the Reign of our Sovgrain Lord King George, and In the Year of our Lord God, one Thousand, Seven hundred Twenty Seven-Eight. I, Francis Layden, of the province of North Carolina, In the County of albemarle, In the precinct of perquimons, Being Verey Sick and weak In body, but of perfect mind and memory, Thanks be

Given unto god; Therefore Calling Unto minde the mortality of my body, and Knowing that It Is appointed for all once to Dye, Do make and ordain my Last will and Testament, that is to Say, principally and first of all I Give and Recommend my Soul Into the hands of God that Gave it; and my body I Recommend to the Earth, to be Buried in Decand and Christian manner at the Discretion of my Executrix, nothing Doubting but at the General Resurection I Shall Receive the Same again by the all mighty power of god; and as Touching Such worldly Estate wherewith It hath pleased God to bless me In this Life, I Give, demise and Dispose of the Same In the following manner and forme:

Imprimis, I Give and bequeath to my Dearly Beloved wife, Elizabeth Layden, whom I Likewise Constitute and appoint my Executrix, the benefit and use of all my Estate, both Real and personal, During her widow hood.

Item, I Give and bequeath to my well beloved Son, William Layden, the plantation I now Live upon, Containing Two hundred and Thirty Seven acres; the Same to Remain free and Clear for Ever, to him and his Heirs.

It is further my will that my Son, William, when possessed of the manor, Shall pay unto his Three younger Brothers, Fraincies, George, and Isaac, the sume of Teen pounds, to Each, In bills. It Is my will that if my Son, William, Should Dye before he Is possessed of the Land that Then It shall become franceis and his heirs.

Item, I Give and bequeath to my well beloved Son, francis Layden, all that Tract of Land Situat, Lying and being In the precinct aforesaid, Joyning to John Stevens Land, Containing one hundred and Six acres; the Same to be possessed by him and his heirs, and to Remain Clear and free for ever; But In Caise he Should Dye before he is possessed of It, Then It Is my will that his Brother George shall have It, and so to Remain to him and his heirs; and Likewise, further my will, that In Caise George Should Dye before he has possessed It, that Then, and in That Caise, my will Is that It be posse'ed by Isaac, and so to Remain to him, his heirs; but In Caise of his Death before possesion, then the Land to be my Daughter marys, and so to remain to her and her heirs for Ever.

It is further my will, that if my son francis, Should Live to possess the Land, that then and In that Caise, he to pay unto his Brother George and Isaac, the Sume of teen pounds In bills to Each, and likewise teen pounds to his Sister mary; and It Is also my will, that after my widow has her Third out of my moveble Estat, that Then, the Remander be Eaqly Divided between my son francis, George and Isaac, and my Daughter, mary.

Item, I Give and bequeath to my Cousin, William Midlton, my musket; and my other Gun to my Son, William.

        FRANCIS LAYDAIN. (Seal)

Signed, Sealed, Published, Pronounced and Declared By the Said Franceis Layden, In Presence of: JOHN STEVENS,
    WILLIAM EVENS.
      his
   WILLIAM X MIDLTON.
      mark.

Proved by ye Oaths William Middleton, & Willm. Evens, Evidences In open Court.   Test: CHARLES DENMAN, Clk.
Letters granted 22th. april, 1728.

Copied from Original Will, filed in the Office of the Secretary of State.

ALEXANDER LILLINGTON'S WILL.

IN THE NAME OF GOD AMEN. The ninth Day of September, Anno. Dom., 1697. I, Alexander Lillington, of Prcint of Pequemons, being Sick & Weak in Body, But of Good & perfect mind and memory, praysed be God, Doe make and ordayne this my Last Will and Testament in forme following: First and principally, I surrender my Soul to Jesus Christ my only Saviour and redeemer trustin his Merritts & Precious ? Death to have full pardon of all my Sinns; and my Body I remitt to the Earth from whence it came to be decently interred according to the Discretion of my Executor hereafter named; and for my wordly Estate, after my Debts and funerall Expenses are paid, I give as followeth:

Imprimis, I give and bequeath unto my Son, John Lillington, and his heirs forever, my plantation whereon I now live, and the plantation which was formerly Stephen Hancocks over agt. mine, and all the Land to each of them belonging, together with my Still & the Implements to them belonging, also my Silver hilted Sword and Belt, the Mills, and my Long Gunn. I give to my Son John my ffeely'. Gunn and Backsword.

Item, I give to my Son, George Lillington, and to his heirs forever, my plantation att Yawpins River, called my Quarter, and my plantation att Little River whereon Francis Penrine lived, w'th all the Land to Each of them belonging. And if in Case that either of my Sons Dyes before they come to age, I give the part of him Soe dying to the Surviver and his heirs, and if both of them Dyes before they come to age then I give my plantation I now live on to my Daughter, Ann Walker & her heirs; and my plantation att Little River to my Daughter, Elizabeth Fendall, and her heirs; and my plantation called my Quarter, to my Daughter, Mary Lillington, & her heirs; and my plantation which was Stephen Hancocks to Sarah Lillington, and her heirs.

Item, I give and bequeath to my Children, Mary Lillington John Lillington, Sarah Lillington & George Lillington, & to Each of them thirty pounds apeece, to be paid them by my executors hereafter named, when they shall Severally come to age or Marriage. I having advanced Soe much already to my Eldest Daughters in Marriage.

Item, I doe Will that my wife, Ann Lillington, have a Decent livelihood out of my Estate Soe long as Shee keeps her sel: a Widow; and that She Shall have the management of my plantation in buying and Selling, Soe as that my Said Wife shall dispose of nothing but of the ground of the Said plantation, and that for and towards the maintenance of her Sel: and my Children, and to noe other use.

Item, I will that my wife shall have the disposall of fifty pounds att her Decease to be paid to whom Shee shall give it to, by my Executors hereafter named.

Item, I will that my children Shall likewise have their maintenance out of the produce of my Stock and plantation Soe long as they live together on the Same.

Item, I will that all the rest and residue of my Estate, be Equally divided among all my Children, to Say, Ann, Eliz. Mary, John, Sarah, and George, and to the survivors of them.

Item, it is my Desire that what I have given to my Daughter Sarah, be laid out to buy her a negro, to be delivered to her att age or Marriage.

Item, I will that if any of my children dyes before they come to Enjoy the Thirty pound I have given them, the same Shall fall to the rest of my Children or the Survivors of them.

Item, I will that my Executors carry on my Son, John, in his learnings as I have begun, and that All my Children be brought up in Learning as conveniently can bee.

I doe appoint my Son in Law, Henderson Walker, ex'tor to John Fendall, dect.

Item, I doe appoint Coll. Willm. Wilkerson & my said Son, Henderson Walker, Executors of this my last Will and Testament and if Either of them dyes before this my will is Executed. I appoint my Son, John, ex'tor in his Roome.

Item, I doe Will that my Executor have the management of my other plantations till my Children comes to age.

And I revoake all other Wills by me made, as Wittness my hand & Seal this Day and year above Written.

       ALEX LILLINGTON (Seal)
    (Impression of Coat of Arms on Seal)

Sealed and Delivered in presence of. CALEB CALLOWAY.
     JOHN BARRON,
     ROBERT HARMAN, Sen.

NORTH CAROLINA WILLS.   287

Att a Genrall Court held S'ber the 8th, 1697, this will was proved by the Evidences Subscribed thereunto By the hono'ble, the Palatin of Court.   N. GLOVER, C. Cor.

NORTH CAROLINA.

Whereas, Major Alexander Lillington is deceased, having made by his Last Will & Testament, a true Coppy whereof is hereunto Annexed, Coll. William Wilkeson and Captn. Henderson Walker, his Executors. These are to impower the Said Wm. Wilkison & Hen. Walker, to Enter in & upon all & Singular the Goods & Chattles, Rights & Credits of the Sd. Alex. Lillington, dc. And a true Inventory thereof to returne w'thin one year after the Date hereof, and the Same to dispose of as by the Sd. Will.

Dated the 9th. day of October, 1697.

FRA. TOMES,
SAML. SWANN,
THO. HARVEY,
DAN. AHEHURST.

Recorded in Will Book 1, page 78. Office of the Secretary of State.

JOHN LILLINGTON'S WILL.

IN THE NAME OF GOD, AMEN. I, John Lillington, of the County of Bath, in North Carolina, Gent., being Sick and weak of Body, but of Sound & perfect mind & memory, and Calling to mind the Sertainty of death and not knowing when it may pleas the Lord to call me out of this life, do make, appoint and ordain this to be my last Will and Testament, in maner and form following, that is to Say, after My Just & lawfull Debts are paid.

Impr's. I give bequeath & Devise unto my Loveing wife, Sarah Lillington, three of my negro slaves, Named, Shippy & Jupiter, two men; and marya, a woman, to her proper use forever.

Item, I give, bequeath & Devise unto my Son, Alexander, one Thousand Acres Land being the one moiety of this parcel of Two thousand Acres of land whereon I now live, to be held of him, his heirs or assignes in fee simple forever.

Item, I give and Devise to my said Son, two of my Negro Slaves, Named Danger & Jack; also Tenn Cowes with Calves by their Sides, and Six Sowes and a Boar, and Six Ews and a Ram, all to be likely and good, and apair of hand mill Cullen Stones, and my large Family Bible, all to be delivered to my said Son, by my Executors hereafter named, when he shal attain to the age of Twenty one years, for his proper use forever.

Item, I give, bequeath & Devise unto my Eldest Daughter, Elizabeth, one of my Negroe Slaves Named Roas, a wench; also Ten likely good Cowes with Calves by their Sides, and One Feather Bedd, bolster and Pillow with a sute of Curten & Vallens, to be delivered to my said Daughter by me Exetrs.

hereafter named, when she shall attaine to the age of Twenty one years or day of marryage, for her proper use forever.

Item, I give, bequeath, & Devise unto my Daughter, Mary, one of my Negro Slaves Named Judy, a Guirl; also Tenn Cowes with Calves by their sides to be likely & good; and one Feather Bedd, bolster & Pillows, with a sute of Curtains & Vallens, to be delivered to my Said Daughter by my Exec'tr hereafter named, for her proper use forever, that is to say, when she shall attain to the age of Twenty one years or day of Marryage.

Item, I give, bequeath & Devise unto my youngest Daughter, Ann, one of my Negroes Named moll, a Guirl; also Tenn likely good Cowes with Calves by their Sides, and a Feather Bedd, bolster and Pilloes with a Sute of Curtains & Vallens, to be Delivered to my said Daughter by me Exesrs. hereafter named, when she shall attain to ye age of Twenty one years or day of Marryage.

Item, I give, bequeath & devise al the rest & Residue of my Estate not before mentioned and given (the better thereby to Inable my sd. wife to bring up my sd. Children in Schooling &c.) unto my afsd. Loveing Wife, for her proper use forever.

And lastly my will and desire is, that all my lawfull debt be paid out of the profits arriseing by the labour of my slaves before nominated & given, and that they be kep together under the Care and ordering of my said Wife, and so to remaine untel all my debts be fully paid & discharged thereby.

I do hereby nominate and appoint my Loveing wife, Sarah Lillington, Maurice Moore, John Porter and John Bap'a. Ash, to be my Exers., Joyntly or Severally to doe and Execute all and every part of this my last will and testament. (Turn over)

In Witness whereof, I have hereunto Set my hand and Seal, this 19th day of March, Anno. 1721/2.

JOHN LILLINGTON (Seal)

Signed, Sealed & Delivered, in presents of us:
  PAT. MAULE.
  SAMUELL COOPPER.
   the mark of
  JOHN I TRANTER

NO. CAROLINA. BEAUFORT AND HYDE PRECINCTS, SCT.

At a court held for the said Precincts, at Bath Towne, on Tuesday ye 2d. July, 1723. Pres't...........? Esqr. His Majesties Justices.

The Last Will and Testam't of Mr. John Lillington, dec'd, was by the Exors. therein named, Exhibited in this Court and proved by the oaths of Sam'll Cooper & John Tranter, two of the Witnesses thereunto, who also deposed yt they saw Patrick Maule, the other Witness evidence the same.

Ordered that notice be given to the Secretary of the Same & that it be Recorded.
     JNO. BAP'TA. ASHE, Cler: Cur:

Copied from the Original Will, filed in the Office of Secretary of State.

WILLIAM LITTLE'S WILL.

IN THE NAME OF GOD AMEN. I, William Little, of North Carolina, do make this my last will & Testament, trusting in Gods great Mercy for my Everlasting State.

Imprim's, I make my dear & loving wife, Penelope Little, my good friends, Christopher Gale, Edmond Gale & Edward Salter, and my brother, John Arbuthnot, Exec's. of this my last will & Testament; and I do hereby give & bequeath to my loving wife Penelope Little, her heirs & assigns, my house in Edenton lately leased to mr. Rice, together with ye gardens, outhouses, pastures, & all the lands, and all appurtenances; She discharging ye hundred pound taken up of ye publick, for which it is mortgaged; also, I give to my sd. wife my negros, Harry, Daniel, Phoebe, Maggy and her child Phibby, & my best horse, and one half of my household goods & furniture; the other half I give to my Daughter, Penelope Little; also, I give to my sd. Daughter, Penelope Little, & her heirs and assigns, my half ye mill att Hoskins bridge near Edenton; & my half ye three tracts of lightwood land att meherrin, patented in John Bonds name, but I pay'd ye purchase & he is to make a title; also, I give my sd. Daughter, my negro Girl Hannah, and I appoint Christopher Gale, Esqr., Guardian of my sd. Daughter, & I do hereby Impower him, or on his decease, ye Survivors of my Exrs. Such of them as shall be in Carolina, to Sell any of her Estate, real or personal, if thought for her benefit, & I would have her still kept at Boston & maintained out of ye Income of her mill, and what Can be made of ye light wood lands & other Estate.

Also, I give my Son, George Little, his heirs & assigns, all my lands in meherrin neck, with what Stock is, or shall, at my decease be thereon, Including also ye land whereon Tayler lived adjacent to ye sd. neck, and whereas in my purchase patent for the sd. lands, there is Included some lands of the Poweys & others, with intent to buy their right out, my will is that out of my debts (or goods to hereafter sold), that are due to me if it shall more than pay ye Debts I owe, that my Execrs. therewith, if to be done at a moderate price, do buy out the Same, or what they can thereof, & if John Ryly wil quit his Claim there, I devise to ye sd. John Ryly & his heirs my land bought of John Badsey? near where Joseph Durds lived, but if not, then I devise ye Same to my Son, George, & his heirs, together with what shall be bought as afsd.

Also, I will that my books lent out, be got in, & all my books sold, & out of ye produce two negros to be bought, viz: one feild negro woman likely for breeding, whom I give to my

Son, George, & one young negro woman or girl of about fourteen years, which I give to my daughter, Penelope.

Also, I give my son, George, my negros Sampson & Scipio only my will is that my Son, Georges negroes be kept att work on ye plantation at occaneechy with ye others, which I hereby give my Son, William Little, viz: Boston, Plymouth, Jock Dinah & her Child, & Jap. I wil that out of ye produce of their labour & ye hoggs & Stears fit for killing, & what Shall be raised, be apply'd towards paying of the four hundred pounds taken up on mortgage from ye Country, viz: two hundred pounds on ye meherrin lands & Two hundred pounds on my Occaneechy land by Edward Hocot.

Also, I give & devise to my Son, William, his heirs & assigns, all my lands in occaneechy & that near ye Court house in Bertie, given my by Wm. Banks, and all my land att Shac & Swift Creek & places adjacent; also ye lands whereon John Pratt lives, and all other my lands & real Estate Whatsoever & wheresoever, Saving yt my wil is, if ye sd. John Prat, who is Considerably in my debt wil Com to a fair acc't & discharge ye Same, I wil & Impower my sd. Exec's., or ye Survivors of them, or Such as shall be in Carolina, to make ye sd. Prat a title in fee, to one half of ye sd. land he lives on, which I bought of Watkins. Also I give my sd. Son, William Little, all ye Stock of Cattle, hoggs, horses, & all tools & utensils att my sd. plantations at occaneechy, Except ye use & produce thereof til 'ye aforsd. publick money be raised & discharged.

in my publick accts. as Recr. Genll. made up a filed in ye Council Office, there is a Smal Ballance of bills now due from me, provided what is outstanding can be got in which has been stopt. but Since that there is much * * * (Illegible) my labour as cheif Justice & holding the courts of oyer & Terminor, which I Expect my   Execr. to receive in proclamation money or Equivalint, and when my debts I owe & Legacyes are payed out of what is due to me, & other my personal Estate as herein disposed of, I devise ye sd. residue of my sd. personal Estate, ye one half to my wife, ye other half to my children, to be Equaly devided between them.

Also, I give my wife ye use & liberty of living on any of my plantations during her widohood & ye use of any Stock or houses for her & her childrens maintenance. And I do appoint her guardian of my young Son, George, & I appoint my friend, Edward Salter, Guradian of my Son, William & his Estate, to let, dispos & manage ye same in ye most beneficial manner, & to Educate him ye best he Can, trusting in his Care & friendship to my dear Child.

Also, I give to my wife ye use of and Service of my molatto Girl, Jenny alt. Jemima, & her negro Girl Bess, till free, with whom I have been at great Expense, & my will is that altho ye sd. Jemima hath no title to any of ye lands intended for her by ye old negro Bunch, yet as there was an Equitable Intent of some benefit to her, I will that there be payd to her & her Sister, at Capt. Bryants, five pounds Each, as they Come of age respectively, in Virginia Currency or Equivall. & I leave it to my wifes discretion do discharge ye sd. Jenny als. Jemima at ye age of Twenty one or to hold her til thirty one years of age after ye Custom of molattos.

Also, I give to my friend, Robert Forstor, my Sword & Cloaths, left me as a legacy by my dear friend mr. Lovick; & ye rest of my Cloaths I leave at my wifes discretion to be disposed among my friends.

Also, I give to   a Mourning ring, and one to each of my execrs. & to my brothers, Isaac Little & John Arbuthnot & my Dear Sister aubuthnot & My Sister Barker; also a handsome ring to mrs. Penelope Lovick, widow of my Dear friend, John Lovick, as a Small token of my Esteemed Value for her.

Lastly, I hereby revoke all other wills by me made, & appoint this my last will & Testament.

In Testimony whereof, I have Signed & Sealed & published ye Same to be my will, this 25th. day of June, 1734.
                                                    WILLIAM LITTLE.

Signed, Sealed & published in presence of us:
    Test: JOHN BOYD.
        JOHN CROWELL.
        JOHN PARKER.

No. CAROLINA. SC.

These may certify That the Reverend Mr. John Boyd, and John Parker, Two of the Subscribing Evidences to this Will, made Oath on the Holy Evangelists, that they saw William Little, Sign, Seal, publish & declare these presents to be & contain his last will & Testament.

Sworn before me the 5th, Septr., 1734.
                                                    GEO. BURRINGTON.

Copied from Original Will, Filed in the Office of the Secretary of State.

JOHN LOVICK'S WILL.

IN THE NAME OF GOD AMEN. I, John Lovick, of North Carolina, being Sick and weak, but of sound mind and Memory & Remembering it is appointed for all Men to Dye, do for the Settling my Estate after my Decease make & Ordain this my Last Will & Testament, after my just Debts are paid.

Impr. I Give & Bequeath to John Lovick, Son of my Brother, Thomas Lovick, the negro Boy called Ned now at the sd. Thomas Lovicks; and also the Tract of Land & Plantation called the Horse Meadow or Pasture adjacent to Plowmans

Land, to him and his heirs; & if the sd. John Lovick Dye before he comes of Age, my Will is that what I Give him, his said Father shall have.

Item, I Give to my said Brother, Thomas Lovick, a mourning Ring and a Suite of mourning.

Item, I Give to the Hono'ble Sir Richard Everard, Bart. & Govn. a Gold Ring, and another to Christopher Gale, Esqr. and another to Edmond Gale, Esqr. & another to Mr. Robert Forster.

Item, I Give to my Friend, William Little, Esqr., a Gold Ring and a Suite of Mourning, and Six of my best Shirts, my best Hat, Wigg, & Sword, my Gold Buttons, all my Law Books & Lord Clarendens History.

I do not mention any Legacy to my Brother, John Galland and because I Leave to my Loving Wife, his Sister who I know will always be ready to do for him while he deserves it.

Item, I Give to my Dear & Loving Wife, Penelope Lovick all the moneys and Effects in George Lovicks hands, and all the Goods I have Sent for & A Legacy due by my Uncle Parrs Will, on the death of Mrs. Fuller, who I hear is Dead, and also all the rest and Residue of my Estate, Real & Personal whatsoever & wheresoever, and of what Nature or kind soever. And I appoint my said Wife Sole Ex'x. of this my Last Will & Testament, desiring her in all affairs of Moment & weight to be advised & Directed by my Friends, Christopher Gale & William Little Esqrs. who, I am Sure will be very Faithful and ready to assist her; I also appoint my sd. Ex'x. to be Executor of the Will of John Plowman, Deceased, to whom I am Exr.; I also appoint my sd. Wife, Ex'r of the Will of Charles Eden, Esqr., Deced., to whom I was Executor, and for as much as the said Charles Eden on his Death Bed did charge me if I met with any Trouble about his Will from Roderick Loyd, or any of his Family, that I should not pay the Legacy of Five hundred Pounds, sterling, in the sd. Charles Edens Will, given to Mrs. Margaret Pugh, I do therefore forbid my said Executrix to pay the same, I having met with great Truuble, Vexation & charge about the said Will from ye Roderick Loyd, and several of his Family, and the sd. Mrs. Pugh having once refused the said legacy too and endeavoured to defeat and overthrow the sd. Charles Edens Will; and also I hereby appoint a joyn with my sd. Wife, Christopher Gale, Edm'd Gale & Wm. Little, to be Executors of the said Will of Charles Eden & of the sd. John Plowman.

And, Lastly, I do hereby Revoke all other Wills by me made & comfirm this to be my last Will & Testament.

In Testmmony whereof, I have hereunto set my hand & affixed my Seal, this 27th. day, August 1727.

J. LOVICK. &a. (Seal)

Signed, Sealed, published & pronounced to be his Last Will & Testament by the sd. John Lovick in the presence of us:
Sign.
ROBERT R WEEKS.
FRANCES F RAZOR
her mark.
WILLIAM LITTLE.
EDW'D HOWCOTT.

NO. CAROLINA. SC.

His Excelly., George Burrington, Esq., Govn. & Ordinary &ca.

These may certify that Edward Howcot, one of the Subscribing Witnesses to the Within Will personally appeared before me this Day, and made Oath on the Holy Evangelists that he saw Mr. John Lovick, Deced., Seal, publish & Declare the within writing to contain his last Will & Testament, that he was of sound mind & no Compulsion offered.

Given under my hand at Edenton, the 10th. Novm. 1733.

GEO. BURRINGTON.

NO. CAROLINA. SC.

Depositions taken De bene esse, to prove the Republication of Mr. John Lovicks Will during his last Sickness whereof he Dyed.

The Deposition of Christopher Gale, Esqr., Sworn on the Holy Evangelists Saith, That John Lovick, Esqr., Deced., as he Las upon his Death Bed, about two Days before he Dyed, taking this Depon't. by the hand desired him very pressingly to assist to assist his wife in the Settlement of her Accounts, and in every thing Else that he could; (and inter alia) he then told this Depon't. that he had got his Will read over since he was Sick (which it was a lond time before then could find), And that there were some few trifling things in it which he could have wished to have altered or added, But that the principal thing in it which the depon't then apprehended from what he had often heard him say was the giving all to his, Will was as he always intended it so that it so that it should now Stand as it was, Or words to that Import.

C. GALE.

Sworn to, March the 9th., 1733.

Before: NATH. RICE, Sec.

NO. CAROLINA. SC.

The Deposition of Doctor Abraham Blackall, Sworn on the Holy Evangelist, Saith, that he attended John Lovick, Esqr., during his ast Sickness whereof he Dyed, and that he being asked by Mr. Little a few Days before his Death if he had made his Will or Settled his affairs, Answered there is a Will but it was made a long time agoe, & Desired Mr. Little to take and Peruse it, which he accordingly did, and being asked by John Lovick his opinion of it, Mr. Little Reply'd he believed it would do well enough or words to that Effect. Whereupon Mr. Lovick, sayd there were a few Trifling things in it which he could wish were altered but that the Principal things in regard to his Wife was as he always intended and therefore he would e'ne let that Will stand as it is, and further said to his Wife, he wish'd that when she Dy'd she would Leave that Plantation he then Lived on, together with four Negroes to Thomas Lovicks Son, and that he would not add it in the Will but wish'd she would do as above mentioned.

And this Depon't further Saith, that the same day or Day after Christopher Gale, Esqr., came to Mr. Lovicks, with Doctor George Allcyn and heard Mr. Lovick request of Mr. Gale to aid and assist his Wife in the

Settling her affairs and accots., & repeated what he had Determined abou his Will much to the same purpose as above mentioned, and Declared i should Stand as it was. ABRAHAM BLACKALL.
    Sworn to, March ye 9th., 1733.
      Before: NATH. RICE, Secty.

No. CAROLINA. SC.

    The Deposition of William Little, Esqr., who being duly Sworn on th holy Evangelists, Sayeth, That some Years agoe John Lovick, Esqr now Deceased, desired this Depon't to draw his Will for him, and gav him directions for several Legacy's, and the rest of his Estate Real an Personal to give to his Wife Penelope Lovick, now his Relict, and accorc ingly, this Depon't drew the Will, wch is the same Will that has bee produced and proved since the sd. Lovicks Death, as his last Will & Testa ment, which this Depon't saw the sd. John Lovick Sign, Seal & Publish this Depon't being one of the Witnesses, And that this Depon't at th time of making the Will & ever since apprehended that the sd. John Lc vick's intent was to give his Lands in Fee to his Wife & so this Dep meant it in drawing the Will tho the word heirs is Omitted.

    And further, this Depon't Saith, that some time agoe about a Year a this Dep't can remember, the sd. Lovick Observed to this Depon't that th word heirs was not Incerted in the Devise to his wife in his Will, signifyin he intended a Fee to her, and asked this Depon't if he thought it woulc and this Depon't told the sd. Lovick, that the words all his Estate rea & Personal in a will, would pass the Fee; and the said John Lovick furthe ask'd this Depon't upon it, Whether it would pass the Lands &c. he pu chased after making the Will as well as before, to which this Depon' reply'd he believed it would as it was there worded; upon which the sc Lovick seem'd satisfyed, signifying that he would have it so.

    And further, this Deponent Sayeth, that in the sd. John Lovicks las Sickness, a few Days before he Dyed, this Deponent ask'd him if he ha Settled his Affairs, to which he answered he had made no other Settlemen but the old Will, that This Depon't Drew, and desired this Depon't t look at it & Read it over to see if it would Do, which this Depon't according ly did. And the sd. John Lovick, ask'd this Depon't with Quickness concern whither it would do, and if it was firm, & this Depon't. told hi he thought it was Firm & Good & Excepting a few Legacys it passed a his Estate to his Wife to which the sd. John Lovick Reply'd, Ay so I woul have it, there is some small Legacy's I would have altered if I had don it over again, but as the Substantial and Main part of the Will is as would have it, It shall stand, I will not alter the Will but it shall stan as it is. And then Speaking to his Wife then present, as followeth: M Dear, I wish when you Dye, you would give this Plantation and fou Negroes to Tom Lovick's Son, I Will not put it into my Will but I wis you would Do it.

    And this Depon't saith, that he several times formerly he heard the sc John Lovick, Express himself so as to Signify he intended the plantatio where he Lived for John Lovick, Son of sd. Thomas Lovick, but doth no Remember he ever heard the sd. John Lovick, Esqr. so particular as t Express how much Lands he should Give him, nor does he Remember t have heard him talk about it since his purchasing the adjoyning Lands.
                                               WILLIAM LITTLE.
Sworn to, March ye 9th., 1733.
    Before: NATH RICE, Secty.

    Copied from the Original Will, Filed in the Office of Secretary of Stat

EMANUEL LOW'S WILL.

IN THE NAME OF GOD, AMEN, the Second Day of the First Month in the Year of our Lord, 1726/7. I, Emanuelle Low, of the prec't of Pasquotanck, & Province of North Carolina, being Sick of Body but or perfect mind & memory, considering that it is appointed for all men once to dye, Do make & ordain this to be my Last Will & Testament, in Manner following:

1st., I bequeath my Soul to Almighty God, my maker; and my body to the Earth to be interred by me Executrix hereafter named, without any funeral pomp, only about Six of my Friends & Neighbours.

2'ly. I Give & bequeath unto my Loving Daughter, Anna Letitia Low, and to her heirs for ever, my Plantation whereon I now Live, w'th five hundred Acres of Land Adjoining to it; also, one negro Girl Called Zilpah w'th her Increase for ever; also, one bed & furniture, to her, the sd. Anna Letitia Low, and her heirs for ever.

3'ly. I give & bequeath unto my Grandson, George Low, Son of my Beloved Son, Nevil Low, Decd., and now in the Kingdom of Great Britain, the Plantation where my Cousin Robinson now Lives & the Plantation called New Abbey, with four Hundred Acres of Land adjoyning to it, to him, the Sd. George Low, & to his heirs for ever; also, one feather Bed & furniture, & one Negro boy called Pompey; also, my Seal Scutcheon of Arms.

4'ly. My Will & meaning is that either my Daughter, Anna Letitia Low, or my Grandson, George Low, they or either of their Heirs, shall be disposed to sell the Lands by me given, that the same shall be sold and disposed of to one or the other of the partyes aforesd, and to no other person or persons whatsoever.

To prevent any Dispute that may arrise after my Decease, by any pretension my Grandson may make as heir to his father, Nevil Low, to the Lands cmmonly called the Town point, Lying on the mouth of the North West side of Newbegun Creek, & now in possession of Jno. Conner; It is my Will that my Daughter Anna Letitia, her heirs or assigns shall keep in possession all ye before mentioned Legacies, w'th Lands & all other things by me bequeathed to him, ye Sd. George Low, in this my last Will, untill he renounce all Such pretensions in Such manner as the learned in the Law shall think proper: but is my sd. Grandson refuse to comply as before mentioned & offer to Molest the Sd. John Conner, his heirs or assings in his Just Right and Title of the Said Tract of Land by me Sold & conveyed to him & his heirs, Then, I Do revoke all that part of this my Will, unto my sd. Grandson, And Do give & bequeath all that Legacy, as Lands, & other things therein mentioned, unto my Daughter, Anna Letitia Low, and her heirs for Ever, she paying him Twenty pounds.

Item, My Will is, that all my Estate, both Real & Personal be & remaine in the possession of my Loving Wife, Ann Low, during Life, the personall Estate to be disposed of by her between my Loving Daughter, Anna Letitia Low, & my Grandson George, as shee shall think most proper.

Lastly, I appoint my Loving Wife, my whole & Sole Executrix of this my Last Will & Testament, to see the Same duly Executed.

In witness whereof, I have hereunto Set my hand and Seal the day and year afosd.

EMANL. LOW. (seal)

Signed, Sealed & delivered in the presence of:
    W. NORRIS,
    EDMD. GALE.
    CHAS. BULL.

A Codicil:

IN THE NAME OF GOD AMEN, The last Will of the afsd. Emanl. Low as follows: Whereas in the former Words of my Will was omitted my Intentions about my Grandson, George Low, therefore to prevent Disputes, My Will is that my Grandson, George Low, Shall not Enjoy the Legacy by me given untill he come to the age of Twenty one Years & in the mean time to continue in the Hands of my Executrix.

Item, I give unto Johanna Pearce, five pounds.

In Testimony whereof, I have hereunto Set my hand & Seal this 8th. Day of March, 1726/7.

EMANL. LOW (Seal)

    Test. WHORRIS JOSEPH JORDAN.
    FILECHRISP JORDAN.

A Codicil:

Item, Whereas, in my last will & Testament, I appointed my loveing Wife my sole Executrix, I doe now no ways to Abbrogate or make Voyde any part of my sd. Sill, but Joine my Daughter, Anna Letitia Low, Executrix, with my loveing wife Ann Low, to See this my Last Will & Testament duly Executed.

Item, Whereas, I am administrat'r to Wm. Vaughn, Decd. I do appoint my said Executrixes to be Executrix's or administratr'xs, giving and bequeathing to my Sd. Executrixs all my right or interest in and to my Sd. Administratorships.

In testimony whereof I have hereunto Sett my Hand and Seal, this 20th. day of Febry. 1726/7.

EMANL. LOW. (Seal)

    Test: JOHN CONNER,
    JOSHUA SCOTT.
            her
    JOHANNA X PEARCE
          mark.

NORTH CAROLINA WILLS.   297

PASQUOTANK PR'CT, COURT.   July 18, 1727.
The Two foregoing Codicile annexed to this Will was proved ye first by the solemn affirmation of Mrs. Filia Chrish Jordan, one of the Evidences thereunto. The other by ye like solemn affirmation of Joanna Pearce, one of ye Evidences thereunto, who likewise attested that she Saw the other Evidences Sign thereunto.
                              Test. THO: WEEKS, Cl. Cur.
PASQUOTANCK. SC.
These are to certify, that on this 24th Day of July, 1727, personally came before me Mrs. Anna Low and Anna Letitia Low, Execxs. to the above Will and made their Solemn affirmation to the performance thereof.
                              Certifyed Pr. Me, JNO PALIN.
NO. CAROLINA. SC.
The above Will was proved in due Form by the Oath of Edmond Gale, Esqr., one of the Evidences, Augt. ye 2d. 1727.
                              Before Me, RICHARD EVERARD.

Recorded in Will Book 3, page 156.

ROGER MASON'S WILL.

NORTH CAROLINA, HYDE COUNTY.

IN THE NAME OF GOD AMEN. I, Roger mason, Sr. being Sick and Week of body, but of perfect mind and memory, Thanks be to God for the same, and knowing that it is appointed for all men once to Die, first, I Recommend my Soull to God that Gave it me, and my body to be Buried in a Christian Like manner at the Discresion of my Executors, hereafter named, first of all, I Give and Bequeath what the Lord hath been pleased in his Infinate marcy to bestow on me of worldly afairs, I Give and Bequeath as followeth.

Item, I Lend my loving wife, mary mason, the use of half my Estate, after the Legaces is paid out, During hur Natural life, and Then to be Equally Divided between my two Sons Benja. mason and Thos. mason. I Likewise Lend hur the use of half my house and plantation During her natural Life and no Longer, and then as follows:

Item, I give to my Grand Son, Christopher mason, one two year old heffer to be in Benja. possession tell he Comes of age

Item, I Give to my Son, Benjamin mason, all Gailars hammocks, and the upper old feild and all that Belongs to it.

Item, I give to my two Sons, Benjamin mason and Thos. mason, all my working tools, and wearing apperill, and negro Boston, to be Equeally Divided Between them.

Item, I give to John Mason and Roger Mason, my two Sons, one Shilling Starling apeace and they therewith to be Content.

Item, I give to my Grand son Roger mason, Jur., my now Dwelling place, if he Lives to the age of twenty two years old, and if he the sd. Roger should Diee before he Comes to the above age, I give it to my Grand Son, David Mason, only my my wife is to have the use of one half During her naturell Life, and to be in my Son, Benjamin Possession tell ther Come to that age.

Item, I give to Thos. mason, my Son, all my Land up Roes Down to the Great Bridges.

Item, I give to my Grand Son, David mason, one peace of Land Caulled the paupoy Ridge, and if my Grand Son Should Die, Roger mason before he Comes of twenty two years old I give the Said Peace of Land Caulled the paupoy Ridge to my Grandson, Samuel mason.

Item, I give to my Grand Son, moses mason, twenty five acars of Land Joyning on his plantation his father Left him, as is marked out by a Line of trees.

Item, I give to my Grand Son, Roger Mason, two Cowes and Calves, and one bed and Covering to it, to be in my Son Benjamin mason possession tell he Comes to the age of twenty two years old; and Eighteen months Schooling.

Item, I give to my Grand Daughter, Susannah mason, twelve months Schooling.

Item, I give to my two Sons, Benjamin and Thomas masons, one half of my estate after the Lagaces is paid out, to be Equally Divided Between them.

I Lastly, Ordain, Constitute and apoint my two Sons, Benjamin Mason, and Thomas Mason, my whole Executors of this my Last Will and Testament, Disalowing and Disanulling and Revoking all former Wills by me Before made, and this to Stand and Remain my Last Will and testament.

as witness whereof I have hereunto Sott my hand and Seall this 23th Day Decer. 1754.

Roger Mason. (Seal)

Signed, Sealled and Delivered in the presence of us to be the Last will and testament of the testator.

   John Tule.
   Jean X Tule.
     her
     mark
   Jacob Tule.

Hyde County, ss.   June Court, 1756.

This may Certifie that the Within Last Will and Testament of Roger Mason, Esqr., of the said County, Decd., was Exhibited to the said Court by Benjamin Mason and Thomas Mason, Exors. of the Within, and proved by the Oaths of John Tuley and Jacob Tuley, who Deposed they saw Jane Tuley Set her Mark as Testamoney as Such; and at the Same time the said Benjamin Mason and Thomas Mason, who are Exors., took the Exors. Oath as is by Law Appointed. Ordered that Mr Secretary have Notice thereof.

Veria Copia Pr. Stephen Denning, Cle: Cur:

Copied from Original Will, filed in the Office of Secretary of State.

JOHN MAULE'S WILL.

NORTH CAROLINA.

IN THE NAME OF GOD AMEN. I, John Maule, of Beaufort County and Province aforesaid, being in a very poor state of Health but of sound & perfect mind & memory, Do make this my last will and Testament in manner & form following, to-Wit: After my decease my Body to be Decently Inter'd at the Discretion of my Executors hereafter mentioned; my just Debts and funeral Expenses to be paid out of my Estate, and the Remainder part of my Estate I Dispose of as follows:

Imprimis, I lend the use of the mannor plantation Whereon I now Live, to my beloved Wife, Elizabeth Maule, with all the Land belonging to the same, which was Given to me by my father, Patrick Maule, Dureing that time that she shall and will continue thereon, and after her Death or Removal from of the said plantation, I give & bequeath the said plantation and Land, to my Son, Moses Maule, to him & his heirs Lawfully begotten for Ever.

I likewise give to my wife aforesd., seven Negroes, whose names are as followeth: Donas, Tom, Cesar, Farewell, Hannah, Venus, and Bess. I likewise give her all my household furniture, and all my stock of Cattle, Except twenty cows & Calves w'ch is to be disposed of in manner hereafter first mentioned.

I likewise give her all my stock of hogs and sheep, and two horses, Jack and lightfoot, to her and her heirs for Ever.

Item, I give further to my son, Moses Maule, six Negroes named as followeth: Adam, Harry, Jem, Crees, Little .... and Phillis; I likewise Give him all my Right & titles to my mill on Blounts Creek, likewise, all the Land that was given to me by my Father, Patrick Maule, which Joyens the Said mill, Except the pine timber on two hundred Acres of Land that joynes walter Evetts line; and my Will is that my Executors shall make John Neal a Deed for sd Land; I also give him 4 cows and Calves.

Item, I give to my Daughter, Elizabeth Maule, my Quarter Plantation and Lands thereunto belonging, which I bought of Moses Nevil, to her and the Heirs of her body for ever. I likewise give her the the following Negros: Frinkalo, gabe, Binah, Beck, Abigal, and Doll; also four cows & Calves, to her and her Heirs for Ever.

Item, I give to my Daughter, Anne, one piece of Land with the Plantation that I bought of John Nevil, and also one Tract of Land which I purchased of William Morris and Katherine, his wife, containing 400 Acres, to her and the Heirs of her body for Ever; also, the folowing Negros, Ben, Asia, Sandy, Ede, & Celia; and also four cows and calves, to her and her Heirs for Ever.

Item, I give to my Daughter, Penelope, the lands I purchased of Susanna Waggonner, Containing 640 Acres, lying on Blounts creek, and also 250 Acres joyning Wm. Morris's Land, to her and the Heirs of her body for Ever. Also the following Negros, Quamans, Nel, Kate, Sid, & Dorcas; also four Cows and calves, to her and her Heirs for Ever.

Item, I give to my Daughter, Jemima, 220 Acres lying on the head of Blounts Creek wch. I purchased of Benjamin Fathree; Also a tract of Land lying on Nevels Creek which I bought of Jacob Giddings lying on Nevils Creek, and two hundred & thirty Acres of Land lying in Pitt County, to her and her heirs for Ever; also the following Negros, Pegg, Tony, Little Ben, Little Hannah, Rose and Kate, also four Cows & calves, to her and her Heirs for Ever.

My Will is further that my Executors cause to be finished my new house as soon as they conveniently can, and that they collect the Debts Due to me as soon as they can, and that they sell my half of a Schooner belonging to me and Capt. Seth Doane, and the money arising therefrom, together with my ready money, be put to Interest, and also the money arising out of the several Legacys given to my Children, Except so much as shall be necessary to Educate and Support them, till they receive their Estate, w'ch shall be at the age of twenty one years or marriage.

I further will, that if any of my before named Children shall die in their minority, or before they receieve their fortunes, that then their fortune shall be Equally Divided between the Surviving ones, and Likewise the Increase of all the negros given to them, shall be Equally Divided amongst them as they come to the Age of twenty one Years or married as aforesaid; and also, all the remainder of my Estate not mentioned shall be Devided in the same manner, lands only Excepted.

Lastly, I nominate and appoint my Beloved Brother in Law, Moses Hare, my beloved and faithful friends, John Patten, Reading Blount, Junr., and Joseph Blount, all of the County aforesaid, to be my Executors of this my last Will and Testament and and I hereby Revoke all former Wills made by me.

In Witness whereof, I have hereunto set my hand and Seal, this 11th. day of December, in the Year of our Lord, one thousand, Seven hundred and Seventy three.

JOHN MAULE (Seal)

Signed, Sealed, Published and Declared, in the presence of:
    WILLIAM GERRARD.
    FORBIS GERRARD.
    JOHN X NEVIL
      his mark.

The above last Will and Testament of John Maule, deceased, was proved before me this 16th. day of Febr'y, 1774, by the Oath of John Nevil, one of the subscribing Witnesses thereto, who swore that he was present and did see the said Testator, sign, seal, publish and declare the same to be and contain his last will and Testament, and that at the time thereof he was of sound and disposing Mind and Memory; and Moses Hare, John Patten, Reading Blount, Junr., & Joseph Blount, the Executors in the said Will named, having qualified agreeable to Law, It is Ordered that letters Testamentary issue thereon accordingly.

Jo. Martin.

Copied from Original Will, Filed in the Office of the Secretary of State.

PATRICK MAULE'S WILL.

North Carolina, Beaford Precinct.

In the Name of God Amen. I, Patrick Maule, of Bath County, Gent., being in my Right Senses do make this my last will & testament, in manner & form following:

I give to my loving wife, Elizabeth Maule, & to her Assigns for Ever, the following Negroes, Vizt: Angus, Hannah, Affrica, Robin, & London, to be delivered after the tar kilns are off & the Crop finished; also, I give unto her the houshold furniture, Except the Eating Spoon & five Silver teaspoons. I give to my wife aforesd., fifteen cows, their calves, ten four year old Steers, & two third parts of the hogs on my Plantation at Rumney Marsh, also the young horse, the foregoing to be delivered after my Interment. And further, I leave my Plantation at Rumney Marsh to my wife during her Natural Life, with a dwelling house to be built for her by my Executors, twenty foot long & Sixteen foot wide; Also, I give unto my sd. wife full priviledge for making tar & Turpintine of my land on Jacks Creek during her Natural Life.

I give & bequeath to my Son, John Maule, his heirs & assigns forever, the following Slaves, Vizt: Cazar, Farewell, Bina, Tom Richards, Young Hannah. I give & bequeath to my Son, John aforesd., my Lands at Smiths point, also my lands at Blunts Creek, also my Saved lot in Bath town, all to him & to his heirs forever. Also, I give & bequeath to my Son, John aforesd., two hundred Acres of Land Adjacent to Roger Kenyons Plantation, to him & his heirs for Ever. I give to my son John, fifteen cows, their calves, at Blunts Creek, with their Increase.

I give to my daughter, Sarah Maule, the following Slaves Vizt: Elleck, great Tom, Peg, Andrew, & Kope; Also I give & bequeath to my daughter aforesd. & to her heirs for Ever, my Land at Tranters Creek, also fifteen Cows & Calves with their Increase.

I give & bequeath to my daughter, Barbara Maule, the following Slaves, Vizt: Chancellor, Jenny, Bess & Nanny; Also,

I give & bequeath unto my sd. daughter my land on Match-
apunga Swamp, as also, I give my sd. daughter, my plantation
at Rumney Marsh; also fifteen Cows & Calves with their
Increase, the lands aforesd. I give to her & her heirs for Ever.

I give & bequeath to my daughter, Mary Maule, the following Slaves, Vizt: Hector, Sue, Mustapha, & Dick; also, I give
to my sd. daughter, Mary, & her heirs for Ever my Lands on
North Dividing Creeks; also my lands on Jacks Creek, also
I give her fifteen Cows & Calves with their Increase.

And as to Lands or any other goods or Chattles not allready
disposed of, I will it, or they, be Equally devided among my
Said Children, and as to the Legacies & fortunes aforesd
they are all payable at the day of Marriage or age of twenty
one years; Also, If any young Negroes shall be born, they shall
be Equally divided among the Children aforesd. And I further
will, that after the marriage of sd. Children they shall not be
Entitled to any Increase of Slaves hapening by births of Negroes belonging to the other Children, Except in Case of
Mortallity.

And I further will, that if any of the Children aforesd. dye
before Marriage or Age of twenty one years, I then will that
their fortuns be Equally divided Among the Surviving Children.

I will that my loving Cusens, John Gray & William Gray, be
Guardians of my Children during their Minority, & have ther
Carefully Educated to best Advantage.

Lastly, I nominate & Appoint my beloved Friends, Mr
John Gray, Mr. William Gray, Mr. John Caldom & Mr
Robert Boyd, to be my Executors of this my last will & testa-
ment, & I hereby revoke all former wills by me made.

In witness whereof, I have hereunto put my hand & Seal
this Ninteenth day of April, one thousand, Seven hundred &
thirty Six.

           PAT. MAULE. (Seal)
Sign'd, Seal'd, Publish'd, &
Declared in Presence of:
    BART. FLEMING.
        her
    ELIZABETH E MONTGOMERY,
        mark.
    NEHEMIAH MONK.

The Last Will and Testament of Patt. Maule, Deceased, was proved in
Open Court, by the Oaths of Barnabas Fleming & Nehemiah Monk, Two
of the Subscribing Evidences thereto. Ordered yt. Mr. Secretary have
Notice Thereof.

Robt. Boyd, one of the Exors. therein mentioned having taken the
Oath by Law Appointed.
        Test. JNO. COLLISON, Cler. Cur.
Lts. issued June, 1736.

Copied from the Original Will, filed in the Office of the Secretary of
State.

WILLIAM MAULE'S WILL.

IN THE NAME OF GOD AMEN, this Twenty first day of February, in the Year of Our Lord, One Thousand, Seven hundred and twenty five. I, William Maule, of the precinct of Bertie, in the Province of North Carolina, Gent., being Sick and week, but of sound and perfect mind and memory, Do make and ordain this my last Will and Testament, hereby revoking and making Null and Void all former and other Wills by me made.

First, It is my Will that all my Debts and Funeral Charges be paid by my Executor.

Item, I Give, Devise and Bequeath to my Wife, Penelope Maule, my Plantation called Scotts Hall, and allso, my Plantation called Mount Galland, to her and hers and Assigns forever.

Item, I Give, Devise and Bequeath to my Daughter, Penelope Maule, all the rest and residue of my Estate, both Real and Personal, to her and her heirs and Assigns forever.

Lastly, I Do hereby Nominate and appoint my Brother, Patrick Maule, Sole Executor of this my last Will and Testament, whom I also Constitute Guardian of my said Daughter, Penelope, hereby Givning him full Power to make Sale of any of the lands before bequeathed to my Said Daughter, for and toward her Education.

In Testimony whereof, I have hereunto Sett my hand & Seal, the day and Year first above written.

WILL MAULE, (Seal)

Signed, Sealed Published &
Declared to be his last Will &
Testament in presence of us:
    ROBT. FORSTER,
    JOHN NAIRNR.
    JONES EAGLES. (?).

NORTH CAROLINA, ss.
    SR. RICHARD EVERARD, BART., GOV:

These may Certify that Robert Foster, Gent., one of the Evidences to the within Will, Proved the Same upom Oath in due form, this 30th. day of March, 1726.

RICHD. EVERARD.

Copied from the Original Will, filed in Office of the Secretary of State.

HENRY McCULLOCH'S WILL.

NORTH CAROLINA.

IN THE NAME OF GOD AMEN, I, Henry McCulloch, Esqr. Secretary of the Province of North Carolina aforesaid, being sick and weak in body, but of sound and disposing mind and memory, praised be God for the same, Do make and Ordain this to be my Last Will and Testament, in manner following that is to say: First and principally, I recommend my Soul into the hands of Almighty God who gave it; and my Body to the Earth to be decently intered according to the discretion of my Executors herein after named: And as for such Temporal Estate as it hath pleased God to bless me with, I Give and dispose thereof as followeth, to wit:

I Give unto my Dear Wife, Mary McCulloch, All that my Real and personal Estate, Goods and Chattels whatsoever and wheresoever, and of what Nature or kind soever, to be divided equally between my said Wife and my four Daughters, Henrietta Mary, Dorothy Berisford, Elizabeth Margaret, and Penelope Martha McCulloch, Share and Share alike, Provided always, and the treu intent and meaning of this my Will is that my sd. Wife shall be at Liberty to pay my said Daughters their several proportions or Shares of my said Real and personal Estate, at their several age or Ages of Twenty one Years, or days or days or Marriage, which shall first happen, and in the mean time, shall, and may reimburse herself thereout the Costs, Charges and Expences she may be at for their several Maintenances and Education.

And Lastley, I Do hereby Nominate, Constitute, and Appoint my said Wife, Mary McCulloch, and my worthy frend John Campbell of Bertie County, in the sd. Province, Esqr. Executors of this my Last Will and Testament, hereby revoking and making Void all other and former Wills by me heretofore made, Declaring this and now other, to be and Contain my Last Will and Testament.

In Witness whereof, I have here unto Set my hand and Seal. The twenty fith day of October, In the Year of our Lord 1755.

his
HENRY HEN:MCL. McCULLOCH, (Seal)
Mark.

Signed, Sealed, Published and Declared, In the presence of us, who have Subscribed our names as witnesses hereto in the presence of the Testator. (the names, Mary, Barisford, Margaret and

Martha, being first Interlined between the Ninth & Tenth Line from the beginning of the Will).
   Wm. Powell.
   Isc. Arthaud.
   Wm. Robertson.

On the 15th. day of November, 1755, the Above Will was proved by William Powell and William Robertson, two of the subscribing evidences, who at the same time made Oath that they saw, Isc. Arthaud, the other Subscribing Evidence, set his hand as a Witness thereto, and then also John Campbell, Execrs. named In the said Will, Appeared & Qualify'd himself by taking the Oath by Law Appointed.
              Arthur Dobbs.

Copied from Original Will, filed in the Office of the Secretary of State.

JOHN McKINZIE'S WILL.

In The Name of God, Amen. I, John McKinzie, minister of Suffolk Parish in Nansemond County, being perfect and sound both in Body and mind, do make and ordain this my Last Will & Testament in manner and form follow'g, that is to say, first, I Commend my soul to my Good and Gracious God of whom I humbly & earnestly beg and trust to obtain mercy and pardon by ye merrits & Intercession of Jesus Christ my blessed Savour and Redemer, in whom alone I put my trust and whom I flee to ye mercies of God hoping he will accept of my sincere Repentance and that he will assist me with his Holy Spirit and Guide me through ye Valley of ye Shadow of Death and Receive me into his Kingdom & Glory.

As to my worldly Goods or Estate, first I give & bequeath to my Eldest Son, John, seven hundred and ninety five Acres of my Land at skeehawkee which I lately purchased of John Spier, joining to the manner place lying in Torril County and three hundred and five acres in the Island of Carorine lying in Bartee County to him and his heirs forever.

Item. I give to my second son, Kenneth, thousand acres of my Land at said Skeehawkee in Including a watermill & ye parcel Land thereto adjoining lying in the County aforesd. together with ye. priveledge of pasturage in the above Name Island of Carorine to him and his heirs forever.

Item. I give and bequeath to my third Son, William, three hundred acres of my land lying on Roanoke River in Bartee County Lately purchased of William Word to him and his heirs forever.

Item. I give and Bequeath to each of sd. three sons one hundred pounds Curt. money of Virginia part of which sum to be laid out and applied towards training & Educating to such crediable calling or mechanick business as shall appear to be most fiting and suitable to their Geneous & Capacities.

Item. I give and Bequeath to my Eldest Daughter, Janet, one hundred and fifty pounds money aforesd. to her & her heirs forever.

Item. I give to my second Daughter, Anne ye. like some of one hundred and fifty pounds money aforesd. to her & her heirs forever.

Item. I will and ordain that ye several sums of money Bequeathed to my said children be settled upon Good security and the Interest thence accruing, if Necessary, to be applied toward their maintenance and Education.

Item. I will and ordain that in case any of my children should die in their menority that then the Deceased portion shall be Equally shared and divided among ye. surviving.

Item. I will and ordain that my Negroes shall not be divided during ye. minority of my children unless my Exrs. shall think fitt to sell one of my fellows Named Bristo & buy another younger in his room, and afterward he be equally shared among them.

Item. I will and ordain that all my cattle hogs sheep crop at ye. Glebe, what sallary may be due to me from Suffolk parish, and whatever part of my household goods, &c., my Exrs. shall fitt to Dispose of for saving ye. Trouble and charges of Transportation to be sold and fifty pounds of the price thereof to be allowed my Exers. towards Defraying ye charges of Removing my family from hence to Carolina & settling them.

Item. I will and ordain that ye Remainder of my household goods be managed at ye Discretion of my Exors. to ye benefit of my family. I will and ordain that my Exors. & family shall have liberty to remove from hence with whatever part of my estate they shall think fit to carry along with them without giving any security in this County.

Item. I constitute and appoint Wm. Gray, my Brother-in-law, Capt. John Hill, of Bartee County, James Pugh and Pasco Turner of Nansemond County, Exrs. of this my last will and testament.

In Witness Whereof I have hereunto set my hand and seal, this second day of March in ye year of our Lord one thousand, seven hundred & fifty four.

JOHN MACKINZIE.

Signed, sealed and delivered in ye presents of
    JAMES PUGH,
    JAS. WRIGHT,
    CHRISTIAN X GOOD
        her
        mark.

At a Court held for Nansemond County Apl. 8, 1754, The Last Will and Testament of John Mackinzie was proved by ye oathe of Jas. Wright and Christian Good, two of ye Witnesses thereto, also by ye oaths of Wm. Gray, John Hill & James Pugh three of ye Exors. therein Named who gave bond with Josiah Riddick, Willis Riddick, and Daniel Pugh, Gent., their securities, Certificate for obtaining Letters Testamentory on ye sd. Will granted unto ye sd. Exors. in due form. Pasco Turner ye other Exor. in ye said Will mentioned came into Court & refused to take on himself ye Burthen & Execution thereof.

Test. LEMUEL RIDDICK, Cl. Ct.

True Copy,
   Test: LEMUEL RIDDICK, Cl. Ct.

Copied from Original Will, filed in the Office of the Secretary of State

JOHN MONCREIF'S WILL.

The Last Will and Testament of John Moncreif, of north Carolina, being weake in Body, but of perfect memory, doe give and demise my Temporal Estate which god of his mercy hath endued me with all, ass followeth:

Imprimis, I give and bequeath unto my beloved wife, Mary Moncrief, The manner plantation dureing her life, and after her decease to my youngest son, george moncrief, Containing one hundred and sixty Acckers of land; and if ye said george moncreif liveth to Come to mans Estat, he shall have the liberty to seat any part of ye Said hundred and sixty Ackers of land not disturbing his Aforesaid mother.

2'ly, I give unto my son, Thomas Moncrief, one hundred and sixty Ackers of land Joyning to the manner plantation.

3'ly. I give to my son, William Moncrief, one hundred and sixty Ackers of land Joyning to my Son, Thomas monerief, land.

4'ly, I give to my son, John moncrief, one hundred and sixty Ackers of land Joyning to my son, William moncrief, land, to them and there heirs for ever; onely if one or more should should die without lawfull heir or Isue, the same land to be Eaqualy devided amoungst ye Rest. Every one of my sons Shall begin at ye pecoson and soe take there due part to ye head line.

Item, I give to my beloved wife, mary moncrief, one Cubard with 3 pewter dishis, 2 pewter poringers, and 6 Inglish spoons, and ye mill and ye peck, and one new fether bed and furniture belonging to it, and one great pot, and ye young bay mare and her Increas, onely my beloved wife, mary moncrief, shall give my son, george moncrief, a young mare of 3 years old when he Comes to age; all ye Aforesaid housalgoods After the decease of mary moncrief shall be given to my son, george moncrief.

Item, I give to my beloved wife, mary moncrief, 2 deep dishi;
and one great bason, and 2 poringers, and 6 spoons, one pae:
of fier tongs, 4 botls, and one fryingpan, and ye great greater
and ye great Chest, and ye litel box with a lock and key t(
it, and one great table, 4 Chears, and one great tankert, on(
iron pestel, one drawing knife and handsaw, and ye Cutin(
knife, one great narow ax.

Item. I give to my daughter, mary moncrief, one fethe
bed, one great Rugg and one paer of sheets and bed stea(d
one Chest that is next to yt of my wifes, one paer of fier tongs
4 Chears, one litel pot, 4 botels, 2 pewter basons, one tankert
to litle flat dishis, 6 Inglish spoons, 2 poringers, 2 pewte
plats.

Item, I give to my son, John Moncrief, 2 pewter dishis, tw(
poringers, 6 spoons, 2 plats, 1 Cheare, one litle Chest witl
lock and key, one Cros Cut saw, one small auger, one adds.

Item, I give to my son, william moncrief, 2 pewter dishis, :
poringers, 3 spoons, 2 Iron wegges, one narrow ax, one litl(
Chest with lock and key.

Item, I give to my son, Tho: moncrief, 2 pewter dishis, :
poringers, 3 spoons, one long pot, and a Chear, one linin be(
and one Rugg, and one paer of sheets and bed stead, one broa(
ax, one great gimblit, 2 Iron wedges, one spade, one grea
Auger, 2 Chisels.

Item, I give to my beloved wife and my son, george, 6 Cow
and 4 Calves, and ye 2 great steers, one yeo and yeo lamb.

Item, I give to my daughter, mary moncrief, 3 Cows an(
Calves, one sow and piggs, to be paid upon her marriage day.

Item, I give to my son, John moncrief, when he Comes t(
age, one Cow and Calfe, and 3 two yeare old hefers, and on
sow and piggs.

Item, I give to my son, William moncrief, one Cow an(
Calfe, and 3 teers, one sow and piggs if ye sows has them.

Item. I give to my son, Thos. moncrief, 4 steers, one so\
and piggs if ye sows has them, and one young horse.

Item, I give to my daughter, mary moncrief, my black mar
yt I sold to Craft if he Returns her, if not ye bill.

as for ye linin and wooling, I give to my wife for ye use o
ye small Children and her own use; and for my wareing Cloaths
I leave ytm to my wifes disposisan, to devide as she think
fitt amoungst ym; and ye Cart and wheels for ye use of ye plan
tation, and all my hoogs I give to my wife to pay my debts
and what debts there is due to me fer her to Receive; the
meale sifters I give to my wife; as for ye wooden ware, devid
it amongst them as you shall think fit.

Item, I give to my son, george, my gun; and my sword to m:
son, Thomas.

And as for all other things yt is not mentioned, I leave t

my beloved wife, mary moncrief, and I doe heareby ordaine, Constitute, and appoint my beloved wife, mary moncrief, to be my only Executrix of this my last will and testament, and I doe heareby Revoke and disanul all former will or wills by me made, ass wittness my hand and seale this 22th. day of June, 1712.

JOHN MUNCIREEF. (Seal)

Signed, Sealed in ye presents
of us: ADAM PEARRY
        THOMAS DAVIS.
               his
        DANIEL OX GLASCOE.
             marke

This Within Written Will was Proved in Open Court in Lawfull Manner the 14th. Day of Ags: Anno Dom., 1713, By The Oaths of Thos. Davis And Dan: Glasco.   Tets. Jos: WILKER, Clk. Cout.

Copied from Original Will, filed in the Office of the Secretary of State.

ROGER MOORE'S WILL.

NORTH CAROLINA, NEW HANOVER COUNTY.

IN THE NAME OF GOD AMEN, the Last will and Testament of Roger Moore, of the Parish of Saint Philips.

Imprimis, I doe give, Devise and Bequeath unto my Son, George Moore, and his Heirs forever the Following Tracts or Parcells of Lands, Vizt., All that Part of my Plantation Called by the Name of Kendall, Bounding to the Southward by the Creek that runs up to my Mill as far as there is a Post to be fixt about three Hundred yards up the Creek above the House where Gready Lately removed from; and from thence a Due west Line to be Continued as far my Lands runs up the Neck, and Bounded to the Northward by Mr. Allens Creek, with the Little Island of Marsh fronting the said Plantation in the River. And all Other my Lands bounding on the said Creek; and all Other my Lands Lying between the Thorofare and Black river, in the Neck known by the Name of Maultby's Point, with all my Lands on the Island Opposite; And One half of the Tract of Land in the fork of the river known by the Name of Mount Misery; the Same to be Divided in Such Manner as my son, George, shall think Proper to Direct; and them my William to Take his Choyce, & that to be Done in One year After my Decease. And five Hundred Acres on the Northwest river, Lying Between the Lands of Mr. Job Howes and the Land that was Mr. Dallisons, Decd.; and all that Tract of Land I bought of Mr. John Porter, Decd., on the No. West River at or Near the Saxapahaw Old fields, being Three Thousand & Twenty five Acres; And the Lott of Land in the Town of Brunswick where Mr Ross at Present Dwells, being five Poles wide & runing from the river as farr as the Street before Doct. Fergu's House, with the Wharf and all Other Improvements thereon.

Item, I doe give unto my Aforesaid Son, George, my Negro man Higate the Carpenter, His wife Rose, with all her Issue & Encrease.

Item, I doe give, Devise & Bequeath unto my son, William Moore, & his Heirs for ever all that my Plantation Called Orton where I now dwell, Joyning on Kendals, as its before Bounded by this my Will, with all my Land Bounded to the Southward on the Creek where My Mill now is, being in all about 2500 Acres; & also, 640 Acres at Rockey Point, bounding on Mr. Allens and the river, and the Remaining half of Fifty five Thousand Acres in the Neck known by the Name of Mount Misery, and all the Tract of Land bounded by the River & Smiths Creek; and 5000 Acres at or near the Haw or Eno old Fields.

Item, I doe Also give, Devise, and Bequeath unto my Said Son, William, One full fifth Part of the Slaves I Shal Dye Possessed of; and its my Will that all my Slaves Shall in One Month After my Decease be Devided into five Equall Parts, as near as mybe, by himself and my Son George, & when so done that my son, William, take his Chance by Lott for such his Part. And I doe Also give unto my said Son, William, all the Stock of Horses & Cattle & Sheep that Shall Properly belong to, & be on my Plantation Orton at my Decease, with all my Plate & Household furniture, Hee, my son William, Paying to my son George, in Two years After my Decease, the Sum of One Hundred Pounds, Proclamation Money or the Value thereof.

Item, I doe give unto my Daughter, Sarah Smith, the Sum of five Pounds, being in full for her Fortune; She having Already recd. from me, with the Legacy Left her by Her Grand Mother, by my Computation, at Least £1600 Sterling.

Item, I doe give unto my Daughter, Mary Moore, the Sum of Eighteen Hundred Pounds, Proclamation Money, or the Value thereof, to be Paid Her, or sure'd to be paid Her, in Two years after my Decease; but on the Condition Only my Exors. then Taking a Release for the Legacy left her by Her Grand Mother, Mrs. Sarah Trott, and Also, that she Doe not Marry but with the Consent of my Exors. & her Aunt, Mrs. Sarah Allen, or the Majority of them.

Item. I doe give unto my Daughter, Anne Moore, the Sum of Eighteen Hundred Pounds, Proclamation Money, or the Value thereof, to be Paid her, or sured to be paid Her, in Two years after my Decease; But on the Same Terms & Conditions as Her Sister Mary before Mentioned.

Item, I doe give unto my son in Law, Mr Thomas Smith, &

his Heirs for ever, all that Lott of Land in the Town of Brunswick where Mr. William Lord at Present resides, Besides with the Building thereon.

Item, I doe give, Devise & Bequeath unto my sons, George & William Moore, and their Heirs forever, all the rest & Residue of my real & Personal Estate, to be Equally Divided Between them, After the Payment of all my just Debts & Legacys, but on these Conditions, that they, at the expence of my Estate, Maintain their Said Sisters, Mary & Anne aforesaid, untill their Legacy become Due, unless they shall Marry before, but Nevertheless, if my Two Sons Shall Choose to pay their Legacy Out of my Principal Estate, they shall be at their Liberty so to doe soe as not more then One third of the same be Paid to Each in Land; & the Lands & slaves to be Vallued to them by Indifferent Persons, to be Choose by each Party, & they on Oaths, there being Twenty Odd Thousand Acres of Land & Near Two Hundred & fifty Slaves, with the Stock of Horses, Cattle, &c., & besides the Debts Due To me not before Bequeathed in this my Will.

Item, I doe Devise & Bequeath unto my Dear beloved Wife, Mary Moore, all the Estate that was her own at the Time of Her Marriage, be it of any Nature and Kind Whatsoever, with the Profits arising Since Such her Marriage; as also the Saw Mill I intend to Build on Brices Creek, with the Slaves & all Utensils that shall Properly Belong to them. And if it shal soe Happen that I shal Dye Before the said Mill shall be Compleatly finished, that She, my said Wife, is to have the work of my four Carpinters now at Nuce, until they be Compleatly Finished; and the aforesaid Land & Mill I doe give unto my said Wife, & Hurs forever, & in full Consideration of her Dower & any Claim She may have by Law to any Part of my real & Personal Estate.

Item, it is my Will that each of my Daughters, Mary & Anne, Doe at their Marriage, take Each their Choyce of any One of the House Slaves, Except the Negro wench Bess, who I leave to Her Liberty to make Choyce of any One of my Children for her Master or Mistress.

Lastly, I doe Nominate and appoint my Two Sons, George & William Moore, Exors. to this my Last will & Testament, Revoaking all Other Wills herefore made by me.

In Testimony Whereof, I have hereunto Set my Hand & Seal, this 7th. Day of March 1747/8.

ROG. MOORE (seal)

Signed, Sealed, Published & Declared to be my Last Will & Testament in the Presence of:
    WM. FORBES.
    RICHD. QUINCE.
    GEO. LOGAN.

A Codicil to this my Last will & Testament: Whereas, it is Apparent from the Late Storm, that the Legacy I have Bequeathed unto my Loving Wife, Mary, The giving her my saw Mill and the Appurtenancys thereunto Belonging, may, Instead of being a Yearly Profit to her, Prove rather an Expence, therefore I doe Absolute Declare that Part of my will soe much as relates to the Saw Mills and appurtenancys thereunto Belonging to be Void and of none Effect; & in Lieu of the Same, do give unto my said Loving Wife, Mary, One Hundred Pounds, Sterling Money, or the full Vallue thereof, to be Paid her Yearly by my Exors. During the Time she Does remain my Widdoe, and noe Longer, and the same to be in full for her right of Dower, & in full for any Claim or Demand of any kind Whatsoever She may have Legully to any Part of my Estate.

In Testimony Whereof I have here unto Set my Hand & Seal, the 30th. Day of June, 1750.

R. MOORE. (seal)

Signed, Sealed & Published in the Presence off us:
WM. ROSS.
REBECCA COKE.
GEO. LOGAN.

Att a Court held at Wilmington, On the Last Tuesday in May, in the Year of Our Lord, One Thousand, Seven Hundred and fifty One. On Motion the Last Will & Testamt. of Roger Moore, late of the Province of North Carolina, Esqr., Deceased, was Proved in Due form of Law By the Oath of George Logan, One of the Subscribing Witnesses to the said Will and Codicil, by which Will George Moore and William Moore are Appointed Exors. of the Last Will and Testament of the said Roger Moore Decd., which said William Moore and George, Appeared in Court and Took the Oath of an Executor According to Law.

Therefore it is Ordered that Letters Testamentary do issue to the said George Moore and William Moore, to Impower them to Take upon themselves the Execution of the said, of the said Roger Moore, Decd.

By the Court. ISAAC FARIES, C. C.
Mr Rice's Ex'or, Dr for this, 16 Cash.

Copied from the Original Will, Filed in the Office of the Secretary of State.

THOMAS MOOR'S WILL.

WILMINGTON, 3d. february, 1735.

I, Thomas Moor, Late of New York, now in Wilmington Being Sick of Body but sound of Judgment, Doe make This my Last Will and Testament.

In Primis, I appoint and Constitute Cosmas Farquharson Doctor of Physic, my Sole Executor and Administrator of all the Debts, Effects and Moneys I Can Lay any Claim to in

North Carolina, in Order that he, the said Cosmas Farquharson, may Remit the Same to New York to be Dispos,d off there as my former Will, in the hands of Mr. Alsop and Carroll there Directs, and this My Last Will and Testament Day And Date foresaid, I have signd, seald and
Delivered in presence of:

THOS. MOOR (Seal)

Witness:
  CALEB MASON.
  SIMON PAYNE.
  RD. HARTLEY.

At a Court begun and Held for the County of New Hanover on Tuedsay the 4th. Day of February, 1753.

 Present His Majestys Justices:

These may Certify that Richard Hartley, one of the subscribing Evidences to the Within Will, appeared in Open Court & made Oath on the holy Evangelist that he was Present and saw Thomas Moor, sign, Seal and Declare the within to be and contain his last Will and Testament; and that the Said Thomas Moor was then & at that time of sound and disposing Memory; and that he also saw Caleb Mason and Symon Payne, two other Subscribing Evidences, sign their names thereto at the same Time: then also appeared Cosmas Farquharson, Executor, in open Court and took the Executors Oath in Due form of Law.

ISAAC FARRIES, Cl. Cu.

Copied from Original Will, filed in the Office of the Secretary of State.

EDWARD MOSELEY'S WILL.

NO. CAROLINA, SC.

IN THE NAME OF GOD AMEN, I, Edward Moseley, of New Hanover County, Esqr., do make and Declare these Presents to be and Contain my Last Will & Testament Rovoking all Other.

Imprimis, I will that all my Debts be well & Truly paid, within Convenient time after my Decease, Out of the Profits arising from the Labour of my Slaves.

Item, It is my Will that as soon as it well may be done After my Decease, a True and Perfect Inventory be made of all my Personal Estate, and that the Same be Returned upon Oath into the Secretary's Office, as also into the Office of the County Court of New Hanover, within Ninety Daies After my Decease.

Item, I give and Bequeath unto my Eldest Son, John Moseley, my Plantation at Rockey Point, where I Frequently reside, on the West side of North East Branch of Cape Fear River, Together with all my Lands Adjacent thereto, Containing in the whole about 3500 Acres, be the Same more or Less, To Have and To Hold the same to him, the said John Moseley, & his heirs male of his Body Lawfully begotten for ever. And for want of Such Heirs then to my Second Son, Edward Moseley, and his Heirs Male of his Body Lawfully Begotten for ever; and for want of Such Heirs, then to the next of my Sons as Shall Attain to the Age of 21 years, intail male as above mentioned; and for want of Such to my right Heir infee Simple.

Item, I give to my Second Son, Edward Moseley, my Plantation where I formerly Dwelt in Chowan County, and the Lands adjacent thereto, Containing by estimation 2000. Acres, be the Same More or Less, To Have & to Hold the Same to him & the Heirs male of his Body Lawfully Begotten infee tail; and for want of Such, then to my Son, Sampson Moseley, & the Heirs Male of his Body Lawfully Begotten infee tail; & for want of Such, then to my Son, James Moseley, infee tail Male as above exprest; & for want of Such, Then to my Fifth Son, Thomas Moseley, and His heirs for ever.

Item, I give and Bequeath unto my Son, Sampson Moseley, and his Heirs and Assigns, all my Lands On the East Side of the North East Branch of Cape Fear River, Lying Between Holly Shelter Creek and the bald white Sand hills, Containing by Estimation 3500 Acres, be the Same More or Less.

Item, I give & Bequeath unto my Son, James Moseley, and his Heirs & Assigns, all my Lands on the East side of the North East Branch of Cape Fear River Opposite to my Rocky Point Plantation, Containing by Estimation 1650 Acres, be the Same More or Less.

Item, I give & Bequeath unto my Son, Thos. Moseley, & his Heirs and Assigns, all my Lands on the North West Branch of Cape Fear River, Vizt: 1280 Acres I had by the Will of John Baptista Ashe, Esq[r]., at Rockfish Creek on both sides the River; and 600 Acres on the East side of the North West branch of Cape Fear River, Near Opposite to the Lands Whereon M[r]. Mitchell Formerly Dwelt.

Item, I give & Bequeath unto my Son, John Moseley, and his Heirs and Assigns, my Lot and Houses in Brunswick where my Habitation usually is at Present, After the Decease of my Loving Wife, to whom I give it During her Natural Life. I also give to my said son John & his Heirs and assigns, my Plantation below Brunswick, Commonly Called Macknights.

Item, I give and Bequeath unto my Son, Edward Moseley, and his Heirs and Assigns, my Lot & house in Wilmington; Also, 600 Acres of Land Opposite to Cabbage Inlet; Also 500 Acres of Land in Tyrrel, Commonly Called Coopers; & 450 Acres of Land in Tyrrel County, Commonly Called Whitemarsh, all these to him & his Heirs & Assigns.

Item, I give and Bequeath to my three Sons, Sampson, James and Thomas, all my Lands on the East side of Cape Fear River on Part. whereof M[r]. Bugnion dwelleth, to be Divided into three Equal Parts, as near as may be; Thom[as] to have his first Choice, and Jam^es the Next, the Division to be made by my Wife.

Item, I give to my Loving Wife, Ann Moseley, During her Natural Life, my Plantation at the Sound which I bought of John Hodgson, Wheron there is a Large Vineyard Planted; Also 3200 Acres of Land in EdgComb, Called Alden of the hill, be the Same More or Less, Lying on a Branch of Fishing Creek, by Some Called Irwins by Other Butterwood; Also 1650 Acres, be the Same More or Less, upon the West side of Neuse River, about Twenty four Miles above New Bern Town. With full Power to her by any Deed or will, to give the first Mentioned to all or any of my Children She pleases, to be held by Such in fee Simple, and the two Last Mentioned Tracks, Vizt: 3200 & 1650, to all, or any of my four Youngest Sons, as She shall think they best deserve or may most want the Same, in Such Proportion as She Shall think Proper, to be held by Such as she shall Appoint, the same in fee simple.

Item, I give and Bequeath unto my five Sons, John, Edward, Sampson, James, & Thomas, & their Heirs & assigns, to be held in Severalty, & to be Equally Divided, my Large Tract of Land in EdgComb County, Called Clur, Containing by Estimation Ten Thousand Acres, be the same more or Less; & it is my Will that in Case Any of my Sons Shall Dye before they attain the Age of 21 Years, or Without Leaving Lawfull Issue, that then the Lands of Such so Dying Shall be Equally Divided Among the Survivours, to be held by them infee Simple, Except those first Mentioned Lands Given to my Two Eldest Sons in tail Male, which in Case of their Or either of their Death is to go as I have before exprest.

Item, It is my Will that no part of my Stocks, Houshold Goods, Slaves, or Other Personal Estate, be Sold for Payment of my Debts; but that the Same Shall be Paid Out of the Money's Arising by Crops or Other Labour of my Slaves; hereby Directing that what Products of the Labour of my Slaves Shall be in being at my Decease, the Same Shall go towards Payment of my Debts, and that my Slaves that work in the field or on Tarr Work &c'^c, to be kept to Labour in Such Manner, on all, or any of my Lands as Shall best serve, to raise most Money for Discharge of my Debts.

Item, After my Debts are Paid by the Labour of my Slaves, I give and Bequeath unto my Dear & Loving Wife, Ann Moseley, these 21 Slaves Following, Vizt: Robin & his wife Dinah & their Children, Little Mustapha, Cæsar & Jonathan; Kate & her Children, Willy & Abram, Simon, Gabriel, Jacob, Primus, Francis, Abigail, Hager, Phillida & her Two Children, Quashey & Billey; Drago & his Wife Nan; and Moll Statiras Daughter.

Item, I give and Bequeath unto my Daughter, Aner Moseley, these Eleven Slaves, Vizt: Sarah, Mustapha's Wife; Hannah &

her Two Daughters Phillida & Bessy; Cudger & his Wife Bolinder & their Daughters Betsy, Sarah & Lucy, Esther Simons wife; and Little Esther, Jennys Daughter.

Item, I give & Bequeath unto my five Sons, John, Edward, Sampson, James & Thomas, these 56 Slaves, to Wit: Manuel & his Wife Maria & their Children, Manuel, Frank, Jenny, and Yauna; Robin & his wife Doll; Judith and her Sons, Henry, Tony, Tom & Ben; Jenny & her Sons, Andrew & Ned; Bacchus & his wife Yanbo & her Children, Jupiter, Sarah and hannah; Mat, a Cooper, & his wife Mercy, & their Children, Mat, Frank & Peggy; Jemmy & his wife Sarah; Tom a Cooper & his wife Jenny; Joe & his wife Doll, & their Daughter Dol; Jemmy & Cooper, Sambo & Cooper, Scipio, Roger, Sandy, Cook, Button, Cyrus, Peter, Zebedee; Flora & Diana, the Daughters of Dinah; Nancey & her Children, Alden, Jacob & Suckey; Cudgeo, Kates son Statara, Peg & her Daughter Sarah Membo; Belindas Daughter Jenny; Esthers Daughters, Cates Daughter Hagar.

Item, I give and Bequeath unto my Loving Wife, Ann, my New Chaise Harness and the Pair of Bay Horses, Smoker and Toby, which I bought of John Hull, Esqr, for that use, I also give Unto her Out of my Stocks, Ten Cows & Ten Calves, Ten Steers of Differant Age's, & Twenty Sheep & the horse Spark.

Item, it is my Will that my said Wife have the Care, Tuition and GuardianShip of my Daughter, Ann; & in Case of her Death, then to my Honour'd Mother in Law, Mrs. Susannah Hasell.

Item, It is my Will that the Slaves now usually kept about the house, shall be kept in the same Employment for my Wifes easier Life, and Care of my Children, untill She Marries, or One of my Sons Arrives at Age of 21 Years, then they are to go to those I have before Bequeathed them.

Item, It is my Will that my Wife Shall have the Use of my Lot & houses in Brunswick; and also of my Dwelling house, Kitchen &c. at Rockey Point, untill She shall Marry or that One of my Sons Shall Attain in the Age of 21 years, She keeping all my Houses in Repair. And when Any of my Sons Shall Attain 21 years of Age, then my wife Shall have her Choice Whether She will Dwell in my houses at Brunswick or at Rockey Point; it is also my Will, that she may work so many of the Slaves on any of my Lands as she Shall choose, along with my Childrens Slaves for which She may Draw a Proportionable Part with Such Slaves of my Children as shall be thought most for their benefit to be worked with hers; The Barns to be for the Use of my Children as well as for my Wife.

Item, it is my Will that after my Debts are Paid, my Sons Slaves Shall be Employ'd on all, or any of my Lands, and no where else, in the Most Beneficial Manner that may be for the Profit of my said Sons; and Annually Accts. to be rendered to the County Court of New Hanover, of the Profits Arising thereby, which Profits are to be Accompted for without Any Charge of Commissions, &ª., Other than the Overseers Share. Nor shall my Children's Estate be made any way Less Under pretence of Commissioners, &cª., But all that I have or shall leave them in this my Last Will is to go Clear to them, Except what shall be hereafter exprest Concerning my Sons Education.

Item, I give unto my Six Children all my Stock of horses Mares, Neat Cattle, Sheep and Swine, to run & encrease for ther Benefit; and I will that proper Slaves be Appointed for Managing thereof of, which increase & profit made thereby of Such as are necesarily to be sold or Killed at Proper Seasons, Accot. to be rendered to the County Court, for my children advantage, without Charges, Deducting first thereout what may be necessary of such kind of Provision for housekeeping for my said wife & Children.

Item, It is my Will that the Profits Arising by the Labour of my Two sons Slaves, & their part of the profits Arising by the Stocks, be laid Out in purchasing Young Female Slaves to be Added to their Stocks of slaves; And it is also my will that if any of the Female Slaves given be my in this will shall breed, in Such Case I give the issue to go along with the Mother.

Item, When it shall be necessary to give all or any of my sons Other Education than is to be had from the Common Masters in this Province; for I would have my Children well Educated, it is then my Will that Such expence be Defrayed Out of the profits of Such Childs Estate & not Otherwise.

Item, I Recommend it to my Dear & Loving Life that one of my sons, as shall be Thought best Qualified for it, be bred to the Law, it being highly necessary in so Large a Family; and to him I give all my Law Books, being upwards of 200 Volumes, which are now or Shall be in My Closet at Brunswick, and are Exprest in a Catalogue of my Own hand Writing, in a Marble Cover Book in my Closet.

Item. I give to my Dear wife, Blomes History of the Bible in folio, 3 Volumes in folio of Arch Bishop Tillotsons Works, four volumes in Octavo of Dr. Stanhopes on the Epistles & Gospels, and all the Books of Physick.

Item, I give to my Daughter, Ann Humfries, 3 Volumes in folio on the Old & New Testament, and I will that my Exors. buy for her, the work of the Auther of the whole Duty of Man. I give to the Eldest of my Sons, that shall not Study the the Law; Chambers Dictionary, two Volumes in folio; Locks Work, three Volumes in folio; Millers Dictionary; 2 Vol^{ms} in folio, and LeBlond of Gardening in Quarto: And the rest of my Books, about 150 Volumes, to be Divided among my Other three ͨ ·

Item, I give & Bequeath unto my Eldest Son, John, my Large Silver Tea Kettle, Lamp, & Server for it to stand on, weighing in all about 170 Ounces. To my Son, Edward, my Large Silver Coffee Pot Pott; to my Son, Sampson, my Large Silver Tea Pot; to my Son, Jam^{es}, my Large Silver Tankard, & to my Son, Thomas, a pair of Large Square Silver Servers; my Cases of Knifes, forks, Spoons, Salts, Casters, & Other my Plate, to be Divided Between my wife & Daughter, my wife to have Two Thirds, & my Daughter One Third. Nevertheless, my wife to have the use of my Children's plate untill She shall Marry, or they respectively Attain to age of 21. But if any shall Depart this life before that Age, such Childs part of the plate or Other Personal Estate I shall & Hereafter in this will give to them, to be Equally Divided among my sons Surviving.

Item, in Case my Wife shall marry, or as Soon as Any of my sons Shall Attain to 21 years of age, which shall first Happen, I will that my household goods & Other Personal Estate not before by me given shall be Equally Divided into four Parts; One thereof to be for my Wife, the Other three Parts among my Six Children.

Item, As there are very Considerable Debts due to me I expect more than Sufficient to pay the Debts I owe, I leave it to my Wife either to Apply the Same for Payment of my Debts, or in Building for all or any Of my Son's as She shall think Proper, if she shall Choose to Apply it in Building, I would have the house at the Vineyard Finished Fit for Use, and as She knows my mind with Regard to a handsome large Dwelling house to be built at Rockey Point, the Foundation whereof is Dugg, She may, if She pleases, Proceed thereon And use all the Materials Already Provided by me, And Also, the Sum of One Hundred Pounds Sterling, or the Value thereof in Products, yearly for Two Years, Out of the Labour of all my Sons Slaves, And all or any parts of the Debts Due to me.

Item. I give & Bequeath unto my very Good Friend, Samuel Swann, Esqr., Major John Swann & my Brother in Law, Mr. Jas. Hasell, Jr., the Sum of Ten Pounds Sterling, each, or in Products; hereby Requesting there Advice & Assistance in having this my Will fullfilled. And to Mr. Jeremiah Vail & Mr. Alexander Lillington, the Sum of Five Pounds Sterling, Each, or Value in Products; & to my Very Good Friend Jas. Hasell, Esqr., & to my Sisters in Law, Mrs. Mary Vail & Mrs. Sarah Porter, I give to Each a ring of two Guineas price; & to Each of the Children of my Sister in Law, Mrs. Mary Vail & of her sister Elizabeth, late the Wife of Collo. Maurice Moor, and to the Children of my Late Brother in Law, Mr. John Lillington, & to Colo. Maurice Moor's three youngest Children, I give to Each a ring of a Guinea price.

Item, I give to my Honoured Mother in Law, Mrs. Susannah Hasell, a ring of three Guineas price.

Item, the rest & Residue of my Estate, Real & Personal, I give to be Equally Divided among my Sons & the Survivours of them.

Lastly I nominate & Appoint my Dearly beloved Wife, Ann Moseley, & my Two Eldest Sons, John & Edward, to be Executors of this my Last Will & Testament (Containing in Eight Pages all of my Own hand Writing)

In Testimony whereof, I have Hereunto Set my Hand & Seal, this Twentieth Day of March, Anno Dom., 1745.

E. MOSELEY, (Seal)

Signed, Sealed, Published, & Declared In presence of:
    ELEAZR. ALLEN.
    ROGR. MOORE.
    WM. FORBES.
    MATT. ROWAN.

August Court, 1749.

A Codicil to the Last Will and Testament of Edward Moseley, dated March 20th., 1745. hereunto annexed.

To my Son William, born since my said Last Will was made, I give & bequeath my two round Silver Servers; Also, the tract of Land in my said Will mentioned, lying in Edgecombe County, called Alden of the Hill, containing 3200 acres, be the same more or less; Also about 300 acres more, contiguous thereto, which I have Entred in Earl Granville's office. To hold the same, about 4000 acres, to him & his heirs forever. It is also my will, that my said Son, William, shall have an equal share of the Slaves & personal estate left to be divided among my other five sons in that my will.

It is also my will, that if I shall have any more children, They shall be intitled to an equal part of my slaves & personal Estate left to my sons in that my Will mentioned, and that all my sons born or to be born, shall have an equal share or dividend of that my large tract of 10,000 Acres called Clur, mentioned in my said will.

I give to my dear wife Ann, my negro woman named Jane, for her better care & management of my children, she having been much employed about them

I give to my Daughter Nancy, Peggy's youngest mulatto child named Abram.

My slaves Mustapha, Cush & Moll having behaved very well I order them to be free, but if it shall not be allowed them, Then it is my will that my executrix shall place them jointly or severally as they shall choose, on any of my lands, to make what they shall judge most for their advantage, rendering one tenth part of the profits to my executrix.

Lastly, I make my dear wife Ann, Executrix, and my two Eldest Sons, Executors, of this Codicil which I will shall be taken & deemed as a part of my last Will & Testament.

In Witness Whereof, I have hereunto set my hand and seal this Nineth day of June, Anno Dom., 1748.

E. MOSELEY (seal)

Signed, sealed, published &
Declared in presence of:
    JOHN COCHRAN.
    JOHN HANCOCK.
    JOHN COOKE.

N B, This Codicil is fixed to the Will by Mr. Sampson's Seal (my Wife's Father) mine being lately lost.

NEW HANOVER COUNTY.   August Court, 1749.

The within Will of the Honb^l. Col. Edward Moseley, Esqr., lately deceas'd was proved now here in open Court by the oath of the Honb^l. Mathew Rowan, Esqr., one of the Subscribing Evidences thereto in due form of Law, and the Codicil hereto the said will annext was Proved Likewise at the Same time by the oath of M^r. John Cook, one of the Subscribing Evidences thereto in open Court also in due form of Law.

Test. ISAAC FARIES, C. C.

June, 1750.

Personally appeared before me Mrs. Anne Moseley, and was duly sworn to the just & faithfull Execution of the within Will & Codicil.

NATH. RICE.

Registered in Book C Fol 741, 742, 743, 744, 745, & 746.

ISAAC FARRIES Register.

Copied from Original Will, Filed in the Office of the Secretary of State.

SAMUEL NICHOLSON'S WILL.

NO. CAROLINA, THE 22 OF YE: 1: MONTH, 1727/8.

Know ye, that I, Sam. Nicholson, am week in body but of parfect mind and memory, thanks be to the Lord for it: Do make this my Last and Testement, Revoking all other Wills heretofore maid by me, first of all, I comit my Soul unto the Lord and by body to the Earth from whence was, to be desently buriad after the discresion of my Executors hereafter named.

Saconly, my will is that my dear and well beloved wife, Elizabeth Nicholson, Shall have the whole Use and Benifit of all my Lands and houses and plantation during har life; and after har dises, my will and pleasure is that my daftor, Elisabeth Anderson, shall have and injoy all my Lands, plantations houses and profits, Shee and her Lawful hares for Ever. Allso, i give to my Said daftor, Elizabeth Anderson, a Negro woman caled bes.

I give to my daftor, Sarah Nicholson, one Neigro boy caled Sesor, during her natuall Life, and at har dises, to fall to them of har Kindred which she may think fitest to Life with. I allso give to my Said Daftor, Sarah Nicholson, a father bed and furniture.

I allso give to my Gran Children, forty shillings a peas, to be pid to them or thare fathers for them.

I allso give to my Friend, Sarah Gloster, as much good fine Silk Crape as will make har a Suit of Close, a pare of good Stays, three yards of m... lin, a pare of worsted hoes, two Yards of Holen, as much fine C...rlick as will make har a Shift.

And as for the Rest of my Estate of what Remains after Lagists and Just debts are duly paid, I give to my Loveing Wife, Elizabeth Nicholson, to be at har disposing. I also make and ordain my Loveing Wife, Elizabeth Nicholson, and my SoninLaw, John Anderson, Executrex and Executor of this my Will.

As witness my hand,

his mark
SAMUEL S NICHOLSON. (Seal)

Witnes by us:
    ZACHARIAH NIXON.
    JOHN KEATTEN.
    ELISABETH S MONTECU.

Proved by ye oath of Mr. John Keatten, and affirmation of Mr. Zachriah Nickson, in open Court.

Test. CHARLES DENMAN, Clk.

Mrs. Eliz Nicholson, one her Solemn affirmation In Open Court, did declare that She would proforme the within will According to ye Law of this Government, She being Executrix.

Test. CHARLES DENMAN, Clk.

Letters granted the 23d. Jan'y, 1727.

Copied from Original Will, filed in the Office of the Secretary of State.

FRANCES OLIVER'S WILL.

IN THE NAME OF GOD AMEN. I, Frances Oliver, of Edenton, in the County of Chowan & Province of North Carolina, the Widow & Relict of Andrew Oliver, deceased, Being weak of Body, But of sound & disposing Mind & Memory, praised be God for the Same, and Knowing that It is Appointed for all Persons once to die, and after Death the Judgment; Do make & Ordain this my Last Will & Testament, in Manner & Form following, (that is to say) First and principally, I Comit my Soul into the Hands of Almighty God, my Heavenly Father; and my Body, I Commit to the Earth, To be decently buryed at the Discretion of my Executors herein after named.

And as for such Worldly Goods & Estate, as it Hath pleased God to bestow upon me, I Give & Dispose there of as followeth, Vizt:

Imprimis, I Order & Appoint that all my Just Debts, Legacyes and Funeral Expences shall be paid, as soon as conveniently may be after my Decease.

Item, I Do hereby Give, Devise & Bequeath unto my Son in Law John Davison, of Edenton aforesaid, Marriner, his Heirs & Assignees for Ever, All my Real and personal Estate of what Nature & Kind so Ever, Scituate, lyeing and being in this Province, and not herein Otherwise disposed off; and my Will & meaning is, With Respect to my Negroe Woman, called Rachel & her Three Grand Children (that now live with me), I Give & Bequeath them all unto the said John Davison & the Heirs of His Body Lawfully Begotten; and in case of His Death without Such Issue, I Order & Appoint that all my said Negroe Servants shall immediately be discharged from all Manner of Bondage & have their Liberty to work for Themselves as Other Free Negros have.

Item, I Give & Bequeath unto Each & Every of the Daughters of my Brother & Sisters in Virginia, All My Wearing Apparrel, both Linnen & Woolen, of what Nature & Kindsoever, To be Equally divided between Them, and to be sent or delivered unto Them by the said John Davison.

Item, I give & Bequeath unto Ichadah Davis, Spinster, (Who now Lives with me) her, Her heirs and Assigns, One Bedstead, & Feather Bed & Bolster, Two Blankets & a Pair of Sheets.

And Lastly, I do hereby Constitute & Appoint the said John Davison, to be the Sole Executor of this my Last Will & Testament, Hereby Revoking & Making Void all former & Other Wills by me heretofore made, and hereby Declaring the within Written Instrument To be my Last Will & Testament.

In witness whereof, I, the within named Frances Olliver, have hereunto set my Hand & Seal, The Twenty Sixth Day of February, In the Twenty Seventh Year of the Reign of Our Sovereign Lord, George the Second, by the Grace of God, King of Great Britain, &c., Annoq Domini., 1754.

FRANCES OLIVER. (Seal)

Signed, Sealed, Published and Declared by the Above named Testatrix, as & for her Last Will and Testament In the Presence of us: ANTHONY CARTEEL.
ELIZABETH El Flood.
her mark
LEONARD COTTON.

October County Court, 1756.
  Present His Majesties Justices:
The Last Will and Testament of Francis Oliver, deceased, was proved in Court According to Law, by the Oath Elizabeth Flood.
                    Test. THOMAS JONES, Cler. Cur.
NORTH CAROLINA. ss.
  Personally Appeared before me John Davison, the within named Executor and Qualified by taking the Oath by Law Appointed for that purpose. Octr. 14th., 1756. Let it be Registered.
                    PETER HENLEY, C. J.
  Copied from Original Will, filed in the Office of the Secretary of State.

WYRIOTT ORMOND'S WILL.

IN THE NAME OF GOD AMEN. I, Wyriott Ormond, of Beaufort County, in the province of No. Carolina, Gentleman, am in health of body and sound mind, therefore put my Last Will and testament in Writing as follows:

I Give and bequeath to my Loving Wife, Mrs. Elizabeth Penelope Ormond, Five hundred pounds, proclamation money; Six Negroes, including those two she had from her Father, that is to say: Stephen, Ben, Lankeshire, Sam, Linda, Mariah; My English Bey Mare, And Such of my furniture as She shall Choose, not exceeding one hundred pounds value, to be assessed by My Executors, or the Survivor of them. And my desire is that My Executors deliver my Said Wife, the above mentioned Legacies as soon as Convenient after my death, which said Several Legacies and every part thereof, I Give to my said Loving Wife, and to her heirs and Assigns for ever.

Item, I Give to My Loving Daughters Nancy Ormond, and Sarah Ormond, the (Remainder) Remainder of my estate both Real and personal (Wearing Cloathes excepted), to them the said Nancy and Sarah, their heirs and Assigns for ever to be Eqully Devided between them, when they or either of them shall arrive to the age of eighteen Years old, or day of either of their Marriage, the said Devision to be Made by my Executors and Executrix or the Survivors or them. Nevertheless, it is my Will and desire that my Exers. or the Survivor of them from time to time, and at any time before such Division to be made between my two daughters, Sell and dispose of any or part of the Estate by me Given to my two Daughters, either Real or personal, at publick or private Sale, as they shall think proper, for the Benefit of my Said Children. And the mony arising from Such Sale, to be put on Interest or purchase likely Young Negroes and hire them out, together with those Negroes which I have herein Left them. And further, I do Impower my Executors or the Survivor of them to transact, And Manage the Estate herein Given to my two Daughters, as they shall think necessary for the Benifit of my said (Daughters) Daughters, without Respect or Controle of the Law.

My principle desire is that of the Education of my two Daughters, which I strongly Rely on the Care of my Executors and each of them, Begging in my Last Moments that they will Continue their Love and Friendship to those little Orphans; And I die Satisfyed, that this request will be put in Execution, and that no Expense be thaught too Great provided it doth not effect the principal of their Estates; I not only mean that part of their Education which Respects their Schooling, but Every Other that Can be had for their Advantage.

My Will is that if either of my Daughters die, before they arrive to the age of eighteen Years of day of Marriage, the Surviver shall have the Whole of the said Estate, to them Given. And if Both of them should die before they Arrive to the age of eighteen years or Day of either of their Marriage, then it shall go, and I Give the same to my Brother, Roger Ormond, and his heirs And assigns forever.

I Give and bequeath my Wearing Cloaths to my Executors, to witt: my Loving Brother, Mr. Roger Ormond, and my Worthy and Honest Friend, Mr. George Barrow; and My Daughters, Nancy Ormond (And) and Sarah Ormond, I also appoint Executrix of this my last Will and Testament.

Signed, Sealed, Published and Declared in the presence of the Witness thereunto Subscribed, March the Ninth, one thousand, Seven hundred and Seventy three.

Wy. Ormond, (Seal)

The above and within Testament of Wyriott Ormond, deceased, was proved Before me this first day of December, 1773, by the Oaths of Richard Caswell, Thomas Respess, and Thomas Rispess, Junr., who deposed that they are well acquainted with the Hand writing of the said Testator and that to the best of their Belief, the same is wholly of his own hand writing.

And Roger Ormond, one of the Executors by him thereby appointed, having qualified, by taking the Oaths agreeable to Law, It is ordered that Letters Testamentary issue thereon accordingly.

Jo. Martin.

Copied from the Original Will, filed in the Office of the Secretary of State.

JOHN PAINE'S WILL.

North Carolina.

In the Name of God Amen. I, John Paine, of Wilmington, in the Province of North Carolina, Merchant, being sick and weak in Body, but of sound and disposing Mind, Memory and understanding, Do make, publish and declare this my Last will and Testament, in manner following, That is to say,

First, I recommend my soul to God who gave it and my Body I desire may be decently Buried at the discretion of my Executors herein after named.

Item, I will, Order and direct that all my Just Debts and Funeral Expences may be paid by my Executors herein after named, so Soon as Conveniently may be after my decease.

Item, I Will, order & Direct that all my real Estate, Lands and Tenements be Sold by my Executors herein after named, if they shall think proper to sell & dispose of the same; And I do hereby Impower them in Case of sale, to give good and sufficient Titles in Law for the same to the purchaser or purchasers.

Item, I Give devise & Bequeath all my Estate whatsoever and wheresoever, unto my Loving wife, Catharine Paine; To my loving Daughter, Catharine Musgrove Paine, and to the Child or Children that my wife now goes with to be equaly divided between them, share and share alike, and to their heirs and assigns for ever; my Childrens Portions to be paid to them by my Executors when they respectively attain the age of Eighteen ——— years or day of Marriage which shall first happen; And if Either of my Children die before they Attain the age of Eighteen years or day of Marriage then, and in that Case, I give, devise and Bequeath the same to my sd. wife, Catharine, to the survivor or survivors of them, and their heirs & assigns; and in Case all my Children die, then I give, Devise & Bequeath all my Estate to my loving wife, Catharine, and her heirs forever.

And whereas there is a Legacy of Nine hundred pounds, South Carolina Currency, directed & ordered to be by me paid, (by the Last will & Testament of my Mother, Mary Brewton, Decd.), to the Children of my Sister, Elizabeth Arthur, wife of Francis Arthur, now in Georgia, I do therefore hereby Will, order and direct that my Executors after named, Do pay or cause to be paid unto the said Children of my Sister Elizabeth Arthur, in Georgia, the said Legacy of nine hundred pounds, South Carolina Currency; together with lawfull Interest for the same till paid, and that the same be paid them so soon as may be after my decease.

Item, I Will, order & direct that my Executors herein after named, within three years after my decease, or sooner if convenient, Do pay into the hands of the church Wardens of every county in this Province, thirteen pounds, proc. money, to be by them distributed amongst the poor Inhabitants of the said several & respective Counties.

Lastly, I appoint, constitute & nominate my Loving Wife, Catherine, Executrix of this my last will and Testament during the time she remains my Widow; and I direct that she may have the Tuition & Guardianship of my Children, But in case she marry, then, I nominate, constitute & appoint my good Friends, Maurice Moore & William Hill, Executors of this my last Will & Testament, and desire they may take possession of my Childrens Estate if they think proper. And I do hereby Revocke all former & other wills by me at any time heretofore made, and declare this Only to be & Contain my last Will and Testament.

In Witness whereof, I have hereunto set my hand & seal at Wilmington, this ninth day of January, in the year of our Lord one thousand Seven hundred & Sixty Seven.

JOHN PAINE. (Seal)

Signed, sealed, published, pronounced & declared by the Testator, to be, and contain his last will and Testament, In presence of us, who in his presence, and at his request, Subscribed our names as witnesses thereto at the same time, (the words, my wife Catharine, being first interlined)

MARY SNOW.
ANN MOUAT.
WILL: MOUAT.

The within last Will and Testament of John Paine was proved before Me, this day, by the Oath of Ann Mouat, one of the subscribing Witnesses thereto, who deposed that She saw the Testator sign, seal, publish and declare the same to be and contain his last Will and Testament and that at the Time thereof he was of sound disposing Mind and Memory. Catherine Paine, the Executrix therein named, Qualified as such agreeable to Law. Letters Testamentary have therefore issued Accordingly.

WM. TRYON.

Brunswick, the 14th. March, 1767.

FRANCIS PARKER'S WILL.

IN THE NAME OF GOD AMEN, the the 26th. day of April, 1746. I, Francis Parker, of Edgcombe County, and Province of No. Carolina, being in health of Body and in perfect mind and Memory, Thanks be given unto God therefore, calling unto mind the Mortality of my body, and knowing that it is appointed for all men once to die, do make and ordain this my Last Will and Testament, that is to say, principally and first of all, I give and recomend my Soul unto the hands of God; and for my body, I reccommend it to the Earth to be buried at the Discretion of my Executor: and as Touching such Worldly Estate wherewith it hath pleased god to bless me with in this Life, I give and bequeath the same in manner and form following:

Imprimis, I will that my Just debts and funeral Charges be paid out of my principal Estate.

Item, I give & bequeath unto my Loving son, Francis Parker, a Pair of Iron wages, to him & his heirs or assigns.

Item, I give and bequeath unto my son, Joseph Parker, one Cow Yearlin, to him, his heirs or assigns.

Item, I give and bequeath unto my Daughter, Elizabeth Foreman, one Cow Yearlin, to her, her heirs or assigns.

Item, I give and bequeath unto my Daughter, Charity Brett, one Cow Yearlin, to her, her heirs or Assigns.

Item, I give unto my Daughter, Catherine Hodges, one Large Painted Trunk, to her, her heirs or Assigns.

Item, I give and bequeath unto my Son, Simon Parker, One Feather Bed, a green rugg and Blanket, and Sheet; and one Oval Table, to him, his heirs and assigns.

Item, I Lend unto my Beloved Wife, Elizabeth Parker, the use of my Plantation where I now Live, and all my Personal Estate, not already bequeathed, during her Widowhood or natural Life.

Item, I give and bequeath unto my son, Simon Parker, the Plantation where I now Live Containing 200 Acres, more or less, after his Mothers Decease or Marriage; and one Tract Containing 80 Acres, where he, the said Simon, now Lives; One Tract Containing 200 Acres of Land, to him, his heirs or Assigns for ever.

Item, I will that all the rest and residue of my Estate, I will that it be Equally Divided between my Loving Children, Francis Parker, Joseph Parker, Elizabeth Foreman, Charity Brett, Catherine Hodges, and Simon Parker, after the Decease or Marriage of my Wife, Elisabeth Parker.

Item, I Constitute and ordain my Beloved Wife, Elizabeth Parker, and my Loving son, Simon Parker, Executors of this my Last Will and Testament, disanulling all former Wills by me before this Time Made, Confirming this to be my Last Will and Testament.

         FRANCIS PARKER (Seal)

Signed, Sealed Published and Pronounced, by the said Francis Parker as his Last Will and Testament in Presence of us:

    GERRARD X WALL, Jurat.
       Mark

    JOHN X KNIGHT. Jurat.
     Mark

    WALTER M^c FORLAN.

Excr: Qualified, SIMON PARKER.

EDGCONB COUNTY. ss. August Court, 1757.

The within Will was in open Court Exhibited by the Exors. therein Named. and proved by the oaths of Gerrard Wall and John Knight, Evidences thereto; and at the same time the Exors. within Named Qualified for sd. office according to Law, which is ordered to be Certified.

Test. Jos: MONTFORD, Cl: Cur:

Copied from Original Will filed in Office of the Secretary of State.

JOHN PFIFER'S WILL.

IN THE NAME OF GOD AMEN. I, John Pfifer, of Mecklenburg County & Province of North Carolina, being of sound mind and memory and considering the uncertainty of life, & knowing it is allotted for all men Once to dye, do make & publish this my last Will & Testament in manner following: first and of all things I recommend my soul in the hands of almighty God who gave it, hoping to find mercy; and as for my Body, I Recommend it to the Earth to be Buried in a decent like manner at the descretion of my Executors hereafter named; and it Is my will that my just debts & Funeral Expences to be duly paid and discharged.

Item, I give, Bequeath & demise unto my beloved Son, Paul Pfifer, the Tract of Land, together with Mills and all other improvements on which I now live, only as sd. Land was not as yet conveyed to me, I therefore, beseech my Honored Father, Martin Pfifer, to Grant & convey unto my sd. son, Paul Pfifer, the above sd. Lands in as full & ample a manner as he ingaged to do to me.

Item, I give, bequeath and demise unto my Beloved daughter, Margaret Pfifer, her Heirs, Executors, Administrators or assigns, a Certain Tract of   Acres of Land lying on both sides of english Buffelo Creek, joining on the upper side of Alexander Penneys Land, being Land Conveyed by John Penney & lying in Rowan County.

Item, I give, bequeath & demise unto my beloved daughter, Anne Elizabeth Pfifer, her Heirs, Executors, admns. or Assigns, two Tracts of Land Lying on big Cold water Creek, nearly joining each other, the one known by the name of the Christopher Wolbirts old place, the other known by the name of the Meeting House Lands.

Item, I give & Bequeath unto my Beloved wife, Catherine Pfifer, during her life, a tract of Land Lying on the Nine mile Branch, being land bought of Mickel Raddought to the end that she, the sd. Catherine, (is to) is to have free Liberty and access to act and do as she shall think fit during her life time, and all profits & advantages to be clear & free to her, provided she does not ask, & demand her Right of dowery in & on any other of my Lands which are Will'd, or to be Will'd, and after her death the sd. Land is to be sold to the best advantage; & the money so arising from such sale, to be equally devided Between the above Said, Paul Pfifer, Margaret Pfifer & Ann Elizabeth Pfifer; and it is likewise my Will that such Lands as are Willed to my sd. Childring as above, is to be leased and Rented from year to Year, & the Rents of each Childs Land is to be applied to the end of Clothing & Schooling them untill they shall come of age.

Itim, I give & Bequeath unto my son, Paul, a Negro Fellow named David; & Also a Negro Wench named Jude, together with their Issue, except the first child the said Jude shall be delivered of, which is to be disposed of as shall be hereafter mentioned.

Itim, I give & Bequeath to my Daughter, Margret Pfifer, a Negro fellow named Charles, & Negro woman named Nanny, together with their Issue that they shall hereafter have.

Itim, I give and Bequeath to my Daughter, Ann Elizabeth, Pfifer, a Negro Boy named Charles & the first born Child of the Body of the above mentioned Jude.

Itim, I Give & Bequeath unto my Beloved Wife, A Negro Fellow Named Wall, & a negro Girl named Dina; also, it is further my will, that if any of my Children should die before he, her or them, shall be of full age, that then & in that case, the Estate of the deceased shall be equally devided Between the surviver or survivers of my Children: and father it is my will, that so long as my sd. Wife does continue to live single, & in Capacity of a widow, she may continue to live on the Premises which I have Hetherto lived on, & have all the profits of mills & Plantation, only to make no destructive use of Timber, except so much as will be wanting for repairing & keeping the fences & Plantation in good Order, and for House use; to the end that she shall Raise my Children; but in case she should alter her station of life & Marry, it is then My Will & Meaning, that my sd. Children shall be under the care and direction of my Executors herein hereafter Mentioned; & that as soon as they shall derect her, my sd. wife, to quit the sd. premises unto them, the Executors of my will, upon which they are forthwith directed to Rent or lease the sd. Premises as above mentioned; and farther, as to touching my personal Estate, It is my will that as soon as my debts is paid, my Funeral expences discharged, and my Executors Each Receive the sum of Six pounds as an Acknowledgement to them, together with a Reasonable allowance for their trouble, that whatsoever there is remaining, if any, it is my will, that the one third part of my sd. personal Estate, be given to my sd. wife, the Remaining Two thirds to be devided equally Between my Children.

It is also my Will, & I do humbly Request my Executors to

take all Reasonable pains to have my before mentioned Children instructed in the Christian Faith, & to have a reasonable Education, & in perticular my sd. son, Paul, to be put through a liberal Education & Colleged, if there should be any sufficiency of my personal Estate left to his Share. Also, I do hereby direct a Tract of Land lying on the head of Little Cold water Commonly Called Cains Place, to be sold & disposed of by my sd. Executors and the Money arrising from such sales to be applied to the End to the End of purchasing of some Vacancy ajoining the land on which I now live, in the name of my son, Paul Pfifer, if to be had from the proprietor, & if not, to be applyed to the use of my son, Paul Pfifer in schooling him or to be declared a part of his Estate.

And I do hereby nominate & appoint my Honoured Father, Martin Pfifer, & my Honoured Father in Law, Paul Barringer, to be my Executors of this my Last Will & Testament, Revokeing all other Wills & Testaments heretofore by me made.

In Testimony whereof, I have hereunto set my hand & seal this 17th. Day of August, 1775.

JOHN PFIFER (Seal)

Signed, wrote & sealed with my own hand and Published as my Last Will & Testament:
 BENJAMIN PATTON,
 WM. WALLACE,
 SAMUEL PATTEN.

NORTH CAROLINA, MECKLENBURG COUNTY, ss.

This sheet contains a just & perfect copy of the Last Will & Testament of Colo. John Pfifer, Deceased.

Given under my hand at Charlotte, the 22 Day of Jany., A.D., 1777.

SAM. MARTIN, Cl. C.

NORTH CAROLINA, MECKLENBURG COUNTY.

I do hereby certify that the Original Will of John Pifer, Esquire, deceased, (of which the above is a True Copy) was Duly proved before the Justice of said Court in their Sessions in Jany. Term, 1777, by the Oath of William Wallace, one of the Subscribing Wittnesses thereto.

Certifyed by me this......day of Feby., 1774.

NORTH CAROLINA, MECKLENBURG COUNTY ss.

AT an Inferior Court of &c. Jany. Seun., 1777.

Whereas, it appears to this Court that Col. John Pfifer, is Dead and hath made a Will in Writing, whereupon proof thereof being made, Nominating Col. Martin Pfifer and Paul Berringar, Esqrs., Executors and Paul Berringer aforesaid by an Instrument of writing relinguishing his right of said Executorship, being produced in open Court Here, It is therefore ordered that Letters Testamentary Issue to Said Col. Martin Pfifer, with a Copy of the will annexed, of all and singular the Goods & Chattles, Rights and credits of the said Deceased, (except in those particular Paragraphs which mention the land whereon the Deceased aforesaid lived, and also some other Articles not being the Estate of the Decd. but the Estate of the said Martin Pfifer) and the same in his possession take wheresoever to be found in this State, and an Inventory on Oath Return into the Court here, within ninety Days from the Date hereof, and all Just Debts of the said Deceased to pay so far as the Estate will extind or amount to.

In Testimony hereof, I have fixed the public Seal of this County, at Charlotte, the 23d. Day of Jany., A.D., 1777.

SAM. MARTIN, C. C.

(Official Seal).

Copied from Will filed in the Office of the Secretary of State.

GEORGE PHENNEY'S WILL.

IN THE NAME OF GOD AMEN. I, George Phenney, Surveyor Generall of his Majesties Customs in the Southern District, on the Continent of America, Do make and Ordain this to be my last will and Testament in manner following:

Imprimis, I bequeath my Soul to Allmighty God, most humbly beseeching him to receive the Same to his Mercy.

Item, I give to Mr. Ralph Noden, of London, Merchant, one hundred Pounds, Sterling, to be disposed of as follows (vizt), That the said one hundred pounds be by him paid unto Elizabeth Kirk, (formerly Eliz. Houghton), of London, and to her only use in such manner as the said Ralph Noden Shall think necessary for her support.

Item, I give to mary, a Negro girl, Daughter of Jettimair, her freedom as soon as she shall attain the age of twenty years, or at the Decease of my Executrix which, shall first happen.

Item, I give and bequeath unto Penelope phenney, my wife one full third part of all my Estate, Real and personal whatsoever (my Debts and Legacys being first paid and deducted), to her sole use and behoof.

Item, I give and bequeath all the rest and residue of my said Estate, Lands, Houses, negros, moneys, goods, chattles, plate and Jewells, unto the sd. Penelope, my wife, for the uses following, (that is to say), if it shall please god that the said Penelope be Delivered of the Child with which She is now pregnant, then my will is that she, the said Penelope, have the use of my said Estate During the term of her naturall Life, and after her Decease I give and bequeath all my Said Real and Personall Estate unto Such child, and to his or her heirs for ever, and if ther should be more than one, then to be equally Divided between them, share and Share alike, But if such Child or Children shall happen to Dye before the Decease of the said Penelope or before he, She, or they shall attain the age of one & twenty years, then, and in Such Case, I give and bequeath unto Joseph Harrison, my Nephew, the sum of five hundred pounds, Sterling, to be paid unto him at the Decease of the sd. Penelope or of Such Child or Children as aforesd, which Shall last happen.

In witness whereof, I have hereunto set my hand and Seal in North Carolina, this twenty third Day of June, in the year of our Lord 1736   G. PHENNEY (his Seal)

Signed, Sealed, published and Declared in the presence of:
>SAM'L JOLLY.
>THOMAS ASHLEY,
>J. BUTLER.

June, ye 23d., 1737.

Came before me Thomas Ashley and made Oath on the holy Evangelists that he Saw George Phenney, Esqr., Deceased, Sign Seal & publish the above as his last will & Testament; that he was of sound & Disposeing mind & memory at that time; & that Sam. Jolly, Esqr., & Thomas Butler, Did Subscribe as witness thereto.   W. SMITH, C. J.

Recorded in Grant Book 4, Will No. 68. Office of the Secretary of State.

GRACE PILSON'S WILL.

NORTH CAROLINA. SS.

IN THE NAME OF GOD AMEN, I, Grace Pilson, of the County of Craven, and province of North Carolina, Widdow, being sick a weak in body but thro' mercy, of Sound mind & perfect memory, & being mindfull of Mortality & desirous to settle my affairs, do make this my Last Will & Testament, as follows: Chief of all, being penitent for my Sins past & in love & Charity with all men, I commend my Soul into the hands of God, my Maker, & Jesus Christ my Redeemer, as every Christian ought to do; and my Body to the Earth to be Interred in Such Decent & Christian like manner as to my Executors shall seem meet, in hopes of the glorious Resurrection of the Last great Day; & as for Such Worldly Goods that providence hath blessed me with, after my just debts, necessary Expences & Acco'ts ballanc'd are contented discharged & paid by my Executors wch I will shall be first honestly done, the Remainder I bequeath as followeth:

First, I will & bequeath unto my well beloved Sister, Mrs. Mary Fox, Living at Perth Amboy, near the Province of New York, Two Negro Men, Named, Will the cooper, & Phillip; One Negro Woman Named Moll; Two Negro boys named Quastree & Boatswain; Two Negro Girls, named Sabona & Phillis; Two Feather Beds & furniture, four Silver Spoons, three Large Looking Glasses, one Small Do. one Silver Cann, Two   , Six Leather Chairs, one Two armed Ditto, Three Dozen of pewter plates, one Doz. of pewter Dishes, Three Oval Tables, Three pr. of brass Candlesticks, One Copper kettle, & all my wearing Apparrell; Also, Three gold Rings.

Item, I give & bequeath unto my Kinswoman, Grace Fox,

Daughter of my Sister Mary Fox, Three Negro Men, Named Beeliford, Caesar, & Thoms; One Negro Girl Named Jane, alias Jenny; One Feather Bed & furniture, One Two quart Silver Tankerd, Two Silver Spoons, one Looking Glass, one Gold Chain & Two Gold Rings.

Item, I give & bequeath unto my kinswoman, Ellinor Fox, Another Daughter of my said Sister, Mrs. Mary Fox, Two Gold Rings, & one pr. of Gold Ear Rings. (Turn over)

Item, I give & bequeath unto Mr. Richard Scott, one Negro Man Named Scipio.

Item, I give & bequeath unto my Brother, Mr. Thomas Fox, one Silver Watch.

And all the Residue & Remainder of my Estate, both real & personal, as horned Cattle, Horses, Hoggs &c. with Goods & Chattles, & all other properties of what kind Soever, to me appertaining, I give, devise and bequeath, to my sd. well beloved Sister, Mrs. Mary Fox.

Item, I Do Constitute & appoint Mr. Richard Bidder, of the province of New York, Marriner, whole and Sole Executor of this my Last Will & Testament; And I do hereby utterly revoke, disallow, & disanul all former requests, Wills and Legacys, by me heretofore in any wise Left or made, declaring & ratifying, & Confirming this & no other to be my Last Will & Testament.

In Witness whereof, I have hereunto Set my Hand & Seal, this seventeenth Day of September, in the Year of our Lord, One Thousand, Seven hundred & forty three.

       GRACE PILSON. (Seal)
       (Coat of Arms on Seal)

Sign'd, Seal'd, published & Declared, by the within named Testatrix, Mrs. Grace Pilson, to be her Last Will & Testament, in presence of us, who Subscribed our Names, in presence of the Said Testatrix.

  GEORGE POPE.
  JAMES WHITING.
  JAMES COOR.

CRAVEN COUNTY. This said 17th. Sept., 1743.

This is to certify, whom it may concern, that whereas, I, Grace Pilson, Testatrix of this Will, have constituted & appointed, Mr. Richard Bidder, whole & Sole Executor of of the Same, It is my further Will & desire, That Thomas Pearson, Esqr., of the County of Craven, and province of North Carolina, Should & do Joyn with the aforementioned Richard Bidder in the Executorship & Due performance of this my Last Will and Testament.

As Witness my hand and Seal, this said 17th. Septemb'r, 1743.
                                    GRACE PILSON, (Seal)
                (Impression of Coat of Arms on Seal)
Sign'd, Seal'd, publish'd & de-
clar'd in the presence of Us:
    JOSHUA ACKIS,
    WILLIAM WEBB,
    JAMES WHITING,
    JAMES COOR.

                                    Edenton, Decr. 23, 1743.
Then the above will was proved before me, And Richard Bidder took the Oath of Executor appointed by Law.   GAB. JOHNSTON.

Copied from Original Will, filed in the Office of the Secretary of State.

SETH PILKINGTON'S WILL.

IN THE NAME OF GOD AMEN. I, Seth Pilkington, of Beaufort County, and Province of North Carolina, Gentn., being sick and weak of body but of Sound and perfect mind and memory, and calling to mind the Certainty of Death, not knowing when it may please the Lord to call me out of this life, do make appoint and ordain this to be my last Will and testament, hereby Revoking all former Wills by me made, in Manner and form following, my desire is to be buried in a Desent and Christian Manner according to Custom, and form, of the Established Church of England.

Imprimis, My desire is that my just debts be punctually paid as soon as Money can be raised as hereafter mentioned.

Item, I give, bequeath and devise unto my loving Wife, Sarah Pilkington, five of my Negroe Slaves, Viz: Jupiter, Fortune, George, Men and Catherine, & Jenny Women. Likewise, one third part of All my household furniture, her choice of two of my horses, and all the stock of Catle and hogs, with one third of the Sheep, on or belonging to her own plantation, known by the Name of Weerenunteh, to her and her heirs or assigns. Likewise, my desire is that she have the use and occupation during her Natural life, or Widowhood, and no longer, the Labour of my Negro fellow named Tom, and Hannah a Girl; and after her decease or Day of Marriage, the afforsaid Negroe fellow Tom, and Hannah a Girl, I bequeath to my Daughter, Winifrid.

Item, I Give, bequeath and Devise unto my Daughter, Sarah Cautanche, Seven of my Negroes, Viz: Lancashire, Dublin, Jack, fellows; Mustapher, York, and Lonnon, boys; and Jenny a Girl; my Silver Watch, and one third part of My Houshold Furniture, to her and heirs and Assignes; likewise, halfe my Horses and Mares, and one third of my Sheep.

Item, I Give and bequeath unto my Daughter, Winifrid Pilkington, ten of my Slaves, Viz: Cato, Derby, Cudgoe, Prince, Men; Cain a boy; Africa, Grace, Betty, Flora, Wenches; Phebe a Girl. Likewise, I Give, bequeath and Divise to my Daughter, Winifrid, the Plantation or Tract of Land whereon I now Dwell, together with all the buildings, Marshes, Meadows, Woods and all appurtenances thereunto belonging; likewise, two tracts of Land Containing twelve hundred and Eighty Acres, Situate on Lemuel Cherry herring runs, and Purchased of Mr. Allexander Lillington; one third part of my houshold furniture, and All my Catle and Hogs belonging to the Plantation aforsd. one third of the Whole stock of Sheep, and halfe the Horses and Mares belonging to me, to her, and her heirs and Assigns in fee simple.

Item, I Give and Devise unto my Daughter, Sarah Cautanche, upon Condition my Daughter Winifrid shou'd die before Marriage, or without Lawfull Issue, all that Part, or Portion, of Land, Slaves, and Stock before mentioned and given to the Aforsaid Winifred; but in case that my Daughter, Sarah, shall die first and without lawfull Issue, that then, the aforsaid Portion of Lands, Slaves, and Stocke, be Equally divided between My Wifes, Daughter and GrandDaughters, Viz: Ann Lillington, Catherine Lockhart, and Mary Evans, and their lawfull heirs.

Lastly, My will and desire is, that what Cash I leave in hand, All bonds, bills, and book debts, be Collected and my Debts punctually paid, and that the Surplus be equally divided between my son in law, Michael Cautanche, and my Daughter, Winifrid. Likewise, my desire is, that my other lands, Goods and Chattells of all kinds not be mentioned and Given be Sold; or Equally divided between my Afforsaid Son in law, Michael, and my Daughter, Winifrid, as they shall think for.

And I do hereby Nominate and appoint my Son in law, Michael Cautanche, to be my Executor, and my Daughter, Winifrid Pilkington, to be Executrix, jointly and Severally, to do and Execute, all and Every part of this my last Will and testament.

In Wittness whereof, I have hereunto set my hand and Seal this Seventh day of October, in the Year of our lord, one thousand, Seven hundred fifty and one, 1751. (the words furniture, and Issue, being interlined before Signing and Sealing hereof.)

         SETH PILKINGTON. (SEAL)

Signed, Sealed and Delivered in presence of:
    JOHN FRY.
    W:M. STUBBS.
    MICHAEL COUTANCHE, JUNR.

BEAUFORT COUNTY, ss.

At a Court held for the sd. County, at Bath Town, on the second tuesday in March, 1754.

Present his Majesty's Justices.

The last will & testament of Seth Pilkington was exhibited into Court & proved by the Oath of John Fry, who swore on the holy Evangelists, that the sd. Seth Pilkington was of sound & disposing mind & memory when he executed the same; & that he also saw Wm. Stubbs & Mich^l. Coutanche, Junr., the other subscribing Evidences, set their hands thereto at the same time: And Michl. Coutanche & Winifred Pilkington qualified as Extor. & Extrix. to the same.

Ordered that the Secretary have notice hereof that Letters Testament may issue. Test. WALLEY CHAUNCY, cl. cu.

Copied from Original Will, filed in the Office of the Secretary of State.

CULLEN POLLOCK'S WILL.

NORTH CAROLINA. ss,

IN THE NAME OF GOD AMEN. I, Cullen Pollock, of Tyrrel County, Gen., calling to mind the uncertainty of ye mortal life & yt all Flesh must dye, Do make & Ordain this to be my last Will & Testament hereby Revoking, disanuling, & makeing void all former Wills & Testaments by me heretofore made.

Imprimis, I Bequeath my soul unto almighty God; And my Body to be decently Buried at ye discretion of my Excrs. hereafter named; And as to what worldly Estate it hath pleased God to bless me with, I Give & dispose of as followeth:

Item, I Give & Bequeath unto my dear & loveing Wife, Frances Pollock, one Plantation & Tract of Land at Matchapungo River, in Hide County; And also, one Lott of Land in Bath Town in Beaufort County, And also, ye Negroes following, (Viz.) Bess & her Seven Children, Harry, Morea, Prince, Caesar, Bristoll, Betty, & Edenbourg, boath the Lands & Negroes, to her Heirs for Ever; with one Sixth part of all my Houshold-Goods, Stocks of Horses, Cattle, Sheep & Hoggs, to her & her Heirs for Ever.

Item, I Give & Bequeath unto my loveing Wife, Frances Pollock, ye use & Occupation of any one of my Plantations, yt she shall chuse, wth ye use of the Negroes following, (viz.) Pappa Seesar & great Rose, Cajo & his Wife pegg, Will & his wife Sarah with their Daughter Moll & Son Pomp, (the Land
[Interlin'd in the original]
& Negroes dureing her life), And after my Wifes death it is my Will & desire yt ye Land & negroes herein left to Her dureing Life (& not to her & her Heirs for Ever.), go to my Children as hereafter directed, yt is to say, to be equally divided betwen my Sons, George & Cullen, wth ye oyr Land & Negroes hereafter given them.

Item, I Give & Bequeath unto my Nephews, Cullen & Thomas Pollock, Sons of my Bror. Thomas Pollock, Deceased, all yt Stock of Cattle at the Plantation on Salmon Creek where my Bror. George Pollock, deceased, about fifty & four head wch were drove to my sd. Nephews Quarters above black-rock; And also the Negroes following, (viz) Frank & his Wife Dinah with their Children, George, Frank, Joshua, old Nanne now old Dicks Wife, Bodwin & his wife Hoope & their four Children Jamie, Seesar, Todge, & Moses, the Boy Dowe, Jamie & his four Children yt he had by his wife Patience, or rather Patiences four Children; Jamie & Hanna, Pat & Mingo: Jack the Cooper, little Rose & her two Children, Dinah, & Seesar, wth their Increas, to be delivered to my sd. Nephews when they arive at the age of twenty & one Years, to them & their Heirs for Ever; But if neither of my sd. nephews shall arrive to the age of twenty & one Years, nor at their Deceas leve any Lawfull Issue, That in such Cases it is my Will that the Legacy hereby given to them goe to my Children to be devided as followeth: yt is to say, two seventh parts to my Son George, Two Seventh parts to my son Cullen, one Seventh part to my Daughter Martha, one Seventh part to my Daughter Frances, & one Seventh part to my Daughter Mary, to them & their Heirs for ever: and I do hereby decree yt ye Legacyes by me given in this Will to my nephews, ye Sons of my Bror. Thomas Pollock, are given in conformity to a Trust lodged & reposed in me by my Bror. George Pollock, the consideration for two Bills of Sales & wch I declared in my answer to Mr. Thomas Blount & his Wife's Petition to the Genll. Court of this Province: and further in conformity to ye same it is my Will yt if any part of my Bror. George Pollock's P'sonall Estate is or shall be recovered by ye suit yt Mr. Thomas Blount, Deceased, & his Wife formerly brought for one halfe of the sd. Estate; or if any part of ye sd. Estate be hereafter recovered by any suit that may hereafter be brought by Mrs. Elizabeth Blount, now Widow of the sd. Thomas Blount, or oy[r] Person on account of Her claim to my sd. Brother's Personall Estate by being his Widow; That in such case the aforsd. Legacyes to my sd. Nephews, Cullen & Thomas, be charged with one halfe yt may be recovered as aforsd. and also one halfe of the Charges yt I have been at in defending ye sd Estate, and also, one halfe of ye like charges yt may accrue hereafter, to be paid out of the Legacyes given to my sd Nephews. And the other halfe to be paid proportionally out of ye Legacyes given to my Wife & Children of my Personal Estate yt is, those yt have litle pay litle, & those yt have more pay more, in proportion to what they have, so as to pay one halfe so recovered, with one halfe the Charges.

Item, I Give & Bequeath unto my Daughter, Martha Pollock, all the Plantation & Tract of Land lying upon a Branch of Trent River, called the halfe way House, in Craven County, containing about Seven hundred & tenn Acres, on wch Jacob Sheets now lives; wth Thirteen Negro Slaves; that is my Negroes or Slaves being devided thirteen in each parcell or Lott, & each parcell or Lott to be as near as possible of equal Value, & my sd Daughter Martha, to have one parcell or Lott, with one Sixth part of all my Houshold Goods, Stocks of Horses, Cattle Hogs & Sheep; all which negroes, wth the Sixth part of the Stocks & houshold Goods aforsd. to Her & her Heirs for Ever.

Item, I Give & Bequeath unto my Daughter, Frances Pollock, one Plantation & Tract of Land in Tyrrel County, called the deaded Woods, contain'd in two Pattents, one in the name of William Milton, ye oy^r in the Name of Richard Milton, & by them sold to Jno. adderly, of whom I have his Deed for 1280 Acres, lying on Coneto Creek in Tyrrel County; and also, thirteen Negroes or Slaves of equal goodness & Value to those I by this Will give to my Daughter Martha, wth one Sixth part of all my Stocks of Horses, Cattle, Sheep & Hogs; and also one Sixth part of all my Houshold-Goods; all which Land, negroes, houshold-Goods, & Stocks aforsd., I give to my Daughter Frances, to Her & Her Heirs for Ever.

Item, I Give & Bequeath unto my Daughter, Mary, one Plantation & Tract of Land in Bertie County, containing Six hundred & forty Acres, on ye Roonaroy Meadows, lying betwen Land yt belonged to my Bror. Thomas, Land yt belonged to Collo Jones, & land that belonged to Collo. Maule, ye Pattent in my Bror. George's name, & dated ye second day of august, anno Dom., seventeen hundred & Twenty Six; And also thirteen negroes or Slaves of equal goodness & value of those yt I by this Will give to my Daughter Martha; And also one Sixth part of all my Houshold-Goods, Stocks of Horses, Cattle, Sheep & Hogs, All wch Land, Negroes, Houshold Goods, Stocks of Horses, Cattle, Sheep & Hogs, I give to my sd. Daughter Mary, to Her & her Heirs for Ever. (vide margin) and it is my Will & desire yt y^e. Legacy herein given to my Daughters be delivered to each of them as they shall arive at twenty one Years or at ye day of their marriage, wch first shall happen.

Item, I Give & Bequeath unto my two beloved Sons, George Pollock & Cullen Pollock, all my oy^r Estate, boath real & Personall, wch is not before in this Will bequeathed, to be equally devided beteem them & each of them to have his equal part to Him & his Heirs for ever; my Son George to have his part when He shall arive at the Age of twenty one Years: And my Son Cullen to have his part delivered to him when He shall arive at ye age of twenty & one Years; & that my Son George have the first choise in the Devision.

Item, It is my Will & desire yt if one of my Sons, either George or Cullen, shall Dye before He arrive to ye age of twenty & one Years, or day of marriage, yt ye Legacy of my Personall Estate by this Will given to him yt so dyeth, be devided amongst my Children surviving as followeth; (Viz), one halfe to my Son surviveing, & ye other halfe to be devided equally amongst my three Daughters aforsd.

Item, It is my Will & Desire yt if one of my Daughters Martha, Frances or Mary shall dye before she arrive to the age of twenty & one years, or day of Marriage, yt ye Legacy of my personall Estate by this Will given to her yt so dyeth, be devided amongst my Children surviveing as followeth: (viz), two thirds to my two Sons, George & Cullen, to be equally devided between them, & the other third to be equally devided amongst my Daughters surviveing: and it is my Will & desire yt if two of my sd. Daughters shall deceas before they arrive to the Age of Twenty & one Years, or day of Marriage, that the Legacyes given them by this Will of my Personall Estate, that so dyeth, be devided amongst my Children surviveing as followeth, (Viz), four fifths to my two Sons George & Cullen, to be equally devided between them & ye other fifth to my Daughter surviveing.

Item, It is my Will & desire yt. whatever Just Debts appear against my Estate (except what I have before directed) yt it be immediately paid out of the ready money yt I leve, or out of ye Debts due to me.

Item, It is my Will & desire that my thre Daughters have as good Education as can be had in this Province, & that my two Sons when they have got what learning they can have in this Province, that they be sent to Boston for farther Education, & their to remain untill they be eighteen Years of Age in ye care of some discrete Person to direct what Education will be most usefull for them; & yt all charges ariseing for & towards Educateing my Children as forsd. be paid out of the Profits of my whole Estate Bequeathed to my Children.

[In the Original here is seventeen Lines erased with the following wrote in the margin, (Vizt) "Note this Clause was Wrote when my Wife was bigg with Mary, my Youngest Daughter, now of no use".]

Item, I Give & Bequeath unto my Daughter, Elizabeth, to her & her Heirs for Ever, Two Thousand Acres of Land to be laid off out of a Tract of Land yt my Bror. George Pollock, formerly Rented to Edward Buxton in Bertie County, The Pattent contains 4700 Acres, & Dated ye 13th. day of May, Anno Dom., 1714: I also Give & Bequeath unto my sd. Daughter, Eleven Negroes to be taken out of the foregoing Legacyes as followeth: (Viz) one from my Wife Frances's part, two from each of my aforsd three Daughters parts, & four from those

Negroes before Given to my two Sons, to be devided, or shared out to Her, in the same manner as before by this Will is Directed for my oy^r Children; And also I Bequeath y.o my sd. Daughter, one seventh part of all my Stocks, of Cattle, Horses, Sheep, Hogs & houshold-Goods, to be taken out of the Legacyes in this Will before Bequeathed to my Wife & Children, So as yt my Wife & Children may each of them have an equal part thereof. Furthermore, it is my Will & desire yt this Legacy be delivered into the Possession of my sd Daughter (if it be a Girl) when She arrives at the Age of twenty & one Years or day of marriage, wch first shall happen, but if She should decease before She arive at the Age of Twenty & one Years, or day of marriage, In that Case it is my Will yt this Legacy be utterly Void, and the foregoing Legacyes remain in every respect as they are.

Lastly, I Nominate & appoint my beloved Wife, Frances, Executrix & my Loveing Bro^r:, Colo. Robert West, Stevens Lee, Esqr., Wm Cathcart, Esqr., & Mr. Robert West, Executors of this my last Will & Testament, hereby revokeing all other Wills & Testaments by me in any ways heretofore made, & hopeing (if occasion be) that my said Executrix & Executors will see the same duely Executed.

In Testimony whereof I have hereunto set my Hand & Seal this 13th day of August, Anno Dom., 1749. The Words (my Daughter Elizabeth to Her) ware interlined before the Sighning, Sealing & publishing of this present Will, as also, Wm. Cathcart, Esq.

CULLEN POLLOCK (L S)

Signed, Sealed, Published & declared in the Presence off:
    ELIZABETH LEE.
    JOHN GOMM.
    WILLIAM HANSARD

NORTH CAROLINA, TYRREL COUNTY.   June County Court, 1751.
    Present his Majestys Justices:

These may Certifie that the within will was proved in open Court by the Oaths of John Gum, and William Hansford, subscribing Evedences thereto, that they saw the Hon. Cullen Pollock, Esq., Deceased, Sign, Seal, Publish & declare the within contains His last Will and Testament; and that he was then and at that time of sound and disposeing Memory; then also appeared Col. Robert West, and Capt. Robert West, Executors to the said Will and were duely Qualified by taking the Oath by Law appointed to be taken by Executors. Ordered that the Hon. Nathaniel Rice, Esq., Secretary of this Province, or his Deputy, have notice thereof that Letters Testamentary Ishue thereon as the Law Directs.

Test.   EVAN JONES, C. C.

Recorded in Will Book 5, page 23.

GEORGE POLLOCK'S WILL.

IN THE NAME OF GOD AMEN. I, George Pollock, of North Carolina, Merch't, being of Perfect Mind & Judgment & Memory, (Praised be god for the Same) Do make this my last Will & Testament, Hereby absolutely revoaking all others, and this to be taken only as my last will & testament.

Imprimis, I give & bequeath my Soul to allmighty God & my Body to the Ground to be Decently Buried by my Executors hereafter named; and for what Estate it hath pleased God to bestow upon me I give & bequeath as followeth:

Item, I give & bequeath unto my Loving Brother, Cullen Pollock, all my land on Salmon Creek & Chowan River, wch is Contained in three Pruchase pattents; also a tract of land on the South Shore, where Loftin lived; also, eleven hundred & forty Acres of land on the South Side of Morattock River, nigh Canaho Creek; also, four thousand, Seven hundred Acres on the North side of Moratock River wch. I had of mr. Thos. Jones; also, two other Tracts of Land adjoyning to ye Land wch. I had of Mr. Thos. Jones, also seven hundred & ten acres of land on ye North side of Trent River in Nuse; all of wch. Land I give & bequeath unto my Brother, Cullen Pollock, to him & his heirs for Ever.

Item, I give & Bequeath unto my two Nephews, Cullen Pollock & Thomas Pollock, five thousand acres of Land at the Haw-Fields, also three thousand, three hundred acres on Tarr River also two thousand, two hundred Acres lying in ye fork of Coor Creek & Nuse River, also two hundred & twenty acres of Land on ye Est. Side of Coar Creek, also one hundred & fifty Acres at Bennys Creek, also five hundred Acres of Land on Wecone Creek, also Six hundred & forty Acres on Morattock Island, all wch. Land I give & bequeath unto my Nephews, Cullen Pollock & Thos. Pollock, to them & their heirs forever.

Item, I give & bequeath unto my Brother in Law, Colo. Robert West, four tracts of Land wch I hold by Entry & Survey upon Trenters Creek & a tract or Parcell of Land wch. I hold by Entry & Survey upon or near to horn Creek, all wch. Land I Give & Bequeath unto my sd. Brother in Law, Colo. Robert West, to him & his heirs for ever, w'th a Sufficient Sum of Money to be paid out of my Estate to purcure Pattents for all the sd. Land and also an Island called Crow Island lying in Currituck, unto him & his heirs for ever.

Lastly, I make, Constitute & appoint my Loving Brother, Cullen Pollock, & my Brother in Law, Collo. Robert West, to be my whole & Sole Execrs. of this my last Will & Testament.

In Witness whereof, I have hereunto set my Hand & Seall this 18 Day of October, Anno Dommini, Seventeen hundred & thirty Six.   GEORGE POLLOCK, (Seal)

Signed, Sealed & Declared to be his last Will & Testam't in ye presence. of:

    THOMAS ASHLEY.
    WILLIAM W FRYLEY.
         his / Marke.
    NEHEMIAH WARRING.

                                        July ye 29th. 1738.

Came before me Nehemiah Warring & made Oath that he Saw George Pollock, Gent., Sign, Seal, publish ye within as he last will & testament, that he was at that time of sound mind and memory, & that Thomas Asheley & William Fryley, Subscribed as evidences thereto.

                                          W. SMITH, C. J.

Recorded in Grant Book 4, Will No. 82.

THOMAS POLLOCK, SR.'S WILL.

IN THE NAME OFF GOD, AMEN, I, Thomas Pollock, Senr., off Chowan Precinct, in North Carolina, Mercht., being off Perfect Memory & Judgem't (Praised be God ffor ye same), Doe make ys my Last Will & Testament, Hereby absolutely Revokeing all others, And this to be Taken only as my Last Will & Testament.

Imprimis, I give and Bequeath my soul to Almighty God; and my Body to ye Ground to be Decently Buried by my Executors Hereafter mentioned; And ffor what Estate it hath Pleased God to Bestow upon me, I Give & Bequeath as Followeth:

Item, As for my Daughter, Martha, Lately maryed to Mr. Thos. Bray, I haveing Given & Delivered to her already Her full Portion, Therefor I Hereby Cut Her of ffrom any part more of my Estate whatsoever, Either By Pretence of Deeds of Gift, or any other wise Whatsoever. And more Especially, I Hereby Make Null and Void and of None Effect, A Deed of Gift to her, Dated June, 1709, Being to Mr. David Henderson, for her use, and recorded by Nathaniel Chevin (?) Esqr., in ye Secretarys Office: Aprill: the 15: 1712: Being therein a Clause Giveing me Power of Revocation and makeing of it Null, Void & of None Effect by any Writing under my Hand & seall.

Item, I Give and Bequeath unto my Son, Thomas, his Heirs & Assigns for Ever, Fifteen Hundred & ffity Acres of Land, Contained in one purchas lying on ye South west side of Chowan River, Between Mr. Kings & Thos. Daniels Old ffield; The Land Lately Purchased of of Thomas Daniel, Lying Between the upper side of the forsd. Land & John Rasberrys Lowest Line; also, ye Land Purchsed of James Wilkeson, Bounded Between ye said Mr. King and the forsd. fifteen Hundred & fifth acres; Also, the Land Lately Purchased of Martin Frederick Rasor, The five Back Tracks of Lightwood Land Between the forsd. Lands & Eastermost Swamp of Samon Creek, The Land where ffirebent Built ye Mill; and also, Eight Thousand ffive hundred on Mill-Creek, with fifteen Hundred acres to be added to ye same; according To a Warrant for ten thousand acres from ye Lords Propiertors to w'ch Now I have ye Right, Lying on Mill-creek in Bath County; and also, two thousand ffive Hundred & sixty acres in the ffork of Raquis, Called Springfield. All which Land I Give & Bequeath to my sd. son, Thomas, his Heirs & assigns for Ever.

Item, I Give & Bequeath unto my son, Cullen, his Heirs & assigns for Ever, Two thousand and ffive Hundred Acres of Land lying on the South Side of Moratock River, Called Canecarora; Also, ye six Hundred & fforty acres of Land Joyning to ye sd. Cullens Lapsed Land on Bridges Creek, at Weekacanaan. A Tract of Land containing Two thousand, Eight Hundred acres Lying on Cassayah, called Rose-field; All ye Land on Moratock Joyning to Where Bowman now Lives; Likewise ye Land Purchased of Richard Rose, Joyning to ye Lower-Side of ye Land Last mentioned; and also, ye Land on the South side of moratock-bay, Where my Negros are now Cleareing; Also, Nine hundred Acres of Land on Neus River fork, Called New-Bern. All w'ch Land, I Give & Bequeath to my sd. son Cullen, his Heirs & assigns ffor Ever.

Item, I Give & Bequeath unto my Son, George, his Heirs & assigns ffor Ever, The Land Lately Bought of Major Robert West, on w'ch I now Live; The Land belonging to me Joyning ye sd. Land where I now Live, and ye Land Joining on yt W'ch I bought of Cary Gobbee; Also, A tract of Land I Lately bought of Thos. West, Joyning to Parrots Land. The Land wher Samll. Edmunds Lived; Wher John Griffin Lived, Neare Bavie swamp; Where Wilson Lived att Weekacoon Creek; And wher John Mainard Lived at Pettishore; also, two thousand ffour hundred acres Called Crany Island; Two-thousand, Two Hundred acres lyeing on ye south-side of Neus River & west-side of Core-Creek; also, Seven Hundred and Ten acres, Lying on the North side of Trent River called, ye Halfe-way House; Two Hundred & twenty acres Lyeing on ye Est-side of Core-Creek; The Land wher Leonard Loften Lived on ye South Shore; Three hundred and sixty acres of Land lying on Boag Sound; Two Hundred and ffifteen acres Lyeing in the fork of Chester Creek On White-Oake River; One Hundred & fifty acres lyeing on ye south-side of Nuse River at ye head of Bennys Creek; Also, five thousand Acres to be taken up to ye southward of Nuse River by a Warrant from ye Proprieters to w'ch now I have a right; also, six-hundred & forty Acres on Nuse River, Called Wilkesons Point, in One Purchased Patent; All w'ch Land, I Give & Bequeath to my Son, George, his Heirs & assigns for Ever.

Item, I give and Bequeath to my son, Thomas, his Exers., admrs. or assigns: Pompey, Molaina, Maneuell, Cate, Scipio & Moll, wth ye Children Ruth, Joe, & Moll; Abraham & Dina his wife; Notoose Cesar, his wife Bess Tody; Scipio & Coylo, Harry, Jack-fiddle, Coffe Jackco, & Joe, franks son; Charls & Becke, tottes Daughter, All w'ch Negroes or slaves, I Give & Bequeath unto my son, Thomas, his Excrs. adms., or assigns for Ever.

Item, I Give & Bequeath to my Son, Cullen, his Exers., admrs., or assigns: Diego, Long Mingo, old mingo, Young mingo, Cajo & Venus, Stevens, George, papa Ceasar, Bowman, Jueda, Long-Dick & Bess, Wife; Little-Dick & Bess, & Debora, Little Bette, West & Ceasar; Cottoes Children, Pattey & Jack; tom's Children, Sarah & Toms Eldest-son next to Jack; & Ruth, Hannas Daughter. All w'ch Negroes or Slaves I Give & Bequeath unto my son Cullen, his Exrs. Admrs. or assigns for Ever.

Item, I Give and Bequeath unto my son, George, his Exrs., admrs. or assigns; Franke, Sambo, Cesar I bought of Gainsbe; Peter, Little-Will & Caramante Will, Dowe, Sharper & Frank, old tom and naney, London & Bettey; Little tom, Mols Son; Little Nane; Little Manewell, Nane's youngest Garle; Venus's Child, Patience; Dina, Jeneys daughter; Tomboy, & Ceasar, his son; and all toteys Children w'ch She will have hereafter; all w'ch Negroes or Slaves, I Give & Bequeath to my Son, George, his Exrs. admrs. or assigns for Ever.

Item, I give and Bequeath to my son, Thomas, his Heirs & assigns for ever, Eight-thousand, Nine-Hundred acres of Land Lying on ye West side of the Eastermost Branch of Salmon-Creek, Reserving free liberty to my son George, to make what Pitch and Tar he sees fitting on ye same, with his hands, for the space of three or four years after My Death.

Item, I Give & Bequeath to my son, Cullen, One hundred pound to be paid in Boston, and also, five thousand foot of plank which I have sent for from Boston.

Item, I give & Bequeath to my son George, his Heirs or assigns for Ever, a Tract of Land lyeing on South-Lancaster, formerly belonging to Coll'll William Wilkeson.

Item, I Give & Bequeath to my son, George, sixty pound to be paid in Boston.

Item, I Give and Bequeath to my three sons, Viz: Thomas, Cullen, & George, all my other Lands, Tenements, Mortgages, Extents, Annuities, annuel Rents, Remainders, Revertions or any Other Heridatements, whatsoever, In what part of ye World soever, Whether here in america, or Scotland, or any other part of ye World, whereunto I have any Right, Title or Interest, To be Equally, Devided by ym & to be Held in Common & not in Joint-Tenancy.

Item, as to all my other Personall Estate, whatsoever, not hereabove Bequeathed, of what Kind soever, Debts Due to me, Negros, Stocks of Horses, cattle, Hogs, &c.; What monay may Be Due to me in New England or any other Place in ye World, Money, Plates, Jewels, Books, Arms, Household-goods; and Every thing else of whatever Kind in Whatever Place or Countery, Properly belonging to me; I Give & Bequeath to my forsd. Three Sons, Thomas, Cullen & George, Equally to be Devided among them.

Item, as to the Warrants for fifteen Hundred acres of Land to my son Thomas, & five thousand acres of Land to my son George, if it be Not Layed out and surveyed to them, & Each of them, their Heirs or assigns wth One year after my Death, Then, that they have a porpotionable allowance from ye others as to ye Quantity of the land they Loose; of the full Value thereof as they Can agree.

Item, as to ye crop Now on ye Ground, and what Pitch & Tar ye hands in ye woods makes until ye first of aprill Next, shall be Equally Divided amoungst my three Sons, Thomas, Cullen & George.

Lastly, I Make, Constitute, & Appoint my three Sons, Thomas, Cullen, & George, my whole & sole Executors of this my Last Will & Testament, and they to pay all my Lawfull & Just Debts; Especially, ten Pound, Ten shillings, that I owe to one Joseph Mills, of Bermudas, Marrimer, Being Part of Twenty four pounds yt I owe him, ye other Thirteen pound, teen Shillings being paid by Captn. David Henderson, unto one Boas Bell, of Bermudas, by his order, & a Receipts thereof given on the Back of my Note to him; also all Charges for ye Building the House at Black-Rock, to be Paid out of ye Tar & Pitch, first made by ye Hands.

Item, To Explain & make more Clere Som Land Willed before to my son, Cullen, Lying on ye south-side of Morattock-River, on both sides Roses Creek, thes are to Certify yt it contains Three thousand five hundred & fifty acres of Land in one Purchase Patent; also ye Land on Casaya River, to Contain Two-thousand, Eight hundred & tenn acres in a purchased Patent; also, ye Land on Moratock Called Conacaroro, to Contaon two thousand, five hundred & sixty Acres in one Purchased Patent, all w'ch Land I have given, & Doe hereby Give unto my son, Cullen, his heirs & assigns for Ever.

THOS. POLLOCK. (Seal)

Signed, Sealed, Published by the sd. Thomas Pollock as his Last will & Testament, in the Presence of us the Subscribers:
    JOHN BURNNELL,
    WILLIAM HARDY, W. his mark.
    JAMES CASTELAW,
    DAVID HENDERSON.
    LAWRANCE SARSON.
    JAMES CASTELLAW.
    ROBERT WICKS, X. his mark.

(the Two Interlineations set Down in ye margin of this Wil was acknowledged by the Testator to Be Done Before the signing, before us the subscribers, this Eighth Day of august, 1721.'
    DAVID HENDERSON.
    LAWRANCE SARASON.
    JAMES CASTELLAW.

And, whereas, Since the publishing of my above writter will and Testament, I have Expended and Laid out for a house at Black Rock (when mr. West the Carpentare is paid what is due to him for his worke there) for my Son; Thomas, Twoe hundred Pound, and also Ten Pound more for New Englanc plank, makeing in all Twoe hundred and Ten Pound,

And, whereas also, I have been out and expended upon a House for my Son Cullen, on the South Shore (when mr West the Carpentare is paid for what worke he hath done ther, (to wit) the covering the house, doeing the Dormant Windoes, and makeing upe the Gavell end of the Sd. House, and when Cullen hath what Glass is in the House that will answer his purposes, and what nailes he will have occasion of for the Said House, The Sume of Three hundred Pounds I Reckon (?) and being willing for my Sons all Equall, so near as I can Judge Doe Therefore by this Codicil, will and bequeath to my Son George, (he haveing no House built) besides his Equall Share of all the rest of my Moveable Estate, Two hundred and eighty Pounds, whereof one Hundred pound to be paid in New England and the other one hundred and eighty to be paid out of my moveable and personall estate here, w'th Twenty Pound that I value the old houses here where I live, will make upe the Three hundred Pound equall to my Son, Cullens. Also, To make upe my Son, Thomas Part, equall w'th cullens, I valueing the Houses at Black Rocke at Ten Pound, doe hereby give and bequeath to my sd. Son, Thomas, Eighty Pound, to be paid out of my moveable and Personall estate in this Provence.

In my accounting above in this codicill concerning Cullens

House standing in Three Hundred Pound, I made a mistake in not mentioning That mr. Coke, the Bricklayer, wages for making, Laying the Bricks in the chimneys, Sellar, underpining, and doeing all the other worke agreed fer, is part of the Three hundred Pound, and is to be paid out of my personall estate. Also, he is to have what lands ar necessary for him for Burning the * * * * * Bricks, or what other worke he hath occasion for, to finish the worke he hath agreed for, wherefore my will is that the Bricklayer aforsd. be paid out of my personall estate befor Shared.

Also, I give and bequeath unto my Son, Thomas, one Third Part of all the vessels, clearances, whether it be in money, * * bils to New England or Elsewher.

also, I give and Bequeath to my Son, Cullen, Six Pound to be paid him in the first goods from New England, at first cost, I owing him so much,

also, I give and bequeath to my Son, George, Twenty Pound to be paid him in the first goods I have come in from Boston, I oweing him so much.

also, Elisebeth Hawkins, wife to Thomas Hawkins at the South Shore, haveing lived with me about twoe year after the Expiration of her time of servitude, Wherefore, I hereby order and appoint my Executors to pay to whomsoever she shall order them to pay, by a writting in her hand in whole or in Part (Her husband not to have   therein) Fourty Pound currant money of this Provence.

in presence of ——— ——— I sett my hand and Seal, 20 day of July 1722:

THO. POLLOCK. (Seal)

Signed, Sealed, and delivered ye as my last will and Testament before the following witness:
THOMAS NEWNAM.
WILLIAM LITTLE.
JOSEPH X SKITTLETHORP.
his / mark

BERTIE PRECINCT. Sc.   February Court, 1722.

The Revd. Thomas Newnam Clark came into Court and made Oath That he Saw Thomas Pollock Sign the above and acknowledge the same as his last Will and Testament.   Test. F. FORSTER, Cler. Cur.

BERTIE PRECINCT. Sc.   Februeary Court, 1722.

James Castellaw came into Court and produced the above Will being an Evidence to Seven Several places in the sd. Will and made Oath that he saw the Sd. Thos. Pollock Sign & publish the sd. Will as his last Will and Testamt. and that the several Interlineations in sd. Will was writ at the time of the Signing thereof   Test. FR. FORSTER, Cler. Cur.

Copied from Original Will, Filed in the Office of the Secretary of State.

THOMAS POLLOCK'S WILL.

IN THE NAME OF GOD AMEN. I, Thomas Pollock, of Bert Precinct, in North Carolina, Being of perfect memory Judgment, (praised be God for ye same), do make this m last Will & Testament, hereby revoking all others, & this to l taken only as my Last Will and Testament.

Imprs., I give & bequeath my soul to Allmighty God; & m Body to the Ground to be decently Buried by my Exec hereafter Named; and for what Estate it hath pleased Go to bestow upon me, I give and bequeath as followeth:

Item, I Give unto my Dear & loving wife, all my plantatio caled Black Rock, during her Natural Life; and after her deces I give & bequeath Said plantation to my Son, Cullen, his hei & Assigns for Ever.

Item, I give & bequeath unto my Son, Cullen, his heirs assigns for ever, my plantation called ye Great quarter, & m plantation called Manuels or Crickits; also, all my othe Land lying between ye Easter most swamp of Salmon Cree & Chowan River.

Item: I give & bequeath to my Son, Cullen, a Tract (Land Adjoining on ye back of ye forsd. Land, Containir Eight thousand, Nine hundred Acres, which Land my Wi is, that my Executors, sell or dispose of as they shall thin best, for my Son, Cullens, interest; & Such part as remaii unsold when my Son Cullen comes to ye Age of one & twent I give to my Son Cullen, his heirs & assigns for Ever.

Item: I give & bequeath to my Son, Thomas, his heirs assigns for ever, all my Land on Trent River in Bath Count Contained in two pattents, one for Eight thousand, five hui dred Acres, ye other for fifteen hundred Acres.

Item: I Give and bequeath to my Son George, his heirs assigns for ever, a Tract of Land Containing two thousan(five hundred & Sixty Acres, Laying in ye fork of Roqui called Springfield; also, all my Land at ye Unaroye Meadow being in two pattents; also, two tracts of Land nigh of Tuskaroi Indian Town; also, three hundred Acres of Land on ye Sout side of Moratuck River; also, two hundred & thirty five Acr(on ye Side of Moratuck River; also, four Tracts of Land La ing one Fishing Creek.

Item, I give & bequeath to my three Sons, Cullen, Thom; & George, these negroes, viz: Tomboy, Becke Rachel, Jane Catto, Pomp, Molany, Crists, Cipeo, Moll, Ruth, Joe Manue

Kate, London, Nany, Dick, Coyler, George, Betty, Frank, Hary, Bess, Bristoll Phillis, Hary, Toby, Betty, Cecero, Jaco, & Abraham; to be equal Divided among my three Sons when they come of Age, by my Executors, or those they shall appoint; & my Will is yt ye Negros aforsd. be for ye Use of my three sons from my deces till they be of Age.

Item, I give unto my Dear & Loving wife, During hir Natural life, these Negro, viz: Charles, & Moll & her Child, Cooper, Bess, James, & two Boys, Cipeo, Nany, Jack, Jane, Will, Dina, Dick, and Nansey; & after my wifes decease, I give ye aforsd. Negroes & their increse to my Sons, Cullen, Thomas, & George, to be equally divided among them.

Item, I give to my Sons, three Negroe viz: Rose, Phillis, & quash, which I had by my wife.

Item, as to the Eight Thousand nine hundred Acres before given to my Son Cullen, I give & bequeath three hundred Acres of yt Tract of Land to Jacob Parat, his Heirs & assigns for ever.

Item, I give & bequeath to John Hailes, his heirs & assigns for ever, a Tract of Land Laying on ye Briery Branch, containing near five hundred acres of Land, begining at a marked pine within ye midle Swamp, runing thence to three marked pines Thomas Yeats, his Corner, & so his Line to John Cokes, So allong other lines till it comes into my own, & So all down ye Midle of ye Main Branch untill they come to ye foresd. markd Pine; which Land is allso to be taken out of ye foresd. Eight thousand, nine hundred Acres given Cullen.

Item, I will & Order & give by this my will, to all Such persons who are Setled on my lands at Trenton, Condition of a Certain writing I give to Jacob Miller, that those already Setled thare, have leases on ye Same termes I promised them.

Item, I give to my Dear & loving Wife, one fourth part of all my Catle, Horses, hogs, & Sheep; & also ye Houshold Stuffs.

Item, I give to my Sons, Cullen, Thomas, & George, three fourth parts of all my Catle, Horses, hogs, & Sheep.

Item, my Will is that if one of my sons Desese before he be of Age of one & twenty, yt then his portion of Land & of ye present Estate, be Equally Divided between ye other two.

Item, my Will is that all my Debts be paid out of ye whole Estate by my Executors.

Item, I give to Mrs. Eliz: Dickson, one hundred pound.

Lastly, I do hereby Nominate & apoint my Loving Brothers, Cullen Pollock, George Pollock, & Robert West, to be my true & Lawfull Exec. to Execut this my last will & testament.

In Witness whereof, I have hereunto Set my hand & Seal this Sixteenth of Aprile, in the Year of our Lord, Seventeen hundred & thirty two, my will Containing one Sheet.

        THOS. POLLOCK. (Seal)

Signed & Sealed in ye presence of:
 GEORGE POLLOCK.
 JACOB JP PARAT.
   mark
 ELIZABETH E DECKSON.
    mark
 FRANCIS FR RASOR.
    mark
 ROBERT R MINOR
    mark

NORTH CAROLINA. ss.   Jany. ye 20th, 1732.

Jacob Parrot, one of the Evidences to this will, came before me & Mad oath that he See Thomas Pollock, Above name, Sign, Seal & publish y foregoing Insturment as his Last will & Testament, & that he was of Soun & Disposing mind & Memory; & that this Deponant at ye Same time i ye presence of ye Said Thomas Pollock, Sett to his mark as an Evidence & yt ye Other Evidences Above named he See at ye Same time Sign a Evidences thereto in ye presence of the Said Thomas Pollock; & also that ye said Thomas Pollock Signed & Executed ye sd. Will in ye presenc of this Deponts & ye rest of ye Evidences whose names are Set thereto a Witnesses.

 Capt. & Jurat. die predict. Coram me
        W. LITTLE Ck: Jur.

Copied from Original Will, Filed in the Office of the Secretary of State

In the Will of Thomas Pollock, is the following Legase
Item, I give unto my dear and loving wife dureing he natural life these Negroes Viz, Charles and Moll and her child Cooper Bess Jamey and two Boys Cipio, Nany, Jack Jan Will Dina Dick, Naney and after my wife deceases I give th aforesaid negroes and thire increse to my sons Cullin, Thcma & George to be equally devided among them
dated the 16th of November 1732.

JOHN PORTER'S WILL

IN THE NAME OF GOD, AMEN. John Porter, of Cape Fai in North Carolina, at present being weak & Ill of body, bu of sound mind and memory, doe make and ordain this to b my last Will and Testament in manner and form following:

Imps. I give and bequeath to my son, John Porter, my negro named Jack and my negro boy named Mars, to be de livered him when he shall attain to the age of Twenty on Years, or day of marriage.

Item, I give and bequeath to my daughter, Sarah Porter, my negro girl named Beck, to be delivered her when she shall attain to the age of Eightteen Years or day of marriage; also a likely young negro man, sound of wind and limb, to be procured out of that part of my Estate which is not Already mentioned, to be given & in like manner as aforesaid, to be deliverd unto my Daughter by my Executrix hereafter mentioned.

Item, I further give and bequeath to my daughter all the increase that shall be hereafter born of my negro wench Nan.

I Give, Devise and Bequeath, to my Dear and Loving Wife, Sarah Porter, all the rest and residue of my Estate not before given, to say, all my lands to Dispose and do with as she shall see proper and convenient, and a Title thereof to make to any person or persons that shall buy or purchase any of my lands of and from my said wife, Also, all the rest of my Goods, Chattels, Rights and Properties, in whatever kind, either here or whereever to be found; and further, that all my lawfull Debts be paid, out of that part of my Estate so coming by this my Will to my loving Wife.

Item, My Will is that in case either of said children should die before they attain to the age above mentioned, or be possessed with the legacies before given them, that then the survivor thereof shall have his or her part of the legacy before given to him or her so Dying, and further my will is, that in case both of my sd. children should die before they attain to the age aforesd. or be possessed with the legacies herein given them, that then, & in such case, their parts or portions herein given shall come to my Loving Wife, Who I make my whole and sole Executrix of this my last Will and Testament.

In witness whereof, I have herewith Sett my hand and seal this Eleventh day of October, 1727.

JOHN PORTER. (Seal)

Signed, Sealed and delivered,
in the presence of:
    SETH PILKINGTON, Jurat
    JOHN WORTH,
    T. KNIGHT,

By the Honoble the Gov'r &c Mr. Seth Pilkington, Personally appeared before me & pr..ved the above Will in due form of Law.
Given under my hand the 6th Day of Janry, 1728.

RICHD. EVERARD.

Copied from the Original Will, Filed in the Office of the Secretary of State.

JOHN PORTER'S WILL.

IN THE NAME OF GOD AMEN. This Twentieth Day of November, In the year of our Lord, One Thousand, Seven Hundred & Fifty one. I, John Porter, of the County of Hide, Being Sick and Weak of Body, but of Perfect Sence & Memory, Blessed be God for it, & Knowing that it is appointed for all men once to Die, Do make & Ordaine this my Last Will & Testament; & first & Principally I Recommend my Soul into the hands of God that Gave it; And as Touching such Worldly Goods as it has pleased God to Bless me With in this Life, I Give & Dispose of the same in the Following Manner & form:

Imprim: I Give & Bequeath to my Son, Willm. Porter, one half the Land Whereon I now live, Including the Houses & Plantation, to him & his heirs for Ever; also, my Gun & Sword.

Item, I Give & Bequeath to my son, John Porter, the Other half of my Plantation above Mentioned to be Divided by Themselves.

Item, I Give to my Daughter, Patience Porter, My Negro Girl Nam'd Phillis, after my Wifes Decease, to her & her Heirs for Ever.

Item, I leave to My Well Beloved Wife, Elisabeth Porter, all the Rest of my Estate, Both Real & Personal, During her Natural Life, for the Education & Bringing up of my Children, & after Her Decease to be Equally Divided amongst said Children, if there is any of my Said Estate Remains * * * Hereby appoint & ordain Thomas Smith & John Smith * * * Executors to this my Last Will & Testament, Ratifying and Confirming this & no other to my be my * * * * Last Will & Testament.

in Witness whereof, I have hereunto set My Hand & Seal the Day & Year above Written.

JOHN PORTER. (Seal)

Sign'd Seald & Pronounced to be The Last Will & Testament of the Testator, in the presence of us, the Subscribers:

THOS. SMITH.
MARY SMITH.
MARY X RHODES.
   her
   mark

HYDE COUNTY.   December Court, 1751.

The within Will was Exhibited into Court and proved by the Oaths of the Subscribing Evidences, the within Thos. Smith, was qualified Exr. persuant to Law. Ordered that Mr Secretary have Notice thereof.

THOS. LOVICK, Clk. Court.

Copied from the Original Will, filed in the Office of the Secretary of State.

JOHN PEYTON PORTER'S WILL.

IN THE NAME OF GOD AMEN. I, John Porter, Of Beaufort !o. & Province of No. Carolina, Gent., being of Sound & erfect Mind, memory & judgement, & calling to mind the ertainty of Death and my Infirmity of body, do by these resents, revoke and make Void all former Wills & Testaments y me heretofore made or Executed, & do by these Presents ake, constitute & ordain, this my Last Will and Testament 1 Manner & Form Following:

Imprimis, I render my Soul to Almighty God; My body to he Earth to be decently Interr'd.

1 tem, I will & bequeath unto my well beloved Wife, Elizabeth Porter, one half of my Plantation Situated on the East Side of Durham's Creek, Commonly Called the Garrison, containing 644 acres, be the same more or less, wth all and Singular, its rights, Priveleges, & appurtenances for & during, the term of her natural lifetime; and it is my Will and pleasure, that after her decease, the said one half descend to my eldest Daughter, Mary Porter, & her Lawfull Issue; & on failure thereof, to my younger Daughter, Sarah Porter, & her Lawful Issue; & on failure thereof to my Sister, Sarah Richardson, & her Lawfull Issue, to posess & enjoy the same for ever.

2 [tem, I Will and bequeath to my eldest Daughter, Mary Porter, the other half of my Plantation aforsd. on the East side of Durhams Creek, Commonly called the Garrison, & to her Lawfull Issue forever; & on failure thereof, to my Daughter, Sarah Porter, & her Lawfull Issue, & on failure thereof to my sister, Sarah Richardson, & her Lawfull Issue for ever.

3 Item, I Will and Bequeath to my Daughter, Sarah Porter, (all my plantation on the East side of Durhams Creek, commonly call'd Hardings Plantation, be the same more or less, and now adjoyning my Plantation called the Garrison), and to her Lawfull Issue forever; & on failure thereof, to my Daughter, Mary Porter, & her Lawfull Issue; and on failure thereof to my sister, Sarah Richardson and her heirs forever.

4 Item, I Will and bequeath, that my tract of land beginning at Snoads line, from thence to the Savanna, from thence to the Horse-penn Swamp, & from thence to the Dismall; be the same more or less, with all and singuler it's

Rights, Members, Privileges and Appurtenances, to be occupied in manner & in form following; Viz., They are to keep my Negroes, Or a suff't Number of them, on said Tract to make Tar, Turpne: &c, in order to raise money to pay my funer'l charges and all other Lawfull demands, that may come ag'st my said Exrs. or agst. the Legattees of my Estate; & that afterwards the same shall descend, to my Eldest Daughter, Mary Porter, & her Lawfull Issue; & on failure thereof to my younger Daughter, Sarah Porter, & her Lawfull Issue; & on failure thereof to my Sister, Sarah Richardson; & her Lawfull Issue forever.

Item, I Will and Bequeath that all my Negroes or a sufft. number of them, togeather with my Horses, Oxen, Cows, Calves, & Sheep, be kept und the care of my Extrs. untill such Time as my aforsd. Debts & Funer'l charges be fuly discharged & satisfied. & Likeways, it is My Will & Pleasure, that all my Hoggs, household Furniture, & other Personall Estate, by sold at Publick Vendue, by my said Exrs., in order to discharge the Charges && Lawfull Debts aforsd; & my will and pleasure is, that w:n those Funerl Charges, & Lawfull Debts are fully & Justly sitisfied & discharged, That then, all my Negroes, Horses, Oxen, Cows, Calves, & Sheep be fairly, Justly, and Equally, divided into three Equal Parts or Proportions (after the Following manner), by my Exrs.—Viz: One third Part or Proportion, I bequeath to my loving Wife, Elizabeth Porter, during her natural Life; one third part to my Eldest Daughter, Mary Porter, her Lawfull heirs forever; & the the Remaining third Part to my younger Daugh:r Sarah Porter, & her Lawful heirs forever,———

Item, I Nominate, ordain, Constitute & apoint by these presents, my Loving Wife, Eliz. Porter, Executrix; together with Mich'l Coutanche, Mar' & Nathan Richardson, Mariner, to be Executors of this my Last Will & Testament.

In Wittness whereof, I have hereunto set my hand & seal this, Twenty Ninth day of April, one thousand, seven hund'd fifty Four.

       JOHN PEYTON PORTER, (Seal)

Signed, sealed & Published in the presence of us:
  THOS. LOUGH.
  WILLIAM TRIPP.
  CHARLES LOWTHER.

BEAUFORT COUNTY, Ss.

At a Court held for the sd. County at Bath Town, on the second tuesday in March 1755.

Pres^t: his Majesty's Justices:

This certifies that the within last will & Testament of Jno. Peyton Porter, decd., was exhibited into Court & proved by the Oath of Will Trippe, who swore that the sd. Jno. Peyton Porter was of sound & disposing mind & memory at the time he executed it; and that he saw Thomas Lough and Charles Lowther, the other subscribing Witnesses, sign their names thereto at the same time; and Eliza Stewart (formerly named Eliza Porter) appeared in Court & qualified as Extrx. and Nathl. Richardson appeared & qualified as Ext'or unto the same; and it was ordered that the Secretary have notice that Letters Testamentary may issue.

Test. WALLEY CHAUNCEY, Cl. Cur.

Copied from Original Will, filed in the Office of the Secretary of State.

JOSHUA PORTER'S WILL.

IN THE NAME OF GOD AMEN. I, Joshua Porter, of Bath County, in ye Province of North Carolina, Esq., being of Sound & perfect mind & memory & Calling to mind ye Certainty of Death, & not knowing when it may Please ye Lord to call me out of this Life. Revoking & by these presents make Void all former & other wills by me heretofore made, do now make, Constitute and Ordain this to be my Last Will and Testament, in Manner & Form following:

Imprimis, I render my Soul to allmighty God; & my Body I Commit to ye Earth to be Buried in a Decent Manner.

Item, I give ye Use & Occupation of all yt Tract of Land & Plantation whereon I now Live, lying on ye East Side of Derhams Creek in Bath County in ye Province afsd., Containing by Estimation four hundred & Seventy five acres, be ye Same more or less, it being ye Lands yt I bought of Mr. Thomas Harding, Deceasd., with all & Singular ye Houses & Appertinance thereunto belonging, unto my Son, John Peyton Porter, & to ye heirs of his Body Lawfully begotten; & for default of Such Issue, I Give ye use & Occupation of ye afsd. Land & Plantation unto my Daughter, Elizabeth Porter, & to ye heirs of her Body Lawfully begotten; & for default of Such Issue, I give ye use & Occupation of ye afsd. Land & plantation unto my Cousin, John Fry, & to his heirs of his Body Lawfully begotten; & for default of Such Issue, I give ye use & Occupation of ye afsd. Land & Plantation, unto my Cousin, Anne Lillington, & to ye hears of her Body Lawfully begotten.

Item, I give unto my Daughter, Elizabeth Porter, One Thousand Acres of Land lying on ye South Side of Deshams Creek, Joying on ye upper Side of Majr. Robert Turners Lands, & Commonly goes by ye Name of ye Sand Hills, to her & her heirs for Ever.

Item, I give ye Use & Service of three Slaves unto my Sd. Daughter, Eliza. Porter, to ye heirs of her Body, Vizt: Patt, Jane, & Simon, I allso give unto my Said Daughter ye first Slave Child yt shall be born in my family after my Decease; but my Will is yt if my Said Daughter should Dye without Issue, yt then I give ye Use & Service of ye Sd. Slaves unto my Son, John Payton Porter, & to ye heirs of his Body Lawfully begotten.

Item, I give my Said Daughter, Elizabeth Porter, fifteen Cows & Calves, & ye Sum of One hundred & fifty Pound, Currant Money of this Province, to be paid her at ye Day of Marriage or when she arrives to ye age of Twenty One Years, which shall first happen.

Item, I give ye Use & Service of One third Part of my Personal Estate unto my beloved Wife, Dorothy Porter, for & dureing her Natural Life & after my Said Wifes Decease, it is my Will & pleasure yt ye afsd. third part of my Estate may be Equally Devided between my Son, John Payton Porter, & my Daughter, Elizabeth Porter, to them & their heirs for Ever.

Item, I give ye Use & Service of all ye rest of my Moveable Estate not herein before given, be it of what kind So Ever, as Negros, Musters, or Indians, & their Increase, unto my Son, John Peyton Porter, & to ye heirs of his Body Lawfully Begotten; & for Default of Such Issue, I give ye Use & Service of ye afsd. Moveable unto my Daughter, Eliza. Porter, & to ye heirs of her Body Lawfully begotten; & for default Such Issue, I give ye afsd. Moveable Estate & Slaves unto my Cusin, John Fry, & to ye heirs of his Body Lawfully begotten; & for default of such Issue I give ye afsd. Moveable Estate & Slaves unto my Cousin, Eliza. Fry, & to ye heirs of her body Lawfully begotten; & for Default of Such Issue I give ye afsd. Moveable Estate to my Cousin, Anne Lillington, & to ye heirs of her Body for Ever.

Item, I give unto my Loving friend Philip Cremer, Ten pound, to Buy him a Mourning Ring.

Item, I give unto my God Son, William Trippe, Ten pound for ye like use.

Item, it is my Will & Desire yt none of my Slaves be removed from my Said Plantation, but yt they be put Under a Carefull Overseer, & kept to work in Order to raise Money to Discharge my Just Debts & Legacies, & it is my further Will & desire yt my Execs. hereafter named see yt my Son & Daughter may be Carefully learnt to read & write & to Cypher, & yt they may be duly Educated, & yt a Sufficient Sum of Money may be raised out of my Estate by me Execs. in Order for my Said Son & Daughters Education as afsd.,

Item, I do nominate & appoint, yt my Loving Brother, Edmund Porter, & my two Brother in Law, Messrs. Patrock

Maule & Seth Pilkington, & my Trusty & Loving friends, Colonel Edward Moseley & Capt. John Trippe, to be Joynt Executors of this my Last Will & Testement.

In Witness whereof, I have hereunto Set my hand & Seal this Seventeenth Day of January, One Thousand, Seven hundred & thirty three.

JOSHUA PORTER. (Seal)

Signed, Sealed & Published in
Ye Presence of:
  CHURCHILL READING.
  JOHN CALOOM.
  WILLIAM WHITFORD.

No. CAROLINA, Sc.

These may Certifie that William Whitford, one of ye Subscribing Evidence to this will, Appeared before us & proved ye Same in due form of Law, Septr. ye 14th., 1734.
          GEO. BURRINGTON.

Recorded in Will Book 3, page 329.

MARY PORTER'S WILL.

NORTH CAROLINA, SS.

IN THE NAME OF GOD AMEN, this 12th. day of November, anoq Domi., 1717. I, Mary Porter, of Chowan Precinct, in the County of Albemarle, in the Province of North Carolina, Widow, being of sound and Perfect Memory, doe make, Constitute and ordain, Declare and appoint this to be my last Will and Testiament, Revokeing and annuling by these Presents all former and other Will or Wills heretofore by me made, In manner and forme following, That is to say:

Imprimis, I recomend my Soul into the hands of almighty God, who gave it; and my body I comit to the earth to be decently Buried at the discretion of my Exors. herein After nominated and apointed.

Item, I give and bequeath unto my well beloved Sonn, John Porter, my Negroe man Knowne by the Name of Sandy, half a dozen Rusia leather Chairs, my large oval Table, one midle Sized Pewter Dish, Two large Pewter basons. & a Shovel and tongs Tiped with brass.

Item, I give and bequeath unto my well beloved Sonn, Edmund Porter, my Negroe man knowne by the name of Oliver, one large Plank Chest, one Silver Drinking cup with Two handles, half a dosen Silver Spoons, one large China bason already (?) in his possession, the large pair of Tongs and Shovel, one Bedstead one couch, the largest of the Small looking ———, the largest Cedar Table, half a dosen painted Chairs, and my whole Stock (?) of hogs that I shall leave at my decease, After my Debts and legacies paid; and one pound of Iron Doggs, fifty pound weight of feathers; and all the money due to me lyeing in the hands of Mr. Welstead and Oliver, Merchts., in Boston, he paying out of the sd. mony, within Six months After the receiving it, unto my beloved Daughter, Eliz: Porter, Six Silver Spoons, each weighing Ten Shillings, Sterling at least; and one Iron pott & pott hooks, and Twelve Soup Plates. But it is my Will and pleasure that if the Said Edmund Shall not be in this Government at my Decease, that then, and in Such Case, all and every of the legacys here left to the Sd. Edmund, shall remain in the Exors. hands hereafter Named, until his arrival here, or until he shall impower any person After my Decease to take and receive the Same, and if it shall happen that ye Sd. Edmund, Shall never arrive here, nor impower any person as Aforsd. after my Decease, then all and every of the legacys Aforsd. I give and bequeath unto my Sons, John Porster and Josua Porter, and to my Daughter Eliz: Porter, to be equaly Divided amongst them.

Item, I give and bequeath unto my Wel beloved Son, Josua Porter, a tract of Land lyeing in Yawpim, bounded by Mr. Clayton's & Mr. Clarks line, to him, the sd. Joshua, and his Heirs for ever; my Negroe woman knowne by the Name of Edy, one Ticken feather bed and bolster, and Two pillows, one feather bed covered with Canvas and bolster, and one Pillowe, three pillow cases Suitable, two pair fine Sheets, Two pair Coarse Sheets, one Set of red watered Curtains and Wallons, one Spotted worsted Rugg, Red Rug, Two pair good Blankets, 1 Flowered Bed Coverlid, Bedsted that Stood in the Hall Chamber, Six Rusia leather Chairs, one one of the large lookeing glasses, and my largest and one midling Iron pott, the large Andirons, a large double brass Skillet and Trevit, one brass Candlestick, one pair brass Scales and weights, one pair of Stilliards, two Diaper towells, a pewter mustard pott, the Coarsest of brass ridles, my Dantzick locks Chests, a lime Sifter, a Case of Knives and forks, a Cross cut Sawe, a writeing Desk, four Pewter Porringers, one earthen Porringer, ten Pewter Plates, 1 Iron pestle, 1 Ash Table, 1 large Soup Pewter dish, one large shall Dito, one midle Sized Dito, 1 large and 1 Small Pewter bason, 2 Earthen bason, and 2 Pewter Dº, one Set of Wedges and Six wooden Chairs, 2 Joint Stooles to wooden turned Chairs, 2 Iron tramels 1   ss butter(?) ladle, 1 Small brass Ketle, 1 pewter Chamber pott,   Mill and   Salt, 1 Iron Chafing dish, a pair
            all my reap
Cloth brush afroe and Currying   and the half of my
Sheep and Cattle, and the half of a   now
        f   and the half of all my Crop now in the

Ground, with a pottle pewter pot and a pint Pewter pott, one Glass Gallon Bottle, and one broad Axe; my Debts first to be deducted.

Item, I give and bequeath unto my beloved Daughter, Sarah Lilington, my Negroe woman call'd Maria, 1 Chest of Drawers, six painted Chairs now in her possession, one pair of Iron fire doggs, one small Cedar table, 1 pair of fine Sheets, two pair Coarse Sheets, and Two pillow cases, Two diaper towells, my largest Quilt, one Lignum Vitae Spice Mortar, one large Soup dish, one midle Sized pewter dish, 1 Small pewter bason, 1 brass Skimer, 1 Small Iron Ketle, the least of my painted Trunks, Two earthen bason, and plates, 1 English Flasket, 1 large glass bottle, 1 Stone Jugg, 1 pewter Chamber pott, 1 bed pann, three of my other which she likes best, and the full third part of the Cotten and Wooll that shall belong to me at my decease.

Item, I give and bequeath unto my beloved daughter, Eliz. Porter, my Indian woman called Judith and her Daughter Named Sukey, 1 Chest of Drawers, 1 oval Table, my best Sett of red Curtains & Valent belonging to my lodging roome, 1 Ticken feather bed and bolster, four pillows, 1 bedstead belonging also to my lodging roome, three pair fine Sheets, Two pair Coarse sheets, four pillow Cases, my Green Rugg made of worsted, 1 pair of the best rose blankets, the least of my Quilts, my Callico Counterpaine and Jester cloath, my Bible, my Spice box, 1 warmeing pann, 1 pair Chamber Doggs with brass, 1 Black Trunk and one painted Trunk, a large brass Keetle and Two Skimers, a Brass Shie(?) and Two Iron potts one linked Tramel, a brass Flam, one Copper Chocolate pott, 1 white rugg, 1 Gridiron, four matted Chairs, my Silver Salt Marked, I P M, and Silver peper box with the Same marke, one large pewter Soup dish 1 Shallow D°, two midling pewter dishes, 1 large and one Small pewter basons, 10 pewter plates, Six painted Chairs, five pewter porringers, 1 pr. brass Candlesticks, Snuffers and Snuff dish, my Smoothing Iron heaters and Frame, 1 Gallon Stone Jugg, 1 Glass Cruit, Two glass cups, one mustard pott, Two pewter Chamber potts, three earthen Bason, 1 large Dish D°., & Two plates, 1 Tin puding pann, 1 Spitt, 1 leaden pann, and 2 painted brushes, a brass Shovel and Tongs, 1 large looking Glass, the best of the Bed panns, 1 pewter Salt, 1 Glass Decantor, 2 tin dish Covers, 1 brass Ridle, a large turned Elbow chair, 1 Drippen pann, 1 Case of bottles, one half of my Sheep and Cattle that shall remain after my Debts and legacys paid and half of the now on foot and half the Crop now in the ground, 12 diaper N   diaper Table Cloath, Two diaper Tow
one Bell mettle Skillett,
 and bequeath unto my G   Porter, 1

Young Cowe, 1 Young Ewe, to run for his Benefit, Increase to be Delivered to him with the increase at his age of one and twenty or Day of Marriage which shall first happen & also my Silver tankard marked I P M, to be delivered at ye same time.

Item, I give and bequeath unto my Grandaughter, Sarah Porter, one young Cowe and one young Ewe at my decease, to run for her benefit, and also Six Silver Spoons Marked I P M, to be delivered to her with the encrease at the age of eighteen years or day of Marriage which Shall first happen.

Item, I give and bequeath unto my Grandaughter, Elizabeth Lilington one Young Cowe and one Young Ewe, and my Smallest looking Glass, to be delivered with the encrease at the age of eighteen Years or day of Marriage.

Item, I give and bequeath unto my Grandaughter, Mary Lilington, one young Cowe, and one Young Ewe, and my Silver Dram Cup. marked I P M, to be delivered to her with their increase at the age of eighteen Years, or day of Marraige, which Shall first happen.

Item, I give and bequeath unto my grandaughter, Sarah Lilington, one Young Cowe and one young Ewe, to be delivered to her with their encrease at the age of eighteen Years or day of Marriage, which shall first happen.

Item, I give and bequeath unto Robert Herrick, if alive, and in this Government at my decease, the Sum of five pounds to be paid out of my Estate.

Item, all the rest and residue of my Estate not herein and hereby disposed of, Debts being thereon first Deducted, I give and bequeath unto my Sonn, Joshua Porter, and my Daughter, Elizebeth Porter, to be equaly Divided between them; and lastly, I doe hereby nominate and appoint my Said Sonns, John Porter and Joshua, to be exors. Jointly and Seperatly of this my Said last Will and Testament; but it is my Will and pleasure, and I doe hereby nominate and apoint my Sonn, Edmund, upon his Arrival in this Government After my Decease Joint Exor. with his Two Brothers.

           Mark
         MARY M PORTER (Seal)

Signed, Sealed and Delivered (the interlineing about the Silver tankard being first made) in the presence of:

   ————— LOVICK. Jurat
  MARY X HENRY.

CHOWAN ss.   Jany, ye 21st. 17—.
 Proved in Open by the oath of ——— ———ick.
            R. HICKS, Clk. Cur:

Copied from Original Will, filed in the Office of the Secretary of State.

NICHOLAS PORTER'S WILL.

In the name of God amen, the twenty forth day of augost, in the yeare of our Lord Crist, one thousand, Seven hundred and forty nine. I, Nicoless porter, being Sick in body, but of Good and perfect memory, thanks be to allmighty God, and Calling to remembrance the uncertain estate of this Life, must yeald unto Death when it Shall please God to Call, Do make, Constitute, ordain and Declare this my Last will and testament, In maner and forme folowing; revoking and annulling by these presents all testements and wills here to fore mentioned, or declared by word, or by writing, and this only is to be taken for my Last will and testement: I do order, give and Dispose of my Estate in maner and forme following, that is to Say, furst, I will that all those Debts and Dewes that in Right or Conscience to any person whatsoever, Shall be well and truly Contented and paid, or ordered to be paid, by my Executors in Convenient tine after my Deceas.

Item, I Give and bequeath, In witness, my maner plantation with one hundred acors of Land belonging to it, laid out at the uper End of the Sd. tract that the plantation is on, to my, to my beloved Daughter, Jeane porter.

I Give and bequeth one hundred and forty fore acors of the Same Tract, Joyning to Jeans, to be Laid out a Cross the Sd. Land, to my beloved Daughter, Elizabeth porter.

I give and bequeath one hundred and forty three acors of the same tract, to be laid out a Cross the Sd. Land Joyning to Elizabeths, to my beloved Daughter, Anne porter.

I Give and bequeeth one hundred and forty three acors of the Same tract, being the Lower End of the Sd. Land, to my beloved Daughter, Agness Porter.

Also, I give and bequeeth my polecat Land to my beloved Son, Samuell porter, it being in two patens.

I give and bequeth my negrow felow toney to my beloved wife, Elizabeth porter. I Give and bequeth all my Stock of Catle, and horses and mairs, to be Equaly devided betwen my wife and all my Children.

In witness whereof, I have hereunto set my hand and Seal.
NICHOLAS PORTER. (Seal)

In witness, I do opint my beloved Wife, Elizabeth porter, and my well beloved and truste James farmer, to be my Executors.

test. NEEDHAM BRYAN.
MARY X DEES.
hir
mark
} Jurat

JOHNSTON COUNTY. SST. Sept. Court, 1749.
Prest. His Majesties Justices:

Then the within Last Will & Testament was proved in Open Court by the Oaths of the within Needham Bryan & Mary Dees; & Likewise the Executrix & Exor. appeared & were Qualifyed Agreeable to Law. Ordered that the Secretary have notice thereof that Letters Testamentory issue, &c.
Test. RICHD. CASWELL, Cl. Cu.

Copied from Original Will, filed in the Office of the Secretary of State.

FRANCIS PUGH'S WILL.

IN THE NAME OF GOD AMEN. The 5th. Day of July, 1733. I, Francis Pugh, of Bartie precinct, In North Carolina, being well and of good Health in Body, and of perfect Mind and memory, thanks be given to Allmighty God therefore, Calling unto Mind the mortalietie of my body, and knowing that it is appointed for all men once to Die, Do make and ordain this my Laste Will and Testements, that is to Say, principally, and first of all, I give & Reccommend my Soule into the Hands of God that Gave it; and my body I Recommend to the Earth to be buried in Decent Christian Buriale at the Discretion of my Executors; Nothing doubting but at the Generale Resurrection I shall Receive the Same again by the mighty power of God; and as thouching such worldly Estate, wherewith it hath pleased God To Bless me in this Life, Doe give, Demise and Dispose of the Same in manner and form following:

Imprimus, I give and bequeath unto my well beloved Wife, three Negroes, viz., Barns, Lymus, and affrow, a wench which is now with Samuell Wiggins, for Ever: and Likewise, I lend the Rest of my Negroes to her Dureing the time She lives a widow, and in order to keep to their buissiness in makeing Corn and Tobacco, towards bringing up my Children at Scoole, and finding them in Cloaths; and if my well beloved Wife should marry, I Desire the reste of my negroes which I have not already Given to my wife for Evee, to be put to work, and what they Gite, put to the Use of bringing up my Dear beloved Chilldren as aforesaid, and Likewise I Desire my well beloved Wife may Live upon the plantation where I now live, dureing her Life, and after her Death to return to my well beloved Son, John Pugh; and likewise, I Desire my well beloved wife may Kill provissions out of my Stock of Hoggs and Cattle dureing the time She lives a widow, and the Rests of my Stock which is Killable yearly, I Desire it may be Sold, and the money to be Laid up, for to be Equally Divided between all my Chilldren; Likewise, I give to my well beloved Wife, two Feather Beds and urniture and half the rest of my House hold Goods.

Item, I Give and bequeath unto my well beloved Son, John

Pugh, the plantation whereon I now live, after the Death of his mother to him and his heirs for Ever

Item, I give and bequeath to my well beloved Son, Thomas Pugh, my plantation at the Emperors fields which I bought of Christian Hitteburgh to him and his heirs for Ever.

Item I give and bequeath unto the Child my wife now goes with, it if is a boy the plantation where Samuele Wiggins Lives at Grindale Creek and if it is a Girl to be Equally Divided between my two Sons John Pugh and Thos. Pugh and likewise if it is a boy I give and bequeathe all the rests of my Lands which I have not already given which lies in Bartie precinct and Edge-Combe precinct, which is already patend and likewise the Entries made, to be Equally Divided between my Sons, John Pugh, Thos. Pugh and the Child my well beloved Wife now Goes with if it is a boy, and if it is not a boy, to be Equally Divided between my Two Sons Jno. Pugh and Thos. Pugh Share and Share alike, to them and there heirs for Ever. and the lands which I have in Virginia, and in Chowan precinct I Desire they may be Sold and the money to be Equally Divided between my Dearly beloved wife and all my Children Share and Share alike, and it is my Desire that all my Stock of Cattle and Hoggs, and Horses & mares may be put out to plantations, and when the Stears Comes of full Grooth to be Sold and what is not made use of by my wife towards bringing up my Children, the money to be Laid up, and Equally to be Divided amongst my Children Share and Share alike, and likewise my Hoggs the Same the Horses the Same, my well beloved Wife all waies haveing an Equale Share with my Children. And it is my will that my well beloved wife Shall have the management of the Ferry where Henry Horne Lives and receive the money towards maintaining her and her Children, Dureing the time She lives a widow, and if She Should Change her Condition, then it is my Desire that the Incomes of the Ferry may be Equally Divided between all my Children, while the Youngest Shall Come of age or marry; and after that I give and bequeath it unto my two Sons John Pugh and Thos. Pugh and all the rest of my personall Estate I Give and bequeath to be Equally Divided between all my Children; and it is my will and Desire that none of my Estate Shall be Sold at publick Vandieu or outCry but that my Executors and Trustees may manage it according to my Will and Desire before Expresst and all my Negroes which I have not allreadye Given to my wife for Ever I give and bequeath unto all my Children to be Equally Divided amongst all my Children, both them and there Increase for Ever to them and there Heirs for Ever.

And as for the Debts which I have now Due to me, I Desire that they may be Received by my Executors and Trustees, and pay all my Just and true Debts, which I am Indebted to any prson whatsoever and the overplus to be Laid out in Young Negroes, and be Equally Divided amongst all my Children and likewise all my Merchantizeing Goods I Desire they may be Sold and the Effects that Comes for it to be Laid out in Young Negroes and to Remain with my Wife Dureing the time she Lives a widow and afterwards to be Equally Divided amongst all my Children.

And it is my will and Desire that if my Sons Should Die without Heirs Lawfully Begotten of their Body, that then the lands which I have heretofore Given may may return to their Sisters Share and Share alike.

And I Do hereby Constitute, make and Ordain, my well beloved Wife, and Colln. Robert West my Sole Executors of this my Last will and Testament, and Mr. Cullin Pollock to be my Trustee to the Same.

And I Do hereby Utterly Disallow, Revoke and Disannull all Every other former Testaments, Wills, Legacies and Bequests, and Executors, by me in any ways before named, Willed and Bequeathed, Ratifieing and Confirming this and no other to be my Last will and Testament.

In Witness whereof, I have hereunto Set my hand and Seale the Day and Year Above Written.

FRANCIS PUGH (SEAL)

Signed, Sealed, published pronounced and Declared by the Said Francis Pugh as his Last will and Testemt. In the presents of Us NEEDHAM BRYAN } Jurats
HENRY HORNE
WILLM. JONES

BERTIE PRECINCT SC   May Court 1736

The above Will of Francis Pugh was proved in open Court by the Oaths of Needham Bryan & Henry Horne Two of the Subscribing witness thereto. And Also Pherebe Pugh Relict Widow and Executrix therein Named took the oath of and Exect by Law Required

Test. JNO. WYNNS d: cler Cou.

A CODICIL to be annexed to the last Will and Testament of Francis Pugh gent.

Whereas since the makeing of my last Will and Testament I have begun to build a Brigantine which is now on the Stocks in Bertie prect.

It is my Will and Pleasure that my Executors in my last Will named, do proceed and out of all & every part of the debts which shall be due to me at the time of my death, and out of the produce of my Stock of Cattle, Horses, Mares, and Hoggs, they finish and Compleat the said Brigantine with Anchors, Masts, Cables, Sails and all other Appurtenances.

Item, it is my will and pleasure that after the said Vessel is finished, my Executors & my Trustee herein named do out of the debts due to me and my aforesaid Stock, purchase a Loading of Tobacco black Wallnut or other merchandize fitt for the British market and that they do send the said Vessel to great Britain from thence to return to No. Carolina, and afterwards to be employed or disposed of as my said Executors & trustee shall think proper

Item, I give and bequeath the said Brigantine to my dear Wife and to my dear Children, both Sons and Daughters, and likewise the Cargo to be purchased as aforesaid, with the profits in trade ariseing thereby, Share & Share alike.

Item, I give to my dear wife, the plantation, & house wherein I now live in Bertie, for and dureing the term of her natural life, and after her death it is my Will the same shall go as by my said Will is directed.

Item, I do hereby constitute & appoint John Montgomery Esqr., Trustee and Supervisor of my last Will and Testament in the place & stead of Cullen Pollock, Esqr.

Item, it is my Will and pleasure that after my Sloop Carolina returns from New England, that my Executors & Trustee do out of her Cargo Inwards, purchase a Cargo and send the said Sloop to the West Indies with the said Cargo, & that the said Sloop & Cargo be there sold for the benefit and use of my Wife and Children, Share & Share alike.

Item, It is my Will that my Trustee herein named may have freight for about twenty Barrels free & clear, and for the usual freight a Carryage for what more he shall desire in the said Brigantine to Great Britain.

Item, It is my Will that my dear wife & Eexcrs. do receive from Captn. Grainger the Cargo now brought in A Schooner into this province which belongs to Mr. Coleman, provided the said Grainger allows to my Execrs. twelve pounds pr. Barrel for good and well pickled pork, vizt., for so much as is produced from my own Stock, and at the same price for the remainder which I paid to others.

In Testimony whereof, I have signed, Sealed & published this as a Codicil to be annexed to my last will & Testament, this twelfth day of April, one thousand, seven hundred & thirty Six.   FRAN (Remainder of Signature is gone)

Signed, Sealed & published, In the presence of:
          JON CHANCEL (?)
                &
          S. PLUMMER
          PETER BRITTON.

October 4th., 1736.

Doctor Saml. Saban Plummer made oath before me that he is a subscribing witness to the within Codicil, and that he saw the within named Francis Pugh, sign, Seal & publish the same as a Codicil to be annexed to his last Will, and that sd. Pugh was at the time when it was perfected of sound understanding.
GAB. JOHNSTON.

1736 Oct. 6th appeared Col. Rob. West and took oath of Executor in due form of Law.
GAB. JOHNSTON.

Copied from Original Will, filed in the Office of the Secretary of State.

CHURCHILL READING'S WILL.

IN THE NAME OF GOD AMEN, the nineteenth day of September, 1734. I, Churchill Reading, of Bath County, being very Sick and weak in body but of Perfect mind and memory, thanks be given unto God, Therefore, calling unto mind the mortality of my Body, and knowing that it is apointed for all men once to Dye, do make and ordain this my last Will and Testament, that is to Say, Principally, and first of all, I give and Recommend my Soul into the hands of God that gave it; and my Body I recommend to the Earth, to be buried in decent Christian Buriel at the discretion of my Executors, nothing doubting but at the General Resurrection I shall receive ye Same again by the mighty power of God; and as touching Such worldly Estate where with it hath pleased God to Bless me in this Life, I give, demise and Dispose of the Same in the following manner and form:

Imprimis, I give and bequeath to my Nephew, Churchill Caldom, my manner Plantation where I now live on, to him and his heirs forever. My Dearly beloved wife, Martha Reading, shall enjoy ye sd Plantation and the profits thereof During her widdowhood.

Item, I give and bequeath to my nephew, John Blount, my Plantation at Swifts Creek, to him and his heirs forever.

Item, I give and bequeath to my nephew, Jacob Blount, the land a took up at Catachney, to him and his heirs forever.

Item, I give and bequeath to Martha Reading, my dearly beloved wife, the land att Cathney, her Father, Robert West gave me, to her and her heirs forever.

Item, I give and bequeath to my nephew, Churchill Caldom, my land att Hickrey Neck, and all my back land Joining upon it, to him and his heirs forever. My Dearly beloved wife, Martha Reading shall have ye Use of ye light wood belonging to the sd. land During her widdowhood.

Item, I give and bequeath to Martha Reading, my Dearly beloved wife, five Negroes named, Jeek, Quamiers, Boston Tom, Dinah and Maud, with all my hushold Stuff, and all my Sheep, and all my Cart horses, and all my Cattle, excepting 8 winter Cows and Calfs to my Nephew, John Blount, to her and her heirs forever. I desire that my Brother, Thomas Reading, shall live with my Dearly Beloved wife, martha Reading, and care may be Taking of him.

Item, I give and bequeath to my Dearly beloved Wife, Martha Reading, three Negroes Named, George, Joan, and Rose, to her and her heirs forever. (carried over)

Item, I give and bequeath Unto my Brother in law, John Caldom, my old white mare and Colt, to him and his heirs forever.

Item, I give and bequeath to my Nephew, Jacob Blount, one young Mare of a black Colour, To him and his heirs forever.

Item, I likewise Constitute and ordain ye persons hereafter named, to be my Sole Executors, Named: Coll. Robert West, my Dearly beloved Wife, martha Reading, Mr. Thomas worsley, Gent., and John Caldom, of this my last will and Testament, and I do hereby utterly disaloaw, Revoke and Disanul all and every other former Testaments, Wills, Legacies and bequests, and Executors, by me in any ways before Named, willed and bequeathed, Ratifying and Confirming this and no other to be my last will and Testament.

In witness whereof, I have hereunto Set my hand and Seal, the Day and Year above written.

CHU'L READING, (Seal)

Signed, Sealed, Published, Pronounced and Declared by the said Churchill Reading, as his last will and Testament, in the Presence of us the Subscribers:
EDW'D TRAVIS.
HARMAN HILL.
EDWARD SALTER.

NO. CAROLINA.

Before His Excelly. Gabriel Johnston, Esqr., His Majestys Governor in Chief, and Ordinary of the said Province:

Personally appeared Harman Hill, one of the Witnesses to the Annexed last Will and Testament of Churchill Reading, who being duely Sworn, Sayeth That he was present and Saw the said Church'l Reading, Sign, Seal, Publish and Declare the Same to be his last Will and Testament, and that he was then of Sound & Disposing Mind and Memory to the best of his knowledge.

And that he saw Edward Travis present & and sign his name as witness to the said last Will & Testament; and likewise that he belives the words, Edward Salter, being the Name of the third Subscribing Witness to be the handwriting of Edward Salter, late of Bath, Deceased.

Given at Edenton, Under my hand the 14th Day of February Anno Dom., 1734. GAB. JOHNSTON.

Likewise appeared John Caldom, one of the Executors of the Annexed Last Will and Testament and took the Oath of Executor as required by Law.

Given at Edenton, under my hand the 14th. Day of February Anno Dom., 1734.
GAB. JOHNSTON.

Copied from the Original Will, filed in the Office of the Secretary of State.

LIONEL READING'S WILL.

No. CAROLINA, BATH COUNTY. Sc.

IN THE NAME OF GOD AMEN, The Twelfth day of July, 1708, I, Lionel Reading, of this County, Esq., being of perfect mind, menory and health, Thanks be given to God, Therefore Calling unto mind the mortality of my body and Knowing that it is appointed for all men once to die, Doe make & ordain this my Last Will & Testament, That is to Say, Principally, and First of all, I give and Recommend my Soul into ye hands of God that gave it & my body I Recommend to the Earth, to be buried in a decent Christian Buriall, at the discretion of my Executors, nothing doubting but at the Generall Resurrection I Shall Receive the Same again by the mighty power of God: And as touchin Such Worldly Estate wherewith it hath pleased God to bless me in this life, I Give, Demise & dispose of the same in the following Manner & Form:

Imprimis, I Give & bequeath unto mary, dearly beloved Wife, One Negro Woman called Joan, the same to enjoy & possess during her naturall Life; and after her decease, the Said Negro woman, with her Increase, to be disposed on to any of the Children born of her Body, as my Dear wife shall think fitt to bequeath the Same thereto. Likewise, I give her one Bed w'h its Furniture; with one third part of the pewter potts and Brass ware that I shall be possessed withall at my Death; and Four Cows & Calves; & also, all the male Cattle wth what hogs and Sheep shall be found on & belonging to ye Plantation I now live on, to be Injoyed during her natural Life, & after her decease to be disposed on to the Child or children of mine, born of her body, as she thinks fitt; & also, three horses; & also, ye Plantation I now live on to Injoy ye Same during her natural life.

Item, I give & bequeath to my well beloved Son, Nathaniel Reading, the Said Plantation after his mother's decease, to him & his heirs for Ever, Provided he returns back from England & personally Enjoy ye Same, But if he should not return from England, to Live on & enjoy ye Same, That then, my Son, Churchill Inherit & possess, to whom I Give and bequeath it, to him & his heirs forever, provided his brother Nathaniell Return not to Claim & Injoy the Same; & Likewise, to my Son

Nathaniell, I Give one Negro Man called George, to him and his heirs for ever, provided he returns (as aforesd.) to Injoy the Same; and one Feather bed with Furniture, with a hand Mill, w'th four Young Cows and Calves, the Said Cattle, Negro and Houshold Stuff, to be delivered to him when he shall arrive at the age of fifteen years, with their Increase, male and Female, to him & his Heirs; and the Same not to be paid out of his own Cattle w'ch are of a different mark from mine, as by Record appears.

Item, I give & bequeath to my Daughter, Sarah, thirty pound, money of this Province, to be paid at my decease; & one Cow & Calf, I bequeath to her first born Child; & ye youngest of my horses now running in the Woods, I bequeath to her husband, David Dupuis.

Item, I Give and bequeath to my daughter Mary, my Negro Man called Jeffery, w'th one Bed & Furniture, one Iron pott, w'th five pound, current money; with four Cows & Calves, ye said Legacy to be delivered her att ye Age of fiveteen Years or att ye day of her marriage with her Mothers Consent.

Item, I Give to my daughter, Ann, one Negro woman called Diana, w'th one bed & Furniture, one Iron pott, w'th Five pound current money; & four Cows & Calves, to be Delivered att the age of fifteen years, or at ye day of her marriage; w'th her Mothers Consent.

Item, I Give & bequeath to my son, Thomas, one Negro Boy called Tom, with a Bed and Furniture; w'th four Cows & Calves, to be paid him att ye age of fifteen years.

Item, I Give and bequeath to my Son, Churchill, one Negro Girl, called Han, w'th one bed and Furniture; & also Four Cows & Calves, the Same to be paid him at the age of fifteen years.

Item, my Will & Intent thereof, is so, That if it should please God that any of my Children should die unmarried & under ye Age, that ye Same part & Legacies to them bequeath'd, Shall be Equally divided & Given to those of my Children yt shall be alive, & likewise wt Estate & Effects to me belonging, not herein mentioned, after my lawfull debts are paid & discharged, I leave to my wife's Disposall & that att her death, to give & leave to any one or more of our Children she shall best approve of.

And hereby, I Constitute & ordain my Dear Wife & Mr. Davis Dupuis, & Mr. Humphry Legg, my Executors of this my last Will & Testament; and I do hereby utterly disallow, disannul & Revoke all & every other Former Will or Testament, Legacies & bequests, or Executors by me made or named, Ratifying & Confirming this my Last Will & Testament.

In witness whereof, I have hereunto Sett my hand and Seal, the day and year above written.

          LIONEL READING. (Seal)

Signed, Sealed, Published, Pronounced & Declared by the Said Lionell Reading, as his last Will & Testament in the presence of us: the Subscribers:
  JAMES LEIGH,
  HENRY BROOK.
  JNO. LAWSON.

(Negro and Houshold Stuff, the Said Legacy, David Dupuis, these Words Interlined before Signed & Sealed.)

SR. RICHARD EVERARD, Barrt., Gov.

These may certify that the within Will was proved upon Oath in due form by the Oath of James Leigh, Esq., one of the Evidences.
Given under my hand, this 18th. Day of Febry., 1725.

            RICHD. EVERARD.

Letters granted with the Will annexed, to Grace Reading, the Widow, the Exors, refusing to Act.

Copied from Original Will, filed in the Office of the Secretary of State.

JOHN REDDING'S WILL.

IN THE NAME OF GOD, AMEN, the Twentyeth Eight day of January, 1754. I John Redding, of Perquimons County, being very Sick and weak in body but of perfect mind and memory, Thanks be given unto God; Therefore Calling unto mind the mortality of my body, and knowing that it is appointed for all men once to Dye, do make and ordain this my Last Will and Testament, that is to Say, Principally, and first of all, I Give and Recommend my Soul into the hands of God that gave it; and my body to be buried in a decent Christian burial at the Discretion of my Executors, nothing doubting but at the general Resurrection I shall Receive again by the Mighty Power of God; and as touching Such Worldly goods and Estate wherewith it hath Pleased God to bless me in this Life, I give, demise and Dispose of the Same in following Manner and Form:

Imprimis, I give and bequeath to Elizabeth Fullenton, my Dearly beloved and Intended Wife, my Plantation and Land next to Jesse Eason's to the Deviding, Together with my horse, bridle and Sadle, & three Cows and Calfs, to her and her heirs for ever.

Item, I Give and bequeath unto my three Sisters all my

Other Lands, Together with all my others Goods and Estate, to be Equaly Devided between them three. and their Heirs for ever.

Item, I Give and bequeath unto my Cousin, John Ellis, one Mare Colt, to him and his heirs for ever.

Lastly, I Nominate and appoint my to Brothers in Law, John Davis, & Joshua Small to be my Executors to this my Last Will and Testament, and do hereby Revoke, Dissanull and make void all other former Wills by me heretofore made, and this Only to be my Last Will and Testament.

In Witness whereof, I have hereunto Set my Hand and fixed my Seal the Day and year above Written;

JOHN REDDING. (Seal)

Signed, Sealed, Published, Pronounced, & Declared by the said John Redding as his last Will and Testament, in the Presence of us the Subscribers,
JESSE EASON,
JOSEPH SKETO.
JOHN HARRIS.

PERQUIMANS COUNTY. ss. April Court, Anno Domini, 1754.
Present his Maiesteies.

These may Certify that the within will was Duly prov'd by the Oath of Jesse Eason, one of the Evidences thereto and at the Same time appeared Joshua Small, Executor, and was duly qualified by taking the Oath by Law appointed. Ordered that the Secutary of Sd. Province have Notice that Letters Testamentory Issue thereon as the Law Directs.

Test. WILLM SKINNER Clr. Cur.

Copied from the Original Will, filed in the Office of the Secretary of State.

JOSEPH RIDDICK'S WILL.

NORTH CAROLINA. Ss.

IN THE NAME OF GOD AMEN. I, Joseph Riddick, of the County of Perquimons, In the Province of North Carolina, planter, being at this time In a weak and Low Condition, but of Sound mind and memory, blessed be the Almighty God for the Same, but Duly Considering the Incertain State of this mortal Life, and being Desirous of Setling and Disposing this, my temporal Estate, which it hath pleased God to bless me with, I hereby make and Declare this present Writing to be my Last will and testament which is In manner following:

Imprimis, I will, order and apoint, that ll my funeral Charges and Expences, together with my Just Debts be truly paid and Satisfied by my Executors hereafter Named, and that the Same be Deducted out of my Estate which I shall Leave behind me at my Decease.

Item, I Leave to my Loving wife, Hanah Riddick, the use of my whom plantation, During her life, with the use and work of two Negros, Named will and Luce, and also, my Riding horse, bridle and Sadle.

Item, I Give, Devise and bequeath unto my Son, Joseph Riddick, the Same plantation, with all the Lands aJoyning to it, which I bought of Thomas Ward, to him and his heirs for ever, and it is my will and Desire that my Wife, hanah Riddick, Do not Debar my Son, Joseph Riddick, from Selling and living on Some part of the plantation and land when he Comes of Lawfull age, without any hinderance or molestation of his mother.

Item, I Give, Devise and bequeath unto my Son, Kadak Riddick, all the tract of land and plantation Which I bought of William Rountree, and moses fields and James Price, to him and his heirs for Ever; and also, I give and bequeath unto my Son, Kadak Riddick, my plantation and all the Lands which I bought of William moor and William Wilson, that Lyes In Balahack, to him and his heirs for Ever.

Item, I Give, Devise and bequeath unto my son, Isaac Riddick, all the tracts of Lands and plantation Which I bought of John Barclif and George Shell, that Lyes over little River upon deep Creek, to him and his heirs for Ever; and also, the Sum of twenty pounds, Virginia money, and all the Stock of Cattle that belongs to the plantation, to him and his heirs for Ever.

Item, I Give, devise and bequeath unto my Daughter, mary Riddick, the Sum of twenty pounds, virginia money, to her and her heirs for Ever.

and It is my Will and Desire that all the Rest or Residue of my Estate, of what Nature or kind Soever, Shall be Equelly Devided amongst my Wife and Children, Viz: Kadak Riddick, and Joseph Riddick, and Isaac Riddick, and Mary Riddick, to them and their heirs for Ever; and If In Case Either of my afore Named Children Should Dye without Isue, it is my will and Desire that all their part or Share of my Estate, then be Equelly Devided amongst the Survivers, to them and their heirs for Ever, and it is my will and Desire that the same two Negros, Named Will and Luce, which I have Left my wife, Hanah Riddick, the use of, after her Death, them and their Increase to be Equelly Devided amongst my four Children, or the Survivors of them, to them and their heirs for Ever.

and Lastly, I Do hereby Nominate, make and apoint my Loving Wife, Hanah Riddick, and my Son, Kadak Riddick, and my Brother, Robert Riddick, my Sole Executrix and Executers of this my Last will and testament, Desiring them to Se the Same fully Executed and performed.

In witness Whereof, I the said Joseph Riddick the testator

have hereunto Sett my hand and Seal, this twentyeth Day of September, In the year of our Lord God, one thousand, Seven hundred and fifty Nine.

JOSEPH RIDDICK (Seal)

Signed and Sealed, Published and Declared to be the Last Will and Testament of the Testator In the Presents of Us:
  JOSEPH PERRY, Jurt.
  BENJAMIN PERRY, Jurt.
  JOB RIDDICK.

PERQMS COUNTY.   October Court, Ann Dom., 1759.
  Present His Majestys Justices.

This that Joseph Perry & Benj, Perry, two of the subscribing Evidences to the within will, appd. in Court and made Oath on the holy Evangelist that they were present & saw Joseph Riddick sign, seale, publish & declare the within to be and contain his Last will and Testament, & that the Joseph Riddick was then & at that time, of Sound & Disposing Memory, then allso appd. Hannah Riddick, as Ex^{ix}. in Court and took the Exor's. Oath in Due form of Law. Ordered that the Hon^l. Rich^d. Spaight, Esqr., Secty. of this Province, have Notice thereof thet Lerr^s Testamenty Issue thereon as the Law Directs, &c.
       Test. MILES HARVEY, Clk: Cr.

Copied from Original Will, filed in the Office of the Secretary of State.

PETER RIEUSSETT'S WILL.

NO. CAROLINA. SST.

IN THE NAME OF GOD AMEN. I, petter Rieussett, of Bath County, In ye provence of Afforsd., being of Scund and perfict Memory, praised be God for the Same, do Make, ordaine this My Last will and testament, In Manner and form following: that is to Say, first and principally, I Commend my Soule to the hand of Almighty God that Gave it, Hoping through the Merrits, Death and passion of My Saviour Jesus Christ have pardon and forgiveness of all My Sins and to Inhearit Everlasting Life; and My Bodey I Commit to the Earth to be Buried att the Discretion of My Executors Hereafter Named; and as tutching the Disposition of all such temporall Estate as it hatt pleased God to Bestow upon Me, I Give and Bequaith In Manner and forme as followeth:
 Imprimis, I Will that all My Just Debts and funerall Charges be first payed And Discharged.
 Itm. I Give and Bequaith unto My Loveing Nice, Ann Galaber, forty pound, Current bills of this province.
 Itm. I Give and Bequaith Unto my Loving Nice, Jean Caila, fifty pound, Current bills of this province.

Itm. I Give and bequaith unto My Loving Nephew, Peter Randown, fortey pound, Current bill of this province.

Itm. I Give and Bequaith unto My Loving Nice, Mary Covee, fortey pounds, Current bills of this province.

Itm. I Give unto the Church att Bath Town, ten pounds, Current bills of this province.

Itm. I Give unto the branch Church in petters Street, In Dublin, five pound Starling, Now in the Hands of Mr. William Espinah, In Dublin.

Itm. I Give and Bequaith unto My Naturell Son, John Bell, In Dublin, one Hundred pound, starling, Now in the hands of William Espinah, and to be Disposed of by my Dearly Beloved Brother, Jno. Rieussett, att His Discretion, for the Best use of my afforsd. Son, Jno. Bell, when He arrives att ye Age of Twenty one years.

Itm. I Give and Bequeath all the Rest and Residue of My Estate both in ye kingdom of Ierland and In ye provence of North Carolina, In Americka, to my Loveing Brother, John Riusett.

I do hereby Constitut and appoint my trusty and well Beloved friend, Thomas Hanes and Vinson Hurrard? my Execttr. of all My Estate in the kingdom of Ierland. I Liekewise Constitut and and appoint my trustey and well Beloved frends, Edward Salter and Oliver Blackburn, My Exetrs. of all My Estate In the province of North Carolina. I do Hereby Revock, Disanull and Make Voide all wills and testaments Heretofore by Me Made.

In Witness whereof, I the sd. petter Riussett, to this my Last will and testament, have hereunto sett my hand and Seal this forthtenth Day of Januarey, In the yeare of our Loard God, one thousand, Seven Hundred and thirty foure, 1734.

         his
      PETTER X RIEUSSETT. (Seal)
         marke.

Signed, Sealed, and Delivered
In presence of uss:
  OLIVER BLACKBURN.
  PETER RANDON.
  MATHIAS COLLIER.

No. CAROLINA.

Before his Excelly. Gabriel Johnston, Esq., His Majestys Governor in Chief of the said Province, and Ordinary of the Same:

Personally appeared Peter Randon and Mathias Collier, Two of the Witnesses to the within last Will and Testament of Peter Rieusett, late of Bath Town, Deceased, who being duely Sworn, Say, That they were present and Saw the Said Peter Rieusett, Sign, Seal, Publish and Declare the same to be his last Will & Testament, and that he was then of sound and disposing Mind and Memory to the best of their knowledge.

And that they saw Oliver Blackburn, the third Subscribing Witness present and Sign his Name as Witness thereunto.

Likewise appeared Oliver Blackburn appointed Executor to the said Last Will and Testament and took the usual Oath of Executor as required by Law.

Given at Edenton, under my hand, the 21st. Day of February, Anno Dom., 1734.

GAB. JOHNSTON.

Copied from the Original Will, filed in the Office of the Secretary of State.

SUSANNA ROBISSON' WILL.

IN THE NAME OF GOD AMEN. Ap. d ye 30th: one Thousand, Seven Hundred & nine, I, Susanna Robisson, being Sick & weak but of Sound & perfect memory, Thanks to God for it, do make This my last will & Testament, In manner & Forme Following; First I Give & bequeath my Soul to Allmighty God my maker & Redeemer, Assuredly beleiving in ye Resurrection of ye dead: & my Body to be buried att ye discretion of my Executor hereafter nam'd.

Imp'. I Give & bequeath To my well beloved Daughter, Elizabeth Bond, one Feather Bed & Covering now in her possession; like unto my well beloved Son, Luke Grace, one Shilling, & for ye rest of my Estate, both real & Personal, after my just debts are paid; be ye same of what nature Or Quality soever, I Give & Bequeath to my well beloved Son, Henery Grace, to him & his heirs, Executors or assignes for ever;

Likewise do Constitute & Ordaine my well beloved, Son Henery Grace, to be my Whole & Sole Executor of this my last will & Testament, utterly Revokeing disanulling & makeing Voide all other wills & Testamts. By me heretofore made.

in Wittness whereof, I have hereunto Sett my hand & Seal ye day & ye year above written.

SUSANNA X ROBISSON.

Signed, Seald & Deliverd In ye Presence of.
EURIAR HUDSON.
ELIZABETH X JENKINS.
JOSEPH JESSUP.

Recorded in Will Book 2, page 13.

JAMES ROBERTSON'S WILL.

IN THE NAME OF GOD AMEN. I, James Robertson, of the County of Pasquotank, in the Province of North Carolina, being of sound and perfect Memory, Do make this to be and Contain my last will and Testament, in manner and form following; that is to saw:

I Give and bequeath to my well beloved son, Mordecai, my manner plantation whereon I now live, containing fifty Acres, More or less, to him and to his heirs forever.

I likewise give and bequeath to my beloved son, Malachi, my Road Plantation, Containing fifty Acres, to him and to his heirs for Ever.

I also give to my son Mordecai, one Ram and one Ewe, two Sows, two Cows, and one beehive, to him and to his heirs forever.

I likewise give to my son, Malachi, two Sows, one Ewe and Ram, two beehives, and one Cow and Heiffer, to him and his heirs forever.

I Give to my Daughter, Euphan, one Feather bed and furniture, three pewter Basons, and one Dish, one Sow, and one Cow, to her and her heirs forever.

I Give to my Daughter, Salley, three Basons, and one pewter dish, one Fethar Bed and Furniture, one Sow, and one Cow, to her and her heirs for ever. I also give to Each of my Daughters one Chest.

I also give all the rest of Moveable Estate to my Dear and Well beloved Wife, Sarah Robertson, and to her Disposal, whom I Nominate my Executrix, and my Trusty friend, Thomas Taylor, Executor to this my last will and Testament, hereby revoaking all other wills heretofore made,

JAMS. ROBERTSON (Seal)

Signd, Seald and Declared, this to be my last will and Testament. the 17th. day of January, Annoq Dom. 1753, in the presents of:

SAMUEL OKELY,
WILLIAM WOODLY.
MARY TAYLOR

NORTH CAROLINA,
PASQUOTANK COUNTY. ss.   October Court, Annoq Dom., 1754.
Present His Majestys Justices:

These may Certifie that that William Woodley, one of the Evidences to the Within Will, appeared in open Court, & made Oath, on the Holy Evangelist, that he was present & Saw James Robertson Sign, Seal, publish and declare the within to be and Contain his Last Will & Testament; and that he was at that time of sound and Disposeing memory; that he also Saw the other Evidences Sign their Names thereto att the same time: then appeared Sarah Robertson, Executrix, and was duly Qualified as Such; ordered that the Honorable James Murray, Esqr., Secretary, have Notice that Letters issue, &c., dated at the Clerks office, the 22d. Day of January, 1754.   Test. THO. TAYLOR, ck. Cu.

Copied from Original Will, filed in the Office of the Secretary of State.

MATTHEW ROWAN'S WILL.

IN THE NAME OF GOD AMEN, I, Matthew Rowan, of New Hanover County, Esqr., in ye Province of North Carolina, being of Sound and disposing mind, Memory & Understanding, do make and Ordain this to be my last Will and Testament in manner following:

Imprimis, I bequeath my Soul to God who gave it; & my body to be decently Interred; & all my just debts and funeral Expence to be first paid.

Item, I give to my Niece, Rose Rowan, daughter of my Brother Andrew Rowan, ye Sum of One hundred and thirty three pounds six Shillings & Eight pence, proclamation, to be paid one year after my decease.

Also, I give to Mathew Rowan, son of my Brother, Atcheyson Rowan, the sum of One hundred & thirty three Pounds, six shillings & eight Pence, proclamation Money, to be paid two years after my decease.

Also, I give to my Niece, Ann Rowan, daughter of my Brother, William Rowan, ye Sum of four hundred pounds, Proclamation Money, to be paid three years after my decease.

Also, I give to Richard Lyon, Esqr., of Spring hill, in the County of Bladen, ye sum of three hundred and thirty pounds, proclamation money, being the remainder of ye Sum I intended to give him with my Niece, Margaret Rowan.

Also, I give ye Negroe Boys named Dickey, Sam, Johney, Hecton and Africa, together with ye Negroe Wenches, named Black Milley, Lucinda, Bella, Maria, Bess, with their Increase, to Mildred Lyon, Daughter of John Lyon, & Mildred Lyon; but in Case ye said Mildred Lyon, should dye before she is married or of Age, then I Give said Slaves to her Sister, Mary Lyon.

Also, I Give & Devise all that tract of Land Situate on ye North East Side of Ye No. East River, Opposite to Stag Park, in New Hanover County, containing five hundred acres, unto Frederick Gregg, of Wilmington, Esqr., to him & his Heirs. I also give unto ye said Frederick Gregg, my Negroe Fellow Ogee & little peg & My Gold Watch. Also, I give & bequeath all those two tracts of Land, ye one Containing five hundred acres, ye other four hundred acres, situate on ye White Marsh, in Bladen County, being land in the possession of Robert Rowan, upon part of which ye said Robert Rowan now lives, & ye following Negroes, Jack, Sanca, Africa, Boatswain, John Lindsey, & Joan a Negroe Wench, unto ye sd. Frederick Gregg, & Richard Lyon, in trust for Esther Rowan, wife of said Robert Rowan, and ye Heirs of her Body Lawfully begotten, to ye Sole use and benefit of ye said Esther Rowan, free from ye power & Controul of her husband, Robert Rowan, nor in any wise subject to his Debts, my meaning in this devise being no more than to vest ye said two tracts of land & Negroes last mentioned in ye sd. Frederick Gregg & Richard Lyon as Trustees for ye use of ye sd. Esther Rowan, so as to bar any rights to ye sd. lands & Negroes last mentioned which ye said Robert Rowan might Claim as Husband to ye sd. Esther Rowan.

Also, I Give ye Sum of twenty six Pounds, thirteen shillings, and four pence, proclamation money, a year, to be paid Annualy out of my Estate not heretofore disposed of, unto ye said Frederick Gregg & Richard Lyon, in Trust for my Daughter in Law, Elizabeth Maclaine, Wife of Archibald Maclaine, of Wilmington, Mercht. to be paid annually to ye said Elizabeth Maclaine, to her sole use, free from ye powre of her husband, Archibald Maclaine, nor in any wise Sibject to his debts.

Also, I Give and devise all my three parcels of land ye. one being on ye South West Side of ye. N. West River, Situate on ye. lower side of land belonging to Henry Simmonds, deceased, Containing 320 acres; ye other on ye No East Side of sd. River, Situate as aforesaid Containing 640 Acres; ye third on ye No East Side of sd. River Joyning ye above, 297 Acres, all in Bladen County, and all that tract on ye No. East Side of ye No. West River, lying betwixt Judge Lenards Land, & Nelltown in Bladen County, aforesaid being 640 Acres; & all that Parcill of Land part of ye Marsh on ye River trent, Opposit to Newbern, in Craven County, containing 197 acres unto my Executors hereafter Mentioned, to sell and dispose of in ye best maner they can, & to apply ye money arising by such Seale in discharge of ye Legacies heretofore given. and lastly, I give & devise all my Estate of what kind soever, both real & personal, not heretofore disposed of after my Death, to John, ye Son of Jane Stubbs, of Bath town, in ye Province aforesaid, & Commonly Called & known by the Name of John Rowan, now of ye Island of Barbadoes, Mariner, & ye Heirs of his body lawfully begotten; and in default of such Issue, then to ye said mentioned Mathew Rowan, son of my brother Atcheyson Rowan, & his Heirs and Assigns. And I do make John Rowan, Frederick Gregg, & Richard Lyon, Executors of this my last will, hereby revoking all former Wills by me heretofore made.

In Witness whereof, I have hereunto set my hand and Seale this 18th Day of April, in ye year of our lord, 1760.

MATT. ROWAN. (seal)

Signed, Sealed Published and declared in ye Presence of us, whose Names is hereunto affixed,

SAM^L. WATTERS.
GEO: GIBBS.
THOS: CLARK.

Personally Came before me Thomas Clark, one of the Subscribing Witness to the above Will, who being duly sworn, deposed that he saw the above Testator, Mathew Row in, Esqr., Subscribe Seal & Publish the above will as his, as also that he saw this in presence of the other Witnesses Saml Watters & George Gibs & farther says to the best of his knowledge the said Testator was perfectly in his Senses. Wilmington, 15 July, 1760.

Given under my hand, Ordered therefore that Letters Testamentary may issue.   ARTHUR DOBBS.

No. CAROLINA NEW HANOVER COUNTY.

These are to Certify that Frederick Gregg and Richard Lyon, Esqrs.. Qualified as Executors to the Last Will and Testament of The Hon'ble Matthew Rowan, Esqr., Deceased, according to Law, before me.

Given under my hand this 19 day of July, 1760.

CORNS. HARNETT, J. P.

Copied from Original Will, filed in the Office of the Secretary of State

THOMAS RYAN'S WILL.

IN THE NAME OF GOD AMEN. I, Thomas Ryan, of the county of Bertie, in the Province of North Carolina, being of a very sick & infirm Body, but of sound & Good Memory. & Calling to rememberrance the uncertainty of Human Life, doe constitute, make & appoint this my Last will & Testament, in manner & form following: First & Principally, I Commend my Soul to God who gave it, in certain hopes of the Resurrection of the Dead; & my Body to the Ground to be decently inter'd & buried at the discretation of my Executors hereafter mention'd. Touching my Worldly Estate, I give, dispose & bequeath of That as follows:

Imprimis, I give, & bequeath unto my Son, David Ryan, two hundred acres of Land, more or less, lying in the Bottom of Cashy Neck, on the thorough-fare, commonly known by the name of The Old House; also four hundred & fifty Acres, being one half of the Land That John Holdbrook liv'd on; also six hundred & forty acres of Land, more or less, lying upon the great Beaver dam; Also four hundred & fifty Acres of Land, more or less, lying upon Cypress Swamp, which Land I sold to William Lane, conditionally, and if the said Lane pays the purchase Money, which is Twenty five pounds, current money of Virginia, which money I give & bequeath to my Son, David aforesd. as a compensation or in Lieu of the said Land sold to the said Lane. But if the said Land makes default of Payment, That then if recover'd by Law, I give the afor'sd. Land to my Son, David, afores'd. Also, I give unto my son, David, foor Negroes, to-wit: Casar, Phoebe & Peter, Taffay. Also, one Bridle & Saddle, & my Shooe & Knee (Buckles) Buckles; & my Will & Desire is That the afors'd Legacies, as well Real as Personal, Which I have here Bequeath'd to my son, David, Be to Him, his Heirs & Assigns for ever.

Item, I give & bequeath unto my Son, James Ryan, three hundred & fifty Acres of Land, or there-abouts, upon Mysattick River in Tyrrell County. Now This Land is conditionally sold to Matthew Thomas, late of Edenton, Merchant, who is to pay the purchase money, to-wit: one hundred & seven pounds, ten Shillings, Current money of Virginia, payable on the Eleventh day of November in the present Year of our Lord, one thousand, seven hundred & Fifty Three. If the said Matthew pay the money due, at the time afor'sd, then my will & Desire is that the said money be put to Interest upon Good Security; The Bond or Bonds which shall be gave as Security or Securities of the said money to be renewed every Year. But in Case the said Matthew should make Default of Payment, it is then my Will & Desire that the said land be in the Possession of my Son, James, aforesd. And Either the said Land, or the said Money (if paid), with the Interest thereof, I give unto my son, James Aforesd., his Heirs & Assigns forever.

Also, I give unto my Son, James aforesd., five hundred & fifty Acres of Land, the Remainder part of Holdbrooks Land & where the said Holdbrook dwelt. Also, four hundred & forty acres of Land lying in Cashy Neck, formerly the Estate of James Castello. Also, one hundred & thirty Acres of Land joyning the Land of Thomas Sutton, deceased. Also, I give unto my Son, James afores'd, Three Negroes, towit: London, Jacob & Ned; Also, a Bay horse which now runs in the woods. All the Legacies aforesaid which I have(here) here bequeathed unto my Son, James aforesd., My Will & Desire is that they Be to Him, his Heirs & Assigns for ever.

Item, I give & bequeath unto my Son, George Ryan, my my Plantation Containing five hundred Acres, lying in Roeguis, formerly known by the name of James Castello's Islands. Also, I give & bequeath unto my Son, George afores'd, my Plantation on the Head of Salmon Creek, together with my water Mill; & also two Plantations lying up Chowan, formerly belonging to John Rogers & John Graves; Also, one hundred Acres of Land lying upon Cashy River, where Garrett Vanupshall now lives, together with three Negroes, to wit: Tom, Jack & Rose. Also, two Mares, the one a Bay, the other a grey Mare. All which Legacies, I have here bequeath'd unto my Son, George aforsd., my Will & Desire is that they, as well Real as Personal, Be to him, his Heirs & Assigns forever.

Item, I give & bequeath unto my Son in Law, Cornelius Campbell, & his wife, my Daughter Elizabeth, my Plantation containing two hundred & twenty five Acres, lying in Tyrrell

County, & upon Albemarle Sound; also, two Plantations in Bertie County, formerly belonging to Thomas Mewbern & William Goodwin. Also, the plantation in Bertie aforesd. whereon John Nicholls now dwells. Now the said Nicholls has made a purchase of this Land & paid some part of the purchase money, but the whole being not paid within the time limited by Agreement, the said John Nicholls has forfieted his Title to the said Land; my Will therefore is that if my son, Cornelius & his Wife, Elizabeth, please, they may either receive the Remainder of the money due from the said Nicholls, as an equivalent for the said Land, or enter upon the said Land, on the surrender of the said Nicholls; Also, two hundred acres of Land lying upon upon the Southside of the Middle Swamp; also, two Negroes, towit: Jenny & Lucy. The Legacies aforesd. which I have here bequeath'd to my Son, Cornelius & his Wife, Eliaabeth, as well Real as Personal, my Will & Intention is that, That they be to them & their Heirs for ever. But with this restriction to the Heirs only of my son, Cornelius begotten of the Body of my Daughter Elizabeth.

Item, I give & bequeath unto my Daughter, Mary Ryan, two Plantations lying on Chowan River, containing five hundred Acres; Also, two Plantations lying on Black Wallnut Swamp, containing four hundred & Eighty Acres; Also, two Negroes, to wit: great Jane & Esther; Also, fifty pounds current money of Virginia, to be paid unto my Daughter, Mary Afores'd, from out of the outstanding debts due to me; Also one Bay horse. All which Legacies, as well Real as Personal, which I have here bequeath'd unto my Daughter, Mary afors'd, My will & Intention is, That they be to her & her Heirs for ever.

Item, I give unto my Loving Wife, Martha Ryan, the Use & Occupation of my Manor Plantation, together with the dwelling house, Utensils, Stock, Smith's Tools & other appurtenances whatsoever, to the said Plantation & House belonging, during her natural Life, together with the profits arising from the Servitude & labour of these three Negroes, to wit: Ben, Bess & Moll, likewise of the indented Servants. Also, I give & bequeath unto my said Wife, my Riding horse Pompey & her own Riding Horse, Ruffin, as also my watch & Sleeve Buttons. Also, One hundred Pounds, Current money of Virginia, which will be due to me from John Hardisson, on the Nineteenth day of December, in the present Year of our Lord, One thousand, seven hundred & fifty three. And my Will is, that the aforesaid horses, watch, money & sleeve Buttons, Be at her own absolute power & disposal. And my farther Will & Desire is, That after the decease of my said Wife, That the Manor house & Plantation aforesaid, shall devolve to my Son, Thomas Ryan, Together with the aforemention'd

Negroes, Benn, Bess & Moll, & their increase, & I doe declare, Will & Desire that the aforesaid Legacies, both Real & Personal, are for, & shall Be, to my Son, Thomas aforesaid, his Heirs & Assigns for ever.

Also, I give unto my son, Thomas aforesaid, One hundred Acres of Land, joyning to David Thompson's & Edward Bird's line upon Cashoak Swamp, & my will, Intention is that these last Legacies also, together with the abovementioned, be to my Son, Thomas aforesaid, his Heirs & Assigns for ever; and I also give to my sd. son, Thomas, & his heirs or assigns forever, four hundred Acres of Land joining to the manor Plantation & known by the name of Jacob Hardy's Old field.

Item, I give a bequeath unto my Worthy Friend, Capt. John Campbell, ten Spanish Pistoles, or their value in Current money of Virginia.

I likewise hereby authorise & impower my Executors, to make Titles unto all Those Purchasers of the Land which I have sold, upon Such Purchasers paying in of the Respective moneys due for the Purchase of such Land. Provided the Legatees of those Lands shall be contented with such payment for & as an Equivalent for their Several & Respective Lands.

My will & Intention farther is, That the Mill which I have bequeath'd unto my Son, George aforesaid, be repair'd & kept in constant repair from out of the profits of my whole Estate, Each Child or Legatee contributing thereto his or her equal Share in proportion, till the said George shall arrive to the age of twenty one Years, And in Consideration thereof each of my Children shall be entitled to the benefit of having their Corn and the like, ground therein free of all toll or expence whatsoever.

Touching the Education of my Children, my Will & Desire is that each of my three younger Sons, to wit: James, George, & Thomas, shall be paid for from out of the Outstanding Debts, But if the Outstanding Debts fall short & are insufficient to discharge my Own Debts & Legacies, that then my whole Estate shall equally contribute towards such their Education. My Will & Desire is That my Wife, Martha Ryan, have the Care & Guardianship of my Children who are not of full Age, untill they shall respectively arrive to the age of twenty one years, But if in the mean time, my Wife should intermarry, then upon such her marriage, my will & Intention is That she shall not any longer continue Guardian, But shall justly account for the profits of, as well also as for the separate Estate, of each Child with & To my Son, David, Their Eldest Brother, who I desire may then have the care, Guardianship & Tuition of his Brothers Aforesaid, and their Estates.

My Will & desire farther is, That the Brig be sold & that the money arising from such Sale, be appropriated to the payment of my just Debts, & That immediately after the Sale, my Executors pay unto Thomas Castello, the sum of one hundred twenty five pounds, current money of Virginia, Exempt from all manner of Deduction or abatement, And after the said Castellow be paid, my will & Intention is That the Residuum or Remainder of that & the Outstanding debts be equally divided betwixt my Wife & Children, share & share alike.

My Will & Intention is, that if any of my Children dye before he or She before such child be of full Age, or Dye without Issue, that the rest of his or her brothers, surviving Shall be entitled to an equal Share of Such Decedents Estate.

My Farther Will & Intention is, That those Negroes, (whose Servitude during the Nat'ral life of their Mistress, Isabella Dyal, I bought of John Holdbrook, to whom such servitude was before made over by Edward Dyal, during the Nat'ral Life of his Wife, Isabella aforesaid), be equally divided betwixt my wife & Children share & alike.

I Likewise Desire & injoyn my Executors to offer no other money than Gold or Silver to any of my Creditors in discharge of my Respective Debts, unless any Creditor should particularly prefer the Proclamation Money, or Commodities of the Country, in lieu of his respective Debt.

And I doe hereby appoint my Loving Wife, Martha Ryan, & my Son, David, Capt. John Campbell & Cornelius Campbell, & Thomas Turner, Executors of This my Last Will & Testament, bearing Date the twenty ninth day of January, in the Year of our Lord, One thousand, seven hundred & fifty three.

THOS. RYAN (T. R.)

Sign'd, seal'd, publish'd & declar'd in the presence of:
  EDWD. UNDERHILL.
  DAVID ALLEN.
  HUMPHRY NICHOLS.

By way of Codicill to this my Last Will & Testament, I now declare that, any Clause whatever in my aforesaid Will to the Contrary notwithstanding that it is my will & Intention that if my Son, Thos. Ryan, Should dye, without Issue, that then my Manor house & Plantation shall fall & devolve to my Son, David Ryan & his heirs forever, & that the sd. Manor house & Plantation shall not be divided as is mentioned in my Will aforesd. but shall immediately divolve to my son, David Ryan, his heirs & Assigns forever,

in witness whereof, I have hereunto set my hand & seal, this twelfth day of February, in the Year of our Lord, One thousand, seven hundred & fifty three.

THOS. RYAN, (T. R.)

February, ye 12th, 1753.

Thos. Ryan, publish'd & declar.d the above Codicill to his Last Will & Testament on the day of the date hereof in the presence of us:

   EDWD. UNDERHILL.
   DAVID ALLENS.
      her
   ELIZABETH I ASHBURN.
      Mark.
     her
   MARY X CAPHART.
     mark.

March General Court, 1753.

The within Last will & Testament of Thomas Ryan, Dec'd., was Proved by the Oaths of Edward Underhill & David Allen, two of the subscribing Witnesses to the same, & The above Codicil Proved by the Oath of David Allen & Mary Caphart, each of which evidences made Oath that the said Thomas Ryan, was at the time of Executing the said will & Codicil of sound and Disposing mind & memory.

And David Ryan, having taken in the Oaths of an Executor, Ordered that Mr. Hand, the Secretary have Notice thereof that Letters Testamentary Issue Accordingly.   JNO. SNEAD, C. G. C.

Copied form Original Will, filed in the Office of the Secretary of State.

EDWARD SALTER'S WILL.

NORTH CAROLINA. SC.

IN THE NAME OF GOD AMEN. The Sixth day of January, in the year of our Lord Christ, one thousand seven hundred thirty, and four, I, Edward Salter of Bath County, in the Province aforesaid, Merchant, being sick in body but of sound and perfect mind and memory, (God be praised) Do make and ordain this my Last Will and Testament in manner and Form following, That is to say:

Imprimis, I Commend and Resign my Soul to Almighty God, my Maker, hoping for Salvation through the Merets of My Blesed Saviour Christ Jesus. My Body, I desire may be decently interred according to the Discretion of my wife and Executors hereafter named.

Item, I will and Desire that all my Just Debts may with all Convenient speed be truly and honestly paid.

Item. I Give and Bequeath unto my loving Wife Elizabeth, (after the payment of my Debts and Legacies), One Third part of all my personal Estate on or after a Just Division by my Executors to be made, but so to be apportioned as that none of the slaves hereafter named by me devised and alloted to be part of the Residue or other Two Thirds of my personall

Estate given and bequeathed unto my Children, be taken or included as part of her said Third part of my personal Estate.

Item. I Give, Devise and bequeath unto my Children, Vizt: unto my son Edward, and unto my Daughters, Sarah, Mary, and Susannah, all the Rest and Residue of my personal Estate Wheresoever being, or to be found, to be Divided among them in and among which, and as Part of the said Residue by me hereby to my Children given. My Will is that the Slaves by me hereafter immediately named shall be accounted, taken and reserved for my said Children. Vizt: Diego, Peter, George, Priamus the Shoe maker, Toney and Black Wall both Coopers, young Priamus, Aberdeen, Cimrick, Tom a boy which I bought of Mr. Pilkington, Moses Nann, a negro woman which I Purchased of Mr. Churchill Reading, Mary Ann a negro woman which I purchased of the Executors of the Estate of Colonel Thomas Harvey, deceased, Violet a negro woman which I purchased of Mr. Cannon, and hannah a negro Girl, together with their increase which shall or may belong to me at my decease, as also my largest Periauger with her Anchor, Cable and Sails. And My Will is That none of these Slaves by me aforementioned and named, be Sold or disposed of on any consideration whatsoever otherwise than to be divided among my Said Children, (as follows) and their respective parts together with the rest of their respective portions or parts of my Estate to be delivered to them by my Executors according to my Direction herein. Vizt:

First, I Bequeath unto my Daughter, Sarah Salter, whatever she hath now in her possession at Cape Fear, together with Sundry necessaries That I have sent for to Mr. George Monk, of Boston, to be Directed to Mrs. Porter for her use, which above articles I desire may not Come into the Division of my Estate.

Item. I Further Bequeath unto my said Daughter Sarah, my Negro man Aberdeen, my Negro man Tom, my negro Girl Named Hannah, also my Negro Girl named Teresa now about Sixteen or Eighteen months old, being the Child of Mary Ann, also Twenty Cows and twenty Calves, Ten (two year old) Cattle, Five (three year old) steers, and Five (one year old) heifers, Two likely young Mares and one likely young Stone horse, also two hundreds pounds (or value) of the said province Bills as their Value now is. And if Madam Sarah Porter of Cape Fear (in whose care my said daughter, Sarah, now is) shall think proper after my decease to continue her Care and Tuition of her, my desire is that my Executors hereafter named may (immediately after my decease, on the motion of the Said Madam Porter), deliver the negroes and other Effects by me bequeathed unto my said Daughter, Sarah, (Excepting the two hundred pounds which is not to be paid till Eighteen months after my decease) unto Madam Sarah Porter, so that the said Madam Porter may have the Labour of the Slaves for the maintenance of my sd Daughter Sarah Salter. My will is that my Executors may take Security of the said Mrs. Porter, for the Delivery of the Slaves and other Effects as above said, unto my said Daughter, Sarah, at her day of marriage or when she arrives to the full age of eighteen years (mortality excepted), and in Case my Said Daughter, Sarah Salter, should die before she be of the age Eighteen years, or day of Marriage; I will that then what Estate she shall own or which of right shall then to her belong shall be equally Divided between her said Brother and said Sisters. Note, my Executors are to Observe that my Daughter Sarah Salter is to be no ways burthened with any of my Debts.

Item. I give and bequeath unto my Daughter, Mary Salter, the plantation which I purchased of Charles Smith, lyeing on Pamplico River, quantity about three hundred and six acres, Called in the patent, Mount Colvert; also twenty Cows and twenty Calves, five (three or four year old) steers, five (one year old) heiffers, two Mares, one young stone horse; all to be branded M S when she arrives to the age of twelve years, also, one hundred pounds of the Currency of this province to be applied by my Executors towards improving the last mentioned plantation to my said daughter, mary Salter's use. My further Will is that my said Daughter Mary may have two able slaves, (one of them being a man the other a woman) not to exceed the age of thirty years each, delivered unto her by my Executors, also one negro boy, and one negro Girl not to Exceed ten years of age each, also one feather bed and furniture, all the above effects to be delivered by my Executors unto my said daughter, Mary Salter, at the day of her marriage or at the time that she shall arrive to the age of Eighteen years.

Item. I give and Bequeath unto my Daughter, Susannah Salter, my Negro woman Mary Ann, and one negro man about thirty years of age, my negro Boy Named Tom (if he should live to the time alloted) if not, another in lieu of him; also, one negro Girl, not under six nor above twelve years of Age; and a good feather bed and furniture agreeable; also twenty Cows and twenty Calves, five (three or four year old) steers, five (one year old) heifers, two mares, and one young stone horse; And in Consideration that she has no Land, my will is that she, my said Daughter, Susannah, shall have five hundred pounds of the currency of this province, as the Value at this time is. All the above mentioned money and effects to be delivered by my executors to her at the day of her marriage, or at the time that she shall arrive to the age of Eighteen years; My Further will is that if my Executors should find that the sum of money bequeathed unto my daughter, Susannah, can conveniently be spared any time after my decease, and a Tract of Land or a plantation should offer for Sale, then it shall and may be lawful for my Executors to purchase the same, and to have sufficient Deeds passed as may secure it to my said Daughter, Susannah Salter, which affair I leave intirely to their Discretion.

My Will is that my wife, Elizabeth may have the use of the plantation whereon I now dwell (which I purchased of Robert Campain), during the time that she remains my Widow, or in case the Child should live wherewith She now is big with, (to whom I shall hereafter give the said Land); also that my said Widow shall not be debarred from having the use of the Back Land which I purchased of John Swann for tar or Turpentine or as she shall think proper. My Will further is that if it shall please God the Child that my wife now goes with, should live, that then my said wife shall have the care and management of the last mentioned plantation for the use of the said Child.

Item. I give and Bequeath the plantation whereon I now dwell, also the Back Land which I purchased of John Swann, of Cape Fear unto the Child that my wife is now big with; if a Boy to be Delivered to him at the age of one and twenty years; if a Girl to be Delivered to her at the day of her marriage, or when she shall arrive to the full age of Eighteen years. But in case the said last mentioned Child should die before it shall arrive to the day of marriage or age of Eighteen years; Then it shall be lawfull for my Executors to take the said plantation and Land into their Care and possession (observing my Directions hereinafter expressed for that purpose).

Whereas, I have sold a negro Girl named Hannah, which I had given to my Daughter, Sarah Salter, in this my Last will and Testament as above, In Consideration whereof My Will is that there may be a likely negro-man, not to exceed Twenty years of age, purchased out of my Estate and given to my said Daughter, Sarah Salter, in lieu of the said negro Girl Hannah.

Item. I bequeath unto my Godson, John Watkins, (son of william Watkins) a negro or Mullato Boy now about eighteen months old (being the Child of my said negro woman Nann, which I purchased of Mr. Churchill Reading), to him and his heirs for ever.

Item. I Bequeath unto my son-in-law, Miles Harvey, one hundred pounds to be paid him in four years after my Decease, being the Value as the Bills now stand at, and no otherwise.

Item. I Bequeath unto my son in law, John Harvey, Ten pounds in order to purchase him a good Beaver hat and a pair of Gloves, which money is to be paid when called for after my Decease.

Item. I bequeath unto my beloved Son, Edward Salter, my

best Saddle and Bridle, and one pair of Silver Spurs and Richard Bloom's History of the Holy Bible, together with all the books that I shall own at my Death (be they Divinity, Law History or Mathematical), which are to be found by the Catalogue, also my Large China Punch Bowl (which I purchased of Mr Edmond Gale). The above Goods I give to my said son, Edward Salter, as a Legacy and not to be brought into the Division of my Estate.

My will is that my Brigantine now in the stocks at John Smith's, be got finished and made fit for the Sea as soon as may be (By Name The Happy Luke) and may (after she is ready for the Sea) be loaden with tar which I have in my hands, belonging to Sundry Gentlemen in Boston, as will appear by my Book and papers, or by a list which I shall leave to inform my Executors; My Will also is that James Rostern proceeds Master of her. My Will further is that my Executors may write two or three ways (before she Sails out of the Port of Bath) to Collo. Jacob Windall and Company, to Insure the sum of Twelve Hundred pounds, (Boston Money) upon the said Brigantine, The Happy Luke, And my will further is, that my Brigantine The Happy Luke, may be Consigned to Collo. Jacob Windall and Company, with positive orders for them to make sale of her to the best advantage for the use of my wife and Children; my will further is, that the money that may arise, by the Sale of the said Brigantine shall be remitted in youngable Slaves, (none to exceed the age of twenty years).

Item. I bequeath unto my Said beloved Son, Edward Salter, all the remianing part of my personal Estate I have not already bequeathed, provided that he or my Executors see my Daughters fully contented, satisfied and paid their above menticned portions, given them by me, their father, Edward Salter.

Item. I further bequeath unto my Said Beloved Son, Edward Salter, all my lands scituate and lyeing on the south side of Pamlico River (excepting what I have before bequeathed to my said loving Daughter Mary Salter) also my whole right, title and interest of all the Lands that I have under Surveys. My further Will is, that the Six hundred and fourty acres of Land lyeing on Bear creek be immediately secured by my Executors on the best terms the country will afford, which Land was formerly Surveyed by William Bartram, whose right I purchased, (Consideration twenty Cows and twenty Calves); also that the Six hundred and fourty acres of Land lyeing and being on the West Side of the Bever Dam of Grays Creek, (whereon John Arrington now dwells my tennant) be secured on the best terms my Executors can have it done. But my will and orders is that my Executors may not neglect upon any terms whatsoever to Secure the two last mentioned

Tracts of Lands to my said beloved son, Edward Salter, let the Costs be small or great to perfect the same.

My will is, that in case any of the aforementioned Children should die before they shall arrive to the age before mentioned, or day of marriage, whatsoever then may be belonging to them by this my will, that then it shall be equally divided among my surviving Children let, them be younger or older which may first happen; but if any of them shall happen to die and leave any heirs Lawfully begotten of their bodies, that their heirs shall have the same right, title, and interest to the Estate as they themselves might have, if living.

My Will and desire is That my last will and Testament may be proved immediately after my death, and Letters Testamentory obtained so a a Division may be made with al possible expedition, that my widdow may have her third part delivered to her after payment of my Debts and Legacies, or her giving good Security to pay her third part of them.

Item. My will, intent and desire is that my Executors have the care, custody, keeping and educating my children aforesaid 'till they shall arrive to the age of twenty one years or their day of marriage.

My will is that all my Children's Slaves may be kept together to labour upon the Land that I have given to my said beloved son, Edward Salter, under the Care of some good honest man Such as my Executors may think proper, for the Support and education of my said Children. My singular will further is, that my said beloved son, Edward Salter, may have a thorough education to make him a compleat merchant, let the expense be what it will. My Will is that my said son, Edward Salter, may have his Estate Delivered him by my Executors, hereinafter named, when he shall arrive to the age of twenty one years, and no sooner.

Lastly of this my Last will and Testament, I Make, constitute, nominate, appoint and order my Trusty and well beloved friend, Colo. Edward Mosely, Mr. John Odeon, Mr. John Caldam, Mr. Thomas Bonner, Mr. William Willis, and Mr. William Adams, Executors. And I hereby utterly revoke and annul all other and former wills and Testaments by me before this time in any wise made.

In Witness whereof, I have subscribed my name and Set my Seal unto this my present will and Testament, the day and year first above written.

EDWARD SALTER. (his Seal)

Sign'd, Seal'd and Published,
In the presence of:
  WALLEY CHAUNCEY,
  BENJAMIN RIGNEY,
  WALTEN DIXSON.
  ROGT. JONES.

No. CAROLINA.

Before his Excelly., Gabriel Johnston Esq., His Majesty's Governor in Chief and Ordinary of the said Province:

Personally appeared Benjamin Rigney and Roger Jones, two of the Witnesses to the within Last Will and Testament of Edward Salter, deceased, who being duely sworn Say, That they were present and Saw the said Edward Salter Sign, Seal Publish and Declare the Same to be his last will and Testament; and that he was at that time of Sound and disposing Mind and Memory: And that they Saw Walley Chauncy and Walter Dixon the two other Witnesses Sign their Names as Witneeses thereunto.

Given at Edenton, under my hand the 5th day of February, Anno. Dom., 1734.

GAB. JOHNSTON.

No. CAROLINA.

Before his Excelly. Gabriel Johnston Esqr. His Maj'tyes Governor in Chief and Ordinary of the Said Province:

Personally appeared Edward Mosely Esqr., and William Adams, Two of the Excrs. as required of the within last Will and Testament & took the Oath of Executors as required by Law.

Given at Edenton under my hand this 5th. February, anno Dom., 1734.

GAB. JOHNSTON.

Recorded in will Book No. 3, p 256, Office of Secretary of State.

RICHARD SANDERSON'S WILL.

IN THE NAME OF GOD AMEN. I, Richard Sanderson, of the Precinct of Perquimons and County of Albemarle, Gent., Being very Sick and weak of Body but of perfect mind & memory, (thanks be given to God therefore) calling unto Mind the Mortality of my body and knowing that it is Appointed for all men once to Die, do make and Ordain this my Last Will and testament: That is to say, Principally, and first of all, I Give & recommend my Soul into the hands of God that gave it; and for my Body, I Recommend it to the Earth, to be Buryed in a Christian-like and Decent Manner at the Discretion of my Executors, nothing doubting but at the General Resurrection I shall receive the Same again by the mighty power of God: and as touching Such Worldly Estate wherewith it hath pleased God to bless me in this Life, I Give, Devise, and Dispose of the Same in the following manner:

Imprimis, I Will & Desire that all my Lawful Debts may be payed & Discharged by my Executors hereafter named.

Item, I give And Bequeath unto my well beloved Son, Richd. Sanderson, ye Island of Ocreecock w'th all the Stock of Horses, Cattle, Sheep & hoggs, thereunto belonging or Appertaining, To be Enjoyed by him & his heirs (Lawfully begotten) for ever; and in Case my sd. Son should die & leave no heirs Male, I Give & bequeath the Said Island of Ockrecock w'th all & Singular the Sd. Stock, Goods & Chattles, thereunto belonging, Unto my Nephews, Joseph & Richd. Sanderson, & their Male heirs (Lawfully begotten) for ever; to be Equally Divided between them two & Enjoyed by them And their heirs for ever.

Item, I give & bequeath unto my well beloved Son, Richd. Sanderson, Four Slaves, viz: three Negros Named Cooper-Jack, Sam, & Sarah; wth one Indian Named Tom, to him & his heirs Lawfully begotten for ever; & in Default of Issue I give & bequeath the aforesaid Slaves, unto my Son in Law, Tully Williams, & his Wife, my Daughter Grace, & their heirs On her body begotten, for ever.

Item, I Give & bequeath unto my Son in Law, Tully Williams, & his wife Grace, & the heirs on her Body begotten, Five Slaves, viz: Curratuck Jack; Commoner; Sandy; Moll, & One Mulattoe Boy named Jack, to them & their heirs for Ever.

Item, I give & bequeath unto my Brother in law, Henry Woodhouse, One Mustee Fellow named Arthur, w'ch is in part of the Money due to him of my Fathers Estate; and I further will & Desire that If in Case that my Son Richd. had rather have the Said Arthur that he pay unto my Brother in Law, Henry Woodhouse, According to the Just Value of ye aforesd Slave, named Arthur.

Item, I give & bequeath Unto my Well beloved Sister, Susanna Erwin, During her Natural Life, Two Negro Slaves named Dye & Kate, Provided, & is to be Understood, So long as She Abides, Dwells & Remains on the Mannour Plantation whereon I now dwell; and after her Decease I give and bequeath the Sd. Slaves & their Increase unto my Son, Richd. & his Lawfull heirs for ever; & in default of Issue, I give & bequeath the Said Slaves & their Increase unto my Nephews, Samuel & Joshua Sanderson, & to their heirs for ever; and I will & Desire that my Sister Susanna, have a Maintenance During her Natural Life on the aforesd. Mannour Plantation; and also a Bed & furniture; a Pot & a Skillet, two pewter Dishes & four Plates; & after her Decease to Devolve unto my Son, Richd & his Lawfull begotten heirs for ever.

Item, I Give & bequeath unto my well beloved Daughter, Elizabeth Pollock; one third part of my flock of Sheep; w'ch be at this time on my Plantation whereon I now dwell.

Item, I give & bequeath unto my Cousin, Elizabeth Dickson, One black Horse now running in my pasture to be Delivered unto her by my Executors hereafter named.

Item, I give & bequeath unto my Nephew, Hezekiah Woodhouse, a certain Tract of Land lying on the Sandy Bank by the name of Point Lookout, to be Enjoyed by him & his heirs for ever.

Item, I Give & bequeath unto my Son, Richd. Sanderson; & my son in Law, Tully Williams, the Mannor Plantation whereon I now Dwell to be by them freely Possessed & Enjoyed for the full Term of Six years after my Decease, wth all profits & Commodities thereby ariseing yearly, or Accruing from the Same, to be Equaly Divided or shared between them, during the Sd. Term of Six years. at the Expiration of w'ch Term the Sd. Mannor Plantation wth. all Buildings, Houses, Messuages & Tenements, as also, Orchards, Gardens; wth. all live Stock or whatsoever els belongs or Appertains unto the Said Plantation, to Devolve wholly to my Son, Richard Sanderson, & his Lawfull begotten heirs for ever; & in default of Issue, unto Tully Williams & his Wife, my Daughter, Grace, & their heirs on her Body begotten for ever to be by them freely Possessed & Enjoyed.

Item, I give & bequeath unto my Son, Richd. One Spay'd Mare branded R:S:

Item, I give & bequeath unto my Son in Law, Tully Williams and his wife, my Daughter Grace, & the heirs on her body begotten, a Tract or Parcel of Land Containing one hundred forty & Seven Acres, Lying Perquimons Precinct bordering on my Son, Richd. his Line; formerly John Willoughby's;

Item, I Give & bequeath unto my Son, Richd. Sanderson, all my Lots in RoanOak Town, wth all the Lands thereunto belonging.

Item, I Give & bequeath unto my Son, Richard, & my Son in Law, Tully Williams, all my Other Lands, Messauges & Tenements, wth all my Rights & Titles to Lands, as by Deeds & Pattents are to be found; to be Equaly Divided betwixt them.

Item, I give & bequeath unto my Son Richd. & my Son in Law Tully Williams, all my Other Stock of Horses, Cattle, Sheep & Hogs, wth all my houshold Goods & Moveables to be Equally Divided betwixt them (excepting what is already Given) or bequeathed in this Will & Testament,

Item, I Give & bequeath unto my Son, Richd. Sanderson, two thirds of the Sea flower, Brigantine, & one third part unto my Son in Law, Tully Williams.

Item, I Give & bequeath unto my Son Richd. Sanderson, & my Son in Law, Tully Williams, the Sloop Swallow, to be Equally Divided betwixt them; wth All appurtenances thereunto belonging.

And lastly, I Constitute, make, Ordain & Appoint my only & well beloved Son, Richard Sanderson, & my Son in Law, Tully Williams, to be my only Executors of this my Last Will & Testament; and I do hereby utterly Disallow, Revoke & Disannul, all & every other former Wills & Testaments, Legacies, Requests, & Executors, by me in any wise before this time Named, Willed & Bequeathed; Ratifying & Confirming this & no other, to be my Last Will & Testament.

In witness whereof, I have hereunto Sett my hand & Seal this Seventeenth Day of August; in the Year of our Lord, One Thousand, Seven hundred & Thirty three.

RICHD. SANDERSON. (Seal)

Signed, Sealed, Published, Pronounced & Declared by the Said Richard Sanderson, as his Last Will Testament; In the Presence of us the Subscribers, viz:

    CLEMT. HALL.
    THOMAS T T TRUMBAL.
            his / mark
    THOMAS T S SNOWDEN.
            his / mark

PERQMS. PRECT:

At a Court held October the 15th., 1733. The within Will of Colo. Richd. Sanderson, was proved by the oaths of Mr. Clement Hall, Mr. Thoms. Snowden, Mr. Thoms. Trumball, whereupon the Executors took the Oathes Injoyned by Law, & Requested Orders for Letters Testamentary. Ordered that Letters Testam'y Issue on Said Will.

Test. CHARLES DENMAN, Clk. Cr.

Copied from Original Will, filed in the Office of the Secretary of State.

MACRORA SCARBROUGH'S WILL.

IN THE NAME OF GOD AMEN, I, Macrora Scarbrough, of Pequimons County, in the Province of North Carolina, Gent., Being in good health of Body and of Sound & perfect Mind and Memory, Praise be therefore Given unto Almighty God for the Same; But Calling to Mind the Mortality of My body, and knowing that it is Appointed for all Men Once to die, but not how Soon or Sudent it May be, Do therefore make & Ordaine this my Present Last Will and Testament in Manner and forme following (that is to Say), first & principally, I commend my Soul into the hands of Almighty God, hoping through the Merits, death, & Passion, of my Saviour Jesus Christ, to have full and free pardon & forgiveness of all my Sins, and to inherit Everlasting life; And my body I commit to the Earth to be decently Buried at the Discretion of my Executors hereafter Named, nothing Doubting but at the General Resurrection, I shall receive the Same again by the Mighty Power of God. And as Touching the Dispossion of all Such Temporal Estate, as it hath pleased Almighty God to bestow upon me in this Life, I Give & Dispose thereof as followeth:

Imprimis, I Will that all my Just debts & funeral Expences be first paid and discharged in reasonable and convenant Time after my Decease.

Item, I Give & bequeath unto My welbeloved Wife, Elizabeth Scarbrough, and to her Disposial, all that part of my Estate that may or will become due to me upon the Division of Mr. William Reeds, (hir former Husbands) Estate. I also give unto my said Wife, the use and Labour of two Negros, Vizt:, Miak a fellow & Pasquotank Rose, a wench, During hir widowhood, And after that, to be Divided as my Other Estate is hereinafter Directed To be. I give likewise unto my said Wife, My Chest of Draws, and the Six Silver Tea? Spoons, Strainer & Tongs, which is more commonly used?.

Item, I Give, bequeath & devise unto my Son, Benjamin Scarbrough, and his heirs forever, the land & plantation whereon I now Dwell, called Springfield, and all other the lands gave to me by Mrs. Juliana Lakers, which may appear By hir Deed of Gift to me, bareing date, ye 20th. day of July, Anno Dom. 1731., reserving only the Use & Occupation of the houses, Plantation and that part of the land whereon I Now Dwell, unto my wellbeloved Wife, Elizabeth, Dureing hir Widowhood, if She thinks fitt to live thereon. I also Give and bequeath unto my Said Son, Benjamin, four Negros, Vizt: Nicholous, Dennis Two fellows, Nann & Venus, two wenches, Six Silver Spoons Marked P., my Silver Headed Cane, Silver Shoe Buckles, Knee buckles, fourteen Silver vest bottons, Black walnut Desk, and all my wearing apparil.

Item, I Give, bequeath, Devise Between my two Sons, Benjamin, and Macrora, and their heirs forever, My Land & plantation at Yawpim, wch I Bought of Thomas Wyatt, and now Called point Pleasant, Divided Between them as followest, Vizt., Beginning at ye Mouth of a Small branch Issueing out of ye River, Neare the Mouth of Yawpim Creek, Thence running up the Middle of the Said branch to a forked Sweet Gum, at the head of ye Said branch, Thence about a west Course thorough the Clear'd ground to a Small Dubble Dick, so along the Same to the End thereof, and from thence a Strate Course about ye middle of the Neck of Land to a Marked tree a Standing between a Small pond & the head of a branch making out of the Beaver Cover, Thence the Same Course until it Intersexs the line of William Wyatts land adjoining thereto; and my Son, Benjamin or his his heirs to have the part binding on Yawpim River, and my Son, Macrora or His heirs, the other part, binding on Yawpim Creek; Both parts of the said land, I give and Devise under This Restriction and Directions, That neither of them nor their heirs, Shall sell or Give their Divident or Part of the land afsd. (unless it be either to one other) or any part or parcell thereof, unless they be or their heirs, joyntly agree to Dispose of the Same, or any part of it, but if either of my two Said Sons, or their heirs shall presume (Contrary to this my Will & Desire), To make any deed or Conveyance Other ways than herein Directed, Then in Such case, I hereby Revocke the Devise of their part in This land, and then I do hereby absolutely give and Devise all the aforesaid land unto him and his Heirs forever, either of which of them my two sons, Benjamin or Macrora, their heirs that shall Com—— with the Conditions of this my Will and Testament.

But if Either of My two Said Sons, Benjamin or Macrora, Should happen to Die before they To the age of twenty one years, Then, and in Such Case, my Will is that the Survivers or his Heirs have the whole tract or Parcell of Land forever.

And further My Will is, That my Son, Benjamin, have the Use & Benefit of that Part of Point Pleasant land which I have herein given unto my Son, Macrora, untill he, my said Son shall come To the age of fifteen years; Unless there be a acasion to Dispose of the Same for the purchase of Other Lands as hereafter Directed, and Provided, he my Said Son, Benjamin, will let his Mother in Law, my wife, Elizabeth, have the Use for the Same time of fourteen yrs. of that part of the plantation whereon I Now Dwell and wch is given to him by his Grandmother, Juliana Lakers, other wise, this bequest to be void. And my said wife, Elizabeth, to have the Use & benefit thereof, the better to Enable hir to bring up the said Child So long as She Shall have the Care of him.

Item, I Give, Bequeath, & Devise unto my Son, Macrora, and his heirs forever, My Oak Ridge land, Containing Two hundred & one Acres, as per the Patent granted to me in the year of Our Lord, 1744. And I also Give and Bequeath unto my said Son, Macrora, four Negros, vizt., Little Rose, Welcome, Grace & Suana; a Quart Silver Can, my Silver Watch, Pinch back headed Cain, one good Black walnut Deask, To be bought for him, if the Same be not don before my Decease, my Copper Still & furniture thereunto belonging.

Item, I Give, Bequeath & Devise Unto my Son, William, and his heirs forever, My land adjoyning the Land of Mr. Harvey, Containing three hundred & Ten acres, which I bought of John Pettiver & Benjamin Talbot, as may appear by their Several Deeds or Conveyances, Now upon record in the Registers Office of Pequimans County, and also I likewise, Give, bequeath & Devise unto my said Son, William, and his heirs forever, the land I bought of Robert Wilson, Containing Thirty acres as by the Conveyance may ——————.
And I also Give and bequeath unto my Son William, four

Negroes, vizt: Sam, Doll, Tamer, and Pasquotank Dinah; a pint Silver Cann, my Silver Snuff box, and Mohogina Desk.

Item, I give, bequeath & Devise unto my Daughter, Elizabeth, and the heirs of her body lawfully Begoten forever; the land & Plantation I bought of Joseph Stewart, Containing Two hundred & thirty Eight Acres, as may Appear by the Patent Thereof Assigned to me by ye said Joseph Stewart, And in the falier of such heirs of my said Daughter, I Give the said land & Plantation unto my Son, Macrora, and his heirs forever. And I also give & bequeath, unto my Daughter, Elizabeth, Three negros, Vizt:, Pompey, Dianna and Margaret, Six Silver Tea Spoons, a creem Spoon, suger Tongs, and a new Straner that came with them.

And further my Will is, and I do hereby Order and direct, That in Case any of the Slaves herein Given to any of my Child afsd. Should Happen to Die or otherwise be lost before they be of Age to receive them, That then they shall be made up unto Them Out of the Negros not herein given By Name, and the increase that may hereafter arise from any of the Female Negroes before They are Delivered to them they may belong, So that every Childs part of Negros, May be made as good In Value to them at the Receiving, as they would have been had there not happened any Death or other misfortune to Them as aforeSaide.

Item, I Give & Bequeath unto my two Sons, Macrora Scarbrough and William Scarbrough, One hundred pounds Starling Money of Great Britain, Equally to be Divided between Them, And to be Disposed of at the Discretion of my Executors hereafter Mentioned towards purchasing Each of them a piece of good land and for no other use whatsoever. Further to make provision for a good settlement of land for my two sd. Sons, I hereby Order and Impower my Exrs. herein Named if Need shall Require (that is if the land that may Happen to be bought is of greater Value then can be had for the Money here allotted), to Sell the land herein Given to Each of my two said Sons, or so much thereof as may be Sufficient for that purpose. And in Case my Exrs. Should happen to disagree, of Differ in Opinion about the Purchase of the said Land as to place or price of the land to be bought, or that wch may be to be sold, in Such Case It is my Will That they Apply to the Court of Pequimons to appoint three of as Honest & indifferent Men in the Matter, and that is of knowledge & understanding, as they can git in the said County, Whose oppinion of any two of shall be binding on my Exrs. as to that Matter.

Item, I Give & bequeath unto the Children of My Cowzen, Mary Atkinson, Twenty pounds Curt. Money of Virginia, or the Value thereof in the Produce of this country, To be paid for and toward Schooling Them of any of them that can git the Opportunity thereof, and no other Use whatever, but In larning them to Read & writing English, and thereby the better to interest them in the principles of the Christian Religion. And it is my Will & Desire there may be all the Care possible takon that That they or   of them May have this———

Item, I Give & bequeath unto my Son in law, ——————
my Black walnut Desk, and   Case of Five, five pint Bottles now in the house at Pasquotank.

And foras Much as the Slaves herein gave unto my two youngest Sons, Macrora & William Scarbrough, are very young and cannot be sufficient for their Edication and bringing up in any Christianlike Manner, Therefore, it is my Will and I do hereby order and Direct That my Melato Fellow Harry, shall be Sold or hired out for Money for their further Support, and that the Dispossion of the Said Slave be under these Restrictions and Directions, That is to Say, in Case the said fellow Can produce the Some of Forty pounds Currant Gold & Silver Money of Virginia, or any friend for him, Then he shall be his Own man, and at his Liberty, But if Neither can be complied with, Then my Exrs. hereafter nam'd, that is the acting ones, are to make Sale of him to any person That will Give fifty pounds of the Currancy Afsd. for him, and if None will do that Then it is my Will for him to be hired out for yearly or Monthly wagers, for So much as can be got for him, Until the Said Sum of fifty pounds afsd. be Accomplished, Then for him to be free and at his liberty, as afsd. And it is my Will and Desire that the money Arising by the sal or wages be applyed to no Other Use then in Schooling & Edicating my two Sons, Macrora & William, and for buying them good & useful Books Such as may Instruct them in Larning and the true Principalls of Christionity.

Item, I Give and bequeath all the rest of my Estate be it of what Nature, kind or Quality Soever (and not herein before given), To be Equeally Divided amongest my Welbeloved Wife & my four Children, Vizt., Benjamin, Elizabeth, Macrora, & William, And I do hereby order & Desire, and it is my Will, That In Case Any of my Children afore Named Should Die before they come to Age or Married, that then the Whole part by this my will given be Equally Divided amongst the Survivers of them.

And in Case the Several Legacys in this Will given to any of my Children of Negros by Name, Shall Happen not any of them to Die before they be received by them they belong to, so that then there will No Accasion of Making any Loss Up, out of the increce as is before Directed, Then it is my will that All Such Increace Shall be Equally Divided amongst my Said Children or the Survivers of them, That shall not before have recaived their Legacys of Negros as afore Said.

And furthermore, my Will and Desire is, That upon a
Division of my Estate, That part comeing or belonging
either of my two youngest Sons, Macrora or William, T]
is by Law Deemed perisable and May Grow Much worse
Keeping untill they come of Age; Be appraised on Oath
three honest Men, apointed by Agreement of my Exrs.
Order of Court, and Kept or Sold by the Acting Exrs. who
to acct. and pay the Same according to the apraisement, eit]
in Money or things of the Same Kind & Equall Value in
Judgment of them, under the Same restrictions as aforesa

And, I Do hereby Nominate, Constitute and appoint 1
Dear and welbeloved Wife, Elizabeth Scarbrough Executrix, a
my welbeloved Son, Benjamin Scarbrough, Macrora Sc
brough, and William Scarbrough, Executors of this my l
Will and Testament, And do hereby Revock, Disanul a
Make Void, all former Wills and Testaments, by me heretof
Made.

But if it shall so happen (which God forbid it Shoul
That my Wife & Eldest Son, who are most likely to be 1
acting Exrs. in this my Will, Should quarel, Differ, Disagr
and Suffer the Adversary to Peace to git the Uper hand of the
so that to render their Joynt Acting as Exrs. Ought to do
the Intrust of Every one concerened in the Will, and there
not to Answer the trust imposed in them, Which in my lif
have too offten Sean, ——————————— where own Motl
& Son as well as other—— They have Spent great part
their own Intrust as well as that of the orphans & Others
ways Concerned In there Differences, Which, I hope in t
God of all Mercy peace & Truth, will not be the Case hea
But if it Should, Then it is my Will and I do hereby Nomina
Constitute & Appoint my loveing Brother, John Scarbrou
my brother in Law, Edmond Hatch, and my friend, Willi
Burgis, Senr., To be overseers or trustees of all that part
my Estate Given by Legace or other ways becoming Due
this my Will to any of my three Children, vizt., Elizabe
Macrora, & William, as also that Legace Given to the Child
of my Cozen, Mary adkinson, Hereby Desireing you my frien
To Accept & take upon you the trust hereby required if
casion Shall be, on the bahalf of Orphans and their Esta
According to the true Intent & Meaning of this my W
Hereby giving & granting unto you all the Power, & Author
So to do as can be Required Either in Law or Equity.

In Witness whereof, I the said Macrora Scarbrough,
this my present last will & Testament have set my hand a
Seal. This 31st. Day of Jan'ry, Anno Dom., 1752.

      Ma'c. Scarbrough (Seal)
    (Impression of Coat of Arms on Sea

The above writing was Signed,
Sealed, Published, Acknowledged

& pronounced by the said Macrora Scarbrough the day & year aforesaid, To be and Contain his last Will and Testament, writ with his own hand and Contained within Two Sheets of paper annexed togeather with three Seals of black wax and Silk Ferreting, In the Presents of us, who was Desired to Signe as Evidences thereto:
WALTER KIPPIN.
JOSHUA HOBART.
his
CORNELIUS X MULLIN
mark
ROBERT AVERY.
MARTHAAN KIPPIN.

NORTH CAROLINA.   Edenhouse, Feby. 18, 1752.

This Day Walter Kippin & Cornelius Mullin, two of the Subscribing Evidences to the last Will & Testament of mcRora Scarbrough, late of Perquimons County, Esq., Decd., which is hereunto annexed, personally appeared before me, Gabriel Johnston, Esq., Captain General, Governor & Comander in Chief in & over the sd. Province, & Ordinary of the same, and made Oath that they saw the sd. Mcrora Scarbrough, Sign, Seal & deliver the same as & for his last Will & Testament, and that they saw Joshua Hobart, Robert Avery & Martha Ann Kippin, sign as Evidences to the said Will.   GAB. JOHNSTON.

Copied from the Original Will, filed in the Office of the Secretary of State.

ELIZABETH SCOLLAY'S WILL.

IN THE NAME OF GOD AMEN, I, Elizabeth Scollay, of the County of Bertie, in the Province of North Carolina, Widow, being low in Health, but of Sound Disposing Mind, Memory & understanding, and Calling to Mind the Uncertainty of this Transitary Life, do make, & Declare this to be my Last Will & Testament; hereby Revoking and Annuling every will Heretofore by me made.

Imprimis, I Surrender my Soul to Almight God that Gave it, and Desire that I may be decently Buryed by the side of my Late Husband, Samuel Scollay, and that a Genteel Tombstone be provided by my Executors to place over me; as to my Worldly Estate, I Give and dispose of it in Manner Following:

Item, 1st. I Give and Devise to my son, Thomas Pollock, my Negro wench Doll, and all her Children (Except a Negro Boy named Charles which I Have herein after otherwise Disposed off), and my Negro Wench Susannah and all Her

Children, Also, all my plate (to Wit) Tea Pott, milk Pott, Tankard, two Salts, three table spoons, & a Large Soop Spoon, and all my Tea Spoons but in Case my said son should die without Issue then and in that Case, I Give the above mentioned Negroes & Plate, to be Equally Divided, the one Half to the Children of Tulley Williams, and the other Half to the Children of Richard Saunderson, share and share alike, I Desire the Negroes & Plate given to my son, Thomas, may be in the Care of Doct^r. Robert Lenox untill otherwise Ordered by the said Thomas Pollock.

Item, 2ndly. I Give & Devise unto my son, Cullen Pollock, all my Books, also a Mourning Ring.

Item, 3rdly. I Give & Desire to Mrs. Fanny Lenox, wife of Doctr. Robert Lenox, my Side Saddle, Cover & Bridle.

4thly, I Give & Devise to Doct^r. Robert Lenox, my Still with the Appurtenances; also my Negro Wench named Moll, and my My Negro Boy, named Charles.

Item, 5thly. I Give & Devise to John Scollay of Boston, in Consideration of a Debt I owe the said John Scollay, my Negro man named Rum, and also Two Bonds now in the possession of Cullen Pollock, (to wit) one of Joseph Robinson's of Perquimons County, and the other one the Honble John Rutherfurd's, and in Case the said John Scollay should not be satisfied therewith, then, I desire the Negro Man Rum may be sold and the above two Bonds may be Collected and so much Money be Remitted by my Executors to the said John Scollay as will pay him the said Debt I owe Him, But in Case Cullen Pollock should Choose to Keep the above two Bonds and pay the said John Scollay so much Money out of the Estate herein after given said Cullen Pollock as will Amount to the same sum, then I desire He may Have his Choice.

Item, 6thly, I Give & Devise to Peggy Cathcart, Daughter of Doct'^{r} William Cathcart, my Negro girl named Ruth.

Item 7thly, I Give & Devise to Sarah Blount, Daughter of Joseph Blount, my Negro Girl named Bridgett.

Item, 8thly, My will & Desire is that all my Household Furniture (not before Given) and all my Stock of Horses, Cattle, Hogs & Sheep be sold to satisfy my Debts, and if any Money Remains, I Give & Devise the same to Cullen & Thomas Pollock, share and share alike.

Item, 9thly, I Give & Devise to Sophia Rasor, Daughter of Edward Rasor, my Negro Girl Named Hannah.

Item, 10thly, I Give & Devise to Fanny Cathcart, Daughter of Doct^r William Cathcart, my Negro Girl named Polley.

Item 11thly, I Give & Devise to Thomas Blount, Son of Joseph Blount, my Negro wench named Sarah and all Her Children.

Item 12thly, I Give all the Residue of my Negroes and other

Estate of all Kind Whatsoever or Wheresoever to be found, to be Equally divided Between Cullen Pollock & Thomas Pollock, share & share alike, They & each of them Paying Mrs. Sarah Vaughan the Sum of Eight Pounds, Proclamation Money, Yearly, & Every Year during her Natural Life.

Item, 13thly. I Remit all Money due to me from Tulley Williams.

Item, 14thly, Whereas, I Have herein Given Sundry Negroes, Legacies to my Kindred & friends, and not to my Children & Perhaps it may be thought some of them might Belong to the Estate of my former Husband Mr. Thomas Pollock, this may Certify all who may think so; that none of the said Negroes so Given Belongs to my sd. Husband, Mr. Thomas Pollock's Estate.

Lastly, I Constitute and Appoint Thomas Pollock, Doctr. Robert Lenox, Richard Saunderson, and Joseph Blount, Executors of this my Last will & Testament.

In Witness Whereof, I have hereunto Set my Hand & Seal the First day of December, In the year of our Lord, One thousand Seven hundred & Sixty Six.

ELIZABETH SCOLLAY. (seal)

Seigned, Sealed & Declared to
be the Last Will & Testament of
Elizabeth Scollay in the presence
of us:
  HARDY HARDISON.
  FREDERICK HARDISON.

The Within Last Will and Testament of Elizabeth Scollay was proved before me this day by the oath of Hardy Hardyson, one of the subscribing Witnesses thereto, who swore that he saw the Testatrix sign, seal Publish & Declare the same to be and Contain her last will and Testament.

Given under my Hand at Newbern, this 12 January, 1767.
WM. TRYON.

Copied from the Original Will, filed in the Office of the Secretary of State.

SAMUEL SCOLLAY'S WILL.

IN THE NAME OF GOD AMEN. As It is appointed for all Men once to Depart this Life, I, Samuel Scollay, being sound of judgment and of Perfect memory, I resign my Soul to him that gave It and my Body to the Ground. I make this my last Will hereby revoking all Wills, Deeds and Grants whatsoever before made by me, and this only to be taken as my last. What Estate it hath pleased God to bestow on me I give and bequeath as Follows:

I Give and bequeath unto my Dear and well beloved Friends, Thos. Gilford, of Busty, Esquire, In Zetland, and to Magnis

Henderson, of Guarde, Esquire in Zetland, and to George Triel, of Broh, Esquire, I Orkney, In the Island of Sandy, Fifty Pounds Sterling, each, to them, or their Heirs Surviving.

Item I give and bequeath unto my beloved Friend, Mrs. Margaret Stewart, Alias Triel, late Lady of Eleoness in Orkney, in the Island of Sandy, or hir Heirs Surviving, Twenty Pounds Sterling.

Item, I give and Bequeath unto my beloved Friend, Mrs. Mary Tulinton, Alias Davis, Spouse of the Deceased Mr. Robert Davis, Shipbuilder, In Leath in Scotland, to hir or any of her Heirs surviving, Fifty Pounds Sterling.

Item, I Give and Bequeath unto my Brother, Jerman Robert Scollay, of Lerwick, Esquire, in Zetland, to him or his Heirs Surviving, one hundred Ponds Sterling, and it is my Will that these legacies be immediately remitted to Mr. Hugh Blackburn at Norfolk, By my Executors, and by the Said Mr. Hugh Blackburn to be remitted to his Friends for an equal Division.

Item, I Give and Bequeath to my loving Spouse all my houshold Furniture and all this Stock of Catle and living Creatures.

Item, I give unto her two hundred pound, Virginia Currant, to be paid out of the first money that rais'd upon these Goods, Now In the House.

Item, I Give and bequeath unto her two hundred Pounds, Virginia Currant, to be paid out of the Pasquotank Debts. Which Debts amounts to in Bills Bonds Eight hundred & twenty odd Pounds.

Item, I Give unto my loving Friend, Doctor William CathCart, one hundred Pounds, Virginia Currant, to be paid out of the Pasquotank Debts.

Item, I Give unto my beloved Friend, Mr. Robert Todd, of Norfolk one hundred Pounds, Virginia Currant, to be paid out of the Pasquotank Debts when Collected.

Item, I Give unto my beloved Sons in Law, Cullen and Thos. Pollock, all the dry goods lately imported from Virginia, excepting two hundred Pounds, Virginia Currant, which my beloved Spouse is to have in Cash or Goods at her Pleasure.

Item, I Give and Bequeath unto my beloved Sons in law, Cullen and Thos. Pollock, The Remainder of the Pasquotank Debts, when my beloved Spouse hath Drawn her Legacy of two hundred Pounds, Virginia Currant, and Doctor William CathCart and Mr. Robert Todd of Norfolk hath drawn theirs two hundred, Virginia Currant, Then I Give and Bequeath unto my beloved Sons in Law, Cullen & Thos. Pollock, the remainder which amounts to about four hundred Pounds. I give and Bequeath unto my beloved Sons in Law, Cullen and Thos. Pollock, Part of a Track of Land containing about seventy Acres, or thereabouts, laying near the Plank Blidge

In Pasquotank. It is my Will that Cullen & Thos. Pollock collect the Debts. clear of all Charges at their own Expence.

Item, I Give unto Tully Williams, his Fathers Sword, also the Stock of Cattle at Kettyhauk. It is my Will that Cullen and Thos. Pollock pay off the ballance of that Bond In Virginia Due to White and Scott.

Lastly, It is my Will that my beloved Spouse, and my sons in Law, Cullen and Thos. Pollock, be Executors to this my last Testamt. my Will contains one sheet of paper.

SAM. SCOLLAY. (Seal)

Signed, Sealed, delivered this 15 Day of December, In Presence of
    Testis. ANN ANDERSON.
        ED. RASOR.
        JOHN NICHOLLS.

Edenhouse, 18 Feby., 1752.

This day Edward Rasor & John Nichols, two of the Subscribing Evidences of the foregoing Will, personally appeared before me & made Oath that they saw Samuel Scollay Sign, Seal & Deliver the same as & for his last Will & Testament, and that he was at the time of his Signing thereof of sound & disposing mind & memory; & at the same time Cullen Pollock & Thomas Pollock two of the Executors appointed by the sd. Will qualified themselves by taking the Oath prescribed by Law for that Purpose.

GAB. JOHNSTON.

Copied from Original Will, filed in the Office of the Secretary of State.

DAVID SHEPARD'S WILL.

IN THE NAME OF GOD AMEN, I, David Shepard, of Carteret County, in the Province of North Carolina, being weak in body, but of Sound Mind and Memory, and calling to mind the Mortality of my Body, that it is appointed for all men once to die, do make and Ordain this my Last Will and Testament, in manner and form following: I committ my Soul unto the Hands of God that gave it, hoping through the Merits and Mediation of my Blessed Saviour to receive free pardon of all my sins; and my body I committ to the Earth from whence it was taken, to be buried in Christianlike manner at the Discretion of my Executors. And as to such Worldly Estate as it has pleased God to endow me with, I Dispose of it in the following manner, to wit:

First, I give and bequeath to my son, Solomon Shepard, a piece of Land on the West side of Black Creek which I bought of Lankisthur Lovett; and a piece joining to it which I took up myself; and a piece of Land on Boague Sound, known by the name of Smiths Hammock whereon he now lives; and a Piece on the head of Broad Creek which I took up myself; and a Negroe man named Sanko, and a negro man named Fryday, and a Negro man named Jim, to him and his Heirs forever, he paying Sixty pounds to my Estate for the said Negro Jim, to be disposed of as hereafter shall be mentioned

2th. I give unto my Grand son, David Shepard, son of Solomon Shepard, One Plantation on Boague Sound, at the Mouth of Goose Creek, which I bought of Thomas Townley, and known by the name of Townleys Point; And a Negro Girl named Seaney, to him and his Heirs forever.

3th. I give and bequeath unto the Heirs of my Son, Jacob Shepard, Deces'D, a piece of Land on Boagues Sound, called Whitehall, and a piece of Land on the South Side of Newport River, known by the name of Mount Pleasant; and a piece on the North side of Newport River whereon John Barber once lived; and a Negro man Named Harry, which said Lands he was possessed of in his lifetime & Disposed of in his Will to his Heirs.

4th. I give and bequeath to my son, Elijah Shepard, the Plantation whereon I now live, and a peace of Land on the South side of Newport River Called Snows Neck, and a piece of Land on Boagues Sound known by the name of Bartroms Point, whereon he now lives; and a Negro man named Cuff, and a Negro man named Darbey; and a Negro man named Felix; and a Negro woman named Rachel, he paying for the two last Negroes mentioned to my Estate the sum Twenty Pounds, to be divided as shall hereafter be mentioned; and if my son Elijah should die without Heirs Lawfully begotten of his Body that then, the Plantation on Boagues Sound whereon he now lives, shall be given to my grand son John Shepard, son of Jacob Shepard Dr and his Heirs forever; and the Plantation I now live on to be given to my grand son, David Shepard, son of Solomon Shepard, to him and his Heirs forever.

I also give unto my Two sons, Solomon and Elijah Shepard, a piece of Land on the South side of Newport River known by the name of Reads Neck; a piece joining to it which I bought of John Harmon, to be Equally divided between them, they paying to my Estate the Sum of Forty Pounds, to be divided as after mentioned.

5, I give and bequeath to my Daughter, Sarah Wallis, a Negro Woman named Cate, and her four Children her lifetime; and after her death the said Negroes, and the increase of them, to the Lawfull Heirs of her Body forever.

6. I give and bequeath to my Daughter, Rebeckah Sanders, a Negro Girl named Savinour, During her Life; and after Death to the Lawfull Heirs of her Body forever.

7th. I give and bequeath to my Daughter, Abigail Ward, a Negro Woman named Tab, and her four children and a Negro woman named Thamer and her child, for her lifetime, and after her death to the Lawfull Heirs of her Body forever; I also give unto my Grand son, David Ward, son of Abigail Ward, one Negro boy named Anthony.

8th. My Will further is, that Wiliam, Wilkins Taylour, have nor Possess no part nor parcell of my Estate as hereafter shall be mentioned. I give unto my Daughter, Elisabeth Taylours Heirs, Lawful of her Body, a Negro Woman named Venus & her Child, and a boy named Abram, and Negro Girl named Cloey, with their Increase. I also give unto my grand son, David Taylor, son of Elisabeth Taylor, One Negro boy named Peter, and if my Daughter Elisabeth Taylor should necesiated for a support, I leave it to the Discretion of my Executors to assist her, out of the Money & others of the Division of my Estate which is left to the Heirs of her Body, and if her Heirs should die before they come of age, or without Heirs Lawfully begotten, that then the above Legacy be divided Equally Between my Heirs.

9th, I give and bequeath un my beloved Wife, One Negro Girl named Tillar, her Lifetime and to be maintained out of my Estate, and after her decease the said Negro girl named Tiller, be given unto my grand sons Absolom, and Solomon Shepard.

10th. I give and bequeath unto my Grandson, David Sanders, Son of Rebeckah Sanders, one Negro Girl named Rhoady.

11th, I give and bequeath unto my Grand son, Solomon Shepard, a Negro Woman named Vilot, and her child; I also give a Negro Woman named Dinah, and her three Children, to be equally divided between my Grand Sons, Absolom and Solomon Shepard.

12, I give and bequeath unto my Grand son, Solomon Shepard, that Tract of Land on Boague Sound which his Father lived on, and which sd. Land I Bought of Habbicock Rustel, and to him and his Heirs forever, but if Solomon should Die without Heirs of his Body Lawfully begotten, that then the said land shall be given unto David Taylor, son of Elisabeth Taylor.

13th, I further Leave one Negro Girl named Annes to be sold by my Executors at their Discretion, and the money for said Negro, together with that afore mentioned, to be paid by my two sons, Solomon & Elijah Shepard, and all other money belonging to my Estate, together with my Houshold Furniture, and moveables, and Stock of Cattle, to be Equally Divided between my Legatees, to wit, Solomon Shepard, Elijah Shepard, Sarah Wallis, Rebecah Sanders, Abigail Ward, the Heirs of Jacob Shepard Deacst, the Heirs of Elisabeth Taylor, & (the Heirs of) Absolom & Solomon Shepard, jr., which sd. Last three mentioned shall in proportion be Equal to one Shear. But if the said Negroes, Felix, Jim, or Rachel should die, or either of them, before Solomon or Elijah should be Pocest of them that then they shall not pay the sum agreed they was valued to.

Lastly, for the better Executing this my Last Will and Testament, I Constitute and appoint Colonel William Thomson, and my two Sons, Solomon and Elijah Shepard, my Executors, and I do hereby Utterly Disallow, revoke & Disannull, All and every other Will or Will by me made, Ratifying and Confirming this and no other to be my Last Will & Testament,

in Wittness whereof, I have hereunto set my Hand and Seal this 30th, day of May in the Year of Our Lord, One thousand Seven Hundred & Seventy four.

DAVID SHEPARD.

Signed, Sealed, Published and Declared in Presence of us:
    CORNELIAS CANADY.
    ELISABETH CANADY. her X mark
    GIDEON CANADY.

The last Will and Testament of David Shepard, deceased, hereunto-annexed, was proved before me this thirteenth day of January, 1775, by the Oath of Gideon Canady, one of the Subscribing Witnesses thereunto, who swore that he was present and did see the said Testator sign, seal, publish and declare the same to be and contain his last Will and Testament; and that at the time thereof he was of sound and disposing mind and memory. And Solomon and Elijah Shepard, two of the Executors in the said Will named, having taken the Oaths of Executors and Qualified agreeable to Law, It is Ordered that Letters testamentary issue thereon accordingly. JAS. HASELL.

Copied from Original Will, filed in the Office of the Secretary of State.

DANIEL SHINE'S WILL.

NORTH CAROLINA, CRAVEN COUNTY.

IN THE NAME OF GOD AMEN The 9th Day of May, 1757.

I, Daniel Shine, being Sick but of Perfect mind and memory thanks be given unto God therefore. I make this my Last Will and Testament, first of all, I give my Soule into the hands of God that gave it, and my Body to the Earth to be Buried after a Christian like Manner at the Discretion of my Executors is as Thuse(?)

Item, I give and Bequeath unto my Son, John Shine, Out of Love and Good Will, One English Shilling.

Item, I give and Bequeath unto my Son, Thos. Shine, One Horse Named Roger, One Bead and furniture, and half a Dozen Puter Plats and Two Sisable Dishes, and One Sisable Iron Pot new; and One Negro Fellow Named Tow, after my Debts are Paid, and all my Wareing Apparell.

Item, I give and Bequeath unto my Son, William Shine, when he Comes to the Age of Twenty One years, One Negro Gurl Named Judah, and One Negro Boy Named Gabriel, and One Horse Named Dolphin, And One Bead yt is Called my Bead and furniture, and One Pot, and Six Puter Plates and Two Sisable Dishes.

Item, I give and Bequeath unto my Daughter, Elizabeth Vaughan, out of Love and Good Will, One English Shilling.

Item, I give and Bequeath unto my Son, James Shine, Out of Love and Good Will, all the Rest of my Personall and Rale Estate as Negroes, Lands, horses, Cattle, Hogs, Household furniture, And Out Standing Debts,

And I make and Ordain my hole and Sole Executors, James Shine and John Oliver, Revocking and Disanulling all Other Wills and Lagacis before made by me.

DENIEL SHINE (Seal)

Sealed, Signed, and Published, Pronounced and Declared, by the Said Daniel Shine, as his Last Will and Testament in the Presence of us the Subscribers:
 GREEN.
  JOHN WILLIAMSON.
   CHARLES SHINEWOLF.

CRAVEN COUNTY ss.   August Court 1757.
 Present his Majestys Justices:

Then was the Last Will and Testament of Daniel Shine Exhibited into Court and Proved at the Oath of Charles Shinewolf, Who Swor that he Saw the Decd. Sign, Seal, Publish and Declare the Within to be his Last Will and Testament. And that to the Best of his Knowledg he was of Sound Mind and Disposing Memory; and that he also saw the Other Evidences Sign as Concuring Evidences with him: at the Same time Appeared James Shine, Executor therein Mentioned, and Qualified by Taking the Exors. Oath. Ordered that Mr. Secy. have Notice that Letters Testamentory Issue Accordingly.
     Test. PETER CONWAY. D. C. C.

Copied from Original Will, filed in the Office of the Secretary of State.

RICHARD SKINNER'S WILL.

IN THE NAME OF GOD AMEN, this 18th. day of May, in the Year of our lord, 1752. I, Richard Skinner, of the County of Perquimans, & Province of No. Carolina, being Sick in body but of perfect mind & memory, Thanks be to Almighty God Therefore, Calling unto mind the Mortality of my boddy and knowing that it is appointed for all men once to die, doe make

& ordain this my last will & Testament, That is to say, principally, & first of all, I give & Recomend my Soul into the hands of God that gave it; & my boddy I Recomend to the Earth to be buried in a Decent & Christian manner at the Discretion of my Exrs. hereafter Namd, Nothing doubting but at the Generall Resurection I shall Receive the same again by the power of Almighty God my Redeemer. And as touching Such Worldly Estate wherewith it hath pleasd God to bless me wth. in this life, I give, Demise & Dispose of the Same in the following manner & form:

Imprimis, I will & desire that as Soon as my Death all my Just Debts, that in Right or Conceine I owe to every person or persons, be dischargd & payd wth. Justice.

Item, I give & Bequeath to my Dearly belov'd wife, Sarah Skinner, the plantation whereon I now live, wth. the liberty of Timber for the plantation's use, but none to be Sold nor Carried Away, During her widdowhood, as farr back as the main Road. And in Case Marrys, my will is that she have the one half of said plantation, wth. the dwelling house, milk house, Smoke house & Kitchen During her Naturall life.

Item, I give & bequeath to my belovd Son, Saml. Skinner, the plantation whereon he now lives wth. the lands belonging thereto, to be Enjoyd by him & his heirs for Ever.

Item, I give & bequeath to my belovd Son, Eavens Skinner the plant'n. whereon John Simpson now lives, Lying in Chowan County, wth. Two hundred & Ninety Acres of Land, to be Enjoyd by him & his heirs for Ever.

Item, I give & Bequeath to my Belov'd Son, Joshua Skinner, my plantation Lying on the Sound Side, formerly call'd Fendells, Containing One hundred & fifty Acres of Land whereon he now lives, Beginning at the Sound Side & Running to the back head line, being the one half of the land I purchasd of Christian Reed, to be Enjoyd by him & the heirs of his Boddy Lawfully Begotten; & in Default of Such heirs to my Beloved Son, John Skinner; & the heirs of his boddy Lawfully Begotten.

Item, I give & Bequeath to my Belov'd Son, William Skinner, my back plantation adjoyning the plantation whereon I now live, from the back head line unto the Main Road, & in case my wife marrye I give the other half of the plantation whereon I now live Unto my Said Son, William, & After her Death I give the Said Plantation wth. the houses & lands belonging thereto, unto my Said Son, William Skinner, to be Enjoyd by him & the heirs of his boddy lawfully begotten; & in Default of Such heir, unto my belov'd Son, Samuel Skinner, & the heirs of his boddy lawfully begotten; And in default of Such heir, unto my Son, Joshua Skinner, & the heirs of his Boddy lawfully begotten; & in Default of Such heir to my Son, John Skinner, & the heirs of his boddy lawfully Begotten.

Item, I give & bequeath unto my Son, John Skinner, my plantation Lying on the sound Side, formerly called Petifers, wth. one hundred & fifty Acres of land, being the other half of the land I Purchased of Chris'r. Reed, to be enjoyd by him & the heirs of his boddy lawfully begotten; and in Default of Such heir unto my belov'd Son, Joshua Skinner, & the heirs of his boddy lawfully begotten.

Item, I give and bequeath I give & Bequeath unto my Dearly Beloved Wife, Sarah Skinner, the Sole use of the plantation whereon Thomas Munds now lives, lying in Chowan County, during her widdowhood, & at or after her Marriage or Death, I give & Bequeath unto my belovd Son, Saml. Skinner, the said plantation wth. one hundred & fifty Acres of land, to be enjoyd by him & his heirs for ever.

Item, I give & Bequeath unto my belov'd Son, Saml. Skinner, my Negro Girl namd Serenah, to be enjoyd by him & his heirs for ever.

Item, I give & Bequeath unto my belov'd Son, Joshua Skinner, my negro Girl Venus, to be enjoyd by him & his heirs for ever.

Item, I give & bequeath unto my belov'd Son, Willm. Skinner, my negro Girl nam'd Hannah, one feather Bed & furniture, four Cows & Calves, Six head of Sheep, two Iron potts & one Ovell Table, to the Value of twelve Shillings & Six pence Virga. Money.

Item, I give & Bequeath unto my beloved Son, John Skinner, my negro boy namd Frank, one feather bed & furniture, four Cows & Calves, Six head of Sheep, two Iron potts & one Ovell Table to the Value of twelve Shills. & Six pence Virga. money.

Item, my will & desire is that my two Negroes, Namly, Sall & Zangoe be Continued in the possession off, & for the use of my wife Untill her Marriage, or death, & then my will is that the above namd two Negroes & their Encrease, if any, be Equally Devided between my five Sons, Namely: Samuel, Eavens, Joshua, William & John, to be enjoyd by them & their heirs for Ever.

Item, I give unto my belovd wife, Sarah Skinner, the use of my Negro woman namd Flora, & her Increase, if any, During her Naturall life, & at her Decease my will & Desire is that the said Negro woman Nam'd Flora, & her Increase if any, be Eaqually Devided between my five Sons, Namely: Samuel, Eavens, Joshua, William, & John, to be enjoyd by them & their heirs for Ever.

Item, I give unto my Dearly belovd wife, Sarah Skinner, the use of all the rest & Residue of my Personall Estate During her Widdowhood; & after her Marriage, to have one third of sd. personall Estate to her own use & Benefitt; the other two thirds of said Estate after my wife's part is taken out, to be

Eaqually Devided between my five Sons, Namely: Samuel, Eavens, Joshua, William, & John, to be enjoyd by them & their heirs for Ever. It is my will & Desire that in case Either one or more of the Young Negroes bequeathed my Sons, Should Die before the Devision of my Estate, or they are possesd wth. them, It is my Desire that the Value of Such Negroes or negro, as may happen to die as afforsd. Shall be made Good unto him or them out of my Estate.

My Will & Desire is that in Case there should hereafter arrise any Disputes or Differences between my wife & Children, or any of them, that Joseph White, John Harvey, & Benjamin Harvey, or any two of them, doe Decide or determine the Same, and they, the said Joseph White, John Harvey & Benjamin Harvey, or any two of them, is hereby Appointed whole & Sole Arbitrators of any Disputes or Differences that may arise between my wife & Children, or any of them, by Virtue of this my Will,

And Lastly, of this my last will Testament I doe Nominate, Constitute, Ordain & Appoint my Dearly belov'd Wife, Sarah Skinner, Executrix, My belov'd Son, Samual Skinner, my Belov'd Son, Joshua Skinner, my belov'd Son, William Skinner, & my belov'd Son, John Skinner, Executors to this my last will & Testament, to See it Strictly fullfill'd in all its parts, Revoking & Disallowing all other will or wills by me made, Ratifying & Confirming this to be my last will and Testament.

in Witness whereoff, I have hereunto sett my hand & Seal, the day & Year Above Written.

RICHARD X SKINNER (Seal)
his mark

Sign'd, Seal'd, Publish'd, Pronounc'd & Declar'd by the Said Richd. Skinner, to be his last will & Testament in Presence off us who are likewise Witnesses to the under written Memdm. at same time

    JOSEPH WHITE. affd.
    PETER JONES. affd.
    JOHN HARVEY.

Memerandum: that it is my will & desire that my Grand Daughter have, & doe hereby Give & bequeath unto my Said Grand Daughter, Sarah Skinner, one Cow and Calf.

As Witness my hand the Date Above Mentiond

RICHARD X SKINNER (SEAL)
his mark

SARAH } Qualified affm
JOSHUA } & WILLM Qualified by Oath

PERQUIMANS COUNTY. ss.   July Court, anno Dom., 1752.
        Present His Majestys Justices:
These may Certifie that the will hereunto annexed and the Memorandum, was duly Proved in Open Court by the affirmations of Joseph White & Peter Jones, two of the Subscribing Evidences thereto, and at the Same time appeard. Sarah Skinner Exx. & Joshua Skinner Exr. who was duly Qualified thereto by taking the affermation by law appointed & William Skinner another Exr. was duly Qualified thereto by taking the Oath by law appointed. Ordered that the Secretary or his Deputy of Said Province have notice, that Letters Testamentary issue thereon as the law Directs.
            Test. EDMUND HATCH, Cler. Cur.

Copied from Original Will, filed in the Office of the Secretary of State.

JOHN SLADES' WILL.

IN THE NAME OF GOD AMEN.

This Sixth Day of September, Anno, Seventeen hundred & forty three. I, John Slade, of Hyde County, in the province of North Carolina, being Sick & weak of Body, but of Perfect Sense & Memory, Blessed be God for it, do Constitute & Ordain this my Last Will & Testament, That is is to Say, first, I Give & bequeath my Soul to God that Gave it me; & my body I Commit to the Earth to be buried in a Chrisitan Like Manner; and as for what worldly Goods the Lord in his Mercy hath been pleased to bestow on me I Give & bequeath as followeth, Viz.:

Imprimis, I Give unto my Eldest Son, John Slade, the plantation he now lives on, with a hundred & twenty five Acres of Land, it being the Land I bought of John Smith, Cooper, to him & his heirs for ever.

Item, I Give to my Son, Benjamin Slade, the plantation I now dwell on with a Line that I have made adjoyning to the Land I bought of John Smith, Cooper, & So running up the Creek to a Pine Markt, & So round to the Said Land that I bought of the Said Smith, to him & his heirs for ever.

Item, I Give to my Son, William Hodges Slade, the remainder Part of the Manner Plantation which in my Patent is five hundred & Eighty Acres, of what is Left out of the Patent of my Son, Benjamin Slade Land, which I have bounded by Markt trees; & Also a tract Land one hundred & fifty Six Acres of Land & adjoining to the former pieces of Land, to him & his heirs for ever.

Item, I Give unto my Son, Hezekiah Slade, the Remainder part of two hundred & fifty Acres as by patent doth appear; & also the remainder part of one hundred & fifty Acres I bought of Francis Banks, it being the remainder part of both parcels I haveing already made a deed of Gift & Given to my Daughter, Mary Jewel, & her husband Ben: Jewel, as by bounds doth appear that I have made be the Same more or Less, & the remainder of the said two parcels of Land I Give unto my Son, Hezekiah Slade, & his heirs for ever.

Item, I have already Given to my Daughter, Mary Jewel, & Benj: Jewel, her husband, two hundred Acres of Land, be the Same More or Less, as by a Deed a Gift More & at Large appears bearing date the Sixth Day of September, Anno, 1737: & also a parcel of Cattle, which is to be there full part & portion of My Estate & I Demise that they shall not Come in for no more.

Item, I Give unto my Son, Hez: Slade, one Gun.
Item, I Give unto my Son, Wm: Hodges Slade, one Gun.
Item, I Give unto my Son, Benjn: Slade, one Gun.
Item, I Give unto my Son, Hez: Slade, one Cow & Calf.
Item, I Give unto my Son, Wm: Hodges Slade, what Cattle is in his Mark which is under Square the Left ear.
Item, I Give unto my Son, Benjn: Slade, what Cattle is in his Mark which is Crop & an under bit & one Slit in the Right Ear.
Item, I Give unto my Daughter, Sarah Slade, what Cattle is in her Mark which is under Square the Right Ear.
Item, I Give unto my Daughter, Kezia Slade, one feather bed & furniture.

Item, I Give unto my welbeloved Wife, Abigal Slade, all the rest of my Moveables within Doors & Without, that I have not already, be it of what kind Soever, or in any wise appertaining to me, to her & her Disposals.

And I will that my Wife, Abigal Slade, be my Sole Executrix of this my Last Will & Testament & that She Satisfie all my Debt that I Justly owe to any Person.

       JOHN X SLADE. (SEAL)
        mark

Signed, Sealed & Pronounced in the Presence of us, to be the Last Will & Testament of the Testator:
  RICHARD LEATH.
  WILLIAM WILKINSON.
  URIAH COLLINS

HYDE COUNTY,   Decbr. Court, 1743. (1743)

The with in will was proved in open Court by the oath of Richd. Leath & Wm. Wilkerson, two of the Subscribing Evedences thereto, ordered that Secretary have notice thereof.

       WM. BARROW, Clk. Cr.

Copied from Original Will, filed in the Office of the Secretary of State.

SAMUEL SLADE'S WILL.

IN THE NAME OF GOD AMEN, I, Samuel Slade, of Beufort County, within the Province of North Carolina, Planter, being in good Health of Body & in Perfect Sound Mind & Memory, praised be God for it, But Knowing the uncertainty of this Life and that it is appointed for all men One to die, Do make, Ordain, Constitute & appoint This to be my last Will & Testament, To Say, First, I Will that all my Just Debts be paid, my Funeral Rights dischrged & satisfied; And as Touching my Worldly Goods I give, bequeath & Devise in Manner following to:

First, to my beloved Daughter, Elizabeth, Wife of William Dunbarr, give my two Female Slaves known by the Names Serey & Judey, but the Child that Serey is at this Time pregnant with I give unto my Grand Daughter, Mary, the Eldest Daughter, of William Dunbarr & my Daughter Elizabeth. I also give unto my Daughter, Elizabeth, aforesaid, One Bed of Feathers, One Pair of Sheets, One Rugg & a Bed stead & three Cows & their Calves. Unto my Grand-Son, Samuel Dunbarr, I give & bequeath all that Tract or Parcel of Land, being & lying on the South Side of Pamtico River, at the Head of Blounts Creek, & on a Branch known by the Name of Good Neighbourhood Branch, & near this Land whereon I now Dwell, which Land was granted Unto me by his Excelency Gabriel Johnston, the Present Governor of this Province.

unto my beloved Daughter, Hanah, the Wife of William Tossyue (?) I give two Shillings, Sterling, with full Value in Current Money of the Province.

unto my Grandson Samuel Blount, son of James Blount, begotten on the Body of my Daughter and his late wife Jane, I give my Negro Male Slave Named Joshawa, that is now a Child about four Years of Age; and also two Cows & their Calves.

Unto my Grand Daughter, Mary Blount, Daughter of James & Jane Deceesed as aforesaid. I give my Negro Female Negro Slave named Charley, now an Infant, an also two Cows & their Calves.

Unto my Dearly beloved Daughter, Susana Slade, I give, Devise & bequeath this my Manner Plantation, whereon I now Dwell with all the Buildings, Houses, Edifices and Improvements thereon & all the Tools, Tackell & utinsils thereunto belonging, with all other my Lands not before given, to be holden to her & her Heirs, as also all the Rest, Remainer & Residue of my Estate as Goods, Chattels, Apperrell, HouseHold Furniture, & Slaves. Especially Jack & Jerome & Sam & Nan, and all other things or Part of my Worldly Estate unto me belonging, or any wise appertaining, all these I give unto my Daughter, Susana, aforesaid.

I Do nominate & appoint my beloved Daughter, Susana, to Executrix & Benjamin Rigney & Jacob Nevell, both of the County, Executors of this my last Will & Testament.

SAMUEL SLADE (SEAL

Signed, Sealed, Published & Declared this Seventeenth Day. of March, in the Year of Our Lord God 1746. In the Presence of:
  RICHARD EVANS.
  THOS. JAMES.
  PHILLIP SHUTE.
  MARY X DUNBARR.
    her
    mark

BEAUFORT COUNTY. ss.   December Court 1746.
 Present his Majesty's Justices:
 These are to certify that the within last Will & Testament of Samu Slade, late of the said County, Planter, Deceased, was exhibited ir open Court & proved by the Oaths of Thos. James & Phillip Shute, Sig ing Evidences thereto, who swear that they see'd the afsd. Deceasd Sig Seal, Publish & Declare the Within to be his last Will & Testament, a that they seed the other Subscribing Evidences witness the Same. Ben Rignie Exor. within named qualified himself by taking the Exor's Oa according to Law. Ordered that the Secrty. have Notice thereof.
     Testis. JOHN FORBIS. Cler. Curill.
Recorded in Will Book 6, page 45.

SAMUEL SLOCUMB'S WILL.

NORTH CAROLINA.   May 8th: 1712.
 IN THE NAME OF GOD AMEN. I, Samuell Slocumb, of Ba County, in ye province of North Carolina, Planter, this bei my last Will & Testamt:
 All my wearing Clothes I Give to my bror: John Slocum I Give to my bror. Wm. Smyth two Cowes & Calves and my bror. Solomn: Smyth, two more Cowes & Calves. And my sister, Isabel Smyth, two Cowes & Calves more. I Gi to my Mother, ten Cowes & One bed tick; And one bed ti to Margt: Davis, the rest of my Estate I Give to my Moth & my bror. John Slocumb & Margt. Davis,to be equally Divid between them.
       his
    SAMLL: X SLOCUMB (SEAL)
       mark
Signed, Sealed & Delivered In
ye presence of:
  WM: BRICE.
  LOVICK THOMAS.
  ANN BRICE.

NORTH CAROLINA. ss.
 By the Honble. the Presidt. &ca.
 It being Certifyed unto me that Samll. Slocumb is Dead & hath ma and put his last will & Testament in writeing, a true Copy whereof hereunto annexed, And not haveing appointed any Execrs. therein;

his Mother, Eliza Smyth, & his bror. John Slocumb, and Margt. Davis, being therein mentioned Genll. Legatees, by wch: they have right to be Admrs. wth ye said Will Annexed. These are therefore to Impower them, ye Said Eliza Smyth, John Slocumb, & Margt: Davis, to enter in & upon, all & Singuler, ye Goods & Chattles, rights and Credits, of ye Said Samuell Slocumb whereever in this Governmt: to be found and ye Same into their possession to take, and a true Inventory thereof, appraised according to Law, to returne into ye Secys. Office within One Yeare after the Date hereof, and all ye Just Debts of ye Decd. to pay Soe farr as ye Said Estate will Extend or amount to. And the remaindr: to dispose of as by the Said Will is appointed, Security being given for ye true performance hereof.

Given und'r my hand & ye Seale of ye Collony, this 3d: day of Augt: 1713. THOS. POLLOCK.

Copied from Original Will, filed in the Office of the Secretary of State.

JOHN SNOAD'S WILL.

NORTH CAROLINA. SST.

IN THE NAME OF GOD, AMEN. I, John Snoad, of the County of Beaufort, Province Afsd., being in Great weakness of body but of Sound & Perfect mind and memory, Doe make & ordain this my Present Last Will & Testament, In manner & form Following, Vizt., First & Principally I Commend my Soul Into the hands of Almighty God, hoping through the Meritts and Death of my Savour Jesus Christ, to have Full & Free pardon of all my Sins, and to Inherit Everlasting life; & as touching the Disposall of all such Temporal Estates as itt hath Pleased Almighty God to Bestow upon my, I give & Dispose thereof in Manner Following:

Imprimis, I will that all my Just Debts shall be paid & Discharged.

Item, I give and Bequeath unto my son, Henry Snoad, my Plantaion I now Dwell on, Containing two Hundred & Twenty Five Acres of Land, to him and his heirs For ever, reserving one third for my wife, ye use & Benefitt of the two front rooms, & the three Front Chambers of my Dwelling House, w'th the Priviledge of the Smoak house to Smoak her meat & the Barn to put her Crope In; & I also Give & Bequeath unto my Son, Henry Snoad, a Certain tract of Land Containing Six hundred and Forty Acres Lying on the West side of the little Beaver Dam, in maules Neck; and I give and Bequeath unto my son, Henry Snoad a Certain tract of Land on the North side of Pamplico River, and on the west side of the herring run, bounding on Sam'le Boutwell Land; & I also Give & bequeath unto my Son, Henry Snoad, a Certain tract of Land Containing Six hundred and forty Acres of Land lying In the County of Beaufort, on the north Side of pamplico River & on the west side of Grindell Creek, & was by me purchased of Mr. Thompson, & by him purchased of Thos. Roper.

Item, I give and Bequeath unto my Son, Wm. Snoad, Certain tract of Land Containing Six hundred & Forty Acr of Land lying on the west Side of the mouth of white o: River, & on Queens Creek, & was taken up by Capt. Jo Martin; & I give & Bequeath unto my Son, Wm. Snoad, Certain tract of Land Containing one hundred Acres Lyi on the North Side of Pamplico River & was by me purcha:s of Thos. Norcom; and I Give & Bequeath unto my son, Willia Snoad, one Moiety of a Certain tract of Land Containi: Six hundred & Forty Acres, lying on the north side of Pampli River & was by me purchased of Wm. Little, Esqr., & by hi purchased of Thos. Roper; and I Give and Bequeath un my Son, Wm. Snoad, a Certain tract of Land Containing S hundred & Forty Acres, lying on the north Side of pampli River and In the Fork of Moy's Beaver Dam.

Item, I Give and Bequeath unto my Son, John Snoad, o: Moiety of a Certain tract of Land containing Six hundred a1 Forty Acres of Land, lying on the North Side of pampli River on the west side of Grindell Creek, & was by me pu chased of Wm. Little, Esqr., & by him purchased of Th(Roper.

Item, I give & Bequeath unto my well Beloved wife, Eliz Snoad, my Negro Man Robin & his wife Africa, my Neg man Aungus & his wife Hannah, & my Negro man London.

Item, I give and Bequeath unto my Son, Henry Snoad, n Mullato man Pompey, and my Negro man Huffey.

Item, I give and Bequeath unto my Son, Wm. Snoad, n Negro man Kent, and my Negro man Salem.

Item, I Give & Bequeath unto my Daughter, Mary Snoa my Negro man Windsor & his wife Rose.

Item, I give & Bequeath unto my Daughter, Anne Snoa My Negro man Will & his wife Venus.

Item, I give and Bequeath unto my Daughter, Elizth Snoa my Negro man Patrick and his wife Martha.

Item, I give & Bequeath unto my son, John Snoad, my tv Negro Children, Vizt: Virgill and Homer.

Item, I give & Bequeath unto my Daughter, Sarah Snoa My two Negro Children, Scanderbeg & Tamerlane.

Item, I Give & Bequeath unto my Son, John Snoad & n Daughter, Sar—— Snoad, my Negro Man Cato, to be Equal Divided Betwixt them.

Furthermore, itt is my will that none of these Legaci are to be Delivered till the Afsd. Children are of Age, or 1 the Day of Marriag.

Item, I Give and Bequeath unto my well Beloved w Elizth Snoad, two of the Largest & one of the Smaller Feath Beds w'th Furniture, & one of the Sack Bottom Bedstea——.

Item, I Give and Bequeath unto my son, Henry Snoad, one Feather Bed with Furniture.

Item, I Give and Bequeath unto my Son, Wm. Snoad, one Feather bed with Furniture.

Item, I Give and Bequeath unto my Daughter, Mary Snoad one Feather bed w'th Furniture.

Item, I Give and Bequeath unto my Daughter, Anne Snoad, one Feather bed with Furniture.

Item, I Give and Bequeath unto my Daughter, Elizth Snoad, one Feather bed w'th Furniture.

Item, I Give and Bequeath unto my well beloved wife, Eliz'th Snoad, All the pewter, brass & Iron potts that I had by her, Likewise the Chest of Drawers Standing In the new Chamber and the table Standing in the New ro'm.

Item, I Give and Bequeath unto my Son, Henry Snoad, Vizt: all the Chairs, Tables, Chests, Chest of Drawers, Desks, Pictures, books, Silver Spoons, Tea Spoons, Pewter, Brass, Iron potts and Kettles & what did belong to me, as also the New Gun hanging over the Middle room Door and my small sword and belt.

Item, I Give and Bequeath unto my Son, Wm. Snoad, My Hangers, Hanging In the new Room.

Item, I Give and Bequeath unto my Son, Henry Snoad. & my Son, Wm. Snoad, all my Cloaths and Saddles to be Equally Divided Between them.

Item, I Give and Bequeath unto my Daughter, mary Snoad, my New Side Saddle.

Item, I give and Bequeath unto my well Beloved wife, Eliz'th Snoad, all the Cattle, horses, Mares, hoggs &c, that Runs at Rumney Marsh, and a third part of the Sheep.

Item, The rest of my Cattle, horses, hoggs, Sheep &c, to be Equally Divided Amongst my Children, Henry Snoad, Wm. Snoad, Mary Snoad, Anne Snoad & Eliz'th Snoad.

Item, I give & Bequeath unto my Son, Henry Snoad, the my Part of the Great Pettiauger.

Item, I Give & Bequeath unto my Son, Wm. Snoad, my little Peteiauger.

Item, I Give & Bequeath unto my Son In Law, John Fry, my black mare Branded |—|—| S.

Item, I Likewise Give & Bequeath unto my Well Beloved wife, Eliz'th Snoad, a third part of Debts that is Due to me at the time of my Decease, the paying a third part of Charges For Collecting; & I give & Bequeath unto my well Beloved wife Eliz'th Snoad, a third part of Merchandize I shall be possest w'th at that time, Either at home or abroad; & a third part of Bottles, Earthenware &c.

Item, I Give & Bequeath unto my well beloved wife, Eliz'th Snoad, one of my plows.

Item, I give & Bequeath unto my Son, Henry Snoad, my three Mills & my Cross Cutt Saw.

Item, I give and Bequeath unto my well beloved wife Eliz'th Snoad, my horse Cartt.

Item, I Give & Bequeath unto my Son Henry, Snoad, my two large Looking Glases.

Furthermore, itt is my will that my son, Henry Snoad, shall pay unto my Children the Sum of Sixty pounds when they are of age or att the Day of Marriage.

Furthermore, itt is my will that my son, Henry Snoad, shall have the Care & Management of the Negroes till the time of Delivery as Afsd., he, ye Sd. Henry Snoad, Allowing his Brothers & Sisters Vizt: Wm. Snoad, Mary Snoad, Anne Snoad & Eliz'th Snoad, a handsome and proportionable maintainance.

Furthermore, itt is my will that my Son, Wm. Snoad, shall be possest w'th the Benefitt of his Negroes att Eighteen years of Age.

Furthermore, itt is my will that all those Legacies that I have given to my Children is to them & their Heirs Forever.

And, I Doe hereby Consitutte & Appoint My Brother In Law, Wm. Martin, my Brother In Law, Walley Chauncey, & my Son, Henry Snoad, Executors of this my last will & Testament; hereby Revoking all former wills by me made.

In witness whereof, I, the said John Snoad, have to this my last will and Testament, Hereunto Sett my hand & Seall, this 21st. day of June, Anno Dom., 1743.

JNO. SNOAD, (Seal)

Signed, Sealed & Delivered In the Presence of us:
   HENRY LUCAS.
   ELIZABETH LEAKS,
   SARAH LUCAS.

NO. CAROLINA.

This day Henry Lucas and Sarah Lucas, two of the Subscribing Evidences to the execution of the within will appeared before me and on the Holy Evangelists made Oath, that they saw the Testator, John Snoad, sign, seal And publish the within Instrument as his last will and Testament; and that the Sd. Testator was then of perfect & sound disposing mind & Memory.

Bath Town, Septr. 1st, 1743.   J. MONTGOMERY, C.

Septr. 1st. 1743.

Then appeared before me William Martin and Henry Snoad, two of the Exec'rs appointed by the within Will and took the Oath by Law appointed to be taken for the qualification of Executors.

J. MONTGOMREY, C. J.

Copied from the Original Will, filed in the Office of the Secretary of State.

HENRY SNOAD'S WILL.

IN THE NAME OF GOD, AMEN. I, Henry Snoad, of the County of Beaufort, in the Province of North Carolina, being Sick & weak in Body, but of Sound mind, do make & ordain this my last Will & Testament:

First & principally, I recommend my Soul into the Hands of Almighty God, hoping thro' the merits & intercession of our Lord & Saviour Jesus Christ, to have full & free pardon of all my Sins & to inherit everlasting life; and as touching all such temporal Estate as it hath pleased him to bestow upon me, I do dispose of it in manner following, Viz:

Imprimis, I will and desire that all my just Debts & Funeral Expenses be paid as soon as possible after my Decease.

Item, I give & bequeath unto my Son, John Peyton Snoad, the Plantation whereon I now live, containing four hundred & fifty acres of land; and also the Plantation I bought of John Lane, together with all the Houses, Fields, Improvements & Appurtenances belonging to both & either of them, to him & his Heirs for ever: Provided, nevertheless, & I do declare it to be my Intent & meaning, that my Sister, Mary Lane, have the quiet use & Occupation of the plantation I bought of John Lane aforesd., during her Life. Likewise I give & bequeath unto my Sd. son, John Peyton Snoad, my Plantation lying on the Herring Run, binding on the Plantation, I bought of John Lane, containing three hundred acres of Land. Likewise, I give & bequeath unto my sd. Son, John Peyton Snoad, my Silver Watch, my Silver hilted Sword (now in the possession of Stephen Cade), my Silver Shoe & Knee Buckles, Six Large Silver Spoons, my Silver Can, my Gold Sleeve Buttons, my Mahogany Desk, & my gilt fram'd Looking Glass, & my large China Bowl.

Item, I give & Bequeath unto my Son, Benja. Snoad, my Plantation lying in the Cow pen Neck, below Wm. Spear's, containing Six hundred & fourty Acres of Land. Likewise, I give & bequeath unto my sd. Son, Benja. Snoad, My Plantation lying at the Mouth of white Oak River, on Queens Creek, containing Six hundred & fourty Acres, to him & his Heirs for ever. Likewise, I give & bequeath unto my sd. Son, Benja. Snoad, my Silver hilted Sword that was my Father's, Six large Silver Spoons, my black Walnut Looking Glass, & all my China Ware that is now at home, excepting what is before bequeathed.

Item, I give & Bequeath unto my Daughter, Ann Snoad, my Plantation lying at the Mouth of Blunt's Creek, conta'ing four hundred & fourty Acres, to her & her Heirs for ever. Likewise, I give & bequeath unto my sd. Daughter, Ann Snoad,

Six Silver Tea Spoons, my Silver Tea Tongs, my Silver Pepper Box, my Tea Table, & all my China Ware & cloaths that were her Mothers, now in Possession of my Aunt Chauncy.

Item, I Give & Bequeath unto my sd. Sons, John Peyton Snoad & Benja. Snoad, all my Books to be equally divided between them.

Item, I give & Bequeath unto my Sisters, fourty Shillings sterl. apiece, to buy each of them a Ring.

Item, I Give & Bequeath unto my Sister, Mary Lane, enough Money to purchase a couple of Slate Grave Stones, for her Son Jno. Snoad Lane, who lies buried in my Orchard.

Item, Likewise, I give & bequeath unto my Friend Walley Chauncey, hereafter named my Executor, my black Stallion, wch I bought of Stephen Cade, together with my best Bridle, Saddle, Case of Pistols, & Gun that was my Fathers; and I also give & bequeath unto his Wife, my Aunt Chauncy, fourty Shillings sterl., to buy her a Ring, & also Five pounds sterl. to be disposed of (as) she shall think fit.

Item, I give & Bequeath unto my Friend, James Bonner, hereafter named my Executor, my Gun & Sword that was my brother William's.

Item, I Give & Bequeath unto William Oglesby, My Apprentice, A set of Carter's Tools, & a new Suit of Cloaths.

Item, I give & Bequeath unto my sd. Children, John Peyton Snoad, Benja. Snoad, & Ann Snoad, all the remaining part of my Estate, wether real or Personal, to be equally divided between them. And it is my Will & Desire, that my Executors hereafter named, keep my Estate together & employ the Same to support, maintain & educate my Children until they, or either of them, shall arrive to the Age of twenty one Years, or marry, then to be divided by my Executors, & each Childs portion delivered, as above bequeathed, unto them; but in case two of my Executors shall decease, before the time, then the sd. Division & Delivery to be made by the Surviving Executor in Conjunction with two of the Court to be appointed for that purpose; but if none of the Executors should Survive then, the sd. Division & delivery to be made by three members of the Court, to be appointed for that purpose. It is likewise my Will & Desire, that what Money arises out of my Estate more than will maintain & Educate my sd. Children, be applyed to purchase young Negores for my sd. Children. Likewise it is my Will & Desire that my Executors sell such of my Lightwood Lands, as shall become useless to my Estate, both the Lands At Brush Fare, & wch I took up in conjunction wth Jos. Hardee, and likewise the perishable Moveables, reserving the Leather Chairs & three of the best Feather Beds & Furniture, & also the Mill situated on the Herring Run. It is likewise my Will & Desire that my Executors bring up my

Son's to some reputable Calling, according as their Genius shall incline. Likewise it is my Desire that my Executors procure Gravestones for all my deceased Friends that ly buried in my Plantaion.

And, I do hereby constitute, authorize & appoint my trusty Friend, Walley Chauncy, my trusty Friend James Bonner, my trusty Friend, John Hardee, & my trusty Friend, Edwd. Salter, Executors of this my last Will & Testament, hereby revoking all former & other Wills by me made.

In Witness whereof, I have hereunto set my Hand & Seal, This 20th day of May, 1752.

HENRY SNOAD. (Seal)

Signed, Sealed, published & declared by the Testator, to be his last Will & Testament in presence of:

SAML. BOUTWELL,
ANN WILLOUBEY.
GRIFFETH HOWELL.

BEAUFORT COUNTY. ss.

At a Court held at Bath Town for the said County, at the Court house, on the second tuesday in December, and 12th. day of the same Month, Anno Dom., 1752.

Present his Majesty's Justices.

These are to certify that Griffith Howell, one of the Subscribing evidences to the within Will appear'd in Open Court and made Oath on the holy Evangelists, that he was present and Saw Henry Snoad Sign, Seal and declare the within Instrument of writing to be his last Will and Testament, and that the said Henry Snoad was at that time of Sound and disposeing mind and Memory; and that he also saw Samuel Boutwell and Anne Willoughby, the other subscribing Witnesses sign their names thereto at the same time. Then Walley Chauncy and John Hardee, Exors. of the said Will appear'd in Open Court and took the Oath of Exors, in due form. Whereupon it was Ordered by the said Court that Mr. Secretary have notice thereof that Letters Testamentary Issue thereupon as the Law directs.   Test. WILL ORMOND, Cler Cur.

Copied from the Original Will, filed in the Office of the Secretary of State.

SETH SOTHELL'S WILL.

IN THE NAME OF GOD AMEN. I, Seth Sothel, of the County of Albemarle, wthin ye province of Carolina, Esqr., being (throug Mercy) of Perfect Mind and Memory, Doe ordaine and Make this my last Will and Testament in Manner and forme following:

Imprs. I give and bequeath unto my Loving frien, Francis Hartley, the plantation where he now dwells for the tearme of five years, wch is to Commence from the day of my death, and two thirds of my Signory, bounding on flatty Creeke and Pasquotank River, for and during the Naturall Live of him the Said, Francis Hartley, and his Wife, and after their disease, to Anna Sothell my Wife, her heirs and assigns for ever.

Item, I Give and Bequeath to Edward Foster, Esqr., my father in Law, all that my Plantation at Cuscopinum, to him, his heirs and assigns for ever; and Thirty heads of Cattle belonging to the Said Plantation, & one Negroe Man.

Item, I Give unto William Duckinfield, Esqe., five pounds to buy him a Gold Ring: Item I give unto William Wilkison, five pounds to buy him a Gold Ring: Item I give unto Mr. Henderson Walker five pounds to buy him a Gold Ring.

Item, I Give unto Edward Wade all y my Plantation where Mr. Thomas Evins now dwells in Little River, to him & his assigns, for and Dureing his Naturall life, and after his disease to Anna Sothell, my Wife, her heirs and Assigns for ever.

Lastly, I Give and bequeath unto my Deare & entirely well beloved wife, Anna Blunt, all my Lands, Plantations, Tennaments, and Hereditaments wch I Now have (in ye Province of Carolina Adjoining or Bounding on Salmon Creek, Kendricks Creeke, Little River, Flatty Creeke, and the River of Pasquotank, to her, the Said Anna Sothrel, her heirs & assigns for ever: excepting the Tearme of five years to Mr. Hartley, and that the Sd. Mr. Hartley and his Wife, and Mr. Edward Wade, may hold all the Lands above bequeathed to them for their Natural lives, and the Said Anna, my Wife, to have it in Reversion, and I Give and Bequeath unto the above Named Anna Sothell, my Wife:

All my Personall Estate whatsoever, to witt., all my goods and Chatteles, Mouvables and Immouvables, Rights and Creditts wthin the abovesaid Province of Carolina, for ever, And I doe make the Said Anna Sothell, my Wife, my Whole and Sole Executirx of this my last Will and Testament.

In Testimony whereof I have hereunto Sett my hand and Seale the five and Twentyeth day of January, one thousand, Six hundred eighty nine. 1689/90

          SETH SOTHELL. (Seal)

Sealed, Signed & Delivered
in the presence of:
  WM. WILKISON.
  HENDERSON WALKER.
  JOHN LOWES.
  WM. WOLLARD.
    Signum
  SARAH X WOLLARD.

Proved by the oath of Sarah Wollard before mee, the Subscriber the 3 day of February, Anno Do: 1693/4.
          WILLIAM WILKISON.

Proved in Court by the oath of Colloll Wm. Wilkison, and Capt. Henderson Walker, ye 5th of Feb'ry, Anno Do., 1693/4.

Attested EDWARD MAYO, Clr.

Whereas Anna Sothell hath upon the 5th day of February Anno Di., 1693, in open Court proved ye above written to be the last will testum of Seth Sothell, esqr., her deceased husband, and shee being thereby constituted sole executrix of the Same, these are to empower the Said Anna Sothell to take into her Possession all & every the estate of the said Seth Sothell wherever in this govenment to be found, and the same to dispose of according to the import and Meaning of of the said last will and testamt.

Given undr our hands, and the Seal of the County, the 26th. day of March, Ano Dim., 1693. regett the 26th of March 1693.

W. GLOVER.

PHILIP LUDWELL.
THO. HARVY.   FRANCIS JONES.
WM. WILKISON.   SAML. SWANNE.
THO. POLLOCK   DANIEL ALKEHURST,
                                        Sect.

Copied from Recorded Copy of Will, filed in the Office of the Secretary of State.

ARON SPRINGS' WILL.

IN THE NAME OF GOD AMEN, I, Aron Spring, of the County Beaufort, and in the province of North Carolina, Calling to mind uncertainty of this Transitory Life, & being well Assured that all men are born to Dye, & not knowing how Soon it may please the Almighty God to Call me out of this present State of Life, Do make, ordain, Constitute and appoint this to be my last Will & Testament, in manner and form as follows:

Imprimis, I Give and Devise & Bequeath to my Son, Robert Spring, the plantation whereon he now Lives, & one hundred Acres of Land belonging to the aforesaid plantation, which said Land I give to my said Son, Robert, & to his heirs and Assigns for ever.

Item, I Give, Devise & Bequeath to my Two Youngest Sons, James Spring, & Abraham Spring, four hundred & forty Acres of Land to be Divided between the two; that is to say, Abraham to have my manner plantation Up the Swamp to the Brink, from thence South to the Back Line; & all the Land on the North side of March, to my Son, James; which said Land I give to my Two Sons & their heirs & Assigns for ever.

Item, I Lend to my beloved Wife, Martha Spring, my manner plantation During her widowhood & no longer. Also, I lend to my sd. Wife, Martha, one Negroe woman called Sew, during the Life of my said Wife & at her Decease, that the said Negroe Wench & her incres to be Eckely Devide between My Two Youngest Sons, Abraham & James Spring. Also, I Give to my Wife, Martha Spring, one Feather Bed &

Furniture, & one Whit horse, & four Cows & Calves, & one small Iron Pott. Also, I Lend to my well beloved Wife, Martha Spring, one Large Bason, & one Large Pewter Dish & four Pewter Plates, & one Large Chist, & one Looking Glass.

Item, I Give & Bequeath to my Son, Robert, one Negroe boy called Daniel, Together with what he has allready in possession, to him, his heirs Assigns for ever.

Item, I Give and Bequeath to my well beloved Dorter Dinah, which is know the Wife of William Jessor, Ninty Acres of Land lying upon the hed of Goos Creeck, and one Negroe Garl called Flory, excepting of the first Child the aforesaid Negro brings, to be given to my Son, James Spring.

Item, I Give, Devise & Bequeath to my Son, Aron Spring, one Negroe Boy called Seasor, & one Feather Bed & Furniture, & Two Cows & Two Earlings, & Two Ews & Two Lambs, & four Sows, and pigs, & one new Gun, one Chist, & one Large Iron pott hooks, I give to my sd. Son Aron & his heirs & Esignes for ever.

Item, I Give, Devise & Bequeath to my well beloved Dorter, Elizabeth Spring, one Negroe Girl called Prudence, & one Feather Bed & Furniture, to her my sd. Daughter, Eliz: Spring, & her heirs & Esignes for Ever.

Item, I Give to my Cusen, James Magee, Two Cows & Two Erlings, to him for Ever.

Item, after the deces of my Loveing Wife, Martha Spring, that then the remander part of my Estate, whih is not all Redy Espeshely Given, I desive & Give the same between my four Children hereafter named, that is to say, Aron & Elizabeth, and James, and Abraham Springs, Which the forsaid Articlkes, I Give Devise & Bequeth to my four Children heretwo Befor mentioned & to ther heirs & Assigns for ever.

I Do appoint my Brother in Law, John Barrow, & my Son, Aron Spring, to be Executors of this my Last Will & Testament.

In Testimony hereof I have hereunto Set my hand & fixed my Seal this 18th. Day of April, in the Year of our Lord God 1755.

ARON SPRING (Seal)

Signed, Sealed, Pronounced, and Declared in the presence of us: THOS. BARROW.
LITTLETON EBORN, Jun.

BEUAFORT COUNTY. ss.

This certifies that at a Court held at Bath Town for the said County, on the Second tuesday in June, Ann. Dom., 1756,
   present his Majesties Justices,

The last Will & Testament of Aaron Spring dec'd was exhibited into court, & Proved by Thomas Barrow, one of the Subscribing Witnesses

thereto, who swore that he saw the sd. Aaron Spring execute the same & that he was at the time of sound & disposing mind & memory; & that he saw Littleton Eborne, Jun. the other Subscribing Witness set his hand thereto at the same time, Whereupon John Barrow, & Aaron Spring qualified as Executors to the said Will according to Law. Ordered that the Secretary have Notice that Letters Testament. may Issue.
      Test. WALLEY CHAUNCY, Cl. Cu.

Copied from Original Will, filed in the Office of the Secretary of State.

SAMUELL SWANN'S WILL.

IN THE NAME OF GOD AMEN, I, saml. Swan, of pequimonds County, Being sick of Body, But of Perfect Mind & Memory, Thanks be to god, Do Make and ordain this my last Will & Testament, Hereby Revoking all Other Wills heretofore By me Made.

Imprimis, My Will and Desire that all My Just Debts Be Paid as Soon as My Exers., hereafter Namd, Can Conveniently Raise the Money Out of Such Part of my Estate as My family Can Best Spare.

Item, the Land whereon I now Dwell, Containing Four hundred an Twenty fove Acres, I Devide, Dispose of In Manner following; I Give to my Son Inlaw, Richard Claton, And my Daughter Mary, the Use of The House they Now Live in, with Ninety Acres of Land on which the House Stands & going Back from the Sound Side for the Said Compliment of Ninety acers, that is To Say, Begining at a Large Scaley Bark oak on the bank to the Eastward of Richard Clatons house, Thence A Direct Line to A Branch, Thence Through the Brance to A Beech Standing on a point of Land on the Westward of Alferds Swamp, Thence up a Branch of the Said Swamp to a beech a Little Above an Old Cart Brige, Thence A streight Course To A beech Catch maids Corner Tree. I give the Use of the above mentioned Ninety Acers of Land to My Son in law, Richd. Claton, and my Daughter, Mary Claton, During their Their Natural Live; and at their Deaths I give the Said Ninety Acers of Land, with The Appurtenances Thereunto belonging, unto the heirs Lawfully Begotten of my Daughter, Mary Claton, To them their Heirs and Assigns forever. Item, I give and Bequeath to My son in law, Richard Claton, all the Land to the Westward Of the Afsd. Deviding Line, above the Afsd. ninety Acers, on Condition of his Paying the Same price pr. acer to my other Six Children, as the Remainder of my Sd. Tract of Land Will Sell for, To him, his heirs and Assigns forever.

Item, My Will and Desire is that after the Death of My wife all the Remainder of my Sd. Tract of Land, and all my ˥k of Cattle, horses, hog & sheep May Be Sold and the

Money arising, equally Devided Between My other Six Children, Vizt., Sarah Ann Elisabeth Martha Jane and Margaret.

Item, I give and Bequeath Unto Jesse hendley, of Pasquotank County, one half of my allegator Land, to him, His heirs and assigns for ever, the other half of The Said Land, with my Young Black pacing Mare and My Riding horse I Desire May Be Sold by My Execurs. and the Money ariseing to be Laid out in Moving the house I now Live in, to a Certain Place I have appointed, and In finishing two Log houses I have Begun.

Item, I Desire that all my Tools, only some for the use of the plantation, May Be Sold and the Money ariseing appropriated to the Moving & Building the Afsd. houses, if Required.

Item, my Will and Desire is that my Negroes, houshold Goods and Stock, Remain in the Possession My wife Dureing her widowhood, and at her Marriage or Death, Be Equally Divided Between My aforenamed Six Children, Sarah, Ann, Elizabeth, Martha, Jane, and Margaret.

Item, I Give to my Daughter, Mary Claton, My pickle Case and Bottles.

Item, I Give To my bror. John Vail, My Silver Seal and Stock Buckle. And Do Hereby Nominate and Appoint my Brothers, Jeremiah Vail and John Vail, Executors to This My Last Will and Testament, Revoking all Other Wills heretofore By me Made.

In Testimony Whereof, I hereunto Set My hand & Seal, this Eighth Day of January, In the Year of our Lord, one Thousd. Seven Hundred and fifty three.

SAMUELL SWANN, (Seal)

Signed, Sealed, pronounced and
Delivered in presence of us:
JOHN SMITH. Jurt.
SUSANNA (HUAIL? VAIL?)
WILLM. X WOLLARDS, Jurt.
mark.

PERQUMANS COUNTY. ss. April Court, Anno Dom., 1753.
Present his Majestys Justices.

These may Certifie that the Will of Samuell Swann, Decd., hereunto annexed was then & there Duly Proved in Open Court by the Oaths of John Smith and William Woolard, Evidences thereto, and at The Same time Mr. John Vail was Duly Qualified thereto as Executor by taking the Oath by law appointed.

Ordered that the Secretary of Said Province have Notice thereof, that Letters Testimentary Issue thereon as the Law Directs.

Test. EDMUND HATCH, Cler. Cur.

Copied from the Original Will, filed in the Office of the Secretary of State.

SAMUEL SWANN'S WILL.

NORTH CAROLINA. Ss.

IN THE NAME OF GOD AMEN. I, Samuel Swann, of the precinct of Pequimans, Esqr., Being Sick and weak of body, but of Sound and perfect mind and memory, praised be God, Do make, Constitute and Declare, these presents to be and Contain my Last will and Testmt., hereby revoaking and makeing void all former and other wills by me heretofore made or Declared.

Imprimis, I Give and bequeath unto my Son, William Swann, an old Bible, and a Seale ring, which was my fathers, in full for his portion, haveing advanced sufficient for him in my life time.

Item, I Give and bequeath unto my Son, Sampson Swann, the Sum of five pounds, in full for his portion, having advanced sufficient for him in my life time.

Item, I Give and bequeath My Land lying between Muddy creek and Marshey gutt, to my Sons, Henry and Thomas, and their heirs for ever, ye Same to be equally divided betwixt them, and my Son, Henry, to have his first choice.

Item, I Give unto my said Sons, Henrey and Thomas, all my Lightwood, that is or shall be pick't up on Grassy pt Land, with reasonable Assistance of my Negroes to help burn ye Same, Also, the use of my Pitch Kettle (if any shall come in), to Boyle ye Tarr. Allso, what Pitch Tarr, as Mr. John Pottiver stands indebted to me by Bill.

Item, I Give and bequeath unto my sd. two Sons, Henry and Thomas, All the Goods, that I have sent for from London, to trade with.

Item, I Give unto my sd. two Sons, Henry and Thomas, what goods I have perticularly sent for, for their use, vizt., as much Shagathee, Shallon, Buttons & Silk as will make each of them a Suit. Also, 4 Shirts & two muslin Neckloaths apiece.

Item, It is my Desire and I Do Earnestly recommend it to my said two Sons, Henry and Thomas, That the produce of the Lightwood and goods, which I have given them, be employed in a Joynt Stock for trade, as being the most likely Course to thrive.

Item, I Do Give and bequeath unto my two Sons, Samuel and John, and my two Daughters, Elizabeth and Sarah, All my moneys that is due to me in England by Bills of Exchange or otherwise. And, it is my Earnest Desire and request That my Loveing Brother Richard Bland of Virginia, Esqr, or his Assignes Do Employ ye Same in one Joynt trading stock for the use and proffitt of my said Children; which said trade-ing Stock is to be Carried on Entire till such time as either of my said Children shall marry of Come of age, which shall first happen, then his or her part, to be Delivered to him or her, and ye remainder to be Carried on for the benefitt and advantage of the rest till such time as they shall severally marry or come of age.

Item, I Give unto my Loveing Wife, Elisabeth Swann, Fifteen pound per. Annum, out of the proffitts which shall arise of the said trading stock, and to be Allowed the said Richard Bland, or his Assignes upon his Accompts.

Item, It is my Will and Desire that the said Richard Bland, Esqr., or his Assignes, Do yearly make up the Accts. of the proffitts of said Stock to my Executrx. hereafter named.

Item, I Give and bequeath unto my said Loveing wife, Elizabeth, My plantation whereon I now live, with all the Land and Houses and appurtenances thereto belonging, for and dureing the term of her naturall Life. And after her Decease, I Give Devise & bequeath the Same to my Son, Samuell, his heirs and Assignes for ever.

Item, I Give, Devise and bequeath my Land on the Sound side, joyning to Normans, to my Son, John, his heirs and Assignes for ever.

Lastly, All the rest and residue of my Estate, I Give, Devise and bequeath the Same unto my Loveing Wife, Elizabeth, whome I make my sole Executrx. for paymt. of my Debts, Legacies, and Christain Education of my Children.

In Testimony whereof, I have hereunto putt my hand & Seale, this Twelfth day of September, Anno Dom., 1707.

        SAMUEL SWANN. ( )
      (Impression of Coat of Arms on Seal)

Signed, Sealed, Published and Declared In presence of:
  ELIZABETH THICKPEN.
  ANN MOSELEY.
  JOHN LILLINGTON,
  FRAN. FOSTER.
  EDWD. MOSELEY.

Att a Genl. Court, holden the .0th. day of Aprile, Ano. Dm. 17.., the above will was proved by ye Oaths of the Hon'ble Edwd. Mosely & Fran. Foster, Esqr.   Test. F. KNIGHT, Secty.

NO. CAROLINA. ss.

Willm. Glover, Esqr., Presid't of the Council and Command'r in Cheife of this Province.

Whereas Good & Lawfull proffs hath bin made of the last will and Testam't of Saml. Swann, Esqr., Decd., a true Coppy whereof is hereunto annexed, and therein hath appointed and made Elizabeth, his wife, Sole Executrix of ye Same.

These are, therefore, to Impower the sd. Elizabeth Swann, in and upon all and Singular, the Goods & Chattles, rights and Creditts of the sd.

Samuell Swann, to Entor wheresoever 't to be found, and the same into her posession to take, and a true Inventory thereof to returne into the Sectys. Office, within one yeare after ye Date hereof, and ye Same to dispose of as by the sd. Will is appointed.

Given und'r my hand and ye Seale of this Collony, this 28th. day of May, Ano. Dm., 1708.   W. GLOVER.

(Official Seal)

Copied from the Original Will, filed in the Office of the Secretary of State.

THOMAS SWANN'S WILL.

The 7th. Day of May, in ye Year, 1733. Be it rememered that I, Thomas Swann, of the preci't of pasquotank and province of North Carolina; being very Sick of body but of Sound & perfect mind & memory, thanks be Given to God, therefore calling to mind ye Mortality of my body, & knowing yt it is appointed for all men once to Dye; Do make & ordain this to be my last Will & testament in manner & form following, Vizt:

1st. I will y^t all those Debts or Duteys y^t I owe to be well & truly Contented & paid in Some Convenient time after my Decease by my Exors. here after named.

2d'ly, I Give & bequeath to my Son, Samuel Swann, ye Plantation were I now Dwell, to him & his heirs for Ever.

3d'ly, I Give & bequeath to my Son, William Swann, my other plantation wch I bought of ye heirs of Robert Wallis, to him & his heirs for Ever:

Butt in Case Either of my sd Sons shall Sell, alien, Mortgage, or any other way convey. Either of ye Sd Plantations hereby Given out of the name cf ye Swanns, that then it shall & may be Lawfull for the other of my sd sons to reEnter & take Possession of ye Same.

Item, I Give and bequeath to my Son, William Swann, my Negro boy Named Jack.

Item, I Give & bequeath to my Son, Samuel Swann, my negro Girl named Dido.

Item, my Will is yt my other plantations at Moyock and in ye prect: of Curratuck, be Sold for money wch I give to my two Daughters, Rebeca & Elizabeth Swann, Equaly to be Divided between them.

Item, my will is yt my part of ye Sloop Swann be Sold.

Item; I will yt a Sufficient quantity of corn be reserved for the family Use & Stock, & ye Remainder be Sold for money.

Item, my will & Desire is y^t my Estate consisting in negrows, other Creatures or whatsoever it may, be & Continue & remain in ye possesion of my Dear & Loveing wife, Rebeca Swann, & ye Use of them for & towards the Maintenance & Christian Education of my Children; & when my sd. Children shall attain to Age, then to Draw out of my Estate there proportionable part, or share of Young Negroes, as shall be raised in their Minority.

Item, I give and bequeath to my Dear & Loveing wife my Best feather bed & furniture.

Item, I give & bequeath to my two sons, William & Samuel Swann, Each of them a feather Bed & furniture.

Item, I give and bequeath to my two Daughters, Rebeca & Eliz^a. Swann, Each of them a feather Bed and furniture.

Item, I give and bequeath unto my two Sons, Samuel & William Swann, Each of them a horse, bridle and Sadle.

Lastly, I will that all ye rest of my personable Estate remain Intirely whole in the Possesion of my Wife, Rebeca Swann, untill my Children arrive to there respective ages, or Day of marrage and then to be Equally Divided among them.

And, I Do hereby nominate and apoint my loving wife, Rebeca Swann and my Respected frend Colo. Edward Moseley to be my whole & Sole Exors. of this my Last Will and Testam't hereby Revokeing & Disanulling all other wills & Testaments heretofore in any wise by me made, Rattifying & Confirming this to be my Last will & Testam't and no Other.

In Witness whereof, I have hereunto Sett my hand & Seal the Day and Year above written.

THOMAS SWANN. (Seal)

Sign'd, Seal'd, pronounc'd and Declared by Thos. Swann, as his Last will & Testament in the presence of:
    BENJA. PRITCHARD.
    MARY EDWARDS.
    SAM^L: WISE.

This Day personaly appeared before me Benjm. Pritchard, who Declared on the Sollemn affirmation of a Quaker that he Saw Collo: Thomas Swann, lately Deceased, Sign, Seal & Declare the foregoing writing to Contain his last Will & Testament, and that he was in his full Sences and no Compulsion was offered; and that also he Saw Mary Edwards & Samuel Wise, the other two Subscribeing Witnesses set their hands thereto. Given under my hand at Edenton the 9th. of Augt. 1733.

GEO. BURRINGTON.

Copied from Original Will, filed in the Office of the Secretary of State.

FRANCIS TOMS' WILL.

I, Francis Toms, of Pequimons, being Sick and weak of Body, but of Sound mind and memory, Do make this my Last will and testament in maner and forme following, Viz:

I will that my Just Debts be paid by my Executors hereafter named,

Item, I Give and Bequeath to my Doughter, mary Newby, the Plantation I Bought of James Thickpen, to her and her Husband for and during their Naturall Lives, and after their Decease to their Son, Francis Newby, to him, his heirs and assigns for Ever; and for want of Such Heirs to the Next of Kinn. And, also, to my Sd. Doughter and to her, Her Heirs or assignes, my Tract of Land on Usess Creek and Bounding on ye Said Creek and the Land he, N: Newby, bought of William More; and allso, to my Said Doughter, the Labour of my Negro Wench named Nan two days in a week, viz: the Days Commonly Called Mondie and Tusday, from the day of the date hereof, to the full End and term of ten Years, My Daughter finding the Said Negro Woman a New Cotton and Woll Coat and Jackit duirng the above terme of ten years, yearly.

Item, I Give and Bequeath unto my Doughter, Elizabeth Phelps, the plantation and tract of Land I had in Exchange from Stephen Gibbons for my Land Called ye Image, to her and her heirs for Ever; allso, I Give to my Said Doughter, Elizabeth, forty Acres of Land lying at ye head of Rachell Barrows Land and that which was formerly Called Clagisters, to her and her Heirs for ever.

I Give and Bequeath unto my Doughter, Priscilla Jones, a Negro Wench named Jenney and all her futer Increse, Save the first Child She Shall Bring, which I Give to my Wife, whether male or female, and when ye Said Jenney does Appear to be with Child, She Shall be Returned to my wife or Relict, and Remain with her till her Child is weanable, and the Wench Naney to Serve in her Stead to my Said Daughter during the Said time.

Item, I Give and bequeath unto my Doughter Margret Tomes, my Land on Both Sides of Long Branch, as far as the head of Bull Branch on ye north Side, and on ye South Side, as far as first big Branch that Comes out Long Branch below Stephen Gibbons Brid, and to the head of the Said Branch to my Said Doughter, Margaret and to her Heirs for ever; Likewise, a Negro Boy Called Jack and, a young Horse Named Smoaker, and a feather beed and furnituer Equivlent to the Beed and Furnituer her Sister Pleasant had.

Item, I Give and Bequeath to my Doughter, Pleasant Winslowe, two hundred acres of Land on Usess Creek, Joyning on ye Land Given to Francis Newby by my father, which two hundred Acres of Land, I Give to my Said Doughter, Pleasant, and to her heirs or assignes for ever.

Item, I Give and Bequeath to my Loveing Wife, Rebekah Tomes my Negro man named Guy, to be disposed of at hir discretion; Likewise the Labour of my Negro Mingo boy, from the date hereof to the full End and term of twelve years, if my Said wife Live So Long, and at ye Expiration of ye abov[e] mentioned twelve years, or at my Said wifes decease whi[ch] Shall first happen, I will the Said Boy to my Son, Franci[s] to him, his Heirs or Assigns. Likewise, I Give to my sai[d] Wife, one hundred Acres of Land I Bought of John Porter, an[d] fifty acres out of the Tract I now live on Joyning to the S[aid] hundred acres of Land; and the one halfe of my orchard, S[he] keeping the same in Repair for and During her Naturall Lif[e] and allso, I Give to my Said wife, the one third of my Moveab[le] Estate, Shee taking what was Hers before our Marige in par[t] of the Said third; and allso, I give my said wife all her wearin[g] apparell; and allso I Give to my Said wife, the Labour of m[y] Negro Naney, Save the two days heretofore in a Week Give[n] to my Doughter Mary, untill my Son Francis be marryed and then I will he may have the one third of the Said Negr[o] Labour; and the Said Negro Naney at his Mother in law Decease. And also, I Give to my said Wife the one halfe [of] my bedding the whole of my Remaining Beding to be Eaqual[ly] Devided betwixt my wife and my Son francis. Allso, I Giv[e] to my Said Wife my horse Named Fox and Side Sadle and Bridl[e] and allso my horse Named Dick.

Item, I Give and Bequeath to my Doughter Pleasant, m[y] Negro Boy named Pompey, to her, her Heirs and assignes fo[r] ever.

Item, I Give and Bequeath to my Son, Francis Tomes, th[e] Plantation whereon I now Live acording to his Granfather Will; and to my Said Son, my Negro Girle named Naney, an[d] One Gray maire I Bought of William Jackson, and my Ridin[g] Saddle, to him his, heirs or assignes for ever.

Item, all the Remaining part of my Estate after my wife'[s] part is taken out, be the Same of what kind or Quality S[o] Ever, or whereEver to be found, I Give and Bequeath to m[y] Doughter, Margret Pleasant and my Son, Francis, to be Eaqual ly Devided amongst them, there, to be devided by the Judgmen[t] of Joseph Jessop, Thos. Jessop, Thomas Winslow and Willia[m] More, or any three of them.

Lastly, I do ordain, Constitute & appoint My Loveing wif[e] Rebekah Tomes, and my Son in Law, Nathan Newby, to b[e] my Executors to see this my will full filled, Revoaking a[ll] former wills by me heretofore made.

as witness my hand, this 5th. of Sept, Ano. Dom., 1729.

FRANCIS TOMS. (Seal)

Witness: J. JESSOP.
RICHD. CHESTON.
RALPH FLETCHER.

Octbr. 7th., 1729.

Proved this will by the Afferm. of Jos. Jessop.

R. EVERARD.

Copied from the Original Will, filed in the Office of Secretary of Stat[e]

JAMES TURNBULL'S WILL.

NORTH CAROLINA.

IN THE NAME OF GOD, AMEN. I, James Turnbull, of Tyrrel County and province Aforesaid, Marchand, being in halth and of sound and disposing mind and memory, do make and ordain this my last will and Tastement in manner and form as follows:

Imprimis, I Give, bequeaf & divise, unto Mr. Yreot ormond and Mr. Thomas Barker, attorneys of this province, one half of my Negrows that is Keept and detaned from me by William Mckey or proviso, tha, the above Said Yreot ormond & Thomas Barber will or do Sue for & Recover the the whole Nunber of negroes and Deliver the Othar half according to my will and clear of all Coste & Charges, in that Case, I will them the above Said half the number of my above Said Negros & their incres, to tham and thair assigns for ever: I mean my Negroe Woman Phebe and har dafter Scotta, and her Sun London, & har dafter Phebe, and har dafter pege, & har dafter ianne. I heared the wench head one boye since, Named Charls, *he is dead by neglect, &c.*

Item, I Give, Bequeaf and divise unto my Nece, Mary Pantry, har two Suns, Robert & James, the one half of the abovementioned Negroes, To be Delevered by Mr. Ormond & Mr. Barker, to tham or thair assigns, Clear of Chargis, if tha Sue & Recover as Aforesaid; if the above Said Mr. Yreot ormond & Mr. Thomas Barker will not Exsept of the above Legasy, in that Case, I give, Bequeaf and divise all the above Said Negrows, to the above said Robart & James Pantry and thair hairs for Ever, and to be Sued for at the Charg of my Estate, and to be Repaid if the Negrows are Recovered. I likewise order, that the above Said Robart, James be mentaned on my Estate if tha will assist to Kepe the plantation in order untill they are at full Age; then, & in that case, tha, the Said Robart & James, Shall have and injoye my Two peaces of Land at Scupernung, Called the Brak oake Land, and the Rich Levils; & one quarter part of my female black Cattle; & one quarter part of my beading and puter; and one quarter part of my horsis. My intent & meaning is, that the Said Robart & James Cume from london hear, at lest, one of tham, or luse thare legasys, but if tha Cum over Sea with Capttn. Dalley, or Otharwise, my Estate must pay thare passage, ten pound Starling for both; if tha parform all that I injoyne, then I Give Bequeaf and divise to the abov said Robart & James Pantry, as above mentioned, to tham and the hairs of thare body lawfully begoten; and for wont of Such, to Eithars hairs; & for want of Such, to the heairs of their

Sister in london; & for want of Such, to my legateas heare in Carolina, I dont mean Mr. Barker nor Mr. Ormond.

Item, I Give, bequeaf, & divise unto mary Turnbull Butcher, one half my parsonal Estate, after the above Legaseys are paid, To har and the hairs of har body lawfully begoten; & for want of Such, to Mary Pantry, har hairs if tha are hear, if not, to har Brother, Bell Butchar, or my hairs.

Item, I give, Bequeaf, divise unto Bell Butchar, all my land not allredy given, I mean Bells gift and gards island, and my land in Edenton, and the Remainder of my Parsonall Estate, to him and his hires of his body lawfully begoten, and for want of Such, one half to the hiars of mary Pantry, and the othar half to the hairs of Mary Turnbull Butchar, or the Surviver of tham to have all.

Item, I Give, Bequeaf and divise unto Mary Butchar, the use of all my Estate both real and Parsonall untill the legates cum to the Age of twenty one years, Exsept har dafter, Mary Turnbull Butchar, She ma keep har Legasy during har life if She pleasis, and the one half of Bells gift land &c., to har use during har life, my intent is that non of the legates Shall have thare legaseys, untill untill, tha are twenty one years olde.

Item, I order & direct that all mu Just debts. be paid by the Sails of my Scooner & paryagor & Conews, and marchanddiz, at vandue for Redy money, or private Sail as my Executrix & Trustte pleasis as Soon as posable, and Collecting my Debts or Sue derectly all that will not Pay on Sight of the list of Debets or the accounts, Since.

My, Will and Desire is that Mary Butchar doth mantain and Edecate all the minors above mentioned as well as She can aford with the use and Intrest above Given Har; if She make any waste of my Estate the County Court is Required to make har give Securyty or tha are derected to appoint gardians for the children or tha chuse them if of age.

Item, I order that nomoney be paid to any parson but Mr. Hanry Jordan that his mothar, Elizabeth Hanmore, left him, nor to him untill my hairs be indamnified from danel Hanmore & his hairs.

Item, I order that the ballance due to the hairs of Mrs. Ann Mountgumry be paid as it Now stands, deducting the quit-rents since paid.

Item, I order that the title and bounds of the land that I now Live on be defended according as the Survaer hath made out a plott and Sartificate agreeable to my deed, which I naver Rec'ved, any consideration for of any Parson, all the foregoing legates Shall beare thare proporationable part of the Charg if Accation, And on thare Refusall, forfit thare Legasey to the Rest of the Legatyes. I order the quitrents of all my land to paid yearly.

I order that my Cloths be made up for Bell Butchar and Robartt & James pantry, if tha are hear as tha want Cloths; likewise, my books and instruments to be divided amoungst tham three boyes.

My will is if my Neace, Mary Pantry should Cum over sea to see me, I order her the Use of my dweling House in Edenton and the Smoke house & oven during har and har huseband, Phillip Pantry, thare natral lives, Rent free, but must Keep the same in good Repare &c.; my intent and meaning is, that my Executrix shall do & parform Every thing and things that I have given, bequeafed, devised, willed ordered and derected as much as lyes in har power, with the advice and concent of my truste hearafter Named. My Truste must be wall paid Every Year for his Truble.

Lastly, I Nominate and appoint Mary Butchar to be my Executrix and William gardnar, Esqr., to be a truste to this my laste Will and Testament.

In witness hear of, I have hear unto Sett my hand and Seal, this twenty Sixth day of September, one thousand, Seven hundred and fifty three.

JAMES TURNBULL. (seal)

Signed and delivered in public presence of : (interlined before signed, bove)
  ANN DENEM.
  JOHN MATHEWS.
  CHARLES DENEM.
  JAMES TATTERTON, Jurat.

NORTH CAROLINA, TYRREL COUNTY. ss.   June Court, 1754.
  Present his Majesty's Justices:

These may Certifie that John Mathews & Ann Denam, Two of the Subscribing Evidences to the Within Will, came into open Court and made Oath on the Holy Evangelists of Almighty God that they Saw James Turnbull Sign, Seal, publish, pronounce & declare the Within Writing to Contain his last Will and Testament; & That he was at the same time in perfect sound mind and disposing memory, and that they also at the Same time, Saw James Tatterton & Charles Denon Sign their Names as Evidences to the said Will. Then also Appeared Mary Butcher, Executric & Quallified herself by taking the Oath as the Law in such Cases Directs.

Ordered, that the Hon'ble James, Murray, Esqr., Secretary of this Province, have Notice thereof, that Letters Testamentory Issue Accordingly. Test. EVAN JONES, Cler. Cur.

Copied from the Original Will, filed in the Office of the Secretary of State.

HENDERSON WALKER'S WILL.

IN THE NAME OF GOD AMEN. I, Henderson Walker, being well in body and of perfect mind & memory, Considering the uncertainty of this life Doe make & ordeyne this my Last Will & testam't.

Impri., I Surrender up my Soul to God yt gave it, believing that through ye prehous death & passion of my Saviour, I shall have full pardon of my Synns, and my body I comitt to ye earth from whence it came to be Interred; and for my Estate, I give as folt:

Imps. I give to Elizabeth Walker, now w'th me, and to her heirs for ever, my Plantation at Yawpim, as alsoe Six Cowes, & Calves, Six Sowes, Six Yewes, one Young Mare, one good Feather Bed, bolster, Hooks, Rugg, Blankett, one Larg Iron Pott & frying pan, two pewter dishes, two plates, and my Negro Frank, all to be delivered her at ye sd. plantation at age or Marriage, but if She dyes before, I give sd. Land to my Executrix & her heirs.

I give to Maj. Swann, my Swoard, and to Samll. Swann, my Seale Ring, and to tenn poore people tenn Barrells of Corne; and Five Pound to ye building of a Church, and Five Pound to ye Minister who preaches my Funerall Sermon. And to John, George, & Sarah Lillington & ye sd. Elizabeth Walker, each of them, a Silver spoone.

And all ye rest of my Estate, bothe reall & personall, whatsoever, I give my wife, Ann Walker, and to her heirs; and this my Will to be taken & looked upon as firme for ye guifts abovesaid as if it were made in ye ample manner as ye law ran.

I devise and I make my said wife Ann, Executrix thereof. Do revoake all others by me made.

Witness my hand & Seale, the 27th. of Octor. Anno. 1701.

     HENDERSON WALKER. (Seal)

Sealed, published & delivered in presence of:
  P. GODFREY,
   The marke of
  ROBT. O HARMAN, SENR.
  GEORGE CHAMBERS

I, the Subscriber do Declare in ye Presents of god & under ye Peanallty of Perjary, that I saw the Hon'ble Henderson Walker, Esqr., Sign, Seale & Publish the within written to be his Last Will & Testament, & that he was then in Perfect Sence & Health to ye Best of my Judgment.

        Sign.
       ROBT. O HARMON

Proved in Court, July 4th, 1704.

By ye Oathe of Mr. Peter Godfrey & Geo. Chambers and ye Subscrition of Robt. Harmon, Senr.   Test: NATH. CHEVIN, Cl.

Copied from the Original Will, filed in the Office of Secretary of State.

ABRAHAM WARREN'S WILL.

IN THE NAME OF GOD AMEN, the 26 Day of Octobr., 1739. I, Abraham Warrin, of ye Provence of North Carolina, in the County of Perquimanes, Planter, being vary Sick and weak in Body, but of Perfect mide and memory, thanks be given unto God therefore, Calling unto mide ye mortality of my Body, and Knowing yt It is appointed for all men Once To Dye, do make and Ordaine this my Last will and testament, yt is to say, Principally, and first of all, I give and Recommend my Soule into ye Hands of God yt Gave It; and my Body I Recommend to ye Earth to be buryed in a Decent and Chrisan mannar at ye Discretion of my Exesetricks, nothing Doubting but at ye General Resurrection I Shall reseive ye Same Again by the Almighty Power of God: and as touching Such worldly Esteate wharewith It hath Pleased God to Bless me in this Life, I Give, Demise and Dispose of ye Same in ye following manner and form:

Imprimis, I Give and Bequeath to my well beloved wife, Sarah Warrin, my Rideing Hors, bridle and Saddle, and three Cows and a bull Stag, ye names of ye Cows are as followeth, winter, red head and pinck; also, I give unto my wife, Sarah Warrin, Six three yeare Old Stares and all my Stock of Hoogs, als, all my Eiarn tools: yet It is true Intent and meaning of this My Last will and testament yt my wife, Sarah Warrin, Pay out of my Stock of hoogs, what hoogs I Oeth to Sarah Sutten and Suseanah Sutten; also, to pay what Pork I Oeth to Jeames Sumner.

Item, I give and Bequeath unto my Son, Henery Warrin, my Plantation and tract of Land I now Live on; also my Little gunn, and Stone Colte.

Item, I give unto my five Children now Born my Rideing mare and my young mare at ye Sound Side, them and there Increce, To be Equally Devided between my five Children.

Item I give unto John Chesson and Jeames Chesson three Pound in Provence bills to be paid them when they Com of age:

Item, I give unto Christopher Denman twenty Shillings, in Provence bills.

Lastly, after all my Just Depts are paid, I Give all ye rest of my Estate to be Equally Devided between my Wife and Children; also, It is ye true intent and meaning of ys my Last will and testament, yt If my Wife be now with Child, yt ye Childe have an Equal part of my Estate with ye rest of my of my Children; also I Doo Constute and ordain my well beloved wife, Sarah Warrin, and my trusty frind, Richard Skinner, Senr., my Sole Exsetrick and Executor of ys my Last will and testament: and I Doo Likewise give and request My trusty and well beloved frind, John Stepney, to be an adviseer and a trustee to my wife and Children. And I Do hereby utterly Disallow, revoke and Disanul, all and Every other formar testaments, wills, bequests, And Executors, by me in any ways named, Willed, and Bequeathed; Ratifying and Confirming this, and No other, to be my Last will and testament.

in witness whareof I have heare unto set my hand and Seal the Day and yeare above Written.

ABRAHAM A^{his}_{mark} WARRIN (Seal)

Signed, Sealed, Published, Pronounced and Declared, By the Said Abraham Warrin, as his Last Will and testament in the Presence of us the Subscribers:

JOHN X^{his}_{mark} CREESE, Juret.

MARY X^{her}_{Mark} CREESE.

JOHN STEPNEY, Juret.

PERQUIMONS COUNTY ss.   July Court, 1740.
  Present His Majestys Justices:
  Came before them in open Court John Creasey and John Stepney, and made oath on the holy Evangelists that they saw Abraham Warren Sign, seal & publish the above as his last will & Testament, and that he was of sound & disposing mind & Memory at that time; & that these deponants Subscribed as Witnesses thereto; at the Same time Sarah Warren took the Oath appointed by Law to be taken by Executors.

Test. JAMES CRAVEN, Clr. Cur.

Sarah Warren Quallified as Exx.

Copied from Original Will, filed in the Office of the Secretary of State.

THOMAS WATKINS' WILL.

NORTH CAROLINA.

IN THE NAME OF GOD AMEN. I, Thomas Watkins, of the County of Perquimans, Being of sound mind and memory, thanks be given to god for the same, and Calling to mind the mortality of my Body, and Knowing that it is appointed for all men once to Dye, Do make and ordain this my Last Will and Testament, that is to say, Principally, and first of all, I Recomend my soul to god that gave it, and my Body to be Buried in a Decent Christain Manner at the Discretion of my Executors; and for what Temporall Estate it hath Pleased god to Bestow upon me, after all my Just Debts is Paid, I give and Bequeath the use as followeth:

Imprimis, I give to my Friend, John Whedbee, all the Ditching that I Cutt for him, and An four Pound, Seven Shillings, and Six Pence, Virginia money, to him and his Heirs.

Item, I give to Richard Whidbee all the Ditching I Cut for him.

Item, I give to John Morris all my wearing Close.

Item, I give all the Remaining Part of my Personall Estate to Samuel Newbey, being near Little River Bridge in Pasquotank County, and I hereby Nominate, Constitute and apoint my loving friend, John Whidbey my Executor of this my last Will and Testament, Holden for Firm this and no other to be my last Will and Testament.

in Witness whereof I have hereunto Set my hand and Seal this 3rd Day of January 1740(?)

THOMAS X WATKINS (Seal)
his mark

Signed, Sealed, Pronounced and Declared by the said Thomas Watkins as his Last Will and Testament In Presence of:
    WILLIAM FOSTER, Jurt.
    POTSEFULL PIERCE.
    MARY WHEDBEE. Jurt.

NORTH CAROLINA, PERQM. COUNTY. Janury Court Anno Dom. 1754.
    Present his Majesty's Justices:

Then was the within Will proved in open Court by the Oaths of Willm. Foster & Mary Whedbee in due Form of Law, at the Same Time John Whedbee, Exor, to the within Will was duly Qualified by taking the Oath by Law appointed. Ordered that Letters Testamentary Issue thereon as the Law directs.   Test. EDMUND HATCH. Cler. Cur.

Recorded in Will Book 6, page 225.

WILLIAM WATKINS' WILL.

IN THE NAME OF GOD AMEN. I, William Watkins, of Pitt County, in the Province of North Carolina, Planter, being in a Week low State of health & calling to mind the uncertainty of this life, Do therefore make this my last Will & Testament, Revokeing & disannulling All other & former Wills by me heretofore made; And first, I Recommend my Soul into the hands of Almighty God that gave it me, hopeing through the Merrits of Jesus Christ to Obtain everlasting Salvation; And my Body I desire to be buried in a Christian like manner; And as to my Worldly Estate, I dispose of it in manner & form following, to wit:

I give & bequeath unto my beloved Wife, Christian Watkins, & to my two Sons, John Watkins & William Watkins, & to my four Sons in Law, Francis Buck, James Cason, William Ormond, & James Jones, all my Ready money that I leave at the time of my Death, to be Equally divided betwean them, Share & Share alike.

And, Whereas, I have Some time ago made & Executed in an open & lawful manner, Deeds of Gifts to my Sons & Sons in Law, for my Land & Plantation & all my Negroes & my Still & Worm, which was then immediately before the Execution of the said Deeds, my Right & Property, & which was done Agreeable to & by & with the free & mutual Consent & Agreement of my aforesaid Wife, & Sons, & Sons in Law, And my said Wife, as I married her a Poor Woman without any Estate at all, at the same time Agreed & Concluded to Renounce & quit all manner of Wright or Dower in, or to, the said Land & Plantation in two of the aforesaid Deeds mentioned, either in law in equity, or any other ways howseover, on Condition that I would leave her at the time of my Death the one third part of all my Personal Estate, except the Negros, the Still, & the Worme; Therefore, I do hereby Give & bequeath in behalf of the said Agreement as also for the love that I bear unto my said Wife, Christian Watkins, to her & her heirs for ever, The one third part of all my personall Estate, of all kinds whatsoever, except the Ready money already Given. (and)

And, I do hereby Give & bequeath unto my said Sons in law, Francis Buck, & James Cason, the other two thirds of all my personal Estate of all kinds whatsoever (except the ready money already given), to be equally divided between them, Share & Share alike. And the reason why I Give no more to my Sons, John & William Watkins, and to my Sons in Law, William Ormond & James Jones, is because I have heretofore provided for them in the before mentioned Deeds of Gifts.

I give & bequeath unto my Daughter, Sarah Buck, one Shilling, lawful money of Great Britain.

I give & bequeath unto my Daughter, Elisabeth, one Shilling.

I give & bequeath unto my Daughter, Ann, one Shilling.

I give & bequeath unto my Daughter, Rachael, one Shilling, And the Reason is because I have provided for them in the name of their Husbands in the aforesaid Deeds of Gifts.

Lastly, I appoint my beloved Wife & my Son in Law, James Cason, Executrix & Executor of this my last Will & Testament.

In testimony whereof, I have hereunto put my hand & Seal, this Ninth day of November, Anno Domini, 1771.

WM. WATKINS (Seal)

Signed, Sealed, published & declared by the Testator to be his last Will & Testament in the presence of us:
CATHERINE — CROFTON.
<small>her mark.</small>
JOHN SALTER.
RANDEL McDANIEL.

The within last Will and Testament of William Watkins was proved Before me, this fourteenth day of October, 1773, by the Oath of John Salter one of the Subscribing Witnesses thereto, who swore that he was present and did see the said Testator, sign, seal, publish and declare the same to be and contain his last Will and Testament; and that at the time thereof he was of sound and disposing Mind & Memory.

And James Cason, the Eexcutor therein named, having taken the Oaths of Executors and qualified as the Law directs, It is Ordered that Letters Testamentary be granted thereon accordingly.   JO. MARTIN.

Copied from the Original Will, filed in the Office of the Secretary of State.

BINGMAN WEEKS' WILL.

IN THE NAME OF GOD AMEN, ys. Ninth Day of November, in the Year of our Lord, One thousand, Seven hundred & Forty Four. I, Bingman Weeks, of Cartwright County, in North Carolina, being very sick & weak of Body, but of Perfect Mind & Memory, Thanks be given unto almighty God for it, & Knowing it is appointed for all Men Once to Die, Do make & Ordain this to be my last Will & Testament, that is to say; First of all I give my Sold into the Hands of God that gave it; & for my Body, I recommend to the Earth to be buried in a Christian like manner at the Discretion of my Executors, Nothing Doubting but at the General Resurrection I shal receive the same again by the mighty Power of God that gave it; And as for Touching such Worldly Estate wherewith it has pleased God to bless me with, I give & Dispose of the same in the Manner & form following.

Item, I give & bequeath unto my two Sons, Isaac Weeks & Jabas Weeks, the Tract of Land that I now dwell on with the Marsh thereunto belonging, to be Equally divided between them and their Heirs & Assigns for Ever. That is to say, my Son Jabas to have that Part of the Land that the Plantation & Houses is on, and Isaac to have the other Part with half the Marsh.

Item, I give to my Son, Theoflis Weaks, on Shilling, Sterling.
Item, I give unto my Son, Archelas, One Shilling, Sterling.
Item, I give to my Son, Bingmam, One Shilliag Sterling.
Item, I give to my Daughter, Lidde Witton, One Shilling Sterling.

Item, I give to my Dafter, Mary Williams, One Shilling, Sterling.

Item, I give to my Dafter, Christian Weake, One Shilling Sterling.

Item, I give to my Dafter, Thankful Hicks, One Shilling Sterling.

Item, my Will & Desire is for my Wife to have the Plantation in her Lifetime.

I give to my Dafter, Elizabeth Weake, one Shilling Sterling.

Item, my Will & Desire is that my two Sons, Isaac & Jabas, do Each of them pay unto my Grand Son Edward Weaks, the Sum of Ten Pounds, current Money of Carolina, & upon Failure thereof to be Dispossessed of the Land before given.

Item, I give unto my well beloved Wife, Mary Weake, Two Beds & Furniture, Two Cows &   , and all other Houshold Goods & all the Remaining Part of my Estate that is not yet given During her Widowhood, She paying all my Lawful Debts. I also Depute and apoint my sd. Wife to be my whole & sole Executor of this my last Will & Testament, Ratifying and alowing this & no other to be my last Will and Testament. Disanulling all other Will formarly by me made.

In Testimony hereunto I have Set my Hand & Seal the Day & Year above written.

BINGMAN B WEAKS (Seal)
his mark

Signed, Sealed in the Presence of us,
JEHOSAPHAT HOLLAND.
FRANCIS BURNS.
THOS. T PERSON.
his mark

CARTERET COUNTY, NORTH CAROLINA.   June Court, 1745.

These may certify that Thomas Person, One of the Evidences to the Within Will, in open Court made Oath that he Saw Benjamin Weeks, Decd., Sign & Seal the same; and that he also saw Jehosaphat Holland & Francis Burns, Evidence the same, And Mary Weekes, Widow, hath taken the Oath of an Executrix, and by the Court admitted to Record. Dated at the Court House the 6th. Day of June, Anno Domini, 1745.

Tess. GEOR. READ, Clk. Cur.

Recorded in Will Book 6, page 62.

THOMAS WEST'S WILL.

IN THE NAME OF GOD AMEN. I, Thomas West, of Bertie County and Province of North Carolina, Yewman, being very sick and Weak in Body, but of perfect mind and Memory, thanks be to God for it, Do hereby make this my last Will & Testament, first and Principally I Commend my Soul into the hands of Almighty God, hoping for Remission of all my sins thro' the Merits of Jesus Christ, my blessed Saviour and Redeemer; and my Body to the Earth to be decently buried at the discretion of my Exors: and as for sutch Worlly Estate and Effects as it hath pleased God to bless me with I Give and bequeath as followeth:

Item, I Give and bequeath to my loving Wife, Elizt^h West, three Negroes. Harry, Tom. Amey, with one third of all my Personal Estate.

Item, I Give and bequeath to my Daughter, Elizabeth West, Merear & Melenor, with one third part of my Estate that is not already given, to her and her heirs for Ever.

Item, I Give and bequeath to my son, William West, Bess and Taffy, with all my lands, to him and his heirs for Ever; also, with one third part of my Estate that is not already Given in this Will.

I do here appoint my loving Wife Executricks, and my Brother Robert West Executricks of this my last Will and Testament, and I Do hereby disallow, Revoak and Disannul all and every other former wills, Testaments, by me made, willed or bequeathed, Ratifying and Confirming this and no other to be my last Will and Testament.

in Testimony whereof I have hereunto set my hand and fixed my Seal, this six Day of November, one thousand, Seven hundred and fifty six.

T. WEST. (Seal)

Sign'd, Seal'd, published, and declared in the presence of:
JOHN CORBERT, Jurat.
JOSEPH WHITE.
WM. FLEETWOOD, Jurat.

BERTIE COUNTY. ss. April Court, 1757.
The above written Will was Exhibited into Court by Elizabeth West, Widow, Relict & Exx. of said Will, and Robert West, Exr. thereof, and proved by the Oaths of John Corbert & William Fleetwood, two of the Subscribing witnesses thereto, and at the same Time the same Exx. & Exor' was Qualify'd for said office in due form of Law, which was ordered to be Certifyed. Test. BENJ. WYNNS, Cl. Cur.

Copied from Original Will, filed in the Office of the Secretary of State.

THOMAS WHITEHURST'S WILL.

NORTH CAROLINA.

IN THE NAME OF GOD AMEN. I, Thomas Whitehurst, Lieutenant in the Royal Navy, being Weak in Body, but of Sound Mind, Memory and Understanding, Do make and Ordain this to be my last Will and Testament in Writing, in Manner and Form, following, that is to say:

First, I Desire that all my Just Debts and Funeral Expences be first Discharged.

Also, I Give and Bequeath the Sum of fifty pounds, Lawful money of Great Brittain, belonging to me in the hands of my Agent, Mr. George Marsh, of Savage Gardens, Tower Hill, London, unto William Grenfell Lobb, Youngest Son of Jacob Lobb, Esquire, Commander of his Majesty's Sloop, the Viper.

Also, I Give and Devise all that peice of Land, Commonly known by the Name of Styles Copp, within Six Miles of the Town of Stafford, in the County of Stafford, in the Kingdom of Great Brittain, (Subject to a Lean made from me unto my Uncle, John Whitehurst), unto My Sister, Ann Whitehurst, her Heirs and Assigns for Ever.

And Whatever Estate, Real and personal, not heretofore bequeathed, I dye Possessed of; I Give, Bequeath and Devise unto my said Dear Sister, Anne Whitehurst, her Heirs and Assigns for Ever.

And I do hereby publish and Declare this to be my last will and Testament and appoint my said Sister, Executrix and the said Jacob Lobb, Executor of this my last Will and Testament, hereby Revoking all other wills by me heretofore Made.

In Witness whereof, I have hereunto set my hand and Seal this Twenty second day of March, in the year of our Lord, One thousand, Seven hundred and Sixty five.

JOHN WHITEHURST.
(Impression of Head on Seal)

Signed, Sealed, published and Declared by the Testator in the presence of us, who have subscribed our Names in his presence, and in the presence of Each other: (the words "not heretofore bequeathed" being previously inserted in the Seventeenth line from the Top).   J. EUSTACE.
THOS. COBHAM.
THOS. MCGWIRE.

NORTH CAROLINA,   Brusnwick, the 23, June, 1766.

Then personally Appeared before my Thomas Cobham, one of the subscribing Witnesses to the foregoing Will, and Made Oath on the Holy Evangelists of Almighty God, that he saw Thomas Whitehurst, sign, seal and Publish the foregoing as and for his last Will and Testament; and that the said Thomas Whitehurst was at the same Time (to the best of His knowledge and Belief) of a sound and disposing Mind and Memory, and that he, the said Thomas Cobham, together with John Eustace, and Thomas McGwire, subscribed their Names as Witnesses thereto in the Presence of the Testator.   WM. TRYON.

Copied from the Original Will, filed in the Office of the Secretary of State.

THOMAS WHITMELLS' WILL.

IN THE NAME OF GOD AMEN. I, Thomas Whitmell, of Bertie precinct, being Sick of Body, but of Perfect memory & Judgment, first Recommending my Soul to God that Gave it and my Body to be buried at the discretion of my Executors, doe make this my last will & testament, this 23d. Day of November, one thousand, Seven hundred & Thirty five.

Imprimis, I will & bequeath to my Dutyfull Son, Thos. Whitmell & his heirs for ever, my Plantation where I now live, on Kesia River, which Contains three hundred & Sixty acres of Land as by Deeds past to me by Gardner, as also three hundred & twenty acres of Land Lying on Buck, it being of a survey by pattent, Dated in Aprill, one thousand, Seven hundred & twenty six; as also half of all my Stock of horses, Cattle & Sheep as also two negro boys (viz.), Jupiter & Caloe, as also one fether Bed and furniture & one Desk; and whereas, there is a Stock ye Original of which was one hundred & fifty pounds, Sterling, Imployd in ye Indian trade by my Son, Thomas, one half of ye sd. Stock I further will and bequeath unto him, with one half of the profits arising from ye sd. Stock, one negro mand Called peter, to him & his heirs for ever.

2d., I will & bequeath to my loving wife, Elizabeth Whitmell all my houshold furniture of what sort so Ever thereunto Belonging, viz., Deds, Sets &c. She * * * (Illegible) my Daughter Martha Whitmell, fifteen pounds, Sterling, Money, at ye Day of her Mrrriage, or when at age By law, and after ye payment of the above Sums, I further will and Bequeath to her, the one half of my Trading Stock in ye hands of my Son, Thos. Whitmell, & one half of the Profits arising from ye sd. Stock, and half of all stocks of Cattle, horses, Sheep, belonging unto me, to her and her heirs for ever, & further, I Leave unto her, for her naturall Life, the use of my plantation where I now Live, & ye Use & Labour of three negro Slaves, Called Mingo, Bess & Peter.

3rd., I will a Bequeath to my Second Son, Lewis Whitmell one hundred & fifty Acres of Land Joyning to my Son, Thomas and John Grays lines; & Three hundred & Twenty acres of Land Lying on Buck Swamp, Being ye other half of the tract of Land bequeathed to my Son, Thomas; & one negro Boy Called Bristoll & one fourth of ye Increase of A negro Woman Called Bess, her first Child Excepted, as also the fourth part of two negro Girls, Called phillis & penney, and one fourth of their increase, to him & his heirs for ever.

4tly., I will and bequeath to my Infent Son, to Be Baptized William, the fourth part of ye Increase of one negro wench, Called Bess, the first Child Excepted & one fourth part of two negro Girls, Called phillis & penny & their Increase, to him & his heirs forever.

5'hly. I will and bequeath to my loving Daughter, Elizabeth Pollock, one Shilling.

6thly. I will and bequeath to my loving Daughter, Sarah Whitmell, thirty pounds, spanish Silver money at fifteen penny weight to the ounce, to be pd. by my loving wife, Elizabeth Whitmell, & one negro Woman Called Bess, her increase Excepted untill Devided, to her and her heirs forever.

7thly. I will & bequeath to my loving Daughter, Martha Whitmell, fifteen pounds Sterling money, and one negro Man, Called Mingoe, to her & her heirs for ever.

8thly. ———— woman called Bess, ———— alive Otherwise, ye first Child that shall be born alive of the sd. Bess, & one fourth part of two negro Girls Called phillis & penny, & their Encrease, to her & her heirs for ever.

9th., I will a bequeath to my Loving Daughter, Mary Whitmell, one forth part of two negro Girls, Called philis & penny & their Encrease, to her & her heirs forever.

Lastly, Constituting my Duty full Son, Thos. Whitmell, & my loving Brother, John Gray, Joynt Executors & my loving wife, Executrix, of this last my will & Testament, Declaring all former wills to be void I doe pronounce & Declare this to be my Last will & Testament &c.

         his
     Thomas T Whitmell (Seal)
         mark

Signed, Sealed & Delivered in the presence of:
  Simon Gale.
  Garrad Van Upstall.
     her
  Mary U Cannaday,
     mark

North Carolina.

Before his Excelly., Gabriel Johnston, Esqr., Govr., and Ordinary of the sd. Province:

Personally appeared before me Simon Gale & Garrard Van Upstall, two of the Subscribing Evidences to the within Will & made Oath on the Holy Evangelists, that he was present and Saw Thomas Whitmell, Sign, Seal, publish and Declare this to be his last will & Testament; & that he also Saw Mary Cannaday sign her name thereto at the same time; he was of Sound mind & disposing Memory at the time he Executed the Same.

And at the Same time, Thomas Whitmell, one of the Executors to ye within will took the Executors Oath in Due form of Law.

Given under my hand, this 17th of Decr., 1735.

           Gab. Johnston.

Recorded in Grant Book 4, No. 22, Office of the Secretary of the State

WILLIAM WICKLIFFE'S WILL.

IN THE NAME OF GOD, AMEN, I, William Wickliffe, of the County of Craven, in the province of No. Carolina, Being of a Sound & perfect Memory, thanks be to God. I Make & Ordain this to be my Last will and Testament, In Manner & form following, that is to Say first,

No. 1, I Give to my God who gave it, & my body to the Earth from whence it Came to be Decently Buried at ye. Discretion of My Executors Hereafter Named; and as following what Worldly Estate God of His Mercy hath Been Bestowed upon me, I Give and Bequeath in Manner & form following:

Imprimis, I Give and Bequeath unto my Loving Son, William Wickliffe, and his heirs, One Negroe fellow Named peter, And one Wench Named Jenny, with her Increase. Likewise, I Give unto my Son, William, all my Wareing Apparel, both woolen & Linnen, and What Silver & Gold I wear in Apparell; all my books, Riding Horse, Bridle and Saddle; Two feather beds with beding and Bolsters; One Desk, one Black Walnut Table that is in House. Likewise to give unto my abovesaid Son, William Wickliffe, the One forth Part of all my Cattle and Horses, mares and Colts, The One forth Part of all the Moneys, household Goods, Merchant Goods, and wares I have, Both at home and aBroad, after my just Debts and Legacies Paid, Exclusive of a Bond Indorsed Over to Jas. Hannis for 208, Two Hundred and Eight Pounds, Proc., and another of £20ulk 8 proc, April 30th. 1754. Dosed.

Item, I give and Bequeath unto my Loving Daughter, Eliz^a. Wickliffe, which is now Eliza Franks, to her and her Heirs, One Negro Fellow named Pompee, One Bed, Bolster and Beding, her Mother Pounk, Likewise, I give unto my aforesaid Daughter, Eliz^a. the Oneforth Part of all my Cattle and horses, mares and Colts. the One forth Part of all the Money's, Household Goods, Merchts. Goods, and wares, both at home and abroad, after my just Debts and Legacies Paid.

Item, I give and Bequeath unto my Daughter, Alce Wickliffe, and to her Heirs, Three Negros: One Negro fellow Named Adam, One Negro wench Named Hannah, And One Negro Girl Named Phillis. Likewise, I give unto my aforesaid Daughter, One Desk with four Draws, One Feather bed, Beding and Bolster, One Chince Gown and a Blue Mantle which was her Mother, One Lining Wheel; the One forth Part of all my Cattle and Horses, mares, and Colts; the One forth Part of all the Money's, Houshold Goods, marchts. Goods and wares, have Either at home or aBroad, After my just Debts and Legacies Paid, Exclusive of a Bond made Over of Mr. Jno. Rice for One Hundred and Forty Pounds, Sterling, and Another of Docter

Bryan, for Two Hundred and Twenty Pounds Sterling, B
tween Alice and Katharine Wickliffe.

Item, I give and Bequeath unto my Loving Daughte
Katharine Wickliffe, and her Heirs Three Negroes, (to wi
One Negro Fellow Named Will, One Negro wench Named Mo
and her Child Named Grace. Likewise, I give unto my af
Daughter Katherine, all her Mother Wearing Cloath's, wi
all the Table Lining, One Chester Draws, One Bed, Bolster, a1
Bedding, One lining Wheel and Wooling Wheel. Likewise,
give unto my said Daughter. the One forth Part of all my Catt
and Horses, Mares and Colts; the One fourth Part of all t]
Money's, Household Goods, Merchant Goods and wares, I ha·
Either at home or abroad, After my Just Debts and Legaci
paid. Exclusive of a Bond of Mr. John Rice for One Hundr(
and forty Pounds, Sterling, and Another of Doctr. Bryan, f
Two Hundred and Twenty Pounds, Sterling, Between Al
& Katherine

Item, I give and Bequeath unto my Grandsones, which
Sons to my Son, William Wickliffe, which is Truly Begott(
After Mariage, Equally to be Divided Amongst them all, n
Lotts, Lands, Houses and Tenements that is in the Province
North Carolina, or in any Other of his Majesty's Dominior
to them or their Heirs forever. But if in Case my aforesa
Son William, Should die without issue as foresaid, then, I gi·
And Bequeath unto my Grand Children, which is Children
my Children, Eliz^a., Alce & Katherine Wickliffe, which
Truly Begotten after Mariage, all my Lotts, Land's, Hous(
and Tenements as above Mentioned, Equally to be Divid(
Amongst them and their Heirs for Ever.

Item, All the remainder Part of my Estate, not before Giv(
of what kind and Nature soever, I give and Bequeath unto n
Loving Son, William Wickliffe, and my Daughters, Alce a1
Katherine Wickliffe, Equally to be Divided amongst thei
their Heirs and Assigns Forever, But in Case any of my Ch
dren should Die in their Minority, that then, their Part of n
Estate Divided to them shall Equally be Divided Amongst t:
Survivors of my above Mentioned Children, William, Alce
Katherine Wickliffe.

Item, I Constitute, Ordain and appoint my well Belov(
friend, my Loving Son, William Wickliffe, and Son in La·
John Frank's, all also my Loving Friend, John Starkey,
Craven County and Province of North Carolina, to be n
Exors. to This my Last Will and Testament. Revoking all Oth
Wills by me Before made. Ratifying and Confirming this a1
no Other to be my Last Will and Testament.

In Testimony Whereof, I have hereunto Set my Hand a1
fixed my Seal this 30th. day of September, In the Year of O·
Lord, One Thousand Seven Hundred and fifty three.

        WM. WICKLIFFE, (seal)

Signed, Sealed, Published, and Declared in Presence of: The words in the Original Will (my Loving friend Jno. Starkey being first Interlined and Samuel Hatch Scratcht. Out.)

    JE. VAIL.
    DANIEL DUPEE.
    SOUTHY REW.

The above Will was Proved before me by the Oath of Jeremiah Vail, who also made Oath that he Saw Daniel Dupee and Southy Rew, Sign the Same as Concuring Evidences thereto. Let Letters Testamentory Issue Accordingly.
Decr. 16th. 1754.   ARTHUR DOBBS.

Att the Same time William Wickliffe and John Frank's were Qualifyed as Exors. as the Law Directs.   ARTHUR DOBBS.

Recorded in Will Book 8, page 127.

THOMAS WILLIAMS' WILL.

IN THE NAME OF GOD AMEN, I, Thomas Williams, of Beaufort County, in North Carolina, Mariner, Do make, ordain and declare this to be my last Will and Testament, being at the same Time of sound mind and Memory.

Imprimis, I Give & devise unto my Wife, Ann Williams, during her Natural Life, half a Tract of Land containing Two hundred Acres Lying on the East side of the Mouth of Bath Town Creek, being the Land that I bought of Wm. Baker, which formerly belonged to Benjamin Forbes. I also give and bequeath unto her, two Negroe Men Slaves, named Chepstow and Cezar, for her use and behoof for Ever.

Item, I Give unto my Eldest Son, Thomas Williams, the other half of the said Tract of Land I have given his Mother during her Life: after her decease I give the same Land unto my Son, Thomas, his Heirs and assigns; and I likewise give and devise unto him one Lott of Land in Bath Town, Known by the number, 39; and my Silver Watch.

Item, I Give one Tract of Land, containing Two hundred and twenty five acres, that lyes in the Fork of Cuckolds Creek, unto my two Youngest Sons, Charles and John, to be equally divided between them, their heirs or assigns.

Item, As I have given unto my Daughter, Temperance, a Negro Boy Named Quamino Ever since he was born, so that She may have no Greater share than the rest of my Daughters, I Will & bequeath unto her only one Bedd and Furniture of the Fourth Choice, and all the Cattle that I have formerly given her, and that she has no further Share with the rest of my Children, In my Estate in North Carolina, the said Legacys to be given her at the Age of Twenty one.

Item. And all the remaining part of my Estate, both real & Personal, may be Equally divided between my wife, Ann Williams, and all of my Children, (Excepting Temperance, my third Child, unto whom I have given certain Share of what I possess in North Carolina as aforesaid, (vizt) Elizabeth Pritchard, Thos. Williams, Ann, Mary, Robert, Charles, Sarah, Hanah and John Williams, unto which Children my desire is that they have them respective their shares when they are Married, but not before they are of Twenty one Years of Age.

and my Will and desire is that my lawful Debts & Funeral Expenses be first paid before my Legacys are paid or any division made of any part of my Estate

Item, And as for what Estate I have belonging to me in England Or Wales, I do Will and bequeath them to be equally divided between my Wife and all my Children as aforesaid, only prefering my Eldest Son, Thomas Williams, to whom I Give a Double Share of my afd. Estate in England or Wales.

Item, I have given my certain Attys. my Wife Ann Williams, and Wyriott Ormond, Esquire, orders to purchase a Tract of Land in the Fork of Nevils Coak, formerly Nichols Garganers, which I give and devise unto My Son, Charles, his heirs and assigns. And the Tract of Two hundred and twenty five acres I have before devised to my son Charles and John (if the sd. Purchase is made) I give to my son John, his heirs and Assigns.

And if please God my wife should be with Child with any more Children by me begotten, not now Born, I bequeath unto it, or them, an Equal share of all my Estate in North Carolina or Else where (Excepting as aforesaid.

And for the Executing of this my last Will and Testament, I do hereby appoint my wife, Ann Williams, Executrix, Wyriott Ormond Esqr., James Ellison, Esqr., Mr. Coleman Roe, & Thomas Williams, my son, Exrs.

In witness whereof I have hereunto set my hand and seale this 17th. Day of Feb'y, 1757.

        THOMAS WILLIAMS. (Seal)

Signed, Sealed & declared to be the last Will & Testament of the Testator in the Presence of us the Subscribers:

  WILLIAM DOWD.
  JACOB NEVIL, Jun.
    Mark
  MOSES O NEVIL.
    his

BEAUFORT COUNTY, ss.   March Court, 1758.
 Present his Majesties Justices:
 This Certifys that the Last Will & Testament of Thomas Williams, Deceased, was Exhibited into Court and proved by the Oath of Jacob

Nevil, Jun., who swore that he was of sound and disposing mind and Memory at the time he Executed it, and that he saw William Doud and Moses Nevil, the other Subscribing Witnesses set their hands thereto: at the same time Ann Williams and Thomas Williams Qualified as Exrs. thereto, by taking the Oath by Law appointed. ordered that the Secretary have notice that Letters Testry. may issue.

Test. WALLEY CHAUNCY, Cl. Cur.

Copied from Original Will, filed in the Office of the Secretary of State.

WILLIAM WILLIAMS' WILL.

IN THE NAME OF GOD AMEN, the 2d. Day of Feb'y, Anno, 1724/5. I, William Williams, of Currituc precinct, In the County of Albemarle, and In the province of North Carolina, Being Very Sick and weak of Body, But of Sound and perfect mind and Memory, praise Be therefore given to almighty God for it, and Calling to Mind the mortality of my Body, and Knowing that Itt is appointed for all men once to Die, Do Make and ordain This my present Last Will and Testament, In Manner and form following: That is to say, first and principale of all, I Give and Recommend my Soul In to the hands of almight God That gave it hopping through my Blessed Saviours Death and passion to have full and free pardon of all my sins which I have Committed In this wicked world; and my Body I Commit to the Ground to Be Buried In Such Decent Christian manner as my Ex'rs hereafter named Shall Think fitt: and as for all Such Worldly Estate as In hath pleased almighty to Bless me in this Life, I give and Dispose thereof as followeth:

First, I will that all my Debts Be paid and Discharged.

Imprimis, I give and Bequeath unto My Son, Thomas Williams, That Tract of Land where I formerly Lived Up Tulls Creek, to him and his heirs for Ever: and also, one Negro Garle I give unto my Sd. Son, Thomas, Called Sew and all her Increase, to him and his heirs and assigns for Ever; and also, my Will and Desire is that my wife Mary Williams, have the profit, Use and possison of the plantation I now Live on During her Widowood, only the New ground, Item, I except for my Son, Stephen williams, and one of the houses to Dwell in; and after my Wife, Mary Williams, marries, my will and Desire is, that she have one third of the plantation aforesaid, and other Two Thirds to my son, Stephen, and after my sd. Wife's Decst.

Item, I give and Bequeath all my plantation and Land Belonging to Itt That I now Live on at the moth of Tull's Creek, Exc'pt part of the Island Called In-the-Woods, at the head Line, Joyning to the Land I bought of Mr. William Swann, to him and his heirs and assigns for Ever; and if my Son,

Stephen, Should Die without Isue, then to fall to my Son, Tulle Williams; and also, I give to my Sd. Son, Stephen, one Negro woman Call'd Bess and all her Increase, to him and his heirs and assigns for Ever, only excepting to my wife her Service During her widowood; and further, my will is that my Son, Stephen, have the Sorrell horse cal'd whipster.

Item, I give and Bequeath to my son, Tulle Williams, Two hundred and Ninty Seven akers of Land that I Bought of Mr. William Swann; and the part of That Island Excepted In the Land given to my Son, Stephen, to him and his heirs for Ever; and if my Son, Tulle, Should die without Isue, to fall to my Son, Stephen, him and his heirs for Ever; and also, my will is, That my Son, Tulle Williams hath one Negro woman cal'd Sylvia and al her Increase, only wife to have her in possion During her Widowood, Tell my Son, Tulle Williams Comes to the age of one and Twenty Years, Then to him and heirs and assigns for Ever: But if my wife shoul Die or marie, Then, my will is That my Son, Tulle, Should medeaintly take her Into his own possison, and all her Increase for Ever; and also, I give to my Sd. Son, Tulle, one young Rone mare Coalt, with a Stare in her face and all her Increase, to him and his Heirs for Ever.

Item, I give and Bequeath to my Three Sons, Thomas, Stephen and Tulle one hundred and fifty akers of timber Land Lying up Tuls Creek cal'd Long Leet, to Be Eaquailly Devided amongst them.

Item, I give and bequeath to my Daughter, Jann Brent, the Use of My Negro Garle Cal'd molle, and the Use of al her Increase, During her Natural Life, only, I Except the first Child the Sd. Negro Garle Brings, for My Grand Son, Johathan Brent, and his heirs for Ever; and after my Daughter, Jann Brents decs. I give and Bequeath to my grand Daughter, Mary Brent, the Sd. Negro Garle, and al the Rest of her Increase, to her and her heirs for Ever.

Item, I give and bequeath to my Daughter, Abigarle Philips, one Negro Boy, cald Jack, and to the heirs Lawfully Begotten of her Body, Body; and for want of Such heirs to fall to Tulle Williams and his heirs for Ever.

Item, I give and bequeath to my Two Sons, Stephen and Tulle, one hundred accores of marsh Lying In the Island Cal'd Gibeses Island, to them and their heirs for Ever.

Item, I give and Bequeath to my Loving Wife, mary Williams, one Negro Man cal'd Glasso, to her and her heirs for Ever, and also the horse cal'd Dick & al my parsonalle Estate, During her Widowood, only, I Except five pounds to pay for my son Tulle's Schooling one year; and further, my Will and Desier is, That if my wife, mary, should marrie or Die that Then, my Two Sons, Stephen and Tulle, Should Each of them, have one Cow and Each two Yeows, a peace, out of my Estate, and Then to be Eaqually Devided amongst them all; and also, I will that a True Inventory of al my Estate, persionalle and that None be Imbasaled. and also I make, ordaine and appoint my Loving wife, Mary Williams, True, Sole and Lawfull Exetrix with my Son, Tulle, of this my Last Will and Testam't.

As witness my hand and Seale, this 2d. Day of feb'y, Anno (?) Domini, 1724/5.

WILLIAM WILLIAMS. (Seal)

Signed, Sealed and Delivered
In the pres. of:
    WILLIAM DAVIS,
          his
    CHARLES C BRENT
          mark
    ROBERT ERVIN.
L'res. Granted 7 Jan'ry, 1725.

Copied from Original Will, filed in the Office of the Secretary of State.

ANN WINRIGHT'S WILL.

IN THE NAME OF GOD, AMEN. I, ann Winright, Of Neuport River, in the County of Carteret, widdow, being of Sound Mind, do make and Ordain this, my last will and Testement in Menner and form following; that is to Say, first I commend My Soul into the hands of Almighty God, and my body I commit to the Earth, to be desently buried, at the discretion of My Executors hereafter Named; and as thouching the disposition of all my Temporal Estate, I give and dispose thereof as Followeth:

Imprimis, I will that my debts and funeral Charges Shall be Paid And Discharged.

Item, I give and bequeath unto Sarah Lovick, and Betsey Lovick, daughters to Thoms. Lovick, the ten Pounds, Sterling, left me by the will of My late husband, James winright, deceased, to be equelly Divided between them.

Item, I give unto Sarah Lovick, that is now wife of Thoms. Lovick, my Gould Rimed Snuff Box, the large loocking Glass and all my Sheep.

Item, I give unto Mary Lovick my large Oval table, and ahalf Dozen of Black Chairs, and a bed, and one Silver Spoone.

Item, I give unto Penelope Lovick, my Second best table, ahalf Dozin of my best Chears, and one of my Best Beads, and two Silver Spoones.

Item, I give unto Sarah Lovick, the Daughter of Thoms. Lovick, My Desk, one Bead, and one Table, and the Small loocking Glass.

Item, I give unto Sarah Benners, And Penelope Lovick,

the Silver that is in John Davisis hands to be made in two large Silver Spoones to be Aquelly divided between them.

Item, I give unto Mary Lovick, Penelope Lovick, and Sarah Lovick, the Remainder of My house and Goods to be Aquelly Devided between them.

Item, I give unto Mary Lovick, Penelope Lovick and Sarah Lovick, all my wearing Aperrell, to be Aquelly Devided between them.

Item, I give unto my Molattah Whinch Named Judy her Freedom after my Desces.

Item, I give unto Thoms. Lovick, My Molatah Boy Named Thomas Harris, to sarve him till the said boy Comes to the Years of one and Thirty, And if the Said Thoms. Lovick should desces before the Said Boy Comes to that eage, the Said Thoms. Lovick Shall leve him to his Daughter, Betsey Lovick.

Item, I give unto Sarah Benners, My Molatah girl Named Cathrin Zift, to Sarve her till the Said Catherin Zift, is of the Eage of one and Thirty, And if Sarah Benners Should goe out of the Cuntry to Carry the Girl with her, if not to leve her, to her mother Sarah Lovick, the wife of Thom's Lovick.

Item, I give unto Sarah Lovick, the wife of Thoms. Lovick, And thair Daughter Betsey Lovick all my hoggs to be Aquelly Devided between them.

Item, I give unto George Phen'y Lovick, my hors.

Item, I give unto John Benners, my Spey Glass.

Item, I give unto Penelope Lovick, My white handle knives and forcks, My Welnitt hood, And all the Tea Spoons.

Item, I give unto Thoms. Lovick, all my Cattle, And all the Rest and Residue of my Personell Estate, goods and Chattles whatsoever, whome I do hereby Make and Appoint Joint Executrixes, with Sarah Lovick, wife to Thoms. Lovick, And Penelope Lovick, of this My Last will and Testament, And I do hereby revoke, disannal and Make Voyd all former wills and testaments by me heretofore made, either by word of Mouth or in Writing.

In witness whereof, I, the Said Ann Winright, to this my last will and Testament, Contained on three Sides of Paper, have Set my hand and Seal this 7 Day of March, 1751.

her
ANN X WINRIGHT
Mark
(Impression of Coat of Arms on Seal)

Signed, Sealed, Published and Declared by the Testator in the Presents of us, and attested by us in the Presents of the Said Testator.   JOHN BENNERS.
         DAVID EVANS.

CARTERET COUNTY,

At a Court of Common pleas, begun and Held at Beaufort Town on the first Tuesday in June, 1751.

Present his Majesties Justices:

These are to Certify, that Mr. John Benners in Open Court made Oath that he Saw Ann Winright, deceased, Sign, Seal, Publish and Declare the Within Insturment of Writing to be her Last will and Testament, & that David Evans were present at the Signing of the said Will and that Thomas Lovick, Esqr., Executor therein Appointed, Qualifyed himself as the Law Directs.   Test.   GEO. READ, Clk. Cur.

Copied from the Original Will, filed in the Office of the Secretary of State.

JAMES WINRIGHT'S WILL.

IN THE NAME OF GOD AMEN I, James Winright, of Carteret County, in the Province of North Carolina, Gentln. Do make and Ordain this my Last Will & Testament, In Manner and form following, (Vizt).

Imps. I Will and Desire that my Just Debts and Funeral expences be first paid and Discharged.

Item, I Will and Desire that all my Lands & Tenements on the North east side of New Port River (lying between Col. Lovicks & Mr. David Shepards Cow pents) with the Stock of Neat Cattle thereon be sold as soon as Conveniency will permit, and That My Beloved Wife, Ann, Shall be paid the Sum of Ten pounds, Sterling, out of the Money Arising thereby, and the Residue thereof Shall be Applyed to the Several Uses hereinafter Mentioned.

Item, I Will and Desire that my Beloved Wife, Ann, shall have the Labour of my Negros During her Widdowhood & not be sold or any other Ways disposed off by her or any person Intermarrying with her, But if so Happen that my sd. Wife should Marry, than Immediately the said Negros be Sold by my Executors and the Moneys Arising thereby to be Applyed as is hereinafter Mentioned.

Item, I Give and Bequeath unto my said Wife & her assignes The Mulatto Girle Called Judy, also all my Houshold Goods, Horses, Sheep and Hoggs.

Item, I Will and desire that my said Wife may have the use & Yearly profitts of a P'cel of Land on Newport River Called NewfoundLand, with the Yearly profitt of the Stock thereon, During her Natural life; and after her decease I give and Bequeath the said Land and Stock Which Shall Consist of Twelve Cows and Calves unto my Nephew, James Malin, & to his Heirs & assignes for Ever; the aforsed. James being the Son of my Sister Sarah, Now in London.

Item, I Will and Desire that my said Wife During her Natura———, May have the Use and Yearly profitts of all my Lands & Houses in Beaufort Town which I bought of John Pindar.

Item, I Will and Desire that a Likely Negro Boy, of the age between Twelve and Twenty, be purchased as soon as Can be after My Decease, to be paid unto Charles Cogdell being the Consideration money due for the Negro Malborough, if not paid before my Decease.

Item, I Give and Bequeath unto my Sister Elizabeth White, now in Boston, the Summ of Ten pounds, Sterling, to be paid as soon as it Can be raised out of my estate.

Item, I Give and Bequeath unto Elizabeth and Susannah Mabson the Sum of five pounds, Sterling, each, to be paid as soon as it Can be Raised out of my estate.

Item, I Give and Bequeath unto Mrs. Ann Blount, ye Wife of Mr. James Blount, the Sum of Five pounds, Sterling, to be paid as soon as it Can be Raised out of my estate.

Item, I Give and Bequeath unto Thomas Flybus, junr., the Son of Thomas Flybus, so much money as shall be Sufficient to pay & Defray the Costs and Charges of Taking up and patenting of One Hundred Acres of Land, Where he may find it in the Province aforesaid.

Item, I Give and Bequeath unto each of my Executors & their Heirs the Sum of Ten pounds, Sterling, after their Lawful Charges are paid.

Item, I Will and Appoint that the Yearly Rents & Profitts of all The Town land and Houses in Beaufort Town, Belonging unto me, with the other Land Adjoining thereto (Which I purchased of John Pindar), after the Decease of my wife Ann, to be Applyed to the Uses hereinafter Mentioned for Ever, (to Wit) for the encouragement of a Sober, discreet, Quallifyed Man to teach a School at Least Reading, Writing, Vulgar & Decimal Arithmetick, in the aforesd. Town of Beaufort, wch. said Man Shall be Choosen and Appointed by the Chair Man (& the Next in Commission) of Carteret County Court, and one of the Church Wardens of St. John parish in the aforesd. County and Their Successors for Ever. Also, I Give and Bequeath the Summ of Fifty pounds Sterling (provided that my estate Shall be Worth so much after my Just Debts and other Legacys are paid and Discharged) to be Applyed for the Building and finishing of a Creditable House for a school & Dwelling house for the said Master to be Erected and Built on Some part of my Land Near the White house Which I bought of the aforesaid Pindar, and my True Intent and Meaning is, that all the Yearly profitts & advantages Arising by the aforesd. Town Lotts and Lands thereunto adjoining as aforesd., with the Use of the sd. Land for Making & Improving a plantation for the planting & Raising of Corn &c. (if the aforesd. Master or teacher of sd. School shall think proper to plant &

Improve the Same) be entirely for the use & Benefitt of ye sd. Master and his Successors During his and their Good Behaviour. Also, that the sd. Master shall not be obliged to teach or take under his Care any Scholar or Scholars Imposed on him by the Trustees herein Mentioned, or their Successors, or by any other person, But shall have free Liberty to teach & take under his Care, Such, and so many Scholars, as he shall think Convenient and to Receive his Reward for the Teaching of them as he and the persons tendering them Shall agree.

Item, I Give and Bequeath unto Col. Thomas Lovick my Shooting Gun.

Item, I Give and Bequeath unto Robert Read the Sum of Five Pounds Sterling, to be paid as soon as it Can be raised out of my estate; and My Rifelled Gun. the sd. Robert being the Son of George Read.

Item, I Give and Bequeath unto George Read all my Books in my Librya.

Item, I Give and Bequeath unto Capt. Arthur Mabson my large Case with the Bottles Therein.

Item, I Give and Bequeath unto my Brother in Law, William White, My Boat and Sails thereto Belonging.

Item, I Give and Bequeath unto George Read my Watch which I now Useth, being a Silver Watch.

Item, I Give and Bequeath unto George Read my Cedar Desk (or Duroe).

Item, I Will and Desire that a P'cel of Land on the West side of Suttons Creek, on Perquimon River, in Perquimon County, be Sold and the money Arising thereby to be Applyed to the Uses of my Legacys.

Item, I Give and Bequeath unto my aforesd. Nephew, James Malin, his Heirs and assignes for ever, all the Rest. and Residue of my Estate, Both Real and personal, (not herein before Devised) When he Shall Arrive to the Age of Twenty one Years.

Lastly, I Appoint my Trusty Friends, Col. Thomas Lovick and George Read, of Carteret County aforesd., Executors of this my Last Will and Testament; and I do hereby Revoke, Disanul & make Void, all former Wills and Testaments by me heretofore Made.

In Witness Whereof, I, the said James Winright, to this my last Will and Testament have Set my Hand & Seal the Thirteenth day of August, in the Year of our Lord, One Thousand Seven Hundred and forty four.

JAS. WINRIGHT. (Seal)

Signed, Sealed, published, & Declared in the presence of us:
DAVID SHEPARD, Jur.
DAVID SHEPARD, Younger.
WILLIAM X DENNIS
mark

No. CAROLINA CARTERET COUNTY   March Court, 1744.
    David Shepard, Junr. and David Shepard, younger, made Oath that they Saw James Winright, deced., Sign & Seal the same and by that Court ordered to be Recorded.   Test. GEO. READ. Clk. Cur.
    Copied from the Original Will, filed in the Office of the Secretary of State.

JAMES WOOD'S WILL.

IN THE NAME OF GOD AMEN, this 25th. day of June, in the Year of our Lord Christ, 1751. I, James Wood, Sener, of the North wess Parish in Northampton County, in the Province of North Carolina, being of perfect mind & memory, Thanks be given to almighty God therefore, calling into mind the mortality of my body, and knowing that it is appointed for all men once to die, I do make & ordain this my Last will and Testament, that is to say, Principally & first of all, I give & recommend my soul into the hands of God that gave it me; & my body I recommend to the Earth to be Buried in a decent Christian Buriall at the discretion of my Executors hereafter named, nothing doubting but at the generall resurrection I shall receive the same again by the mighty power of god; and as touching such worldly Estate wherewith it hath pleased god to Bless me in this life, I give, demise & dispose of the same in the following manner and form:
    Imprimis, I Lend to my beloved wife, Elezabeth wood, two Negros Named Pompy & Hanner, induring her widowhood, and after her marriage, I give pompy to my Daughter, Elezabeth Wood, & hanner to my Daughter, Susannah Wood; and I give unto my Wife all my share of the stock of hogs that John Parker leves for me and the rent of that Plantation whereon he now Lives. I likewise Lend to my Wife, Elezabeth Wood, one bed and furniture, one Iron pott & pott hooks, one peuter dish & Bason, two Plates, Six Spoons & five cows & calves, Induring the time of her Naturall Life; & after her decease I give it to my Youngest Daughter, Mary Wood.
    Item, I Give unto my beloved Son, Jame Wood, the Plantation whereon he lives, with all my Lands lying upon the North Side of Cuttowhisky marsh & half the pasture; & I give unto my Son, James wood, another tract of Land lying upon Cuttowhisky Swamp, begining at the mouth of tare arse Branch, and runing up the swamp to the head Line, the down the branch to the first Station, containing 250 acres, be the said more or less; and I give unto my Son, James Wood, a Plantation lying on the head of Tar River, on both sides of the river, with all the Land belonging thereto; & five Negros named will and tony & Bob and dick & young peter; and one Shilling Serling.

Item, I give unto my daughter, Mary Outlaw, one Shilling, Sterling.

Item, I Give unto my Daughter, Sarah Duffield, one Shilling, Sterling.

Item, I Give to my Son, Moses Wood, one Shilling, Sterling.

Item, I Lend to my Daughter, Rosannah Bond, one Negro Girl named Jude she and her increase, during of her Naturall Life, then to the lawfull Heirs of her Body; & for want of such heirs shall return & be equally divided between my three sons here named, James, Joseph & Jonas; & I give to my Daughter, Rosannah Bond, one Shilling, Sterling.

Item, I Give unto my Son, Joseph Wood, a tract of Land lying upon Cuttowhisky Swamp, containing 650 acres of Land, be same more or less, begining at the mouth of the hog pen branch and runing along a line of markt trees to horsky marsh, & the including all the lands up the said marsh and swamp to tare arse branch; and Six Negroes, old peter and Cader, roben & rose, pat and fillis, they, and their increase for ever; and twenty pounds in cash; and one Bay horse and my great trooping Saddle.

Item, I give unto my Son, Jonas Wood, Plantation whereon I now Live, bounded as followeth: begining at the mouth of hog pen branch, runing aforesaid line of marked trees to ahorsky marsh, and all my land on the South side of Cuttowhisky marsh, and half the pasture; Likewise, Six Negros, named Cudger & Venus, & Jack, & pegg, nead & nan, they, and their increase for ever; and one Horse, & my rifield gun, and my still; & if either of my sons, Joseph Wood or Jonas Wood, dies without heir, the Land to fall to the other.

Item, I give unto my Daughter, Elezabeth Wood, two Negros named Tom & Jenny, they, & there increase for ever.

Item, I give my daughter, Susannah Wood, two Negros named hardy & Cate, they, & there increse for ever.

Item, I do leave my Plantation and land at the head of Coniritratt to the use of my three sons, James, Joseph and Jonas.

Item, I give unto my daughter, Winny Wood, 50 Pounds in Cash, and two Negros Nel & Scipio, the, & there increse for ever.

Item, I give unto my Youngest daughter, Mary Wood, 50 Pounds in Cash, and two negros named wicket & lucia, they, & there increase for ever.

Item, I lend unto my sister, Sarah Killingsworth, one negro Girl named dinah During her naturall life, she and her increase; and after her decease I give the said Girl to her two Youngest Daughters, Ann & Charity, to be equally divided betwen them.

and all the rest of my Estate, Stock of Creatures, Household

Goods, Debts & moveable effects, I leave to be equally divided amongst my Children here named: Joseph & Jonas Elezabeth & Susannah, by my Executors which are my two Sons, Joseph Wood and Jonas Wood, whome I constitute & make and ordain Sole Executors of this my Last Will and Testament, and I do hereby utterly disallow, revoke and dis annull, all and every other former Testaments, wills, leagaces bequeaths and Executors, by in any ways before named Willed and bequeathed, ratifying and confirming this, and no other, to be my last Will and Testament.

In Witness whereof, I hereunto set my Hand and Sealed the day and year above written.

JAMES WOOD W (L S)
his
Mark

Signed, Sealed and Delivered by the said James Wood as his Last Will and Testament in the Presents of us the Subscribers:

BARNABA X BAGGOTT.
his
mark

JOHN X PERKER.
his
mark

WM. FRYER.

In Obedience to your Excellency's Command I went to the Hous of William Fryer and took the Deposition of his Oath as followeth; William Fryer, aged about forty five years, first sworn, and then saith: I was a the hous of James Wood in July or August, in the year one thousand, seve hundred & fifty one, & James Wood was in a Low State of health and h told me he had made his will and he desired me to Witness it, he told m he had two witness to it and they never had heard it read, and he ordere his son to fetch the will and Read it to me, and to the houshold, and afte it was Read he takes the Will and Laid it down and took the pen and sai to me that was his Last will and testament, and in the presents of th said Fryer he signed, Sealed and acknowledg this to be his last will an testament, and that he see Barnaba Baggotts mark and John Perkei mark before he witnesseth, and then he witnesseth underneath and tha he acknowledged that to be his hand, and further saith not. March 1
1752.   Taken before me, JOHN ALSTON.

NORTH CAROLINA,   Edenhouse, 26 March, 1752.

I, Gabriel Johnston, Esqr., Governor and Comander in Chief, &c., i and over the sd. Province of North Carolina, do hereby Certifie that th day Personally appeared before me John Perker, one of the Subscribin Evidences of the within last Will & Testament of James Wood, late of Northampton County, Decd., and made Oath that he saw the sd. Testat sign, Seal & deliver the same as & for his last Will & Testament, and tha at the signing thereof he was of sound and disposing mind & memor and likewise at the same time the annexed Deposition of William Frye taken by Virtue of a Dedimus to John Alston, Esq., of Chowan Count directed was produced to me as farther proof of the sd. last Will & Test ment of the sd. Testator, the sd. William Fryer being another of the Ev dences thereto; and likewise at the same time Joseph Wood one of the Executors appointed by the said Will, qualified himself as Executor, by taking the Oath appointed by Law for that purpose.

GAB. JOHNSTON.

Copied from Original Will, filed in the Office of the Secretary of State.

LOVICK WORLEY'S WILL.

NORTH CAROLINA. SS.

IN THE NAME OF GOD AMEN. I, Lovick Worley, of the County of Tyrell, being Sick and weak in Body, but of Perfect Memory and Judgment, thanks be Given to God, Therefore do make and Ordain this to be my Last Will and Testament, First of all I Recommend my Soul to God that Gave it; and my Body to the Earth, to be Buried in a Christian Like Manner at the Discretion of My Executors hereafter Mentioned; And as for my Worldly Estate, I Dispose of the same in Manner and Form as followeth, Viz:

Imprimis, my Will is that my Two Negro Girls (Viz.) Moll and Bess and their Increas (If any they should have), be not Divided untill my Loving Daughter, Ann Gray Worley, be Twenty One Years Old or Married, &c.

2d'ly, I Give and Bequeath to my Loving Wife, Ann Worley, after My Just Debts are paid, the One Half of all My Personal Estate, to her, her heirs and Assigns for ever. I also lend to my Said Wife the use of My Lands and Plantation whereon I Now Live During her Natural Life.

3d'ly, I Give and Bequeath to my Loving Daughter, Ann Gray Worley, (after my Just debts are paid) the one half of all my Personal Estate in case she Lives to be Twenty One Years of Age or is Married; and if in Case my sd daughter should die before she is Twenty One Years of age or Married, I Give and Bequeath to my Loving Brother, John Worley, his Heirs and Assigns, Ten Pounds Lawful Money of great Brittain, to be raised Out of that Part of my Personal Estate I have Given to My sd Daughter; and the Remainder of that Part of My Personal Estate, I Give and Bequeath to my Loving Brother in Law, William Gray, and my Loving Sisters in Law, Lucretia Gray, Amelia Gray & Louisa Gray, to be Equally Divided Amongst them Share & Share alike, to them, their heirs and assigns for ever.

4thly. I Give and Bequeath to my Loving Daughter, Ann gray Worley, all my Lands that I am Now Possessed of, on Proviso she lives to have a Lawful Heir begotten of her body and her said heir lives to the Age of Twenty One Years or is Married, On such Provisoes, I Give her the sd. Lands; Otherwise, I Give and Bequeath unto my Loving Brother, John Worley, all My sd Lands, to him and his heirs forever.

Lastly, I Constitute and Appoint My Loving Wife, A₁ Worley, My Executrix, and My Loving Brother in Law, Willia Gray, my loving Uncle, James Blount, and My Loving frien Thomas Whitmell, My Executors to this My last Will a₁ Testament, Revokeing and Disanulling All former Or Other Wi by me made, acknowledging and Ordaining this to be my la Wil and Testament.

In Witness whereof, I have hereunto set my Hand and affix₁ my Seal, this 24th. Day of January, Anno Dom:, 1754.

LOVICK WORLEY. (Seal)

Signed, Sealed, Pronounced and Declared by the said Lovick Worley to be his last Will and Testament Before us:

Test.   DAVID JERNIGAN.
         THOMAS KINSY, Jurat.
         DAVID CANADAY, Jurat.

TYRELL COUNTY. ss.   March Court, 1754.

Then was the within Will duly proved in Open Court by the Oath Thomas Kimsey and David Canady, Two of the Subscribing Witness thereto; and at the same Time William Gray & Ann Worley was du Qualified as Exor. and Exrx. thereto as the Law Directs. Ordered that t Honble. James Murray, Esqr., Secretary, have Notice, that Letters Test mentary Issue thereon accordingly.

Test. EVAN JONES, Clk. Cu.

Copied from Original Will, filed in the Office of the Secretary of Sta

WILLIAM YEATES' WILL.

IN THE NAME OF GOD AMEN. I, William Yeates, of t] County of Bertie, & Province of No. Carolina, being sick a₁ weak in Body, but of sound & perfect sence and memor thånks be to Almighty God for it, and calling to mind t] uncertainty of This Transitory life, Do Make and Ordain th to be my last Will and Testament, in manner & form follov ing, that is to say, first I give and Bequeath my Soul to Almigh God that gave it; and my Body to be buryed in a Decent man by my Exctr. hearafter named.

Item, I Give and Bequeath to my Daughter, mary Yeate one negro Boy calld. Jupiter, to Hir & Hir Heirs for ever, onl if my sd. Daughter Mary should Dye Before She Marrey then, the sd Negro Jupiter to Belong to my Son, Richd. Yeate

Item, I Give to my Daughter, Susanah Pipkin, one neg Boy Named Nearo, to Hir & Hir Heirs for Ever.

Item, I Give & Bequeath to my Son, William Yeates, fi˙ Pound, Currt. money of Virginia, to be Paid him by my Exct₁ hearafter Named.

Item, I Give & Bequeath to my Son, Robert Yeates, One Hundred Acres of Land lying in Bertie County, Begining at Pottecasie Creek, at a high Island; from Thence Runing Up A flat Branch to a small marsh; from thence up a little Branch to a markd white Oak; from thence to a small Branch runing out of the Indian marsh to where Bryan Hare's path Crosses; from thence along the sd. Path to Bryan Hares Line, to him and to his Heirs for Ever.

Item, I Give and Bequeath to my Daughter, Martha Langston, one Negro Boy Named Joe, to Hir & Hir Heirs for Ever.

Item, I Give & Bequeath to my Son, Richard Yeates, One Hundred Acres of Land Lying in Bertie County, Begining Att Blew Water Branch at the old Bridge; from thence Up A Little Branch to a marked white Oak standing On the Chapel Path; from Thence Runing to a Little marsh call'd the Rackcoon Marsh; from Thence to Bryan Hares Corner Tree. Allso, one negro man called Pompy after the Death of his Mother. Allso, One Gray Horse Calld Daulphin, his choice of my Guns, and a feather Bed and furniture to it.

Item, I Give & Bequeath to my Son, Charles Yeates, one hundred Acres of Land Lying in Bertie County, Begining On Cuttewhiske Swamp at A Little Branch; from Thence Runing Up the sd. Branch to a Marked Pine, then to a Red Oak Standing On Carters Path, then Along the sd. Path to Bryan Hares Line. Allso, One feather bed and furniture to it, One Gray Coult Runing with his Dam calld. Tibb, two Cows & Calves, one Gun, one Iron Pott, two pewter Dishes & three pewter Plates.

Item, I Give and Bequeath to my Son, Daniel Yeates, My Plantation I Now Live Upon, with All the Remainder Part of my Land Undisposed; One feather Bed & furniture to it; One Bay mare calld. Jone, One Iron Pott, two pewter Dishes & three Pewter plates, & all my Cooper's Tools.

Item, I Give and Bequeath to my Daughter, Judith Yeates, one negro Boy named Catoe, and two Cows & Calves, to Hir & Hir Heirs for Ever.

Item, I Give & Bequeath to my Daughter, Amy Yeates, one Negro Boy named Seesar, two Cows & Calves, two Pewter Dishes and three Pewter Plates.

Item, my Will is that if my Daughter Judith, or Amy Yeates, Or Either of them, should Dye Before they, Or Either of them, should Marrey, then there, Or Either of there Negros Given to them by me, shall fall to & Belong to my son, Robert Yeates. Likewise, if my Daughter Mary Yates, Should Dye Before She Marreys, then the Negro Boy Given to her by me Shall fall to and Belong to my Son, Richard Yeates. Likewise, if My Sons, Richard, Charles Or Daniel Yeates, Should Dye Before they come to Lawfull Age, Or Without Issue, then the Land given to them, Or Either of them, By Me is to fall to and Belong to the Surviveung Brothers and So To Redown to them As Long as Either them Lives.

Item, I Lend to my Beloved Wife, Mary Yeates, the Use of One negro Man Named Pompy, & One Negro Woman named Venus, dureing hir Natural life, and after hir Death, my sd. Negro Pompy to Belong to my Son, Richard Yeates; and my Negro Woman Venus and hir Increase to Belong to my two Sons, Charles and Daniel, and there Heirs for Ever.

Item, I Give and Bequeath to my Beloved Wife, Mary Yeates, All the Rest of My Personal Estate, Both Moveable and Unmoveable. I Allso Appoint my Beloved Wife, Mary, and my Son, Richard Yeates, my Whole & Sole Executors of this my Last Will & Testament. Hearby Disannulling all Other Wills by me Made Or Directed to Which Said Last Will and Testament I have Hearunto Sett my Hand and fixt my Seal, This Twenty third day of December, Anno Domini, one Thousand, Seven hundred and fifty one.

WILLIAM YEATES (L S)

Sign'd, Seal'd, Publish'd, & declared in Presants of Us:
    JNO. BRICKELL.
    ISAAC CARTER.
    BRYAN HARE.

BERTIE COUNTY   May Court, 1752.
    Present his Majesty's Justices

The last Will & Testament of William Yeates, Decd., exhibited into Court by Mary Yeates & Richard Yeates, Executx. & Executr. of the sd. Will, & proved by the Oaths of Jno. Brickell, Isaac Carter & Bryan Hare, the Evidences thereto; at the same Time the sd. Executx. & Executr. qualified themselves by taking the Oath appointed by Law for that Purpose. Ordered to be Certified By Order of Court

Test. SAML. ORMES, Cl. Cur.

Copied From Original Will, filed in the Office of the Secretary of State.

JOHN HARDY'S WILL.

IN THE NAME OF GOD AMEN. I John Hardy of Chowan in the Collony of North Carolina &C Being weak in body Butt in perfect & sound mind and memory praise be therefore given to all mighty God Do make and ordain this my present last will & Testam^t in manner & form following (That is to say) first & princapally I commend my Soul into the hands of All mighty God hopeing through the merritts death & passion of my Saviour Jesus Christ to have full & free pardon & forgiveness of all my Sins And to Inherritt Everlasting life, And my body I committ to the Earth to be Decently buried att the descretion of my Exceutors hereafter named, And as touching the Deposision of all my Temporall which itt hath pleased allmighty God to bestow on me I give & Dispose as followeth

Item, I give unto my Loving Brother William Hardy one Black hors of five year ould, And the best shute of Cloaths I have, Allso my Buckanear gun

Item, I give unto my brother Thomas Hardy one hundred acers of Land out of the tract where he now Dwell on the upper side of the line Joyning to Lewis Davis begining on the pocoson then running up to the head of the line And one gray broad cloath coate

Item, I give unto my brother Jacob Hardy one gray drugett coate

Item, I give unto katherine Stancell Widdow one cow & calfe

Item, I give unto Richard Pickering one young mare two years ould

Item, I give * * * all Johnson other * * * John Butler a certain debt of twenty two pound for which I have his land mortgaged, And I do hereby give him the said debt And allso Discharge the said mortgage

Item, I give & bequeath unto my loving Daughter Elizibeth Hardy both my plantations lying on casiah river where Thomas williamson now Dwell And contayning Six hundred & forty Acers Each as appears by the pattents bearing date november the forth 1707, Allso another tract of Land over casiah river called Hendersons folly contayning four hundred & forty acers as appear by the pattent bearing date aprill the first 1719

Allso I give unto my Daughter Elizibeth another tract of Land on the East side of rockquess contayning four hundred and twenty four acers Excepting the one hundred acors given to my brother Thomas

Item, I give unto my Daughter Elizibeth one tract of Lightwood land Lying on bucklesbury swamp so running back to

Esq⁽ʳ⁾ Duckinfield line contayning five hundred acers as appear by the patent bearing date octor 20ᵗʰ: 1717

All which said lands I give unto my said Daughter Elizibeth And to her heirs Lawfully begotten of her body

Item, I give unto my beloved daughter mary hardy This my maner plantation where I now dwell contayning Six hundred and forty acers as appear by the patent bearing date november 11ᵗʰ 1707 And allso another tract of Land Lying on the head of my said plantation And running to John Marshalls line contayning Six hundred & forty acers as appear by the patent bearing date the 20ᵗʰ: of July 1717 John Hardy

Allso I give unto my Daughter mary one plantation Lying on Casiah river on the East side contayning six hundred & forty acers as appears by the patent bearing date november the first 1712 Allso I give unto my Daughter mary one plantation in the fork of Casiah river where mary Lee now Dwell contayning Two hundred & five acers as appear by the conveyance from the patent All which lands & plantacons I give & bequeath unto my said Daughter mary and her heirs Lawfully begotten of her body

Item, I give unto my well beloved wife Rebecah Hardy one tract of Land Lying aLong the pocoson or Bucklesbury swamp contayning four hundred & seventy acers as appear by the pattent bearing date october 19ᵗʰ: 1716 And called the gum swamp As allso another tract of land between David Hicks line & John Marshalls so along the pocoson side contayning Six hundred & forty acers as appear by the patent bearing Date the 20ᵗʰ day of July 1717 All which said land I give unto my wife Rebecah and to her Dispose

Now in case my wife Rebecah should be with child & Delivered within nine months from the date hereof: Then in such case being a son I give him this my manner plantation And also the other tract on the head of itt both willed to my daughter mary And allso both my plantations on cashia river both willed to my Daughter Elizabeth And in case itt shold be a daughter I give her one plantation Lying on the East side of cashia river willed unto my daughter mary Allso one tract of Land over cashia river called Hendersons folly willed unto my Daughter Elizibeth And in case of the Death of Either my Daughters or a child that may be born in the time above mentioned the sirvivers shall Equally Divid the part of the Deceased both personall & Reall between them

Item, I give unto my Daughter Elizibeth these negroes hereafter mentioned—Viz Scipio: grace: Sharpor: Mall & Morea with all their Increase unto her my daughter Elizibeth

Item, I give unto my Daughter mary these negroes herafter mentioned Viz kent Joane quasha & toney with all their Increase unto my said Daughter mary

Item, I give unto my wife Rebecah these negroes hereafter mentioned Viz Jack: Nanney george & Dido And my half of hector & qommsorer(?) and in case of a son or Daughter born as above mentioned the said son or daughter to have an equall share with the other children of all my personall Estate

Item, my money in England I give Equally to be Divided between my wife & the children Each child having an Equall part with my wife

Item, I give all my horsis cattle and sheep to be Equally Divided between my my wife and the Children Each having an Equall part, And while my wife shall remain a Widdow she has hereby Liberty to kill out of all or any the stock of Cattle or Sheep for her family use

Item, I give all my houshold Stuff and Toles both within and without I give all Equally to be Divided between my wife & Children Equally

Item, I give unto my Daughter Elizabeth thirty pound in publick money to pay the publick dues & quittrents of her Lands

Item, I give unto my Daughter mary thirty pound in publick money to pay the publick dues & quittrents of her Land

Item, for all the rest of my publick bills With my debts by bill account or any other ways whatsoever I wold have all Reserved to all my Just debts from me due to any person Now here I would itt understood I wold have all my Just debts paid in pitch & not in paper Excepting Elliotts debt And that not Excepting they sue for the same And all over & Above paying my debts I give unto my wife Rebecah Hardy

And in case my wife should marry I wold have the negroes belonging to the Children & Imployed on their own Lands & plantations wholy for their own benefit And the rest of their Estates to remain in their mothers hands: Except my Executors see apparent cause to take itt away

Lastly, I do hereby nominate and appoint my well beloved wife Rebecah Hardy Excutrix: And my well beloved Brother William Hardy And my trusty and well beloved friend Thomas Pollock Junior And my Trusty and well beloved friend Major Robert West my true & Lawfull   *   *   *   *   *
these my forementioned friends all joyntly my true and Lawful Executors to this my last will & Testament hereby Declaring owing & Confirming this as my Last will & Testament Revoking & Disanulling all other wills & Testaments for null & Voide

In Witness whereof I have hereunto Sett my hand and fixed my Seall this nineteenth day of January And the year of our Lord one thousand seven hundred & nineteen And the sixth year of the Reign of our Soveragn Lord king George, of Great Britton ffrance and Ireland King Defender of the faith

Contained in thre sheetts of paper   JOHN HARDY (Seal)

Signed Sealed Declared and Published as my last will & Testament in presence of
  HOLLBROOK
  LAURENCE SARTON
  JOHN LUERTON

NORTH CAROLINA ss   By the Honble the Governor

John Holbrook came before me and made Oath that he see Mr John Hardy Signe Seal and publish the within will to be his last Will and Testiam^t Given under my hand this 16th day March 1719
            CHARLES EDEN

Copied from Original Will, filed in office of Secretary of State.

INVENTORIES.

AN INVENTORY of the Estate of William Bartram Senr Deceased Taken by the Administrators:

25 old Books of Diferent sorts & percil of other old Books
30 New pewter plates
18 old puter plates & 26 spoons
11 puter Basons
5 puter Dishes 1 Tin pan
14 Earthen plates
1 Salt Sellar & peper Box
3 Tea Kittles
4 Tea pots & one Coffee pot
12 Tea Cups & sassers
4 Candel Sticks & 1 pair Snuffers
3 Earthern butter pots & 1 pan
2 pair fire Dogs & 1 old one
2 pair fire Tongs & 2 Shovels
8 Iron Pot & 2 Iron Kittle
4 pair pot hooks 1 pot Tramel
1 Flesh fork & Skimmer
2 Skillets & Frying pan
1 Iron Spit & Gridiron
1 Iron trivet & bread Tester
6 Wine Glasses & one Decanter
12 Knives & Forks
2 punch bowles & 1 Case & Bottles
6 Beads & furniture 4 bead Steads
7 Chests & 11 Chairs & 14 Sickels
1 pair of Stillards & Scales & Weights
2 Brass Morters & 1 Iron Morter
3 Tables & 1 Safe & 4 Jugs
2 Wier Sives & 2 pair flat Irons
2 Looking Glasses & 1 Desk
3 pails 2 piggens & 1 tub
2 Churns & 2 Keelers
1 pair of hand Mill Stones
1 Grinding Stone & whet Stone
1 Avil Bellos & 2 Vices
3 hammers 1 Sledges & 2 Service plates
3 pair of tongs & a percil of files
1 Rost Meet hook & Melting Ladle
1 pair of Brass button Molds
1 pair of Spoon Molds
1 pair of Shot Molds
2 Big wheals & 2 Little Wheals
2 pair of Cards & 1 pair Tow Combs
2 Hackels & 1 pair wosted Combs
3 pair bar plow Irons
2 Flacks Iron without Colters
6 pair of Iron Traces
12 Weading hows & Six axes
3 Iron Wedges & 1 frow
1 Cross Cut Saw & 1 Tennent Saw
3 hand Saws 6 Chissels 1 gaug
1 Ads & 2 Augers & 2 old Cross Cut Saws
1 pair Timber wheals & 1 pair Cart wheals

2 Ox Chains & 1 Timber Chain
2 Grubbing hoes & 3 Spaids
1 Still & worm
1 Iron Cotton Gin & 1 Coffee Mill
6 old Gun Barrels
2 Iron Cart hoops & 3 small Boxes
3 old Guns & 1 Cookin Iron
7 Rasors & a percil of Snipe Bills
1 Good Mill Saw & 5 old Mill Saws
2 Cooper howels & 6 pair Bridel bits
1 Surveyers Cumpas & Chain
4 pair of Sturrip Irons & one odd one
1 pair of Money Scales
3 old Swords & 3 Trupers Pistols
2 horse Locks & 1 pair tooth Drawers
1 pair Dore hinges 1 pair of Window Ditto
1 Gun Lock & Staples & ring for Ox Yokes
6 Ox or horse Bells
1 piece & ½ of gert webing
1 Cag with some powder & a peice of Lead
1 Shoe Maker hammer & pinchers & Some other Shoe Maker Tools
1 old Steal Mill
1 Set of Brass for a Gun
8 New bells Not Brased
1 Mouth peice to put on Negros
1 pair Iron hoppels for Negros
1 hand vice & 1 peice of old Copper Kittle & 4 plow Clevis
1 Glue pot & a percil of Glue
2 puter quarts & 1 puter Tankerd
1 pair of Leather Bags
1 peice of old Crank & a percil of old Iron
5 Hogsheads & 2 Powdering Tubs
2 yards of Black Cotton Velvit
1½ yards of Snuff Colered Velvet
63 head of hogs of Diferent Sorts
11 two year old Bulls
14 Barren Cows
4 three year old Bulls
8 year old heffers
34 Cows & Calves
8 two year old heffers
2 one year old Bulls
2 three year old stears
6 for year old stears
2 five year old stears
3 two year old stears
11 working Oxen
3 Stallions
5 Mairs
3 one year old Mairs
1 two year old Mair
1 Mar & Colt
4 plow horses
3 Riding horses
1 four year old horse
1 horse sold by W Bartram Junr
23 head of Sheep
2 Guages & 1 hand Saw 2 Chissels
3 Augors 2 Drawing knives
2 Ox or horse Bells

1 Curring knife & Steal
2 Flats one in the river the other in the Mill pond
1 old pair of Timber Wheals
1 old pair of Cart Wheals
4 Ox Yokes 1 pruning knife
3 horses
4 Barrels Locks instead of pad locks
1 Harrow with 10 Iron teeth
1 Iron Instrument to Make Lines or Ropes & a parcil of Gun Worms
1 Little Old Conno
1 two foot Scale
11 Negro Men & Boys
8 Negro women & Girls
3 Negro Children
8 Negro Children Boys & Girls
  percil of Notes of hands & orders if Can be recovd to the Amount of
  £143: 11: 1:¼
To a proved Account £20: 14: 8
To 23 pounds in Cash
To a percil of Sundrey Book Account unSettled the Amount Not known
To Some horses & Mairs & Some Cattle Supposed to be runing in
  the woods the Number Not known
17 Thousand feet of Marchint Lumber
5 Thousand feet Marchantbb in town
A percil of Slaves the number Not known
About 240 Bushels of Indian Corn
9 head of Cattle killed for use
11 head of hogs killed for house use

The within is a Just & true Inventory taken by us to the best of our Knowledge

                    WM. BARTRAM
                    THOS ROBESON Junr

AN INVENTORY of the Estate of Wm. Bartram Junr Deceased

	Acres
To 1 peice of Land at the Wacanaw Lake Containing	120
To 1 peice of Land at the Lake known by Bartram Lake Containing	320
Ditto to 320 Acres on Bartram Lake	320
To 1 peice on the Bluff at the Sugar Loaf Containing	215
To 1 peice of Land Called ashwood Containing	640
To Ditto 1 Peice on the No. Est side of the river Called ashwood Containing	640
To 1 peice of Land at Bartram Low or Lake Containing	150
To 1 peice at the white Marsh Containing	120
To 1 Peice at the White Marsh Containg	100
To 1 Peice at the White Marsh Containing	100
To 1 peice at the Mouth of Donohue Creek Containing	3
To 1 peice of land on the No Est side of the River containing	500
To 1 peice adjoining to Ashwood Containing	150
To 1 peice adjoining to Hezeck Davis Containing	50
To 1 peice on plummers run to be taken at two thirds the Value	
To 2 peices on Carvers Creek & belonging to the Mill Containing of Land	490
& Mills & Iron works & Utentials belonging to them	
To 1 Lot in Wilmington bought of Kinny 23 feet front 33 feet Back	

To 1 Lot Leased to Burgwin
To 2 Lots from Isaac Hill
To other Lots the Deeds in one Keen Name
To 1 Lot in Campbelltown
To Docter Books & Docter's Medicens & Vials & pots the Number unknown & aiticels to me
To Some Docter Instruments
To a percil of Docter Drugs the Article & Do Not known
1 Rifel Gun Ditto 1 Smooth Gun
1 Good Saddle Ditto 1 Midling Saddle
1 Silver Watch
1 Pair Silver Shoe Buckels Ditto 1 pair Nee Buckels
1 Stock Ditto 1 Hone
1 Hown harne & 2 razars & a Case
To a percil of Book Accounts for practise of Phisick
1 Iron Tea Kittle 1 Chest
1 Large Cutto knife
1 pair of Shot Moles
1 pair of Bullet Moles
To a percil of wearing apperil
To 1 Mouth peice for a Negro
To 1 Rat Trap
to 1 pair Iron Traces
To 1 Fleshing knife
To 1 Iron to Bake Bread

A Just & true Inventory taken by
To the Best of my Knowledge
Thos. Robeson Junr Administrator
(Filed Nov. 17, 1772.)

Albemarle August 2d 1680

Wee the Subscribers being Ordered by the Grand Councell for th appraismt of ye Estate of Capt. Vallentine Bird Deceased wee doe In orde hereunto appraise the sd Goods and Chattles as is brought before us 1 the best of our Skill and Judgment:

Imprimis 3 pr fine holland Sheets at 50 Shillings per paire	07:10:00
3 Pr of Course Ditto att 30 s pr	04:10:00
1 Ditto Course at	01:05:00
2 Prs halfe worne Ditto 15 s Pr	01:10:00
3 browne Orsenbrigg Sheets at 5 s	00:15:00
1 Pr worne Sheets	00:08:00
11 pillows at 2s 6p	01:07:06
6 Ditto at 2s. 6p	00:15:00
4 Cubboard Cloathes	00:16:00
1 fine Holland Cubboard Cloth	00:08:00
1 Dozn Daipr Napkins & Table Cloth	01:10:00
1 Dozn and 9 Daiper napkins	01:18:00
3 Table Clothes	00:18:00
6 course Table Clothes	01:10:00
2 dozn & 4 Course Napkins	01:10:00
16 Course Towells	01:10:00
1 fine holland Towell	00:05:00
1 Tankard and 1 Dozen Silver Spoons	13:07:04
1 Sett Curtains vallens & Counterpans	01:10:00
1 Sett of old Curtains and Vallens	00:10:00
1 fringed Shoulder belt	00:10:00

INVENTORIES. 473

1 gray Shagd Rugg	00:10:00
1 green Shagd Rugg	01:00:00
1 Shagd Rugg	01:05:00
1 Ditto att	01:02:00
1 Dark Cullowed Rugg Shagd	01:00:00
1 Large Black Trunck	00:15:00
1 Smaller Ditto with Drawers	00:15:00
1 small Chest	00:10:00
1 Iron bound Chest	01:00:00
1 Iron bound Ditto	01:00:00
1 New ffeather and boulster	06:00:00
1 ffeather Bed and Boulster	04:00:00
1 Hammacker	00:18:00
1 bed boulster and pilloe	05:10:00
1 bed boulster Coverlet & pillow	04:10:00
1 Looking glass	00:05:00
1 Glass Case	00:10:00
1 dressing box	01:00:00
1 Warming Pann	00:10:00
1 Bed Stead	00:08:00
One Pcell of books	06:00:00
2 hair Brushes	00:01:06
23 Round and Square Bottles	00:12:00
15 yd of Keirsey	01:17:06
11 Prs plain Shoes at 3:s Pr	01:13:00
1 Black walnut Table & frame	01:00:00
10 Chairs	02:10:00
1 Couch at	01:00:00
1 Table and frame	00:13:04
1 Table Cloth	00:06:08
1 Striped Carpet	00:05:00
1 Whip saw	01:00:00
1 bed stead and Cradle	00:10:00
1 fowling piece	01:10:00
1 musket and fowling piece	01:15:00
2 Smoothing Irons att	00:10:00
1 pair of Stilliards and pea	00:08:00
1 Dozen pewter plates	01:10:00
1 Dozn Ditto	01:04:00
19 pewter poringr at	01:08:06
6 Small Salts	00:06:00
2 Large Ditto at	00:06:00
2 pewter Candlesticks	00:05:00
3 Sawsers at 1s 3p per lb	00:04:06
51 Pewter Dishes at	03:03:09
4 pewter Basons	01:12:00
3 old pewter plates	00:05:00
2 Large brass Candlesticks	01:10:00
A parcel of Tining ware	02:00:00
2 pewter Chamber potts	00:08:00
1 pewter Tankard	00:03:00
1 paire Tongues & Fire Shovell	00:05:00
1 brass Kittle: 32 pound at	02:00:00
3 skillets at 18 shillings	00:18:00
6 bell mettle mortor & pearsell	00:10:00
1 posnet at	00:04:00
1 brass (?) and Ladle	00:05:00
1 frying pann at	00:06:00
3 spitts	00:10:00
1 paire andirons	00:15:00

3 paire pothooks	00:06:00
1: paire racks	00:03:00
1 iron pott wt 50 lb at 4p pr lb	00:16:08
1 ditto wt 36 lb at 4p pr lb	00:12:00
2 dittoes wt 33 lb at 4p per lb	00:11:00
1 Lignum vitee punch bowl	00:15:00
1 Lignum vitee mortor	00:02:06
1 flesh forke	00:01:00
1 Cradle	00:05:00
Negro men; (vizt: Mingo at	40:00:00
Andrew and Thom: at 35 lb Sterling pr each	70:00:00
women: negroes Hanna; Betty; Betty; & Bess at 30 lb Sterling each	120:00:00
Mary ye Indian	20:00:00
Negro boy mustapha	20:00:00
1 Small Ditto named Robin at	15:00:00
1 small negro Girl named Jane	15:00:00
1 Negro Child George	10:00:00
1 Woman Servant named Ann ffarmer of 4 years to serve	08:00:00
1 hand Mill	06:00:00
1 sett of wedges	00:10:00
7 weeding howes at 1s: 6p:	00:10:06
8 hilling howes at	00:07:00
2 old Axes at	00:02:00
1 spaid att	00:06:00
1 Trowell at 2s: 6p:	00:02:06
1 broad ax at	00:04:00
1 hand saw at	00:02:00
1 Lathing hamer at	00:01:06
1 coopers adze & rift	00:03:00
22 sheep at 10s:	11:00:00
plantation and housen	80:00:00
12: old Sowes	09:00:00
30 Shotes	07:10:00
6 barrows and board	05:05:00
12 cowes and calves at 30s	18:00:00
6: 2 year old beasts	06:00:00

Total is 583 lb—01s—03p

SAMUELL DAVISS
WM. NEVELL
JNO DIE
    Signum
    Tobacco lb

By 2000 pounds of tobacco Due from Capt Zacha Gillam &c 2000

 I the Subscriber Doe present In humble Manner this as A True Inventory of the Estate of Capt Bird of this County Late Deseased I being his Executrix The Debts of ye Estate being drawne up; I forgott to Bring them; which I humbly Crave Leave to the Next Session of ye Grand Councell; for presentmt of them and that to this Inventory Credits they may bee annexed; November 8th 1680

                MARGARET BIRD

 The pettionar is Lt Allowed for ye Bringing in of the Debts
        ROBT JOHNSON HOLDEN, Secrata

INVENTORY of the Real & Personal Estate of Richard Blackledge Esqr. Deceased taken October 20th 1777 Vizt:

15530 Acres of Land or there About 49 Negroes 320 Head of Cattle or there Abouts ½ Lott No 108 Lott No. 46 Do 36 Do 404 Do 405 Do 406 & Do 236 with Half a Front Lott held with Mr Neale where the Slaughter House Stands Salt Works as they now Stand at the Mouth of Cour Creek being 50 Acres of Land with a Salt Pann Abt 2-3 done 14 by 18 feet Squair about 1700 wt Barr Iron & a Suffciency of Plates to finish the Pann About 700 wt Lead 8 Kittles fixed for Boyling 3 Yoke of Oxen 2 Carts 1 Set of Smiths Tools 3 Boats 2 Cows & Calves & Sundry Tools Consisting of Axes, Hoes, Spades, Saws &c &C for the use of the Works with some Little furniture for use of the Works People Beds &c abt 20M Bricks to put the Pann up with & Abt. 4 M of Lumber to make Resurvoys &c Half the Brigg Ann with Capt. Stephen Williams now Abt Cadiz or up the Straits & Half her Cargo out of which Stephen Williams has Remitted three Hundred Pounds Sterling ¼ of 5-16 of a Schooner called the Beaufort on a Voyage to the West Indies Commanded by Capt. Annible 1-6 of a Brigg now Building at Beaufort by Peter Nowe & Robert Walpoole 3-16 of a Schooner Called the Ellinor now Building at Otter Creek by Mr. Adam Tooley 60 Head of Sheep 250 Head of Hogs or there Abouts Crop on the Grounds 10 Horses 1 Riding Chair & 1 Sulkey One Womens Saddle 1 Silver Mounted Gun 1 P Pistols & a Small Sword 3 Pr Timber Wheels & 2 Screws, 2 Scows belonging to the Mills & 1 Canow, 2 Canows belonging to the Plantation &1 Old Bay Boat 1 Set of Smiths Tooles 1 Set of Gun Mounting a Parcell of Old Iron belonging to Batchelors Creek Mill abt 200 wt 4 Spare Saws & 1 Dozen Files, 3 Pistil Locks 3 Barrs of Run Steele 6 Scythes 2 Cane Knives 2 Old Pistol Barrells, 15 Old Gunns & Gun Ball. 22 Bayonetts, 3 Old Mill saws 2 Sets of Steele Jinn Rowlers 8 Sets of Wooden Ginn Rowlers 1 Ginn 50 wt Nails 1 Pr Hayforks 53 wt Iron Hoops 80 pains of Glass 1 Crucible 4 Jamaca Mill Cranks 41 Iron Mill Rounds abt 250 wt Iron 200 wt Nail Rods abt 550 Sides of Leather in the Tan Yards 1 Copper Distill abt 50 wt Old Brass 1 Small Old Still 1 Old Tea Kittle 3 Pair of Hinges 8 Narrow Axes Pr Wedges 2 Broad Axes 1 Iron Tooth Harrow 5 Grubing Hoes 15 Weeding & Hillin Hoes 1 Dutch Fann 1 Brass Swivill 3 Bitts 2 Pr Styrup Irons 2 Mens Saddles 1 Bryer Hook 7 Cart Boxes 7 Flecke Plows 5 Barr Plows 3 Grind Stones 4 Setts of Plow Geers & 2 Snaffle Bridles 1 New Coopers Axe & 1 Set of Coopers Tools & Some Spair Truss Hoops 2 Brass Cocks 2 Trucks 2 Carts some Old Blocks a Parcel of Brick Moulds abt 400 wt Old Iron Consisting of Axes, Hoes Plows &c the Sweeping of the Smiths Shop Abt 500 wt Old Iron that came out of Mill that was Burnt belonging to Wm Blackledge Pr Worsted Combs 3 Stone Oil Jarrs & Abt 30 Gallons of Oil 7 Pr Cards 6 Woolen Wheeles 2 Linnen Ditto 2 Lumes 3 Pair of Harness 5 Stays 2 Pair of Stulyards & P Scales & Weights 3 Hackels 1 Wire rim Sive 1 Pr Sheep Shears 1 Ginn Case & Abt 6 Doz Qt Bottles 2 Dozen Flat 2 Gallon Ditto & 2 Dozen Round 2 Gallon Do 1 Gallon Pott 1 Qt Pott Funnell & Libra of Books Abt 70 Barrells of Pork 1 Set of Tools for use of the Tan Yards & for Currying

Household Furniture &c Vizt

6 Silver Table Spoons 1 Soop Ditto 12 Tea Do 1 Punch Ladle 1 Set of Caster with four Stands 1 Tea Chest 1 Glass Stand 7 Syllabub Glasses 2 Decanters 10 Wine Glasses 1 Large Tumbler 3 Small ditto 3 Looking Glasses 3 Hash Dishes 1½ Dozen Chinae Plates 3 Chinea Bowls 2 ditto Tea Potts 1 Do Milk Pott 1 Stone Tea Pot 1 Coffee Pott Queens Ware Six Chiney Coffee Cups & Saucers 6 Do Tea Cups & Saucers 1 Queens China Sallet Dish

2½ Dozen Queens Chinea Flatt Plates 2¼ Dozen Do Soop Ditto 4 Large Queens Ware Dishes 4 Small Ditto 1 Stone Dish 1 Queens China Chocolate Pott 10 Large Case Knives & forks 6 Breakfast Knives & forks

1 Queens China Boat 2 Delf Bowls 11 Butter Potts 1 Japaned Sugar Dish 3 Earthen Pans & 14 Tart Molds 2 Chests 2 Trunks 1 Port Mantau Trunk 1 Dining Table 2 Tea Tables 12 Winsor Chairs 1 Couch 1 Candle Stand 1 Pr Hand Bellows 4 Pr Hand Irons 2 Shovels & 1 Pr Tongs 4 Large Pewter Dishes 6 small Ditto 5 Pewter Basons 25 Pewter Plates & Iron Potts 1 Small Iron Kittle 1 Large Brass Kittle 1 Small Ditto 3 Frying Pans 1 Bell Mettle Skillit 1 Iron Do 1 Pr Waffle Irons 5 Pr Pott Hooks 3 Trammells 1 Pr flatt Irons 3 Candle Sticks 2 Pr Snuffers 1 Wire Sive 2 Milk Pans 3 Salts 1 Pewter Tureen & 1 Cullender 1 Close Brush 3 Suits of Curtains & 5 Feather Beds & Furniture 6 Beadsteads & Chords.

Richd Blackledge, Exr.

AN INVENTORY of all the Goods & Chattels belonging to the Estate of Daniel Blinn Deceas'd 1753.

4 Feather beds & Bolsters
5 Pilloes 3 Pillowbers, 1 Rugg
2 Quilts 3 Counterpins 2 Blankets
4 pr Sheets 4 Bed steads
4 Cane Chairs 3 Trunks 1 large Chest
1 Old Warming pan 1 Close Stool & pan
1 Hatt Case 3 Earthen Chamber pots
1 Small looking Glass
1 Pr Chamber hand Irons
1 Low Chair
2 Large looking Glasses
1 Large Walnut oval Table
1 Small Do 1 Mohogginey Tea Table
1 China Bowl & 6 Cups & Saucers
1 Block Tin Tea pott & Milk pott
15 Chairs 1 Arm Chair
1 Chest of Drawers, 1 Desk 1 joint stool
14 Pictures 1 Decanter, 1 Cruitt
7 Drinking Glasses: 1 Jelly Glass
4 Tumblers: 2 Glass Salt Cellers
14 Punch Bowls, 2 Pockett Bottles
1 Mustard pot: 3 Earthern wash Basons
4 Earthen plates
2 white Earthen Bowls
5 White Cups & Saucers
1 Box Iron & heatters: 1 Lawn Cive
1 Coffee Mill: 1 Tea Chest
1 Case with 9 Bottles
1 Large Vicar Bottle
1 Gallon Glass Bottle
7 Douz Glass Bottles 1 Pr Bellows
2 Tea Canisters 2 old Do
1 Sugar Tubb: 1 Pint Silver Mugg
1 Old Sloop & Sails: 1 large Grater
3 Silver Spoons: & 6 Teaspoons
1 Gun: 3 Cloth Bruches
1 Broad Cloth Sute of Cloaths
1 Pr Cloth Breeches
1 Red Cloth Jacket
1 Double Night Gown
3 Holland Shirts 2 Cravits
4 Pr Stockings: 1 Pr hand Irons
3 Pr Tongs: 1 Iron Slice 1 Fire Shovel
1 Dozn & Ten Pewter plates: 8 Dishes
1 Pewter Bason: 1 Small brass kettle

INVENTORIES.

4 Brass Skillets: 1 Iron Do
4 Iron Pots: 1 Iron Driping pan
2 Frying Pans: 3 Spitts
1 Pr flesh forks & Ladle
2 Sauce pans: 1 Chaffin Dish
1 Iron Gridle: 1 Grid Iron
2 Iron Tramels: 6 Milk pans
1 Pudding pan: 6 pattey pans
6 Earthern Pickel pots: 3 butter pots
1 Three Gal Jugg; 2 Tea Kettles
1 Pestle & Morter: 1 brass Morter
1 Jack: 3 Axes: 1 weeding hoe
3 Matts: 1 Bread Tray
1 Grind Stone: 1 Saw: 2 hammers
2 Brass Candle Sticks: 2 Iron Do
1 Hand Mill: 1 Pr Stilliards
1 Pr of Scales: 1 Meal Tub
1 Basting Ladle: 1 Mans Saddles
1½ Dozn Knives: 1 punch Strainer
4 Table Cloths: 8 Diaper Napkins
3 Hackabuch Napkins
2½ yds of Bear Skin: 8 old Barrels
1 Beer Cask: 4 old pipes
1 old Cable: A Parcell of old Iron
2 Cows: 1 heifer: 1 two year old heifer
1 Yearling Steer: 1 horse & Cart
1 Canoe: 40 lb Wool
1 White Dimity Jacket
1 Pr Silver knee Buckles
1 Shagareen Case Watch
1 Pr Brass Shoe Buckels
1 Castor Hatt: 1 Bucket
1 Pail: 1 Piggin: 1 Pr Shoes
3 Small Baskets: 1 pewter pint pot
1 Leaden Tobacco Box
1 Wash Bason Stand
3 Fatt Pots: A Parcel of old Tubs
2 Pr Snuffers: 1 Tin ½ pint pot
1 Gill pott: 1 Small butter Chirn
11 Tin Candle Moulds
1 Lanthorn: 1 Tin pepper Box
1 Large Earthen pan
3 Small Baskets: 1 Iron Sledge
1 Cutlass: 1 Oyl jarr
1 Sea Compass
6 Iron Scures
1 Box & Parcl old Books
1 Bible: 1 Sermon Book
1 Shot Bag & powder horn
A parcl old Blocks
2 Indian Barks
1 White Stone Tea pot
1 Glass pint Mug
3 White Mettle Spoons: 6 pewter
5 Blue & white Stone Tea Cups & Saucers
1 Woolen Wheel
1 Negro Man Named Prince
1 Negro Wench Named Rose
1 Negro Girl aprentice Named Sal
1 Pr Money Scales

June 4th—1753   MOURNING BLIN Extx.

———————COUNTY
April 17th 1753.

AN INVENTORY of the goods and Chattels belonging to the Estate of William Brice Decd as follows Vizt:

7 Negro men 3 Do Women 13 Do Boys & Girls in all 23 and 51 head of Cattle 18 Sheep 20 Hoggs 5 horses 3 guns 7 fether beds 2 Desks 4 Tables 3 Chests 8 Chairs a persil of old pewter a percil of Chaney and Delf Wair 1 Looking Glass a persil of Old Books_____ Tee_____ 8 Iron pots 1 bell mettle Scillit 3 Brass Candle Stick 1 pair Iron Doggs 1 pair Tongs 1 hand Mill 2 Chest 3 be_____ 2 Tarkills Ready Sett 5 Spinning Wheels 1 Hanger 1 Cross cut Saw 1 Grindstone
Returned in May Cort 1753

Pr NATHAN SMITH Exectr.

A INVENTORY of Anne Bryan Estate Dect

7 Negros 3 Feather Beds & Furniture 1 Chist of Drawers 1 Desk 2 Tables 2 Chist 1 Case of Bottles 3 horses 16 head of Cattle 12 Sheep 20 Head of Hogs 3 Iron Pots 2 Brass Kittles 1 Iron Do 6 Puter Dishes 4 Basons 18 Plates a Parcell of Delf and Glass 6 Chaney Cups & Soycers 3 Brass Candle Sticks 2 Iron Do 1 Case of Knives & forks 1 Tea Chist 6 Silver Table spoons 6 Do Tea spoons Straner & Tongues A Parcell of Old Books 2 Bee Hives 2 Gunns 33 Bbl of Indian Corn 13 Bushels of Wheat 1 Cart & Wheals

A Parcell of Old Plows & Axes 1 Spice Morter A small Stock of Cattle on Hatterass Banks 1 Boor Iron 1 Trivett & Gridle 1 Large Looking Glass 17 pounds Prock

JOHN BRYAN Extr

NORTH CAROLINA ss

John Bryan Executor of Ann Bryan deceased maketh Oath and Saith that the above is a true Inventory of the Effects of the said Anne Bryan come to the hands power or possession of this Deponent

Sworn this 28th day of May 1773 Before me
Jo MARTIN

JOHN BRYAN

INVENTORY of the Estate of Mr. Edw: Bryan Decsd.

16 Negros
14 Head of Horses
13 Head of Sheep
6 fether Beds
6 Ruggs 8 Blankitts
1 Bed quilt
10 Sheets
1 Dusk 1 Table
10 Cheears
4 Cheests
1 Cobard
4 Bed Stitts
3 Cords
1 Case of Bottels
11 puter Basens
10 Dishes
32(?) plats
2 puter potts
1 panger
35 Spoons
3 Tee Canestors
1 pound Tee & Canesters

1 Steel trapp
8 Iron potts
3 Kittels
3 Skilitts 1 Brass Do.
1 Tee Kittell
1 pees Girts Wad ?
6 pair poot hoocks
1 Cut Lash
3 Spining Wheeals
5 par of Cards
1 pack of Cards
2 Grind Stons
2 pair Mill Stones
3 plows 1 harrow
1 fery flatt
410 pound pott Iron
1 Iron Rack
2 Cros Cutt Saw
1 Hand Saw
1 whip Saw
1 pees Cloth & trim
1 par wosted Hos

INVENTORIES.

1 Small Compus
4(?) frien pans
1 warmen pan
1 Hand Bales
1 pr: tongs & Shuvell
2 Candell mold
3 Candell Sticks
7 Locks
1 Hatt & Case
1 Bar: Brown Shuger
1 Grater
1 Box Iron & heete'
4 Cheests old
5 Saddels & Bridels
and a parsell of Axes
and Hoes quenty not known
165 Head of Cattel

2 pair Stilards
1 pair Scales
1 womens Sadell
5 Razer 1:1 hone
5 pound Indego
6 pound powder
50 pound Shott
Sum Rements of Goods
a pasell of Coopers tuls
and Carpentors Tooles
and a small parsel of nales
a parsell of Glass & Earthen ware
a parsell old Hogshets
and Barrells and old Iron

Bill money.............................L 539: 15: 00
Vorgina Cur:............................ 44: 2: 09
Debts Recd:............................ 20: 11: 6

1 Spise morter
4 mear Sifters
a parsell of Books
8 fills ?
2 Graters
a parsell of Hoggs
a parsell of Knives and forks
a pair of Cart wheeals
a parsell of woll and
Cotten flax and hamp
1 Ink Glass & Tabel Lining
2 Guns and waren apparell
a parsell of wooden ware
7 Combs 1 pair of hackells
325 Deear Skins
16 Ditto 6 Stocks of Bees
1 Looken Glass 2 Hids
170 Emtey Barells
2 frows
    Erows Excepted

HARDY BRYAN Execr.
LEWIS BRYAN

A SECOND INVENTORY of the Goods which is Com to my hands Sence the the first which I Gave in be Longin to the Estaet of Edwd: Bryan Deesed—

3 Tarkills which was Seet
1 Tarkill halled to Gather
1 Steedr & 13 Sides of tand Lather
3 Skins & 2 Shew Lastes
1 pair of money Scales
2 Iron wedges and 1 trowell
a parcell of old Rotten Dear Skins
100 tarr Barrells in four hoops
    Debts Recd. £ 2262-04-2 ½ old Bills

HARDY BRYAN Exr.

march the 15 day 1749/50
    Red Sence.......................£ 10:00:00 old tenner
    Debts Recd.....................   03-07:-6 old tenner

NORTH CAROLINA, CRAVEN COUNTY.

A TRUE & PARFECT INVENTARY of the Estate Goods & Chattles o
Willeam Bryan late of this County Decesd: 1747 as followeth Viz--

Three Negro Men Three Negro woman Two Negro Children Sixty Si: pounds One Shillings & Eleven pence Virginia Currancy Thirty pound Thirteen Shillings & Ten pence Bill Money five Beds & furniture On Chist of Drawers Two Ovil Tables Two Small Square Tables Two Smal Round Tables One Silver Tankard Eight Silver Spoons One Desk On Large Looking Glass Two Large Brass Kittles One Small Brass Kittl Two bell mettle Skillets four Large Iron pots Three Small Iron pot One Small Iron Skillet Two Iron Cittles Three pistles four Smooth Bord Guns One Rifle Barrell Gun Two Chists One Large Old Trunk On bell mettle Spice Morter & Pessell One Box Iron & Two heaters Six Gallo1 Basons Thirteen Dishes Twenty five plates Two Three Quarts Bason Two Two quart Basons One pair of Small hand Irons One Grid Iro1 Two Trammels four pair of pot hooks Two pair of Tongs & One Shovel One brass Candle Stick Two Iron Candle Sticks One pair of Snuffer One hand Mill of Cullen Stones One hand Mill of Shell Stones One Spi one Brass Ladle One Old Iron Driping pan One frying pan One Ditt Old One Whip Saw One Cross Cut Saw One hand Saw One Tennan Saw One Broad axe One Old Ditto One Case of Bottles One Smal Case with five floward Bottles Three Stone Jugs Three Gars One ol puter Churne One puter Limbrick Two warming pans Eighteen Blacl Bottles Two Small Case Bottles Thirteen punch Boles Delph Ten Delpl plates One mettle Tea pot Thirteen Delph Tea Cups Seventeen Delpl Sasers four Delph Tea pots One Spoon Boat One canter One pint Blac Jack Ten Tumbler Glasses Seventeen Wine Glasses One Delph Disl One Vinegar Cruit one Glass mustird pot three Stone Butter pots Tw Earthen Butter pots One Delph Cream pot One Chamber pot one Larg pair of Stillyrds One Small Ditto One Jack Spit One pair of Small mone Scales Two pair of Scales & weights of Other Sort Two Wooling Wheel Two Lining Wheels Two pair of Old wool & Cotten Cards Two meal Sifters One Grind Stone One pair of Brass Shot Molds One pair Spoo1 Molds One Match· Lock One flat Break One Case Knives & forks On Safe One Slate One Large Church Bible and a parsell of Other Book Two Brushes Thirteen Chairs Two peper boxeses One Nutmeg Grato1 One Two quart pot One pint one funnel all of Tin One half pint pot o puter forty Six head of Sheep four Riding horses One mair & Colt fiv Bed Steeds Three plows One Tap borer One Carpenter Adds Three Gimb lets four Augres One froe Three horse Bells One house Bell Two Drawin Knives One Trowell Two Corking Irons Three goughes One Saw Se One Round Shave Eight Chissells One Gun Stocking plain Two Smal plains One hand Joynter four Reep hooks Two Small hammers One Smal Sledge hammer Eight files One Box Rule One paur of Carpenters Cum passes One pair Nipers One Set of horse flegms One pocket Cumpas On gun Scraper One hone One razor Two Coopers Axeses Two Addses On trowell One Joynter Stock & Iron One Crose ? One Iron Pessel Two Grul hows five Old weeding & hilling hows Three Old Narrow Axeses Twent head of Cattle & a parsell of hoggs Two mens Saddles & bridles On womans Saddle & bridle Twenty nine pound wt old puter & a half fou Viols & Two pocket Bottles One Glass Salt pot One Brown pint mu one flesh fork One Scimmer One Still Thirteen puter Spoons a parse of pails Tubs & peggins One pair of Spring Tongs one pair Tailors Shear One Iron Ladle & A parsell of Old Lumber

March 9-14th 1747/8—

JOSEPH BRYAN
Pr ANNE BRYAN

INVENTORIES. 481

A TRUE AND PERFECT INVENTORY of the Goods and Chattels of Mr Levy Creecy Deceas'd.

Nine Negroes, to Wit Cato, Will, Peter, London, Cate, Dinah, Dorcass, Priss, Gene, Two Boys Namely Jacob & Squire, Ten Children Vitzt Venus, Rachael, Nan, Esther, Rose, Phillis, Cloe, Sam, James, Zango, in all Twenty one. Eighty three Pound Eight Shillings and two pence Proclamation Money, Notes with their Interest to the Amount of Three Hundred & Sixty three Pounds Proc. some unsettled Accompt. Five good Feather Beds one old do. Six Bed Steds Four Hides two Mats five Cords Eleven Pillows Ten pair Sheets Nine pair of Pillow Cases three good Homespun Counterpanes one old Do. Four new Bed Spreads, one Rug, three Bed Quilts three Dutch Blankets five Homespun Do. one large Diaper Table Cloth four Homespun Do. four Napkins Six Towels, one Maple Desk one Square Walnut Table, one do Oval Two do Tea Tables, one pine Table four Chests one old do. Six Walnut Chairs Damask Bottoms, one Arm'd Do one dozen maple flag Bottom do Five Walnut do. flag Bottoms, three low Chairs, one Childs do. one large Glass one small Do one Beaufat three Earthen dishes Twenty white Stone Plates Ten earthen do, five China Bowls one Dozen China Cups & Saucers, four Tea pots Seven Cups Nine Saucers five Glass Tumblers Six Wine Glasses, three Cruets, three Salts, three Cream pots, one Pitcher, one Spice Mill, two mustard pots, one pocket Bottle one pair Silver Tea Tongs one Dozen Silver Table Spoons one do Tea, one Silver Soop Ladle one do punch do, one Silver Watch, one Pair of Silver Shoe & knee Buckles, one pair Clasps, one pair of Silver Studs with Gold Tops Twenty Seven New Pewter plates Six old do, Six pewter dishes Nine pewter Basons, one old Dish Six Pewter Spoons, one Can one fifteen Bottles Case, one do Ten do, one small Trunk, one small Cubbard, one Safe, one Large Flower Chest, one Comb, four Stays & Girts two linnen wheels, two old do, three Woollen do one pair of Cards, four do one small Sein unhung one Litt nett four stone Juggs one earthen do four Stone Chambers Pots two & half Dozn. Round Bottled three Brass Candlesticks two Iron do one Brass Kittle one Iron Tea Kettle one old Copper do, one old Copper Pott one Tin Funnel, three Skillett, two pair of Iron dogs, two pair of Stiliards one Box Iron & Heaters one pair of Flat Irons one dozen knives & Forks four Guns three pair Tongs two Shovels, one poker, one spice morter & Pestle three large Iron pots, five small do, three Iron pot trammels, three pair Pot hooks, one Frying pan, one Spit, one Gridiron, one Iron Ladle, one pair flesh forks, three Iron Spindles, one pair of Sheep Shears, Six reap hooks, two Sythes, two Whip saws, one Cross cutt Do, one Hand saw, one Currying knife & Shel, Forty two sides of Leather in Tan, three Calf Skins, one mans Saddle, one old do. three old Bridles, two Broad Axes, Six falling Axes, five Weeding Hoes, three Grubbing Hoes, two Carpenters Adzs. one Coopers Do One_____ Howel, one Sett of Shoemakers Tools, Six old Chisils two Gauges two old Planes two drawing knives, two old Claw hammers, three old Augers one Smiths Anvil & two Hammers, one Vise, Twenty Pounds Feathers two ox Chains three rings & Staples one large Canoe, four washing Tubs two Pails, two piggens one Can, two Sugar Tubs, two Churns, three small rundlets, two meal sifters, one Tin Cullender, two fine Hackles, three Cyder Barrels four half Barrel Cags one old do. five old Barrels, one Tierce, two old Hogsheads, one Iron Harrow, three wheat Sieves, four trays, one pair of old Cart wheels two old Gyggs one dial one pair of Horse phlegms one lancet, two Brass Locks, two half Bushels one Iron square & one pair Compasses one whip saw, file one hand mill one Grind Stone one Still, one pair of Scales, & weights, one pair of Taylors Shears, one old Spade, one hat Bush three mats for dishes, one Church Bible, three Sermon Books, one spelling Book, three small Bibles now old Books Five Stocks of Bees two mares & Colt one Horse six Cows & Calves three three year old Heifers, three two year old Stears, one two year old Bull, three Cows, three three year old Stears one two year old

31

Heifer seven yearlings one yoke of Oxen, three two year old Heifers Thirty six ewes & Lambs, Fourteen other Sheep thirteen three year old hogs Twenty four year old do fifteen breeding Sows thirteen Shoats Six pigs seven Tann'd Sheep skins one Hatchet two old Axes, five Bar plows, & Coulters three weeding do & five Coulters two Iron wedges Six old Hoes, his wearing apparel seven Pound of Coarse pull tow Spun, seven pound Coarse yarn, Eighteen Pound fine do, Twenty one pound Cotton Warp, five pound of Pick'd Cotton, Ten pound Cotton for filling seven yards white linnen, two yards home spun Cloth, three yards of woollen home spun Cloth, seven pound of Flax, Seventy five pound Coarse wool Wash'd Seventy Six do fine unwashed Forty Eight Barrels of Corn Twenty Acres of wheat Growing a parcel of Fowl Twelve midlings Bacon Two & twenty Hames & Shoulders Four Cows & Calves one Cow & Heifer three yearlings one two year old Stear, one two year old Heifer one yoke of Oxen, Eleven hundred and fifty Feet of thick white Oak plank, Fourteen hundred and fifty three feet of thick pine plank Ninety Feet of Broad Cypriss Plank five Quarters thick, Six Bushels of Salts Six Bushels of Peas, one Bushel of Beans, three small Baskets one Good meal Bag two old do four Bushels of wheat, a small Quantity of Rum Sugar, Molasses & Hogs Lard a parcel of Scantling saw'd to Build a Barn. one Large Black Smiths File, A Small Parcel of tow & Cotten, Sum Flax Not Broke

CHOWAN COUNTY.

June 17th 1772 Personaly Apeard Mary Creecy before me and Provd this Inventory to be Just and True before   EDW VAIL

AN INVENTORY of the Personal Estate of the late Mrs. Jean Corbin Deceased, token 13th April 1775.

Negro Slaves.

(Peter, free) Nancey, Johney, Pleasant, Mingo, Lucretia, Effey, Lars, Innes, Victoria, Barbara, Jenny Cooper, Ben, Sinclear, Exeter left to Dr. Holloway, Monroe, little ones at the Point, Cabin, Patty, Will, Jude, George, Lucretia, Jenny Pollard, Charles, Cain, Sarah, Cudjoe, Douglas, Sam, Nanny, Lucretia, Nede, Stephen, Amelia, Clarissa, Jack, Pegg, June, Kingston, Dolly, Bella, Delia (old), Young Delia, London, Nelly, Ovid, Mary, Phillis, Victoria, Sabina, Harry 2 days old, Quanimo, Nanny, Gray, old James, James, Cumlock, young Quanimo, Belinda, Jameboy, Carolina, Jenny, Sandie, Statira, Dinah, old Cæsar, Dinah,
Buk
Maizey, young Cæsar, Toney, Harry, old Celia, Josie, Buck, little George, Hannah, Cumber, Kuffey, Cato, Kennisby, Billey Murray, big George the Cooper, Nanney, old Murray, Jamaica, old Davis, old Solomon;——— (Will, it appears was Sold to Doctr. Ferguson).* * *

Negroes at Edenton—not in my possession but as I am informed hired out by Dr. Ferguson by Mrs. Corbins order—Rutherford, Ross, Anthony, Caithness, Charles, Violet, and Supposed Six Children, uncertain whether 5 or 6

In all 97 Negroes, big & little, taken before us.
This list taken before

    JOHN LARKINS   WILLIAM LARKINS (formerly overseer)
    JAMES LARKIN.   WILLIAM LARKINS.
                    DAVID POLLOCK overseer

Furniture &c &c.
Plate.

12 large Table Spoons, 12 small do. 1 Pint Mugg, 1 Marrow Spoon, 4 Salt shovels, 4 Extinguishers, 1 P small silver Candlestocks, 1 P Branch Candlestocks with Snuffers & Extinguishers, 1 P Cruet tops, 1 P Butter

Boats, 1 Salver, 1 Sauspan, 1 Milk pott & Sugar Tongs, 1 Quart Tankard,—(The above was Bought by Mrs. Corbin at the Sale of the Estate of Mr Corbin).—1 Caudle Cup, 1 Coffee pot, 2 Butter boats, 4 Salts, 2 small Salvers, 1 P Snuffers & Stand, 6 Forks, 2 P Candle Sticks, 3 Castors, 10 Tea Spoons, 1 P Sugar Tongs, 3 Cruit tops, 1 old punch ladle, 6 table spoons, 1 Soup spoon, 3 glass Cruets with Silver tops, 14 Silver Knives, 20 do. forks, 1 Gold Watch, 1 broker gold Seal, 2 Diamond Rings, 2 Mounring, 1 plain do, 1 green? stone do, 1 P old Stone Buckles, 1 Silber Broach, and 1 Stay hook.

China.

6 Punch Bowls, 6 pint do, 1 small Mugg, 3 Tea Potts, 17 Tea Cups, 25 Saucers, 12 Coffee Cups, 1 Sugar Bowl, 1 Turene, 15 plain plates, 11 Soup do. 7 small do. 5 Dishes, and 1 Bason.

Glass.

8 Looking Glasses, 4 Tea Bottles, 6 Decanters, 10 Tumblers, 4 Water Glasses, 8 Beer do. * * * 5 Mahogany dining Tables, 1 Tea Table, 3 dressing Tables, 12 Leather bottom'd Chairs, 8 Callicoe do. do. 1 Arm Chair, 2 Mahogany Bed Steads, 1 do. Tent do. 1 Sett dble Curtains, 6 Feather Beds, 2 Mattrosses, 4 Bolsters, 8 Pillows, 1 Chest of Drawers, 1 old do., 1 large linnen Chest, 1 eight day Clock, 1 Backgammon Table, 3 round Mahogany Tea Trays, 1 Spy Glass, 2 empty Knife Cases, 1 tea Chest, 33 petty panns, 2 Setts Scales & weights, 1 long Table, 1 Straw bottomed Chair. * * *

5 P Sheets, 6 Blankets, 12 large Table Cloths, 6 Small do. 6 Pillow Cases, 5 Cover lids, 15 Towels, 2 Setts Window Curtains (one of them muslin, & the other Callicoe window Curtains)—8 Chair covers of Callicoe,

1 Musket without a lock, an old fowling piece with contrivance to lock it to the mantle piece, 1 Grate, 1 Fender, 4 P broker Tongs, 4 do. Shovels, 1 P Bellows; 3 P doggs

4 Hand Basons, 9 (?) Pewter Dishes, 2 Pewter Fish Trays, 15 Pictures, 3 Mapps, 2 Punch strainers, 1 Filtering Stons, 2 Milk bowls, 1 milk Dish, 1 small Mahogany Chest of Drawers, 1 Dressing Box (bought of the Vendue of Mr. Corbins Estate).

The above Inventory of the plate furniture &c taken in the presence of Colo. James Moore, Colo. Robert Schaw and Saml. Graham, and the names of the Negroes Called over And negroes on the Spott examined &c.

Plantation Stock. at Point Pleasant

1 Small Horse, 12 head of Cattle little & big & 3 young Calves, (others in the woods have not been seen these 12 months) 200 Bushels of Shelled Corn, 10 Hoggs big & little, 5 Ewes & Lambs, 1 P Mill stones, 1 Grind Stons, a few Carpenters Tools, 28 Candle Moulds, 1 Canoe, 2 Geese, 2 Turkey Cocks, &—but very few fowls, a few old Plow Irons, and some old Iron, 9 Hoes, 3 Axes, 1 small bag of Cotton, 2 do Wooll, 1 P Kitchen Doggs & 1 P Racks, 1 Dutch Oven, 5 Pot hooks, 2 Brass Kettles, 1 bell metal skillet, 1 Stew pann, 1 frying pann, 1 small marble mortar broke 1 warming pann, 1 grid Iron, 2 Spitts, 2 Box Irons, 4 flatt do, 1 Sauce pann, 5 Iron Potts, & 5 cast Iron Backs, 71 Vol. of bookes—In Mr. Corbins pocket book was £ ten pounds two shillings & six pence proc. money—1 old porto folio

Planta. Stock at Long Creek and tooles

19 head of Cattle, 6 oxen & 6 Calves, 2 Mares, 1 horse, 1 Mare & horse in the Woodes about Billie Campbles Mills run Wild—1 sow, 5 Shoates, 3 piggs

25 hoes, 25 Axes, 1 plow, 1 Cart & yokes, 2 Iron Cahines, 1 doz old Sickl(
2 Rice Seives 20 bushels Rough Rice, Corn about 40 bushels, about
bushels pease & 2 P Mill Stones and at another planta. on Long Cree
about 20 bushels of Corn & 20 bushels pease not threshed out 1 X Cut saw,
Whip saw, & some Coopers tooles 8 Chipping axes 4 Iron Wedges * *
                                             JNO. RUTHERFORD

 The above Inventory sworn to before me in due form
  SAML. CORNELL

 AN INVENTORY of the Goods and Chattels Belonging to the Esta(
of his Excellency Arthur Dobbs Esqr. deceas'd

Negro Men

 Prince, Carrick, Bellenure, Billy, Quago, Sambo.

Negro Women

 Molly, Cloe, Betty—

Negro Children

 Joan, Abram, Daphne.

1 Six Oar Canoe wth. auning Irons
6 Bushels Salt
3 Sows
1 Easy Chair, 1 Elbow Do. ½ Doz walnut Do. Leather Bottoms
1 Bed, Boulster, 2 Pillows, Curtains, and 3 window Do. wth. rods
10 Counter Panes 2 Matrasses 10 P Sheets
7 Pillow Cases, 23 Diaper Table Clothes,
11 Small Diaper Napkins, 17 large Do.
1 large Diaper Layover
6 Towels 5 Jelly Hands, 4 Doz. Jelly & whip Syllabub Glasses
4 Doz. wine Glasses, 1 Doz, Large cut wash hand Glasses
1 Doz. Small Do.
1 large Shagreen Case wth. one Doz. old silver handle Knives and fork
 1 small Do.
1 Doz. small empty Canisters, 1 large Tin Do.
3 old Brass chafing Dishes
1 small Brass Scales & Weights
3 Japan Bread Baskets, 2 Tripods, 1 Japan Plate Stand,
1 Small Teackle & Lamp—1 Small tea Kettle, 1 Do. large
2 Doz. Petty Pans, 2 Doz. pewter Plate
8 pewter Dishes, 2 Tin Pudding Pans, 1 Warming pan
2 P Copper Candle Sticks
2 Doz. Green Stone Plates, 8 Dishes
1 Doz. China Soop Plates
1 Doz. flat China Plates
½ Doz. China Dishes
1 Oyl floor Cloth
3 Woollen Carpets
1 large Japan Tea Board 3 Small Do.
1 Doz. white Stone Plates
½ Doz. Do. Chamber pots
1 Copper Coffee Pot
1 Straw Plate Basket

2 old Screens
1 large Copper frame Lanthorn
2 Glass Lamps
2 Doz. China Cups & Saucers
2 Copper Plate Tea Pots
1 pocket Lanthorn, 3 old hand Bells
1 house Bell with Wires & Springs
1 Brass Tender, 1 Doz. Claret, ½ Doz. Port,
1 Mahawgany Dressing Table with Drawers
1   Do.   Do. wth only one Do.
1   Do.   Chest of Drwaers
1 Desk, 2 middling Frame Gilt Looking Glasses
1 Small half Frame Gilt   Do.   Do.
2 Quilts, 1 Copper Cloths Kettle & Tripod
2 Mahawgany Tea Chests, 3 flowerd Sugur Boxes
2 P pint Decanters, 3 P. Quart Do.
2 P Steel Snuffers, a large Bottle Drainer with 12 Doz. empty Bottles
Sundry Pickle Bottles, Sundry Sweetmeat pots
Sundry Stone Jugs, Sundry Butter Pots
1 Hand Coffee Mill, 2 Loaves Sugar
1 Large Bible and 3 Prayer Books
3 foot Carpets, 2 small work Baskets
1 Card Table and Japan Box wth Ivory Fish & Mats
4 Window Callico Curtains in the Drawing Room and Rods
1 Large chac'd Silver Waiter, 2 small hand Do.
1 Doz. Silver Table Spoons ½ Doz. Desert Do.
1 Doz. Silver Tea   Do.
1 Silver Stand, 2 Silver Pint Muggs
2 Chas'd silver Butter Boats
1 large Do. chas'd Coffee Pott
1 Silver Milk Pot, 2 P Silver Salts
2 P Silver Salt Spoons, 1 Silver chas'd tea pot
1 Shagreen Tea Chest wth Two Silver Canisters and
1 Sugar Dish
2 China Punch Bowls 2 Small Do.
½ Doz. Tumblers, 1 P Silver tea Tongs
2 Silver tea Strainers, 1 Silver Punch Ladle
6 large old Trunks, 1 large Mohawgany scollop'd tea Table
4 Small red Leather Trunks
a few broken Volumes of difft. Books
1 Old Umbrella, 1 painted Candle Box
A few old Maps, Do. Magazines
2 China Tea Pots, 1 Doz. Coffee Cups
1 P old Bellows 1 Pewter Bason
1 Silver Punch Strainer
        In Proc. Money found in the Desk ....   70..12..4
        In silver 169 Dollars
            Gold   12 Half Johannahs
                    38 Pistoles
                    10½ English Guineas
        Due by Bond from sevl. Persons .... 885..13..3
        Due by Note from sevl. Do.   ....   80..17..11
        Sums due to the Estate not yet ascertain'd
1 Safe done wth Oznabrigs
1 Bag Wool, 1lb Hyson Tea 3lb Green Do.
1 three gallon Licker Bottle
                                    JUSTENA DOBBS

July 23d. 1765 Sworn to Before
    THOM DAVIS J P.

His Excellency's wearing Apparel
1 half worn Hat
2 old wigs
1 Suit of Gold Lac'd broad Cloth half worn
1 Plain Suit of Paduasoy   Do.
1 Plain Do. Coarse Broad Cloth   Do.
1 Cloth Coat and silk Gold lac'd Jacket—worn out
6 New Shirts, 6 old Do. , 6 Stocks
1 Black Velvet Cap, ½ Doz Handkerchiefs
8 Pair Silk Hose half worn & 6 P worsted & thread Do.
1 flesh Brush, 1 Shagreen Case wth Razors &c
1 Shaving Box & Brush, 1 Silver Stock Buckle
1 Silver traveling Spoon & Ivory Knife & fork in a Shagreen Case
1 Tooth Pick Ebony Case, 1 P Pinch Back Shoe & knee Buckles,
1 Hone, 1 P Spectacles
1 old Case with 2 old Lancets
1 P old Gold Sleve Buttons
1 Small Mohawgany Travelling Chest, with a Broken looking Glass in the lid—
A Parcel of Rubbish of little or no Value

AN INVENTORY of Sundry belonging to the Personal Estate of Richard Eagles Deceased, 29 march 1769

House hold Furniture vizt:
    1 Eight day Clock
    1 doz best hair bottom Mahogony Chairs
    2 Square mahogany dining Tables
    1 Round Ditto Tea Ditto
    1 Square Ditto Side Ditto
    1 Round Ditto dining Ditto
    1 Fine mahogony Book Case & desk
    6 old Ditto framed Leather bottom Chairs
    6 old beach fram'd Chairs—1 Arm Ditto
    6 Beach fram'd Callicoe bottom Ditto
    1 Do   Do   Arm   Do   Do
    2 large Mahogony fram'd Lookg Glasses, with Scaunches
    1 Do   Ditto   Do   do   without Ditto
    1 small Dressing Glass 1 perspective Glass with a Mahogony fram'd & pictures Compleat
    2 old looking Glasses
    1 Mahogany desk 1 old Walnut Ditto
    2 old round Walnut Tea Tables
    1 round mahogony Ditto
    2 Mahogany Close Stool Chairs
    1 large Walnut Chest O'Drawers
    1 Mahogany Spy Glass
    2 old flagg bottom Chairs
    2¼ doz. Gilt frame pictures, newest Fashion
    10 plain Gilt Frame Ditto old Ditto
    3¾ doz plain   Do   old Do
    2 Boxes Glass, 200 feet
    1 Shagreen Case, contg 1 doz knives, 1 doz forks with Silver handles, 1 doz Silver Table Spoons
    1 doz Silver Tea Spoons, 1 pair Sugar Tongs & Strainer in a Case
    ½ doz. old, Silver Table Spoons, ½ Doz. Tea Ditto, 1 Strainer & Tongs
    1 Soup Spoon, 1 punch Ladle & Strainer
    1 Silver Coffee pott & Silver Stand for it 1 Cut top Crewet Stand

INVENTORIES. 487

18 Wine Glass, 8 Beer Ditto, 2 Cydar Do. 11 Jelly Do
11 Syllabul Ditto, 13 Glass Tumblers, 3 large Tumblers
12 Sweet meat Glasses, 8 Sweetmeat Cups
4 Glass Salt Sellers, 4 Silver Ditto with Shovels
1, 1 gallon Decanter, 2, ½ galln Ditto, 2, ¼ gall Ditto
3 large Tumblers with Tops to suit, 3 Glass Mugs w. Ditto.
1 China Water pott, 1 doz. China Cups & Saucers, 2 Pt China bowls
3 doz. large China Cups & Saucers, some been broke & mended
3, 1 gall. China Bowls, 4, ½ gall. C. Ditto, 3, ¼ gall Ditto
9 China plates, 5 China Coffee Cups, 1 China Sugar dish
2 flower potts, one with a piece broke out, 5 delf pint bowls
2 doz. Shallow white Stone plates, 1 doz. Soup Ditto
1 doz. Stone dishes, 1 Stone Tareen, 2 Wicker bottles
1 delf wash bason & bottle, 1 delf Coffee pott, 8 Stone Jugs
2 pr large brass Candle sticks, 5 small ditto, 1 plate warmer
1 Mahogony Waiter, 2 do Tea boards, 3 Japan Waiters
2 Small broken Waiters, 2 Water Jugs, 3 Jars
1 Rum Case with 1 doz. bottles, 47 doz. quart bottles
6 dimijons, 1 Broken Crewet Stand wt. pepper box & Crewet
15 old Tin Cannisters, 1 Tin Funnel
1 old Tea Chest, 1 Tea Kettle, 2 Iron Backs
1 pr large Dogs, Tongs, Shovels & logger head, 1 hone
3 Umbrella's, 3 pr. Gartering, 1 lb. Copperas
1½ gross thr'd Laces, 1 pr Chintz, 1 pr Brocade, 1 Case & 2 Lancets
1 sml. hair Trunk 1 portmantea do, Gilt Trunk
1 Small Gilt Trunk, 2 hair Trunks
8 mattrasses, 5 Feather Beds, 7 Boalsters, 4 Bed Steads
2 Suits Callicoe Curtains, 4 Suits windo Ditto
1 Suit Gause Ditto 7 Bed quilts 1 old dubbell Blankets
6 pr Dubbell Blanketts, 1 Counterpin, 8 pillows, 1 Rose Blankett
8 pr Sheets, 2 pr Oznab Sheets 1 Old Counterpin
12 old pillow Cases, 9 Oznab Towels, 8 sml diaper Table Cloths
6 large Ditto, 6 Oznab Ditto, 2 Suits old Curtains
3 pr Sad Irons, 1 Box Iron, 1 pr old Dogs, 1 back Gamn Table
1 pr old wool Cards, 2 Crocus Bags, 2 Bags Feathers
1 Bed Cord, 1 Warming pan, 1 Bird Cage, 3 hair Trunks
1 Leather Trunks, 1 mattrass 2 pillows, 1 boulster, 2 Oznb Sheets,
2 Blankets & 1 old Quilt 4 Chinese pictures,
20 yd painted paper, 1 dripping pan
1 Case, 15, 2 Galls of Rum, 1 Do 16, 1½ gall Do of Rum
1 Tin Grater 1 pr Scales, 1 Earthen pott
6 pewter dishes, 12 new plates, 1 old dish & 7 plates
4 Cover dishes, 1 Tin Funnell, 1 Tin Kettle
1 Brass Kettle, 1 broken Iron pott, 4 Iron potts
1 Spitt, 1 frying pan, 1 Grid Iron, 1 old pott
1 pestle & morter, 1 Sifter, 2 Rat Traps
1 Large Copper 2 Spinning Wheels, 1 Chafing dish
1 Bell mettle Skillet, flesh fork, 4 stone potts
2 Stone potts full of Butter, 16 Milk pans, 2 Setts ———
2 Large Stone Potts, 1 Stone Jugg, 1 Fish Kettle
2 Small Churns, 12 Candle moulds, 1 Wicker Bottle,
1 Earthen Jar, 3 small Cases, 28 Bottles, 4 Brass Screws
2 doz buck handled Knives & forks, 2 doz. bone Ditto Ditto
1 hone 1 Jogging Iron, 2 Coffee Mills, 1 old Tin Jack
1 Bed Stead, 1 Cork Screw, 1 pine Case with 7 2 Gall bottles
3 Crocus Bags, 2 Bags Cotton, 1 Case, 1 Raisor Case
23 Balls Candle Wick, 8 Stone potts, 18 Tumblers, 4 sml bottles
6 Chamber potts, 2 Earthen potts, 1 Stone Jugg, 16 new pattapans
1 Case & 12 Bottles, 5 Botll wt Jin, 1 Case & 14 bottl, 1 Gall each
   wt Rum

Books.
  2 Annual Register for 66 & 67, 1 Compleat house Wife
  2 Vols. Ulloa's Voyages, 1 Universal Dictionary, 4 Vols. of the Connection of the old & new Testament, 1 Vol. The new State of England
  4 Vols. South Sermons, 1 London Magazeen, 62 Second Edition of the Life of Bernard Gilpin, 4 Vols of the Paraphrase of the Epistle & Gospels, 1 Vol of Benjn Bayley's Sermons, 2 Vols of the Continuation of W Raleighs history of the World, 1 London Magazeen, Bates Dispensatory, 1 Vol. the Sum of Christian Religion, 1 Book of an Instituion of the Laws of England, 1 Family Dictionary, 1 do Bible, 1 Common prayer Book, 2 Vols. discourses preached at the Temple Church, 1 Traveler's pocket Farrior
  1 Book of An Introduction to a Devout Life
  The Life of a Mehomet, Practical Navigation, 1 Vol a true notion of Moderation, Thoughtson military,
  4th Volume of Parmela, 1 Satyre, 1 Sermon Book,
  A Token for mourners, 6 Vols of the history of England
  A parcel of old torn Books
Warring Apparell
  2 Cut velvit Jackets, 1 Red laced Ditto, 1 flannel Do
  1 Corded paduroy Do with Gold Buttons, 1 pr Single Channel pumps
  1 pr Men's Gloves, 1 Suit Sky blue Cloth Cloaths, 1 Suit blk Ditto
  2 Sagathy Coats, 1 blk Velvet Do, 1 old Jacket, 1 old Cloth Coat
  8 pair old breeches, 2 quilted petticoats, 1 Do Red Silk Petticoat
  1 quilted purple Petticoat, 1 blue damask Sack & Coat, 1 Yellow Do & Do
  2 pr Sattin Shoes, 1 blk Callimanco Shirt, 1 Taffaty Sack & Coat
  1 Chintz Sack & Coat, 1 Chintz Gown, 2 old quilted petticoats
  1 pr Sett Shoe Buckles, 1 pr Silver Ditto, 1 paste necklace & Earings,
  1 gold Watch, 1 pr Silver buckles, 1 pen knife
  2 mourng Rings, 1 pr Gold Sleve buttons, 2 plain Rings
  19¼ yds Cap Lace, ¾ yd Silver Lace, 1 Silk Lace
  5¼ yds Gimp, 1 Wach Compass, 2 Fans, 2 yds blk Lace
  1¾ yds White Lace, 1 pr Silk Garters, 4 Whip Laces
  6 Silk Watch Strings, 1 pr blk Shoe buckles, Ivory Memo book
  1 pair Men's Gloves, 1 pr Gauze Ruffles & hand. with Lace
  2 pr Lawn Ruffles, Round Cap with Lace, 1 blk hood
  1 Gause flounced Apron, 1 Lawn hand. & Tucker Laced
  1 flowered Apron, pr Silk Mitts, 2 Silk Stomagers
  15 pr men's thread hose, 6 pr Worsted Do, 8 Linin Jackets
  5 pr drawers, 2 pr Oznab Mitts, 6 Silk handn
  5 Old Cravats, 1 Bag for the hair, 9 old Shirts, 1 Wrapper
  107 Sticks Mohair, 53 do Cruwel, 4¾ doz Horn buttons
  20 doz large & 20 doz sml. mohair buttons, 4 yds striped Linin
  3¼ yd Callicoe, ½ yd Cloth, Some Starch, some Ginger some bluestone, 9 Skains Silk, 1 Case Fishg lines
Saddles & Bridles &c Vizt
  1 man's Saddle & Bridle, 1 Curb Bridle
  1 Woman's Do with Furniture Compleat, 1 Man's do with Furniture compleat, 1 Boys Sadle
  1 Woman's Sadle, 1 Man's Do
  1 Chair with harniss Compleat
Guns & Amunition &c vizt:
  2 pretty good good Guns, 1 Gun Lock
  1 Brace pistols with holsters, 1 pr Shot moulds
  112 lb Shots, 5 Bars lead, 1½ Keg Powder 37 lb
Sundry
  17¼ yds Crocus 35 lb brown Sugar 20 loaves Sugar 181——
  176 lb Soap, 104 lb myrtle wax Candles, 303 lb myrtle wax
  25½ lb coffee, 5 lb Brimstone, 6 Bottles Vinegar

8 Bottles Maderia & 10 Do Port Wine, 6 Bristol Beer
1 Bottle pickles, 4 Bottles honey, 3 Sml bottles Cordials
1½ flask Oil, 1¾ lb Tobacco, 384 lb Smoked Bacon
77 lb Pork, 1 Bushl ground flower, 70 lb bolted Ditto
354 lb Rice, 3 hhds pork for Capt. Gray, A quantity salt
1 hhd. Rum wantg 6 Ins. to be full

Wareing Apparel
   3 pair Women's best Stays, 4 Dos Silk hatts, 1 Man's hatt
   11 new Shirts 6 new Shifts, 4 pr Strip'd Trousers, 6 Gravats
   2 Striped Jackets, 1 Stout Coat
   1 pr Linen No 2 25 yards, 1 pr Ditto 25 yds No 7, 1 paper pins
   5 doz Shirt Buttons

Plantation Utensils vizt.
   1 Box Physick with weights & Scales, 320, 20d nails
   3 pad locks, 2 old Stock Ditto, 1 Chizell, 7 Planing Irons
   5 Joint Irons, 1 large Gauge, 3 Sml Ditto, 1 plain Stock
   3 pr Dividers, 1, 2 foot Rule, 2 Sliding Gunters, 7 dowlg. Bitts
   1 pr Pincers, 1 pr marking Irons, 5 Rice Seives, 1 Sythe & Cradle
   1½ Doz hoes, 1½ doz falling Axes, 14 Spades, 5 Grubbing hoes
   15 pr Screws to role Tar, 1 doz Sickles, 1 Sythe, 16 new Spades
   5 Iron Wedges, 7 Cooper's Adzes, 4 Doz Axes, 3 howells
   3 drawg Knives, 4 Jointer Irons, 1 Coopers Compass
   2 Crow Stocks & Irons, 2 Cross Cutt Saw files, 1 Broad Axe
   4 Augors, 1 Square, 2 adzes, 1 Jointer plain, 5 Chizzels
   1 Bung borer, 2 Cross Cutt Saws, 2 new drawing Knives, 2 Brass Boxes
   2 Cooper's Axes, 1 Joiner's Hatchet, 1 pr Hl hinges
   17 falling Axes, 2 Jointer Irons, 2 Frows, 1 old plow Stock
   1 parcel of old Iron, 3 old & Cut Saws, 3 pr hand mill stones

Saw Mill Utensils
   3 new Saws, 8 Iron Dogs, 1 Dog Chain, 2 Crow Bars
   2 Saw mill Stirrups

Grist Mill Utensils
   3 Bolting Cloths, 1 pr new Stones, 2 pr old Rope

   2 Canoes & Arning with Irons Compleat, 1 Arning Iron
   1 Flatt

Black Smith's Utensils
   1 pr Large Bellows, 2 Anvils, 2 Vellrs, 1 Sledge Hammer
   1 nail tool, 2 sml hammers, 1 Screw plate

Men	Lads	Women	Girls
Old Larry	Nally	Maggy	Betty
Young Ditto	Joe	Bettey	Phoeba
Nedde	Simon	Young Phillis	Tray
young Thorn	Dick	Do Sarah	Mariah
Frank	Boatswain	Hagar	Doll
Prince		Nelly	Bessy
Shampane		Rachael	Beck
Old Montrally	Dimbo	Dyner	Liddy
Young Ditto	Jammey	Rose	Grace
Old Simon	Abrahame	Cumbo	Hannah
Thom Bell	Cane	Young Dianna	Sapho
old Jammy	George	Old Ditto	Willoughby
Old Casar	Nedde	Clarinda	Lucy
Andrew		Judah	Peggy
Jack	*Boys*	Amorita	Mary
Toney	Bobb	Peggy	Rachael
Young Jammey	Tomey	Joan	Phoebe
Sam	Natty	Old Phillis	Betty
Charles	David	Nanney	Sabyna

Men	Boys	Women	Girls
Guly	Sammey	Old Sarah	Nanny
Neroe	Phill	Catey	
Catoe	Prince	Doll	*Young Children*
Old Will	Christmas	Nancy	Wonney
Young Casar	Quath	Cloe	Cattina
Peter	Johnney	Flora	Jacob
Old George		Elsey	Isaack
Young Ditto		Bella	Gibby
Billy		Nanny	Charlotte
America		Hannah	
Dowey		Bess	
		Old Jenny	
		Old Lucy (at Walkers)	
		Young Ditto	

Total
30 men
33 Women
11 Lads
10 Boys
20 Girls
 6 Young children

Tot. 110

Horses, Cattle, Sheep & Hogs
 11 Horses, unbroke, 19 mares do 6 yearlings, 12 Colts
 3 Bulls, 13 oxen broke, 32 Cows, 18 Calves, 15 year olds
 8 two Year old 4 Steers
 31 Sheep
 27 Hogs &c
July 1 1769 Sundry Cattle Hogs & Horses in the Woods, Quantity unknown.
Cash
 33 Half ——— 12 Guineas, 17 half do 2 moidores 1 mill'd Pistole In Proclamation Bills to amot of £54.1.1
 Sundry Accompts on his Books not yet settled

Robert Shaw Esqr Executor of Richard Eagles, personally appeared & made Oath that the foregoing List contained in two Sheets of Paper is a true & perfect Inventory of the personal Estate of the Testator as far as hath come to his knowledge.

ROB SCHAW

Sworn to before me this 8 day of January 1770

——— BURGWIN

(Filed 25 Apl. 1770)

AN INVENTORY of the personal Estate of Doctor John Eustace deceased which hath come to the knowledge or possession of Margt. Eustace his Addministratrix, that is to say.

Books, & first Folios

Universal dictionary of Arts & Sciences 2 Vol
Independant reflection

Quarto

Brayer's French & English Dictionary, Historia Universalis, Jeffrey's Voyages Stich'd, Ainsworth Latin & English Dictionary, Laws of North Carolina, South Carolina Justice (missing)

INVENTORIES. 491

Octavo

Johnson's English Dictionary Abridged, Bellamy's English Dictionary, Foster's discourses, Sharp's Intriduction to Un: History, Brook's Garettur, Schrivelle's greek & latin lexicon, Salmon's grammar, present state of Europe, Puttendorff de Officio &c. Walshe's theory of the Earth, Oeconomy of Love a Poem, Jolliamed; or discourse between an Indian Philosopher & French missionary, Jermippers redivivus; or the Sages? triumph &— Salmon's Chronology, Baker on learning, Smith's moral Sentiments, War of the Beasts, Thompson's Seasons, Philosophy of revelation, Derham's Phisiotheology, Complete angler, Holmes's latin grammer, Poisies diverses, American Magazine for 1745, London Magazine for 1757 & 1761, Universal Magazine 3d & 5th Vols, Smollet's Continuation 2d & 4 Vols, Howels state of England, Compleate Housewife, Nelson's Justice, Antidote against popery, Guliver's Travels 1s Vol, Joubert's french & latin dictionary, Christian faith asserted &c.

Duodecimo &c

Synonymorum Sylva, Salmon's Garetteer, Last Will of Basil Valentine, 9 Vols Voltaire's works in blue Paper, Cleora; or the fair inconstant, Young's Night Thoughts, Fisher's Young man's best Companion, Gordon on the Rebellion, Montesquieu's lettres persanes, Brightlands English Grammar, Memoirs of Brandenburgh, Gentleman instructed 2 Vol, Swift's Works 2d Vol, Six Voyages de Cyrus, Theobalds Shakespear 8th Vol, Passion of the Soul bt DesCartes, Latin Bible, Memoirs sur les Artis &c, Familiar Coloquies greek & Latin, Manyngham's discourses, New treatise of Natural Philosopy, Human Prudence, Bayse's Pantheon, Sherlock's discourses 4 Vol, Relation de la Cour de Rome, Garth's dispensary, Traders sure guide, Spectacle de la nature 7 Vol, Rudiments of ancient History, Pope's Homers Iliad, Hume's Essays– 4 Vol, Brown's estimate of manners &c, British Apollo 2 & 3d Vol, Manners, Gray's poems, Table of the Beers-? 2 Vol, Lives & Characters of Classical authors 2 Vol, Steel's Christian Hero, Pope's Epistles, origin of Evil, School of Man, Existence of God demonstrated, Paradise Lost, Smart's Horace– 2 Vol, News readers pocket Book, D'Argens's philosophy– 2 Vol, Literaires Nouvelles &C, Tristram Shandy, a full Set, Groece Gramatics, Select Scotch & English poems, Court Register 581-63 inclusive 6 Vol, Companion to the Almanack 1768, Minute Philosopher, Ramsay's Poems, The Woman-hater, a Novel 2 Vol, Musicale Miscelany, Piregrim Pickle– 4 Vol, Coloquies french & Latin, Tom Jones– 3 Vol, Old Woman's Magazine 2nd. Vol, Farquhar's Works– 2 Vol, 3 Vol Plays, Sir Launclot Greaves, Bische's art of poetry 1st 2d & 4th Vol, Londin in miniature, Joseph Andrews– 2 Vol Spectator 2d Vol, Female Spectator 4th Vol, Roderick Random 2 Vol, catesbys letters, Letters of Abilard & Heloise, Universal passion, stiched Otways Works 1st Vol, Man of Taste & Court of Lilliput, Martin's Introduction to English, Compendious History of England, Boyer's compleate french master, Steele's plays, a new set of pocket maps, 2 prayer books, Littleton's dialogues of the dead (missing), original poems, British antidote to Scotch poison; or caracaturas of the times 4 Vol stiched.

Books on Physick Surgery & Anatomy &c
Folio
[Anatomical Tables
Quarto

Renodoeus's dispensatory, Shaw's Boer haave 2 Vol, Lewis's Materia Medica, Heister's Surgery, Disertatio medica by Weshart & others, Le Febure's chemistry, Meade's medicinal works.

Octavo

Medical observations, Effects of air on human bodies, Huxham on fevers, Van Swieton's Commentaries, Mihles aliments of Surgery, Astruc's pathology, Sharp's critical inquiry   Langrishe's theory & practice of Physic, Brown's institutions in Physick, Burton's midwifery, Strother on Sickness & Health, Fullers Pharmacopoeia, Lee on botany, Hillary on Air, Petit on the bones, Turner on the Venereal disease, Lobb on painfull distempers, Groinvelt's rudiments of physic, Quinton's observations, Preternatural state of the animal humors, Gaubi's pathology, Flemyng's Phisiology, James's Dispensatory, Celsus de medicina, Thompson's Anatomy, Surgical Pharmacy, Morgan's philosophical principles of medicine, Paxton's Phisics–medical directory, Le Dran's cases in Surgery ——— Observations in Surgery, Chine's theory of fevers, Elaboratory laid open, Lind on the Scurvy, Arbuthnot on Aliments, White on the nerves, Quincy's Lexicon, Pringle on the diseases of the army, Gooche's cases in Surgery, Brooke's introduction, Barry on digestion &c Home's principia medicenoea, Chiselden's anatomy, Life of a Boerhaave, Aprorismi practici, Sharp's Surgery, Gaubi's medicinal forms, Sprengells' Hippocrates, Morgan's practice of physic, Van Sweiton's Commentaries abridged, Brooks's practice of physic, De Moneky on diseases in W. India Voyages, Hatter's phisiology, Quincey's dispensatory, Swan's Syednham, Hillary's inquiry, Account of inoculation, Smelly's midwifery, The Ladies pysical directory, Le Clerc on bandiges and dressings, dissertated medica by Gowdie, The way to health, long life &c.

Duodecimo &c.

Councill's Midwifry, Essay on the Government of Children, Theobald's dispensatory, Boerhaave's materia medica, Lommius's medicinal observation, latin same in English Demettrodo discendiartum medicam, Friends' chemistry, London dispensatory, Boerhaave's aphorisms, Russel on Sea water, Culpepper's dispensatory, Basil Valentine's Triumphal chariot of Antimony, Boyle's Chemistry, Hipporeatis's aphorisms, * * * contractus Lasher's dispensatory, Keill's Anatomy, Best method of preserving health, Boerhaave's praxis medica 3 Vol, * * * Historia plantarum, Hattur's physiology, Chirac's Surgery, Monro on the bones, rational reconomy of human bodies, Strother's Pharmacopoeia, Barthalon's Lexicon, Boerhaave's consultations of medicine,

Pamphlets

Dominicetti's appology, Thompson's discourse on the small pox, Friends prelutiones chymica, Essay on wamr bathing, Stork's essay on hemlock, Ludwig on Vegetables, Tennent's epistle to Dr. Mead, Dissertation on Inocluation, Chandler's treatise on the disease called a Cold, method of treating gun shott wounds, Treatise on the virulent gonnorrhea, Cowper on Peyser's medicine for the Veneral disease, Huxham on Antimony, method of curing fevers, Essay on circulation of the blood, * * * on dry zripes?, Abstract of Berkley on Tar-water, Dissertatis medica de incubo, * * * de pluonalbo, De anima medica protectio, Aphorismi botanici, Quiotionum et responsionum chirurzicarum &c. Dissertatio medica by Gowdie, observations on Night shade

Household furniture & other Articles

3 bed steads wt. Sacking bottoms & screws, 2 sets of Bed curtains worsted and calicoe & curtain rods for two of them, 3 feather beds with bolsters & pillows, a sett of Check Curtains & windoe curtains, a pair of sconces, a

pier Glass, a dressing Glass, a dozen mohogany chairs, an easy chair, a Windsor chair,
a large dining table, a small ditto } all mohogany,
a tea table, a Stand,
3 pine Tables, an ironing table, a mohigany dressing table, a chest of drawers, a writting desk, a pr. andirons shovel tongs & fender, a pr. andiron shovel and tongs, a pr. of Kitchen do.—do. 1 Japan'd Tea board, 1 small do., a pine cupboard, a hair safe, a shop table with drawers, 7 doz bottles, a glass Lanthorn, a brass Kettle, 2 Tea Kettles 2 sauce pans 3 iron potts 5 com: chairs, 1 Copper sweet meat sauce pan, a Copper baking pan, a large Tea Kettle, an old ditto, 2 Spits, 2 Trammels, 3 white wash brushes, a Quilting frame, a basket & candlestick, 2 cheese toasters, a Coffie mill, a mustard mill, a plate basket, 3 brass Candlesticks, a window brush, a scowring brush & hair broom, a chocolate mill, 1 doz large & 1 doz small patty pans, a bread grater, a brass skimmer, a brass ladle, a rubbing brush, a Copper chaffing dish, 2 Brass ditto, a Slate, 3 Cloths lines, 2 sieves, a red china coffee pott, a ½ Gallon decanter, a burnt china coffie pot, 2 glass crewets, 1 large stone Jugg, ½ doz cups & saucers, a small stone Jugg, 3 small Jarrs, 2 large stone bowls, 2 small ditto, a doz stone plates, 7 stone dishes, a child's craddle, 6 perspective views, a print of Mr. pitt, 8 small pictures, a canvass floor Cloth, a woolen ditto, a case with 12 bottles, a large washing tub, a powdering tub, 4 glass candlesticks, a Gun, a pair of pistols, a cutlas with a pistol, a tinder box, a pocket microscope, a small spy glass in a shagreen case, a chamber bell, a horse whip, a razor Hone, a sallad dish, a large glass salver with a doz Glasses, 5 water glasses, 4 wine glasses, 3 tumblers, 4 large common tea pots, 2 dusting brushes, 2 pudding pans, 4 smoking Irons, a pinckbeck watch, 1 doz Cloak pins, 1 punch strainer, a china butterboat, a flower pot, 2 brass branches, 1 trivet & gridiron, 1 Perimson damast-window curtains, a frying pan, an old do., a warming pan, a flesh fork, a pr. Snuffers, a chamber bellows, ½ doz large cannisters, a doz Knives & forks, a water Jarr, a brass candle box, a large brass mortar & pestle, a small do. do., a small do. do., a glass do. do., a maple desk, a large Silver Salver, 2 small do. a Silver Tankard, 3 silver castors, 2 silver mugs, a large porringer, 2 silver Salts, a Silver soop spoon, 6 Silver table spoons, 18 silver Tea spoons & sugar tongs, 3 blue worsted window curtains, 4 Iron rods for window curtains with staples, a bullet mold, a Cloath's brush, a hearth brush, a window brush, a tin Coffie pott, 2 small decanters, 2 glass crewets, 4 doz blue China plates, 3 large family pictures, a wicker hamper, a wicker basket, a large Cloaths Chist, a doz Tea Cannisters, a green Sugar Canister, 3 Trunks, a ps of shell work, a Japan spice box, 4 bed quilts, 4 blankets, 2 flannen sheets, 12 Table Cloths, 10 pr. Sheets, a doz napkins, an etching of Henry Jenkins, a doz plain linen Towels, 1 doz oznaburgs ditto, 3 small magnifying glasses, 2 Ivory table Books, 2 do letter folders, a red leather letter case, a burnt china strawbery dish, a Set blue china, 10 Chocolate cups china, 8 blue & white Coffee cups china, a blue china tea canister, 4 small china bowls, 2 china milk pots, a store room table, wearing apparel of different kinds, a mustard pot, an Umbrella, a pr. of snuffers, an Axe, a hand saw, a hammer, a small spy glass ivory, 2 nests of drawers, Shop table with drawers, 2 standishes, 24 gallipots, 8 painted pots with tin covers, a small syringe, a tin funnel, 8¾ll Salts,

Sundry medicines which with the articles following (the last excepted) were sold for twenty four pounds proclamation money to wit

3 Shop tiles, a large salvatory, a small ditto, 58 painted bottles, 28 bottles 2? bl. flint with glass stoppers, 18 common pots large & small, 18 gallipots, 44 comon vials, 2 pr scales & weights, a gilt measure, 2 ounce & ½ ounce maesure, a funnel, a set pocket instruments, 5 tooR? instruments, a catheton, a pr. forceps, a scalpel, 10 lancets & cases, a gum lancet, 11

surgical needles & case, an electrical machine, a Skeleton & Case, Skins, crucibles, Pr of probe scizzors, sundry Book debts outstanding which cannot yet be settled & ascertained

MARGT: EUSTACE

Sworn to the Eighth day of april 1769 (Eleven lines being previously cancelled) before me
BENN: T? HERON.

No. CAROLINA, CRAVEN COUNTY

AN INVENTORY of the Estate of Martin Francks late of the County & Province aforesd Deceased as farr forth as is come to the Hands of the Executors & Executrix of the last Will & Testament of the Said Martin Franck taken this 14th day of June Anno Domo 1745

Seven negro man (to wit)
Toney
Jack
James
Sambo
Johno Hector
Tobey
Four Negro Women (to wit)
Rachael, Phillis, Kate
Four negro Boys (to wit)
Pharoah, Peter Joseph & Samuel
Two Negro Girls (to wit)
Kate & Rachell
Six Feather Beds 3 good ones
& three ordinary ones
One Catt Tail Bed
Nineteen sheets
Two Blankets—Six Bolsters
Eight Pillows
One Sett of Callico Curtains
One Sett of Old Curtains
One Bed Quilt
Six Ruggs 3 Diaper Table Cloths
Seven Napkins, Two Coarse Towells
One fine Towell
Three pairs of fine Garlix pillow Cases
Three Course Pillow Cases
One Course Table Cloath
One Old great Desk
One Small new Desk
One Looking Glass
Two Old Sconce Glasses
One Picture, One Maple Table
Two Old Cases & fourteen Bottles
Three Old Chests
Six Old Boxes
Two Old Plank Tables
One Little Candle Box
Two Old Leather Chairs
One Old Large flagg Chair
One Little Leather Chair
One Bench or form
One Silver Tankard—abt quart
One Silver Peper Box

Five Silver Spoons
One pair of Silver Knee Buckles
Thirteen Pewter dishes
Twelve Basons
Two Doz & Eight Small Pewter Plates
Six Pewter Poringers
One Pewter Tankard
Ten large Soop Plates
One Pewter Salt Seller
Fourteen Pewter Spoons
One Pewter Pint Pot
One Pewter half pint Pot
One Pewter Gill Pot
On Old Pewter Quart Pot
Two Brass Candlesticks
One Iron Candlestick
Six China Cups & Sausars
Three Earthen Tea Pots
Six Delph Cups & Sausers
Three White Tea Cups & Sausors
Two Razers & one hone
Six White Mettle handle Knives
Five Forks, One Stone Pot
One large pair of Hand Irons
One small pair of Ditto
One large & one Small Brush
Two Chamber Pots
Three Copper Kettles & One Brass Ditto
Two Small Brass Kettles
Two Bell Mettle Skilletts
One Brass Skillett
One Brass Tea Kettle
One Iron Skillett
Four great Iron Potts
Two little Iron Pots
Two Iron Kettles
Three old Iron pans
One Grid iron
One Chafin Dish
Three Iron Pot Racks
Three pair Pot Hooks
One Waffell Iron
Two pairs of Tongs
One Iron & one Brass Pot Lid
Two Bell Mettle Mortars
One Brass Skimmer
Two Iron Laddles Two Spits
One Rosting Hook
Two Brass Ladles
Five old Sifters
One Rice Sifter, Three Iron flesh forks
One Iron Egg Slicer
Two Saddles one old
One Old Buck Skin Seat Saddle
One Box Iron & Heaters
Two flat Irons
One Iron Stand
One Pair Spoon Moulds
One Iron Chopping Knife
One Curry Comb

Two Pairs of Steelyards
One Old Iron Shovell
One Grind Stone
Four Bed Steds Three Testaments
Three Psalters Fifteen Dutch Books
One Candle Mould Two Stone Pots
Four Earthen Pots fourteen Qt Bottles
One Earthen Pitcher One Ditto Jugg
Two Tin Funnells
Two three Gallons Juggs
Four old Cannisters One Coffee Pot
One Stone Pitcher One Stone Mugg
One Pepper Mill, One Sugar Box
One Glass Qt One Gill
Four Little Cups
One Half pint Cup
One Small Stone Jugg
One Nutmeg Grater
One Tin Pepper Box
One Tin Sauce Pan
Two Glass Bottles
One Old Tin Lanthorn
Two Small Dutch Saws
Six Ditto Spinning Wheels (Linen)
Two Large Spinning Wheels
One White Sugar Pot
Two Small Brown Pans
One Small Old still
One Old pair of Nippers
One Tap Borer
Six Branding Irons
One pair of Sheep Sheers
One pair of Taylors Sheers
Two Old Guns
Three pairs of Cards
One Earthen Churn
One Wooden Churn
Twenty Six Milk Keelers
Three hackels one old do
One Copper Pan One Sythe
Four Old Hogsheads
Two Pair of Old Cards
One old Iron Skimmer
Two Old locks
Two Fleshing Knives
four Old Graters
One Cross Cut Saw Old
Two Whip Saws Old
One Small Tennant Saw
Three Butter Tubs
Five Old barrells
One Old Pewter Bottle
Twenty yds of Duroys
One Warming Pan Old
Eight Earthen Plates & One Dish
Fifteen Yds Worsted Damask
Two Snuff Boxes
Two Glass Salt Sellers
One Tea Spoon Case & four Spoons

Three new Reap Hooks
One Old Ditto
Two Old Hand Saws
Two Drawing Knives
One Old pair of Money Scales
One New Pair of Money Scales
One pair of Old Scales
Four Hilling Hoes
Three Weeding Hoes
Five Old Axes & Two New Ditto
Two Grubing Hoes
Three Set of Old Plow Irons
Eleven Brass Cuppin Cups
Two Horse Bells
Three Small Bells
One Bullett Mould
One Carpenters Adz
One Powder flask
One Old Broad Axe
Three Iron Wedges
Two Gimbletts
Two Chisells & One Gauge
One Barr of Steel
One Old Wimble Bitt
One Small piece of Lead
One Coopers adz
One Howell
A parcell of Old Iron
Forty Eight Cows & Calves
Fifteen Calves & Yearlings
Eight Barren Cows
Twelve two Year Old Heifers
Six Three Year Old Steers
Eleven Yearling Heifers
Twelve Yearling Stears
Sixteen Two Year Old Steers
One Five Year Old Steer
One Six Year Old Steer
Two Bulls
One Year Old Bull
Two Cows & Calves
One four year old Steer
One Three year Old Steer
One Two year Old Steer
One Year Old Steer
One Two year Old Heifer
One Yearling Steer
One Two year Old Bull
One Yearling Bull
One Two year Old Heifer
One Yearling Bull
Six Two year old Steers
Two Two year old Heifers
Two two year old Steers
Two Yearling Heifers
One Barren Cow
One four year old Steer
One three year old Steer
Three Mares & Colts

Three mares & Yearlings
Four young horses
Two Two year old mares
One Spaid Mare
Five old Horses
One Sorrell Horse
Eleven Lambs
Seventeen old Sheep

29th of June 1745　　　　　　　　　　　CIVILLA FRANCK Executrix

NORTH CAROLINA, BERTIE COUNTY.

I TRUE INVENTORY of all & Singular the Goods Chattles & Credits of John Gray Deceas'd &c.

Two Pounds Eighteen Shills. & Eight pence Virginia Currency, £15, 1, Procl. Money, £ 29, 17, 6, Old Bills his Wearing Apparell, 80 Books, 2 Pocket ditto, Sundry book Accompt irregularly Book'd & unsett'd, Debts due by Notes of hand to the Ammount of £ 28.8. Sterling, Draughts to the Ammount of £ 375.4.3. Old Bills, Sixteen Negroe Slaves, Six Feather Beds, Six Bolsters, Six Pillows, 4 Ruggs 2 Quilts, 5 Blankets, 2 Setts Curtains, 30 Sheets, 10 Pillow Cases, 8 Bed Steads, Two Matts &: 5 Hides, Seven Bed Cords, Two Bolster Cases, Three Pillow Teak's, 2 desks, Three Walnut tree Tables, Two pine ditto, Eight Chests, Two Trunks, One Wig Box, One Walnut ditto, Fourteen Chairs & 1 Safe, Three Cases & Seventeen Bottles, One Linnen Wheel, three Woollen do. 3 pair Cotton Cards, 1 pair ditto Wool, 1 Chaffing dish, 26 Quart Bottles, 3 Brass Kettles, 6 Iron Pots, 2 Frying pans, 1 Gridiron, 3 pr. Pot hooks, 2 Pot tramell's, 1 Iron Skillet, 1 Bell Mett. ditto, 11 Pewter Basons, 24? dishes, 44 Plates, 7 Porringer, 32 Spoons, 13.℔ 7 oz. Old Pewter 6 Brass Spoons & a Case, One pr. Hinges, One Spring Lock, 4 Iron door Bolts, 3 Cooper's Adzes, 2 Chest Locks, 3 Chizels, 2 Iron Staples, 9 Gimblets, 2 Taper Bitts, 6 doz. Pipes, 3 Box Irons & 4? Heaters, 1 Flatt Iron & 2 Stands, 3 Cross Cutt Saw Files, 1 Case Razors, 7 Razors without a Case, 3 Bunches drum line, 2 Side Sadles & bridles, 1 Mans Sadle & Bridle, 25 Bunches bobbing, Eight Sticks Mohair, a parcel of Buttons, One Closs Stool, One Silver hilted Sword, One Brass hilted ditto, 4¼ Yds. Grogrum, 3¼ Yds. Duroys, 2 Yds. Narrow broads, 13 Yds. Corded Demmitty, 9 Yds. 7/8 Checks, 8 ¾ Yds. ¾ Garlix, 1 Tea Kettle, 1 Punch Bowl delf, 9 Earthen Porringers, 1 Box wt. a parcel of Old Joiners Tools, 4 Guns, 1 Sauce pan, 3 Graters, 1 Spit, 1 Pewter Qrt. pot, 1 drudgeon Box, 1 Loom, 5 Slae's, 2 Setts Harness, 5 Shuttels, 1 Branding Iron, 1 Sun dial, 1 Tin funnell, 1 Churn, 4 Sieves, 1 Stone Butter Pot, 1 Butter Tub, 1 Meal ditto, 1 Earthen Jar, 1 Woodem Tray, 1 Wooden Bowl, 3 Pails, 1 Bucket, 2 Tubbs & 1 old Lanthorn, 1 Cain, 3 Pr. Fire Tongs & 1 Shovel, 1 Pr. hand Iron's, 2 Brushes, 1 Pr. Candle Snuffers, 6 Candle Sticks, 1 Pr. Sheep Shears, 1 Pr. Small Taylors ditto, 1 doz: Case knives, 21 forks & 2 Butcher knives, 1 Clasp ditto, 2 Tobacco Boxes, 2 Pr. Tobacco Tongs, 2 Setts knitting needles, 1 Pr. Pinchers, 2 Tooth Brushes, 3 Cork Screws, 25 Silver Twist Coat Butts., 1 Pr. Money Scales, 2 Pr. horse fleems 1 Ink Pot & 1 ditto horn, 6 Pr. Small Scissors, 2 Pencils, 9 Viols, 1 Mug, 6 China Cups & Saucers, 1 Pewter Tea Pott, 1 flint ditto, 6 Silver Tea Spoons, 1 large Silver ditto. 1 Decanter, 1 peper Box, 1 Salt Sellar, 2 Glass Tumblers, 2 Wine Glasses, 1 Vinegar Cruit, 2 Small Glass Bottles, 7 delf Plates, 2 ditto Saucers, 1 dusting Pan, 2 Tin Canisters wt. Tea, 6 Gallipots, 1 Earthen Butter Pot, 2 ditto Chamber Pots, 1 Pewter ditto, 1 Tin dish Cover, 1 Tin Coffee Pot, 1 Candle Box, 1 Reel, 1 Gunturs Scale, 1 Gauging Rod, 7¾ Bees Wax, 4 1℔ 6 Oz: Tallow, 1 Pr. Small Stillards, 1 Pr. large ditto, 4 Earthen Lard Pots, 1 pewter Serings, 2 Diaper

table Cloaths, 4 ditto Napkins, 3 Linnen Table Cloaths, 5 Towels, a small qty. Powd. & Shott, 1 Pr. Pistols & Holsters, 1 doz: drum Hooks, 19 Sheep, 2 Mares & 1 Colt, 4 Horses, 1 broad Axe, 6 Narrow ditto, 2 Grubbing Hoes, 5 Weeding ditto, 2 Narrow ditto, 1 Cross Cutt Saw, 1 Whip Saw, 1 Looking Glass, 5 Hammers, 2 plows, 1 Flewk ditto, 2 Skimmers, 1 Wooden Can, 2 Coopers Axes, 1 Crow Iron & Stock, 1 ditto Wtout Stock, 2 drawing knives, 1 Wimble Stock & Bitt, 1 Coopers Vice, 1 Jointer, 3 hand Saws, 1 Frow 3 Iron Wedges, 60 head Cattle, 1¾ Yd. Silk Damask, 2 Yds. Muslin, 2 Yds. Irish Linnen, 6 Yds. White Calicoe, 5/8 of Yd. Searsuchers, 1 Glister Pipe & 1 Oz. Thread, 9¼ Yd. Cap Fringe, 6 pound Feathers, 1 Meal Bag, 1 piece Narrow Binding, 3465 hhd. Staves, 300 ditto heading, 89 head of Hogs, 2 hand Milns, 10 Sides Tann'd Leather, a parcel Oister Shells, a Small parcel Old Iron, 1 Sett of Surveyrs. Instrumts., 1 Small parcel of Wool, 1 Small ditto Cotton, 1 Small ditto Flax, 1 Bottle British Oil, 7 Basketts, a parcel old Casks, Some horses & Cattle in the Woods the Quantity unknown, 2 Lancets, 1 Currying knife, 2 hand Saw files, 1 Gun hammer, 29 Taylors Thimbles, 3 Augurs, 2 Bells, 1 house ditto, 4 Reap hooks, 1 Grind Stone, 1 Small Tar kill, a parcel Corn, 2 Cow hides, 7 Bushels Salt, 1 Small Qty. Wheat, a Small do. Peas.
Errors Excepted
February 14th, 1750/1

Pr. ANN GRAY Exetrx.

This day Came before me Ann Gray Executrix of the last Will and Testament of John Gray Deceased and Proved the bove Innotary according to Law Let it be Recorded
Certified under my hand the 14th day of february Anno Dom 1750.

NEEDHAM BRYAN—

JNO. HECLEFIELD'S INVENTORY.

A TRUE INVENTORY of all the Goods and Chattells belonging to the Estate of Colo. Jno. Heclefield Deceased as was produced by the Exec. Mr. Edmond Gale and Mr. George Durant and was Sold at publick Outcry and praised by us the Subscribers being qualifyed according to Law August ye 15th. 1721 Imprimis One poor Mare 3 years old Two Yearlings an Horse and a Mare Two Stears of three and four years old Five Cows Two Heifers Two Calves Eight Ewes Seven Weathers Two Rams most very old Two Barrows Three Sows 3 Years old Five Sows and a Barrow of two Year old Seven less than Yearlings Seven little piggs One Silver Tankard Weighing 1: 1: 15: 16 Eight Good Spoons Two Dram Cups one little Spoon One do broke One Do. large melted a Seal 9: 3— Total of the Weight 1–10–18–16 One Silver Hilted Sword one pair of Buckles not weighed four Diamond Rings two plain Do. One Negro Man called Luke Do. Cuffe a Negro Girl Bess. In province Bills 554: 8: 0 One Bed and Furniture £10: 5: 0 One Do. £10: 1: 0 One Do. 8 £ One Do. 6: 15: 0 One Do. 6 £ One old Saddle £1: 2: 6 Ten Black Chairs £1: 10: 0 Nine Common Chairs £1: 4: 6 Frying pan Andiron and other old Iron £1: 5: 0 Grindstone pestle Adds Froe Chafin Dish 15Shll. Thirty Eight Shooles £1: 6: 0 One Buckaneer Gun £2: 5: 0 One old Do. £1: 5: 0 Two milk Tubbs 4shll. One pair of Stylards 12 shll. One pair Do 12shll. 6 One large pot £2: 8: 0 One Do. Smaller £1: 1: 0 One Do. 7shll. One Iron Kettle 15shll. One old Chest of Drawers 8shll. One Square Table 15shll. One Do. 14shll. Two old Chests £1: 2: 6 A Side of Sole Leather a pair of old Slippers

6shll. One pair of Sheets £1: 13: 0 Do. £1: 1: 0 Do. £1: 1: 0 Do. £1: 11: 0 Do. 11/6 Do. 11 shll. Six pillow Cases 13 shll. One Table Cloth and Six Napkins £ 1: 10: 0 Three Table Cloths 19 shll. Three Do. £ 1: 5: 6 Seven Towels £ 1: 5: 0 Two Bolster Cases 4 pillows Cases 12 shll. A Looking Glass 11/6 Do. broken 5/6 One Dozn. plates 16/6 Fourteen Do. £ 1: 3: 0 Ten Soop plates and Six petty panns £ 1: 9: 0 Four Dishes & Six plates £ 3: 5: 0 One pair of Candlesticks 8 shll. One pair Do. 12/6 Two old Do. 8/6 Spice Mortar 12 shll. Old Bread Sifter 1/6 One Do. 1/8 A large pewter Bason and other old pewter 16 shll. Four Dishes £ 1: 5: 0 Five Do. £ 1: 15: 0 Six Do. & one porringer £ 2: 13: 0 Two Chamber potts 7/6 Two old Do. 3 shll. pot Racks and Crooked Irons 10/6 One pair Do. 7/6 a punch Bowl 6/6 One pair of sheep sheers 3/6 Some old Brass 6 shll. Three Butter potts 5/3 a Warming pan £ 1: 10: 0 a Mill £ 2: 10: 0 a form for a Table 6 shll. a Colt 15 shll. a Bedsted 12 shll. a Round Table £ 1: 16: 0 A little Table 3 shll. Five Knives and 8 Forks Old 3/6 a Copper pot 6/6 Two old Broken Iron potts 6 an Old Cupboard 16 shll. Four old Cask 2 Canns a Runlet and Some Chalk 12 shll. Two Juggs 2 Case Bottles 9/6 A spade 6 shll. an Hamper 2 Baskets 1 old Scales Candle Boxes 6/6 piggin and full of Molasses and Jug 6/6 Some old Axes and Hoes 11/8 Three old Barrels Two Boxes 7/6 Old Hogsheads and Coolers and old Barrels £ 0: 9: 0 Wastecoat and Britches Cheredary 17 shll. a Hammack 18/6 Thirty one lb of Cocoe £ 1: 3: 3 Eleven lb Do. 8/3 a little old Table 2/6 Tea pot Cups and Sawsers 9 shll. Money Weights and Scales 10shll. Five shirts at 12/6 each 3: 2: 6: Two Brushes 1shll. Three old Barrels 4/1 Black Coat Wastecoat and Britches £ 4: 10: 0 Drugget Coat lined with Silk and Stockins £ 6: 5: 0 Knife Basket Salt Seller and Broken Brush 4 shll. Two pair of shoes 7/6 an old Quilt 15 shll. Some Cotton Wick 5 Gally potts 1/6 Three wedges Hammer and other old Iron 10 shll. Drinking Glass /10 Two drinking Juggs 1/5 four Dozn. Bottles 14 shll. a seel skin Trunk 3/6 Sr. Walter Rawleigh's History with 25 other Small Do. 4 £ One Chest with Inside Drawers 12/6 Twenty Six lb of Wool £ 1: 19: 0 Two pair of Thread and Silk Stockins one one pair worsted 1 £ Six and ½ Bush. Wheat £ 1: 6: 0 One Silk flowered Apron 1£ Two Handkerchiefs 15 shll. Two Do. 10 shll. Nine Remnants of Ribondyt. 23 yds. £ 1: 15: 0 One Barrll. Corn Bills 10 shll. Do. other pay 10 shll. Case of Lancetts 5 shll. Four Bushl. and 1 peck of Salt at 4/1 17/4 1/4 Half a Bush Do. 2 shll. Half a Bushl. Corn 1 shll. Three old Barrels 716 To the Benefit and encrease of the Corn Field 2£ Some Dirty Corn 5 shll. a pott sold to Mr. Jno. Bateman 10 shll. Total £ 698: 0: ¾——RICHD SANDERTON ATHO: HATCH THOMAS T PENRICE THOMAS B BARCLIFT——

BEAUFORT COUNTY

AN INVENTORY of the goods and Chattles of Harman Hill Deceast taken 30th day of May 1755

6 negroes named sip & sall Cuff & cesar Quock and Jack 4 feather beds & furniture, 1 Walnut Desk, 4 Chests & 3 Ovell tabels, 1 square table & 8 Chairs, 2 Casses of bottles, 3 Iron pots & 1 brass kittle, 2 Iron Skillets & 1 tea kittle, 2 frying Pans & 2 pair of pot hooks, 1 Bail & 3 Iron hooks, 2 Candle Sticks, 1 pair of Snuffers 3 pair of sisors, 1 pair of Sheep Shairs, 1 hand Bellos 1 hour glass, 1 grid Iron 1 pair of stillards, 1 spie glass & 2 Looking glasses, 1 Slate & : 1 Standish 1 broad ax, 9 Club Axes 2 weed hose & 19 old hose & 1 hiling ho, 2 Pales & 2 tubs & 1 half bushel, 1 Pigin & 1 Can & 1 fat tub, 1 Rum Hodgsed & a Parsil of old wooden Lumber, 1 Spice morter & 61 Chunk bottles & 3 Delfe Punch Bowls, 12 plats & 4 Stone mugs, 13 guns, 5 glass tumblers & 1 Stone Jugg, 1 Spade 3 drawing knives, 2 Coopers Addes, 3 howels and other for a Cooper, 1 Small Box and som cord winders tools & a Small parcel of Carpenters tools, 1 Drinkin

glass 1 glass salt sellar, 1 pocket boottle & 2 Vilos, 1 mistart pott & peper boox, 5 knives and & forks, 1 flesh fork 3 Sids of tand Leather 1 Pair of Mil sones, 1 tea poott, 4 Screens 3 Cups, 4 Bridel Bitts 1 Curb bitt, 7 Earthen pans 1 cullandar 1 Earthen beare pott, 3 butter poots 1 Sithe, 1 Cross Cutt Saw 1 Whip Saw & a parcel of old files, 1 brass Cook, 1 tin funnel, 6 Puter Dishes, 5 puter basons, 26 plates, 1 tan cord, 1 Quart Pott, 1 Chamber pott & 10 puter spoons & 8 ocome spoons, 2 Earthen pitchers, 3 porngers 2 half pints Cups, 2 Chamber potts, 1 pair of Iron wedges, 3 Plows 1 pair of fire toungs, 1 Bocks Iron and heaters, 1 Cury Comb, 1 Bad ———?, 2 mens Sadels and bridels, 1 womans Saddle, 1 Lume & 5 Seets of harnes, 1 flatt & 1 Sale conough, 1 pair Leather Bags, 3 Cloath baggs, 1 Wollett, 3 yards of ozenbrigs, 1 Cutlash, a small of Books, 3 Razors, 3 hones, 2 Combes one horn 1 Ivory, 1 Small Cake of bees wax, 1 Small Cake of mirtle Do. 2 grinStones, 1 Cotten gin, 20 weight of Rope, 1 Shugar Box, 1 pair of money Scales & Weights, 50 gallons of Rum, 4 Barrils of Sider, 1 Cagg Vinigar, 1 Wier Sive, 3 Riddles, 2 meal Sives, 2 Splits Baskits, 9 head of Sheep, to small percel of nails, 96 Weight of Cotten and small parcl of wool, 1 table Cloth & napkins, 2 towels & 2 Canesters, 1 pint of Swet oyl, 62 Weight of raw hide, 50 Weight of raw Dear skin, 60 Weight of tallow, 3 raw Skins besides 1 peace of Bar Iron, 1 Linning Wheal & 1 Woolin Do., 3 pair of Cards, Small percel of old Iron, 3 Siutes of Plow tacklin, 1 Silver Sock buckel, 1 of knee buckels Silver 3 Reap hooks, 1 Cart & Wheals, 1 frow, 1 Branding Iron, 1 Small hatchet 1 fish gigue, 1 tobaco box, 1 quier of paper, 4 Dozen of pipes, 1 Seal, 1 pair of horse fleams, 1 Lansett to a percel of flax, to Six pounds Seven Shillings & Six pence prock and 14 Shillings & Eight Pence Prock, 1 Small Box, 1 old Bread Tray, 3 fishing nets 1 half hough Seas. of Salt, 36 groun hougs, & 25 Small piggs, 15 Cows 8 Calves, 10 yearlings, 6 groun Sears, 1 Bull, 3 Stears, four year old, two steers three year ould, 1 Stear two year old, 1 heifer two year old, 2 Work horses, 3 old, mares and 2 young mares, 1 Iron Spitt,

         SARAH HILL
         JOSEPH SLADE Exec——
         J? BARROW

AN INVENTORY of the Goods & Chattles belonging to the Estate of Christian Isler late of Craven County & Province of North Carolina deceased—(To wit)

Twenty three four year old steers—Twenty five Cows & Calfes—Fourteen three year old steers—Twenty four dry Cows—Twenty two year olds—One two year old steer, Three Bul's— Three Pounds Cash Equal to Twenty four Pounds in Province Bills—

     FREDERICK ISLER
     JOHN ISLER   Executors
     WILLIAM

AN INVENTORY of all the Goods, Chatles, Rights Credits & Estate Personal of the late Gabriel Johnston Esqr. Deceased. vizt

      Household furniture at Eden house

  9 Bedsteads, 9 Beds 9 bolsters
 18 pillows 20 pair of sheets
 20 pillow Cases, 18 Blankets
  6 quilts 3 french covers
  4 matresses 8 Sett bed Curtains 1 Sett Window Do.

4 Dining tables, 4 Card Do.
2 Dressing tables 2 Tea Do.
1 Wryting Do. 1 Card Do.
5 Small Do. 2 Scrutores.
2 Buroes, 7 Chests,
3 Corner cupboards
1 Book Stand, 6 glasses gilt frames
1 Do. Black Do. 1 Dressing Do.
1 Couch, 38 Chairs different Sorts, 9 Wedford Do.
5 Stools, 2 Clocks
1 Basone stand, 1 Marble table
24 Table Cloths 36 napkins
24 Towells

Plate vizt:

1 Silver Tea kettle & Lamp
1 Do. french plate
1 Coffee pot. 2 Cups.
2 Tankards, 2 pint muggs
4 Candle Sticks, 4 waiters,
1 Tea board, 3 Milk potts,
2 Setts of Castors 4 Salt Sellars
2 Butter Cups, 2 Salt Shovels
2 punch ladles, 1 Tea pott.
2 Canisters, 17 Tea spoons
2 pr. of tongs, 1 Snuffer Dish
27 Table Spoons 1 large Soop Do.
11 forks, 11 Sweet meat Spoons
1 Doz knives & forks
1 marrow Spoon, 1 punch Strainer
1 Shaving Basone & Ewer
1 China Jar & Stand Sett in Silver
3 Bread Baskets
2 Decanter stands
2 knife Trays   6 China bowles
5 Do. Dishes, 6 muggs
2 Doz. of China plates
5 Basons Do. 6 Tea potts
2 Doz. Cups and Saucers
1 Sugar Dish 6 Coffee cups
3 Decanters. 15 Drinking glasses, 2 watter Do.
1 Doz. of Jelly Do.
2 glass muggs
2 Doz. of Ivory knives & forks
7 Pr Doggs 4 Pr. Tongs
2 Shovels, 1 fender
3 house Brooms 2 hearth brushes
1 Terrestial & 1 Celestial globe
1 Chair & harnis, 1 Chaise & Do.
1 Bay Boat, & 2 Canoes.

Kitchen Furniture

17 pewter Dishes
5 Do. Covers, 2 fish Dishes
8 Doz: of Plates, 1 Jack
1 Driping pan, 6 Sauce pans
2 Stew pans

INVENTORIES. 503

13 potts 5 pott lids
2 Tea kettles, 2 Chacolet potts
1 Coffee pott, 4 Brass Candle Sticks,
1 Brass Drudgers
1 large Copper kettle
1 Small Do. 2 grid Irons
3 Spitts, 1 Chafing Dish
1 Cheese Toaster,
2 mortars & pestills
1 Shovel, 1 pr. Tongs 1 pr Doggs
1 Warming pan, 4 flat Irons
1 Box Do. 1 Brass Candle Stick
2 Brass plate warmer molds
1 Small Still, 3 Lanthorns
2 pair of Scales
3 Spinnins Wheels
9 milk panns, 4 pails
3 washing tubs Some glasses
17 Garden Spades
1 Chest Carpenters tools
a quantity of Bottels & nails & old Iron

Cloaths vizt.

5 Coats 5 pair Breeches
8 Waist Coats
3 wiggs
12 Shirts & 12 neck Cloths
6 pair of Stockings
4 pair Shoes, 4 Swords
4 Pr. Pistols 1 Do. Holsters
3 Sadles & Bridles &.

Stock & Tools att Eden house viz:

4 horses, 1 Mare about
45 Sheep About
80 head of Black Cattle Including Calves About
60 head of Swine Including piggs &ca.
11 Broad Hoes, 4 narrow Do.
3 axes 3 Spades, 3 fluke & 1 plow,
Some sheet lead and 1 iron press Lying in the Barn

An Inventory of goods at Mount Galland vizt.

5 Bed Steads, 6 Beds
6 Bolsters, 7 Pillows
3 french Covers, 9 Blanketts
1 Coloured quilt, 9 pillow Cases, 7 pair of Sheets,
4 Tables, 20 Chairs, 1 Chest,
1 Clock, 1 Couch, 1 rugg, 1 Decanter, 1 Cruet 1 rummer 2 Watter glasses, 9 wine Do. 3 punch Bowles, 3 Small Do. 4 hand Basons, 2 porrangers 7 Chambers potts 1 Butter Do. 1¼Case Silver handled knives & forks, one fork wanting, 5 Ivory handled knives & forks 1 Tea kettle 1 Copper Sauce pan 1 Spitt 1 grid Iron 1 Mortar 4 Small brass Cocks, 2 Do. larger 1 Chafin Dish 1 large Copper kettle 1 Box Iron, 2 heaters 1 juggs, 1 rope 1 Bung borer 1 large Funnel, 6 earthen pans 7 Rulers 1 large Copper pot 1 Coffee Pott, 6 Candle-Sticks 1 pair snuffers 1 Drudger 1 Tea pott, 1 Milk Do. 1 pepper Box, 8 Pewter Dishes, 11 Soop plates, 27 flat Do. 1 quart mugg 1 half pint Do. 1 Butter Boat 1 fish Strainer 2 wine tubs, 2 Covers for Dishes, 3 watter pails 1 Washing Tub——

Stock &. Tools &ca at Mount Galland

153½ Barlls Sound Corn, 34 Barls Do. rotten, 3 Iron potts, 1 frying pan, 4 Iron Wedges. 2 ox Chains, 1 share & Coulter 2 plow hoes, 14 broad & 8 narrow hoes, 4 grubing Do. 2 Bells, 11 axes, about 50 head of Black Cattle Including Calves about 100 head of Swine most of them young, Shoots & piggs 4 horses, 1 Mare & 1 Colt.

Stock & Tools &ca at Fishing Creek

36 Barls of Corn, about 50 head of black Cattle Including Calves, about 80 Swine Including piggs &ca 4 horses & Mares 1 Colt 3 broad hoes, 3 narrow Do. 2 grubing Do. 4 axes, 1 small Share & Coulter 1 fluke hoe 1 Drawing knife 1 Sett of Wedges—

Stock & Tools at Possum Quartr.

43 Barls Sound Corn 4 Do. rotten, about 5 head of black Cattle 36 Swine Including piggs 4 broad hoes 4 narrow Do. 2 grubing Do. 4 axes.

Stock & Tools &ca. at Conahoe.

188 Barls Sound Corn 13 Do. rotten 11 broad hoes 6 narrow Do. 5 axes 1 frow, 1 hand saw 1 Drawing knife 1 Shovel 2 Augures 1 Chisel, 1 gun, 2 plows, about 30 head of black Cattle Including Calves, about 68 Swine most of them piggs 2 Horses.

A List of the Negroes

Nim, Waltham, London, Carolina Boatswain Taffie Cato Quash Charles Eden George Malch Virgil Sambo Jack Jammey Mingoe Joe Galland Hamstead Coltrain Caesar Cato Titus Benn Eden Indian Johnny Gregory Dick Sambo Dromo Glasgow Scipio Cain Peter Coldin In all 35 men. Dinah Tetimah Diana Baban Grace Sella Moll Teresa Rose Diana Kate China Tamar Lucey Sarah Betty Quasheba Phebe Sukey Rachel Baubas, Juba Jenny old Bess Sellah Nancy Hagar Dinah Bess. In all 29 women. Titus Charles James Cato Homer Dromo Coot Pounce Will Jack Dick Piramus Jupiter Waltham Cupid Sandie Jack Aaron Timothy Arther In all 20 Boys many of these born since the Goverors Death & some since.—— Polly Sarah Grace Beck Jude Hannah Betty Teresa Kate Slip slap Bett Venus Cloe Priscilla Peggy Jenny Dinah Many of these Born Since the Govrs Death In all 19 Girls One Negroe Girl named Titty not Included in the above List being expressly given to me by Will . . .

Books not Included The same by Will being left to Doctr William Cathcart Mr Samuel Johnston and I chusing any number not exceeding 40 Vols. neither is Watches Included &ca. Given by the late Governor before His Death and By Will:,—

N. B. The above Inventory was taken in May 1753, Since which time Eden House was burned and the following things were thereby lost.

Lost by the fire at Eden House since this Inventory was taken.

8 Bed Steads,/ 4 Beds, 6 Bolsters, 16 pillows, 10 pair of sheets/ 6 pillow Cases/, 16 Blankets, 6 quilts, 2 french Covers, 1 Matress 6 Setts of bed Curts, 3 Dining Tables, 1 Waiting Do., 1 Card Do., 4 Small Do., 1 Scrutore, 5 Chests, 1 Corner Cup board, 3 gilt framed glasses, 11 Chairs, 9 Windsor Do., 5 Stools, 1 Clock, 10 Table Cloths, 3 China Dishes, 1 mugg, 1 Doz: of Plates, 5 Bassons, 3 Tea potts, 1 Doz. Cups & Saucers/ 6 Coffee Cups, 1 Decanter, 5 Drinking glasses, 1 Doz of Jelly glasses, 2 glass muggs, 1 Doz: of Ivory knives & forks. 3 pair of Dogs, 1 pair of Tongs, 3 house Brooms, 2 Hearth Brushes, 12 pewter Dishes, 4 Do. Covers, 1 fish Dish, 5 Dozen of plates, 2 Brass plate warmer molds. 1 Small Still, 1 pair Scales, 1 Spinning Wheel, 9 milk pans, 17 Garden Spades, 1 Chest of Carpenters tools, 1 Salt Spoon.

Cloths &ca.—

4 Coats, 5 pair Breeches, 4 Waist coats, 8 shirts, 5 neck cloths, 6 pair Stockings, 4 pair Shoes, 4 Swords, 4 pr. pistoles, 1 pr. Holsters, 2 Sadles & Bridles.

In Silver and Gold In the House at the Governors Death.—as pr. accot. Credited. Three hundred and eighty Six pounds eight Shillings and two pence Virginia money. In Proclamation Bills one hundred and ninety five pounds five shillings and eight pence alsoe Credited. In Accot. as like ways is the Tobacco's and whatever has been Sold from off the Plantations, and now remains unsold belonging to the Estate.

Jewels Belonging To Miss Johnston are as follows vizt. five gold Lockets, 1 garnet necklace Sett in Silver one Bristol Stone Necklace sett in Silver, one Gold Watch & Chain, one Sett of Gold Tweezers, these excepting the Gold Watch she used to wear In her fathers life time. The Gold Watch was made a present off to the late Mr. Chief Justice Hall and afterwards exchanged by his late Excellency on Accot. of His Daughter, for a large Silver Repeating Watch given to Mr. Hall In lieu Thereof. The following Rings were given to Mrs. Rutherfurd one large Gold Diamond ring one plain Do. one Gold Diamond hoop ring two mourning Gold rings of which Miss Johnston now has at WilliamsBurgh with her, the Gold Diamond ring the Diamond hoop Do. and one mourning ring) The remainder of Miss Johnstons Jewels are as follows. one Mother of Pearl Snuff box Sett in Gold one Gold Girdle Buckle one Bristol Stone Do. Sett in Silver, one Small Picture Sett in Gold. The Gold Repeating Watch Sent to Scotland agreeable to Will to Mrs. Ferrior.

What articles were for the use of the family are not Sett down In the Inventory as not advised usual or necessary no accot. was taken of these things, therefore the particulars not Remembered as Inconsiderable excepting about one hhd. & a half of West India and not quite one hhd. of Jamaica Rum.————

The Chapel plate 2 Silver flaggons 1 Silver Cup two Silver Salvers not included in the Inventory

JNO. RUTHERFURD
FRANCES RUTHERFURD.

NORTH CAROLINA, ss.

John Rutherfurd Esqr. and Frances his Spouse severaly make oath on the holy Evangelists that the foregoing is a just and true Inventory of the Estate the late Gabriel Johnston Esqr taken as exactly as the Situation of the Estate would permit and that there is not to the best of their knowledge any material omission to the prejudice of any party

Sworn Feb 20th 1756 before me
JA MURRAY J. S. C.

(The following affidavit is to a former Inventory, of which the above Inventory is an exact copy.)

NORTH CAROLINA ss.

John Rutherfurd Esqr for and in behalf of Frances Johnston (?) the Executrix of the last Will & Testament of His late Excellency Gabriel Johnston Esqr. deced maketh Oath that the within & above, to the best of His this Deponents knowledge & belief contains a just and true Inventory of all & Singular the Goods & Chattels of the said deced

JNO. RUTHERFURD

Sworn the 29th day of July Anno Domini 1754 & filed in my Office
JA MURRAY Sec.

Accot. of Lands left by Will To Miss Penelope Johnston his Daughter.

Counties

County	Description	Acres
Bertie	Eden house planta.	900
	Back of Do. Salmond Creek.	2,000
Northampton	Mount Galland planta.	560
	Lovicks Island.	640
Edgecomb	Lovicks field.	4,500
Craven	Mouth of Swifts Creek (disputed)	640
Granville	Fishing Creek.	3,200

12,440

Northampton	Small Island opposite to Mount Galland planta.	154 Acres

12,594

County	Description	Acres
Bladen	To Sam'l & John Johnston's.	7,654
Craven	To Henry Johnston.	1,000
	To Carolina Johnston.	988
	To Penelope Johnston.	450
	To Mrs. Johnston now Mrs. Rutherfurd	
Tyrrel	Conahoe old feildes.	855
Granville	Possum Quarter.	1,250
	Salmond Creek I believe it is.	320

2,425

25,111

In all About twenty five thousand one hundred & Eleven Acres of land Left to the above named persons——

Accot. of the Rights & Credits of the late Gabriel Johnston Esqr. not included in a former Inventory Given in to the Secretary's Office.

10,439½ Acres of Land in Orange, Bladen & New Hanover Counties to be disposed of by Will 200 acres more in New Hanover County for which Mr. Saml. Johnston Sayes he made a deed to the late Govr.— no Such deed has yet appeared

1 Lott in Newbern Disputed

Due by the Crown to the late Govr.	13,462.19.2
by Do. in part of the late Chief Justice Smith's Salary.	251.5.0
Two Notes of the late Robert Forsters bbls ?.	7.16.0
Jno. Tinnings Note.	7.00.0
Benjn. Wynn Clk of Edgecomb.	6.15.0
Wm. Ormond Clk of Beaufort.	6.00.0
Stephen Cade Clk of——.	8.00.0
Thos. Robeson Clk of Bladen.	60.00.0
Due on two Patents.	.10.0
by Edwd. Underhill P Note.	16.00.0

By the late Nathl. Rice's Estate Sum unknown
By Patents in the Secretary's office unknown
By Clks of the different Counties unknown

13,826.05.2

By james Abercrombie Esqr of London to be applied towards Recovery of Arrears of Salary P his Accot.	114.06.0

13,940.11.2

In all When Reced the Sum of thirteen thousand Nine hundred & forty pounds 11.2 Str. money. besides the above unknown Sums.

JNO. RUTHERFURD.

The above Inventory of the late Govr. Johnston's Credits was given in Sepr 28th 1754 by John Rutherfurd Esqr upon Oath before me
JA MURRAY Sec

INVENTORY of the Estate of William Kennon deceased this 8th of
   Octbr: 1777

Schooner Nancy, Lumber, Staves, Sloop Robert, Sloop Sally, Brigantine Hector, Schooner Dispatch, ½ of the Brigantine Dobbs, ½ of the Brigg Sally, 1/3 of the Brigg Mariane, 1/3 of the Sloop Caswell, 14 Horses & Mares, one Coach, one Phaeton, one Chariot, one Chair, 2 Waggons, Severall refuse Store Goods, 1000 Bushels Salt (Supposed) 1 Carpett, 1 doz Chairs, 4 Mahogany Tables, 6 Looking Glasses, 2 Setts tea china, 9 Windsor Chairs, 1 Castor, 2 Cups,—? Waiters, 4 plated Candlesticks, 1 doz Spoons, Almost 2 Setts of table china, 6 Beds, 5 Bedsteads, 12 pair Sheets, 7 Table cloths, 3 pair Curtains, 3 Pair Musquito Nets, 12 Pillow Cases,   In Bills drawn by the President of Charleston to the amou of— 8584 Dollars
In other money and Notes about 600 Dollars
   The above is en Inventory of the forementioned Estate as far as can be at present ascertained, there shall be an exact Inventory of the remainder made as soon a possible by me.
PRISCILLA KENNON Administratricks

Sworen to before me this 8th Day
Octr. 1777
   WM. PURVIANCE J. P.

INVENTORY of the Goods and Chattels, Rights and Credits of Pierre
   Le Blanc late of Brunswick deceased at the Time of his Death on the 9th of August 1766 taken by the Administrator (Fountain Etwin) to said Estate.

Proclamation Money & Specie £4—2 (Four Pounds & two Pence)
a Silver Watch with two seals and a Key
a Book of Accounts, a Pocket Book and Sundry Papers
an Hair Trunk with Padlock & Key, containing the following

Cloaths

A Coat and Waistcoat, Second Mourning Cloth, trimmed
Coat and Breeches, Silk and Worsted, brown Colour
Do. and   Do   Brown Cloth
Two Frocks, One Waistcoat & 2 pr. of Breeches (all Fustian)
a Waistcoat, Red Cloth; another, Black Silk knit
a Pair of Red Stocking Breeches
   Do   Black   Do   Do
   Do   Buff   Do   Do
   Do   Leather   Do
a Pair of Boots, 5 pr. of Old Shoes, One pr. Shoe Buckles, One Hat,
Two Razors and a Case, an old Gold Hat Lace with Loop,
a pr. of red Worsted Garters, Four Old Black Cravats, a String of Black Beads, an Ink Stand, 14 White Metal breast Buttons
a little White Thread & Black Worsted, a small Piece of Fustian

Linnen

Twenty Shirts (most of them very bad)
Seventeen Stocks (Do   )
4 Linnen Waistcoats
9 Handkerchiefs
16 Pair of Stockings, (most of them very bad)
12 Linnen Night Caps
a Pair of Check Linnen Bags; another Check Linnen Bag

Books,

Histoires francoises, Gallantes & Comiques
Les Vrayes Centuries & Propheties de Maitre Michel Nostra Damus
a French Prayer Book
2 Volumes, Comte de Warwick
a Grey Gelding, Bridle & Saddle, and a Pair of Spurs

Credits

Due from His Excellency Governor Tryon for Wages to the 9th Aug 1766 the Sum of Thirty Seven Pounds fifteen Shillings & Eight Pence Sterling, Say £ 37, 15, 8 Sterling
Newbern the 16th December 1766

FOUNTN ETWIN Adminr.

sworn before me the 17th December 1766
JAS HASELL Csc

AN INVENTORY of the Goods and Chattels of Mr. Richard Lovett Late of Craven County Deceased that came to the hands of the Admrs taken and given in by John Starkey one of the Said Admrs.

To Wit Negroes

Lamrick, Perro, Stepney, Dublin, Peter, Jackson, Casar } Men 7

Moll, Hannah } Women 2

Essex, Nimrod, Perthena, Quash } Children 4

In all 13 Negroes

Horses Black, Gray, Hard bargin, Fly } in all 4 Horses

Mairs in the Woods not known
Catle 5 Cows, 4 Yarlings, 3 Calves } 12 in all

What Catle in the woods not known
Hogs—3 Sows and Pigs and some in the Woods not known
1 Ox at Doctr Bryans
1 Ox Cart and Chain at Mis Harrolls
1 Tar kil old Cart and Pott in the Woods 99 Tar Barrells
1 Hand mill in the Woods
Some Plantation tools as in the Acct of Sales 5 hoes 2 axes 1 Drawknives only
1 Chair and Harness
5 Leather Chairs
1 Small Desk
3 Tables
3 Iron Potts and Hooks
5 Do Skillets
1 Frying Pan
2 Iron Dogs
1 Do Trefoot
Some Woodn Ware
Do Earthen Wares as Pr Sales
Do Glasses Tumbler only
2 Table Cloths
Some Wearing Cloths as by Sales Coat and Breeches only
Also Books as by Do 21 Books in all
3 Pewter Dishes 6 Plates 5 Spoons

INVENTORIES. 509

3 Feather Boxes and Furniture
1 Cow and Yarling at Mr. McCubbins's
¾ Parts of Scooner Gabriel
Some old Hewd Logs Brick
and other Small things as by Acct: of Sales
¾ of 80 foot Red Cedar
1/6 of a Nett for Fishing
Debts Received in all £33.03.10 Procln.

An Acct what moneys are not Collected belonging to Mr Lovetts Estate this 7th Janry 1754

	£ s. d.
Samuel Ratcliff and others for Negro Dublin Bon......	21.05.0
Samuel McCubbins for Cow and Yarling..............	1.10.0
Arthur Johnston for Negro Essex part...............	10.13.6
Edward Franks part of Note given for Vendue........	3.00.0
George Kornagee part of Note for Vendue............	29.15.8
Nathan Smith for Wm Brices Estate note for Vendue..	39.00.0

505.04.2 in all

I am told of five pair of milstone, left at Core Sound found but not come to hand yet

Also one Abram Sheperd owns he is in debt two dollars also a small debt or two I have warranted for not not determined yet

An Inventory of the Goods and Chattels of Richard Lovett of Craven County Deceased and the Prices they were sold at Publick Vendue Septr 21st and October 2d 1752 By John Davis Vendue Master in order to Enable Elias Legardiere and John Starkey Surviving Admrs: to pay the Deceased just Debts.

To Wit

To John Kilbee	£ s.	
a Horse and Chair	20.10	
Negro Lemrick	66.00	
		86.10.0
Charles Adams		
Black Horse	16.10	
Small Cart	1.12	
Negro Stepney	50.	
Negro Child	18.	
2 Books	.08.06	
Iron Pot	.04.08	
		86.15.2
Edward Griffith		
Bay Horse	5.00.00	
Negro Casar	22.	
		27.
Terimy Veal		
A Bay Horse	3.15	
Negro Woman and Child	63.00	
		66.15.0
Elias Legardiere		
¾ of a Scooner	257.00	
Boys Bed and Bedstead	1.10	
Iron of hand Screw	.14	
Iron Pot	.12	
2 Books	.08.06	
12 Pin Stocks	.04	
		260.08.06

John Clatherall		
Negro Peter	50.10	
Negro Moll	41	
		91.10
Stephen Lee		
Negro Boy Nimrod	30	
		648.18.08
Brought Over		648.18.08
Thomas Lovick		
Negro Peroe	51.00.00	
Arthur Johnston		
Negroe Essex	35.10	
William Brice		
Negro Ralph	64	
John Bryan		
Ox and Yoke	2.12.00	
Cart and Chain	1.17	
		4.09.00
Samuel McCubbins		
Cow and Yarling		1.10.00
Edward Franks		
A Tar Kiln	8.15	
Hand Mill	0.04.04	
5 Leather Chairs	2.10	
		11.09.04
Joseph Balch		
Small Iron Pot		03.00
Joseph Caruthers		
8 Books	0.17.04	
5 Hoes 2 Axes & 1 Drawknive	0.07.00	
A Parcell Brick	1.02.00	
		2.06.04
George Kernegee		
99 Tar Barrells	4.19	
Negro Jackson	57.	
1 Book	.19	
12 Cattle at Home	6.	
Cattle in Woods unknown	6.	
Right to Mares in Woods	2.	
Hogs unknown	3.	
Small Dish	.18.06	
A Table	1.12.06	
Bed and Furniture	1.00.04	
3 Pewter Dishes } 6 Plates 5 Spoons }	1.00.04	
Two Square Tables	5.	
Pair Iron Dogs	6.06	
Skillet & frying } Pan Trypod }	2.06	
Coat and Breeches	4.	
Table Cloth 3 Knives & forks	.03	
Glass Tumbler	.01.08	
		89.15.08
Totall		909.02.00

INVENTORIES.

Brought Over		£909.02.00
John Starkey		
Bed and Furniture	4.06	
8 Books	2.11.10	
	6.17.10	
Negro Dublin Sold at Johnston Court		21.05.00
John Snead		
1/6 Part of Nett	.17.02	
Mr. Kilbee		
¾ of 80 Foot Red Cedar	2	
Totall of things Sold	£940.02.00	
Debts Received		
From Doctr Bryan for Negroes work	7.02.10½	
From Capt Spers	24.01	
From John Williams	2.	
Whole of Debt	33.03.10½	
Amount of whole	£ 973.05.10½	

N B it is sayd there is 5 pair of Mill Stones left at Core Sound but not come to hand

Also Abram Shepard owns he owes two Dollars and one or two Small Debts of hand Warranted for but not Determined yet

An Acct of Titles to Land Belonging to Mr Lovetts Estate Delivered to Mr. Elias Legardiere to keep he having Thomas the Eldest Son.

To Wit A Patent for 66 Acres on Trent River joyning John Murpheys
Do for 130 Do on Do Joyning the Land he formerly lived upon
Do for 320 Do on Acron Branch between Nuce and Trent River
a Deed from John Slocumb for 640 Acres on Contentay Creeks also the Patent
Do from Martin Franks for 640 Acres Atkins up Nues sold for the use of the Publick also the Patent and Mortgage for the Same
Do from John Becton and Wife for 200 Acres on Trent where Mr. Lovett Died
Also Deed from Adam Moore to George Motts for some Land
Deed from James Wimble to Widw Harwood for Lott in Wilmington No 132
Deed for Lot in Newbern No 45
A Bundle of Papers and Deeds for 6 Lotts in Brunswick
Warrant for 640 Acres on White oak

An Acct. how the said Estate has been Administred and pay'd away to the Several Creditors following as by Vouchers by John Starkey Admr

Paid to Doctr Robert Moor Acct........	10.02.04	
John Foster Acct....................	14.07.06	
Fountain and Davis Acct..............	24.08.01	
John Williams Acct...................	2.11.04	
Richard Cogdalde Acct................	13.10.08	
Richard Casewells Acct...............	5.01.01	
Lawrence Donolson Acct..............	8.11.01	
James Davis Acct.....................	1.09.08	
Doctr. Henry Heylin Acct.............	2.03.06¾	
John Starkey Bond...................	58.	
		140.05.03¾

Ebenezer Young Bond	32.00.08	
William Wicklife Bond	39.08.00	
William Wicklife Acct	1.13.00	
Edward Griffith Bond	46.06.01½	
Mrs. Mary Moor Bond	30.13.04	
John Kilbee Acct	87.02.06	
William Coale Acct	2.09.08	
Rice and Company Acct	8.03.02	
John Grandine Bond	3.09.03½	
Revell Monroe Acct	17.02.00	
		268.07.09
David Smith Note	4.16.06	
George Minot Note	7.01.09	
John Grandins Note	8.14.½	
James Wilnot Acct	1.00.05	
James Craven Note	1.15.10	
Ann Needland Acct:	2.00.08	
Sheriff for Taxes	4.12	
Charles Adams Acct:	18.05	
Edward Franks Acct	4.18.	
John Leat Acct Signed	14.07.10	
		67.12.½
Stephen Lee Acct	10.06.06	
Wilkins and Wards Note	3.06.08	
George Johnstons Acct	11.17.04	
Arthur Johnstons Acct:	10.05.	
Francis Coddingtons Acct:	3.13.10	
Joyn Clatherall Note	19.14.05	
		59.03.09
Total	£	535.08.10¼
Brought over		535.08.10¼
William Nicholsons Acct & Note	3.04.06	
John Stephensons Acct:	8.03.09½	
John Fonville Acct:	2.02.08	
Mr. Samuel Johnstons Acct	6.13.04	
Doctr Francis Stringer Award	13.17.08	
Ann Higgens Act:	2	
Capt. Beaton Portage Bill paid	26.18.00	
David Bumpas Acct Sign'd	4.17.10	
Samuel Cornelle Acct	15.00.09	
Mrs. Mary Moors Note	8.11.06	
		91.10.—½
Elias Legardiere Acct:	38.05.	
Williams and Company Acct	3.05.10	
Do for Burial and for Estate	30.16.09	
Joseph Baleh Estate Acct	107.18.03½	
Widdow Pearsons Note	6.18.08	
Henry Chew Acct	4.06.08	
Saml Chadwicks Estate note	6.13.04	
Joseph Falford Junr Acct	3.17.01	
Robert Hogs Estate Acct	2.04.08	
Mr Phillips New York Acct	60	
		264.06.03½
Donolson expences Vendue	3.19.00	
Charles Adams 2 Vendue	.12	
Fees for Patents in Office	4.16.	
Mr Jno Davis as Vendue Master	5	
Fees Letters and Court fees	1.06.08	

Freight of Negro Ralph from West Indies.	1.15.10	
Charg and expense to Negro Dublin at Johnston Court......................	1.05.00	
My Forrages expenses and ——— very many times at Newbern and Johnston and elsewhere.......................	6	
Mr Swann 3 fees for Suit brought against the Estate..........................	6	30.14.06
	Total £	921.19.08¼
Whole Pay'd to Deter. 1753............	921.19.08½	
Amount of the Sale and some Debts Received..........................	973.05.10½	
In hand when all is Collected..........	51.06.20¼	
To 1 fee paid Mr Swann Estate Agt Arthur Johnston.....................	2	

More Debts I have the Acct: but not yet payd because there are Suit against Estate Depending to a Large Sum

John Holden N. Y. Acct................	8.08.
Mr Willm Heretage Acct................	5.01.01½
Also for Mr Roberts Estate............	4.08.
Stephen Dare Acct.....................	6.10.02
Nathan Yeoman about.................	11.
William Davis says....................	9.10.09
Doctr Duncan says....................	26.06.08
Frederick Keble says..................	7.18.11½
Zachary Fields says...................	20.13.04
John Isler says.......................	1.10.
Richard Canady......................	1.09.04
Danl Dupee he says...................	3.14.01
Thomas Braine N York................	33.07.00
some more tho not proved Totall £	139.17.05

N B of the £139.17.5 yet Claimed I have a deal of it not due so shall pay the most Equitable as far as the within Ballance will go when the Law Suits are ended

Querie should not some be retain'd to Defend any Suits that may come hereafter

N B in the within Acct no Commissions Charged nor Clerkships

NORTH CAROLINA BEAUFORT COUNTY Decr. ye 22d 1773

AN INVENTORY of the Personal Estate of John Maule Esqr Decd. Vizt. 35 negros a parcel of Cattle the number unknown a parcl of hogs the number unknown 44 head of Sheep Six horses Six feather Beds & furniture one Desk one case of flasks three Tables ten Chairs a parcel of puter five Iron pots 2pr. of fire tongs on shovel one frying pan one Loom and weaving gear one riding Chair one Copper Still one Cart and 3 pair wheels four Plows and several Axes and hoes the Exact number not known Some Coopers tools some Carpenters Ditto. two Chests a parcl of China a parcel of Delf ware parcel of stone Ditto pr. of hand Irons two guns some wearing Apparrel one hogshead of Rum a small Quantity of rum in another hogshd two hogshead with a small Quantity of molases in Each a parcel of salt Exact Quaty not known a parcel of Corn the Exact Quantity not known one half of a Schooner with her Rigging &c a small Quantity of Saw'd Lumber at the Saw mill, one womans saddle two mens Do 2 Bridles a small parcel of Books 2 Tea Kettles half Dozn Silver Tea spoons pr. Silver tongs a parcel Chunk Bottles parcel Juggs five Barrs of Iron small Quantity of Powder in a Kegg one Silver watch Sixteen Shillings in Silver one hundred an twenty Seven Dollars & five half Johannas; one saddle housing

NORTH CAROLINA ss.

Moses Hare John Patten Reading Blount Junr. & Joseph Blount Executors of the last Will and Testament of John Maule deceased severally make Oath that the above account contains a true & perfect Inventory of the Goods & Chattels of the said John Maule come to the Hands custody power or possession of them these Deponents any or either of them.

READING BLOUNT JUNR
JOSEPH BLOUNT
MOSES HARE
JOHN PATTEN

Sworn this 16th day of Febry 1774 Before me
 JO. MARTIN

A TRUE AND PERFECT INVENTORY of all the goods, and Chattles, Rights and Credits, that were of James Milner, Esqr. deceased, So far as they have come into the Hands or Possession of Joseph Montfont and Andrew Miller Executors of the said James———Vizt.

One Fosters Crown Law, 1 Burrows Reports, 1 Wilsons Reports, 1 Hales Pleas of the Crown, 1 Gilberts C. Pleas, 1 Elements of Criticism, 1 Burke on the Sublime, 1 Voltairs Essay on Crimes & Punishments, 1 Builders Pocket Treasure, 1 Thompsons Works, Money found in the House £ 157,11,8 Currency of No Carolina, 1 Powdering Machine, 1 Set of Curting Irons, 1 Negro Boy named Bob, 1 Folding Screen, 1 Memorandum Book, 1 Clarinda Cathcart, 1 Pair of Shoes, 1 Portmanteau, 1 Negro Woman named Ester, 1 Horse Bald Eagle, 1 Horse Young Black, 1 Grey Horse, 1 Pair of Pistols, 1 Magazine Pistol, 1 old Cart, 1 Gallon of Wine, money found in the House £ 17,14,1 Currency as above, 1 Memorandum Book, 3 Gallons Rum, 1 Fire Screen, 1 Negro Man named Jamaica, 1 Negro Boy named Phil, 2 Spades, 10 Sickles, 1 Cheselden's Anatomy, 1 Tytlers Enquiry, 1 Fordyces Sermons, 1 Voltairs Philosophy, 3 Sticks of Black Wax, 1 Pair White Silk Breeches, 3 Pair Russia drill Breeches, 3 Pair of Shoes, 6 Stamped Handkerchiefs, 6 Pair Thread Stockings, 1 Pair Raw Silk Stockings, 3 Pair fine white Silk Stockings, 1 Jacobs law dictionary, 1 Attorney's Practice C. C. Pleas, 1 Attorney's Practice C. K. Bench, 1 Every man his own Lawyer, 1 Attorney's Pocket Book, 1 Attorney's Practice Epitomized, 1 Rules of Pleading, 1 Reflections on the Study of the Law, 1 Mairs Bookkeeping, 1 Smelling Bottle, 1 Hair Pin, 1 Negro Woman named Susan, 1 Lawyers Gown, 2 Spades, 1 Iron Pot 1 Bason, 18 Bottles of Arrack, 2 Grubbing Hows, 2 Plew Hows, 1 Lock, 3 Grubbing Hows, 2 Grubbing Hows, 2 Weeding Hows, 2 Axes, 2 Weeding Hows, 4 Axes, 2 Iron Wedges, 2 Pair Sheep Shears, 9 Hogs, 19 Pigs, 1000 lbs of Fodder, 2 Weeding Hows, 1 Cross Cut Saw, 5 Barrels of Corn, ½ a Bushel of choice Pease, 2 Weeding Hows, 2 Weeding Hows, 1 Hand Saw, 1 drawing Knife, 1 Frow, 1 Gouge, 1 Chissel, 1 Stone Jug, 1 Grindstone, 1 Red Cow, 1 Yearling, 1 Wide Horn Cow & Calf, 1 Brinded Cow & Yearling, 1 Red Cow white Face, 1 Lock, 1 Sithe, 1 File, 1 Rake, 1 Bridle, 2 Bells, 1 Garden Line, 18 Barrels of Corn, 6 Barrels of Corn, 1 Table, 8¾ Bushels of Wheat, 7½ Bushels of Pease, 10 Barrels of Corn, 4 Barrels of Corn, 1 Bushel of Pease, 500 lbs Fodder, 9 Sheep,——
Green Hill Plantation, 5 Barrels of Corn, 1 Fry pan, 1 Pail, 1 Tub, 3 Bushels of Pease, 1 Brinded pied Cow & Calf, 1 Negro Woman named Sarah

INVENTORIES.   515

with her 4 Children, 5 Bushels of Pease, 90000 Bricks, A Negro Man named Squire & his Wife deb, 1 negro lad named Sam, 1 mulatto Girl named Nancy, 1 negro Man named Tom & his Wife Phebe, 5 Negroes & negress's, Will, Pat, Sam Psilla & Sally, 1 Mare and 1 Colt, 1 Historical Law Tracts, 1 Sorrel Horse, 1 Negro Man named Jacob, 1 Mulatto Lad named Aaron, 1 Horse named old Black, one Horse named Slim Black, 1 Horse named Blaze Black, 1 Horse named pacing Bay, 1 Horse named Buffelo, 1 Black Horse named unlucky, 1 Muses delight, 1 Fools Works, 1 Don Quixote, 1 Phoedrus, 1 Vicar of Wakefield, 1 Sermonis Mewrsic, 1 Musical miscellany, 1 Musick Book, 1 Pair of Stockings, 1 Chain Ring, 1 Pair of Gloves, 1 Comb, 1 Memorandum Book, 9 Small Books, 15 Prints, 3 Blank Books, 1 Set Mathematical Instruments, 1 German Flute, 5 Musick Books, 1 Spy Glass, 1 Muroscope & Apparatus, 1 Magnet, 1 Prism Glass, 1 Camera Obscura, 1 Solar Telescope &c. 1 diagonal Machine, 1 Political Essays, 1 dictionary of Arts & Sciences, 1 Annual Register from 1758 to 1770, 1 Clio & Euterpe, 1 New dispensatory, 25 Volumes of the Critical Review to 1768, 1 Johnston's Dictionary, 1 Small vocabulary, 1 Quincey's Elements of Physick, 1 Mackenzie on Health, 1 Swifts Works, 1 Beauties of History, 1 Tristram Strandy, 1 Humes Essay on Several Subjects, 1 Armstrongs Miscellanies, 1 Yoricks Sermons, 1 Cambray's dialogue, 1 Man after Gods own Heart, 1 Portmanteau Trunk, 1 Observations on Gardening, 1 Indentured Servant named Jno. Chavis, 1 Laws of No Carolina to 1765, 3 Blank Books, 4½ Quire of Bonds, Bill & Indentures, 4 Quires declarations, 1 Miller's Gardners dictionary, 1 Adventures of a Guinea, 1 Tissot on Health, 1 Wyld's Art of Surveying, 1 Effusions of Friendship, 1 Ferguson on Civil Society, 1 Thompsons Seasons, 1 Churchills Works, 1 pair of dice, 2 Books Gold Leaf, 1 Small Flute, 1 Celestial & Terrestrial Globe, 1 Prism Glass, 1 Bureau, 1 Walnut Book Case, 1 Mahogany Folding Table, 2 large Walnut Tables, 1 Walnut Folding Table, 1 Walnut dressing Table, 1 Hair Bottom Chair, 6 Mahogany Hair Bottom Chairs, 6 Hair Bottom Walnut Chairs, 1 dressing Glass, 1 Walnut Washing Stand, 15 Copper plate Pictures in Frames, 1 Back Gammon Table, Box & dice, 1 Whip, 3 Pair Stockings, 3 Brass Knob Locks, 1 Whip, 1 Piece Leading Line, 1 Cartridge Box, Some Rope & Twine, 22 Yards of, Tweels, Some Buttons & Button Moulds, 1 Piece Blue Stroud, 1 Set Black Buckles, 1 Pair shoe Pincers, 1 Sithe, 1 dwelling House Out Houses in which Mr. Milner lived at Halifax with the Severel Lots thereunto belonging, that is to say Lot No 16. 17. 18. 38. 39. 57 & 58 and 4 Acres of Land, 1 Corderius, 1 Etwee Case 1 Knife, 1 Fine Knife, 1 Ink Stand, 1 Knife, 3 Pair Stockings, 1 Table 3 Yds Cloth & Trimmings 1 Grindstone & Screw, 1 Vernons Cases, 1 Hawkins's C. Pleas, 1 Cunninghams Law dictionary, 1 Woods Institutes, 1 Abridgt. Cases in Equity, 1 Bacons Abridgt. of the Law, 1 Bunburys Reports, 1 Viners Evidence, 1 Hardurick's Cases, 1 Comyn's digest, 1 Peere Williams Reports, 1 Bernadistons Reports K. B. Principles of Equity, 1 Crokes Reports, 1 Kelynge's Reports, 1 Atkyns's Report of Cases, 1 Modern Reports, 1 Vezey's Cases, 1 Sir William Jones's Reports, 1 Rastells Entries, 1 Cokes Reports, 1 Jacobs Law dictionary, 1 Lillies Conveyance, 1 Levinzs Reports, 1 Cokeen Littleton, 1 Lillies Entries, 1 Vincer's Abridgment, 1 Swinburn of Wills, 1 Barlows Justice, 1 Tremaine's Pleas of the Croin, 1 Lilly's Register, 1 Repertorium Juridicum, 1 Fitz gibbons's Reports, 1 Rudiments of Law & Equity, 1 Kebles Reports & Table, 1 Kebles Reports & Table, 1 Raymonds Reports, 1 Saunders's ditto, 1 Salkelds ditto, 1 Carthews ditto, 1 Stranges ditto, 1 Registrum Brevium, 1 Precedents in Chancery, 1 Comyn's Reports, 1 Brownlows Entries, 1 Jones's Reports, 1 Yelvertons Reports, 1 Bulstrodes Reports, 1 Wingates Maxims, 1 Blackstones Commentaries, 1 Observations on the Statutes, 1 Statues at large Ruff head, 1 Sheppards. G. abridgt. 1 Pleader, 1 Brevia Judiciala, 1 Orphans Legacy, 1 Burns Ecclesiastical Law, 1 Blackstones Law Tracts, 1 Burns Parish Officer, 1 Barnes's Practice, 1 Hales Crown Pleas &c. 1 Wentworth of Executors,

NORTH CAROLINA WILLS.

1 Law of Evidence, 1 Gilberts Exchequer, 1 Law of Uses & Trusts, 1 Law of Tenures, 1 Treatise on distresses, 1 Cokes Reports, 1 Jacobs Conveyancer, 1 Instructor Clericalis, 1 Laws of the Admiralty, 1 Instituteo Legalis, 1 Morgans Pleader, 1 Attorneys Practice, C. C. Pleas, 1 Attorney Practice C. K. Bench, 1 Crown-Circle Companion, 1 Officeum Clerici Pacis, 1 Astrys Charge, 1 Hawkins's Abridgt. 1 Law of Exchange, 1 Harrison's Practice Chancery, 1 Law of Securities, 1 English Pleader, 1 Doctrine of demurrers, 1 Trials per Pais, 1 Law of Inheritance, 1 Praxis Almae, 1 Crouches Customs, 1 Copious Index to the Law, 1 Clerks Associate, 1 Gilberts Reports, 1 Maxims of Equity, 1 Cases in Chancery, 1 Formulae, Bene, Placetandi, 1 Moores Reports, 1 Gilberts Law of devises, 1 Clerks Manuel, 1 Hawkins Abridgt. of Coke, 1 Andrews Reports, 1 Raymonds Reports, 1 Nelsons Lutuyche, 1 Modern Entrees, 1 Cays Abridgt. 1 Hobarts Reports, 1 Ventrees ditto, 1 Common Law Common placed, 1 Vaughans Reports, 1 Blackstones Commentaries, 1 Brownlows Reports, 1 Frederican Code, 1 Gilberts Cases in Law, 1 Doctor & Student, 1 Jacobs Statute Law Common placed, 1 Rules of Practice, 1 Essay for Gen. Regulations of the Law, 1 Attorney's Pocket Companion, 1 ditto, 1 Attorneys Pocket Book, 1 Woods civil Law, 1 Kelyng, Charles 2d. 1 Hales Natura Brevium, 1 Spirit of Laws, 1 Erskins Institutes, 1 Practice in Chancery, 1 Practical Register, 1 Virginia Laws, 1 Hales of Parliament, 1 Judical Authority of the Master of the Rolls, 1 Bacon's Law Tracts, 1 Impartial Lawyer, 1 Cursons Compendium, 1 Law of Ejectment, 1 Law of Executions, 1 Law of Evidence, 1 Lawyers Office, 1 British Antiquities, 1 Cases in Equity, Talbots Time 1 Jacobs Treatise of Laws, 1 Finches Common Law, 1 Justices Case Law 1 Noys Reports, 1 Young Lawyers Recreation, 1 Virginia Laws, 1 Practical Part of the Law, 1 Bohun's English Lawyer, 1 Wood of Civil Laws, 1 Hales of Parlements, 1 Lawyers Magazine, 1 Hales History of the Common Law, 1 Virginia Laws, 1 Cerpus, Juris Civile's, 1 Jacobs Law dictionary, 1 Terms of Law 1 Noy's Maxims, 1 Law of Covenents, 1 Laws of No Carolina to 1752, One Cookes Reports & Cases & Rules C. Pleas, 1 Register Common Pleas, 1 Law Quibbles, 1 Students Companion, 1 Analysis of the Laws of England, 1 Dyers Reports, 1 Virginia Justice, 4 Blank Books, 7 ditto, 1 Ink Stand, 1 Pen Knife, 1 Parcel of Musick 1 ditto, 4 Prints, 1 Pair of Shoes, 1 Bridle, 3 Sursingles, 1 Walking Stick, 1 Velvet Cap, 1 Pair black silk gloves, 1 Humes History of England, 1 Tom Browns Works, 1 Tom Jones's Works, 1 Memoirs of Several Ladies, 1 Bolingbroke on History, 1 Fordyces Sermons, 1 Rices art of Reading, 1 Aconomy of Human Life, 1 Fable of the Bees, 1 Turnbull on Education, 1 Williams's Gummery, 1 Cambray on Existence, 1 Huxham on the Air, 1 Meads Medical Precepts, 1 Parcel of Blank books &c. 1 Halshams Lectures, 1 Pair Celestial Hemispheres, 1 German Flute, 1 Hymn to the Creator, 3 Musick Books, 1 Bed Stead with Curtains, 1 dodsley's Fables, 2 Carpets, 1 Trunk, 1 Small Pistol, 5 Padlocks, 1 Saddle Bridle &c., 1 Piece of Trace Roop 2 5/8 Yds Satinet, 1 Shovel, 1 Poker, 1 Pr. Tongs, 1 Pair dog Irons, 1 Herveys Meditations, 1 Ignorant Philosopher, 1 Steths History, 1 Biblia Sacra, 1 Religious Philosopher, 1 Virgil, 1 Ovids Epistles, 1 Gauger, 1 Juvinel & Perseus's Satyrs, 1 Fusten, 1 Clarks Introduction, 1 Sallust, 1 Caesars Commentaries, 1 Court Calender, 1 Angler, 1 Beaver Hatt, 8 Quire of Paper, 1 Ream Paper, 8 Blank Books, 1 Ivory Memorandum Book, 1 Parcel of Playing Cards, 1 Bag of Triffles, 1 Eolian Harp & Maps, 2 Brushes, 1 Candle Box & Lanthern, 1 Bag of Trifles, 2 Curtains 7 Curtain Rods, 4 Window Curtains, 1 Chocolate Pot, 1 Window Curtain, 2 Presses, 1 Bed Stead with Curtains, 1 Close Stool Pan, 1 Cheese Toaster, 1 Coat, a Parcel of Brass Pins, 1 Walnut Bedstead, a Parcel of Large Nails, Some Window Glass, a Box of Old Iron, a Parcel of Barrels, a Parcel of Bricks, 2 Save alls, 1 Ball of Blacking, 18 Yds Callico, 1 Riding Chair & Harness, 1 Velvet Cap, 13 Pair Hinges, 4 Yds Black Persian, 1 Key Swivel, 2 Windsor Chairs, 1 Elemt's of Navigation, 1 floor Cloth, 1 Mahogany Writing Desk, 1 Garden Scraper, 1 Smiths

INVENTORIES. 517

Moral Sentiments, 1 Bakers Remarks, 1 description of Animals, 1 Fletcher of Salton's Works, 1 Charles 12th, one Instructions for young Ladies, 1 History of Philosophy, 2 Southern Hemisphers, 1 Common Flute, 3 Musick Books, 5 Ink Pots, 1 Pounce Box, 1 Ink Stand, 1 Sand Box, 1 Box of Red & White Wafers, 1 dum Waiter, 1 Rat Trap, 1 Fan, 3 Tortoise Shell Combs, 1 diamond Ring, 1 Fan, 1lb Hyson Tea, 1 Paste Necklace, 1 Pair of Stone Knee Buckles, 1 Gold hat Lace, Some Silver lace, 2 Snuff Boxes, 1 Whiplash, 1 Flower Pot, 1 Oil Hat Cover, Blanks, 1 Quire Marble Paper, 1 Box Fish & Counters, 1 Pair of Gloves, 2 Pair of Silk Stockings, 11 Caps, 23 Canisters, 1 Ink Stand, 1 Nocturnal, 1 Quadrant, Some Snuff, 2 Sets Quadrille Boxes & Fish, 3 Japan Waiters, 1 Extinguisher & 2 Snuffer Stands, 1 Case of Knives, 1 Tea Chest, 2 China Mugs, 1 Bag of Triffles, 1 Brass ℔ Weight a Parcel of Hat Pins, 1 Tea Kitchen, 1 Curtain, 2 Pair Bottle Sliders 2 Glass Sugar dishes, 1 Pine Table, 1 Tea Kettle Stand, 1 Air Pump, 1 Chest, 2 pairs Silver Candlesticks, 1 Trunk, 1 Shot Bag, 1 Powder Horn, a Parcel of Watch Strings, 1 Set of Pinch beck Buckles, Watering Pot, 1 Trussel, 1 Portmanteau, 1 Plew Hew, 1 Ax, 1 Pair Brass Candlesticks, 2 pair of Snuffers, 1 Pair of Spectacles & Case, 1 Masons Companion, 1 Johnston's dictionary, 1 Blank Book, 1 History of England, 1 Rule, 28 little Books Blank, 1 Sand Box, a Parcel of large Paper, 1 Ring, 1 ditto, 1 ditto, 1 Gold Broach, 1 ditto, 1 Pocket Book, 1 Book, 1 Powder horn, 2 pair Sleeve Buttons, 2 Ink Pots, Some Pencils & Trifles, 3 Pair of Stockings, 3 Bottle Sliders, 1 Brass Kettle, 1 Pattern for a Jacket, 1 Pattern drab Cloth, 2 pair of Stockings, 3 Trunks, 1 Pair of Pistols Shot Bag &c. 1 Rope & Twine, 7 Yds Jeans, 3 pair Nut Crackers, 1 Pair Pistol Holsters, 5 Broken Candlesticks, 4 Cakes of Blacking, 1 Hatchet, 1 Hammer, 1 Mattress, 1 Pillow, 1 Pair Blankets, 1 Grammar, 1 Collier's directory, 1 Clarks Attributes, a Parcel of Cut Paper, a Parcel of Quils, 1 Bed Stead with Curtains, 1 Fine Fan, 1 Pocket Book, 3 Knives, 2 Cork Screws, 2 Pair Scissors, some Watch Keys & a Ring, 4 Brushes, 1 Snuff Box, 1 Pearl ditto, 1 Quire of Marble Paper, Some Blotting Paper, 8 Towels, 1 Pair of Money Scales, 3 Money Weights, 1 Pair of plyers, 1 Bag of Trifles, some Pearl Barley, 1 Coffee Roaster, 1 China Bowl, 5 China Coffee Cups, 1 Press, 1 Cooler, 1 Fry Pan, 1 Griddle, 1 Trunk, 1 ditto, 1 Set Connoisseur, 1 Francis's Horace, 1 Seaches Light of Nature, 1 dodsleys Poems, 1 Hutchisons Philosophy, 1 Sherridans Lectures, 1 Blank Book, 1 Common place Book, 3 Blank Books, 1 Idler, 2 Blank Books, 1 Rude's Enquiry, 1 Laws of Virginia, 1 Morgans Phisico Theology, 35 Small Blank Books, 1 Rule, 1 Ream Quarto Paper, 1 Ream of Paper, 7 Stocks, ½ Ream Gilt Quarto, 1 Trunk, 1 Barometer, Thermometer, & Hydrometer, 2 Barometer Glasses, 1 Portmanteau, 3 Pair of Stockings, some Worsted Binding, 2 Pocket Books & Pen Cutter, 7 Shirts, 1 Bag, 1 Raven grey Coat, 1 Jacket & Breeches, 1 Pair of Boots 7 Rush Bottom Chairs, 1 Chair, 1 Kellys Scotch Proverbs, 1 Pair of Half Boots, 1 Whip, 2 Cases of Razors, Shaveing Implements, 1 Sithe, 1 Piece of Linen, 3 Yds ditto, 1 Stock Lock, 1 Pair Bellows, 1 Brush, Sundry Small Articles, 1 Churchills Works, 1 Brackens Farriery, 1 Essay on Husbandry, 1 Laws on Oratory, 1 Ray on the Creation, 1 System of Oratory, 1 Rollins Belle Lettres, 1 Knoxes Sermons, 1 Watts Logick 6 Vo. Select Plays, 1 Muschembrock's Philosophy, 1 Bacons Natural History, a Quantity of Plank & Scantling, 19 little Blank Books, 1 Rule, some Folio Post paper, 6 Books, 12 ditto, 12 ditto, a parcel of ditto, a Parcel of Scotch Magazines, a Parcel of Universal ditto, 1 Art of Preaching, 1 pair gold Sleeve Buttons, 1 Convex Glass, 1 Parcel of Triffles, 1 Box Shaving Powder, 1 House & Lot in Halifax No 56. 3 Comb Brushes, 1 Bayonet, $9\frac{5}{8}$ Yds linen, 1 dozen Packs of Cards, 1 Memorandum Book, 1 Bag of Trifles, 1 ditto, 4 Jugs, a Parcel of China, 6 Coffee Cups, 1 China Tea pot, 1 Japan Teaboard, 2 decanters, 1 ditto, 1 Westons Bookkeeping, 2 Windsor Curtains, 1 Pruning Chissel, Hook &c. 2 Sithes, 2 Reap hooks, 7 Cruppers & Whip lashes, 2 pair Straps, 2 Cruppers, 3 Girths, 1 Bridle, Whip lashes, 1 Farriers dictionary, 4 Curry

Combs, 3 Brushes, 3 Horse Combs, 1 Grubbing Ax, 1 Riding Belt, 1 Piece of Girth Web, 1 Pair Screwdees, 1 lb Crewel, 18 Yds of Blue & White Calico, Black Hat band, 2 Set pinch beck Buckles, 2 Pair of knee buckles, 1 Pair of Nail Cutters, 2 Silver Smiths Tools, 2 pair Chimney Brasses, 1 pair Pistol Holster, 1 Table Cloth, a Parcel of Metal Buttons, 1 Pair of dog Irons, 1 Shovel, 1 Pair Tongs, 1 Back Iron, 1 Tea Kettle, 1 Pair Curling Tongs, 1 pair Bellows, 2 Brushes, 1 Hand Bell, 1 Coopers Anatimy, 1 Brook's Practice 1 Brooks's Introduction, 1 Bible, 1 Prayer Book, 1 Spelling dictionary, 1 Prayer Book, 1 Frances's Horace, 1 Westminsters Jests, 1 Set Homes Plays, 1 Collection of Songs, 5 Small Blank Books, 1 Critical Spelling Book, 1 lock on Human Understanding, 1 Reflections on Education, 1 Juvinels Satyres, 1 Holmes Rhetorick, 1 Jones's Mathematicks, 1 Newtens Optics, 1 Everards Gauging, 1 Terences's Comedies, 1 Clarks Grotius, 1 Epictitus, 1 Horace, 1 Sallust, 1 Blank Book, 1 Pomfrets Poems, 1 Grotius de Vendate, 1 Etropheus, 1 Mairs Introduction, 1 Plume Volant, 5 Silver Tea Spoons, 1 Strainer & Tongs, 2 Snuff Boxes, 1 Pocket Compass, 5 Books, 4 Trifles, a parcel of broken Brass Cocks, 1 lb of Chalk, 1 Piece drum line, 3 Handkerchiefs, 1 dozen Whip lashes, 4 Coat Straps, 2 pair Window Curtains, 1 Calico Bed Cover, 1 Quins Jests, 1 Whip, 1 pair Brass Candlesticks, 1 Pair White Silk Gloves, 1 Silk Neck Cloth, 1 Theodolite with a Chain &c. 4 Windsor Chairs, 1 Kitchen's Map of Europe, 1 Stone's Mathematical Instruments, 1 Emerson's Astronomy, 1 James on Gardening, 1 Treatise on Agriculture, 1 Fergusons Astronomy, 1 Machiavels Works, 1 Stewarts Political Oconomy, 1 Umbrella, 1 Moores Fables, 1 Bacons Essays, 1 Friar Gerund, 1 Masons Poems, 1 drummonds Hisy. of Scotland, 1 Greys Hudibrass, 1 Emersons Mechanicks, 1 Shaftsbury's Characteresticks, 1 Smiths Optics, 1 Mustons Astronomy, 1 Conversation & Behaviour, 1 Palaso's Maxims Compass rectified, 1 Geographia Classica, 1 Fergusons Lectures, 1 Fine Gun, 1 Old laced Hat, 1 Powder horn, 4 Skins of Parchment, a parcel of Views & Prints, 1 Celestial hemisphere, 4 German flutes, 1 Fiddle Bow, 2 Musick Books, 3 ditto, 1 Camera Obscura & Prints, 2 Ink Pots & a square, 2 Pair of dice, 1 Ink Stand, 1 Box Wafers, 1 Bundle White Sheet Wafers, a Parcel of Gilt Paper, ditto, 1 Mahogany Writing table, 1 Bed Stead with Curtains, 12 Books, a Parcel of Latin Books, 1 pair of Slippers, 1 pair of Garters, 1 Hair Pin, 1 Knife, 1 Seal & phial, 1 Silver Punch Ladle, some Sewing Silk, 1 Button loop &c. 1 leather Snuff Box, 3 Purses, a parcel of Medals, 1 Ring dial, 1 Candle Shade, 1 pair Silk Breeches, 1 Suit of Livery, 1 Table Cover, a Parcel of Blanks, ditto, 1 Quire gilt marble paper, 1 parcel of paper, 1 Bevel, 1 Square, 6 Handkerchiefs, 6 New Shirts, 12 Stocks, 1 dark Lanthorn, Sundry Tipes, 1 Brass Pen, 1 pair dividers, 1 Magnet & Case, 1 Pair Money Scales, 1 dodgion & Case, 2 Curtains, 5 Castors, 1 Walnut Table, Some Silver Binding, 1 Whip, some Thread & Twist, 2 Tin Measures, 1 Grater, 3 Grass Sithes, 7 Yds Russia drill, 1 Hank of leading line, 1 Set of Pinch beck buckles, 1 Queens China Tea & Sugar Pot, 1 Parcel of Painted Room Paper, 5 Tiles, 1 Bullet Mould, Some lead, a piece of Pocket Fustain, 3 Padlocks, 1 Keg Containing a Variety of Iron & Brass, Some Screws, 1 Book, 1 Tweezer Case, 1 Cork Screw 2 Rings, 1 Surtout, a pair of Riding breeches, 1 Hussar Cloak, 2 pair of Stockings, 2 Aprons, a Riband & 1 Square, 1 Cooler, 1 Book, 1 Stone Jug, 1 Pocket Book, 1 Lot N 99, Granville Street Halifax, 1 Hammer, 1 pair Sheep Shears, 1 Saw, 1 Gimblet, Remnants of Cloth, 1 piece Swanskine, 2 Old Sadles, 1 Table Cloth, 3 Hinges, 2 Saw Sets, some old Carpet, 1 Blanket, 4 Pair Stockings, 4 Padlocks, 1 Academy of Complements, 1 Philpay's Fables, 1 Vol. Shinstone, 1 Guardian 1 Persian Tales, 1 Sheep Skin dressed, 3 Pieces Bed Tyck, 11 Window Bolts, 5 Brass Knob Locks, 1 Old laced Hat, 3 Thumb Latches a Parcel of Soals, 12 Yds of Jeans, 1 Scotch Almanack, 1 Cotton Velvet Coat & Breeches, 1 Coat, Jacket & Waiscoat, 1 Pair of Buckskins Gloves, 17 Stocks 1½ Yds Irish Sheeting, 1 Chest of drawers, 1 Prayer Book, 1 Pair of Blankets, 1 Pair

INVENTORIES. 519

Silk Mitts, Remnents of Cambrick, 1 Pair Silver Buckles, 3 Ink pots, 1 Silk Jacket & Nankeen Breeches, 1 Coat & WesCoat, 2 pair of Stockings, 1 Sugar Canister, 1 Coffee pot, 2 Jugs, 2 ditto, 4 ditto, 1 Canister, 3 Bottles, 1 Tea Board, 4 Plates, 1 dish, 6 China Cups & Saucers, 3 Cups & 4 Saucers, 1 Knife, 1℔ Wheted Brown Thread, 9 Gimblets, 2 Pair Silk Breeches, 2 Stamped Linen Handkerchiefs, 2 ditto, Some tobo. a Livery Lace, 1 Scrubing Brush, 3 paint Brushes, 1 Coffee pot, Some Vermilion, a Bag of Trifles, a Parcel of locks, some nails & Tacks, a Parcel of Oil & Paint, 1 Chocolate Pot, 1 Coffee Mill, 1 Ironing Box, 2 Clamps, 1 Funnel, 2 Bowls of Paint, 1 Table, 1 Cart, 1 Bottle Case, 1 Pair of Blankets, 1 piece of Sheeting, 1 Table Cloth, 1 Sugar Canister, 1 Stone Stock Buckle, a Parcel of Buttons, a Gauze Handkerchief, 2 pair Breeches, 2 pair drawers, 2 pair Stockings 2 handkfs, 2 ditto, 6 Towels, 5 China Cups & Saucers, 4 Cups, 3 China Saucers, 1 Bed Cover, 1 Pewter dish, 1 Tin Pan, Some odd Knives & Forks, 2 Vests, 1 pair drawers, 1 Green Coat, 3 Shirts, 1 Piece Buff Cloth, 2 Waistcoats, 2 pair Tongs, 1 Piece White Cloth, 1 Piece Flannel durant, 1 Piece White silk, 1 Pocket Book, 1 Knife, some Watch Strings, Parcel of Combs, a Coat & Jacket, 2 pair Breeches 1 Pair Gloves, a Pair Stockings, 1 Pair Bellows, 1 Box of Wafers, 2 pair Silk Stockings, 1 piece Shalloon, 1 Coat, 2 Vests, a Set of Pinchbeck Buckles, 6 Funnels, 1 Cheese Toaster, 1 Velvet Cap, 1 Rollins Ancient history, 1 Parsons Analogy, 1 Historical Dictionary, 1 Annual Register, 1 Lelands demosthene's, 1 Smith on Government, 1 Martins Philosophy, 1 Fergusons Institutes, 1 Letters to Married Women, 1 Voltaires War, 1 Fitzosborns Letters, 1 Addisons Works, 1 La Belle Assemblee, 1 Elements of the History of France, 1 Lovell, 1 Salmons Grammar, 1 Sterlings Virgil, 1 Gil Blas, 1 Map of the World, 1 Map of America 12 Wine Glasses, 1 Velvet Cap, 1 Pair white silk Gloves, 1 Shagreen Case & Tooth pick, 2 Bullet Moulds, 2 Fenders, 1 Feather Bed, 1 Bolster & Pillow, 9 Childrens Books, 1 Hoyle's Games, 1 Complete Gamster, 1 Fender, 1 Parcel of deeds, 1 Chess Board & Men, 1 Fine Hat, 2 pair Silk Garters, 1 Counterpane, 1 Websters Book keeping, 1 Pair Silk Stockings, 2 pair Scissor, 1 Green Coat, 1 Black Coat, 2 pair of Worsted Stockings, 2 Pair of Gloves, 3 China Bowls, 5 Japan Waiters, 10 Wine Glasses, 1 old Table, 3 Slates, 1 Fool of quality, 2 Fountain Pens, 1 Pencil, 1 Grindstone, 1 Fine Hat, 1 Knife, 4 Bottles Snuff, 1 Tea pot, 1 Sugar Dish, 1 Milk Pot, 2 Presses, 3 Pewter Ink Pots, 9 Masons Glasses, 8 Plates, 2 Spoons, 4 Knives, 7 Forks, 1 Pair Steelyards, 1 Shovel, 1 Pair Tongs, 1 Pair Bellows, 1 Candle Box & Lanthern, 3 Foils, 1 Ramsays Songs, 1 Blank Book, 3 Ink Pots, 1 Parcel of Screws, 1 Chair Bridle 1 Bag of Trifles, 6 Window Bolts, 1 Scale, 2 Spelling Books, 1 Monroes Anatomy, 1 Farmers Guide, 1 Letter Writer, 2 Town & Country Magazines for 1769 & 1770. 4 Vols. Newbery's Sciences, 1 Hattons Merchants Magazine, 1 Leyburns dialing 1 Flute, 1 Parcel of Musick, 1 ditto, 1 ditto, 1 ditto, Two Silver Bases, 6 Musick Books, 1 Box Black Wafers, 1 Ream Quarto Paper, 4 Knives, 1 Pair Silver buckles, 6 Silver tea Spoons, 1 pair silver Sugar Tongs, 3 Sleeve Buttons, 1 Grater, 4 Ink Pots, 1 Spectacle Pocket Glass, 1 Jacket & Breeches, 1 Pair Buckskin Gloves, 1 Pair Cotton ditto, 1 Pair Brass dividers, 2 Pair Spectacles, 1 Tobacco Box, 2 Hair Bags, 1 Cushion, 1 Pot, 2 Lead Canisters with Snuff, a Parcel of Queens China, 2 Bags of Trifles, 1 ditto, 1 ditto, One ½ ℔ Brass Weight, 4 Window Curtains, 7 Mason Glasses, a Parcel of Paper 17 Vols. Travels, 1 Pair of White silk Gloves, 1 Shovel, 1 Pair Tongs, 1 Pair White Silk Gloves, 1 Pair of money Scales, 1 Lock on human Understanding, 1 Shaftsburys Characteristicks, 1 Robertsons History of Scotland, 1 Gordons Accountant, 1 Cambray on Eloquence, 5 Musick Books, 1 Rosseau Eloisa, 1 Blacklocks Poems, 1 Letters from the north, 1 Pair of Pistols Key & Bullet Mould, 4 Irons for Sithes, 1 Key Swivel, 1 Shakespears Works, 1 Essay on Shakespears Learning, 1 Peregrine Pickle, 1 Book Stand, 1 Set Spectators, 1 Sentiments of Pamela, 1 Pair old Sheets, 1 Pair ditto, 1 Something new, 1 Tissot on Sedentary deseases, 1 Natural History, 1 History of England, 1 Art of

Speaking, 1 Dowglas on the Muscles, 12 lb Quick Silver, 1 Set Select Plays, 1 Cuns Euclid, 1 Borchave's Medicine, 1 State of Britain, 1 Sharps Surgery, 1 Court Plaister, 1 Method of Studying Medicine, 1 Le Cat on the Senses, 1 Lobs Compendium, 1 Pantheon, 1 Paths of Virtue, 1 Masons Companion, 1 Van Sweetens Abridgt. 1 Ledrans Surgery, 1 Parcel of Medicines, 7 Quire blue & blossom Paper, 1 Tully's Offices, 4 Musick Books, 1 Pocket Book, 1 Virginia Laws, 1 Pocket Book, 1 Knife, 1 Hair pin, 1 Rule, 1 Knife, 2 Pair Scissors, 1 Silver Seal & Chain, 1 Chain, 1 Seal, 1 Pr. Scissars, 1 door Stopper, 1 Lock, 1 Box of Rose Shells, Some Nitre & some nutmegs, 1 Gold Lace for a hat, 5½ Yds Gold Lace, 2 Snuff Boxes, 1 ditto, 1 Coat, 1 Pair Breeches, 1 Waistcoat, 1 Cloth Cloak, 1 Silk Vest, 1 Pair Breeches, 4 Pair of Leggings, a Parcel of White Gloves, 2 pair Stockings, 3 Shirts, 9 Towels 1 Pair Money Scales, a quantity of Rotten Stone, 2 Tooth Brushes, 2 Chamber Pots, 1 Pocket Microscope & Glass, 2 Canister of Snuff, 2 Blinds, 2 Brushes, 1 tea pot sugar dish etc., 5 decanters, 1 bag of trifles, 1 brass fender, 1 iron pot, 1 gold medal, 1 silver medal, 1 Seal, 1 Book, 1 Brush, 2 Bags Grass Seeds, Some Sulphur, 1 Pair Stirrup Irons, 1 Garden Scaper, 1 Cutting Box, 1 Cutting Knife, 1 Counterpane, 1 Pair dog Irons, 1 Shovel, 1 Pair of Tongs, 1 Pair ditto, 1 Pair dog Irons, 1 Poker, 1 Feather Bed, 1 Bolster, 1 Feather Bed, Bolster & Pillow, 1 Feather Bed, Bolster & Pillow, 1 Bed Stead with Curtains, 1 Set of Cups & Saucers, 1 Set of Coffee Cups, 1 China Bowl, 1 ditto, 1 ditto, 1 Pair dog Irons, 1 Shovel, 1 Pair Tongs, 1 Poker, 1 Shovel, 1 Poker, 1 Molls Atlas, 1 Youngs Night Thoughts, 1 Ainsworth Latin dictionary, 1 Bell, 1 Ruler, 1 History of England, 1 Maclaurins Algebra, 1 Sainte Bible, 1 Emmersons Fluctions, 1 Brightlands Grammar, 1 Telemaque, 1 French Grammar, 1 Pistol Mounted Hanger, 1 Fan & Case, 1 Pair silk Stockings, 1 Pair leggings, 3 Pair Stockings, 1 Silk Handkerchief, 1 Brush, 2 pair breeches, 1 Pair drawers, 1 Volo. Blackstone's Commentaries, 2 Parcels of Silk, 2 Yds Linen & some Buckram, 1 Ink Stand, 1 Small Flute, A Parcel of Fig Blue, 6 Leather bottom Chairs, 1 Lot & House in Halifax No. 50, One Lot in Halifax N 28, with the Stables thereunto belonging, 1 Box of Spermacete Candles, 1 Sand Box & Wafers, 1 Pair of Sheets, 1 Pair ditto & Pillow Case, 1 Fiddle & Bow, some Fiddle Strings, 1 Punch Ladle, 2 pair of Stockings, 32 Bottles Wine, 2 Coolers, 2 Glass Constables, 6 Beer Glasses, 5 Window Curtains with Rods, 1 Prayer Book, ½ lb Hyson tea, 1 Pair knee Buckles, 1 Pair Scissars, 1 Smelling Bottle, 1 Housewife & Thread &c., Some Remnants of Linen, 1 Raven Grey Coat, 2 Pair Breeches, 1 Pair ditto, 1 Jacket & Breeches, 1 Coat & Waiscoat, 2 Waiscoats, 1 Surtout, 2 Pair of Stockings, a Parcel of Paint & Pencils, 1 Sword Belt &c., 1 Prayer Book, 1 Old Beaver Hat, A Bag of Bullets, Shot Buttons &c. 1 Roderick Random, 1 Set Mallets Works, 1 Penknife, 1 Pair of Gloves, 1 Knife, 1 Dressing Table, 1 Bible, 1 Pestle & Mortar, 2 Queens China Mugs, 1 Turine, a Parcel of Queens China a Parcel of Nails, 3 Jugs, 8 Wine Glasses, one Tea Board, 1 Stewpan, 1 Stand, 1 How, 1 Snuff Box, 1 pair Blankets, 2 Table Cloths, 1 Phial Red Ink, 1 Box Wafers, 1 Coverlet, 1 Fan, 4 Caps a Breast Cloth &c. a Parcel of Queens China, 1 Book Stand, 1 Geographical dictionary, 1 New Italian Master, 1 Gays Fables, 1 Practical Geometry, 1 Tacitus 1 Simpsons Convick Sections, 1 Potters Mathematicks, 1 Gerrard on Taste, 1 Aristotles Ethics, 3 Pillows, 1 Pasts Comb, Some Remnants of Silk, 2 Ink Pots, Piece Non so pretty, a Broken Box of Pipes, 1 Towel, 1 Set of Cups & Sawcers, 1 Parcel of Queens China, 1 Piece of Huckaback, a Tea Board &c. 1 China Bowl, 12 Wine Glasses, 1 Pine Table, 1 Chaffing dish, 1 Popes Works, 2 plays, 1 Blank Leger, 1 Bellisarius, 1 Sidney Biddulph, 1 Steths History of Virginia, 1 Testament, 1 Ben Johnston's Tests, 1 Beaver Hat, 1 Old Hat, 1 Map of Great Britain & Ireland, 1 Silk Vest, 2 Striped Waistcoats, 4 Shirts, 2 Table Cloths, 1 Warming Pan, 4 Glass Tumblers, 1 Table Cloth, 1 Pair of Sheets, 1 Sharps Geometry, 1 Martins Trigonometry, 1 British Grammar, 1 Set Humes, Britain, 1 Barrows Euclid 1 Gordons

Grammar, 1 Shervins Fables, 1 Wards Mathematicks, 1 Martins Logarithms, 1 Parcel of Paper, 1 MalCombs Book keeping, 1 Wrights Arithmetick, 1 Simpsons Euclid, 1 Sacred Classicks, 1 Freeholder, 1 Wise Mans Grammar, 12 Copy Books, 1 Letter Writer, 1 Young Mans Companion, 1 Fishers Arithmetick, 1 Brookes Natural History, 1 Ink Pot, 2 Pounce Boxes, 7 Ink Powders, 1 Phial Red Ink, 1 Box of Wafers, 1 Bed Cover, 1 Bed Carpet, 1 Towel, 1 Pocket Book, 1 Knife, 1 ditto, 1 ditto, 1 Pair knee buckles, 1 Purse & Pocket, 1 Ring & Seal, Some Flints, a Snuff Box, 1 Silk Coat, 1 Vest, 1 Parcel of Blanks, 1 Case of Instruments, 3 Pair of Stockings, 2 Rulers, 2 Folders, 1 Ink Pot, 1 Parcel of Trifles, 1 Bag of Trifles, 2 Glass Constables, 2 decanters, 2 Salts, 1 Pair Stone Buckles, 1 Loves Surveying, 1 Apothems of the Ancients, 1 Knife, 1 Snuff Box, 1 Postlethwaits dictionary, 1 Fine large Piere Glass, 1 Map of North America, 1 Map of Europe, 2 Celestial Hemisphers, 1 Sand Box, 1 Parcel of Paper, 1 Looging Glass, 3 Watch Chains, 3 Keys, some rt & Vest Buttons, Cravats & Stocks, 2 Brushes, 4 Leggings, 7 Pillow Cases, 1 Chafing dish, mats & Basket, 4 Japan Waiters, 1 China Bowl, 1 ditto, 10 China Cups, 3 Glass Constables, 8 Beer Glasses, 11 Wine Glasses, 2 decanters, 1 Chest, A Small Iron Pot & Hooks, 5 Books, 6 ditto, Parcel Latin Books, 1 Pair Silver Spurs, 1 Fan, 1 Black Riband, 1 Fine Seal, 1 Paste Pin, 1 Watch Chain, 1 Ring with a Seal 1 Silver Watch, 1 Fan, 2 Silver Pens, ½ ll Hyson Tea, 1 Pearl Necklace, 2 Packs Message Cards, 1 Knife & Fork, a Parcel of Gilt Paper, 6 Books, 12 ditto, 6 ditto, ½ll Hyson Tea, 1 Knife and Fork, 6 Books, 1 Pair of Tongs, a Parcel of Ribands, 4 Pieces of Worsted Binding, 1 Ink Pot, 1 Parcel of declarations, 1 Book of Precedents, a Parcel of Blanks, a Parcel of ditto, 1 Quire Blue Marble Paper, a Parcel of Blanks, 2 Magnets, 1 Book, 1 Pair Silver Buckles, 1 Pair gold knee Garters, 2 Pieces of Black Riband, 1 Piece of Silk Binding, 3 Pair of Worsted Stockings, 1 Stamped Linen Handkerchief, 1 Pair of Stockings, 2 Pair of Silk ditto, 3 Shirts, 5 Coffie Cups, 2 Jugs, 1 Ball of Twine, a Parcel Of Quart Bottles, 1 Table, 1 Chair, 1 Bruss, 1 Queens China Tea pot, 1 Queens Chinia Sugar Pot, 1 Press, 1 foot Rule, Cloaths & Trimmings for 2 Suit Cloaths, 3 Hhds under Tobo, 1 Martins Philosophy, 1 Fergusons Astronomy, 1 Reflections on Ridicule, 1 Po & Odyssy, 1 Dialogues Moral & Political, 1 Thomsons Antonim, 1 Rambler, 1 Lady Marys letters, 1 Ossians Works, 1 Smollets history of all nations, 1 World, 1 Miltons Paradise lost, 1 Youngs works, 1 Ladys magazine, 1 Plutarchs lives, 1 Oconomy of Life, 1 Sir Charles Grandison, 1 Marmontell, 1 Gays Poems, 1 Guthries General history, 1 Seamans Astrology, 1 Wrights Arithmetick, 1 Lawyers Wig, 1 Universal Arithmetick, 1 Treatise on Algebra, 1 Lillys Grammar, 1 Watts Logick, 1 Law Grammar, 1 Vaux Mathematicks, 1 Wilsons Trigonometry, 1 Boerhaves Aphorisms, 1 Boerhaves Institutes, 1 Hallers Philosophy, 1 Walkers Particles, 1 Cornelius Nepos, 1 Rudimans Grammar, 1 French Rudiments, 1 Boyers Dictionary, 1 Boyers Grammer, 1 Ciceros Oratory, 3 Latin Books, 1 Heniciis Antiquitys, 1 Rohauls Physicks, 1 Quintius Curtious, 1 Gradus ad Parnassus, 1 Plautius Comedies, 34 Latin Books of different kinds, 1 Brographica Britanica, 1 Suit White Cloaths, 1 Suit of blue Laced, 1 Suit white Laced, 1 Laced Jacket, 2 Suits of Black Silk, 1 Jacket, 1 Silk Suit, 1 Jacket, 3 Jackets, 3 Pr. Breeches, 2 Suit Cloaths, 2 pair Breeches, Jacket, 5 Jackets, 1 Pr Breeches, 2 Jackets & 1 Bag, 8 Jackets, 1 Tract of Land on Miery Branch, 1 Bureau, el of Hebrew and Greek Books delivered to the R r Wylie as Bequeathed, A Number of Book Debts, Judgement Notes and other Specialtys due to him amount uncertain, 1 Parliamentary History, 1 Parliamentary Debates, 1 Biographica Britanica, 1 Thesarius Brevium, 1 common place Book, 1 Puffendorf, 1 Arnoldi Vereci, 1 Heneciis Commentary, 1 Godolphin abridged, 1 Jacobs Merchants Companion, 1 Retorna Brevium, 1 History of the Law, 1 Modus Instandi 2 Vols, 1 Burlamaque Elements, 1 Complete Sollicitor, 1 Law of Errors, 1 Juris civitatis &c, 1

Rules of Pleading, 1 Bacons Elements, 1 Observ: Theo: Prae: ad Panda, 1 Hawkins Abridgement, 1 Prin-Legis et Equitatis, 1 Clerks Associate, 1 Littletons Tenures, 1 Blackerbys Reports, _____1 Bay Mare, Strayed away_____200 Acres of Land in Guilford county, formerly the property of Husbands

NORTH CAROLINA ss.

Andrew Mi   one of the executors of David Milner deceased   Oath and saith that the above account contains a true & perfect Inventory of   singular the Goods chattels & Effects of his said Testator come to his Hands custody po   or possession or into the Hands custody power or possession of Joseph Montfort one other of the Executors of the said deceased to his Knowledge or Belief.

ANDW MILLER

Sworn this 17th day of Decemr. 1773 Before me
JO. MARTIN.

AN ACCOUNT OF SALE of part of The estate of Thomas Nelson deceased, Sold at public vadue, on May the 22 by Order of The Court, 1751

1751

		£	s	d
	An Anvil, Sledge, hammer, Brick-iron and bellows	7	12	00
	34 Ox hides	6	07	01
	A Linen-Wheel	0	16	00
	A Linen-Wheel	1	00	00
	A Rell	0	03	00
	A Woollen Wheel	0	05	00
	A Woollen Wheel	0	06	00
	An old hand Mill, Frame & Stones	0	03	00
	An hand Mill, frame and Stone	0	09	06
	A pair of Millstones	0	10	06
	A padling Canoa	0	08	10
	An hand Mill, frame and Stone	0	08	06
	A Stock of Bees	0	13	11
	2 Stocks of Bees	1	07	00
	A Grinding Stone	0	12	08
	A large Pereauger and furniture	7	13	06
	A Small Trading gun	1	01	00
	A Gun	1	01	00
	A Musket	1	02	00
	A Buckeneer Gun	1	05	06
	An Old Gun	0	12	00
	A Gun	0	09	00
	A Gun	0	10	06
	6 Hooks	0	02	10
	6 Do	0	02	10½
	6 Do	0	02	10
		£	s	d
2.	Brought from The other Side	35	08	00½
	6 Hooks	0	02	10
	6 Do	0	03	00
	2 Do	0	10	00
	3 Do	0	01	03
	A Case and 12 bottles	1	06	00
	A Case and 15 bottles	1	11	00
	A Case and Eleven bottles	1	01	00

INVENTORIES.   523

	£ s. d	
27 Yards of Coarse Linen @ 3 Pr	4.01.00	
A Case and 15 bottles	1.01.06	
An Old Chest	0.06.06	
A Chest	0.14.06	
A Saine, and furniture	3.05.00	
A Box of pipes	0.11.00	
A Chest, and a parcel of Lumber	1.10.11	
A pair of Silver Shoe Buckles, a Silver Neck buckles, & a pr of Brass Shoe buckels	1.08.00	
A Chest, and a parcel of Lumber	2.04.02	
68 lb of Feathers at 1/4	4.10.08	
A Coat, jacket and breeches	2.12.00	
2 Coats, and A pair of breeches	0.08.09	
3 linen Jackets and a pair of breeches	0.15.06	
A pair of leather breeches	0.18.00	
A pair of Do	0.14.03	
An hand Saw	0.06.00	
A parcel of Coopers Tools	1.16.00	
A pair of Boots	0.04.00	
A Brick Trowel	0.03.02	
A large Willow Bottle	0.10.06	
A Dozen glass bottles	0.02.08	
A pair of Old Wool Cards	0.01.00	
9 glass Bottles	0.02.07	
A flax breake	0.02.06	68.02.03½
Brought from the other Side	68.02.03½	
3 Shirts	0.10.00	
A pair of Small Stillyards	0.06.05	
A pair of large Do	0.17.02	
A pair of Still-yards	0.11.00	
half hour glass and Cann	0.02.09	
A Nocturnal Quardrant	0.16.02	
An Ox Bell	0.03.07	
A Saw	0.06.06	
A Coffee Mill......?	0.05.09	
A drinking Glass, 2 Cruits, and Tumbler	0.01.03	
A Hackel	0.10.06	
4 Old Chairs	0.04.06	
A gauging rod and brush	0.08.00	
A box Iron, and a pr of Cotton Cards	0.07.02	
A slate	1.06.00	
A Brass candle Stick, & pr of Snuffers	0.03.00	
A Dizen of pewter Spoons	0.00.04	
A pair of fire tongs	0.04.00	
A Silver Watch	4.10.00	
A Great Coat	0.12.00	
A Whip Saw	1.12.00	
A Cross Cut Saw	1.10.00	
A Cross Cut Saw	1.08.00	
A Remnant of bending linen	0.07.00	
A pair of Scales and Waites	1.07.08	
7 pair of Cards	0.11.00	
24 yards of Canvass	3.06.00	
A Box and a parcel of Old lumber	0.08.00	
A parcel of Sickles and Augures	0.05.06	
A Shirt lancet	0.02.01	
A Chizle, a pr of Sheep Shears & 6 Spurs	0.02.08	£ s. d 90.04.05½

	£ s. d	
Brought from The other Side............	90.04.05½	
129 lb of Tann'd leather...............	0.13.07	
A Pea jacket.........................	0.05.02	
190 Sheafs of flax....................	1.11.06	
A flax breake........................	0.06.00	
A parcel of Unbroke flax..............	0.15.00	
A Sadle and bridle....................	1.02.07	
A Chest.............................	1.02.00	
A parcel of earthen Ware..............	1.11.00	
A pair of Turns for Lines..............	0.03.00	
A large butter pot, & 1 Small Do.......	0.05.01	
A large butter pot, & 1 Small Do.......	0.06.00	
A large butter pot, & 1 Small Do.......	0.04.06	
A Carpenter's Adds...................	0.06.11	
4 earthen pans.......................	0.03.06	
3 Clubs, Axes, & 1 brad Do............	0.12.06	
A Narrow How.......................	0.04.04	
A Roll of Spun Yarn..................	0.05.00	
A Pot rack...........................	0.07.00	
A broad Hough.......................	0.07.00	
5 Old broard houghs..................	0.16.00	
5 Old hoes...........................	0.05.00	
An old Gun..........................	0.15.06	
2 Ploughs, and A harrow..............	1.01.00	
18 Yards of Striped Holland at 4/0.....	3.12.00	
A Weaver's Loom.....................	0.18.06	
2 Suiters of Slays and gears...........	0.17.06	
A Parcel of old rope...................	5.00.00	
A pair of Oyster Tongs................	0.07.00	
100 lb of Wool at 10d½...............	4.07.08	
100 lb of Do. at 10d½................	4.07.06	£ s. d
	123.03.07½	123.03.07½
Brought from the other Side............	123.03.07½	
100 lb of Wooll at.....................	3.15.00	
100 lb of Wool at 8...................	3.06.06	
100 lb of Wooll at 7d..................	2.18.04	
100 lb of Do at 7d....................	2.18.04	
98 lb of Do at 6½d...................	2.13.01	
100 lb of Cotton at 6 in the Stone.......	2.10.00	
100 lb of Do at 4½d in The Stone......	1.17.06	
100 lb of Do at 4d in Do..............	1.13.04	
73 lb of Do at 4d in Do................	1.04.04	
A Still and all The Appurtenances thereunto belonging.....................	36.00.00	
A Copper Kittle......................	18.00.00	
A brass Kittle........................	17.10.00	
A Small brass Kittle..................	3.00.00	
29¼ lb of Pewter at 3/— Pr..........	4.07.09	
15 lb of Do at 2/4....................	3.15.00	
A Quart, a Pint and a Tumbler.........	0.13.00	
A Quart & a Tea Pot..................	0.10.00	
A Tea Kettle.........................	1.08.00	
A Bell Mettle Spice Mortar & Pestle and a Copper pot.......................	1.10.00	
An Ink Stand, 2 Tin Funnels, 2 Tin pepper boxes, and 1 brass Do..........	0.07.00	
15 lb of Pewter at 2/.2d..............	1.12.06	
A Gun a braod Hough, a parcel of Pewter................................	2.04.00	

	£ s. d	
A Feather Bed, and furniture	16.00.00	
A Bed, pillow, Sheet & Blanket	7.00.00	
A Bed, Boulster, Sheet and Rugg	7.10.00	
A Bed, blanket, Sheet and Boulster	4.00.00	
A Bed, Sheet and Blanket	4.18.00	
A Sea Bed and Boulster	2.00.00	
A Bed, 4 blankets and a Boulster Case	5.01.00	£ s. d
		283.06.05½
Brought from the other Side	283.06.05½	
5 Pots and 2 Kittles and 2 Pot Hook	3.01.06	
1 large Pot and Hook	1.05.00	
a brass Stew Pot, a brass Skillet and a brass Sauce Pan with a Tramel. A Chafing dish, and a file	1.05.02	
A Marriners Compass & Speakg Trumpet	7.00	
176 lb of old iron at 5d pr.	3.13.00	
An Oval Table	2.00.01	
A Parcel of Wooden Ware	1.14.06	
3 Frying Pans	0.15.06	
A large Gun	7.15.01	
		£305.03.07½

JOHN DAVIS Vandue Master.

DARBY O'BRIAN INVENTORY.

August ye. 5th 1725.

AN INVENTORY of the Estate of Darby Obrian deceed To 4 Head of Cattle £4:10:0 To an Horse 4 £ To 21 Head of Hogs £ 6:6:0 To one old Bridle and Sadle 8 shll To a parcel of pewter and a tin funnel 10 shll. To a parcel of Glass Ware 8 shll. To a stone jugg 3 shll. To one Brass Skillet a Brass slice and Brass Box 2/6 To an Handsaw 6 shll. To an Ivory Comb 1/8 To a Hone Razor Vial and Knife 4/6 To a parcel of old Iron 15 shll. To one old Coverlid 5 shll. To 3 pair of old Breeches 7/6 To 2 shirts 12/6 To an old Coat 10 shll. To an old Hat Cap and Jacket 4 shll. To one pair of Yarn Stockins 3 shll. To an old Lock and Key 21 shll. To an old Chest 12 shll. To a parcel of Leather 8 shll. To one Bee Hive and Bees 5 shll. To 100 lb. of dried pork & Beef £ 1: 5: 0 To 1 Bushl. ½ Corn 3 shll. To 6 lb Hogs Fatt 2 shll. To a pair of Stillyds. £1: 5: 0—Antho. Hatch Jno. Bateman This Inventory was proved by the Oath of Wm. Evans the 13th of Septbr. 1725. before Me Geo. Durant.

INVENTORY of the Estate of Seth Pilkington Decsd taken by Michl Coutanche Feb. 27th 1754.

In the Store
  1 Whip Saw
  3 old Siths
  about 60 lb of old Iron
  1½ busa wheat
  in a Chest 11 pair yarn stockings
  1 Doz Clap Knives
  19 quire paper
  23 printed handkershiefs
  14½ yd Shalown
  18¾ yards checks

9½ yds Broad Cloath
1 Doz pair mens Stockings
94 Ells of ozenbrigs
1 Soldiers Coat
1 pr Stockings
1 Cotten handkershief
26½ yds read Plains loope
1 Conoo Sail
8 Black Walnut Chairs & bottoms
18½ yd Candele Cottens
31 yd Dito

14½ yd Coarse Blanketting
11 Smal Blanketts
1 Cadis
4 Small Ruggs
32 felt hatts
1 Powder Canister
3 White tea pots
1 White Strainer
1 Carving Knife
1 old Canister
10 round botels
2 Jointer Irons
1 plane Iron
a Yalow Jackett
2 Club Axes
1 pr Silliards
4 Narrow hoes
1 Shugr Tub
36 lb Shot & buletts
1 mans fine new Saddle & brd
1 old Chest
6 Turpentine hatchets
1 trowell
1 Inck stand
1 Narrow Chizzell
1 Crossing Iron
3 Small Gimbletts
1 Saw Sett
6 pegging Awls
8 Corke Screws
5 Doz Butts.
12 sticks Mohair
10 Doz Shirt Butts
4 Large files
6 Whimble Bitts
6 Smal files
2 Basketts
11 lb bees wax
5 Curried Calves Skins
1 Calf Skin not Curried
2 pices Lather
37 lb Powder
about 15 lb of Cotten in the Store
1 Large Chest
1 oyl Jugg
1 Linning Spinning Wheel
1 4 Gll Jugg
6 Chain Plates
66 lb Talow
35 lb of Dear Skin
3 loaves Shugr
1 old half bushell
in the Celler
Remd of a hhd Rum 11 In
d molasses 14 Inches
18 Sides of Lather
1 lb Cyder
64 botels fayall wine
1½ doz round botels
3 Case Botels

6 Empty barils
⅓ of a baril Pork
1½ baril fine Salt
1 pot hoggs fatt
½ of Smal Tub Butter
½ pot butter

1 tin Gallon Pott
1 Pewter pint pot
1 funnell 1 Cag
1 Small Iron Pot with fatt
in the Store Loft
2 hand saws
1 frame Saw
1 Cross Cut Saw
2 Whip Saws
1 adds
2 Broad Axes
3 Augers
1 old Club ax
2 Drawing Knives
4 Chizells
1 Gough
1 Saw Sett 4 files
1 Grindstone 3 planes
1 old Cooper adds
1 plow shear & Coulter
1 old bed steed
1 Lathing Hammer
1 Grubing hoa
In the Kitchen
2 old Ladles 1 peck
2 Plows 1 Garden Pot
1 Cullender 4 Pewter Dishes
4 Tubs 1 frying Pan
5 Iron Potts 1 Ketle
1 Large Brass Ketle
1 Brass Scillet
1 Grid Iron 1 Spit
4 pot tramells
2 hooks 5 pr pot hooks
1 pair hand Irons
1 pair Tongs
1 Wooling Wheel
3 washing Tubbs
4 Water pails
2 pair old wool Cards
1 Smal funnell
1 flesh fork &——
1 Brass Scimmer
1 Kitchen table
out of Doors
1 Plough 1 large pitch ketle
4 Bay boat bars
1 Bay boat
2 Canoos 1 flat
1 Large boat anchor
1 pair hand Screws
1 Grindstone 1 hhd Lime
1 flax Brake

in the Barn
  about 40 lb Corn
  27 bus Pees 4 bus small
  1 lb & 2/3 of fine salt
  about 6 bus Coarse Salt
  11 old hhd 11 old bb
  about 12 bus beens
in the house
  2 Silver Salts 2 Silver Spoons
  1 Silver Pepper Box
  2 Glass Canns 6 Wine Glasses
  1 China Jack 2 Decanters
  2 Delph Punch Bowls
  1 Black Pitcher
  2 Glas Viniger Cruits
  1 Glass tankard 6 beakers
  6 China Chocolate bowls
  6—— 1 tea Pot
  Silver tongs & 6 teaspoons
  1 pr hand Irons
  1 fire Shovel & tongs
  1 Clock 1 Great Chair
  6 flagg Chairs 1 Elbow Dito
  4 Blak walnut framed Chairs &c
  1 maple table
  1 Black Walnut Do 1 Oak Desk
  1 Broken looking glass
  2 pr money scales in the Desk
  1 pr shot mouls 1 pr Knipers
  1 Shoe hammer 1 Pr Marking
      Irons
  1 pr bullet Moulds 1 brass Cock
  1 pr Shoe Pincers 1 pr Spoon
      Moulds
  5 awls & 2 Gimbletts
  1 Seringe 1 hoan 2 Rasors
  1 Rasor strap about 500 Needls
  horse flems 1 fountain pen
  2 Sticks hair 11 Doz shirt butt
  2 pr Sleave butts 3 mend Books
  2 Smal files 1 pr Compasses
  2 Westband Buckely
  2 Doz butts. 2 pen Knives
  2 pr Specticals 1 burning Glass
  2 Inck glasses 1 Gunter Scale
  12 feet Rule 1 pr thumb screws
  1 botel Batemens Drops
  1 pr nail Cutters Some Rats been
  about 3 Doz fish hooks
  1 glass Ink stand
  1 Sand Box 1 Sliding Rule
  2 Saw Setts 1 Pocket Book
  1 Pr Silver Shoe buckeles
  1 Silver Watch
  2 Lancetts 1 pr Silver Knee
      buckles
  14 Silver Jackett butts
  1 Silver Neck buckle
  13 Silver Small buttons
  1 piece of Silver watch chain

1 Smal pad lock 1 Silver Knee
    buck
1 Green Silk Purse
10¼ pisterins
1 pr Smal Scales
1 pr bellows in Back Room
1 Smal White Table
1 Black walnut Do
1 Warming pan
1 Close Stool 3 old Chairs
1 Large Bed & furniture
1 Smal Bed & Dito
1 Chest Drawers 1 looking glass
    Smal
1 pr hand Irons
1 pr Shovel & tongs
1 black tea Pot 1 black Jack
1 earthen bowl 3 Glasses
1 pint mugh 1 Pitcher
1 tea pot 1 tea Chest
1 Canister 3 Doz round botells
1 Case with 28 botels
½ gal pot 6 lb Soap
6 fayall Basketts
2 Box Irons & heaters 1 Stan
½ gl Peuter Pot 1 Chest
1 Cotton Mill 3 pr Snuffers
4 brass Candle Sticks
2 Guns 2 hammers
2 Spinning Wheels
3½ Doz tin Candle Moulds
1 pr boots 1 Smal Stilliard
1 pr old boots 1 pr stilliards
1 Case & 12 botels
1 tin Candle Box
1 hatchett 1 Coffee pot
1 pickle Pot 2 tea Ketles
1 Grater 1 Copper Sauce pan
1 Cannister 2 Shoe brushes
1 Doz Case Knives 1 D forks
4 pr shoes
1 new Suit Broad Cloth
5 flanell Jacketts
3 Coats
3 bever hatts
1 Read Jackett & britches
1 gray Jacket
1 morning gown
9 pr Stockings
3 pair gloves
1 pair Lather bridches
8 white shirts
2 check Dito
1 par Garters
3 neckleths
4 doz & 8 plates
7 Dishes
1 Gl Bason
3½ Gal Dito
3 3 pint Do

2 2 quart Do
1 Doz milk pans
1 Doz Chairs at Bath town
1 Great Coat D.
⅓ of 3 New Cables D
⅓ of 3 Anchors Do
5 Volumes Doctr. Scots Sermons
1 Map North America
the Compleat Surveyor 1 Vol
Laws of Virginia 1 D
The Athenian Oracle 1
Beveridge thoughts on Crist Life
A Geographical Dictionary   1
Bishop Hoadlys Sermons   1
John Hill Arithmetick   1
16 Sermons by Durham   1
new Calender
feast & fast of the Church
Etimological Dictionary   1
Cores Exposition
Merchants Magazine   1
Wells Geography   1
Popes Essay on Man
Practice Piety
Stanupe on Salvation
Smal Book of Rates
2 Psalm Books
Henrey's Sermons
New Atlantis   1
testement
Etinuler's Practice of Phisick
Decimal Arithmetick
2 old Epitome 1 old grammar
Geography of Children
familiar Letters
Margl of Argyle Instr to his son
Doctr Hammon works 2 Vol
Introdn to the Lord Supper
Marriner Compass
Instruction for the Indians
1 Large Common Prayer
3 Small Common Prayer Books
1 Large Bible 2 Small Dito
4 Ledgers A B C D & Sundry
    Day Books
3 Canes 1 Gauging Rod
about 5 m New Engld Bricks
6 Dry hides 1 Calf Skin
1 horse Bell 2 ox Belles
2 wheel Barrows 18 plant axes
12 hoes 2 pr Iron Wedges
2 Grubing hoes 3 Carts
1 pair of Oxen
6 Cows & Calves
4 Cows not Calves
22 young Catle to 3 years old
4 horses & 1 mare
29 Sheep & 7 Lambs
10 Breeding Sows & 9 Pigs

20 Shoats 1 Large Iron Pot
16 new Oak Barels 2 hand mills
1 Conner table up Stairs
6 Chairs flag bottoms
1 Trunck ½ minute glass
5 Bed & furniture
1 trunk 1 pair tongs
1 Small looking Glass
2 Chest 3 Sifters
5 pair Cards 4 Bowls
1 Suit Curtains 6 old barils &
    Cags
1 buckett 1 pr Lather Bags
3 bags 6 Bowls
4 pint mugs 6 half pints D
a Small persell wool Cotton & flax
yarn & Cotten Spun a Small quan-
    tity
3 Chamber pots 1 Small Box Wind
    Glass
1 Cedar Desk 8 pair Sheets
1 pr Blanketts 2 bed quilts
1 Rugg 4 Diaper Table Cloths
4 Linnen Table Cloths 6 Tow-
    ells D
6 Diaper Napkins
6 pr thread Stockings
Negroe Men
    Jupiter, Lankeshire, Catto
    Darby, Cudgo, old Tom
    young Tom, Jack, Pomp,
    Fortune, George, Dublin,
    Noridge
Negro Boys
    Mustifer, Cain, York,
    London, Bristol,
Wenches
    Africa, Grace, Jenny Florra
    old Betty,
Girls
    Jenny, Pheby, Hannah,
White Boys
    4 prantices
at Plantation Warynunty
7 Cows & Calves
Cows   ⎫
Steers   ⎬ yett unknown
Steers   ⎭
2 Plows
1 P Cartwheels 1 horse
2 mares & Colts
1 ax 1 hoe
at Plantation up the River
Cows & Calves ⎫
Steers   ⎬ yett unknown
Hogs   ⎭
Tar at the Landing
163 bb on floyd Creek not filled
1 Large Tar Kill running off

2 Smaller to runn off	James Event for 0.10.0 Vir cur
& about 200 bbSett up for Tar	Abram Tyler 6. 0.0
2 Iron Potts at Tar Kill	Griffin Floyd for 28bb* * *
Notes of Hand	John Campbell 1.17.6 Vir
Willm Ballard for £4. 5.0 Proc.	Charles Pringle 3.16.6 Vir
John Porters for 12. 6.9 Sterling	John Knowis Ball 2. 1.6 Proc

MICHL COUTANCHE Exectr
WINIFRED PILKINGTON

INVENTORY of Sundreys the Goods & Chattels Rights & Credits of Captn. James Pollard & Anne his wife both Desct. taken by James Innes Administrator to Said Estate, Viz as it is found to his knowledge.

1750, June 11th.

Lucretia ⎱ Negero Women
Jenny   ⎰

Sam'll ⎫
Nanney ⎬ three Do Children
Charles ⎭

Nine Cowes
five Calfes
two old Steers
Six three Yeer Old Do
three Mares
two Yearling Coults
two Horses
One Yearling horse Coult
One Do winning in two years
three Breeding Sowes
Sixteen Shotes
One Iron Pott
One Large Copper Kittle
One Small Iron Skillett
three Spitts, One Cliver, One Bill
One flesh fork, One P Tongues
One Pr. Iron Dogs.
Six Pewter Dishes ⎱ Old Pewter
twinty Do Plates ⎰
3 Tunnells, three Baisons
One Small Dish
One Cotton Counterpinn
two pair & one Odd Sheets Linnen
One Demety Quilted Coat
One Old Gown, One Do Cloack
One Scarlett Do
One Chintz Gown, One Do Camblett
Four Table Cloaths
Two Small Do, Two Towells
a paper containing ten P Brass Slive buttons
Two Owy Nuns thread & head wears
Two ps Bobbings
Two pr Speek—— & Sealing Wax
One Quilted Gown
One Callico Do
One Quilted Silk Coat
One Flowed Gown Do
two Under Coats

Twelve Shirts
Nine Aprons
One Bed Gown
Five Lased Capes
three Do Eadgin
Eleven plain Do
Six white Handkerchefs
three Hoods
One Velvett hood & Bonnett
One pair Lasd Ruffels
two pair Pocketts
One Linnen Handkerchef
two pr Silk Stockings two Pr Thread Do
One Pray Book
One pair Everlasting Shooes
Six Pillow Cases
thre Small Do
Some Scraps Velvett
A paper with some thread
One Gold workt Knott
two plain Do
Two Old Fanns, One pin Cushing & Pins
7 Yards Striped new Stuff
A Meddarl & pockett Book
two silver Spoons, One Childs pap Spoon ⎫
Six Teaspoons, Tongues & Strainer
One peper box, One punch Ladle
One Silver childs nipple
One Stone Girdle Silver Buckle ⎬ Silver Work
One Gold Ring 1 Ps Do Silver
One Silver Snuff Box
Halfe —— of Eight, Eight —— & three Bits ⎭
One Bugle Hatt Band, One Tobacoa Box
One Tea Kettle ⎱ Copper
One Coffee Pott ⎰
One Brass Chafing Dish
three Do Candle Sticks Snuffers & Stand
One Flatt Tinn Candle Stick
two Pinte Glass Decanters
One Small Tea Board
three Glass Salts
One Milke Pott
Twelve Small Plates ⎱ Earthern ware
two Dishes ⎰
Eight Large Tea Cups China
Nine Sawsers
thre Small pleats
three large Cupps
Six Coffee Cupps One three pinte Bowell
One Pint Do
One Stone Tea Pott
Two Earthen quart Bowels
Two Wine Glasses
One Chamber Pott
One Mahogeney Tree
One Brass, two Leaden Weights
Six Knives Six forks
One Dressing Glass
four Picturs

One Tea Chest with a litle Tea & Coffee
Eight Books
a japann Cabinett
A Small Oak Table
One Ellbow Mohogeney Chair & Cushing
One Cane Do
Six Do Chairs without Bottomes
One Old Deske
One pair Brass Scales
Six Candle Moulds
One Earthen Butter Pott
four Straw Bottome Chairs
One Small hand Bell
One Powder Box & beads
two Bed Steads
One pr Vallance Curtings & Rods
One Feather Bed
One Boulster & three Pillows
two Small pillows
two Quilts
One Couch & Bed for ye Couch
One Counterpine One Old Hoop
two Cloaths Brushes
One Small Jarr
One Box hand & 3 heaters
1 pr hand mill stones
two Hoggs in Backon
One Small old Table
One Old Lanthorne
One Grand Stone
three Iron wedges
three old axes
five old Hoes
One Spaid
One Small Pestell & Morter
One Woomans Side Saidle
One large Mogoheney Table
One Chest of Drawers
The Plantation containing two hundred and fifty acres of Land Lightwood gaithered for a Small Tar Kill

JAMES INNES

October 16th 1750.

Then appeared before me James Innes Esqr. and made Oath on the hold Evangelists that the within is a just true & perfect Inventory of the Goods & Effects of James Pollard Deceased as far forth as have come to his hands or Knowledge JOSEPH BALEH

Recorded in filed in H folio 16

AN INVENTORY of the Estate of the Honble. Cullon Pollock Esqr: Decd: Viz:

Names of Negroes.

West	Little Scazar	Salley
Rachael	Cate	Moll
Sam Hannah	Hannah	Jack Do
2 Children	Kilah	Toddgy

Franks Child	Mannewell do	Tom
Beck Hopeey	Dinah	Scipio Do
Sally	Joe Do	Ruth
Young Rachael	Cate Do	Cutto Do
Janey	Mannewell Do	Anthony
Catoe	Charles Do	David Venuce
Stevens	Cate Do	Joe Jack
Sarah	George Do	Charles
Young Stevens	George Do	George Do
Betty	Charles Do	Mingo
Henry Robin	Molenah	Judith Do
Sarah	Exbeah	Dick Nancy
Hoopey Do	Bodwell	Jamemy
Abraham	Dowey	Mingo Do
Sipico	Joshway	Stohan Jenny
Marmuwell	Hannah Do	West Do
Primas	Patience	Popo. Scazar
Frank	Rito	Rose
Ned	Betty do	Dinah
Johnny	Judge	Scazar
Juda	Will	Jane
Young Primas	Sarah	Adam
Boman	George Do	Eve
Scazar	Moll Do	Rose
Donas	Pomp Do	Peter
Scllah	Young Will	Frank Do
Betty Priscilla	Suah	Suokay
Jack Venice	Sam	Betty Do
Jenny	Malenah	Nancy
Betty	Cutto	Cate
Joe	John Dide	Nancy Do
Tinker	Nancy 2 Children	Simon
Bess	Toe	Scazar
Harry	Peggy	Mingo
Young Scazar	Bess Do	Dick Billy
Brister Betty	Harry	Tom Thum
Taffey	Steven Do	Tom Foot
Edenburah	Nancy	Sam
George	Grave	Jack Do
Prince	Con	Caskey
Morear	Patty	George Moses

150 Negroes in all
176 head of cattle and Some out Lying Cattle
Part of thirty nine head of Cattle Part of 43
head of Hoggs part of 20 head of Sheep 34 sheep
46 head of Hogs
7 horses and Two old Mares
37 hoes 13 Grubing hoes 19 axes
12 Grubing hoes do about 130 Bushalls of Salt
Two Sets of Black Smith Tools 2 pairs of
Bellows 2 Vices 2 Anvells 2 Beaking Irons
and as many other Tools as make the Sett
3 Branding Irons 23 Barrels of Beef
5 Barrels of Pork 1 Thousand lb of Tallow
55 hides 2 Barrels of Tallow one Book Case
with a parcill of Books 4 Guns 23 Leather
Chears 10 old Chears & parcil of old frames
2 old chists of Drawers one Desk one Bofet
one small Desk 2 Black Walnut Tables

2 old Black Walnut Do one old Cedar Table
one pine Plank Table 3 old Trunks
1 Old Safe 3 cases with about 16 bottles
1 Large Looking Glass 3 Small Do
2 Puter Glasses 6 Bear Glasses duble flint
2 Glass Decanters 4 Glass Tumblers
a little flowerd Bottle 11 Dram & wine glasses
1 Glass Punch Bowl 2 Glasses Vinigar Cruats
2 Glass Salt Sellers 10 Chany Chocolate Cups
16 Cheny Tea Cups 15 Saucers 9 Vials
29 Bottles of Wine 21 Round Bottles Emty
1 Box with some Glass 4 Earthen Bowls
7 Earthen plates 1 Chocolate Cup Earthen
2 Tea kettles 2 Mettle Tea pots 4 Gelly pots
4 Silver Tea Spoons 1 Silver Strainer
1 Silver Tea Tongs 2 Silver Salt Sellers wt. £1:10:3
2 Silver Cups wt £1:17:6 1 Silver peper Boxes wt £2:7:0
1 Silver Poringar W. £3:7:01 16 Silver spoons Wt £7:17:8
2 Silver Tankard Wt 3:8 oz by the stellards
3 old Beds Wt 34 30 & 20, 4 beds 4 boulsters
3 pillows 3 bags of feathers W 43
3 Rugs 7 Blankits 2 Quilts 2 Sets
of old Curtons 2 Cover Lids 2 pairs of Old Cotton Sheets
3 pairs of Lining Sheets 1 bed Do
1 pair of Do
5 pillow Cases 5 Towels
2 Napkins 4 Daiper Table Cloths
3 Course Table Cloths
5 Bead Steads 1 pair money scales
1 old Do 1 Burning Glass
1 hone Rasor sheths 2 old floots
1 pair Bulet Mould some fishing
lines half a Doz pound Shot
½ pound of Powder 7 files
1 Sord & Scabard 3 Jack
lead Knives 10 Gimlets 1 Steal
1 pack of Cards 1 Dozn Case Knives
and forks 1 pair Spoon moulds
4 Puter Dishes 12 puter plates
8 old puter Dishes 4 old Puter basons
some old Puter 3 Comes
8 Iron pots 1 Stone pot 2 Iron
Kittles 1 Iron Skillet 1 Bell
Mettle one Brass Kettle some
brass some cotton Spun some
unspun about a pound of fyl (?)
3 or 4 yds of Dimmeto 11 yds of Checks
3 yds of Cambrick 2 yds of muslin
3 Silver Seals a Little Spun thread
3 Stone Judgs 3 Jarrs 3 Stone
Pots parcill of old Barrels & Lumber
Some Sorry Leather, half a fagot
of steal 50 wt of London Steal
4 wt 200ᵐ:3:14ʷ Iron 1 pair of Stellards
some Ruffage Iron
4 Wooling Wheales 3 pairs of old
Cards 4 Lining wheals
2 Looms Slays & Harness 7 yds corse
Lining 5 pair of Cart wheals & 2 Carts

3 pair of mill stones 1 set of Carpenters
Tools 1 Set of Coopers Tools 8 plows and
Tackling 2 oxen Chains 1 Grindstone
percill of useless nales and Piggins
1 Set of Shomakers Tools — Pot Hooks
and Trammels some meat for house
use & Corn about two Barrels of Molasses
& Ten Gallons of Rum some Turkeys and Geese fowls
£ s d   £ s d
32:7:9 Cash 769:12:6 old bills
1 pair of Silver Shoe Buckles and Knee Buckles
1 pair of Silver Sleve Buttons 3 gold Breast Buckels
10 Bottles of Wine 1 Small pot of Brown Sugar
6½ loves of Sugar some Lemmon and nutmegs
Mace spices Quarter of Pound Salt Peter
1 Spaid 2 Tin pans 1 old frying Pan
3 little Hone mugs 1 cart 2 Sets of Iron wedges
1 old Tennet Saw 4 sets
1 hand saw 1 pair Sheep Shears 4 Reepn Hooks
1 old Broad ax and auger
a percill of old Lumber about 3000 pound,
due as appears by the Books
3 Cannews one Peteauger (?) wearing apparel
                         Given by me ROBERT WEST Exr

NORTH CAROLINA TYREL COUNTY   September County Court 1751
     Present his Majestys Justices
     These may Certify that the above Inventory was proved in open Court by the oath of Capt Robert West Executor of the last Will and Testament of the Honle. Cullon Pollock Esqr. late of the sd said County deceased, in due form of law
     True Copy same   Test EVAN JONES C C
         EVAN JONES C C

AN INVENTORY of the Estate of Mr. John Peyton Porter Desd. Vizt:

One Negro Man Cuffey
one Ditto do Mingo
one do do Blackwall
one Do do Limas
one Do do Will
one Do do Tome
one Do Boy Will
one do do Ben
one Do Wench edy
one Do do Sarah
one Do Girl Gilley
one Do do Lucy
one Do do Lidia
one Do do Child Dinah
one Gray Gelding Horse
one Ditto Do Do
one Mare & Colt
Three Oxen
Nine Cows
Two Yearlings
Seven Sows & Piggs

Five Small Shoats
One Boar
Eight Sheep
Furniture
One Desk
one Maple Leave Table
one Bl Wallnut Do
Nine Leather Bottom Chairs
Six Rush Do do
One Trunk
One Sma Tea Chests
one pr Iron Doggs
one Case Drawers
Twenty four Pewter Plates
Thirteen Do Dishes
Seven Do Basons
one Do Pint Cann
One Do Tea Pott
one Do Cream Pott
Two Coats
one Jackett

INVENTORIES.

one pr Britches
one Great Coat
Two Chests
one Lead Ink Stand
one old Razor
2 Bibles } Books
1 Whole Duty of Man
1 Broken Looking Glass
1 pr Fire Tongs
one Tea Kettle

one pint Tinn Funnel
one Qa Do Do
Six Quart Bottles
one Tinn Egg Slice
Three Butter Potts
Three Salt Potts
Four Feather Beds
Four Do Bolsters
Two Do Pillows

INVENTORY (of Mr. John Peyton Porter his Esta:) Continued

One pr. Blanketts
one Bed Quilt & 2 Bed Matts
one Do Counterpaine
one Do Rugg
One Pr Holland Sheets
Five Cotton Sheets
one Pr Bellows
one Gunn
Two China Bowls
Some Cupps & Saucers
3 Earthen Plates
Three Wooll Wheels
Three Linnen Wheels
one Warming Pan
one Cradle
one Safe
Two White Tables
one Grid Iron
Three Bedsteads
One Bread Tray
one Sona (?) Bell Mettle Kettle
Two Earthen Panns
one old Saddle

Two Trammels
four Iron Potts
one Iron Kettle
one Do Skillet
Three Pr pott Hooks
Three Raw hides
one Ironing Bod & 2 Heaters
one Pr Stilliards
One Pr La: Stilliards No poiz
one pr Scales one, 4. 1½ Weights
Three Hand Mills
one Iron Candlestick
Two Ploughs
one Bee Hive
one Broken Case & Eight Bottles
one Salt & 1 Pepper Box
one Hoane
Some Shoe makers Tools
one pr Silver Shoe Buckles
Fifteen Yards Striped Linnen
Two Iron Spitts
one Branding Iron J P

Charles Lowther his promsy note............................. 2. 2.0
George Gerrard His Do Do.................................. 3.13.4
Willm. Trippe his Do Do................................... 2. 8.8
One Canoe ———
                ELISABETH STEWART
March ye 13th 1755

INVENTORY of the Estate of Mr. John Swann Porter taken the fourteenth of November 1773

1 Mahogany Tea Table
1 Iron Kettle
1 do Trivit
1 Flat Iron
1 small brass mortar & Pestle
2 Candle Moulds
6 new Pewter Plates
7 old do do
4 do do soup do
4 Pewter Dishes
1 old Soup Dish

1 small Pewter Bason
2 brass Candlesticks
1 Girdle Pan
1 old frying Pan
3 milk Pans
1 Earthen Pot
1 small brass Coffee Pot
1 Iron pot & hooks
1 do Skillet
1 old brass Tea Kettle
6 milk Coolers

2 fire Locks
1 Pistol & Holsters
1 milk paile
2 do   do
2 small Stone Juggs
1 do do Crack'd
3 Earthen ware Juggs
1 pair Cotton Cards
2 pair Sheep Shears
6 Panes of Glass
49 Quart Bottles
1 Auger broke
   old Iron
1 Stock Lock
1 Curry Comb & Brush
1 Bed Cord
1 Ship Pump
2 horse Whips
1 Pr Gilt frame looking Glasses
1 large black Trunk
1 small   do
1 do red do
1 House Broom
1 small Slate
1 Mahoganey Tea Ches &
   Cannisters
1 square Mahoganey Dining
   Table
1 Desk
1 marble slap
2 small Pine Tables
1 Mahoganey Tea Tray
1   do   waiter
1 small Case of Bottles (lock'd)
1 large Kitchen Table
1 pair Iron char: Dogs
1 pair Tongs & Shovels
1 pair sadle Baggs
1 large Delph Bowl
2 smaller   do
1 small China Bowl
5 blue & White China Tea Cups
6 do do do Saucers
6 Burnt China Tea Cups
4 do do Saucers, 2 do broke
1 blue & white China Sugar Dish
5 stone Juggs about 3 Gall's
   (each)
6 Soup Plates
1 Tea Pot (broke)
6 Coffee Cups
1 butter do
1 mustard Pot
1 flour mug
1   do   milkpot (broke)
1 Decanter   do
2 black Tea pots
1 Vinegar Cruet
3 Glass Tumblers
4 wine Glasses

2 Silver pint Cannes
2 do   Salvers
3 do   old Table Spoons
6 do   Tea Spoons
1 Straw bottom Elbow Chair
1   do   do
1 Elbow Chair
4 old Straw Bottom Chairs
2 pretty good
1 Tin Cullender
6 Buck handled knives
6 do   do   forks
3 do   do   old knives
4 do   do   old forks
1 hearth brush
1 Dictionary
1 brush
1 pair old Scissors
½ Doz. reaping hooks
1 Dollar (Cash)
22/6d Proclamation money
An order on G. Moore Esqr for
   £22
38 head of Sheep young & old
2 Geldings (Cook & Belby)
1   do white
1 mare & colt
10 Hoggs all large
2 Horse Carts Collares & Traces
1 Hoe Harrow
1 Bridle & Grinstone
1 Sulkey (Broke) & harnass
1 Feather bed a Bolster & 3 pillows
2 ozna briggs Mattresses
1 old
1 pair brown Sheets
3 white   do
3 Strip'd Blankets
1 Rope do
1 Counterpane
1 Bed Steed
1 pair furc: Check'd Curtains
1 Claret coloured Cloth Coat
1   do   Bear Skin Coat & Jacket
1 blue Silk Coat
1 white fustian Coat & Jacket
1 oznabgs Coat
1 pair woolen Trowses
1 pair coarse thread stockungs
2 silk handkerchiefs
2 Damask breakfast Cloths
3 oznabgs   do   do
1 old Towel
2 Car Ploughs & fleuks
2 parcel of old Casks
2 Raw Cow hides
2 old Surtouts 1 blue great Coat
4 Pr Striped Linen trowses
1 Linen Wrapper
4 Shirts, 3 Stocks

INVENTORIES.

1 Linen Jacket
2 pair old Shoes
1 Diaper
2 Oznabriggs Towels
2 Hats
1 pair Silver Shoe buckles
1 Sett Stock buckle
2 Saddles & Bridles
Jemmy
Else
Tom, Joe
Sam
Will
Hannah
Mercy
4 Cows & Calves

Filed 5th March 1775

2 dry Cows
2 Steers
2 do
4 good weeding hoes
6 old do do
5 good Axes
6 old do
3 grubbing hoes
— Coopers Ax
— do Adze
1 Drawing knife
1 Iron wedge
3 old Bushel Baskets
1 new drawing knife 1 do
1 broad Ax 1 Saw 1 Spade

AN INVENTORY of the Goods, and Chattels, Rights and Credits of The Reverend Mr. James Reed Deceas'd Vizt.

17 Negroes Vizt.

Jack)
Pompey |
Ben |
Neptune } 7 Fellows
Achilles |
Cuppy |
Tom)

Sam } 2 Boys
Jim

9 Males

Sappho)
Abigail |
Nan } 4 Wenches
Sall)

Sabina)
Temp |
Dinah } 4 Girls
Chelsea)

8 Females
9 Males

17 Negroes

HANNAH REED.

Four Horses
27 Head of Cattle large and small

Newbern Nov. 26th, 1777.
Sworn to before me
   JOSEPH LEECH, J. P.

1 Mahogany dining Tables
A Walnut side Table
A Walnut dining Table
A Walnut Dressing Table
2 small Maple Tables
A Round Mahogany Tea Table
An old Chest of Drawers
An old Cedar Desk
21 Mahogany Chairs
7 flag bottom Do
6 Windsor Do
3 Mahogany Bed Steads
1 Walnut Do
1 common Cord Do
3 large Looking Glasses
1 small Do

An Eight Day Clock
7 Mezzotintto Prints
7 common Do
A Close Stool Pan and Chair
2 Cotton Couterpanes
2 Callico Do
8 Pr Sheets
11 Blankets
2 Setts Callico Curtains
2 Setts common Scotch Lawn Do
3 Diaper Table Cloths
2 Linen Breakfast Do and 10 Napkins
2 old Chests
4 Beds and Bolsters
4 Pillows and 6 Pillow Cases

Library containing Vizt.

Seckers Sermons	10 Volumes
Seckers Lectures	1
Seed's Sermons	4
Ditto Ditto	2
Moss's Sermons 8 Volumes the 7 missing is	7
Tillotson's Sermons 10 Volumes 6 & 8 Do is	8
Conybeaux's Sermons	2
Clarke's 18 Sermons	1
Hoole's Sermons	2
Lucas's Sermons	3
Blacknall's Sermons	1
Spratt's Sermons	1
Weston's Do	1
Hickmann's Do	1
Roger's Do	2
Headley's Discourses	1
Fleetwood's Sermons	1
20 Sermons on the Social Duties	1
Jephson's Discourses	1
Balguy's Do	2
Life and Reign of David, King of Israel	2
Dr. South's Sermons	6
Hervey's Do	1
Prideaux's Connection	4
Bragge, on the Parables	2
Scott's Practical Discourses	2
Scott's Christian Life	5
Echard's Evangelical History	2
Wilkins Gift of Preaching	1
Foxcroft's Sermons	1
Hall's Treatise on the Old Religion	1
Frees' Antigallican	1
Frees' Sermons	1
Lucas's Do	2
Orr's Do	1
Pierce's Do	1
A Collection of Sermons	2
Mayhews's Sermons	2
West, on the Resurrection	1
Leland's View of Deistical Writers	2
A Defence of the Christian Religion 3 sets	3
Clarke's Paraphrase on the 4 Evangelists	2
Hickes' Discourses	1
The Husbandman's Spiritual Companion	1
Doddridges Sermons	3
Romaine's Treatise upon the Life of Faith	1
Abernethy's Discourses	2
Barrone's Sermons	6
Sherlock's Discourses	4
Ditto Ditto	2
A System of Divinity and Morality	5
Benson on The Epistles	2
Locke's Paraphrase on Pauls Epistles	1
Heylyn's Lectures	1
Foster's Discourses	2
Snape's Sermons	3
Stanhope's Do	2
Warburton's alliance between Church and State	1
Thompson's Treatise	1

Archbishop of Canterbury on the Catechism	1 Volume
Clergyman's Companion	1
Fordyces Sermons to Young Women	2
Dunlop's Sermons 2 Vols. 1st missing is	1
Blackwall's Sacred Classics	2
Clarke's practical Essays	1
Burnet's Like of God in the Soul of Man	1
Instruction for understanding the Lord's Supper	1
Nature and End of the Lord's Supper	1
Pearson on the Creed	1
Burnet's 39 Articles	1
Stackhouse on the Creed	1
Stebbing's Polemical Tracts	1
Hammond's Paraphrase on the new Testament	1
Stanhope on the Epistles	4
Edwards on Original Sin	1
Edward's Enquiry	1
Stackhouse History of the Bible	2
Holy Bibles	3
A large common prayer Book	1
Small common prayer Books	3
History of England	6
The World	4
Spectator	8
Satirical Letters	1
Belisarius	1
Garth's Ovid	2
London Magazine for 1769	1
Nelson's Abridgement of the Statutes	3
Laws of North Carolina	1
Heister's General System of Surgery	1
English Dispensation	1
Huxham's Essay on Fevers	1
Turner's practical Dissertation	1
Turner's Discourse	1
The London Practice of Physic	1
Brooke's Practice of Physic	2
Ainsworth's Latin Dictionary	1
Dyche's English Dictionary	1
Boyer's French Grammar	1
Plutarch's Lives of Demosthenes and Cicero, Latin	1
Philosophical Questions Do	1
M. T. Ciceronis de Officiis Do	1
Clarke's Homer Latin and Greek	2
Hutchinson's Xenophon Do	1
Patrick's Greek Lexicon	1
M. T. Ciceronis Orationis	1
Apparatus ad linguam Graecam	1
Trapp's Virgil English	3
Lucians Dialogues Latin and Greek	1
Juvenal's Satires Latin	1
Greek Grammar	1
Sallist, Latin	1
Hugo Grotius Do	1
Ellis's 39 Articles Do	1
De Praecipius Greek and Latin	1
Roman History, Latin	1
Sallust, English	1
Gregory's Astronomy	2

Pamphlets
Helsham's Lectures in Natural Philosophy........ 1
Waterland's 8 Sermons......................... 1
Collier's Discourses............................ 1
Mayhew's Sermons............................. 5
Smith's Do.................................... 1
Indifference for Religion Inexcusable............. 1
Conversion of St. Paul......................... 1
Miseries and hardships of the Inferior Clergy...... 1
Lectures in Experimental Philosophy............. 1
Disertation on the Hebrew Vowel Points......... 2
Propositions Mechanicae Latin................... 1
De Animi Immortalitate Do..................... 1
A Caution and warning......................... 1
Conduct of the Presbyterian Ministers............ 2
The Love of God to Mankind................... 2
An Answer to those who receive not the communion................................. 1
An earnest dissuation from Intemperance......... 1
The Trial of the Witnesses of Jesus Resurrection.. 1
Bishop of London's Charge to his Clergy.......... 1
A Second Defence to a Disenter................. 1
Predo Baptism................................ 1
Form of Prayer................................ 1
Divine Dialogues............................... 1
A Legacy to the World......................... 1
History of Jacob and Esau...................... 1
Verses on Dr. Mayhew......................... 1
Considerations on Election & Reprobation........ 2
The Christianity of the new Testament........... 1
Hill's Poems................................... 1
Society Instructions to Missionaries.............. 2
Smith's Oration................................ 1

32 Society Sermons
91 Pamphlets of Sermons
70 small Society Pamphlets
A Book Case

16 Pewter Basons
35 Do Plates
12 Do Dishes
1 Do Water Dish
1 Do Funnell
50 Wine Glasses
8 Tumblers
31 Syllabub Glasses
1 Vinegar Cruet, 1 Mustard Pot & 1 P Salts
3 Quart Decanters
6 China Dishes
46 China Plates
1 P China Butter Boats
2 Do Bowls
2 Do Tea pots
12 Do Saucers and 14 Cups
5 Do Coffee Cups
2 Queens ware Tea pots
1 Cream pot

19 Queens ware and stone tea cups and 4 Saucers
6 Ditto Coffee Cup
8 White Stone Dishes
6 Do Plates
6 Queens Ware Plates
1 Wood and 1 Marble Waiter
4 Japanned Do
1 Clean Plate Baskett
1 Fowl Plate Do
1 Silver Puch Ladle
1 Do Sou Spoon
11 Do Table Spoons
17 Do Tea Spoons
4 Do Salts and Spoons
1 P Tea Tongs
1 Brass, and 1 Copper Coffee Pot
1 Pestle and Mortar
1 Tea Urn
3 Tea Kettles

INVENTORIES. 541

1 Tin Candle Box
4 P Fire Dogs
1 Shovel and 4 P Tongs
1 Frying Pan and 1 P Bellows
4 Skilletts
2 Spits
3 Iron Pots
A Fish Kettle
A large Copper Kettle
A Pine Ironing Table
2 Small one Do
2 dozen Knives and Forks in Cases
8 Forks and Knife Box
6 Brass, and 2 Iron Candlesticks
2 P Snuffers
1 Cloaths Brush
1 Iron Box
8 Bee Hives
8 Grubbing Hoses
7 Weeding Hoes
2 Brod & seven narrow Axes
2 Shovels and 1 Spade
2 Augers, 1 tap Borer, and 2 Spike Gimblets
1 old Coopers Ax, 2 Chizels, and 1 Gauge
1 Carpenters Adze, 2 drawing knives and 3 Trowels
1 P Stirrup Irons, 1 Frow, 1 Hammer, & 3 Iron Wedges
2 Cross cut Saws, and 2 hand Saws
3 P Steelyards and a large Tin Scale
1 P common Scales, 1 P Money Scales and an old Tea Chest
a Bed Pan, a house Bell, and 3 P Sheep Sheers
2 Fowling Pieces
2 large Cotton Wheels
2 Flax Wheels
1 Cotton Gin
A Loom and set of Gears
A Cart and Cart Saddle
A Runner Mill Stone & 1 hand Mill Stone
4 Sets Iron Traces
A Portmanteau and Mail Pillon
3 Bar Plows
2 Flook Plows
2 Grindstones
15½ doz. Quart Bottles
A Single Horse Chair and Harness
A Post Chaise and Harness
A Chest with a Parcell of old Iron &c & C
144 Barrels of Indian Corn
3000 Wt Fodder
260 Barrels of Turpentine

HANNAH REED

Newbern Nov. 26, 1777.

Sworn to before me
   JOSEPH LEECH, J. P.

Debts.

An Account against Carteret County for	28.14.06
James Parratt's Note, Ballt. due thereon	16.14.10
David Marshall's Note for	8.05.04
William Forcs Note for	0.04.06
Mr. McClean's Rect. for 40 Dollars	16.00.00
Thomas Lovett's Note for	1.00.00
D'Arcy Fowler's Note for	50.00.00
Mr. Thos. Thomlinson Rect. for £10. Stg. Excla. 75 P. Ct is	17.10.00
Vestry Order of Christ Church Parish in favour of Mr. Reed for his Salary for the Year 1774	133.06.08
Due from said Parish for 2 Years Salary Commencing 17th April 1775 & ending 17th April 1777 at £133.6.8 P	266.13.04
£	538.09.02

A TRUE INVENTORY of the Personal Estate of Joseph Sanderson Deced taken the 9th April, 1774.

1 Negro Man Named Peter
2 Negro Women Namely Rose & Sall
2 Negroe Boys Namely London & Sambo
4 Negroe Girls Namely Esther, Nan, Grace & Philis
3 Maires
1 Young Horse
2 yoke of Oxen
1 Bull
4 Cows
2 Heffiers 11 Yearling 1 Calf
A Parcell of Hogs the number unknown
4 Feather Beds with Common furniture
1 Do without furniture
2 Mens Saddles
2 Bridles
1 Womans Saddle
2 Ox Yokes with Chains
21 Bar Ploughs
1 Chip Do
2 Fluke Do
3 Pair of Trases
4 Grubbing Hoes
7 Bee Hives
6 Baskets, 1 Razor
10 Weeding Hoes
5 falling Axes
2 Hatchets
1 Cart
2 Augars 1 Drawing Knife
1 Chisel and Gauge
4 Bells
1 Grind Stone
1 Plane
2 Taper Bits
5 Small Gimblets
1 Pr Bullet Molds
1 Pr Horse Fleams
2 Reaping Hooks
Sundry Shoe Makers Tools
3 Files
1 Pr Spoon Molds
3 Guns 1 Gun Lock
4 Set of Mustering Accutriments
1 Weaving Loom
6 Weaving Slays
5 Pr Do Harness
1 Hackel
5 Linnen Wheels
1 Woolen Do
1 Quill Do
2 Sives, 1 Sugar Box
2 Pad Locks
4 Bed Steads with Cords
5 Pots, 1 Skillet, 1 Frying Pan
3 Chests
1 full Case of Bottles &c
1 Do Containing 5 Bottles
1 Table, 7 Chairs
1 pair of Steelyards
8 Chunk Bottles
7 Delph Bowles
13 Small Cups, 6 Saucers
2 Earthen Pots, 3 pocket Bottles
2 Earthen Plates, 1 Tea Pot
3 Juggs, 4 Cyphering Slates
1 Small Grater, 1 Candle Stick
3 Pewter Basons, 2 Do Dishes
½ Dozen Plates, 15 Spoons
1 Tin Bucket, 13 Old Barrels
1 Meal Tub, 1 Churn
1 Stone Pot, 3 Pales, 2 Tubs,
3 Piggins
3 Treys, 1 half Bushel, 1 Small Trunk
1 Old Desk, 1 Pr old Chards
a Quantity of Flax, Rough
a Barrel of Cotton ———
1 Small Bible, 1 Do Testament
2 Psalters, 3 Spelling Books
6 other Books
5 Knives & 12 Forks
1 old Lock, 2 pr Pot hooks
1 Pr Iron Wedges 26 Geese
about 2 sides of Tann'd Leather
2 Small Hides
Warping Bars Box & Rake
Box Iron & heaters, 1 hand Mill
1 Reel 3 Pr Winding Blades &
1 Pr Loom Brushes
2 Gun Barrels 1 Pepper Box
1 Note of hand of 1.13.4

NORTH CAROLINA ss.

Edward Whitty and Jesse Sanderson Executors of the last Will and Testament of Joseph Sanderson deceased severally make oath and say that the foregoing account contains a true & perfect Inventory of the Goods and Chattels of the said Joseph Sanderson come to these Deponents Hands custody power or possession.   EDW: WHITTY
JESSE SANDERSON

Sworn this 16th day of April 1774 Before me
    JO. MARTIN

INVENTORIES. 543

AN INVENTORY of the Estate of Richard Sanderson Esquire Late of perquimans County Decd. taken the 17th day of July 1772 by Talle Williams & Andrew Knox Administators.

14 Negroes, to wit,
Sam, Glasgow, Dick ⎫
Tango,   ⎬ Fellows
Dave   ⎭
George ⎫
Robbin ⎬ Boys
Sam   ⎭
Doll, Rose---Wenches
Sarah, Jenny, Moll---Girls
5 Beds of furniture
1 Sea Bed & Some furniture
2 Pair Andirons
2 pr fire Dogs
11 Pots & Kettles
4 Pot Trammells
3 Tea Kettles
1 Handmill
4 Work Steers
2 Young Do unbroke
32 Head of Cattle at the Plantation
  & three for family use
91 Head of Sheep
66 Head of Hogs
  some left for family
10 Goats
9 Horses Mares &c
One third part of the Sloop Charming Betsey
a Small Vessel on the Stocks
1 Set Carriage Boxes & some old Iron
1 Carriage Chain
4 Rope Irons
5 Plows, some of them old
1 Large Earthen Jar
26 window Springs & Some Catches
15 Bottles
1 Ax Chisel & Bolt
Some old Iron
a piece of old Cable
1 Box & 4 old Cags
2 Churns
some window Glass &c
1 old Trussel
3 Servers
9 Stone plates
3 China Bowls & some Cups & Saucers & 2 Tea potts
1 Stand
2 Holders, 2 Coffee potts
1 China Tea pott
6 patty pans & Canister
5 Bottles & two Cannisters
2 Beaufats
1 Clock
6 Tables
1 Back Gammon Table
1 Looking Glass
2 Desks
8 Pictures
21 Books, besides some lent out & not Ret'd
1 Chist of Drawers
1 Tea Chist
3 Cases & some bottles
1 Cannister
1 Riding Chair & Harness
1 Watering Pott
1 Ox Cart & Wheels
1 Horse do & Wheels
1 Blunderbuss
2 Guns
1 Brass Kettle
1 Gridiron, Gridle morter & pestle
2 Box Irons
2 Candle Moulds
3 pair Stilyards
1 Hand saw
1 Lanthorn
1 Spade
1 Cheese Toaster
1 Cag and Sifter
1 Shaving box
1 Case and Razor Strap & Hone
1 pair of Shell Milstones
1 Grindstone
a parcel of Ceder Timber
6400, 18 Inch Shingles
Some Wharf Framing
1 Powdering Tub
a Parcel of Old Casks as Pr Acct of Sales
1 Old Canoe
9 Oars and two masts
481 feet 2 Inch plank
1 Arm & 6 Walnut Chairs
1 Horse Whip
27 lb Ocum
7 Chairs
1 pr Cart wheels
1 Sett of Black Smiths Tools
Some Iron in the Shop to be worked up
1 Grind stone in the blacksmiths Shop
1 Iron Tooth Drag
5 Axes
6 Hoes
5 Sythes
10 Reap hooks
1 Dutch Frame (?)
1 Cutting Box & Knife
4 Setts Hems and Traces

1 Saddle & Bridle
1 Coffee Mill
1 Coffee pott
1 pair of Pocket Pistels
1 Ox Chain & 2 yokes
2 Dozan Pewter plates
1 Pewter Turene
3 Silver Table Spoons & Punch Ladle
2 Salt Sellers some of which is old & broken
6 Silver Tea Spoons & 1 pair Tea Tongs
1 Case Knives and forks
6 Pewter Spoons
3 Table Cloths
7 Pewter Basons
3 Ditto Dishes

Some Stock at Allegator, also Sundry Articles which we expect is not come to hand, which we intend to Inventory hereafter

Debts due the Estate which we must refer to the Settlement of our Accots.

PERQUIMANS COUNTY

The above Inventory was proved According to Law, the 20th day of July, 1772 by the Oath of Talle Williams & Andrew Knox

Before me THOMAS HARVEY

A TRUE INVENTORY of the good and Chattles belonging to the Estate of David Shepard Deceased Which come to the Hands of the Executors March 1st 1775

Negroes, Peter, Felix, Rachel, Fillis, Annis, Cuff, Darbey, Jem, Dinah Peter, Jem, Antoney, Rhoda, Cate, Hanner, Sam,
25 puter plates 8 Basons
1 puter Quart 1 Pint pot
1 ½ pint 1 Jill 10 puter Dishes
6 puter spoons 4 Mettle spoons
34 Knives & forks 1 Puter Tankerd
9 Chests 1 Chest Drawers
2 Desks one Small the Other large
2 Looking glasses 7 feather Beds
————Furniture 6 Bedsteads & cords 5 Tables 4 Plows 1 Loom
9 Iron Pots 2 Kettles 8 pairs hooks 1 pair flesh forks
5 reap hooks 2 fish Giggs
3 Grindstones 2 Linnen Wheels
1 Cross cut saw 8 Chiping Hatchets
3 Round Shaves 1 Iron scraper
1 Mortis Ax 1 Branding Iron
1 horse Bell 3 Saddles 3 Bridles
1 Side Saddle 1 Jointorestock
2 Iron wedges 3 Oil Jars
1 Iron spit 3 Iron scrapers
24 Axes 9 pair Harnesses
4 Slays 1 sail Cloath 2 Barrels
Cotton 2 fish Nets small
Quantity of Wool
1 side Sole lether & some Curred lether
Small quantity of Nai.s
small quantity of Flax
2 pair Lether Bags 3 Iron hoops
3 Cart boxes 1 Bung bore
3 Hammers 1 Broken frow
1 Saw sett 4 Chizels 1 Gaige
2 Iron Squares 1 wood Square
1 Carpenters Adds 5 Augres

2 large Gimblits 3 Hatchets
1 Broken Ox Chain 2 Trowels
2 fire shovels some old Iron
1 plain 1 Pr. fire tonges 1 pair sharp sheares 1 Hatchet
1 box iron 1 flatt Iron 2 heators
1 pair Hand Irons 5 Trammels
1 Spice Mortor Wooden & Pessell
1 Tea Kittle 6 Punch bowls
5 mugs 4 Earthen Plates 3 Teapots 2 wine Glasses 2 Brass Candlestands 4 Iron stand 2 pair stillards 1 skillit some small Bowls some Earthen Pots 3 mice traps 2 hand saws 1 small saw 1 Slaight
1 Stow 20 Cheirs 6 Juggs
1 Raisor & hone 1 pair shot moulds 1 pair bullit moulds 3 pair Single Bullitt moulds 2 pair spoon moulds
2 pair marking Irons
2 files 2 lancets & case
1 pair Compasses 1 Rule
2 pair Iron Hinges 3 gimblets
3 Cases & 13 bottles 2 Tin funnels
2 Cags 4 Sifters 1 stone pot
1 Brass lock 2 guns 1 Real
1 Lanthorn warping Bars
1 stone pot Earthen pan
1 frying pan 1 Churn 1 keelor
7 Tubs 6 pails 2 pigions
6 Earthen pots 2 Vinigar cruets
1 Sault stand 1 pepper box
1 Drawing knife 5 Conoes
1 hand mill 12 Spools 3 Woolen Wheals
3 pair Card,
4 Boxes, 1 Iron Spindle 5 Canistors
1 Line 1 Sareh 2 pair Silver Shoe Buckles 1 pair Silver knee buckels 4 sugar boxes 5 Gimblets 2 pair Mettle Shoe Buckels 1 pair Bridle bits
7 Bridle buckels some small Nails 1 Cannistor 10 files
1 pair Brass scales Small quantity of Powder & shot
6 small led weights 22 Gun flints 2 Combs 2 pair Spectakles some Sealing wax & wafers 2 pocket books some Chunk Bottles
Small quantity of thread
Small quantity spun Cotton
1 Sugar pot 1 pair Curtain 2 frows 1 Chizel 1 Set of Cuppers Tools lacking Drawing knife 1 Dowling bit some Brimstone 1 snuf box some Bridle Buckels 2 pocket knives
Small quantity old puter
Small quantity of Palmasity
Some girt web 4 Sadlers Irons

35

Some Shoe Tools Remnant of
homspun Cloath Small Quantity
of White Lining small quantity
of Tobaco Some pipes Small quantity of yarn & Toe some
Table Lining 1 half Bushel
1 Jack 1 Small wheal 2 pair
winding blaids some shoe
lasts 1 pair shears 1 shoe
Bench 2 Bibles 1 Drilling
Coat
21 of Other Books 6 bushl.
1 peck Sault 36 Drey barrels
1 pair horse gears 1 Cart
4 ox yoaks 2 Chains & Rings
& Staples 14 Hogshead 7
pine Barrils 5 Tar Barrls
Some Coopers Timber 4
Jointer stocks 6 Irons 6
Cuppers Axes 3 adds 2
Howels 2 Compasses 1 Dowlin
bit 2 Crows Stocks 23 year
old hogs 3 Two year old hogs
4 sows & pigs 12 Sheep 2 pair
Baril Screws 42 hoes 2
Combs 3 Sheep Skins 5 old hoes
Some Leather in Tann 21 lb of
Feathers 1 hat Case 3 Caskets
3 Lining Bags 7 Swarms
of Bees 1 Sundell 1 hand
mill 1 year Old hog 1 hour
glass 1 greator 1 Brass
cock 1 Choping knife
1 yard ¾ Cloth Spotted
1 Brass Cock 2 small Baskets
5 sugar boxes 1 Carpenters
Adds 1 Iron pot 35 lb of Dry Beef
52½ lb Bacon 9 Barrils Corn
22 Barrils Corn   £ s p
To Note hand against John Starkey for 21.8.0 Proc.
with Intrest til paid Taken
the 15 day of may 1772   £ s p
To Note hand against Jacob Shepard for 232:10:0
To Judgment Note against
John Thomlinson for £57:17:11
with Intrest Till paid
To Judgment Note against
William Fulford for £5.0.0
with Interest till paid
To Note hand against Robert
Read for £4.9.4 To Note hand
against Nevel Bell Senr. for
£3:18:0 with Intrest till paid
To Note hand against Edward
Dill for £4.0.9 with Interest   £   s p
To Note hand against William Gaskill for..   6:10:0
To Note hand against Joseph R————
for £2:2:0 with Intrest
41½ Joaneses Supposed to be.............   131:04:0
paper Bills the amount..................   148:03:0
111 Milled Dollars......................   44:08:0

INVENTORIES. 547

7 Cob Dollars..........................	2:16:0
Small Silver to the Value.................	12:00:0
91 Coppers.............................	7:7
Small Debt Book Acct....................	6:09:9

21 Stears 4 Bulls 9 Heffers
22 Drey Cows 24 year Olds
33 Cows & Calves
2 yoak of Small Oxen 34 Bushels potatoes
Some Waring Cloaths

Then Was the Above Inventory proved to be Just & True by the Oath of Elijah Shepard to the Best of his Knowledge
August 11th 1775
Before me ———(?)WALLIS

November the 30th day 1753.

INVENTORY of the goods belonging to the Estate of David Shepard Junr. decd.

1 Negro man Called Nero	2 guns, 3 Axes
Bill Money to the Value of £49.12	5 Weeding Hoes
2 Mairs	1 Hand Saw
1 Horse	2 pr Pott Hooks
2 grown Steers	1 pr fire Tongs
1 Cow	1 Skillet, Some Cooks
2 Heifers	½ dozen knives & forks
1 Calf	2 pr Cards
21 Sheep	2 Sifters
19 Head of Hogs	½ dozen Quart bottles
1 Tarr Kiln	2 Juggs & other Earthen Ware
2 Beds and Furniture	Some Barrells Stubs
2 bed steads	1 bell Mettle Morter
1 Sett of copers Tools	1 Safe two pails 1 Cradle
1 Sett of Cordwainers tools	3 Basketts
Some Lasts	1 Slate
1 Saddle, 2 Bridles	1 pr Stilleards
1 Desk, 2 Chests	2 fish Lines
2 Tables	1 Rope
2 Small Boxes	A percel of Cotten
1 Trunk	A Percel of flax &
8 Chairs 2 Spining Wheel	1 pr Winding Blades
four Pewter Dishes	A Small Quantity of Ammunition
five Basons	A Quantity of Pine
16 Plates	Barrell Timber
1 pint Pott	1 Pr Wooden Scales
A parcel of Pewter Spoons	A Small Quantity of tin ware
1 fish gig	1 Bread Tray
1 pr Money Scales	5 Stocks of Bees
a Percel of old Iron	2 Sides of Leather
1 Hand Mill	3 Cags & 1 Cann
3 Iron Potts	1 Turpentine Bucket
1 frying Pann	1 Broad Cloth Coat and other wearing Aparrel
1 Iron Kettle	
1 Tramel	1 Silver Clasp

March the 11th 1754

This day Came Frances Shepard (Widdow, and made Oath upon the Holy Evengelist that this is a just & true Inventory of her late Husband Mr. David Shepard Junr. decd Estate. JO. BELL

Recorded in the Sec. office in Book H Page 223.

A TRUE INVENTORY of the Goods Chattels & Moveable Estate of Jacob Shepard Deceas'd taken in the Town of Beaufort in Carteret County to September the 7th, 1773.

Pr JOHN SHEPARD Executor

1 Piece blue broad Cloth 14 yards
1 piece Claret Clourd Do 6½ do
1 piece of Wilton 17½ do
1 piece Jarman Sarge 3¼ do
1 piece Superfine Sagathy 30 do
1 piece Damag'd Do 30 do
1 piece deep blue Do 4½ do
1 piece Nap blue Frys 24 do
1 piece blue Duffells 18¾ do
1 piece blue fearnot 7 do
1 piece Light Colour'd do 14 do
4 eight Quartered Spotted Ruggs
3 Indian Blanketts
1 Supr. fine Flanders bed bunt
1 piece Blue Shalloon 30 yds
1 piece Do 25¾ do
1 piece Yellow Tamme 7¼ do
1 piece Blue Shalloon 7¼ do
1 Remnant Do 1¼ do
1 Remnant Durrant 1½ do
1 piece of Brown Tamme 10 do
1 piece Do 7 do
1 piece blue Shalloon 10½ do
1 piece Clarret Colour'd do 8 do
1 Remnant brown do 4½ do
1 Do light colour'd do 8¼ do
1 piece Red Durant 20 do
1 piece black Calaminko 29 do
1 Remant blue Do 14½ do
1 piece Joan Spining 19½ do
1 piece Crimson poplin 17¾ do
1 piece Superfine Tabinet 36 do
1 piece Silk black Taffety 10¾ do
1 piece blue Silk Tafety 9 yds
1 Remnant Strip't Holland 1½ do
1 Ps black silk Persian 9 do
1 piece blue Do 11 do
1 Remant Strip'd do 3½ do
1 Pr silk Mozeen 30 do
1 Remant Silk Susee 2½ do
1 Bolt of Ozenbrigs 114 do
2 Do of Do 158 do
1 Remant Do 40 do
1 piece of Brown Rool 34¾ do
1 piece of Brown Sheeting 21¼ do
1 piece of Do 74 do
1 Remnant white do 4½ do
1 piece 7/8 Lining 21 do
1 piece Do 26 do
1 piece Do 25 do
2 piece Do 50 do
1 piece Do 25¼ do
1 piece Do 25 do
1 piece Do 23 do
1 Remnant of Do 22¼ do
1 Do Do 20 do
1 Do Do 18½ do
1 Do Do 15 do
1 Do Do 15 do
1 Do Do 16 do
1 Do Do 6 do
1 Do Do 4¾ do
1 Do Do 1¼ do
1 Do Do 3¾ do
1 piece of Huckerback 18 do for Table Cloths
1 piece of Dowlas 3¾ yds
1 Remant Do 7½ do
1 piece of Rusha Drillings 17¾ do
1 piece of Do 24¼ do
2 Do of Do 48½ do
1 piece of Do Sheeting 40 do
1 piece Brown Holland 37 do
1 piece of Do 24½ do
1 piece of Brown Holland 36 do
1 piece Stripd bedtick 22 yds
1 Remnant Check lining 2½ do
1 Do of Do 1¼ do
1 Do of Do 9 do
1 Do of Do 5¾ do
1 piece of Do 34 do
1 Remnant of Do 5 do
1 piece of Do 28½ do
1 piece of James 21½ do
1 piece of Dyed Pillow —— 23¾ do
1 piece of Nankeen Light Colour'd
6 Dozn. Britches Paterns Worsted
1 Remnant of Humins 2½ yds
1 do of do 1 do
1 Do of Do 0¼ do
2 piece Strip flowerd Lawn 20 do
1 remnant of Do 1 do
1 piece of Calicho 6 do
1 piece of Do 7 do
1 pice of fine Do 7 do
2 pieces Do 12 do
1 ps Do 11½ do
1 piece Clouded Gingham
2 do purple Calicho 18¾ do
2 do darkground 14¾ do
1 do striped & spotted linen 13 do
1 ps calico 6
1 ps Calicho 6 yds
1 Remant printed Lining 4 do
1 Do Calicho 1¾ do
1 Do Stamped Lining 3 do
1 Do Lawn 2⅓ do
1 Ps Cambrick 8 do
1 Remant Do 2¼ do
1 Do Do 6½ do

INVENTORIES.

1 Do Do 4¼ do
1 piece Lawn 8 do
1 Remant Do 3½ do
1 piece Cambrick 8 do
1 Pc. Lawn 8½ do
8 Bazalonu Silk Handkerchiefs
4 silk and Bark Do
1 Black Baxalony Do
3 Do
13 Black Curvatts
2 Black Bazalony Handkerchiefs
1 silk Do
4 Silk Caps
7 Silk Handkerchiefs
11 Lawn Do
7 do do
7 do do
3 do do
5 do do
7 do do
6 Red Spoted do
5 do   do
15 Romall do
15 do do
8 Check'd do
10 Do lining do
12 Do   do
4 Do   do
29 Do do
12 Lining Check Handkerchiefs
12 Do
24 Do
23 Do
22 Do
4 Diaper Table Cloths
1 pair of Kidskin Gloves
7 pair of Do
7 pair of Blue do
12 small Cutto Knives
12 pair of Knee Garters
3 Bunches Tape
2 Do Do
1 Broaken Do
3 small bunches Do
50 Skanes sewing Silk
47 Do Do
14 sticks of Brown Mohair
2 Do of Blue do
50 do of do do
44 Do Light Coloared
10 Douzen Mettal Buttens
7 Dozn ¼ of do
7 Dozn & 4 do
9 Doz of do
2 Dozn & 3 Black Glass do
10 Dozn & ½ of do do
2 Box's of Wafers
3 Douzen of Jews Harps
17 pair of Sissers
11 Parcell of Sewing Needles
27 Sett of Knitting Needles
71 Brass Thimbles
1 pair of Sissers
4 Ink Potts
1 Tin Water Pott
1 Cooper Lamp
10 Ivory Combs
13 Do
6 Do
13 Horn Combs
5 Common Prayer Books
1 Testament
9 Primmers for School Children
11 Pair of Flattery Shoe & Knee
  buckels
11 Pair of Pinch Back Do
12 Pair of Brass Do
11 Pair of Do
11 Pair of Do
1 Pair of Broaken Specticcls
12 Pair of Block Tin Buckels
12 Do of Brass
5 Do of White Mettal
11 Pair of Knee Buckels
12 Womans Fanns
1 Do
11 Cards of Sleave buttons
17 pair of Brass do
5 dozn pair of Glass Do
15 Pair of Do
15 pair of Brass Do
6 Dozn of small Saddle & bridle
  buckels
2 Dozn of Larger do
½ Dozn of do
40 Douzn of Shirt Buttons
11½ Dozn blue baskett buttens
3 Dozn Vest do
2½ pieces of Quality Binding
3 baggs Silk & hair buttens pr
  Invoice
7 Dozn 7 blue Mohair Buttens
9 Dozn & 3 Clarret Colour'd do
6 Dozn Vest do
6 Dozn & 5 black Basket Buttens
2 Douzn Vest do
3 Douzn black britches do
8 Douzn blue Coat do
10 douzn blue Vest do
3 Dozn & 3 do
3 Doz & 1 do
1½ Douzn light Colourd do
3 Douzn & 3 D o Do vest
4 Brass Cocks
2 pair Candle Snuffers
2 Thousand 8 Oz Tacks
1 Chest Lock
4 Thousand 14 Oz Tack

11½ Douzn of Wood Screws
3 gross of Shoe Tax
1 Parcell of Saddle Tacks
1 Parcell of Smaller do
10 Douzn of Awl Blades
15 Pepper Boxes
7 Padlocks
8 Iron Candle sticks
12 Curry Combs
2 Coffee Mills
6 Pad Locks
4 Cases Shambuck knives & forks
2 Do   Do
5 Real Buck   Do
22 Shoe knives
6 pair Sheep Sheers
12 Pair of Shoe makers Nipers
6 Pair of Do Pinchers
2 large Stock locks
2 Do   Do
6 Do   Do
4 Do   Do
2 Do   Do
5 Shoe Hammers
8 Brass bolts & Latches
10 pair of Brown Thread Hoes
2 pair of black   do
8 Pair of Grey   do
37 Quire of Writing Paper
3 Packits of Pins 4½ pound
2   Do   Do 4 do
7 Thousand   Do
5   do   Do
1 piece of Buckram 11 yds
10 Womans Hatts
4 Puding Pans
5 Tinn Coffee potts
1 half Gallon Tinn pott
3 Quart do
14 Tinn Potts
6 Tinn Tea Cannisters
7 Tinn Tonnells
4 Tinn Boxes
1 Lanthorn
11 small Locks
8 Locks
8 Chest   Do
4   Do   Do
2½ pair Hl Hinges
1 pair small do
7 pair of   do
18 Chest Hinges
20 small do
12 Do   Do
5 Box Irons
8 pair Sturrup Irons
7 Mice Traps
6 Window Bolts
8 Cross Cutt saw files
11 half Pound   do

10 Mill saw files
20 Plain Irons
4 Pair of marking Irons
5 Gimbletts
8 Gimblets
10 pair of Taylors Shears
1 Pair of Handle & screws for a Chest
1 door Latch & Cetch with Uentials
2 Iron Chaffing Dishes
12 Reaping Hooks
3 Pair of Cotten Cards
4 pair of Wool   do
100 fish hooks
100   do
100   do } Different sizes
100   do
1 Parcel do   do
21 Nutmeg Graters
10 Raizers
6 do
30 Pen knives
12 do Barlow
3 Bufflow Handle do
12 Mettle Spoons
12 Tea   do
12 Cutto Knives
3 Douzen & 9 burnt Bone do
12 Cutto ——— do
6 Pistel Handle   do
21 small Cutto   do
10 pair Carpenders Compases
8 pair Dufftail Hinges
1 Parcel of Brads No unknown
2 pair of Bridle bitts
2 douzen of knives
¾ lb of Ozenbriggs Thread
1 lb of Cloth Colowrd Do
1   do   do
1   do   do
½ do Ozenbriggs   do
2½   do Coloured   do
1½ Scotch ounce   do
½ lb Scotch Thread
½ lb do   do
¼   do   do
¼   do   do
¼   do   do
⅛   do   do
⅛   do   do
1/16   do   do
1/16   do   do
¼ do Ozenbriggs do
5 Ounces of White do
1 Box of Wafers
12 fine Ivory Combs
24 Horn   do
12   do   do
12 bunches Tape
2 Packs playing Cards

16¼ yds of White Ribin
1 peice Black Sattin do
1 do white do
1 do red do
¾ yd of Ribbin
¼ do of Red do
½ do of black do
1⅓ do of do do
3¾ do of White do Narrow
3 do of pale blue do
3¾ do of black do
6¾ do of do do
8 pieces of Remnants do
9 pocket looking glasses
9 Papers Ink powder
2 pieces Gartering 36 yds
1 Gross of Thread Laces
2 lb of Cruel
2 Gross of Shoe binding
2 do of do
2 do of do
5 Gross of Quality Binding
4 Remnants of Shoe Do
4 Pair of Red Garters
2 do White do
7 do Striped do
4 pieces do do
1 Slate
3 do
7½ Skanes Twine
22 Yds of Black Lace
1 piece Black Fringe do
1 do Gemp do
2 Douzn Cups & Sawsers
4 Tea Potts
4 Sugar Dishes
4 milk potts
6 Egate Tea potts
1½ Douzn Wine Glass's
10 Glass Sault Sellers
1 Pewter Inkstand
21 Large Delph Bowls
85 smaller do
2 Cooper Tea Kettles W 2½ lb
½ Douzn Galln Pewter Basons
4 half do do
46½ pound Pewter Dishes
26 do do plates
2 Beaver hatts
11 Beaver Writts
5 fine Wool hatts do
4 do
16 Felt do
7 do do
8 do do
6 do do
5 do do
8 do Bound do
5 Felt do
3 Frying Pans

51¾ lb buck Shott with the bagg
47¾ Bristor do with 2 do
117¾ do
20 lb do
2 Cases & Bottles
27 lb of 4d Nails
49¾ of 20d do
61½ of do do
143 of 6d do
6 lb of Cooprus
13½ lb of Allum
1 Parcell of Pipes in a Cask
3 Steel plated Hand saws
4 Iron do
6½ lb of Chockalat
3 Ounces of Linement
10 do of Mace
6 do of Cloves
2 lb 3 do of Nutmeggs
14¾ Black Pepper
30 lb of Allspice
3 hair Brooms
1 Scrubbing Brush
1 Box of Glass
1 Parcell of Gun flints
1 pair of Cart wheel Box's
5 Iron Squares
1 Drawing knife
5 do
1 do
1 Large Steel Trap
1 small do
2 pair of Flatt Irons
1 Narrow Ax
15 Iron Hoes
1 Broom
26 lb of Gun Powder
26 lb of Gun Powder
33 lb of Bohea Tea w lb the bagg
74 lb of Coffee
11 Damifyed Sives
2 Syths
1 Piece of White Flaning
5 yds of Bairskin
1¼ yard of Cloath
11 yd of do
27¾ yd red Flaning
20½ yd of Devon Carsey
1 piece of Red Bays
2 good spotted Ruggs
1 Damag'd do
2 pair of Dutch Blanketts
3 Spaids
167 lb of Flax
230 lb of do
40 Barrells of Turpentine
21 small black Juggs
11 large Pitchers
7 Black Pickle potts
8 Earthen butter potts

31 Loaves of Sugar	275	lb
4 Camp Ovens		24½lb
1 Iron Pott Wt		24½lb
1 do	do	13
1 Do	do	25
1 Do	do	13
1 Do	do	45
1 Do	do	35
1 Do	do	24½
1 Do	do	12¼
1 Do	do	35
1 Do	do	43
1 Do	do	24
1 Do	do	30
1 Do	do	41½
1 Do	do	31

22 black Juggs
11 Earthen Milk pans
7 Iron Skillets
24 Broad Weeding Hoes
17 Large Chunk Bottles
54 half Gallon do
1 Large Jugg
2 small do
1 Iron Pott Wt 12½ lb.
1 Do do 24
1 Butter pott
90 lb of New Rope
55 lb do
10 lb do
1 Fraim Saw
1 Gun
1 Cask of Wine 22 Gallons
1 Hogshead of Molasses 109 Gall
1 Do 116 do
1 Do 117 do
1 Parcell of Blown sault
1 Hogshead of Rum Wt India
1 Main sail fore sail & Gibb sav'd from the Stranded Scooner Dove
Three Anchors & two Cables
a Parcell of Ropes & Rigging
a Parcell of Blocks & Straps
Pumps pears & Box's & old Iron
110 lb of Bees Wax

4¾ of Mirtle Wax
43 Deer skins W 124 lb
2 Cattles Hydes do 21 lb
1 Otter skin
In Cash £160.5.8
Bill money 115.12.4
Notes of Hand 103.5.8
Household Furniture
3 Ovel Tables & 6 Leather Chairs
6 old Flagg bottom Chairs
1 Looking Glass 1 dressing Do
4 Beds & furniture 1 Sea do
1 Spy Glass & old Desk
6 Large Trunks & 1 small do
6 new knives & forks Ivory Handle
6 old do do Bone do
a Parcell of Earthen & Pewter Dishes & Plates
a Parcell of Iron potts Kettles &ᵃ Dutch Ovens with some other Kitchen Furniture
a Parcell of Chainey & Glass Ware
One Negro man Named Harry
One Negro Woman Named Kate
One Negro Woman Named Cose
One Negro boy Named Thom
One Negro Girl Named Jane
One Negro girl named Dinah
One Negro Boy Named Jere
Half douzen Large Silver Spoons
Eight small do
one Large silver Supe Spoon
one Silver Ladle
one Silver Pepper Box
Too pair Silver sugar Tongs
3 pair of Iron Hand Irons
1 Wooling Wheel 1 Lining do
1 Hand mill 1 Cart & Harness
1 Rideing Chair & Harness
2 Horses & 1 Saddle
1 Cow and Calf
1 Sailing boat Sail Oars & Anchor
4 Pair of Window Kirtins
Book Debts £528.18.5¾
A parcell of book for the family use

NORTH CAROLINA ss

John Shepard Executor of Jacob Shepard deceased maketh Oath aɴ Saith that the foregoing Account contains a true and perfect Invento of the Goods Chattles and Effects of his said Testator come to this D ponent's hands custody powor or possession

Sworn this 24th day of
Dec. 1773 Before me
   JO. MARTIN
   (Carteret Co.)

                        JOHN SHEPARD

March th 1758

then Sold the following things of Daniel Shine Descst aCordin to advertisment

to John Oliver two Cows & Calves..............	1: 5:00
To James Shine three stears....................	3:15:00
To Mrs. Crispin three Cows & Calves...........	4: 1:00
To thomas Shine one Bull & steare............	1:10:00
To John Berry one hose......................	3:00:06
To John oliver six plats......................	0: 3:00
To John oliver one table.....................	0: 5:06
To James Shine two glassis...................	0: 3:04
To Francis Dawson two glasis................	0: 3:04
To William Bryan one Chist of Drawers and old Books..................................	0:11:04
To James Shine one Broad ax.................	0:12:06
To William Vaughn three chissils.............	0: 5:00
To James Shine one Desk.....................	2: 8:00
To John Beswick one table...................	1:11:00
To anne Bryan one table.....................	0: 7:04
To Francis Dawson 4 augors & one plain.......	0:12:08
To James Shine one ax & howel...............	0: 9:04
To James Shine one ax & adz.................	0: 4:00
To James Shine one Bocks Iron...............	0:13:04
To James Robards one paire of Stillards........	0: 5:04
To James Shine one Sough....................	0: 4:04
To Francis Dawson 4 Chears..................	0: 8:00
To James Shine a 11 Chears...................	0:15:04
To Francis Dalamare one whip Saugh..........	2: 5:00
To Francis Dawson one Saugh.................	0: 5:07
To John Biswick one Saugh...................	1: 0:02
To John Biswick one Saugh...................	0: 4:00
To Francis Dawson one pare of han Irons......	0:17:00
To Francis Dawson one Spit & Squrs..........	0:10:06
To James Shine Six Chana plats...............	0:10:10
To John Biswick two Iron pessils..............	0: 1:06
To James Shine one table.....................	0: 8:04
To James Shine tee Chist.....................	0:10:04
To John oliver two dished & one Basin.........	0: 5:08
To thomas Shine one Sose pan.................	0:10:04
To Francis Dawson 3 Bras Candil Stiks........	0: 6:08
To John olivour one hakil....................	0: 2:04
To John olivour Six plats & one dish...........	0: 9:04
	32:12:09
To James Shine Six plats.....................	0: 8:08
to thomas Shine plats........................	0:11:02
To james Shine 2 dishes......................	0: 8:06
To john olivour one tee pot and Castor..........	0: 4:08
To Salvanas Justic one putor pot..............	0: 4:10
To thomas Bakor one Wollin Whele............	0: 5:00
To anna Bryan on Skillet.....................	0: 2:04
To anna Bryan one Cittle.....................	1: 5:06
To Francis Dawson one Kittle.................	0: 2:04
To John Bushop one pot......................	1: 2:00
To James Shine one Pot......................	0: 5:04
To John olivour one pare of Sheep Shears.......	0: 1:08
To John olivour griddle Chafin dish & flesh fork.	0: 4:06
To John olivour two Reap Hucks..............	0: 2:00
To Francis Dawsin one Bras Kittle............	0:12:00
To James Shine one Iron Basin................	0: 3:06

To John Biswick one bellows & Lanton & Collonder...	0: 4:00
To John olivour one small wheal...	0: 5:00
To John Bushop one Real...	0: 1:00
To John Biswick one pot...	0: 8:00
To James Shine one Negro man Dick...	13: 5:00
To James Shine one Small wheal...	0: 8:01
To John Bishop one pare Spon mols...	0: 4:00
To Francis Dawson one glas...	1:15:02
To James Shine one Spie glas...	0:15:04
To Solomon Euerton one hone...	0: 5:08
To Elesabath vaughn one Negro Wench Juday...	3: 2:04
To James Shine one pare of han Irons...	5: 8:01
To James Shine one Spade...	0: 4:06
To John Bishop one Shovil...	0: 2:00
To James Shine one pare of tramels...	0: 8:01
To James Carraway one pare of tramils...	0: 8:00
To John Bishop one pare of tongs & Shovel...	0: 4:06
To John Bishop three Bottles...	0: 1:00
To John Bishop one JJgg...	0: 2:06
To James Shine one case...	1: 5:00
To Francis Dawson one Roug...	1:11:04
To James Shine one Roug...	1:11:06
To John olivour one pare of Shears & two cocks..	0:10:05
To Francis Dawson 3 chests...	0:13:04
To John Bishop one pare of cales & wats...	0:11:08
To James Shine Six tee Spones & tongus...	1: 2:06
	37: 3:11

Sold at vandue aCordin to advertisement october 3 1767 the a State of Dannil Shine Descst

To John olivor one negro man tom...	30: 5:00
To James Shine one negro man Jo...	22: 2:00
To William vaughn one negro man Boston...	5: 5:00
To James Shine a negro wench Luse...	63: 1:04
To John Edmonson one Bad...	4: 2:00
To William Spight one Bad...	4: 3:00
To John Bushop two Diches...	2: 6:00
To John arthur Six plats & one Dish...	1: 1:04
To Francis Dawson one Cheast...	1: 3:04
To Joseph Crispon five Books...	0:11:00
To James Carraway five Books...	0: 7:00
To John Bishop one Cofe mill...	0:16:00
To William vaughn one Wator pot...	0: 2:00
To Francis Dawson one pare of tramils...	0: 8:00
To John Edmonson one pot...	1:10:06
To William Spight one table...	1: 5:00
To fornafull green one Kittle...	0: 5:08
To John olivour Sundry trifels...	0: 4:04
	138:13:06

Sold by me in behalf of Mr Curryrthers Sc

JAMES CARRAWAY Jurat

INVENTORIES.   555

AN INVENTORY of the Estate of Mr. Charles Simpson, Mercht., Deceased taken by Michael Coutanche & John Ricasset Administrators * * * * *

BEAUFORT COUNTY, March Court 1748. Present His Majesties Justices
These are to Certifie that John Ricasset Esqr and Mich'l Cotanch Merchants, admors of the estate of Charles Simpson late of Bath town in the sd. County Mercht. deced, returned upon oath the within, as a true & perfect Inventory of the estate of the aforesd. deeced, so far as is yet come to their hand, and that the Secretary have notice thereof, and that the same be recorded in the orphan book, the Same is recorded accordingly.

Test (?) JOHN FORBES Cler. Court

In his Store House
  5 pieces ¾ Garlix
  5 pieces ⅞ ditto
  1 piece ¾ Check Linnen qt 35½ Ells
  1 piece ozinbrig qt 73 Ells
  1 piece Ditto —— 114 Ells
  1 piece Green Tamy 36 yard
No 1: 10½ yards yard wide Holland Checks
  2: 6 yards Ditto
  3: 10¾ yard yd Wide Check
  4: 10¾ yard ¾ Check
  5: 5½ yards Ditto
  6: 4 yards Ditto
  7: 36 yards ½ Ditto
  8: 23¾ yards Ditto
  9: 35½ yards Striped Holland Course
  10: 18¼ yard Ditto
  11: 2¼ yard ⅞ Garlix
  12: 15¾ yards ¾ Ditto
  13: 23½ yards ¾ ditto
  14: 18¼ yard ¾ ditto
  15: 5 yards Holland
  16: 28¼ yard ozinbrigs
  17: 111 yards ditto
  18: 15½ yards Tow Cloth
  19: 24 yards Wrapper
  20: 4¾ yards Ditto
  21: 1 piece Callicoe
  22: 4 yards Ditto
  23: 24¾ yards Half thick
  24: 14 yards Ditto
  25: 18¾ yard German Serge
  26: 14 yards Blue Broad Cloth
  27: 9½ yards Coating
  28: 31 yards Kersey
  29: 26¾ yards Ditto
  30: 36¾ yards Red & Blue Cottons
  31: 20½ yards Green Callimanco
  32: 31¾ yards Blue Tamy
  33: 16 yard Red Tamy
  34: 26¾ yards Green Shalloon
  35: 2¼ yards Blue Callimanco
  36: 11 Silk Handkerchief
  37: 4 peices romol Handkerchief
  38: 10 Romol do
  39: 26 Mill- Caps
  40: 3 Doz: Blue & Red Worsted Caps
  41: 16 Red Worsted Ditto
  42: 15 Boys Caps
  43: 1 Doz: Yern Stockings
  44: 10 pair Blue Worsted Ditto
  45: 10 pair yarn Ditto
  46: 3 pair Black Worsted Stockings
  47: 3 pair Nobbs. Do Ditto
  48: 3 pair Childrens Stockings
  49: 10 peices Gartering & 4 Remnants
    30 pad Locks
    14 Stock Locks
    7 Pair Tow Cards
  50: 20 Necklaces
  51: 15 m Pinns
  52: 10m Ditto (Damnified)
  53: 7 peices tape
  54: 8 Packs Cards
    13 Bed Cords
  55: 23 Doz. Large Mettle Buttons
  56: 13 Doz: & 10 Small Ditto
    8 Bags Containing Sundry Mohair Buttons
    2 lb 10 oz Mohair
    2½ Nunns Thread
    7 lb Could; Ditto
    6 lb Browne Ditto
    1 Ream Paper 5 Snuff Boxes
    5 ounces Sowing Silk
    6 horn Combs
    2 Pewter Dishes & 6 plates
    1 peice fenetinge
    11 Doz: & 4 round Mettle Buttons
    6 Iron Candlesticks
    3 half hour Glasses
    2 Drawing Knives
    1 Coopers Ax
    2 Doz: Ivory Combs
    2 Doz: pen Knives
    8 Butchers Knives

1 Shoe Knife
1 Shoe Hammer
1 Paire Shoe Pinchers
1 pair Nippers
1 Shoemakers Last
4 Pair Stilliard
44 peices Earthen Ware
4 Reap hooks
2 Quintel Fish
2 Jarrs Oyle
4 lb Oz 0 Shotts in Bags
6 lb Shotts in 3 Bags
2 Bags Flax Contg.
4 Tinn 2 quart Potts
1 Large & 1 Small tinn, Sauce pans
1 Box Iron & heaters
1 Cutlass & Belt
½ lb Tea
1 New Wigg
3 Sifters
8 Frying Pans wt 62 lb
5 Ditto   32
9 Ditto   66
20 Ditto   139
1 Cask Gun Powder wt 100 lb Gross
1 Basket Feathers wt 5½ lb Gross
1 Spinning Wheel
1 Case with 6 Small Bottles
2 Club Axes, 2 Paire Sheers
6 Barrs Lead wt 74 lb
1 Barrel Sugar wt 161 lb Gross
1 Barrel Ditto wt 120   do
1 Barrel Ditto wt 180   do
1 Cask 30d Nails wt 80 lb Gross
1 Cask 8d Ditto wt 75 lb do
1 Cask 20d Ditto wt 332 lb do
1 Bag Bullets wt 21 lb
1 Box Mirtle Wax Candles wt.
                 62 lb Gross
1 Box Ditto   62   Do
50 Raw Deer Skins Wt 126 lb
20 Racoon Skins
2 fox & 1 Otter do
6 Hides wt 153 lb
1 Side Upper Leather
1 Ditto Sole do
26½ lb Bees Wax
A Box Contaig. About 3 Groce
   Long & Short pipes
¼ Hogshead Mollasses 1 Gaugd-
                 100 Gall-
1 Hogshead New Engd Rum Gaugd
                 108 Gallons
1 Hogsd; Ditto ——— 92 Gall-
                 6½ Inches Out
3 Ullage Barrels Syder
1 Barrel Tallow wt; 214 lb Gross
35 lb Loose Tallow
1 Empty Hogshead A Barrel a teirce
   4 Cagg

274 lb Junk
28 lb Oacum
39½ Bushells Salts
6 oz: Indigo In A Box
2 Sugar Boxes
1 Box Wafers
1 Small Look g. Glass
4 Watch Keys
1 paper Ink Powder
1 Small Spy Glass
A Parcel Auls & Tax
A Parcel Needles
A Parcel Buttons
1 Pair Spectacles
4 pair Sizars
A parcel Hooks & Staples
2 Bolts
1 Pair Shott Moulds
A Sugar Box
A Dram Cup
3 Gimblets
2 Silk Purses
1 Pocket Book
4 Vials
1:5 Bladed Knife
1 Knife
1 Brass Pencil
1 Brass Cock
1 Brass Snuff Box
1 Whip Thong a Shot Punch &
   Shot in it
1 Old Tinn Tea Cannister
1 Chest No: 59
A Coat German Serge Lind. with
   Red Tamy
A West Coat Broad Clothe Lind;
   with Red Alapine
3 Old Coats
5 Ditto Jackets
6 Old Pair Breeches
6 pair Old hoes
1 Woolen Cap
6 Linnen Ditto
5 Musline Cravats
1 Stripd. Holland Banyan
2 Necks
4 White Shirts
2 Check Ditto
2 pair Gloves
3 Wiggs
14 oz Haire
1 Pair Ozinbrigs Sheets
1 Powdering Puff
A Parcell Old Linning
A Crape
9 Ounces Spunn Cotton
14 oz. Candle Week
2 Leather Baggs
2 Towels
1 Great Coat

INVENTORIES. 557

2 Pictures
A Hatt Case
3 Beaver Hatts
1 Pair Plain Silver Shoe Buckles
1 Pair Steele Ditto
1 Comb
1 Dram Glass
1 Steel Pencil
1 pad lock
1 pair Old Gloves
A Bucket with 66 lb Old Iron
1 Case with Bottles
6 Quart Bottles
1 Hand Saw
1 Hatchet
1 Adz: 1 Brandg. Iron
1 Tap Borer 1 Gimblet
1 Hatt Brush
1 powder horn
1 Sauce pan
1 Pocket Bottle, 1 Cannoe Sail
1 Horse Collar
2 Guns
1 Long Spy Glass
1 Shovel
1 Pine Writeing Desk
  Books
3 Chests
3 Chaires
A Barbers Block
1 Iron Kittle
5 lb Loafe Sugar
A Hickory Stick
1 four pound Lead Weight
1 Sadle & ———
1 Bridle   1 old Sadle
2 pair Mill Stones

A Parcel Barrel Staves (In Town)
A Wheel Barrow
A Cannoe
⅛ of a Petiaugre
A Horse Namd Shoemaker
A Negro Man Named Phill
A Ditto Named Nimble
A Negro Woman at Jno Hardy
171 Barrels of Tarr Pr Mr. Coutanche
£6:8:0 Bill Money receiv'd of Nicholas Smith
A Black Wallnut Desk
£607:1:0 In Old Bills
    9:6:0 In Procklimation Bills
    1:5:4 In Cash Virginia Currency
A Silver Watch
0:19:4 In Boston Currency an English ½ Penny
A Pair Money Scailes & Weights
2 Razors
1 Silver Knee Buckle
2 Brass do
1 Brass Tobacco Box
A Red Leather Trunk & Pad Lock
2 Pen Knives 1 Sand Box
1 Ink Glass
2 Old Ivory Books
1 Leather Pocket Book
1 pair Stone Buttons Sett In Silver
1 Box with Some Wafers
A Parcel Blank Bills Lading
A Pair Double Channel Pumps
1 Pair Hair Cloths
2 pr Stilliards
1 Pewter ½ Gll Pott
1 Pr Scales & Weights

Bath, March 15th, 1748/9

JOHN RICASSET
MICHEL. COUNTANCHE
Admrs.

Beaufort: Filed Mar. 1748/9 Chargd.
Recorded in Book H Page 169

SNOAD

INVENTORY of Goods & Chattels of the Estate of Henry Snoad Esqr late of Beaufort County decd taken the 25th day of Febry 1753 Vizt by Walley Chauncy

1 Coat of Arms 14 Bottles cents ½ pt: 1 pair of old leather baggs 1 tin pepper box 1 wooden Sugar box 6 feather beds 5 blankets 4 bed steds, 3 bed boulsters, 2 baskets 1 pair of Cart boxes 1 Sacking bed sted 1 Steel Breeches buckle 1 tin Candle box 1 Wooden bucket 1 dozen maple Chairs with leather Bottoms & tops, ½ dozen do with wooden backs ½ dozen flag bottomed Chairs, 7 red ordinary ditto, 1 large China bowl, 1 middle & 1 small ditto, 3 large cups and Saucers Do, 7 Cups and 5 Saucers do (mixed), 1 tea Chist, 1 Case cent 11 bottels, 2 tin Canister, 1 Counter pain, 1 Sett of Callicox Curtains, 2 old table Cloaths, 1 Do pillow Case, 1 Chest 2 pr wood Cards, 2 old Cloaths, Coats, 1 Mohogany Desk, 2 delph

Soop plates, 6 shallow blue ditto, 2 Do 1 Do tea pot, 2 large bowls Do, 1 small Do, 1 Case of Drawers 1 pair of brass drawers (a Compasses) 7 earthen porringers, 1 pudding pan large & 1 small Do 2 Candle potts Do, 1 Shallor pudden pan Do 1 pitcher Do, 4 broken crates of liverpool earthen ware 1½ dozen peices of Charlestown Do, 1 small ink Jugg, 2 brass & 1 Iron Candle Stick, 1 Cork Screw, 2 brass Chafing Dishes, 4 Chizels, Crop of Corn about 50 bbs, 3 hhd and 3 bbs of pease, 1 small land Compass (pocket) Sundry flint ware viz 1 butter boat, 1 Do dish, 2 Do tea pots, 3 glass flasks 1 pr of fencing files 1 pr of horse fleems, 1 large looking glass set with sconses, 1 plane black walnut looking glass large 1 walnut stock'd fowling peice, 1 maple Do, 1 rifle gun, 1 gun Scowrer, 7 wine glasses, 1 large and one small decanter, 1 glass cream pot 2 tumblers, 1 glass mustard 1 pepper pott, 1 large Japan'd looking glass, 1 glass salt, 1 Spying Glass, 1 Small Looking Glass, 2 Sashes for folding Doors, 1 Nutmeg grater, 2 gouges, 6 Grindstones, 1 Shoe hammer, 1 nail hackle for flax, 1 earthen Tar, 1 old flannel Jacket, 1 Do Cloth, Sundry iron ware vizt 1 Pr of large hand irons 4 potts, 3 Pr of hooks, 3 kettles, 2 Skillets 1 Spits, 1 old frying pan, much worn and full of holes, 1 gridiron, 1 small Morter 1 flesh fork 2 potts wrack or trammels, 1 Small Pr of tongs, 1 leg broken 6 £ of old Iron Viz horse shoes broken hinges, &c, 5 case knives & forks, 1 drawing knife 1 tea kettle, 1 brass Do, 2 Chest Locks (no keys) 1 broken Spring door ditto, 2 Small brass pad locks for portmanteaus (with one key) 1 loadstone, 1 Coffee mill, 1 brass morter (small) and 1 pestle 1 wooden half bushel, 1 peck and half peck Do., 4 large pictures in black frames viz a plan of Kingington gardens, King Charles Tryal 1 Map 1 Sea peice, 21 Metzotincete ble frames pretty much defaced by the Cock roaches, 1 pair of Pincers, 9 earthen butter potts, 1 Do pitcher, 1 pickel pott 7 picture viz, Map of New York Do of the four quarters of the world, 2 battle pieces 1 picture of the Statues of King Charles 1 & 2nd on horse back (with ble frames) all of them pretty much Sullied with Smoak & some of them torn, 2 pictures viz 1 Map 1 Hystory piece of hudebrass, a small parsel of melted Pewter 2 tin Gallon potts, 1 half gall Do 1 quart and 1 pint Do 15 flat pewter plates, 11 soop do, 5 Soop Dishes, 5 flat Do diferent Sizes 4 Do basons 6 Spoons & 1 Can, 11 pattle pans, of tin, 1 pigging (of wood) 2 Pr of small Stillyards 1 Joint Stool, 1 pr of silver Spurs, 18 pr of Sheets, 1 dozen large Silver spoons 5 small tea Do., 1 Do Scimmer (broken) 1 Pr Do tongs (broken) 1 Do pepper box, 1 Do Can 1 Scithe, 1 Pr of taylers Sheers, 1 pr larg brass old Scales, 1 small hand Saw, 1 Silver Neckbuckle, 1 Pr small money Scales, 1 wooden Sand dish, 1 Small Slate table mustard &c without the glass 11 leather trunk, 1 tin tinder box, 2 old Wigg woolen Spinning wheel 1 Linnen Do, 3 small sticks of redwood, 1 dark bay Stallion called Duke 3 work horses, 2 yoke of oxen, 2 Ox Carts, 9 Negroes & 1 Mullatto Slave in Windsor, Pomp (a Mullatto) Lanceeshire, Cuffey, Kent, Simon Davey, and Peter (Men) Dinah a negro woman, Sarah her child Do Sundry negros 1 put Security, Special Bail &c &c viz Ben a Negro man Jenny a Negro woman and her Child, Clemey a negro girl, Sundries brot from boston P Capt Stephen Brown Feby 1t 1753 viz Beaver hat & 2 wiggs 1 Cane 1 pr Pistols & Holsters, 1 leather pocket book, Sundry books and papers, 1 blu Cloth Coat, 1 brown Do 1 fustain Do, 1 flowered Wastecoat, 1 blew grate Coate, 2 Pr of breches, 2 Pr of Drawers ruffled Shirts 2 holland Jackets, 5 Pr of Stockings, 1 towel, 2 diaper Napkins, 1 Damask Napkin, 1 pillow Case 17 Holland Caps, 4 Cravats, 1 white handkercheif, 1 bag of herbs 1 bridle Sadle and housing, 1 Violen, 1 Silver Watch, 1 pen knife and lancet, 1 Pr of Silver Shoes and knee buckles, 1 Pr of Sleve buttons (Stones) 1 Mourning Gold ring, 1 ink Stand, 1 Small feather bed and 3 pillows, 1 Pr of Sheets, 1 Cotten Counterpain, 1 Blanket, a box cont a few Mediceins) what was left after his death) 1 earthen dish and two plates, 1 doz and three bottles 1 Case with 7 bottles, 1 Raizor, 1 Pr of Garters, 1 Pr of old Gloves, a Sword 1 Negro boy named Jack.

WALLEY CHAUNCY Executor

AN ADDITIONAL INVENTORY of the Goods & Chattels belonging to the Estate of Henry Snoad Esq decd

Sundry Books, viz
  Doctr Evans Sermons 1 Vol 8 vo
      Sherlock on Providence 1 vol. 8 vo
      ditto discourse concerning Death 1 vol. 8 vo
  Cun's Euclid 1 vol 8 vo
  Tayler's Rule of Conscience 2 vol 8 vo
  Plutrach's Morals 1 vol 8 vo
  Gordon's Geography 1 vol 8 vo
  Marcus Antoninus Meditations 1 vol 8 vo
  Hale's Contemplations 2 vol 8 vo
  Government of the Thoughts 8 vo
  Goodman's Sermons 1 vol 8 vo
  Journey through England 1 vol 8 vo
  Godfrey of Bullogn 1 vol 8 vo
  ———— Discourses Moral & Theological 1 vol 8 vo
  Boyer's French Grammar 1 vol 8 vo
  Nature delineated 1 vol 12m
  Hobb's State of Nature 1 vol 12 mo
  Derhams Physics Theologia 1 vol 12 mo
  Proverbial Sayings 1 vol 12 mo
  Evelyn's Gardner's Almanack 1 vol
  Art of being easy at all times 12 mo 1 vol
  Short Introduction to the Lord's Supper 12 mo 1 vol
  Tillotson's Sermons 1 vol 12 mo
  Common Prayer Book 1 vol 12 mo
  ditto 1 vol 8 vo
  Poems on several Occasions (a Pamphlet)
  Leyborn's Gunter's Line 1 vol 12 mo
  Colson's Mariner's Kalender thin Quarto 1 vol
  Book of Instruments for Attorneys 1 vol 8 vo
  Corderius' Colloquies 1 vol 12 mo
  Cato's Dislich's 1 vol 12 mo
  Milton's Paradise lost, 1 vol 12 mo
  Latin Grammar 1 vol 12 mo
  Davids Harp 1 vol thin fol
  Art of War 1 vol (half lost) fol
  Doctr Clark's Sermons vol 1 and 6
  Guardians 2 vol. Thompson's Seasons 1 vol Parnel's Poems 1 vol
  Doctr Young's Poems, the 2d 3d & 5th vol of Tatlers

N. B. These last ten Volumes are the Books wch came from Boston with Mr. Sneads things mentioned in the last Inventory given in at March Court but not set down particularly.

1 Silk Gown, 1 Chints Ditto, 1 white Callicoe ditto, 1 stuff, & 1 Callicoe ditto 1 silk quilt, 1 Pained ditto, 4 Aprons, 1 Linnen Coat, 1 pair of Stays, 2 pair of silk & 2 pair of Worsted Shoes, 1 pair of silk Stockins 1 pr of thread ditto, 1 Velvet Cap, 1 pair of Kid Gloves, 1 Mask, 1 Tippet, 1 Snuff Box, 1 pair of Rockets, 1 Stomacher 1 Hufsey, 1 Jacket, 1 Hoop Petticoat, 1 Pin Cushion 7 Caps, 1 pair of Ruffles, 1 laced Hankn 1 Silk ditto, 1 Gauze ditto, 2 small remnants of Silk 1 small remant of Velvet almost ⅛ yd but not whole Breadth the silk 1¼ yd both of them) 6 Ribons 2 Girdles, 1 white wax glass Necklace, 1 pair of Gold Buttons, 1 pr of Ear Rings 2 Gold Rings, 1 pair of Silver Shoe Buckles, 1 do Small, 1 ditto Girdle Buckle, 1 small round paper Box, 1 little Basket, 1 Trunk, 1 two quart China Bowl 11 gal do 1 pt do 8 Axes, 2 Grubbing Houghs, 4 Weeding ditto, 2 Hillin ditto, 1 Spade, 1 Canoe, 1 Hand Saw, 3 Ploughs, 8 Cows & Calves, 2 Cows & Yearlings 3 five year old Steers 2 four old Bulls. 2 Ditto of a year old. the peat Brush Fare. the following at home 3 Yearlings. 2 dry Cows. 1 three year old Heifer, 1 two year old ditto. 2 Cows & Calves.

                        WALLEY CHAUNCEY Extor

AN ADDITIONAL Inventory of the Estate of Henry Snoad Esqr decd taken by Walley Chauncey Exr Sept 20th 1754 viz:

Nelson's Justice in 2 Vol in ye hands of Jno. Hardee Esqr
1 Boar
1 painted Tea Table & Sundry Acct Books
Some Silver plate belonging to the Estate of Benj Peyton decd viz
A Silver pepper box, do Salt Cellar, 1 do pint Can, 1 do small cup 1 do Salver, 1 do large Soop Spoon 2 Smaller Silver Spoons, 1 do Neck buckle in all weighing thirty eight Ounces, one quarter & one penny weight.
& some Acct: Books
Errors excepted
P WALLEY CHAUNCY Exr

No CAROLINA

In Obedience to an Order of the Right Honoble Lds proprietors Deputies we whose names are hereunder written being mett att the house of Seth Sothrell Esqr Deseased att Salmon Creeke have upon Oath appraised the sd Seth Sothrells Estate as it was prsented to us by Mr John Hawkins att the Sd place vizt

One Negro Man named Emanuel ffrank his Wife....................................	40:00:00
1 Negro Man being very old named Charles att	00:20:00
1 Indyan Woman named Dina very lame & with child	15:00:00
1 Indyan Boy named Harry at..............	12:00:00
300 Gallons of Rumm & 18 Gall of Spirritts whereof Mr. Hawkins alleadges that 2: Hogsheads of the Rum came in since Madam Lears Death...................	47:14:00
21 Bush Salt att 3s Bush...................	03:03:00
45 lb Boar Skins att........................	00:07:06
1 Pr Milstones.............................	01:00:00
97: Dress Buck Skins att..................	09:14:00
126 Dress Doe Skins......................	09:09:00
29 ffawne Skins...........................	01:10:09
14 lb of Beaver att........................	02:09:00
14 ffox: & 14: Wild Catt Skins att..........	00:14:00
600 lb Shot att............................	10:00:00
50 lb. powder att..........................	03:25:00
7: ½ Doz: Glass Bottles att................	01:00:00
12: prs: Door Hinges att...................	00:18:00
A prcell of Iron: Old Block & Riggin........	05:00:00
8 Gunns...................................	08:00:00
203 lb Nayles att..........................	08:00:00
3 Horses att...............................	12:20:00
	192:05:03
A parcell of Hoggs the most part being as we judge raised Since Mr. Seth Sothrells Decease att..	30:00:00
About 200 Sheep..........................	40:00:00
300 lb of tobb.............................	01:05:00
1 Great gUnn att..........................	01:00:00
In the Hall which Mr Hawkins alledges was by Coll Lear given him	
1 old Bedd: 2: Sheets &..................	02:00:00
Blanketts att.............................	
2: Tables & prcll of old chairs.............	03:00:00

INVENTORIES. 561

In the dairy house in like Manner given		
1 pann att....................................	01:00:00	
1 plough Share & Collor att.................	00:10:00	
In the Chamber ———		
1 Bedd & Boulster att......................	02:00:00	
6 Chairs att...............................	01:00:00	
2: prs: Old Andirons.....................	00:16:00	
in the Kitchen given as before		
3 old iron potts, frying panns.... ⎫		
1 pr Andirons: 1: pr: pott Hooks. ⎬	04:00:00	
1 spitt ⎭		
A Small parsell of old pewter...............	00:06:00	
A Small parcell old Brass att................	00:10:00	
1: hand Mill & 1: Grindstone...............	01:00:00	
	———	88:07:00

We the apprisors whose names are under written did appraise the above prmses as we judged them Worth in Currant Country Commodities according to Act as Wittness our hands this 9th day of July 1695:

        Ed: Smithwick
        Hanniball Hoskins
        Geo: D. Deare
         his marke
        Wm X Bembry
         his marke
        ——— Sommory
 Test &   Nicho. Semmons
   Jno Porter, Junr.

I the Subscriber do hereby acknowledge to have ——— all the above ——— Goods according to the above apprisment amounting to Two hundred & Eighty pounds twelve shillings & three pence I Wts of John Porter junr as Wittness my hand this 9th day of July 1695

            Tho: Pollock

 Testrs Edward Smithwick
     Nath Chevin

In Tho: Pollocks Hand.....................	281:12:03	
In Wm Duckinfields Hand.................	020:00:00	
	———	301:12:03

Six prs: Blanketts & 1 Rug & a Remnant of Satton

INVENTORY of ye Sundrie Goods & Chattels of the Esta of Jeremiah Vail Esqr Deceased Late of Newbern in the County of Craven in No Carolina taken ye 17th day June 1760 by Jno. Starkey Admr:

Five Negroe Men	Household Furniture
Four Negro Boys	4 Beds & furniture
Three Negro Women	12 Leather Bottom Chairs
Two Negro Girls	6 straw Bottom Chairs
Three Negroe Children	Two Desks
IN All Nineteen	one Book Case
Cattle in Town	Three Oval Tables
4 Cows & 3 Calves	one Tea Table
2 Stears	Two Cases and Bottles
Cattle at Plantation	Some China & Delph ware
25 head of horn'd Cattle	one Large Looking Glass
19 head of Sheep	Two Pr Dogg Irons
50 or 60 head of Hoggs	Two Brass Kettles
6 Horses and Mares	one Skillett

36

one Pott Trammell
Four Iron Potts
Two Pott Hooks
one Iron Kettle
one Tea Kettle
one Copper Coffie Pott
Two Iron spitts
Three pr. Brass candlesticks
Two Dutch ovens
one Copper Still & Worm
Three Hand Mills
Five stone Juggs
Six pewter Dishes
Eighteen pewter Plates
Two pewter Basons
One Siler Watch
one Silver Punch Ladle
Six Silver Tea Spoons
one Pr Silver Tea Tongs
Three Glass Decanters
   Wine Glasses
one Tea Chest
Six Dozn Bottles
one Water stone
Two Pr Stilliards
two sets money scales & weights
Five Gunns
one P of Pistolls & houlsters
one Cutlass
one small sword
four chests
one Leather Trunk
one square Table
four spinning wheels
one Cotton Ginn
some wooden Vessells
Plantation tools
  Four Ploughs
  six Hoes
  seven wood axes
  one Broad Ax
  two hand saws
  three Wedges
  two Reap Hooks
  two froes
  three grubbing hoes
  two hammers two Ox chains & Yoakes
  two Brans
  four scyths
  one bill hook
  two wire Sives
  two Carts and Gear
  Five Augers
  Five Ads
  two Cutt saws
  four Chizzells
  one square
  one Howell
  one file

one drawg knife
one gauge
one Cooper Ax
Two Grinstones
Some Wearing Apparrell
Mr. Merricks Bond for £266.13.4
     in Bills About 10.00.0
At Cape Fear
  Five head of Cattle gentle
  some wild cattle in ye Woods
  one Iron Pott
  five Do Wedges
  three old hoes
  two old axes
  one old trap and Chain
  one Plough share
Law Books
  Cooks Reports
  Cooks Institutes ye 1st part
  Cook Upon Littleton
  Wingate Maxims
  Kibbles Reports 2 Volls.
  Modern Entries 2 Volls.
  Cowells Law Dictionary
  Danvers Abridgment 3 Vol.
  Finches Reports
  Nelsons Abridgment 3 Voll
  Larkutts Reports 2 Voll
  Levints Reports 3 Volls
  Cases in Chancery
  Woods Civil Law
  New Abridgment 2 Volls.
  Jacobs Law Dictionary
  Carters Reports
  Province Laws
  Conneticut Laws
  Plewdens Comentaries
  Pufendos Law of Nature & Nations
  Hughes Abridgment 2 Voll
  Hobarts Reports
  State Tryalls 2 Voll
  Stattutes 1 Voll
  Stattutes Abridged 6 Voll
  Hawkins Crown Law 2 Voll
  Jacobs Statutes Abridged
  Tryalls P Pais 2 Book
  Boham Cursus (?) Commellarius (?)
  Compleat Attorney
  Attorney Practice 2 Vo
  Lutwich Reports
  Law of Evidence
  Stiles Practical Register
  Jacobs Common Law
  Kilbourns Justice
  Claytons Reports
  Attorney Pockett Book 2 Voll
  Jacob Treatise of Law
  Boham Institatis Clerricus
  Boham —— Cancellaria
  Fitz Harbertes Natura Brevum

Presidents in Clerkship
Law Quibbles
Woods Institutes 2 Volls
Law of Errors
Shepherds President of Presidents
Godolphins Orphan Legasy
Carry Reports in Chancery
Godolphins Admiralty Jurisdiction
Modern Conveyency
Coest (?) Scriveners Guide
Moores Cases Abridged
Morgans Modern Pleader 2 Vo
English Liberties
Kinchin on Courts
Melloy ? Jure Maritime
Marsh's ? New Cases
Gilitons Law Epitomied
Hales Pleas of the Crown
Magna Charta with notes
Law Abridged
Pleaders Abridged
Argument abt Ship Money
Book of Presidents
Presidents of Indictment
Wingates Common Law
Practice of Chancery 2 Voll
Jacob Law Dictionary Abridged
Modern Entries
Topick on ye Laws of England
Dawsons Origina Legam
Books of Divinity
  A Large Bible in folio
  One Do Do Quarto
  One Prayer Book
  Bish W——— on ye Trinity
  Religious Philosipher 3 Voll
  Barrows Sermons
  N England Psalms 2 Books
  Peters Revelation Revealed
  Scripture Sufficiency
  View of Popery
  Doctrines of Originall sin
  Mahews Sermons 2 Volls
  Religion in Nature Delineated
  Rellbewells Practical Believer
  Lock on Education
  Essay Against Popery
  Blackmore on Job
  Course of Catechising
  Hammons Practical Catechism
  Watts Hymns
  English Manual
  Thoughts on Education
  Essay on Man
  Youngs Poems on ye Last Day
  Defence of ye 3 Letters
  Some Loose Sermons
History &c &c
  Bundys Roman History

Gages Survey wth Notes
Telemachus
Marriners Jewell
Jenkins Tracts
History of Pirates
Bailies English Dictionary
Cole Do Do 2 Books
Chubs Tracts
Plutrachs Lives
Wars of Ittaly
Oats Narrative
Echards History of England
Bacons Silva Silvanum
Lattin Dictionary
Hattens Merchants Magazine
Ovids Epistles Latin
Euclid Elements
Thompsons Seasons
Plutrachs Morralls
Ciceros Morralls
Life of King David 2 Voll
Hammons Surveyor
Present State of England
Latin phrase Book
Letters on Several Ocassions
Ovid in Latin
Discourse on ye Revenue & Trade
Walkers English Particles
Salmons Surgery 2 Volls
Echards Classical Dictionary
Latin Rudiments
Hadneys Trigonometry
Cicero Orationis
Marcus Antonius
Annals of King George 6 years
Lelands Works
Locks Letters
Derhams Lectures
Mallbranch after Truth
Turkish Spy 7 Voll
Rapines Critical work 1st Voll
Toland Philipic Orations
Etheringedels Works 2 Voll
Popes Poems
Virgil in Latin
2 Greek Lexicons
History of Georgia
English Gramar
King of ye Heathen Gods
Greek Grammar
History of ye Popish Plots
Mageas French Grammar
Virgils Travettae
Present State of Europe 3d Voll
                State of
Perigrine Pickle 2 Voll
Cato's Letters 6 Voll
Joe Anderson 2 Vo
Ovid in Latin
Cockers Arithmetick

Spanish Dialogues
Marsays Travells
Escharts Discription of Ireland
Corderi Latin
Journey through England
Lucans Pharsalia
Marshalls Epigrams
De Clerks Surgery
Drydens Poems

Latin Tragodys
Lives of Illustrious Men Latin
Meade on Poisons
Ingarties Guager
Brevium Concillium
Romand Antiquities
Mathematicale Dictionary
Bohuns Geographical Dictionary

John Starley Esqr. Admr of all and Singular the goods & Chattels rights & Credits that were of Mr. Jeremiah Vail deceased personally appeared before me & made Oath in due form of Law, that the above is a just & true Inventory of the Goods & Chattels above mentioned that have come to his hands. FREDK JONES

NORTH CAROLINA, PITT COUNTY

AN INVENTORY of the Goods and Chattels of the Estate of William Watkins Deceasd.

one Case & Eleven Bottles 1 Case twelve 1 Do twelve 1 Do Nine Bottles 1 Desk 2 small tables 1 square table 2 Chests 14 Chairs 1 small Loking Glass 1 Slate 3 tin Canesters 1 pickle Bottle 1 tin Candlestick 2 Do iron 2 Hackkles 1 oyl flask 1 pair Stilyards 1 Lantern 1 Iron Ladle 1 pair fier tongs 1 pair hand Bellows 1 Box Iron 2 heater 2 hors bells 1 Gunshot Bag powder horn 1 pr Candle snufs 2 Bibles 1 psalter 1 prayer Book 1 sermon Book 1 old Book 1 almanack 1 kee hole saw 1 half hour Glass 1 Courriers knife & steal 1 Box & old Irons 1 tin Collender 1 Chafen dish 5 files 4 Rasps 1 saw set 4 spike Gimblets 3 plaig Irons 1 pr Pinchers 1 pr Nippers 2 Cross saw files 1 ink Bottle 1 Shoe knife 5 shoe awls 3 Small Bottles 2 Small Vials 1 Cowshen 11 Gimblets 1 Carpenters Rule 1 file 3 pr. Money Scales & Weights 1. Griddle 3 Spectacles 1 paper fish hooks 2 peice Sealling wax 1 paper awl blades 1 pack Cards 1 Nutmeg greater 4 pen knives 2 pr. harness 6 stays 14 Earthen Bowles 1 flask Bottle 1 Pr hors fleams 1 Leather pocket Book 1 Bridle Bit & Spur 1 Stock Lock 8 Candle molds 6 Earthen Dishes 6 gallon porrengers 14 teaspoons 12 stone Cups & 10 Sausers 1 gallon Porrenger 6 Earthen plates 2 Quart pots 2½ pints 1 pint 1 Gil pot 4 tea pots 1 sugar bowl 1 muster'd pot 1 Salt seller 1 peper Box 2 horn tumblers 1 horn Drinking Glass 2 Dippers   5 mugs 1 Tea kittle 1 Coffee pot 1 Copp sauce pan 3 old mugs 7 tumblers 4 Drinking Glasses 6 Small Bowls 8 Club Bottles 2 stone mugs 1 Butter Boat 5 silver teaspoons 1 silver sugar tongs 1 Glass milk pot 6 Chainy Cups 5 saucers 1 tea strainer 1 peic hour glass 2 Enjoin pots 1 pan 1 pint Scilet 12 Case Knives 21 forks 2 gack knives 2 Earthen Butter pots 2 sugar Boxes 2 sugar tubs 1 wood funnell 1 Brass Ladle 1 Chopping knife 1 Dryping pan 6 Stone Jugs 4 Stone pickles 1 stone pitcher 1 Earthen pitcher 1 small Earthen Dish 25 pewter plates 13 pewter Basons 6 pewter Dishes 14 pewter spoons 3 Earthen pans old pewter Dishes &c 1 yellow porrenger 1 tea cup 2 hones 1 Rasor 2 small Vials 1 pr. Spoon molds 1 Copper Cock 5 Large Drum Hooks 2 Dawlen bits 2 knife Cases 1 Girt & web 1. Bag peper 1 Bag alspice senek snakeroot 1 Bag Coffee 1 pr. Iron Dogs 3 old Sifters 1 old search 3 Cakes Chocolate & 2 pieces 1 Cork scrue 5 Rep Hooks 9 pr. old Cards 1 Coffee mill 1 Pr Leather Bags 3 Straw Baskets 2 baskets 1 Linning wheel small matter yewpon 2 Buckets 1 old Real 1 Flower tub 1 old powdering tub 4 pr wood scales 1 peice Cholk 6 Bedsteds 6 Beds 2 Rugs 3 Bed Quilts 3 Blankets 5 Mats

INVENTORIES.

1 hide 10 Sheets 5 Bolster 4 pillar 4 table Clothes 4 Napkins
9 Bolls yarn 8 Bolls tow 3 Combs 1 Bunch Cord line 3 Money Bags
7 old knives 13 pipes 1 Lump Allom parcel old Almanacks 2 fishing lines
1 paper salt peter 1 Cork scrue 1 Cork scrue 33 Bols Cotten 1 Bob hook
4 peices Brimstone 2 Lancets 2 Iron Scillits 13¾ yards homspun
Cloth 1 sword 1 small Baskets 47 fowls 18 Sheep 7 Geese thirteen
pounds five shilling & eight pence prock money
4 Iron pots 2 frying pans 3 Club axes 1 Broad 2 Grubing
4 weeding hoes 2 hilling hoes 2 pr pot hooks 3 Rack hooks 1 horse 2
mares 1 New saddle 1 old Do 1 halter 1 Bridle 1 old halter 1 hand saw
2 old Coopers axes 1 Croze 1 trowel 1 Bung borer 2 azdees 2 Draw knifes
1 hatchel Lathen hamer 1 pr. wood Compasses 4 augers 5 Chizels
1 gauge 1 Rown shave 1 pr Sheep Shears 1 pr old Shears 1 vice
1 hand Jointer 1 Brand Iron 1 taper bit 1 pr Lead Lines 1 old ax
3 old hoes 2 Iron Ring 2 Iron handles 2 harrow hoes 1 Loom 4 shkels
1 pr tempels 1 Iron Spit 2 scures 2 pr hand Irons 2 old Linning wheels
1 Cloth Rake 2 Cowpers Gointrs 2 woolling wheels 1½ Barrel salt
4 old Barrels 1 old keg 1 Do 1 Dying tub 1 Vinegar Barrel 1 Chest
with tobacco 1 Saddle Cloth some oyl 1 Dowlen bit 1 frow 4 Iron wedges
1 steal trap Cros cut saw Carpenters adze 3 peices Sea Cow hide
4 fishing lines 29 tras hoops 4 Brick molds 1 Gord with trumpery
5 Iron Hoops 1 whip saw 1 square 1 Rope 4 piecies Large parcel
wool parcel tow parcel flax in the straw 2 Cags Feathers 3 sider
Barrels 1 old Barrel 2 peicies Drift Leather 2 peicies Leather
9 small mugs 1 pewter tankard 5 small pitchers 1 Brass pepper box
1 Egg slicer 1 stone mug 1 butter pot 1 pickle tub
2 winding Blades 2 sider Barrels 2 Large fat Gords
2 Earthen pecies 1 peice Beas wax few peicies tallow 1 old Riddle
2 old Bowls & 1 old tray 2 old Earthen pots 1 powdering tub 2 fat gords
3 Gallon hogs fat 2 midlens bacon peice Barrel soap
1 hand mil 2 tubs 2 pales 1 piggen 2 small ropes 2 Cart Bodies 1 pr wheels
2 Cart saddle 1 pr hames 3 pieces Leather 5 Raw hides 1 Rope 7 Baskets
2 Riddles 22 sider Barrels 4 old hogsheads 6 old Barrels 1 old keg
1 Large Gord 5 trus hooks 1 Large Box 1 worping Box & Bars
8 trushooks parcel Green tobacco 1 Garden Rake trifle Cedar
parcel peas in hull 3 Bushels peas about five Bushels wheat about 2
Bushels Flax seead 1 Byshel Beans about 3 Barrels Corn 2 Grind
stones 1 sider trough & Basket 1 ferry flat 2 Flax Brakes 2 old Barrels
1 peck Lime 1 keg white oak Barrel timber 2 plows 1 Still tub 1 Gallon
Molasses 4 pound Brown sugar 2 Do Loaf Sugar 1 half Bushel
2 Barrels Brandy 1 Do with twenty eight Gallon 2 Bottles Rum
7 Bottles Brandy 1 Bottle 1 flat iron 1 Bag 8 Candles half
a Bushel of flor half a bushel of risce a parsel of
Cotton Som broke flat 3 Chamber pots 5 sides of Lather 1 yarling
skin and 2 peceis of Lather 1 pack of ingons 1 wollet 2 gallons of
honny monney 5 shillings and a pence quart of oyle 3 skanes and 1 ball
of yearn a smal remnent of spun Cotten and tow, a few oyster shells a
few Bricks, fother in Stacks
16 head of Cattle 63 head of hogs 64 barrels 2 Bushels of Corn
62 Bushels of Poaters &
a Small parcel of Powder and Shot   JAMES CASON

NORTH CAROLINA ss.

James Cason Executor of the last Will and Testament of William Watkins deceased maketh Oath and Saith that the foregoing Account contains a true and perfect Inventory of the Goods and Chattels of his said Testator come to this Deponent hands Custody Power or possession
        JAMES CASON

Sworn this 4th day of November 1773 Before me
   JO. MARTIN
(Pitt Co.)

A JUST AND TRUE INVENTORY of the Goods and Chattels Rights and Credits that were of Sarah West at the time of her Death, taken the 25th day of January, 1758, Vizt.

Four Houses and Lots on Pollocks Street, No. 360, 361, 362, 363
Fourteen Pounds, Eight Shillings in Silver
Five Pounds Sixteen Shillings and six Pence in Bills
Four Feather Beds and four Bedsteads
Two Rugs and four Blankets
Four Gownes, Six Petticoats
A Piece of Country Cloth
Patter for a Gown
1 Callico Bed Gown
1 Flannel Bed Gown
1 blue Broad Cloth Cloke
1 yard ½ Calico
1 Silk Bonnet & 1 check'd one
Quarter of a yd Country Cloth
2 Shifts & Caps, 4 Ribbands
2 Silk Handkerchiefs
1 Checked Apron, 2 Pair of Stockings, 2 Pair of Shoes,
1 Pair of Leather Gloves
1 Pair of Silver Sleeve Buttons
3 Mats, 1 small Trunk, one Chest,
6 new Dishes and 4 old one, 12 new Plates,
and 6 old ones, 2 new Basons and 4 old ones,
6 new blue and white Earthen Plates
4 Pewter Spoons, 5 Earthen Dishes, 4 Earthen plates 2 Earthen
Pans, 3 Earthen Butter Pots, 1 Earthen pitcher
7 Earthen Coffee Cups, ½ Gallon Earthen Jug, 6 Coffee Bowls
2 Stone Muggs, 2 Earthen Pint Muggs, 1 large stone jugg
9 Iron Potts, 1 Iron Kettle, 1 Skillet
Five Tongs, Box Iron & Heaters

1 Tea Pot, 6 Cups & Sasers	a House Lock
4 Punch Bowls	Four Dozen Bottles
7 Glass Tumblers	1 large Tray
2 drinking Glasses	2 Butter Tubbs
1 Funnel 2 Pepper Boxes	2 Sifters
2 Pair Pot hooks	2 Pair Scales & Weights
1 Pot Rack	8 lb spun Cotton
2 Candlesticks	1 Water Pail
6 Tea Spoons	2 Sugar Boxes
a Sun. Dial	8 wooden Trenchers
8 Kn[l]ives & 5 Forks	2 Wooden Bowls
old F[l]esh Forks	1 Wooden Ladle
2 Linnen Wheels	Twenty Barrels
2 Woolen Wheels	One Bear Barrel
3 Tables	1 jill Pot
8 Cheers	1 Tin Sauce Pan
5 Stools	1 Butter Churn
1 Looking Glass	half a Bushel
1 Chamber Pot	1 Pair Pockets
2 Pair of Cotton Cards	Shoe Buckles
2 washing Tubs	Two Combs
1 Spice Mortar	1 Pair of Spectacles
1 Iron Pesel	1 Iron Ladle
2 Axes 2 Hoes	one Pound 11 Shillings that was owd
1 Hand Mill	her at her Death, unpaid
8 Basketts	33 yeards of Cloth
1 Tea Canester	3 quarters of a yd of Linnen

Quarter yd of Calicoe
2 Pocket Books
1 Cow Bell
1 Hamer
6 Pounds & half and 5 ounces
   of Cotton
1 pair of winding
Blaids

1 Bawl of yarn
2 Rowling Pins
and a small quantity of Nails
Three yeards and better of Country
   Cloth
Nineteen Fowls
Two Gimbletts
6 Books

AN INVENTORY of the Goods in Store, Household, Goods Negroes, Horses, Cattle and other Effects belonging to the Estate of the late Coll Caleb Wilson of Currotuck in North Carolina Deceas'd as taken August the 30th 1754

Goods in Store
Rum 4 Hogsheads
Tallow 10 Pounds
Wax 75¼ Pounds
Gunn Powder 3½ Pounds
Salt Petre 26¼ Pounds
Allom 29¾ Pounds
Leather Chairs 1 Dozen
Small Trunks Two
Still Worm, &c a Capp One each
Spinning Wheels Three
Scythe & Stone One
Scikles Eight
Vicos Two
Brass Cocks Three
Case of Bottles Two
Tinn Funnels Four
Fishing Scein One
Fish Giggs Two
Iron Barrs Three
Nails Double Tens Ten Thousand
Old Gunns Three
Heaters One pair
Razors 2 Doz 4 r
Spectacles Three pair
Snuff Box One
Clasp Knife One
Shoemaker Awls 4 Doz & 10 awl
Gimbletts 2 Doz & 1 G
Dowling Bitts Four
Plaining Irons Ten
Candle Snuffers Four pair
Croze Irons Two
Files Five
Augers Eight
Chizel One
Drum Hooks Four
Marking Irons One pair
Womens Thimbles 6 Doz & 10 ths
Sewing Needles Eight Papers
Knitting Needles Five pair
Crane One
Old Mill Stone One pair
Slaizos Four

Fishing Hooks Five
Ink Stand pewter Two
Measures pewter three
Gunn Flints 240
Leaden Weights 14, ¾ Pounds
Scales Large One pair
Money Do & Weights One Pair
Earthen Bowls large Forty Six
   small Twenty four
Cups & Saucers 1 Doz & ½
Dishes Fifteen
Plates 12 Doz & ½
White Linnen 6 pieces & 17 yards
Brown Holland 6¼ yards
Flower Chints 6¼ yards
Callico 1¾ yards
Muslin 1¾ yards
Buckram 1 piece & ½
Tape 10 small Bunches
Silk Laces Fourteen
Old Fann one
Stockings worsted Two pair
   Negroes 26 pair
Wadding 13 Yards
Duroy 9 Yards
Shalloon One Yard
German Serge One Yard
Paper 3 Rhme: 18 Quires
Playing Cards Six packs
Testament One
Ginger 44 Pounds
Bradds 200
Thread 12 Pounds
Buttons Mettal Large 61½ Doz
   Small 24 Doz
Mohair Large 32 Doz
   Small 10½ Doz
Mohair 1½ Pounds
Hatt Bands Two
Woman's Short Cloak One
Spades Two
Stillyards One pair
Chalk 71 Pounds
Old Iron 520 Pounds

Old Lead 91 Pounds
Pork 109 Barrels
Salt a large Quantity the Number of Bushels as yet unknown
Cork Wood 3½ Pounds
Small Paterera One
Deer Skin Drest Two Pounds
Raw 1¼ Pound
Old Chest One
Old Cases without Bottles Two
Beans 8 Bushels
Sheep Sears Two pair

Negroes.

Men	Women	Boys	Girls
Harry	Vinor	George	Pender
Pomp	Phillis	Bristol	Rose
Coffee	Moll	Phillip	Suckie
Ocra	Beauty	Ambrose	China
Phillip	Nany	Jo	Patience
Charles	Dinah	Sam	Abba
No 6	Sarah	Tom	Dinah
	Amber	Ishmael	Sarah
	Tallakin	Affrica	Rachell
	Rachell	Daniel	Rachel
	Kink	Ned	No 10
	No 11	Peter	
		Jeffry	
		Tom	
		Will	
		Davy	
		Dick	
		No 17	

The Whole Number being 44

Household Goods Stock &c
  Beds with Furniture Seven
  Beds with Sheet & Rugg Three
  Chest of Drawers One Sett
  Desk One
  Desk with Looking Glass One
  Looking Glasses Four
  Chair Leather Six
    Cain Ten
  Leather Couch One
  Tables Oval Five
    Square Two
  Chests Cedar Two
  Trunks Leather Two
    Small Five
  Silver Tankard One
    Spoons large Twelve
    Tea Eight
    Watch One
    Hilted Sword One
  Gold Button Sleeve four pair
    Rings Six
    Bobs Two pair
  China Bowles Three
    Plates Eleven
  Cupps and Saucers Five
  Milk Pott One
  A Small parcell of Glasses
  Pictures with Frames Three
    Without Eleven
Chairs Flagged Three
Candlesticks Five
Warming pan Brass One
Spice Mortar One
Cold Still One
Pewter Basons Five
  Dishes Eight
  Plates 2 Doz & 11
  Tea Pott One
Iron Kettle One
  Potts Six
  Pestal One
  Spitts Three
  Doggs Two pair
  Pot Hooks Five pair
  Pott Tramels Four pair
Box Iron & Heater One
Flatt Irons One pair
Augers Eight
Knives Seven
Forks Ten
Ladle, Grid Iron, Frying pan, One each
Flesh Forks One pair
Fire Tongs One pair
Toaster & Bird Spitt
Axes Nine
Cards Three pair
Hoe's Weeding Twelve
    Grubing two

INVENTORIES.   569

Pad lock Three
Cross Cutt Saw and File One
Saw Rest One
Plows Weeding Four
     Sheer two
Brass Kettle old One
     Skellett One
Candle Molds Seven
Tinn panns Eight
     Cannisters Four
Gunns Three
Pockett Pistols One pair
Spinning Wheels Three
Saddle & Bridles Mens Two
Still Cap & Kettle old One
Tinn Funnell One
Spoon, Button & Bullet molds
     One pr each
Razors Two
Stone One
Old Iron A Small parcell
Carts old Four
Gauging Rod One
Wooden Pails Two
     Piggins Two
     Cann One
Waiter One
Flower & Soap Tubbs One each
Basketts Two
Large Bottles Two
Carboy One
Juggs Stone Two
Butter Potts Six
Measures Wooden Three

Grind Stones One
Search One
Sifters Two
Chamber potts Two
Chocolate grater One
Books of Difft Sorts One Doz:
Ladle tree One
Money Scales old One pair
Earthen Bowles Ten
Cask Hogshds 38
   Barrells 43
   Small Nine
Chest & Box old One each
Leather Nine sides
Cow Hides Three
Smiths Tools A Parcell
Coopers Tools A Parcell
Horses Ten
Mares Eight
Colts Four
Sheep 142 Hd
Cows and Claves 51
Other Cattle 192 Hd
Hoggs, Sows, Shoates Barrows,
   piggs &c 454 Hd
        £ s d
Cash 20:19:4
Steel Trapps Two
Case Bottles Five
Pettioger, Anchor & Cable, One
   each
Cedar posts for House Framing,
   Fourteen
                SARAH WILSON
                DANIEL SWEENY

September Genl Court 1754

The within Inventory was Sworn to by Sarah Wilson & Daniel Sweeny in open Court ordered to be Certified   JNO SNEAD Clk

INVENTORY of the Estate of William Wilton Decd Taken Newbern 14th January 1773

One Negro Woman & Child
One Map
three Bedds, 2 bolsters, 1 Pr
   pillows
5 Blanketts, 2 Pr Sheets
1 Coverlaid, Curtain Teaster &c
   not Compleat
2 Bedsteds
1 Large Mahogony Square Table
1 Walnut Tea Table
1 Small Maple Table
1 Pine Ironing Table
6 Rush Bottom Cheers
1 Winsor Chair
1 Pr of Large brass headed hand
   Irons

1 pr brass headed Shovel & tonges
1 pr Common hand Irons
1 pr Do Tongs
1 Warming Pan
1 Large heir Trunk
1 Small Trunk Gilt
1 Mehogony Tea Chist
1 Large Painted Sygar Cannister
7 Silver Table Spoons
6 Silver Tee Spoons
1 Pr Silver Tea Tongs
1 Sett of Chinea Cups & Saucers not
   Compleat
3 Stone Teapots & 1 Coffee pott
3 Delph Bowls
3 Glass Tumblers

1 Small Looking Glass
1 Pr wine Glasses
6 Yellow Stone Plates
2 Pr of Brass Candle Sticks
3 Smoothing Irons
1 Iron Tea Kettle
2 Iron potts; & pott Hooks
1 Small Iron Kettle
1 Large Brass Wash Kettle
2 Smaller Brass Kettles
1 pr of Pott Racks
5 pewter dishes
2 pewter Basons & 1 porringer old
5 Soop Plates pewter
6 flatt   Do   Do
1 pewter Quart Mug
1 Frying Pan
1 Grid Iron
1 Iron Dutch Oven
1 baking Iron or Griddle
5 white Stone Oval dishes
4 wt Stone Plates
2 pr Stilyards
1 Tin Cullender
1 Saftre
1 Wollen Spinning Wheel
a parcel of Old Books
Lex Mercatorie in follo New
1 Walnut Cradle
1 pr of Chair Wheels Old
3 Handsawes
4 Cart Wheel boxes
1 Hilling Hoe
5 Narrow Axes (New
2 Broad Axes (Old
1 Hatchett & 1 Wood Axx
1 Cooper Ades 1 Howel
3 Drawing knives
5 Spoke Shaves
1 Cooper Crose Iron & Stock
10 Augres of different Sizes
2 broad Chizzels, 1 Wimble
5 Iron Hinges Old
4 Rasps 3 files
1 House Bell
1 Iron Dogg for timber
4 Narrow Chizzells
1 Pr Coopers Compasses
2 Goughes 1 Spike Gimblet
2 Steel Gun Chargers
3 Brass Cocks 2 old do
the Remains of an Old Clock
Some Old Iron Trumpery
a Parcel of Slate Pensils
2 Lead Weights
3 Barrells of Oakam
1 Small box of Indigo
2 Old Tea Kittles
1 Watering Pott 1 Spare Girt
1 Mans Saddle

1 Chollar & Hames old
1 pr Joyners Compass
6 Jarrs & Crocks
6 Juggs wth Vinnegar &c
2 Willow Baskets 1 Tap borer
a Parcel of Bottles
4 Wooden Tubs & pails
2 Keggs
1 Gun
1 Large Steel Mill
1 Gray Horse
1 Mare
35£ Cash or Prock in Mrs. Jane Wiltons hands
——— Thirty five Pound.
From St. Eustatia Came to hand the 8 of April 1773 A chest Containing
1 Silver watch
1 pr Goold buttons
2 Silver table spoons
four Do. Tea Spoons
one pr Silver Knee buckles
two Silver Stock buckles
one Brass Cock
a burning Glass
one Cloth & one bucke brush
a Case with 4 Razors 1 old bottle
one Hone & one pr Suzors
two small Hammers
three old Coats
five pair old breeches
1 Sutuit Coat
five linnen westcoats
one Cloth   Do
three pair drawers
one Pr white Gloves
Eight White Shirts
two Check   Do
two pr trowsers
four Hand towels
Four Stocks
one Linnen & two Woollen Caps
one pair Mitts
Seven pair Thread Stockings
three pair worsted Do
three pieces bed Curtains
twenty two feet light Colrd Silk
twenty two Do dark brown Do
twenty one Do Muslin
a Gown & two Sheets
one Table Cloth & one Old Hatt
one Cut & two tail wigs
one pr Books
a pair Shoes & pr Slippers
a Cott feather bed pillow & blanket
a Chart for the English pilot
a Do for the W India Do
a Callender
two pocket Books with papers

two pilloe Cases
two linnen Handns
one Silk Do
one Old Gun

three pieces Chec
one Remnant Do
A Pair Silver Shoe buckles
a Tunick

Personally appeared before me William Rumsay the Acting Executor the Wife of William Wilton deceased and made Oath on the Hold Evangelist of Almighty God that the foregoing Account contains a true Inventory of the Estate & Effects of his said Testator as has as yet come to his Hands powor or possession   Jo. MARTIN

Sale of Sundrys belonging to the Estate of William Wilton decd. Sold at Venue this Eleventh day Feby. 1773.

1773 Goods Sold.	To Whom
69 weight okam at 20s P	Mr Thos Haslen 13.9
2 Narrow Axes	do 6.0
2 Old Axes	Martin Worsley 4.1
2 broad Axes	do 3.
1 Grubing hoe & 1 axx	Thos Haslen 8.
1 Old hand saw	Cash 2.7
1 do do	Timy Clear 2.10
1 do do	Ednd Wrenford 3.6
2 Drawing knives	Cash 3.4
1 do do	Martin Worsley 1.6
1 Gimblet & 1 Tap borer	William Ramsey 1.5
2 Augers	Timy Clear 2.
2 do	Timy Clear 2.
2 do	Cash 2.7
2 do	Cash 2.3
2 do	Cash 2.
2 do	Wm Ramsey .4
4 Spoke Shave	Cash 2.
3 Small Chizells	Timy Clear 1.
2 do. do.	Wm Ramsey 1.2
2 Compasses	Counsil Bryan .9
1 Chizzel &c	Martin Worsley 1.4
4 Brass Cocks	do 7.
1 gun Charger &c	Council Bryan .7
1 Small bell & Charger	John Edge Thomlinson 3.
1 Pewter Pint & Pr Sheeres	Martin Worsley 2
Parcel of Old Tasps & files	do 1.2
2 Old Tea Kittles	Martin Worsley 2.
1 Cooper Compass & Howell	do 3.
1 Croze	do 3.10
1 Adds Wimble &c	do 2.4
1 Grubing Hoe	Timy Clear 2.
2 Lead wieghts	Martin Worsley 2.7
1 Hold fast & tasp	Timy Clear 1.6
1 Pair of fire Tongs	Martin Worsley 3.6
5 Old Hinges	Counsil Bryan 3.7
1 Draw of broken ware	Martin Worsley 1.4
1 Girt, Mallet & Hammar	Bazil Smith .8
1 Old Jack	Timy Clear 3.6
Parcel Slate Pensills	Bazil Smith 2.9
Carried over	£5.16.1

Brought forward		£5.16.1
1 Box of Fish Hooks & flints	Counsil Bryan	1.
1 Pr of Cart Boxes	Bazil Smith	1.6
1 Pr do	Timy Clear	1.
1 pr of mens Old boots	do	.6
1 Pott Trammel	Martin Worsley	5.
1 Pr of Steelyards	do	5
1 pr do	do	10.1
1 pr of pott Trammels	do	5.5
1 Hoe & garden rake	Council Bryan	3.9
1 Spit & old frying Pan	Martin Worsley	4.
1 Mans Saddle	Bazil Smith	9.6
1 Pr Iron Hand Irons	Edmd. Winford	8.6
1 Pr Chollar & Hames	John Kennedy Sr	2.10
1 Woollen Wheel	Jno Harris	6.10
5 Empty Cask at 4d	Martin Worsley	1.8
1 Old Chair Wheels & body	Council Bryan	2.16.0
1 Gray Horse	Timy Clear	8.0.0
Some old books	Mr. Hatch	1.4
2 Books No Carolina Laws	Timy Clear	1.10
1 Lex Merestorie	Wm Rumsey	1.0.0
2 old Books	do	2.2
1 old Case	do	1.1
1 Bed & furniture	Jane Wilton	3.0.0
1 Bed bolster & Pillows	do	3.5
1 Bed	do	2.0.0
1 Large Mehogony Table	do	2.15
1 Sugar Canister Tea Chest & Trunk	do	1.0.0
1 Pr brass head Hand Irons, Shovel & tongs	do	1.6
1 Warming Pan	do	1.0.0
1 doz Rush bottom Chairs	do	1.1
1 Small Case & bottles	do	5
1 Walnut Tea Table	do	1.6
1 Small Table	do	.6
1 Old Pine table	do	.2.4
7 Silver Table Spoons at 17s pr	do	5.19.0
6 Tea Spoons & a pr of Tonges	do	2.7
½ doz Yellow Stone Plates	do	0.3.6
a parcel of Trumpery on the Mantle piece	do	0.10
1 Hair Trunk	do	17.8
Some Old Delph Bowles &c	do	3.4
Carried forward		£48.11.1
brought forward		£48.11.1
1 Map & Small Looking Glass	Jane Wilton	0.2.4
3 white Stone dishes & Cheese toaster	do	0.10.4
½ doz white Stone dishes & plates	do	.4
2 Pewter Dishes	David Evens	6.8
1 do do	cash	2.4
5 do Soop plates	Davd Evens	9.4
7 do flat plates	Jane Wilton	7.4
1 Pewter Bason &c	do	2.6
1 Porringer & 1 decanter	do	1.0
1 pewter Quart & Some Patty pans	do	2.8
1 pair Brass Candlesticks	David Evans	10.8

INVENTORIES.

1 pair do	Jane Wilton	4.4
1 Griddle	do	2.4
1 Iron Tea Kettle	do	2.0
1 Dutch Oven	do	6.8
1 Iron Pott	do	5.0
1 Iron Do.	do	2.0
1 Griddle Bearer	do	.8
1 Brass Kettle	do	7.4
1 large Do.	do	2.0.0
1 Old do	Levy Gill	2.5
1 Frying Pan	Jane Wilton	5.6
1 Washingtub	do	3.0
1 Grid Iron	do	2.8
3 Smothing Irons	do	6.8
1 Hammer & Funnil	do	1.6
1 Safe	do	6.6
1 Cradle,	do	12.4
1 Chest	do	2.4
1 Trunk & Water pail	do	1.0
2 doz Empty bottles	do	at 2d pr 4.0
1 Bedstead & Cord	do	5.0
the remains of an Old Clock	William Tisdale	3.0.0
1 Silver Watch	Jane Wilton	2.11.0
1 Pr Gold Sleeve buttons	do	1.6.4
2 Silver table spoons	do	1.3.0
carried over		£67.16.5

Brought Over		£67.16.5
4 Silver tea Spoons	Jane Wilton	14.0
1 pr Do Shoe buckles	do	14.8
1 Cloth & buckle brush	do	2.10
1 Case Razors &c	Captn. James Roberts	1.0.4
2 Hammers	Jane Wilton	2.6
a parcle of Old Clothes &c.	do	2.2.6
2 piecis Silk	} Claim'd by Jane Wilton	
7 yds. Muslin		
1 Cut & 2 tail wiggs	James Aront	2.10.0
1 pr Books	John Duff	14.0
1 pr Shoes & Slippers	Jane Wilton	10.0
1 Cott, Feather Bed, pillow, & Blanket	do	2.0.0
2 Charts & Calander	Capt. James Roberts	1.1.0
1 Silver Stock buckle	Jane Wilton	6.10
1 Gun	Timothy Clear	17.4
1 Do	Jno. Council Bryan	17.1
1 piece Checs 33 Elles is 39¾ yds	Jane Wilton @ 21d yd	2.19.6¾
1 piece do 34 Ells is 42½ yds	John Rumsey @ 21½ yd	3.16.1½
1 ps do 34 Do 42½ yds	Edward Franks 22 yd	3.17.11
1 doz Tea pots	Council Bryan	13.1
1 doz do	William Rumsey	12.7
1 doz Do	Do	12.6
1 doz do	Do	12.6
1 doz do	John Johnston	12.6
1 doz plain do	William Rumsey	7.6
1 doz do	do	6.0
1 doz do	do	6.0
1 doz do	do	7.0
1 doz do	do	6
4 Tea pots	do	1.10

5 Butter boats	Jane Wilton	4.0
14 Cups & Saucers	John Davis	4.0
2 Sugar Dishes	Jane Wilton	4.2
2 Wash Basons	do	2.6

	£97.15.11¼
Sheriffs Commission at 2½ P C Deducted	2. 8. 8¼
	£95. 7. 3
	Wm. Bryan Sher

AN INVENTORY of the Estate of Mr. James Winright decd Taken the 21st Day of Maye 1745 and Appraised by us the Subscribers Vizt.

one old Negro Man Called Paul	£80
One Man York	150
One Ditto Newton	200
One Ditto George Runaway if found & Returned sound & good	250
One Boy Bedford	150
One Woman, Moll old	100
One older Ditto Pegg	000
One Mulatto Wench Judy bound until she be 30 years old	25
One Horse Diamond	40
One Ditto Prince a Stallion	20
One Ditto Brandy	30
One Ditto Spring	25
One Ditto Squirrel	17
One boat	25
One petty Augre	20
One large Connoe	8
One Silver Watch	—
One old Rifled Gun	2
One looking glass	15
Two Oval Tables	10
One old Desk	5
One old Ditto Cedar	8
One large Case of Bottles	10
8 ews and Lambs	24
7 Rams	10.10
4 dry ews	8
3 Weathers	6
a Pecl of fish hooks	3.18
a Pecl of Books old	10
13 quires of paper	3
part of Two Setts of Surveyors Instruments	40
One Small looking glass, one brass hilted Sword & one large Seal	6
Three old Guns one no lock	5
One Bullett Gun	10
One pair of Money Scales & weight	3
two pocket pistolls	5
Two bridle Bits, one pair of Shot moulds, two files old pr Small Stylliards	3
Carried over	£1353

INVENTORIES.

Brought Over............................	£1353
7 old chairs,	3.10
2 pair Stylliards old, one large & one Small	4.0
3 old pewter dishes & 1 doz plates	7.0
3 Razors one brass cock, 2 lancets, one tap borer &c	6.0
2 New Sails for a boat not finished	16.0
½ Doz knives & forks & pr Sheep Shears	3.0
One pair of Small Hand Irons & 2 Smoothing Irons	2.10
2 brass Candle Sticks 2 pr Snuffers	1.10
One large Pott, Three Small Do & a pair of trammels	9.0
Two old Beds one Sea Bed old Three Ruggs & Two Blancketts	45.0
a Peel of Earthen Ware	5.0
One old Warming pan one Spy glass 2 old Chests one old Grindstone	4.10
One old Saddle and Bridle	1.10
6 Cows and Calves	48.0.0

One Cow & Yearling		9.0.0
2 Three year old Heffers		18.0.0
2 Three year old Stears	at New found land plantation.......	14.0.0
One ——— Bull		3.0.0
——— Hefers		4.0.0
2 Yearling Heffers		4.0.0
9 Cows and Calves...................		72.0.0
3 Cows and Yearlings................		27.0.0
6 Dry Cows.........................		36.0.0
3 four year old Steers...............		27.0.0
2 yearlings.........................		8.0.0
One Two year old...................		4.0.0
One old Bull........................		7.0.0

£1742.10.00

13 barrels of Turpentine in the woods if full & Trimed................................ 19.10
————— £1762.

A MABSON
DAVID SHEPARD
CHAS COGDELL
THOS AUSTIN

Brought Over.......................	£1762.00.0
131½ pounds Course Musco Sugar at 4d P pound.................................	26. 6.0
14½ gallons Rum at 3s P Gallon.............	21.15.0
In paper Currency........................	171. 1.0

————— £1981.2.0

No. CAROLINA, CARTERET COUNTY

These may Certifie that Col. Thomas Lovick and George Read Exrs of Mr. James Winright decd Came before me One of his Majesties Justices of the Peace and made Oath that the above is a just Inventory of the estate of the aforsd James deced. And in the Hands of the Widd
Given under my Hand the 19th Day of June Anno Domini 1745
A MABSON J P

(Recorded in Book H Page 112)

September the 8th Day——1750

A TRUE AND PERFECT INVENTORY of the Goods and Chattels of John Worsley Juner Decd.

Wearing Apparell
1 Whitne Coat
1 Dorged (?) Dito
1 Ozbrs. Dito
1 Home Spun Dito
1 Pr of Duroys Breeches
1 Pr of home spun do
1 old Green Cotton Vest
4 Pr of Stockings
2 Country Cloath Vests
1 Caster Hatt
1 old Rackcoon Hatt
3 Shirts
1 Pr of Silver Shoe Buckels
1 Pr of nee Buckels Dito
3 feather Beds
3 Boasters
3 Rugs
4 Pr of Sheets
3 tabels
1 Chest of Drawers
1 Chest
1 Dozn of Black Chears
1 Coffee Mill
1 Looking Glass
4 Bed Steeds
3 Linnen Wheels
2 Woolen Ditto
2 Pr of Cards
1 Case with Eight Bottles
4 Guns
1 Weaving Loom
3 Stays
1 Pr of Worping Bars and Boxes
3 Gallon Basons
3 Large Supe Dishes
4 flatt Dishes
1 Small Supe Dish
12 Plates Pewter
1 Box Iron
2 heetors
2 Weeding hoes
2 hilling hoes
1 Grubing hoe
4 Club axes
1 Broad ax
2 Coopers axes
3 Cooppers add'es
2 Drawing Knives
2 Coopers Joyners Stocks & Irons
1 Pr of Coopers Compass
1 Croes and Iron
1 Round Shave
1 Dowling Stock & Bitt

1 hand Saw
½ a Cross Cut Saw
2 hand Mills
1 Pr of Mill Stones
15 Sides of tan'd Leather
2 Water Pales
2 Piggons
5 Iron Potts
2 Iron Skillets
1 frying Pan
1 Scimer
1 Pr of flesh forks
3 Pr of Pott hooks
2 Pr of Pott tramels
1 Copper tee Kittel
1 Iron Spitt
1 Large Stone Buttor Pott
1 Earthen Pott
1 new Saddel
1 old Dito
2 Bridels
1 horse Cart & Wheel
2 Punch Boles
6 Chyne Sasors
3 Cups Dito
1 old Brass Candelstick
2 Earthen Jugs
1 flax hackel
1 Pr of Stillard
1 Pr of Sheep Shears
1 flack Brake
1 Small Ink Jugg
4 old Vollums of Books
1 Spaid
1 Chesel
1 frow
3 old hogsheads
3 old Barrels
1 Syphering Slate
1 Large Cannue
1 Weeding Plow
1 Shear Plow
7 mares
5 horses
14 Cows
7 Calves
7 year Olds
2 too year old heffors
2 4 Year Old Stears
2 three Year Old Dito
3 too year Old Dito
2 Bulls
2 hogs young & old
8 yews
8 Lambs

INVENTORIES.

2 Weathers
3 Negro fellors
1 Negro Woman
2 Negro Boys
1 Negro Garl
1 Meal Sifter
1 Pare of hand Irons
1 Box Iron Stand

1 Branding Iron
2 Old awgers
4 Reep Hooks
1 Rasor
1 Grindstone
1 Brass Cock
1 pair of Wedges Iron

MARY WORSLEY admr

Marey Worsley Porduced this within Inventory upon oath in Cort ordered that the Secretary have Notice thereof

Test PHILL PRITCHETT C Cort

Filed 16th Novr. 1750. Recorded in folio 26, Book H.

INDEX

	PAGE.
Adams, Abraham	7
Allen, Eleazar	8
Allen, Sarah	9
Andrews, John	13
Arenton, William	19
Ashe, John Baptista	15
Bailey, David	20
Baker, Henry	23
Barclift, John	25
Barrow, William	29
Bartram, William, Inventory	469
Bartram, William, Jr., Inventory	471
Batchelor, Edward	30
Bates, Henry Lawrence	34
Bell, Thomas	36
Benbury, William	38
Bennet, John	39
Bird, Valentine, Inventory	472
Blackledge, Richard, Sr.	41
Blackledge, Richard, Inventory	475
Blinn, Daniel, Inventory	476
Blount, Benjamin	49
Blount, Edward	51
Blount, Elizabeth	52
Blount, James	53
Blount, John	56
Blount, John	60
Blount, Thomas	63
Blount, William	65
Blunt, James	55
Bond, John	67
Bond, Vinyard	70
Bond, William	73
Bonner, Henry	74
Bonner, John	76
Bonner, Thomas	78
Boone, James	79
Boozman, Ralph	82
Boyce, William	83
Boyd, Thomas	85
Brice, William, Inventory	478
Bryan, Ann	87
Bryan, Ann, Inventory	478
Bryan, Edward	89
Bryan, Edward, Inventory	478
Bryan, Hardy	92
Bryan, Simon	97
Bryan, William	98

	PAGE.
Bryan, William, Inventory	480
Bryant, John	95
BURIAL GROUNDS:	
Allen, Sarah	12
Caswell, Richard	118
Bundy, Benjamin	99
Butler, John	101
Calloway, Caleb	104
Carr, William	106
Carruthers, John	112
Cartwright, William	107
Chauncey, Edmud	114
CHARITABLE, EDUCATIONAL, AND RELIGIOUS USES, BEQUESTS FOR, BY:	
Bennet, John	39
Duncan, Alexander	164
Harvey, Thomas	231
Innes, James	265
Paine, John	325
Rieusett, Peter	374
Walker, Henderson	436
Winright, James	456
Casewell, Matthew	122
Caswell, Richard	118
Clifford, Thomas	124
Collins, John	125
Conway, Mary	127
Corbin, Jean	134
Corbin, Jean, Inventory	482
Cotten, John	129
Cotten, John	132
Courtney, Robert	136
Craven, James	139
Creecy, Levy, Inventory	481
Crisp, Nicholas	142
DeRossett, Moses John	144
Dobbs, Arthur	145
Dobbs, Arthur, Inventory	484
Douglass, James	148
DuBois, John	150
Dudley, Christopher	154
Duckenfield, Nathaniel	155
Duckenfield, William	161
Duncan, Alexander	163
Durant, George	165
Durant, George	167

	PAGE.
Eagles, Richard	168
Eagles, Richard, Inventory	486
Eaton, William	171
Eborn, Henry	177
Eborn, Nathaniel	180
Eden, Charles	176
EDUCATIONAL (see Charitable, etc. Purposes).	
Eubanks, George	182
Eustace, Dr. John, Inventory	490
Evans, Barwell	182
Evans, Richard	184
Falconer, Thomas	186
FAMILY PICTURES DEVISED BY— Jones, Wm. Harding	278
Fendall, John	188
Figures, Bartholomew	189
Fonvielle, John	192
Fortsen, Mary	196
Francks, John Martin	197
Francks, Martin, Inventory	494
Fry, Thomas	200
Goodlatt, Alexander	201
Grainger, Caleb	202
Gray, John	207
Gray, John, Inventory	498
Green, Farnifold	210
Griffin, Edward	212
Grist, Richard	214
Hardy, John	465
Hare, Edward	216
Harrell, John	219
Harrell, John	222
Harrington, Humphrey	226
Harris, John	225
Harvey, Thomas	228
Harvey, Thomas	230
Hassell, John	251
Hatch, Anthony	233
Haywood, John	234
Hecklefield, John	236
Hecklefield, Jno., Inventory	499
Henley, Peter	237
Heritage, William	239
Hill, Harman	247
Hill, Harman, Inventory	500
Hill, Isack	249
Hodges, James	253
Holebrough, Joseph	256
Hoskins, Thomas	257
Hunter, Isaac	258
Hyrne, Henry	261
Innes, James	265

	PAGE.
INVENTORIES:	
Bartram, William	469
Bartram, William, Jr	471
Bird, Valentine	472
Blackledge, Richard	475
Blinn, Daniel	476
Brice, William	478
Bryan, Ann	478
Bryan, Edward	478
Bryan, William	480
Creecy, Levy	481
Corbin, Mrs. Jean	482
Dobbs, Arthur	484
Eagles, Richard	486
Eustace, Dr. John	490
Francks, Martin	494
Gray, John	498
Hecklefield, Jno.	499
Hill, Harman	500
Isler, Christian	501
Johnston, Gabriel	501
Kennon, William	507
LeBlanc, Peirre	507
Lovett, Richard	508
Maule, John	513
Milner, James	514
Nelson, Thomas	522
O'Brian, Darby	525
Pilkington, Seth	525
Pollard, James and Ann	529
Pollock, Cullen	531
Porter, John Peyton	534
Porter, John Swann	534
Reed, James	537
Sanderson, Joseph	542
Sanderson, Richard	543
Shepard, David	544
Shepard, David, Jr	547
Shepard, Jacob	548
Shine, Daniel	553
Simpson, Charles	555
Snoad, Henry	557
Additional	559-560
Sothell, Seth	560
Vail, Jeremiah	561
Watkins, William	564
West, Sarah	566
Wetton, William	569
Wilson, Caleb	567
Winright, James	574
Worsley, Jno., Jr	576
Isler, William	265
Isler, Christian, Inventory	501
Jenore, Joseph	268

	PAGE.
JEWELRY (see Plate and Jewelry).	
Johnston, Gabriel	269
Johnston, Gabriel, Inventory	501
Johnston, Samuel	272
Jones, Frederick	273
Jones, James	277
Jones, William Harding	278
Kennon, William, Inventory.	506
Knight, Lewis Alexander	279

LAND ENTAILED BY—

Adams, Abraham	7
Barclift, John	26
Bennet, John	39
Blackledge, Richard	45
Blount, James	54
Blount, John	56
Blount, John	61
Blount, Thomas	64
Boozman, Ralph	82
Bryan, Edward	89
Dudley, Christopher	154
Duckenfield, Nathaniel	155
Durant, George	166
Eaton, William	173
Green, Farnifold	210
Hardy, John	466
Harrington, Humphrey	227
Harris, John	225
Harvey, Thomas	228
Heritage, William	240
Hill, Isack	249
James, Turnbull	434
Jones, Frederick	274
Knight, Lewis Alexander	279
Lear, John	282
Moseley, Edward	313
Porter, John Peyton	353
Porter, Joshua	355
Pugh, Francis	364
Ryan, Thomas	381
Sanderson, Richard	390
Shepard, David	404
Skinner, Richard	408
Swann, Samuel	425
Swann, Thomas	429
Toms, Francis	431
Williams, William	451
Worley, Lovick	461
Lawson, John	280
Lear, John	281
LeBlanc, Peirre, Inventory	507
Leydon, Francis	283

	PAGE.
LIBRARIES OR BOOKS BEQUEATHED BY—	
Allen, Sarah	11
Blackledge, Richard	43
Collins, John	125
Craven, James	140
Durant, George	167
Falconer, Thomas	186
Hare, Edward	217
Hatch, Anthony	234
Hyrne, Henry	263
Innes, James	265
Johnston, Gabriel	270
Jones, Frederick	275
Jones, Wm. Harding	278
Lillington, John	287
Little, William	289
Lovick, John	292
Moseley, Edward	317
Pollock, Thomas, Sr.	345
Salter, Edward	388
Scollay, Elizabeth	400
Swann, Samuel	427
Winright, James	456
Lillington, Alexander	285
Lillington, John	287
Little, William	289
Lovett, Richard, Inventory	508
Lovick, John	291
Low, Emanuel	295
McCulloch, Henry	304
McKenzie, John	305
Mason, Roger	297
Maule, John	299
Maule, John, Inventory	513
Maule, Patrick	301
Maule, William	303
Milner, James, Inventory	514
Moncrief, John	307
Moore, Roger	309
Moore, Thomas	312
Moseley, Edward	313
NEGROES (see Slaves and Negroes).	
Nelson, Thomas, Inventory	522
Nicholson, Samuel	320
O'Brian, Darby, Inventory	525
Oliver, Frances	321
Ormond, Wyriot	323
Paine, John	324
Parker, Francis	326
Pfifer, John	328
Phenney, George	331

	PAGE.
Pilkington, Seth	334
Pilkington, Seth, Inventory	525
Pilson, Grace	332

PLANTATIONS:

	PAGE.
Adderson's Island	123
Arden of the Hill	315
Ashewood	16
Atkins Banks	240
Aunt Sarah's	208
Back Ridge	123
Ballards	95
Bartrom's Point	404
Batts' Grove	143
Bayes'	74
Bell's Gift	434
Black Rock	348
Bowser's	173
Brak Oake Land	433
Brick House	140
Breffit's Island	123
Brin's	74
Broad Creek	178
Butterwood or Irwin's	315
Cabbin Neck	63
Cain's Place	330
Canecarora	343
Chinpin	197
Christopher Wolbert's Old Place	328
Clagister's	431
Clur	315
Collenn's Creek	248
Conahoe	269
Cooper's	314
Crany Island	343
Crickets or Manuel's	348
Cumboes	173
Deaded Woods	338
Faulk's Point	228
Fendals	143
Fendell's	408
Folek's Pint	231
Folly	21
Fort Barnwell	241
Gards Island	434
Garrison, The	353
Goshan	66
Goshen	58
Goulds	173
Great Quarter, The	348
Gum Swamp	465
Halfe Way House	338
Halfe-Way House	343
Handcocks	42

PLANTATIONS—*cont.*:

	PAGE.
Hardings Plantation	353
Harrow	240
Hendersons Folly	465
Holes, The	225
Holes'	74
Holley Neck	99
Horse Meadow	291
Hunting Quarter	22
Hughes	173
Image, The	431
Irwins or Butterwood	315
Jennings Neck	240
Jones'	74
Jno. Fryers	126
Judys Branch	169
Kendalls	309
Kits Neck	98
Lillingtons Quarter	285
Lilliput	12
Little, The	110
Little Town	23
Log House	123
Manuels or Crickits	348
Morerts	111
Matthews Point	36
Maultbys Point	309
Meeting House Lands	328
Mount Calvert	386
Mount Galland	303
Mount Misery	309
Mount Pleasant	404
Mush Island	175
New Abbey	295
New Bern	343
New Germany	89
New Hyrnham	261
New River Banks	16
Nottingame Point	210
Old Boz Neak	73
Old House, The	379
Orton	310
Pagetts	140
Paradice	90
Paupo.' Ridge	298
Petifers	409
Piners	68
Piney Point	21
Point Pleasant	265
Point Pleasant	393
Pollucks Bever Dam	95
Possum Quarter	269
Quarter, The	229-231
Rayborns	173
Reads Neck	404

	PAGE.
PLANTATIONS—*cont.*:	
Red Banks	123
Rich Levels	433
Rose-field	343
Salmon Creek	14
Sandey Run	110
Sand Hills	355
Scotts Hall	303
Springfield	239
Springfield	343
Springfield	348
Springfield	393
Smiths Hammock	403
Snows Neck	404
Stump Island	16
Ticers Rich Land	66
Ticers Rich Neck	58
Tower Hill	147
Town Point	295
Townleys Point	404
Trewhetts Old Place	44
Turkey Point	16
Wallins	138
Walnut Hill	120
Whitehall	404
Whitemarsh	314
Wilkersons Point	344
Windleys	143
Youngs	173

PLATE AND JEWELRY BEQUEATHED BY—	
Allen, Sarah	11
Andrews, John	14
Ashe, John Baptista	17
Barclift, John	27
Batchelor, Edward	30
Bates, Henry Lawrence	34
Blackledge, Richard	43
Blount, John	59
Blount, Thomas	64
Blount, William	67
Bond, William	73
Bonner, John	77
Boyce, William	84
Boyd, Thomas	86
Carruthers, John	112
Conway, Mary	127
Craven, James	140
Crisp, Nicholas	143
Dobbs, Arthur	146
DuBois, John	150
Durant, George	167
Eden, Charles	176
Fonveille, John	195

	PAGE.
PLATE AND JEWELRY—*cont.*:	
Frank, John Martin	197
Grainger, Caleb	203
Hare, Edward	216
Harvey, Thomas	229
Harvey, Thomas	231
Hecklefield, John	236
Henley, Peter	237
Heritage, William	246
Hill, Harman	248
Hodges, James	253
Holebrough, Joseph	257
Hoskins, Thomas	258
Hyrne, Henry	262
Johnston, Gabriel	270
Jones, Frederick	274
Little, William	291
Lovick, John	292
Maule, Patrick	301
Moseley, Edward	318
Pilkington, Seth	334
Pilson, Grace	332
Pollock, Thomas, Sr.	345
Porter, Mary	357
Ryan, Thomas	379
Scarborough, Macrora	393
Scollay, Elizabeth	400
Snoad, John	417
Snoad, Henry	419
Swann, Samuel	426
Swann, Samuel	427
Walker, Henderson	436
Williams, Thomas	449
Winright, Ann	453
Winright, James	457
Pollard, James and Ann, Inventory	529
Pollock, Cullen	336
Pollock, Cullen, Inventory	531
Pollock, George	341
Pollock, Thomas, Sr.	343
Pollock, Thomas	348
Porter, John	350
Porter, John	352
Porter, John Peyton	353
Porter, John Peyton, Inv.	534
Porter, John Swann, Inv.	535
Porter, Joshua	355
Porter, Mary	357
Porter, Nicholas	361
Pugh, Frances	362
Reading, Churchill	366
Reading, Lionel	368
Redding, John	370
Reed, James, Inventory	537

	PAGE.
RELIGIOUS USES (See Charitable, etc., Uses).	
Riddick, Joseph	371
Rieussett, Peter	373
Robisson, Susanna	375
Robertson, James	375
Rowan, Matthew	377
Ryan, Thomas	379
Salter, Edward	384
Sanderson, Joseph, Inventory	542
Sanderson, Richard	390
Sanderson, Richard, Inventory	543
Scarborough, Macrora	393
Scollay, Elizabeth	399
Scollay, Samuel	401
Shepard, David	403
Shepard, David, Inventory	544
Shepard, David, Jr., Inventory	547
Shepard, Jacob, Inventory	548
Shine, Daniel	406
Shine, Daniel, Inventory	553
Simpson, Charles, Inventory	555
Skinner, Richard	407
Slade, John	411
Slade, Samuel	412

SLAVES BEQUEATHED BY—

Allen, Sarah	11
Arderne, John	14
Ashe, John Baptista	16
Bailey, David	20
Baker, Henry	23
Barclift, John	25
Batchelor, Edward	30
Bates, Henry Lawrence	34
Bell, Thomas	37
Blackledge, Richard	42
Blount, Elizabeth	52
Blount, John	60
Blount, Thomas	63
Bond, John	68
Bond, Vinyard	71
Bond, William	73
Bonner, Henry	75
Bonner, John	77
Boone, James	79
Boyd, Thomas	85
Bryan, Anne	87
Bryan, Edward	90
Bryan, Hardy	92
Bryan, Simon	97
Bryant, John	95

	PAGE.
SLAVES BEQUEATHED—cont.:	
Bundy, Benjamin	100
Butler, John	101
Calloway, Caleb	104
Carruthers, John	113
Cartright, William	110
Chancy, Edmud	114
Caswell, Richard	118
Collins, John	125
Cotton, John	129
Cotten, John	132
Corbin, Jean	134
Craven, James	140
Crisp, Nicholas	143
Dobbs, Arthur	146
DuBois, John	152
Dudley, Christopher	154
Duncan, Alexander	163
Eagles, Richard	168
Eaton, William	171
Eden, Charles	176
Eborn, Henry	178
Eborn, Nathaniel	180
Evans, Barwell	182
Evans, Richard	185
Figures, Bartholomew	189
Fonvielle, John	192
Frank, John Martin	197
Grainger, Caleb	202
Green, Farnifold	210
Griffin, Edward	212
Grist, Richard	214
Hardy, John	466
Hare, Edward	216
Harrell, John	219
Harrell, John	222
Harvey, Thomas	230
Hassell, James	252
Hecklefield, John	236
Henley, Peter	237
Heritage, William	240
Hill, Harman	247
Hodges, James	253
Hoskins, Thomas	258
Huntor, Isaac	258
Hyrne, Henry	262
Isler, William	265
Johnston, Gabriel	269
Johnston, Samuel	272
Jones, Frederick	273
Jones, Wm. Harding	278
Lear, John	282
Lillington, John	287
Little, William	289
Lovick, John	291

INDEX.

	PAGE.
SLAVES BEQUEATHED—*cont.*:	
Low, Emanuel	295
McKenzie, John	306
Mason, Roger	297
Maule, John	299
Maule, Patrick	301
Moore, Roger	310
Moseley, Edward	315
Nicholson, Samuel	320
Oliver, Frances	321
Ormond, Wyriot	323
Pfifer, John	329
Phenny, George	331
Pilson, Grace	332
Pilkington, Sarah	334
Pollock, Cullen	336
Pollock, Thomas, Sr.	344
Pollock, Thomas	348
Porter, John	350
Porter, John	352
Porter, John Peyton	354
Porter, Joshua	355
Porter, Mary	357
Porter, Nicholas	361
Pugh, Francis	362
Reading, Churchill	366
Reading, Lionel	368
Riddick, Joseph	372
Rowan, Matthew	377
Ryan, Thomas	379
Salter, Edward	384
Sanderson, Richard	390
Scarbrough, Macrora	393
Scollay, Elizabeth	399
Shepard, David	404
Shine, Daniel	407
Skinner, Richard	409
Slade, Samuel	412
Snoad, John	416
Springs, Aron	423
Swann, Samuel	426
Swann, Samuel	427
Swann, Thomas	429
Toms, Francis	431
Turnbull, James	433
Walker, Henderson	436
Watkins, William	440
West, Thomas	443
Whitmell, Thomas	445
Wickliffe, William	447
Williams, Thomas	449
Williams, William	451
Winright, Ann	453
Winright, James	455
Woods, James	458
Yates, William	462

	PAGE.
Slocumb, Samuel	414
Snoad, John	415
Snoad, Henry	419
Snoad, Henry, Inventory	557
Additional	559-560
Sothell, Seth	421
Sothell, Seth, Inventory	560
Springs, Aron	423
Swann, Samuel	425
Swann, Samuel	427
Swann, Thomas	429
TESTATORS:	
Adams, Abraham	7
Allen, Eleazar	8
Allen, Sarah	9
Arderne, John	13
Arenton, William	19
Ashe, John Baptista	15
Bailey, David	20
Baker, Henry	23
Barclift, John	25
Barrow, William	29
Batchelor, Edward	30
Bates, Henry Lawrence	34
Bell, Thomas	36
Benbury, William	38
Bennet, John	39
Blackledge, Richard, Sr.	41
Blount, Benjamin	49
Blount, Edward	51
Blount, Elizabeth	52
Blount, James	53
Blount, John	56
Blount, John	60
Blount, Thomas	63
Blount, William	65
Blunt, James	55
Bond, John	67
Bond, Vinyard	70
Bond, William	73
Bonner, Henry	74
Bonner, John	76
Bonner, Thomas	78
Boone, James	79
Boozman, Ralph	82
Boyce, William	83
Boyd, Thomas	85
Bryan, Ann	87
Bryan, Edward	89
Bryan, Hardy	92
Bryan, Simon	97
Bryan, William	98
Bryant, John	95
Bundy, Benjamin	99
Butler, John	101

INDEX.

TESTATORS—cont.:

Name	PAGE
Calloway, Caleb	104
Carr, William	106
Carruthers, John	112
Cartright, William	107
Casewell, Matthew	122
Caswell, Richard	118
Chancy, Edmund	114
Clifford, Thomas	124
Collins, John	125
Conway, Mary	127
Cotten, John	129
Cotten, John	132
Corbin, Jean	134
Courtney, Robert	136
Craven, James	139
Crisp, Nicholas	142
DeRossett, Moses John	144
Dobbs, Arthur	145
Douglass, James	148
DuBois, John	150
Dudley, Christopher	154
Duckinfield, Nathaniel	155
Duckenfield, William	161
Duncan, Alexander	163
Durant, George	165
Durant, George	167
Eagles, Richard	168
Eaton, William	171
Eden, Charles	176
Eborn, Henry	177
Eborn, Nathaniel	180
Eubanks, George	182
Evans, Barwell	182
Evans, Richard	184
Falconer, Thomas	186
Fendall, John	188
Figures, Bartholomew	189
Fonviclle, John	192
Fortsen, Mary	196
Francks, John Martin	197
Fry, Thomas	200
Goodlatt, Alexander	201
Grainger Caleb	202
Gray, John	207
Green, Farnifold	210
Griffin, Edward	212
Grist, Richard	214
Hardy, John	465
Hare, Edward	216
Harrell, John	219
Harrell, John	222
Harris, John	225
Harrington, Humphrey	226
Harvey, Thomas	228

TESTATORS—cont.:

Harvey, Thomas
Hassell, John
Hatch, Anthony
Haywood, John
Hecklefield, John
Henley, Peter
Heritage, William
Hill, Harman
Hill, Isack
Hodges, James
Holebrough, Joseph
Hoskins, Thomas
Hunter, Isaac
Hyrne, Henry
Isler, William
Jenore, Joseph
Johnston, Gabriel
Johnston, Samuel
Jones, Frederick
Jones, James
Jones, William Harding
Knight, Lewis Alexander
Lawson, John
Lear, John
Leydon, Francis
Lillington, Alexander
Lillington, John
Little, William
Lovick, John
Low, Emanuel
McCulloch, Henry
McKenzie, John
Mason, Roger
Maule, John
Maule, Patrick
Maule, William
Moncrief, John
Moore, Roger
Moor, Thomas
Moseley, Edward
Nicholson, Samuel
Oliver, Frances
Ormond, Wyriot
Paine, John
Parker, Francis
Pfifer, John
Phenney, George
Pilkington, Seth
Pilson, Grace
Pollock, Cullen
Pollock, George
Pollock, Thomas, Sr. 3
Pollock, Thomas 3
Porter, John 3

PAGE.		PAGE.
TESTATORS—cont.:		TESTATORS—cont.:
Porter, John 352		Weeks, Bingman 441
Porter, John Peyton...... 353		West, Thomas 442
Porter, Joshua 355		Whitehurst, Thomas 443
Porter, Mary 357		Whitmell, Thomas 445
Porter, Nicholas 361		Wickliffe, William 447
Pugh, Francis 362		Williams, Thomas 449
Reading, Churchill 366		Williams, William 451
Reading, Lionel 368		Winright, Ann 453
Redding, John 370		Winright, James 455
Riddick, Joseph 371		Woods, James 458
Rieussett, Peter 373		Woods, James 458
Robertson, James 375		Worley, Lovick 461
Robisson, Susanna 375		Yates, William 462
Rowan, Matthew 377		
Ryan, Thomas 379		Toms, Francis 430
Salter, Edward 384		Turnbull, James 433
Sanderson, Richard 390		Vail, Jeremiah, Inventory... 561
Scarbrough, Macrora 393		Walker, Henderson 436
Scollay, Elizabeth 399		Warren, Abraham 437
Scollay, Samuel 401		Watkins, Thos. 438
Shepard, David 403		Watkins, William 439
Shine, Daniel 406		Watkins, William, Inventory 564
Skinner, Richard 407		Weeks, Bingman 441
Slade, John 411		West, Sarah, Inventory...... 566
Slade, Samuel 412		West, Thomas 442
Slocumb, Samuel 414		Whitehurst, Thomas 443
Snoad, John 415		Whitmell, Thomas 445
Snoad, Henry 419		Wickliffe, William 447
Sothell, Seth 421		Williams, Thomas 449
Springs, Aron 423		Williams, William 451
Swann, Samuel 425		Wilson, Caleb, Inventory.... 567
Swann, Samuel 427		Wilton, William, Inventory.. 569
Swann, Thomas 429		Account of sales...... 571
Toms, Francis 430		Winright, Ann 453
Turnbull, James 433		Winright, James 455
Walker, Henderson 436		Winright, James, Inventory.. 574
Warren, Abraham 437		Worley, Lovick 461
Watkins, Thos. 438		Worsley, Jno., Jr., Inventory 576
Watkins, William 439		Yates, William 462

www.ingramcontent.com/pod-product-compliance
Lightning Source LLC
Chambersburg PA
CBHW060907300426
44112CB00011B/1371